P9-APL-791

RENEWAL THEOLOGY

RENEWAL THEOLOGY

The Church, the Kingdom, and Last Things

J. Rodman Williams

ZondervanPublishingHouse
Academic and Professional Books
Grand Rapids, Michigan
A Division of HarperCollins*Publishers*

RENEWAL THEOLOGY: THE CHURCH, THE KINGDOM, AND LAST THINGS

Requests for information should be addressed to:
Zondervan Publishing House
Academic and Professional Books
Grand Rapids, Michigan 49530

Library of Congress Cataloging in Publication Data
(Revised for volume 3)
Williams J. Rodman (John Rodman)
Renewal theology
"Systematic theology from a charismatic perspective."
Vol. 3– has imprint: Grand Rapids, Mich.: Zondervan Pub. House.
Includes bibliographies and indexes.
ISBN 0-310-24890-6
Contents: [1] God, the world, and redemption — [2] Salvation, the Holy Spirit, and Christian living — [3] The church, the kingdom, and last things.
1. Theology, Doctrinal. 2. Pentecostalism. I. Title.
BT75.2.W54 1988 230'.046 88-912
ISBN 0-310-24290-8 (v. 1)
ISBN 0-310-24190-1 (v. 2)

Edited by Gerard Terpstra
Cover design by Art Jacobs

Printed in the United States of America

92 93 94 95 96 97 98 / / 10 9 8 7 6 5 4 3 2 1

This edition is printed on acid-free paper and meets the American National Standards Institute Z39.48 standard.

To My Wife

CONTENTS

Abbreviations 9
Preface 11

Part One
THE CHURCH

1. Definition 15
2. Scope 25
3. Description 49
4. Functions 85
5. Ministry 159
6. Ordinances 221
7. The Church and Civil Government 265

Part Two
LAST THINGS

8. The Kingdom of God 289
9. The Return of Jesus Christ 297
10. Signs 317
11. The Manner of Christ's Return 385
12. The Purpose of Christ's Return 397
13. The Millennium 421
14. The Last Judgment 445
15. The Consummation 479

Bibliography 509
Index of Persons 517
Index of Subjects 521
Scripture Index 523

ABBREVIATIONS

AB	*Anchor Bible*
ASV	American Standard Version
BAGD	Bauer, Arndt, Gingrich, and Danker, *Greek-English Lexicon of the New Testament*
BSC	*Bible Student's Commentary*
EBC	*Expositor's Bible Commentary*
EDT	*Evangelical Dictionary of Theology*
EGT	*Expositor's Greek Testament*
HNTC	*Harper's New Testament Commentary*
IB	*Interpreter's Bible*
IBC	*International Bible Commentary*
ICC	*International Critical Commentary*
ISBE	*International Standard Bible Encyclopedia, Revised Edition*
JSNT	*Journal for the Study of the New Testament*
JSOT	*Journal for the Study of the Old Testament*
KJV	King James Version
LCC	*Library of Christian Classics*
LXX	Septuagint (Greek Old Testament)
MNTC	*Moffatt New Testament Commentary*
MT	Masoretic Text
NASB	New American Standard Bible
NCBC	*New Century Bible Commentary*
NEB	New English Bible
NIGTC	*New International Greek Testament Commentary*
NIBC	*New International Bible Commentary*
NICNT	*New International Commentary of the New Testament*
NIDNTT	*New International Dictionary of New Testament Theology*
NIV	New International Version
NPNF	*Nicene and Post-Nicene Christian Fathers*
NRSV	New Revised Standard Version
NTC	*New Testament Commentary*
RSV	Revised Standard Version
TDNT	*Theological Dictionary of the New Testament*
TNTC	*Tyndale New Testament Commentary*
TWOT	*Theological Wordbook of the Old Testament*
WBC	*Word Bible Commentary*

PREFACE

This volume of *Renewal Theology* is divided into two parts: "The Church" and "Last Things."

Part 1 begins with a definition of the church. Then such matters as the scope of the church, various descriptions of the nature of the church, and diverse functions of the church are considered. This leads to a discussion of ministry in the church, the ordinances (or sacraments), and the relation of the church to civil government.

Part 2 begins with a brief study of the kingdom of God and after that focuses on the return of Jesus Christ. From the perspective that the return of Christ is *the* great event yet to occur, such matters as the signs, manner, and purpose of His return are considered next. Finally, after reflection on the millennial question, the book concludes with a study of the final judgment and the consummation in the new heaven and new earth.

Renewal Theology: The Church, the Kingdom, and Last Things is the third in a series of volumes. The first two are subtitled, respectively, *God, the World, and Redemption* and *Salvation, the Holy Spirit, and Christian Living*. This present volume brings to a close a study of the full round of Christian doctrines.

I again extend gratitude to Regent University for helping to make this book possible: to Pat Robertson, Chancellor; David Gyertson, President; George Selig, Provost; and Jerry Horner, Dean of the College of Theology and Ministry. I am particularly grateful to my faculty colleagues Charles Holman, Jon Ruthven, Joseph Umidi, and Owen Weston, and to Herbert Titus, Dean of the College of Law and Government, for reading various portions of the material and offering many helpful suggestions. Mark Wilson has again rendered invaluable service by the initial editing of the book, and Daniel Gilbert, my graduate assistant, has likewise been of much help in checking Scripture and bibliographical data. I am also thankful to the students at Regent University in my course Church and Last Things for their lively input.

I also extend appreciation to Gerard Terpstra of Zondervan Publishing House, who for the third time has done the final editing of *Renewal Theology*.

My gratitude to my wife, Jo, is unlimited. She has put all the material on computer and continued to encourage me over the long process. To her I gladly dedicate this volume.

Part One

THE CHURCH

1

Definition

The word *church*[1] is the usual translation of the Greek word *ekklēsia*.[2] The word *ekklēsia* (plural: *ekklēsiai*) occurs 114 times in the New Testament, and, with four exceptions in the Book of Acts[3] and one in the Book of Hebrews,[4] is translated throughout as "church" (or "churches"). In the Gospels *church* occurs only three times, all in Matthew;[5] nineteen times in Acts; in Paul's letters sixty-two times (most frequently in 1 Corinthians, twenty-two times); in Hebrews, James, and 3 John five times; and in the Book of Revelation twenty times. The word *church* does not occur in Mark, Luke, John, 2 Timothy, Titus, 1 and 2 Peter, 1 and 2 John, and Jude. It is apparent that the word belongs largely to the period following the life and ministry of Jesus.

I. BACKGROUND

A. The Old Testament

In the New Testament there are two places where in reference to the Old Testament the word *ekklēsia* is usually translated "assembly" or "congregation": Acts 7:38[6] and Hebrews 2:12.[7] In the former, Stephen spoke of "the *ekklēsia* in the wilderness," referring

[1]Our English word *church* (also, e.g., Scottish *kirk,* German *Kirche*) is derived from the Greek word *kyriakos*, meaning "belonging to the Lord" (*kyrios*). This Greek word, however, was never applied to the church in the New Testament. The closest approximation is 1 Corinthians 11:20, "the Lord's [*kyriakon*] supper" and Revelation 1:10, "the Lord's [*kyriake*] day." In post-Apostolic times *kyriakos* was applied to the church; *kyriakon* referred to a church building. Even though *kyriakos* does not in the New Testament specifically relate to the church, surely the church does belong to the Lord!

[2]In many Romance languages a direct connection with *ekklēsia* has continued. Note, for example, French *église*, Spanish *iglesia*, Italian *chiesa*. In English we maintain the connection through descriptive terms such as "ecclesiology" and "ecclesiastical."

[3]Acts 7:38; 19:32, 39, 41. I will discuss these passages later.

[4]Hebrews 2:12 (the KJV alone translates it as "church").

[5]Matthew 16:18; 18:17 (twice).

[6]The NIV reads "assembly"; the NEB has the verbal form "assembled"; RSV and NASB have "congregation." The KJV translation "church" is somewhat misleading, since the church as such did not exist in Old Testament times.

[7]The NEB reads "assembly"; RSV, NIV, and NASB have "congregation." The KJV again translates it as "church."

particularly to the occasion at Mount Sinai when Moses received the Ten Commandments. Moses, alluding to that event in Deuteronomy 10:4, spoke of the Ten Commandments as given "out of the midst of the fire on the day of the assembly."[8] Thus the *ekklēsia* was the coming together, the assembling, of the people of Israel. It was the congregation of Israel understood in a dynamic sense as the assembled gathering.[9] Hebrews 2:12 reads: "I will proclaim thy name to my brethren, in the midst of the *ekklēsia* I will praise thee." This is a quotation from Psalm 22:22: "I will tell of Thy name to my brethren; In the midst of the assembly[10] I will praise Thee" (NASB). *Ekklēsia* in both Acts 7:38 and Hebrews 2:12 refers to the active assembly of the people of Israel whether for hearing the law or offering up praise.

B. The Greek State

The word *ekklēsia* was also used in the Greek world of New Testament times to refer to political assembly. The assembly consisted of the citizens of a Greek city. In this connection *ekklēsia*, translated "assembly," occurs three times in Acts 19. The citizens of Ephesus had rushed together to defend their goddess Artemis against the gospel: "Some cried one thing, some another; for the assembly was in confusion" (v. 32). The town clerk finally quieted the crowd, gave some advice, and added, "But if you seek anything further, it shall be settled in the regular[11] assembly" (v. 39). After a few more words, the clerk "dismissed the assembly" (v. 41).

The "assembly," *ekklēsia*, in this incident obviously conveys the note of coming together. The "regular assembly" refers more to official occasions when citizens in a Greek city were called from their usual duties to meet together to act on civic and political affairs.

C. Summary

It is significant that the references in both the Old Testament and Acts 19 to the *ekklēsia* allude to an assemblage of people. The Israelites and the Greeks were called from their regular activities and ordinary responsibilities into assembly. While the *ekklēsia* primarily refers to the ongoing congregation of Israel and to a regular assembly of Greek citizens, there is also the dynamic and active sense of a people called for a particular purpose and activity.

II. THE CHURCH AS "CALLED"

Let us now move on to the predominant use of *ekklēsia* in the New Testament, where the translation is invariably "church." We may properly define the church as "the assembly of the called."

[8]The Hebrew word is *qāhāl*. *Qāhāl* is "especially an assembly for religious purposes" (TWOT, 2:790). See also Deuteronomy 5:22; 9:10; and 18:16 where *qāhāl* is also used for "assembly."

[9]Another Old Testament word, *'e<u>d</u>âh*, is most commonly used to signify the "congregation." This could apply to the people of Israel in all their functions apart from their coming together in assembly. For example, the LORD says to Moses, "Speak to all the congregation of Israel. . ." (Exod. 12:3 NASB). These words simply refer to the people, or community, of Israel and not to any particular gathering or assembly. Incidentally, wherever the Septuagint (LXX) has *ekklēsia* it is invariably a translation of *qāhāl*, not of *'e<u>d</u>âh*.

[10]The Hebrew word is *qāhāl*. The KJV, RSV, and NIV translate it as "congregation"; NEB and NASB, as "assembly." The translation "assembly," I believe, better retains the active note of coming together.

[11]The Greek word is *ennomō*, translated "lawful" in KJV and NASB. The NIV reads "legal"; NEB, "statutory."

A. Called Out

The church consists of those who have been "called out." This is its basic meaning. The word *ekklēsia* is derived from two Greek words, *ek*, "out," and *kaleō*, "call"; hence the church is composed of "called out" people.[12] However—and here is the great difference—the calling is not from ordinary responsibilities but from the dark situation of sin and evil.

In this connection Paul writes the churches (the *ekklēsiai*) of Galatia that Christ "gave Himself for our sins, that He might deliver us out of [*ek*] this present evil age" (1:4 NASB). The church accordingly is composed of those "delivered out," hence "called out" ones. Peter, while not speaking of the church by name, speaks similarly in describing his readers ("God's scattered people"[13] [1 Peter 1:1 NEB]) as "a chosen race, a royal priesthood, a holy nation, God's own people," and then adds that God has "called[14] [them] out of darkness into his marvelous light" (1 Peter 2:9). Thus the church consists of those "called out" of darkness into light. Two other references in Paul's letters are noteworthy. He writes Timothy that God has "saved us and called us with a holy calling"[15] (2 Tim. 1:9). Hence "saved" ones are "called" ones; thus they are the *ek-klēsia*. Paul begins his first Corinthian letter with these words: "Paul . . . to the church of God which is at Corinth, to those who have been sanctified in Christ Jesus, saints by calling"[16] (1 Cor. 1:2 NASB). The church is composed of those "sanctified" in Christ, that is, "saints" through their call from God. To sum up, the church by definition consists of those called out of the world—delivered, saved, sanctified—whatever the terminology. The church is the *ek-klēsia*.

This is apparent likewise from the perspective of the church on the Day of Pentecost. Peter proclaimed to the assembled multitude, "Be saved from this perverse generation!" (Acts 2:40 NASB). His was a call to come out of the perversity and evil of the world: it was a call to salvation. Hence when some three thousand persons that day "received his word were baptized" (v. 41), this signified their salvation. Truly this was the establishment of the church in Jerusalem:[17] a "saved" people. They

[12]According to Thayer, *ekklēsia* is "from ἐκκλητος, called out or forth, and thus from ἐκκαλέω." TDNT raises some question as to whether such etymology was in the mind of New Testament writers when they spoke of *ekklēsia*; however, these words are added: "Εκκλησία is in fact the group of men called out of the world by God even though we do not take express note of the ἐξ" (3:531). I submit that in light of both the Old Testament references and early Greek city-state usage, but most of all because of New Testament appropriateness, *ekklēsia* may be properly understood to mean "called out."

[13]The Greek phrase is *parepidēmois diasporas*, literally "sojourners of the dispersion," referring to believers scattered throughout "Pontus, Galatia, Cappadocia, Asia, and Bithynia," all in Asia Minor (present day Turkey).

[14]The Greek word is *kalesantas*, from *kaleō*.

[15]The Greek word is *klēsei*, a cognate of *kaleō*.

[16]The Greek word is *klētois*, a cognate of *kaleō*. "Saints by calling" is a better translation than "called to be saints" (KJV, RSV) or "called to be holy" (NIV). These translations may suggest that sainthood or holiness is a future calling, something yet to happen. Paul's point, however, is that the church is composed of saints by virtue of their calling.

[17]The word *church* is not used in Acts until some time later (see Acts 5:11). However, there can be no question that the church is referred to in Acts 2. Incidentally, by "establishment" I do not mean the origination of the church. Later, I will discuss an earlier

came out of the past into a new life in Christ.

The church thus is characterized by an event. It consists of those who have actually made the transition from lostness to salvation. Such people are the church—the called-out ones. Clearly if this event of calling out has not occurred, there is no church; the word *church* is evacuated of all meaning. The church in its very being is constituted by an event:[18] the event of salvation.

The important thing to bear in mind is the dynamic character of the church. People who constitute the church have been "called out" from sin and lostness, and as such are the *ek-klēsia*. Again, if this event has not occurred, there is no church, whatever claims a gathering of people might make for themselves. Moreover, individuals may be called "church members," but if they have not been called out, they do not truly belong. The church is the *ekklēsia* of the redeemed.

B. Called Together

In addition, the church is the assemblage of those who are called. Like the Israelites who came together in assembly, so also is the church an assemblage of believers. The church is the gathered community of believers. Paul, in writing to the Corinthians about a certain matter, says, "When you come together as a church. . ."[19] (1 Cor. 11:18 NIV, NASB). The church is the assemblage itself. Paul speaks of "the church of the Thessalonians" (1 Thess. 1:1; 2 Thess. 1:1), which emphasizes that the church is the actual gathering of the believers in Thessalonica. The church obviously is not a building or even a place; it is the assembly of believers wherever they come together.

This does not mean that there is no continuity. The Greek citizens were an *ekklēsia* only when they assembled; after that the *ekklēsia* ceased to exist until the next occasion.[20] There was no *ekklēsia* in the Greek city-state between the called meetings. Unlike this, Paul speaks of the church "at Corinth" (1 Cor. 1:2; see also 2 Cor. 1:1) or "in Corinth" (NIV)[21] and "the church in Cenchrea" (Rom. 16:1 NIV). In Acts there are references to "the church in Jerusalem" (8:1; 11:22) and "the church at Antioch" (13:1), and in the Book of Revelation there are messages to "the church in Ephesus" (2:1) and elsewhere.[22] Thus although the church has the being of an event and is basically an assemblage of believers, there is continuity. The church in Corinth, and elsewhere, has an abiding reality.

Further, the church, while being an assemblage of believers, is more than just a collection of individuals. This was surely true of the Old Testament assemblage: it was a people, a nation, who gathered at Mount Sinai. They met together as a corporate entity. As a people they had been brought out of Egypt, and as a people they gathered on "the day of assembly." Similarly the

---

beginning. My point now is simply that the church in Jerusalem by definition consisted of those who had received and acted on the injunction "Be saved from. . . ."

[18]Karl Barth speaks of the being of the church as "the being of an event" (*Church Dogmatics* 4.1.652; cf. "the church as event" in NIDNTT, 1:298).

Note: Publication data for this and other works cited in this volume may be found in the Bibliography.

[19]Literally, "in church" or "in assembly" (*en ekklēsia*).

[20]Recall the words of Acts 19:41 to the effect that the town clerk "dismissed the assembly."

[21]The Greek preposition is *en*. "In" may be the better translation.

[22]See Revelation 2 and 3 for messages to the other churches—those in Smyrna, Pergamum, Thyatira, Sardis, Philadelphia, and Laodicea.

New Testament depicts the church as a redeemed people. For example, Paul speaks of "the church . . . which He purchased with His own blood" (Acts 20:28 NASB). Thus the New Testament *ekklēsia* is called together as those who have been redeemed by Jesus Christ and are corporately united in Him. In Ephesians Paul addresses the saints as "the faithful in Christ Jesus" (1:1–2 NIV), "in" signifying that the believers were "incorporate in Christ Jesus" (the NEB translation).[23] Thus the church is not only "saved" individuals coming together in assembly; it is also, and more profoundly, a people whom God has redeemed who come together unitedly as His church.

To be more specific, we may observe the situation in Acts on the Day of Pentecost. After Peter's message "Be saved from this perverse generation" had gone forth and people responded in faith and baptism, "there were added that day about three thousand souls" (2:41). The relevant matter is the expression "there were added," "added" referring to the approximately one hundred and twenty believers (see Acts 1:5) to whom they were now joined. The Scripture does not say that as a large group of individuals the new believers added themselves to, or joined themselves to, other believers. Rather, they "were added" to the body of believers by the very fact of salvation. Moreover, it was the Lord's doing, not their own. Later in the Acts narrative, after the addition of the three thousand to the one hundred and twenty, a description is given of the life and activity of the Jerusalem church (2:42–47). This concludes with this statement: "And the Lord added to their number[24] day by day those who were being saved" (v. 47). It was still a matter of the saved being added immediately to the church, but here the emphasis is that it was the Lord's doing.

Hence, salvation is into the body, that is, the already existing community of believers. As a believer, one does not have a solitary life. The *ekklēsia* was, and is, the believer's life from the beginning. Further, salvation means that believers are joined not only to Christ but also to one another. A person is added by the Lord to others on the very occasion of salvation. Thus there is no genuine Christian life outside the church.

C. Called For

The church is called for obedience to Jesus Christ. Israel, as we have noted, was "the assembly"—the *ekklēsia*—before God at Mount Sinai, gathered to hear the law. Also the assembly, after hearing the law, expressed obedience to God by saying, "All the words which the LORD has spoken we will do" (Exod. 24:3, 7; see also 19:8). Israel was called to totally obey the Lord. Likewise—but with even more reason because of the great work of redemption—the New Testament *ekklēsia* is called for total obedience to Jesus Christ.

In his first epistle Peter writes, "To God's elect,[25] strangers in the world,

[23]According to F. F. Bruce, the phrase "in Christ Jesus" is "incorporative—that is to say, it does not point to Christ Jesus as the object of belief but implies that the saints and believers are united with him, *partakers together* of his new life" (italics mine) (*Epistles to the Colossians, to Philemon, and to the Ephesians*, NICNT, 251).

[24]The KJV reads "added to the church." Although the word church has little manuscript evidence (on this see Bruce, *The Acts of the Apostles*, 102), the KJV correctly understands the thrust of the text, namely that the addition was to "the church."

[25]The Greek word is *eklektois*, God's "chosen." Without using the word *church* Peter

scattered throughout Pontus, Galatia, Cappadocia, Asia, and Bithynia . . . chosen according to the foreknowledge of God the Father, through the sanctifying work of the Spirit, for obedience to Jesus Christ and sprinkling by his blood" (1:1 NIV). "For obedience to Jesus Christ" is the calling of the elect of God, the church. Paul writes the Romans, "We have received grace and apostleship to bring about the obedience of faith for the sake of his [Christ's] name among all the nations, including yourselves who are called[26] to belong to Jesus Christ"[27] (1:5–6). Those in Rome[28] were called, along with all nations, to faithful obedience to Jesus Christ. Also, Paul's opening words to the Corinthians are relevant: "To the church of God which is at Corinth . . . saints by calling, with all who in every place call upon[29] the name of our Lord Jesus Christ, their Lord and ours" (1 Cor. 1:2 NASB). The church consists of those who call on the name of Jesus Christ as Lord wherever people are. This means the acknowledgment of His lordship and obedience to His name and purpose.

Here let us step back and observe that in the first recorded words of Jesus about the church He refers to it as His church: "I will build my church" (Matt. 16:18). Thus the church belongs to Him; He is its Builder, and to Him total obedience is due. This is all the more apparent from the fact that the church was later purchased by the blood of Christ. Paul speaks in Ephesians about how Christ "loved the church and gave himself up for her" (5:25). Christ is both Builder and Savior of the church: He is indeed its Lord. As we have previously observed, it was also the Lord who added to the church daily those who were being saved. Thus He continues to add to, hence, to build, His church. It is His church, and He is therefore Lord of it.

Again, this means obedience. The church exists to carry forward the will and work of Jesus Christ. The church is His representation on earth. At every moment in the church's life the one critical factor is total obedience to whatever He has commanded[30] and will command. Truly the church is called to give total obedience to Jesus Christ. He alone is Lord of the church.

III. THE DUAL ASPECT

It is apparent that the church has a dual aspect: it is both a spiritual and a social reality.

---

views "the elect" corporately (recall 1 Peter 2:9—"You are a chosen race, a royal priesthood, a holy nation . . . called . . . out of darkness"). Thus they are the *ekklēsia*.

[26]The Greek word is *klētoi*. Recall the connection with *ek-klēsia*.

[27]The KJV and NASB read "the called of Jesus Christ." The Greek phrase is *klētoi Iēsou Christou*; hence those readings are quite possible. However, the RSV reading above (likewise NIV) more likely captures Paul's meaning. Paul uniformly speaks of God the Father as author of the call (cf. Rom. 8:30; 11:29; 1 Cor. 1:9; 2 Tim. 1:9). Thus John Murray writes, "They are the called of Jesus Christ in the sense of belonging to Christ" (*Epistle to the Romans*, NICNT, 14).

[28]Paul does not use "church" in these opening verses. Rather, after the words quoted above, he writes, "to all God's beloved in Rome" (v. 7). However, it is surely the church that Paul is addressing (note also Rom. 16:16: "All the churches of Christ greet you"—obviously a greeting to the sister church in Rome).

[29]The Greek word is *epikaloumenos*, literally "calling upon."

[30]In the Great Commission to the apostles, and thereby the believing church, Jesus declared that this included "teaching them [the nations] to observe" all that He had "commanded" the disciples (Matt. 28:20). This implies that the church, prior to such teaching, was already committed to obeying Christ's every commandment.

A. Spiritual

The church is composed of persons whose common basis for existence is spiritual. Paul declares that "our citizenship[31] is in heaven" (Phil. 3:20 NIV, NASB). The church has been called out of the world—out of darkness into light. To use the language of Jesus in John 3, the church consists of those who have been "born anew" (vv. 3, 7), or "from above,"[32] and are like the wind that cannot be seen. Like the wind, this spiritual reality is invisible, but it can be sensed and felt. People "called out" may even look like everybody else, but there is an unseen, spiritual depth. The church is "from above"; its origins lie in God and its essential life in a realm not open to observation.

Indeed, the church is the only body on earth that has its roots beyond the earth, and thus is sure to be victorious. Even, Jesus declared, "The gates of hell shall not prevail against it" (Matt. 16:18 KJV). The church has its spiritual being from beyond itself: it is "the *ekklēsia* of God."[33] In essence it is an invisible, spiritual reality.

It is important to emphasize the spiritual essence of the church. Often people who constitute the church fail to bear in mind its divine origins. They view the church as just another human organization—one among many—that serves a valuable moral and social purpose, but it is little more. What is spiritually invisible, the church rooted in God, is totally unknown to them, and great is the loss.[34] Surely many Christians need to recapture the eternal significance of the church as a supernatural entity on earth that has come down "from above."

B. Social

The church is also a social reality. It is the assembly of those on earth who belong to the Lord; hence it has an empirical social dimension. This was true of the assembly of Israel in the wilderness and of the Greek citizens who came together for civic duties, and it is likewise true of the Christian church. The church exists on earth as one social entity among many others. Significantly Jesus, who had referred to the spiritual dimensions of reality in His statement "I will build my church; and the gates of hell shall not prevail against it" (Matt. 16:18, KJV), says later in regard to a rather mundane matter, "Tell it to the church" (Matt. 18:17). The church, while from above, exists on earth and definitely has a visible shape and form.[35] "Tell it to the

[31]The Greek word is *politeuma*. In its article on *πολίτευμα*, BAGD quotes M. Dibelius as saying, "Our home is in heaven, and here on earth we are a colony of heavenly citizens."

[32]The RSV and NIV margins.

[33]"The church of God" is a frequent New Testament expression. See 1 Corinthians 1:2; 10:32; 11:22; 2 Corinthians 1:1; Galatians 1:13; 1 Timothy 3:5, 15 ("church of the living God"). Also note "the churches of God" in 1 Corinthians 11:16 and 2 Thessalonians 1:4; "the church of God in Christ Jesus" in 1 Thessalonians 2:14.

[34]C. S. Lewis in his *Screwtape Letters* depicts the senior devil Screwtape writing his nephew Wormwood, a junior devil. At one point Screwtape says, "One of our greatest allies at present is the Church itself. Do not misunderstand me. I do not mean the Church as we see her spread out through all time and space and rooted in eternity, terrible as an army with banners. That, I confess, is a spectacle which makes our boldest tempters uneasy. But fortunately it is quite invisible to these humans" (p. 15).

[35]In this way there is some parallel to the Incarnation. Christ, while having a divine, even invisible, nature, was also a human being with a visible, tangible body and lived in a specific place. To deny His humanity was the heresy called Docetism (see "Real Man" in *Renewal Theology*, 1:332–34). Accordingly, to overlook or downplay the church's tangible social reality would be a kind of ecclesiastical Docetism.

church" means to tell it to a tangible body of believers existing in a specific place.

The church as a social entity is the concrete expression of the church in its spiritual depth. Accordingly, it includes only believers—those called out of the world. It is true, however, that again and again the institutional church[36] will have unbelievers in its midst. Some who are attached to the church profess faith in Christ but are not truly "called." In this connection Jesus' parable about the good seed and tares (or weeds) is quite relevant. He speaks of sowing "good seed" of wheat, which "means sons of the kingdom" (those who receive the word and truly believe), but along with this the enemy, the devil, sows tares—"the weeds are the sons of the evil one" (Matt. 13:24–30; 36–43). The true church accordingly will often have evil in its midst, namely, unbelievers. However, they are by no means a genuine part of the church: they still belong to the enemy, the evil one. The visible church may include such persons, but they are not truly the assembly of the "called out" ones.

We may ask, "Then what is to be done about unbelievers attached to the *ekklēsia*?" For by their very presence unbelievers bring an alien element into the church as a social entity. Should the true believers seek to have them removed? The answer is no.[37] In the same parable of the wheat and the weeds Jesus speaks against trying to get rid of the tares: "No . . . because while you are pulling the weeds, you may root up the wheat with them. Let both grow together until the harvest [the end of the age]" (Matt. 13:29–30 NIV). There is such an intertwining of weeds with wheat, such an admixture of the "sons of the evil one" with the "sons of the kingdom," that only the Lord Himself can some day accomplish the task. Jesus' words also imply that, because of the admixture, true believers may not always be able to discern clearly between wheat and weeds. To attempt this separation could do more harm than good. "The Lord knows those who are his" (2 Tim. 2:19). That is sufficient for now.

Thus it is a serious mistake for believers to withdraw from a given church in an effort to create or find a perfect church. The enemy will always infiltrate ("sow tares," which is his business) the purest church on earth. Hence the proper attitude is to recognize this fact and seek to move ahead under the lordship of Christ.

Now to return to the main point: the *ekklēsia* is both a spiritual and a social entity. It has an invisible, transcendent spiritual aspect; it also has a social and empirical dimension. On the one hand, it originates in God and is from above; on the other, it exists on earth as a visible assemblage of believers. Indeed, in the latter sense the church is a human institution not unlike many other social institutions. From this perspective the church is an organization with authorities and forms, certain practices and activities, and various cultural and linguistic expressions. It is, from the human side, one social entity among many and is subject to social analysis. However—and this must not be forgotten—the basis and source of the *ekklēsia*, its lifeline of vitality and direction, does not stem from anything of earth. The

---

[36]By "institutional church" I refer to the church of professing members, whether or not they are true believers.

[37]This is a different matter from the exercise of church discipline. The "sons of the kingdom," true believers, may often need discipline even to temporary exclusion from the church (see the sec. "Exercising Discipline," pp. 120–23). Such discipline is not the same as the attempted removal of unbelievers.

church is ultimately the church of the living God.

EXCURSUS: THE CHURCH AS "INVISIBLE" AND AS "VISIBLE"

Since Reformation times there has often been a distinction made between the "invisible" church and the "visible" church. For example, John Calvin declares that "the Scriptures speak of the Church in two ways . . . the Church as it really is before God—the Church into which none are admitted but those who by the gift of adoption are sons of God, and by the sanctification of the Spirit true members of Christ." Again, "by the name of Church is designated the whole body of mankind scattered throughout the world, who profess to worship one God and Christ. . . . In this Church there is a very large mixture of hypocrites, who have nothing of Christ but the name and outward appearance."[38] The former is the invisible, the latter the visible church.[39]

The basic problem with this distinction is that it is foreign to the Scriptures. As we have noted, there are invisible and visible dimensions of the church. But these dimensions refer to the church—the *ekklēsia*—in both its invisible spiritual and its visible social reality. The invisible and the visible church are one and the same viewed in dual aspect. As we have observed, the church may indeed have an admixture of alien with good elements; but it is unwarranted to designate such as the visible church in distinction from the invisible church. The believing church itself as both invisible and visible has this admixture within it. The Scriptures do not depict a church invisible "into which none are admitted but the sons of God" and a church visible with a "very large mixture of hypocrites." One danger in this distinction is that it may mislead people to forego membership in the visible church because they think of themselves as participants only in the pure, invisible church. Calvin did not, I hasten to say, counsel such, for he adds that "we are also enjoined to regard this Church which is so called with reference to man [the visible church], and to cultivate its communion."[40] Surely Calvin is correct in saying that we are to cultivate communion with the church regardless of its admixture of evil. The mistake lies in the separation between the invisible church as composed only of true believers and the visible church as the church in which evil dwells. There is the real danger, despite Calvin's admonition, of viewing the invisible church as the true believer's home and of giving up on the visible church as a sordid mixture of believers and hypocrites.

The one and only church undoubtedly has both invisible and visible dimensions. There is the invisible dimension of not belonging to the world: the church is *ekklēsia*— "called out." There is also the visible dimension of being totally in the world and sharing fully in it as a social entity. It is important to maintain this distinction that the one church of Jesus Christ as such is both invisible and visible. This recognition enables us to participate in the one church on earth with full devotion.

---

[38]*Institutes of the Christian Religion*, 4.7.288 (Beveridge trans.).
[39]See context in the *Institutes*.
[40]Ibid., 4.7.288.

2

Scope

We turn next to a consideration of the scope of the church. Our concern is with such matters as the extent and range of operation of the church. Where is the church to be found?

I. UNIVERSAL

The church may first be viewed as *universal*. Its scope is not limited to any one place: it is worldwide. Although there is much to be said about the church as local[1] and particular, we need first to view the church in its universal expression.

Surely the best place to begin is with Jesus' statement "I will build my church" (Matt. 16:18). In these words Jesus was not referring to a particular church, but to the universal church: it is not "my churches" but "my church." This is the universal church of Jesus Christ.

Paul refers to the universal church in his address to the elders from Ephesus when he speaks of "the church of God which he obtained with the blood of his own Son" (Acts 20:28). This is not simply the Ephesian church but the whole church of Christ. In his Ephesian letter Paul again speaks of the universal church. Although this letter may begin with Paul's salutation "to the saints who are at Ephesus"[2] (1:1 NASB), hence referring to a particular church, reference throughout is to the church universal. God "has made him [Christ] the head over all things for the church" (1:22); "that through the church the manifold wisdom of God might now be made known" (3:10); "to him [God] be glory in the church and in Christ Jesus to all generations" (3:21); "Christ loved the church and gave himself up for her, that he might sanctify her . . . that he

---

[1]See the next section.

[2]I say "may begin" because a number of early Greek manuscripts do not contain "at Ephesus." "Ephesus," however, is included in KJV, NIV, NASB, and NEB. F. F. Bruce states that "the weight of documentary evidence indicates that the phrase 'at Ephesus' is not part of the original wording" (*Epistle to the Colossians, Philemon, and the Ephesians*, NICNT, 249–50). Bruce suggests that a space may have been left in the original letter to be filled in for each church to which it was sent, e.g., "at Philippi," "at Laodicea," etc. This idea of a circular letter may be appropriate in light of the fact that no references are made in the letter to persons in Ephesus or in any other particular church. (For a fuller discussion of this whole matter see EGT, 3:227–33.)

might present the church to himself in splendor" (5:25–27). Paul may indeed be writing to a local church, but the central theme is the universal church. Similarly Paul writes the church at Colossae that "he [Christ] is the head of the body, the church" (Col. 1:18) and later speaks of "his body, that is, the church" (v. 24). These again are references to the church universal. Likewise we note Paul's statement in 1 Corinthians that "God has appointed in the church first apostles, second prophets, third teachers. . ." (12:28). This clearly goes beyond the Corinthian church into the universal church. Finally, in the Book of Revelation some of the closing words are "The Spirit and the Bride say, 'Come'" (22:17). "The Bride" undoubtedly refers to the universal church who, along with the Spirit, extends the invitation.

We now focus on various attributes of the universal church. Let us examine four of these.[3]

A. Oneness

The church is essentially one. As surely as God is one and Christ is one, the church is one. It is "*the* church of God," "*the* church of Christ," hence one church. Shortly after speaking of "glory in the church and in Christ Jesus" (3:21), Paul in his letter to the Ephesians declares, "There is one body and one Spirit . . . one Lord, one faith, one baptism, one God and Father of us all" (4:4–6). The "one body" specifically refers to the church. Indeed, such images of the church as "the body of Christ" and "the bride of Christ"[4] declare the oneness of the church. For certainly Christ as the head has but one body, even as the bridegroom has but one bride.

According to the Fourth Gospel, Jesus speaks of "one flock." He declares, "I am the good shepherd . . . I lay down my life for the sheep. And I have other sheep, that are not of this fold; I must bring them also. . . . So there shall be one flock, one shepherd" (10:14–16). "The sheep" doubtless were those around Him—His Jewish disciples; "other sheep . . . not of this fold" refers to the Gentiles. All together, Jesus was saying, Jews and Gentiles will compose one great flock under Him, the one Shepherd. Although Jesus does not use the word *church*, His language implies it.[5] There will be one flock, not two or more, however many folds there may be or however far scattered the sheep. Clearly the "one flock" parallels the Pauline images of one body and one bride.

Next we observe that there are, of course, a multiplicity of churches. In addition to the singular "church," Paul refers to "the churches of God" (1 Cor. 11:16; 2 Thess. 1:4), "the churches of God in Christ" (1 Thess. 2:14), and "the churches of Christ" (Rom. 16:16). Such language points to geographical diversity: Corinth, Thessalonica, Rome, etc. The point, however, is that all such churches are expressions of the one church. They are the one church of God, of Christ, assembled in a given place. Thus it is, for example, "the church of God which is at [or in] Corinth"; it is the same

[3]The four attributes (sometimes called "notes") to be discussed follow the pattern of the Creed of Nicea-Constantinople (popularly known as the Nicene Creed, A.D. 381). In this creed is the affirmation "We believe . . . in one, holy, catholic, and apostolic Church" (see, e.g., John Leith, *Creeds of the Churches*, 33). The Nicene Creed is generally accepted throughout Christendom as representing the orthodox Christian faith.

[4]See "The Body of Christ" and "The Bride of Christ," pages 65–77.

[5]Compare Paul's words about "the mystery" now "revealed to his [Christ's] holy apostles and prophets by the Spirit . . . [that] the Gentiles are fellow heirs, members of the same body" (Eph. 3:4–6).

church that meets in a great diversity of places.

Simply put, wherever people who have been "called out" assemble, this is the *ekklēsia*. They make up the one church that belongs to Jesus Christ. They may be, and are, from countless nations, languages, and cultures. But they still represent the one church of God in Jesus Christ. Accordingly, there is a oneness of believers around the world.

This given fact of oneness, however, is often threatened by division. What is essential unity may become disunity. In his epistle to the Ephesians, just prior to his words about one body, one Spirit, one Lord, etc., Paul encourages his readers to be "eager to maintain the unity of the Spirit in the bond of peace" (4:3). There is a given unity of the Holy Spirit that may be threatened. This threat sometimes exists in the local church. Nowhere in the New Testament is this more strikingly depicted than at Corinth, for the unity there was severely threatened by growing factionalism. Some were saying, "I belong to Paul"; some, "I belong to Apollos"; some, "I belong to Cephas [Peter]"; some, "I belong to Christ"[6] (1 Cor. 1:12). Thus the given unity was threatened by disunity, possibly even to the splitting apart of the church. Paul cries out in vigorous protest, "Is Christ divided? Was Paul crucified for you? Or were you baptized in the name of Paul?" (v. 13). Paul's point is unmistakable: If the Corinthians would only recall that Christ, and no one else, was crucified for them, and that they in faith were baptized in the name of Jesus, and no one else—indeed, that *they all* belong to Christ,[7] and no one else, then dissension and division would quickly end. As far as we know, this party spirit at Corinth was kept in check, perhaps overcome, and the church maintained its unity in Christ.

The tragedy is that often this has not been the case. Many a church has allowed party spirit, dissension, and rivalries to split it apart. Christ has thereby been divided and His cause severely damaged. To be sure, if it is for the purpose of multiplication, division is good—as in the case of cell division, in which true growth occurs. Indeed, congregations often become too large and need to divide into smaller bodies. But splitting, or schism, is an entirely different thing and can only cause harm to the cause of Christ. The oneness, the unity, of the church is broken. To any church threatened by the specter of division—even for seemingly justifiable causes—Paul's further words should ring in the ears of all: "I . . . entreat you to walk in a manner worthy of the calling[8] with which you have been called,[9] with all humility and gentleness, with patience, showing forbearance to one another in love, being diligent to preserve the unity of the Spirit in the bond of peace" (Eph. 4:1–3 NASB). Knowing that we are an *ekklēsia*, people "called out," there should be a spirit of gentleness, patience, love, and forbearance (yes, in even the "stickiest" of matters!), all of which should make for an eagerness and a diligence to preserve unity.

Let us now go behind Paul and his great words in Ephesians to the words of Christ Himself in the Gospel of John concerning oneness and unity. We have

---

[6]Literally, in each case "I am of Paul, . . . I of Apollos," etc.

[7]The party that said, "I belong to Christ," in this context is apparently a faction also. "I belong to Christ" would seem to be what all should be saying; however, here there is a touch of superiority in these words. I am reminded by this of some denominations that lay claim to the name "Christian"—we are "*the* Christian Church," "*the* Church of Christ," etc.

[8]The Greek word is *kleseōs*, from *kaleō*, hence referring to the calling to salvation.

[9]The Greek word is *eklēthete*, likewise from *kaleō*.

already noted Jesus' statement "so shall there be one flock, one shepherd." Later He prayed to the Father both for His disciples and for believers after them "that they may all be one; even as thou, Father, art in me, and I in thee, that they also may be in us. . . . The glory which thou hast given me I have given to them, that they may be one even as we are one, I in them and thou in me, that they may become perfectly one, so that the world may know that thou hast sent me and hast loved them even as thou hast loved me" (John 17:21–23). Oneness is essentially a given fact for all who are in Christ, but it is also something that continually needs perfecting. That believers have allowed disunity and separation to intrude is both a denial of their oneness with Christ and the Father and a resulting barrier to the world's coming to faith.

But now something else must be said. There is one legitimate reason for separation, namely the situation of unbelief or apostasy. If a so-called church is merely a gathering of unbelievers—those who have not been "called out," hence know nothing of salvation—it is a church in name only. Paul writes to the Gentiles in the church at Rome: "You stand fast only through faith. . . . If God did not spare the natural branches [the Jews], neither will he spare you. . . . You too will be cut off" (Rom. 11:20–22).[10] In the extreme situation of such disbelief, indeed apostasy, there remains no church.[11] Separation truly is necessary.

Caution is needed here. It is far too easy to allow differences such as minor doctrinal matters, liturgical practices, and social orientations to bring about separation. The one fundamental matter is that the church is an *ekklēsia*—it is "called out." If this has not happened, the most orthodox theology, the most impressive forms of worship, the most noteworthy ethical activities are in vain. *They are all operating in a void.* Wherever there is an assemblage of called out—that is, saved—persons, the church exists, and nowhere else.

Let us recall the formation of the Jerusalem church on the Day of Pentecost. After Peter had proclaimed the gospel with such power that thousands were "cut to the heart" (Acts 2:37), he then urged his hearers, "Repent, and be baptized . . . for the forgiveness of your sins" (v. 38). He continued shortly after with the exhortation, "Be saved from this perverse generation!" (v. 40 NASB). As a result, "those who received his word were baptized, and there were added that day about three thousand souls" (v. 41). Thus the church in Jerusalem came into being. They had been told enough about God's act in Jesus—His death and resurrection—to bring about conviction, repentance, and faith. Thus they were "called" to salvation. It was only after this event that the Scripture adds, "And they devoted themselves to the apostles' teaching [or 'doctrine']" (v. 42). They would need much teaching to clarify their thinking, which until then had been traditionally Judaistic. But prior to any such teaching, the three thousand had already become a part of the *ekklēsia*.[12] This matter needs emphasis, for it demonstrates that what constitutes the church

[10]The pronoun "you" is in the singular throughout these verses. However, Paul is not addressing a particular person but the Gentiles collectively ("Now I am speaking to you Gentiles" [v. 13]).

[11]According to the Westminster Confession, "the purest churches under heaven are subject both to mixture and error; and some have so degenerated as to become no churches of Christ, but synagogues of Satan" (15.1).

[12]I say "a part" because they were "added" to the others (the one hundred and twenty at Pentecost); thus the *ekklēsia* was already in existence.

is the event of salvation and not a fully formed theology. They were now united in Christ, whatever else may have been their differences. Increased doctrinal formulation was important, but it was secondary to the primary event of salvation by which they had become an *ekklēsia*.

Nothing I have said is intended to denigrate the importance of doctrine. Clearly, essential doctrine is involved in proclaiming the gospel—namely, what God has done in Jesus Christ and how to receive His work of redemption. But there still is no *ekklēsia* until people respond in faith. Thus the most orthodox theology will not suffice. Indeed, there is always the danger of an orthodoxy that tends to substitute doctrine for salvation. For example, the Athanasian Creed[13] declares, "Whosoever will be saved: before all things it is necessary that he hold the Catholic faith . . . and the Catholic faith is this: that we worship one God in Trinity and Trinity in Unity, neither confounding the Persons nor dividing the substance." Finally, after many further, still more technical statements, the Creed continues, "He therefore who would be saved must think thus of the Trinity." If this were really the case, nobody would have been saved on the Day of Pentecost! To be sure, the Triune God was at work in the whole event. But orthodox formulation of the doctrine was by no means yet at hand.

Now let us return to the main point: that the church is one. This is primarily to be understood as a spiritual oneness. The church as represented by true believers—the genuine *ekklēsia*—is one throughout the world. There are many differences in doctrinal formulation, worship practices, organizational forms, and the like, but the church is still one. Oneness is *not uniformity*, but it is unity in the one Lord who has redeemed His people. This oneness, this unity, is there even if many institutional churches have split apart and have little or no fellowship with one another. The one church continues to exist in and through many denominational expressions, for wherever "called out" persons are gathered, there is the church.

I quickly add, however, that this spiritual oneness needs more and more to take on visible expression. The church, as earlier noted, has an empirical, social dimension and therefore needs to express its spiritual unity by a common recognition that every true *ekklēsia* is a part of the one church of Jesus Christ.

This means, first, an openness and harmony of believers with one another in all churches and denominations. Recognizing the oneness of the *ekklēsia* throughout the world, believers should be ready to share in worship, in fellowship, and in ministry. If separate denominations continue to exist, it should be clear to all their members and to the outside world that the church is in unity.

Second, this also means an increasing emphasis on the need for visible unity in the church and among churches everywhere. If it is true that there is only one church of Jesus Christ throughout the world (as I have earlier stressed), that the church universal is His one body—in that sense organically united to Him—then the church needs likewise to be in visible and outward unity wherever it exists. When Jesus prayed for future believers that they would "all be one," He meant surely not only spiritual but also visible and tangible unity. For, as noted, Jesus immediately added, "Even as thou, Father, art in me, and I in thee." Out of

---

[13]One of the three creeds (the other two are the Apostles' and the Nicene) widely used in Western Christendom to express the orthodox faith. The date of the creed is uncertain.

this unity of being should flow a like unity in the universal *ekklēsia*.

The church is one universal *ekklēsia*, and the more we express that oneness, the more we are at harmony with Christ and with one another, and the stronger our witness becomes to the world. For it is only as we become "perfectly one" that the world is fully able to believe.

B. Holiness

The second attribute of the church is holiness. Peter addresses "God's scattered people"[14] in Asia Minor, declaring them to be "a chosen race, a royal priesthood, a holy nation" (1 Peter 2:9). In language borrowed from Exodus about Israel—"you shall be to me a kingdom of priests and a holy nation" (19:6)[15]—Peter refers to the dispersed believers collectively. They are "a royal priesthood, a holy nation." Since such believers are the church, the church is a holy nation, a holy people.

The church is holy, first, because it is separated from the world. The word *holy* in the Old Testament,[16] implies separation, apartness. Israel as a nation was separated from all other nations. So the church, the *ekklēsia*, has been called out, separated from the surrounding world. Jesus spoke to His Father of the apostles as men whom the Father had given Him "out of the world" (John 17:6); by implication this includes later believers, hence the church.

The church essentially is holy in that a distinct separation has occurred. The "holy nation" is composed of people who, in Peter's continuing words, have been "called . . . out of darkness into his marvelous light." Thus they have been separated from the realm of darkness into the realm of light and are therefore "a holy nation."

The church may also be described as a sanctified people. Indeed, Peter begins his letter by addressing the believers of the Dispersion as those "chosen and destined by God the Father and sanctified by the Spirit" (1 Peter 1:2). "Sanctified by the Spirit," they are "a holy nation." Similarly Paul addresses "the church of God which is at Corinth" as "those sanctified in Christ Jesus" (1 Cor. 1:2). This, of course, does not mean that the church was without sin, for the Corinthian church in particular was laden with immorality. Nonetheless, the church was God's church, and the people, whatever their sinful activities, had basically been separated from the world to be a holy people. Thus Paul later adds, "You were washed, you were sanctified" (6:11). It is this basic sanctification, this separation from the world, that made all the more reprehensible their many sinful activities.

The separation of the church is a profoundly spiritual matter. In the Old Testament Israel was separated from other nations in a geographical, political, and cultural sense; however, there was no radical spiritual separation. There were, to be sure, God's given laws and ordinances, the sacrificial ceremonies, and the continuing call to holiness; but no interior change occurred. In the New Testament the church is a people no longer separated from other nations physically, but spiritually—namely, from the principalities and powers of darkness that dominate this world. The church undoubtedly is a long way from perfection; nonetheless, there has been a break, even a transition, from the old order to the new. The church is a holy nation.

Second, the church is holy because of the holiness of her Head, Jesus Christ.

[14]Recall the NEB translation in 1 Peter 1:1.
[15]See also Deuteronomy 7:6; 14:2.
[16]*Qāḏôš*. See *Renewal Theology*, 2:83, n.2 for more detail.

Through faith in Him believers have become united to Christ and are therefore partakers of His holiness. In this vein Paul further writes to the church in Corinth: "You are in Christ Jesus, who has become for us wisdom from God—that is, our righteousness, holiness,[17] and redemption" (1 Cor. 1:30 NIV). Christ is "our holiness." Surely we have been sanctified by Him,[18] but, even more, the Christ with whom we are united continues to impart His holiness, even as the head through all the body.

One of Paul's most extraordinary statements about Christ's headship over the church is found in these words: "[God] has made him the head over all things for the church, which is his body, the fullness of him who fills all in all" (Eph. 1:22–23 NRSV). Since Christ is truly "the Holy One,"[19] His holiness is shown forth in the church, which is His fullness on earth. This means, further, that however important the holiness of individual believers is,[20] it is only the church, the collective body of Christians that can reflect the fullness of Christ's holiness. The church is "the fullness" of her head, Jesus Christ.

Hence, for example, when the church comes together for worship, it does so as a holy people. Its purpose is to worship the Lord "in holy array" (Ps. 29:2). It is to allow His holiness to cleanse the sins and evils that have accumulated, perchance to hear the words, "your guilt is taken away, and your sin forgiven" (Isa. 6:7).[21] It is to go forth as a people renewed in holiness to fulfill the Master's will and to live out His holiness.

Here let me give a word of caution: the holiness of the church does not mean a kind of material holiness that relates to a building or to certain objects. The church is not a building and surely not any of the objects it contains; it is therefore a serious mistake to view a church edifice as a holy place or to speak of holy vestments, holy water, and holy beads. *The church is not where believers meet, but the meeting of believers itself.* Hence holiness cannot attach itself to anything material, indeed not even to certain designated persons. Ordination, for example, confers no holiness upon any church functionary—be he priest or pastor. No individual, properly speaking, is either a "holy" or "reverend" person.[22] The church itself as a body under the sole headship of Jesus Christ is a holy people.

This also means that the whole body of believers is holy; there are no levels of sainthood. We have earlier noted Paul's address to the Corinthians as "those sanctified in Christ Jesus, saints by calling" (1 Cor. 1:2 NASB). The whole church (even in Corinth!) by virtue of its call to salvation was composed of "saints" and holy people. Sainthood therefore is not a higher level

---

[17]The KJV, RSV, and NASB read "sanctification." The Greek word *hagiasmos* can be translated either way.

[18]Recall 1 Corinthians 1:2.

[19]Recall Peter's words: "You are the Holy One of God" (John 6:69).

[20]See *Renewal Theology*, 2:83–117 (chap. 4, "Sanctification"), for a discussion of this matter.

[21]These words were spoken to Isaiah the prophet against the background of the mighty seraphim crying forth, "Holy, holy, holy is the LORD of hosts; the whole earth is full of his glory" (v. 3).

[22]Psalm 111:9 in the KJV reads: "holy and reverend is his name." This, of course, refers to God, not to any man.

of Christian attainment or recognition;[23] for all of God's people are holy ones. To be sure, there should be growth in saintliness, but there are none who are uniquely saints. The church—not just a higher echelon or a selected few—is holy.

Now, saying that the church is holy does not deny that the church is also called to holiness. Holiness—even sainthood—is a given fact, but there needs to be continuing sanctification and purging. Here the words of Paul in Ephesians are quite relevant: First, "Christ loved the church and gave himself up for her, to make her holy, cleansing her by the washing with water through the word." This is the basic sanctification, or being made holy. Second, Paul adds, "and to present her to himself as a radiant church, without stain or wrinkle or any other blemish, but holy and blameless" (5:25–27 NIV). This is the holiness—not a higher level of sainthood—that Christ intends for His church.

Accordingly, the church can never rest in its essential holiness. Indeed, far too often the church falls into the way of the world and needs deep repentance and change. Surely the church, "the saints" of Corinth, needed it so much that large sections of Paul's first letter are devoted to admonition and to a call for repentance. Likewise, the church in our own day—leaders and people alike—often needs serious examination of its worldly ways and pursuits so as to represent more truly the holiness of her Head, Jesus Christ. The church is holy—and ever called to holiness.

Third, the church is holy because of the indwelling Holy Spirit. Here the words of Paul are to the point: "Do you not know that you are God's temple[24] and that God's Spirit dwells in you? If any one destroys God's temple, God will destroy him. For God's temple is holy, and that temple you are" (1 Cor. 3:16–17). In this context, Paul is speaking of the church,[25] not the individual,[26] though it is true that the Holy Spirit also dwells in each believer.[27] The Holy Spirit, the Spirit of God Himself, makes His dwelling in the church. In the Old Testament God's particular dwelling was the inner shrine, the Holy of Holies, of the tabernacle and later of the temple. Now both have been replaced by the church as God's dwelling place. The church therefore is essentially holy because the Spirit of God dwells within it. The significance of this is so vast that

[23]As, for example, in the Roman Catholic Church, where sainthood belongs only to certain departed ones who are elevated by the church to a higher level through a process of beatification and canonization (see article "Canonization" in EDT). See also *Renewal Theology*, 2:83. n.20.

[24]The Greek word translated "temple" is *naos*, meaning "shrine"—the inmost sanctuary or Holy of Holies, of the Old Testament temple. Another Greek word, *hieron*, refers to the temple, including all its precincts. Hence, although "temple" is the usual translation for *naos*, the idea of God's shrine or Holy of Holies should be kept in mind.

[25]Earlier in this chapter Paul writes to the Corinthians: "You are God's field, God's building" (v. 9). Verses 16–18 follow immediately after the description of the church as God's building (vv. 10–15).

[26]In 1 Corinthians 6:19–20 Paul does speak of the individual when he writes, "Do you not know that your body is a temple of the Holy Spirit within you, which you have from God? . . . Glorify God in your body." Here the context of Paul's statement deals with personal, sexual immorality (see v. 18).

[27]This is the basic fact of the believer's life. So Paul writes in Romans: "You are not in the flesh, you are in the Spirit, if in fact the Spirit of God really dwells in you. Any one who does not have the Spirit of Christ does not belong to him" (8:9).

if anyone destroys[28] God's temple (i.e., the church), God in turn will destroy[29] him. This shows the truly awesome nature of the church as the dwelling place of the Holy Spirit: he who destroys[30] the church will himself be destroyed.[31] The church, whatever its flaws, is sacred and holy because God's Spirit dwells within it.

The church as the dwelling place of God's Spirit is also described by Paul in Ephesians 2. There Paul speaks of the church as "the household of God, built upon the foundation of the apostles and prophets, Christ Jesus himself being the cornerstone, in whom the whole structure is joined together and grows into a holy temple in the Lord; in whom you also are built into it for a dwelling place of God in the Spirit" (vv. 19–22). The household of God consists not only of believing Jews but also of believing Gentiles ("you also"). And in Christ Jesus the comprehensive church is God's holy temple, God's holy dwelling place. In earlier times the temple was viewed as peculiarly a structure for Israel, the Gentiles having access only to the outer courts. But now in Christ Jesus all has changed: the temple is no longer an earthly building whose inner shrine, the place of God's dwelling, is limited to the Jews. It has now become a spiritual temple in which both Jews and Gentiles are built together for God's habitation in the Holy Spirit. The church, not limited to any race or people, is now the unique place of God's holy dwelling.

In regard to this last point, the church is holy, not because its members have reached an exalted level of holiness and righteousness; rather, Jews and Gentiles alike are growing "into" a holy temple and thereby, as being built into it, are God's holy dwelling. The church is holy because the holy God makes it His holy dwelling place.

We move on to observe that Peter, like Paul, depicts the church as a holy edifice. Peter speaks of it as "a spiritual house." He describes Christ first as "a living stone" and then adds, "You also, as living stones, are being built up as a spiritual house for a holy priesthood, to offer up spiritual sacrifices acceptable to God through Jesus Christ" (1 Peter 2:4–5 NASB). Shortly after that Peter declares, "You are a royal priesthood, a holy nation" (v. 9). Peter does not directly refer to the church as the dwelling place of God's Spirit; how-

---

[28]The KJV has "defiles" instead of "destroys." The Greek word *phtheirei* can mean "ruin" or "corrupt," hence "defiles." However, according to BAGD and TDNT, "destroys" is the proper translation in this context.

[29]The Greek word is *phtherei*.

[30]Paul does not say how one may destroy the church. Probably he is referring to those who were attempting to divide the church in Corinth (1:10–13; 3:1–4) and thus render it a mortal blow: to divide would be to destroy. It is sometimes suggested that Paul may be referring to some of the immoralities in Corinth, to be discussed later. However, this is less likely, for even in the worst case of incest, the offender, says Paul, is to be delivered "to Satan for the destruction of the flesh, that his spirit may be saved in the day of the Lord Jesus" (5:5). This perpetrator of incest was not therefore ultimately destroyed, for he did not destroy the church despite his gross immorality. Thus it seems clear that Paul is referring to the dividing of the church, God's holy temple, as the cause for God's final destruction (see next footnote).

[31]According to BAGD, "destroy" (in "God will destroy") means to "punish with eternal destruction" (see ψθείρω, 2.c.). That this is the meaning is all the more apparent from the preceding verses about the church as God's building. One may even build poorly upon the foundation, namely Christ, and still "be saved, but only as through fire [consuming the hay, wood, and stubble]" (v. 15). But to destroy the church, God's holy dwelling place, can only result in eternal destruction.

ever, the imagery of "a spiritual house"[32] strongly suggests a holy temple. Moreover, the rest of the language, "a holy priesthood" and "spiritual sacrifices," clearly depicts the church as a temple in which the members are holy priests who offer up spiritual sacrifices.[33] Again, the church is holy because God's Spirit dwells within and all its members are a holy priesthood, not because of the degree of holiness its people possess.

To sum up this section: The church is separated from the world by the holy God. Its head is the Holy One, Jesus Christ, and it is indwelt by the Holy Spirit. The church is a holy church.

C. Catholicity

The church is also catholic. The word *catholic* is a transliteration of the Greek word *katholikos*, which means universal or whole.[34] *Katholikos* is not a biblical term; it was first used by Ignatius of Antioch in his letter to the church in Smyrna (ca. A.D. 112): "Wherever Jesus Christ is, there is the catholic church" (8:2), hence the universal or whole church.

The word *catholic* in this sense refers first to the universal[35] extension of the church. The church is worldwide; it is "ecumenical." *Oikoumenē*, from which "ecumenical" is derived, means literally "the inhabited earth,"[36] but it is usually translated in the New Testament simply as "the world."[37] For example, "this gospel of the kingdom shall be preached in all the world [*oikoumenē*] for a witness unto all nations" (Matt. 24:14 KJV). "Ecumenical" actually refers both to the universal proclamation of the gospel and to the goal of this proclamation: in both cases all the inhabited earth.[38] Hence the church, which is the result of this proclamation, is worldwide, or ecumenical.[39] In this sense the church is catholic: it extends over the whole earth.

The word *catholic* also refers to wholeness. For example, the epistles of James, John, Peter, and Jude are sometimes described as "catholic epistles" because they are addressed to the early Christian church at large, hence to the whole church. The church as catholic therefore does not refer to a certain section of the church, or to particular churches, but to the whole of Christ's church. Catholic therefore also means comprehensive: to be whole is to be comprehensive.[40] Thus the church cath-

---

[32]The Greek phrase is *oikos pneumatikos*.

[33]I will discuss the nature of these spiritual sacrifices at a later place (see "The Primacy of Worship," pp. 87–90).

[34]*Katholikos* is a combination of *kata*, "through" or "concerning," and *holos*, "whole" or "entire."

[35]Recall our previous discussion of "universal" at the beginning of this chapter.

[36]*Oikoumenē* is derived from *oikein*, "to inhabit."

[37]E.g., see Luke 4:5; Acts 11:28; Romans 10:18; Hebrews 1:6; Revelation 3:10. *Oikoumenē* occurs fifteen times in the New Testament.

[38]Paul writes to the Colossians about a universal proclamation of the gospel: "the gospel which you heard, which has been preached to every creature under heaven" (1:23; cf. Rom. 10:18). F. F. Bruce suggests that this is a "prophetic prolepsis [anticipation]" (*Epistles to the Colossians, to Philemon, and to the Ephesians*, NICNT, 791).

[39]The word *ecumenical* describes the early universal councils of the church, e.g., the councils of Nicea, Constantinople, and Chalcedon. These were councils of the whole undivided church, hence ecumenical. Ecumenical is now more commonly associated with a movement—the "ecumenical movement"—that seeks to restore the visible unity of the church. See "Excursus on the Ecumenical Movement," pages 43–48.

[40]The word *catholic* in a nonecclesiastical context is often used to refer to a comprehensiveness or broadness in attitude and orientation—"in sympathies, understanding, apprecia-

olic includes people of every place and region, of every age and condition. In Revelation 5:9 a "new song" contains these words to the Lamb: "Thou wast slain and by thy blood didst ransom men for God from every tribe and tongue and people and nation"—thus from every ethnical, cultural, social, and political group in the world. Truly the church catholic is comprehensive, including all the configurations of mankind.

The word *catholic* in the history of the church has taken on two additional meanings. First, by the time of Augustine (A.D. 354–430) catholic had also come to include the idea of "orthodox."[41] Hence the catholic church was not only universal but was also the church adhering to the true faith. Second, from the sixteenth century to the present the word *catholic* has increasingly become associated with the church related to Rome. Thus there is the title, "the Roman Catholic Church" or, still more commonly, simply "the Catholic Church." This, I must quickly add, is a quite unfortunate development. "Roman" used in conjunction with "catholic" is a contradiction, for catholic, as noted, refers to the universal, whole church. Even though the Roman church is spread over much of the world, it is only one part of the whole church. Catholic cannot properly refer to Rome or to any other branch of the church,[42] for this implies that the rest of the church is not truly the church. The church is catholic or not the church at all.

Some Protestant churches in using the Nicene Creed or the Apostles' Creed substitute the word "universal" or "Christian" for "catholic," thus seeking to make clear that their creedal affirmation does not refer to the Roman church. Such a substitution is unfortunate for the simple and basic reason that Protestants generally do recognize the whole church and not one particular configuration. Thus to affirm that we believe in "one, holy, catholic church" (Nicene) or "the holy catholic church" (Apostles'), rather than affirming Rome, does quite the opposite. It is to declare that we believe in the catholic (small *c*), namely the universal, the whole, church wherever it exists.

Who then is "a catholic"? That person is one who affirms the church of Jesus Christ throughout the world. In a sense it is to say with Ignatius that "wherever Jesus Christ is, there is the catholic church." For truly Jesus Christ is wherever His church is found—those who have come to new life in Him. Personally I am glad to confess that I am a catholic, a member of Christ's universal church.

D. Apostolicity

Finally, the church is apostolic. This attribute of the church points to the criterion of the church's life—namely, that the church always stands under the normative character of the original apostles' instruction and direction. Christ Himself, according to Hebrews, is "the apostle" (3:1)—as the One originally sent from God.[43] The apostles, in turn, were those specifically sent by Him. Jesus "chose . . . twelve, whom he named apostles" (Luke 6:13). They were under His teaching and

tion, and interest: not narrow, isolative, provincial, or partisan" (*Webster's Third International Dictionary*). The latter part of this definition could be used specifically of a truly catholic church.

[41]See, e.g., *The City of God*, 18:51, where Augustine speaks of the Catholic Church as over against various heresies.

[42]Hence also such designations as "Greek Catholic" and "Anglo-Catholic" are improper.

[43]"Apostle" is derived from the Greek word *apostellō*, "send out, or away." Christ was the first to be sent by the Father.

guidance throughout Jesus' ministry and were given instruction by Him for forty days between His resurrection and His ascension.[44] As soon as the three thousand converts in Jerusalem had come to salvation, they "devoted themselves to the apostles' teaching" (Acts 2:42). The early church was under the instruction and guidance of the apostles; it was therefore an apostolic church. Paul was later added to the original apostolic group by virtue of a special revelation of Jesus;[45] hence, his teaching and direction also became authoritative for the Christian church.

The church, of course, no longer has the early apostles in its midst; however, it does have the apostolic writings in the New Testament.[46] Hence, by recognizing these writings as authoritative and normative and seeking to be guided by them, the church remains apostolic. Since the apostles were the original witnesses of Christ and received direct instruction from Him,[47] their writings have a unique and irreplaceable role in the life of the church.

None of this signifies a disregard for the authority of the Old Testament. Indeed both Jesus Himself and the apostles draw without hesitation on the Old Testament Scriptures as God's written Word. For example, in John's gospel there is the testimony of Jesus that "the Scripture cannot be broken"[48] (10:35 NIV). Peter declares about the Old Testament that "no prophecy of scripture . . . ever came by the impulse of man, but men moved by the Holy Spirit spoke from God" (2 Peter 1:20–21). Paul speaks of "the holy Scriptures" that Timothy had known "from infancy" (2 Tim. 3:15 NIV)[49] and then adds: "All Scripture is God-breathed and is useful for teaching. . ." (v. 16).[50] All these references to the Old Testament make clear that a church that is apostolic gives full weight likewise to the apostolic affirmation regarding the Old Testament.

Let us now discuss a certain error that must be guarded against—the theory of "apostolic succession." By the late second century the view began to be advanced that apostolic authority and teaching were guaranteed by the bishops of the church.[51] According to

---

[44]Acts 1:2 speaks of the risen Jesus "until the day he was taken up . . . giving instructions through the Holy Spirit to the apostles he had chosen" (NIV).

[45]Paul inquires rhetorically: "Am I not an apostle? Have I not seen Jesus our Lord?" (1 Cor. 9:1). A basic requirement for the apostleship was that of having seen Jesus in His resurrection. See Peter's words in Acts 1:22—"a witness to his resurrection."

[46]This is not to say that all the books in the New Testament canon were written by the apostles (e.g., neither Mark nor Luke were apostles). However, they were either written by an apostle or carried apostolic authentication.

[47]Paul again is included, for though he did not know Jesus during the days of His ministry, he was given the gospel by special revelation, "I did not receive it [the gospel] from man, nor was I taught it, but it came through a revelation of Jesus Christ" (Gal. 1:12).

[48]Or "annulled" (Bruce's trans., *The Gospel of John*, 234). The Greek word is *luthēnai*. Although in this context Jesus was referring to a particular psalm (see context), His statement clearly refers to the whole of the Old Testament. (Cf. also Matt. 5:17–18).

[49]A clear reference to the Old Testament. Paul was writing to Timothy when he said, "From infancy you have known the holy Scriptures." New Testament Scriptures, of course, came many years later.

[50]Here the reference may include the New Testament as well. Peter, for example, speaks of Paul's letters as Scripture: "His [Paul's] letters contain some things that are hard to understand, which ignorant and unstable people distort, as they do the other Scriptures" (2 Peter 3:16 NIV).

[51]Irenaeus (ca. 130–200), bishop of Lyons, in his struggle against heresies wrote that the

this view, the bishops were in a direct line of succession from the original apostles. Presumably the apostles had laid hands upon certain believers and they upon others after them to insure that authentic teaching and practice were maintained. These persons, designated as bishops, were increasingly viewed as being lineal successors of the apostles and thereby guaranteed apostolic perpetuation. "Apostolic succession" therefore became essential to the life of the church. Thus the attribute of apostolicity no longer meant standing under the authority and tutelage of the original apostolic witness but under their episcopal[52] successors. This led increasingly to the Roman idea of the church as *magisterium*, i.e., that the bishops of the church are the authentic teachers and, especially where gathered in council, have the authority and capacity to define apostolic truth for the whole church.[53] Ultimately, in the Roman church—which claims that the pope is in lineal succession from Peter, who is viewed as chief of the apostles—the succession climaxes in the pope's presumed infallible teaching office. Hence, together with the pope—and never without his consent—the bishops as successors of the apostles have supreme authority over the church.[54]

It is apparent that the above view of apostolicity is far removed from the position that the church as apostolic stands under the teaching and authority of the original New Testament apostles. Actually there is no suggestion of apostolic succession in the New Testament. The closest approximation might be Paul's words in 2 Timothy 2:2: "What you have heard from me before many witnesses entrust to faithful men who will be able [or 'qualified' NIV] to teach others also." Here is a nonapostolic succession of three: Paul, Timothy, then faithful, qualified men. But there is no suggestion that either Timothy or those after him had Paul's apostolic authority. Paul did lay hands on Timothy to confer some gift—"I remind you to rekindle the gift[55] of God that is within you through the laying on of my hands" (2 Tim. 1:6)—but this was by no means to perpetuate apostolic authority. Paul, along with Barnabas, did appoint elders in various churches—"they had appointed elders . . . in every church" (Acts 14:23), but the elders' responsibility was altogether local, that is, for a particular church. Indeed, elders were also described as "bishops"[56] but, to repeat, their sphere of authority was within the local church. In the New Testament there are no bishops over churches, and surely those who were designated elders, or bishops, had no apostolic credentials to define the faith. It is interesting that

---

apostles had established a line of succession through the bishops, who by their teaching authority could determine the truth.

[52]The word *bishop* is derived from the Greek word *episkopos*.

[53]According to Vatican Council II (1962–65) of the Roman church, "by divine institution bishops have succeeded to the place of apostles as shepherds of the church, and . . . he who hears them hears Christ, while he who rejects them rejects Christ and Him who sent Christ [cf. Lk. 10:16]" (*Dogmatic Constitution of the Church*, chap. 3, "The Hierarchical Structure of the Church, with Special Reference to the Episcopate," sec. 20).

[54]"The order of bishops is the successor to the college of the apostles in teaching authority and pastoral rule. . . . But this power can be exercised only with the consent of the Roman pontiff. For our Lord made Simon Peter alone the rock and key-bearer of the Church" (ibid., sec. 22).

[55]The Greek word is *charisma*, a "gift of grace." See *Renewal Theology*, 2:345–46, "Excursus on the Word *Charisma*."

[56]See, e.g., Titus 1:5, 7 where elders and bishops (or "overseers") are unmistakably the same persons.

there is nothing said about Peter or any others of the Twelve appointing successors,[57] nor does early church history attest to any such succession.[58] Rather, in the early church, long before the present list of New Testament books was fully recognized by the church at large,[59] the letters of Paul and others, as well as the gospels (or portions of them), were circulated throughout the churches and provided the basic apostolic authority and guidance.

To sum up: The church is apostolic because it is based on the witness of the New Testament apostles. The church is apostolic when it is faithful to the apostles' teaching and direction and allows no teaching from without (heresy) or tradition from within (e.g., "apostolic succession") to dilute or expand the New Testament apostolic authority.

In the Book of Revelation "the holy city," the glorified church, had "a great, high wall. . . . And the wall of the city had twelve foundations, and on them the twelve names of the twelve apostles of the Lamb" (21:12, 14). The church was, is, and will be apostolic so long as it remains founded on[60] and faithful to the original apostles.

II. LOCAL

Besides being universal, the church is *local*. The church universal is invariably expressed in the local church. For the church is always a gathered body of believers in a particular location. Paul writes "to the church of God which is at Corinth" (1 Cor. 1:2). He does not address "a church of God" but *the* church *at* Corinth. Then Paul, a few words later, adds, "together with all those who in every place call on the name of our Lord Jesus Christ, both their Lord and ours" (v. 2). "In every place" signifies other places where the church exists. Wherever the local churches are, they come together to call on the name of Christ.

The local church, accordingly, is not just one part or fragment of the church universal. It is not somehow a lesser, perhaps even inferior, assemblage of the whole church. Rather, it is actually the total church in its individual expression.[61] Every local gathering, however small or large, is *the* church of Jesus Christ and is therefore complete in Him. The church is local or it is not the church at all.

We may now observe how the New Testament speaks of various locations of the church.

A. In a House—The Home *Ekklēsia*

We begin with the smallest, thus most local, setting of the church: in a house. Paul makes several references to a house church in his letters. Twice he refers to a church in the house of Aquila and Priscilla. He writes to the church in Corinth: "The churches of Asia send

---

[57]This is all the more strange in light of the aforementioned Roman dogma that "the order of bishops is the successor to the college of the apostles"!

[58]"This theory of succession did not arise before A.D. 170–200" ("Apostolic Succession," EDT, 73)—the time of Irenaeus (see n.51).

[59]Not until A.D. 367 was the present New Testament canon of twenty-seven books fully accepted.

[60]Two final comments here: (1) Paul speaks of apostles and prophets as the foundation—"the household of God, built upon the foundation of the apostles and prophets" (Eph. 2:20; see chap. 5 in this volume for a discussion of prophets); (2) ultimately Christ Himself is the foundation, as Paul says in 1 Corinthians 3:11–12; however, he may also be called "the chief Cornerstone" (see continuance of Eph. 2:20 NASB). In any event, the apostles are foundational to the life and ministry of the church. (For more on apostles and prophets see pp. 165–74).

[61]A. H. Strong writes, "The local church is a microcosm, a specialized localization of the universal body" (*Systematic Theology*, 892).

greetings. Aquila and Prisca [Priscilla], together with the church in their house,[62] send you hearty greetings in the Lord'' (1 Cor. 16:19). Later Paul writes to the Romans: ''Greet Prisca and Aquila . . . to whom not only I but also all the churches of the Gentiles give thanks; greet also the church in their house'' (Rom. 16:3–5). In the former instance the house church was probably in Ephesus, the latter undoubtedly in Rome. In his letter to the Colossians Paul writes, ''Give my greetings to the brethren at Laodicea, and to Nympha and the church in her house'' (4:15). The church in Nympha's house was probably in Laodicea, for a little later Paul refers to ''the church of the Laodiceans'' (v. 16). Finally, Paul writes a letter addressed ''to Philemon our beloved fellow worker . . . and the church in your house'' (Philem. 1–2).

In all these references it is significant that the word ''church'' is used in reference to home assemblies. Such gatherings were not simply home meetings of believers in distinction from a church meeting in a perhaps larger and more formal gathering. No, the gathering in a house or home was equally an *ekklēsia*. Paul can say (as we have noted), ''The churches of Asia send greetings,'' and then immediately add, ''Aquila and Prisca, together with the church in their house, send you hearty greetings.'' There is no suggestion that the house church is somehow less a church, or only a part of the large church. Even more pertinently, the church in a house was not viewed as some schismatic group that had broken away from the larger church. It was simply believers—''called-out'' people—meeting together; therefore, it was truly a gathering of the *ekklēsia*.

The Book of Acts has many references to the early Christians assembling in homes. Indeed, at first it was both in the temple and in homes. In the earliest description of the believers in Jerusalem Luke writes that ''all who believed'' were ''day by day, attending the temple together and breaking bread in their homes''[63] (2:44, 46). Both temple and home were therefore believers' assemblies, hence *ekklēsia*. So when the text later reads, ''The Lord added to their number day by day those who were being saved'' (v. 47), this was an addition to the church[64] whether meeting in temple or home. Temple and home are again mentioned where Acts records about the apostles that ''every day in the temple and at home[65] they did not cease teaching and preaching Jesus as the Christ'' (5:42). Temple and home were both gatherings of the church. Later when ''great persecution arose against the church in Jerusalem,'' the text reads that ''Saul began ravaging the

---

[62]The Greek phrase is *kat' oikon autōn* and can be translated literally ''at their house.'' The NIV so translates it and reads, ''the church that meets at their house.'' *Kat' oikon* is likewise the Greek phrase in Romans 16:5; Colossians 4:15; and Philemon 1–2 (also quoted in this paragraph).

[63]The phrase (as in 1 Cor. 16:19 and others) is again *kat' oikon*. The translation ''from house to house'' (KJV, NASB), while not literal, does convey a helpful picture that these were not just families breaking bread in their individual homes but believers meeting in one another's homes, hence the phrase ''from house to house.''

[64]In fact, the KJV reads, ''The Lord added to the church [rather than 'to their number'] daily. . . .'' The word ''church,'' *ekklēsia*, however, does not appear in the earliest ancient manuscripts (see chap. 1, n. 24). Nonetheless the KJV translation does properly convey the truth that these gatherings in the temple and in homes were the *ekklēsia* to which God added people day by day. (The word *ekklēsia* is not used until Acts 5:11.)

[65]The Greek phrase again is *kat' oikon*.

church, entering house after house"[66] (Acts 8:1, 3 NASB). Since it was no longer possible to meet in the temple, the church truly was none other than the meetings held in various homes; therefore, to "ravage" the church was to ravage the gatherings of believers in individual homes.

To sum up: The house church was simply believers meeting in a home and therefore an *ekklēsia*. The house church was more than just a Christian household consisting of a nuclear family of believers—for example, parents, children, and perhaps grandparents, relatives, and servants. Rather, it was the coming together of a number of believers in a particular home. They knew themselves in such a gathering to be the church of Jesus Christ.

B. In a City—The Urban *Ekklēsia*

The most common New Testament designation of the church's location is in a given city. In the Book of Acts the first use of the word "church" follows upon the deaths of Ananias and Sapphira: "And great fear came upon the whole church, and upon all who heard of these things" (5:11). The "whole church" refers to all the believers who had been meeting in the temple and in their homes. The next reference to the church concerns "the church in Jerusalem": "Great persecution arose against the church in Jerusalem" (8:1). Up to this point that church geographically comprised the whole church. It is interesting that the next specific reference to the church in a given city is to "the church at Antioch" (13:1), the first church to include Gentiles in its fellowship. Throughout Acts there are a number of references to "the church" and "churches," each referring to a given locality.

We have earlier noted Paul's references to the local church "in Corinth," the church "in Cenchreae," "the church of the Laodiceans," and "the church of the Thessalonians"; likewise the messages in the Book of Revelation were directed to "the church in Ephesus," "the church in Smyrna," and so on. All such references likewise point to the urban *ekklēsia*. So, again, the critical point is that the universal church is invariably local and often has the designation of a given city. This means, further, that all the believers in a given city were viewed as the church in that locality. As we have observed, a house church (possibly house churches), as well as a larger gathering, may also have been in a certain city, but all made up the urban church.[67] Hence whenever believers met in a city, whether as one body[68] or as smaller groups, it was the church in a given city.[69]

There is no suggestion in the New Testament of division or competition between the house church and the urban church. Whether it was the larger meeting, possibly in some public facility

[66]The Greek phrase is *kat' tous oikous*.

[67]Recall, e.g., reference to Laodicea where Paul mentions both "Nympha and the church in her house" and "the church of the Laodiceans."

[68]In writing to the Corinthians Paul speaks at one point of the "whole church" coming together—"If . . . the whole church assembles" (1 Cor. 14:23). This suggests that, in addition to gatherings of the whole church in Corinth, there were also smaller assemblies.

[69]In one sense this means that there was only one church in a given city; however, this is quite different from a particular church in a city calling itself "the local church" to the exclusion of all other churches. I refer here particularly to the Local Church movement, founded by Witness Lee. Headquartered in Anaheim, California, it claims "one city, one church," thereby designating itself "the Church in Anaheim" (similarly "the Church in Seattle," etc.). All other "churches" are viewed as pseudo-churches. See Neil T. Duddy and the SCP, *The God-Men: An Inquiry into Witness Lee and the Local Church*; also Jack Sparks, *The Mind Benders*, Part 3, "The Local Church of Witness Lee."

or in someone's home, both gatherings were equally the church. It was basically a matter of logistics: the size of the facility that was necessary to accommodate the assemblage of believers. The larger gathering did not view the smaller group as somehow being less a church, nor did the smaller gathering view itself as somehow more truly the church. "All those who in every place call on the name of the Lord Jesus Christ" (to quote Paul again) is the key. Wherever this took place, the church was—and is today—truly in operation.[70]

C. In a Larger Area—The Regional *Ekklēsia*

The New Testament also designates the church as existing in a larger area. The most distinctive statement in this regard is Acts 9:31: "So the church throughout all Judea and Galilee and Samaria had peace and was built up; and walking in the fear of the Lord and in the comfort of the Holy Spirit it was multiplied." Note the singular—"*the* church"; thus the churches in Judea, Galilee, and Samaria are viewed collectively as the church. There are, in addition, New Testament references to the churches in a given area: "the churches of Galatia" (Gal. 1:2), "the churches of Christ in Judea" (Gal. 1:22), and "the churches of Asia" (1 Cor. 16:19). Thus a vital sense of their corporate unity exists; "the churches" are "the church" in a specified region.

However, this corporate picture of the church by no means implies a church somehow above the individual churches. The regional *ekklēsia* is nothing other than the assemblies in a given area. Whether they are urban churches or house churches, it is always the gathering of believers in a particular place.

III. TRANSCENDENT

The church also consists of the saints in heaven. The letter to the Hebrews declares, "But you have come to Mount Zion and to the city of the living God, the heavenly Jerusalem, and to myriads of angels, to the general assembly[71] and church of the first-born who are enrolled in heaven, and to God, the Judge of all, and to the spirits of righteous men made perfect" (12:22–23 NASB). This extraordinary statement, which refers symbolically to the worship experience of believers as coming to Mount Zion, depicts in heaven, in addition to innumerable angels, "the church of the first-born."[72] This phrase portrays believers in heaven as the transcendent *ekklēsia*.[73] Thus the

[70]It is quite significant that shortly after Jesus refers to the church in Matthew 18:17, He declares, "Where two or three are gathered in my name, there am I in the midst of them" (v. 20). The two or three accordingly are an *ekklēsia*. According to EGT, the wording in Matthew 18:20 "is a synonym for the new society. The *ecclesia* is a body of men [people] gathered together by a common relation to the name of Christ" (1:241).

[71]The NIV reads, "thousands upon thousands of angels in joyful assembly" (similarly RSV). The "general assembly" or "joyful assembly" can refer to the angels (so F. F. Bruce in *The Epistle to the Hebrews*, NICNT, in loco); however, I am inclined to the NASB (similarly KJV and NEB) translation because of the overall context.

[72]"The first-born" refers to Christ. See Hebrews 1:6 (also cf. Rom. 8:29; Col. 1:15, 18; Rev. 1:5).

[73]The phrase "the church of the first-born" has also been interpreted as referring to angels (e.g., see EGT, *Hebrews*, in loco) as well as to those who died "in faith" prior to Christ's coming. (Calvin speaks of the phrase as referring to the patriarchs and other renowned saints of the ancient church [*Commentaries, Hebrews*, in loco].) Bruce in response to both such views writes that "more probably the reference is to the whole communion of saints,

church is not limited to the earth but consists also of those who have passed on into glory.

The church, accordingly, is not only the redeemed people of God on earth but also the church in heaven. It exists there in purity and holiness: "the spirits of righteous men made perfect." This calls to mind the statement of Paul that Christ's intention for the church is to "present to Himself the church in all her glory, having no spot or wrinkle or any such thing . . . holy and blameless" (Eph. 5:27 NASB). Although these words doubtless apply to the church in the final consummation, there is also the possible implication of a purified church in glory that even now fulfills Christ's final purpose. There may be a further suggestion of this from the scene in the Book of Revelation where there is great joy in heaven: "Let us rejoice and be glad and give him the glory! For the wedding of the Lamb has come, and his bride has made herself ready. Fine linen, bright and clean, was given her to wear" (19:7–8 NIV). That this is a heavenly scene is further shown where John writes, "I saw the holy city, new Jerusalem, coming down out of heaven from God, prepared as a bride adorned for her husband" (21:2). Once again, although this is a picture of the consummation,[74] heaven is unmistakably the background. There is a church in glory even now.

This, however, is not a church different from the church on earth that is universal and local. It is the same, yet now "a glorious church"[75]—a purified church, a truly holy church. This church in glory is the heavenly Jerusalem.[76] It is surrounded by myriads—thousands upon thousands—of angels; it is the transcendent church of perfected saints. While the church on earth is sometimes called "the church militant," its heavenly counterpart is referred to as "the church triumphant." Its battles on earth are over; the victory has been won![77] However, the important thing is that the church in heaven is the church radiant with the divine glory.

The church in heaven is truly the transcendent church. We cannot behold the heavenly church; however, in worship we come very close to it. Spiritually, as Hebrews describes it, we come to "Mount Zion," and perhaps we sense the myriad hosts of angels and "the church of the first-born" there assembled. Most of all, in times of high praise we may even envision the myriads of angels also praising God[78] and the glorified church joining them.[79] It is good

---

including those who, while 'militant on earth,' are enrolled as citizens of heaven" (*Epistle to the Hebrews*, NICNT, 376–77). While Bruce provides a good answer to the prior views mentioned, I do not believe his statement clearly enough differentiates between the church "militant" and the church in heaven. It is interesting that in a footnote to the words I quoted, Bruce affirmatively refers to some words of B. F. Westcott: "Christian believers in Christ, alike living and dead, are united in the body of Christ." This statement clearly distinguishes between the believers living and dead, hence, by extension the church now on earth and the church in heaven. Hebrews 12:23, I submit, refers to the church in heaven.

[74]Revelation 21 begins, "I saw a new heaven and a new earth."

[75]The KJV translation in Ephesians 5:27.

[76]As depicted both in Hebrews and in Revelation.

[77]L. Berkhof writes, "If the Church on earth is the militant Church, the Church in heaven is the triumphant Church. There the sword is exchanged for the palm of victory, the battle-cries are turned into songs of triumph, and the cross is replaced by the crown" (*Systematic Theology*, 565).

[78]For the continuing praise given by angels see especially Revelation 5:11–13.

[79]Also in Revelation 5:13 John declares, "I heard every creature in heaven and on earth . . . saying 'To him who sits upon the throne and to the Lamb be blessing and honor and

to know that both on earth and in heaven the worship of God never ceases! Still, the church above is not visible.

Moreover, I must now add, even our richest spiritual experience does not—indeed cannot—include direct contact with the church in heaven. There is no biblical suggestion that we may make contact with the church in glory. The expression "the communion of saints,"[80] while it may include the church in heaven,[81] is not a communion with departed saints. The church in glory may indeed be aware of our praise and activity,[82] but contrariwise there seems to be no biblical evidence of the glorified saints making contact with saints on earth. Still—it is important to add—it is the one church of Jesus Christ on earth and in heaven.

EXCURSUS: THE ECUMENICAL MOVEMENT

One of the most significant features of church activity in the twentieth century has been the ecumenical movement. *Ecumenical*[83] is often used to describe the movement that seeks to foster cooperation and unity among all churches.

The usual date suggested for the beginning of the ecumenical movement is 1910 with the convening of the World Missionary Conference in Edinburgh. This was the first truly international and multidenominational conference. Its purpose was to discuss the growing problems connected with disunity and division, even competition, of churches on the mission field. The conference led some to the vision of a united church, and out of it came a call from Edinburgh to the church at large to confront divisive issues of doctrine and practice. One result was the first world conference on Faith and Order that convened in Lausanne in 1927. Rather than being a gathering of missionary societies as at Edinburgh, this was formally an interchurch assembly. As before, it was a Protestant gathering; however, many evangelical churches did not attend. The conference at Lausanne was con-

---

glory and might for ever and ever!' " Every creature in heaven surely includes the glorified church. Some interpreters view the twenty-four elders in heaven who frequently offer praise (Rev. 4:4, 9–11; 5:8–10; 11:16–18; 19:4–5) as representing the glorified church (the twelve Old Testament patriarchs plus the twelve New Testament apostles; cf. Rev. 21:12–14). In any event the church in glory is a praising church.

[80]In the Apostles' Creed just following the affirmation "I believe in the holy catholic church" are the words "in the communion of saints." The last phrase has sometimes been understood to refer to a heavenly/earthly communion, so that, for example, one may pray to the saints in heaven. There is no biblical basis for such an understanding and practice. (For further discussion of "The Communion of Saints" see pp. 82–83.)

[81]Karl Barth writes, "To the *communio sanctorum* belongs not only the *ecclesia militans* but also the *ecclesia triumphans* . . . therefore the communion of the blessed who have gone before us" (*Credo*, 194).

[82]If the elders in Revelation represent the glorified church, they seem to be aware of what is happening on earth. Note particularly Revelation 7:13–14, where one of the elders speaks knowingly of "the great tribulation" on earth and of the persons in heaven who have come out of it. Hebrews 12:1–2 depicts the Christian life as a race of perseverance, which begins by affirming that we are "surrounded by so great a cloud of witnesses." While these witnesses may refer primarily to Old Testament men and women of faith, they could also include New Testament believers who have passed on into glory. Leon Morris writes that "perhaps we should think of something like a relay race where those who have finished their course and handed in their baton are watching and encouraging their successors" (*Hebrews*, EBC, 133).

[83]See note 39.

cerned primarily with doctrinal questions that divided the churches.

At another world conference on Faith and Order convened at Edinburgh in 1937 came a call for the formation of a world council of churches. As a result, 148 denominational groups gathered in Amsterdam in 1948 and founded the World Council of Churches. The intention was not to create a superchurch, but to serve all the member churches in various ways, including the promotion of visible unity. A brief statement of theological basis was adopted: "The World Council of Churches is a fellowship of churches which accept our Lord Jesus Christ as God and Savior."

In 1961 at New Delhi the World Council of Churches was enlarged beyond its basically Protestant constituency to include the Russian Orthodox Church and two Pentecostal churches from Chile. Also, for the first time, Roman Catholic observers were officially present. Likewise, the International Missionary Council, which had been formed in 1921 as one of the results of the World Missionary Conference in Edinburgh, merged with the World Council. Further, the original doctrinal statement was expanded to read: "The World Council of Churches is a fellowship of churches which confess the Lord Jesus Christ as God and Savior according to the Scriptures and therefore seek to fulfill together their common calling to the glory of the one God, Father, Son, and Holy Spirit."

Another striking ecumenical development occurred with the convening of the Roman Catholic Vatican Council II (1962–65). Sessions were presided over by Pope John XXIII and his successor, Pope Paul VI, with some 2,500 bishops from around the world officially present. The expressed intention of the Council was to renew and update various areas of the church's faith and life. Along with this was a strong emphasis on ecumenism. For one thing, even as Roman Catholic observers had been present in 1961 at New Delhi, both Protestant and Orthodox observers were invited and so attended all the sessions. Most importantly, one of the deliverances of the Council, the "Decree on Ecumenism," called for "the Catholic faithful to recognize the signs of the times and participate skillfully in the work of ecumenism."[84] For the first time it recognized non–Roman Catholic Christians as "brothers in the Lord," though "separated," for "it is through Christ's Catholic Church alone . . . that the fullness of the means of salvation can be attained."[85] The Eastern Orthodox Churches were fully recognized as churches and Protestant churches were designated as "ecclesial communities."[86] For Rome these were large ecumenical steps. At the end of Vatican II in December 1965, Pope Paul and Patriarch Athenagoras, head of Eastern Orthodoxy, issued a joint declaration removing the mutual excommunication of A.D. 1054 that had divided the Roman and Eastern churches and expressing a desire for restoration of full communion in faith and sacramental life. Also, a

---

[84]Section 4.

[85]Section 3. This sounds, however, as if non-Roman brothers are still deficient. Nevertheless, for Roman Catholics, this was a big step ahead from the days when they recognized no "brothers in the Lord" outside the Roman fold.

[86]I.e., not fully churches. One of the reasons given was this: "The ecclesial communities separated from us lack that fullness of unity with us [and] we believe that especially because of the lack of the sacrament of orders [in which priests alone participate] they have not preserved the genuine and total reality of the Eucharistic mystery" (sec. 22). Although this is a very limited statement from the Protestant perspective, it is a far cry from the older exclusivist Roman position.

permanent Secretariat for Christian Unity was created. Since that time numerous conferences and dialogues between Roman and non-Roman churches have been held.[87]

Since New Delhi numerous bilateral dialogues between denominations,[88] ongoing Faith and Order conferences,[89] and an increasing number of denominational mergers[90] have taken place. There is undoubtedly a growing conviction among many denominations that the former multiplication of divisions should now move in the direction of cooperation and unity.

Evangelicals on the whole have been hesitant to participate in the ecumenical movement. Since the shift after Edinburgh, 1910, from missionary societies seeking harmony in the mission fields to official church gatherings ultimately seeking union, many evangelicals have drawn back. Another group that emerged from Edinburgh—in addition to Faith and Order—was Life and Work. One of its early mottos was "Doctrine Divides, but Service Unites" (Stockholm, 1925). This is the kind of trend that evangelicals have been wary of: the dilution of doctrine. Even though Faith and Order has been devoted primarily to issues of doctrine and the World Council of Churches presently has a strong Christological and Trinitarian confessional basis, evangelicals have feared insufficient concern for the full orthodox Christian faith. Also, many evangelicals have questioned the commitment of the ecumenical movement to evangelism and missions as well as to the need for a personal experience of regeneration. Further, evangelicals are concerned about the support that the World Council has often given to Third World leftist movements.

The emphasis of evangelicals has been more on cooperation than on visible union. On the American scene, for example, over against the Federal (later National) Council of Churches (founded in 1908), which sought unification of churches on a federation model and espoused various liberal causes, a number of evangelicals formed the National Association of Evangelicals (NAE) in 1942. The NAE drew up an orthodox confession of faith, stressing certain fundamentals that are required for churches and de-

[87]This has also included dialogue of the Vatican with representatives of the charismatic movement and Pentecostal churches since early meetings in 1972. The dialogue has continued to prove fruitful in fostering better understanding between the Roman church and the Pentecostal renewal.

[88]See, e.g., H. Meyer and L. Vischer, *Growth in Agreement: Reports and Agreed Statements of Ecumenical Conversations on a World Level*. In the United States one of the most extended has been the Consultation on Church Union (COCU), which began in 1960, that seeks to bring together several denominations into the Church of Christ Uniting ("uniting" signifying an invitation to other denominations to come into the union).

[89]One of the most significant was the meeting in Lima, Peru in 1982 that finalized a consensus on baptism, Eucharist, and ministry (all highly critical points of traditional differences) as part of a program to set forth a statement of apostolic faith for today that all could agree on.

[90]Some of these have been interdenominational mergers, such as the Methodist Episcopal Church and the Evangelical United Brethren to form the United Methodist Church, and the Evangelical and Reformed Church and the Congregational Church to form the United Church of Christ. Others have been intradenominational, such as the Presbyterian Church UPUSA and the Presbyterian Church, U.S. (a cleavage going back to the Civil War), to form the Presbyterian Church, U.S.A., and the merger of the Lutheran Church in America (LCA), the American Lutheran Church (ALC), and the American Evangelical Lutheran Church (AELC) to form the Evangelical Lutheran Church in America (ELCA).

nominations to confess if they wish to belong, and has developed a program of action in such spheres as evangelism, Christian education, and missions. Members of the NAE have also worked with evangelicals in other countries to organize the World Evangelical Fellowship (beginning in 1951). "Fellowship" suggests more concern for working together and mutual support than for church union. Conferences on evangelism and missions have become increasingly the orientation of evangelicals, such as a World Congress on Evangelism in 1966 in West Berlin sponsored by *Christianity Today*, a leading evangelical Protestant magazine; a Congress on World Evangelization in Lausanne in 1974 convened by 142 evangelical leaders under the honorary chairmanship of Billy Graham; and Lausanne II in Manila in 1989.

Lausanne I in 1974 produced a widely acclaimed Lausanne Covenant that stressed the need for "the church's visible unity in truth" along with the mandate for world evangelization. Lausanne II met in Manila with over 3,500 participants from 186 countries present. Facing the last decade of the twentieth century, they sought to lay out strategies for a worldwide evangelistic endeavor. Beginning with Berlin in 1966, these have all been ecumenical conferences in the sense of being worldwide—across "the inhabited earth." But the emphasis has been on cooperation for a worldwide task rather than achieving a recognizable Christian unity.

In many ways the mainline ecumenical movement—sometimes called the conciliar movement (World Council, Vatican II Council, National Council, etc.)—and the evangelical cooperation movement run side by side. For example, in the same year (1989) that Lausanne II, the evangelical Conference on World Evangelization, was being held, the World Council of Churches had a Conference on World Mission and Evangelism in San Antonio, Texas. Moreover, there are some evangelical churches in the World Council of Churches,[91] and a number of World Council member churches have groups within that are active in evangelical meetings and activities.[92] So there is overlap, and perhaps an increasing convergence, between the interests and aims of the two movements.

A brief reflection: the concern of this excursus has been primarily on the ecumenical movement and its connection with the unity of the church. I am convinced that this is very important. Cooperation among denominations in evangelism and missions (and in many other ways) is an important first step, but it should not be the final one. Since 1900, multiple denominations in America have sprung up. No matter how much they may work together (often they do not), there is still the stumbling block, the scandal, of divided churches seeking to evangelize the world. The chief evangelical thrust is missionary, namely, to bring the world to faith in Jesus Christ, yet one of the greatest barriers to this is the church's own disunity. It is only, according to Jesus Himself, as we become "perfectly one"—or are "perfected in one"[93]—that the world can believe.

Evangelicals often say that their chief opposition to the ecumenical movement is the matter of truth. I agree that in many denominations affiliated with the movement there has been doctrinal

[91]E.g., Pentecostal churches, mentioned earlier, that are affiliated with the World Council.

[92]Almost all major denominations affiliated with the WCC and/or the NCC have minority groups within that are strongly evangelical—for example, the Presbyterian Evangelical Fellowship (PEF).

[93]The literal translation of John 17:23—*"teteleiomenoi eis hen."*

weakness. However, as noted, the World Council of Churches is strong in its declaration of Jesus Christ as "God and Savior" and its statement on the Trinity—"one God, Father, Son, and Holy Spirit." Also, many of the denominations involved affirm such ancient orthodox creeds as Nicea, Constantinople, and Chalcedon (the nonaffiliated Roman church does the same). These creedal statements include such additional "fundamentals" as Christ's virgin birth, vicarious atonement, and bodily resurrection. Evangelicals do well to stress the need for doctrinal purity, but they often fail to recognize adequately its existence in the ecumenical movement.

There are doctrinal problems, of course; however, the really divisive issue, I submit, is not theological but existential. Thus it is not primarily a matter of doctrine but of Christian experience.[94] Does the ecumenical movement place sufficient stress on the nature of the church as *ekklēsia*, "called out" of the world together with other believers to Jesus Christ? Its members may make quite correct theological statements about Jesus Christ and the Triune God and confess adherence to orthodox formulations of faith, but none of this is the church's essence. Even Satan knows that Christ is God and that there is Father, Son, and Holy Spirit, but he surely does not belong to those who are "called out." Hence when the way to visible unity is viewed largely as the way of doctrinal affirmation or practical expression, this is not sufficiently fundamental. The real issue is calling, without which the church does not exist at all. Hence the fundamental matter is salvation—whether defined as effectual calling, regeneration, justification, or initial sanctification.[95] One may applaud efforts of the churches to unite, but one must also recognize that without the undergirding of salvation there is nothing that can unite them except outward forms.

The primary concern in the ecumenical movement should be with the spiritual vitality of the churches seeking to unite. It is good to know that there is some increasing doctrinal convergence—also progress on such matters as ministerial orders, sacraments, and church polity.[96] But the heart of the matter is still missing if there is not the fundamental, even driving, concern to face up to the issue of salvation in the churches. One may be grateful for the outward witness of the World Council of Churches in seeking to bring churches together and for the fact that the Roman church is becoming more ecumenical in relation to Protestants and has removed a thousand-year-old ban of excommunication regarding the Eastern church. Yet one needs to be aware that the truly critical issues have not yet been dealt with.

This might even mean a call for the conversion of the church! I do not intend to suggest that there are not true believers in all churches—Protestant, Roman, and Eastern—who consequently form a salvific core and are the true church. For indeed there are many. Nor do I intend to imply that all efforts that seek to achieve outward unity should cease. For making these efforts is far better than seeking to maintain old walls of isolated enclaves of churches.

---

[94]This is not to deny that there are serious theological differences, indeed in many cases increasing apostasy from established creedal and confessional standards. However, the root cause of this is existential—the failure to experience the realities to which historical creeds and confessions refer.

[95]See a discussion of these matters in *Renewal Theology*, volume 2, chapters 1–4.

[96]Such discussions continually go on.

Nor again do I intend to suggest that the whole church will ever be completely converted. Among the "wheat" there will always be "tares" that cannot be rooted out. But the basic question must be faced: *Whom are we seeking to unify?* The church in Jerusalem, according to Acts 2, knew tremendous unity; they were together in many ways. But this happened only because they were a saved people and others being saved continued to join them: "The Lord added to their number day by day those who were being saved" (v. 47). Thus there needs to be the unmuted call of the church to inward transformation. As the ferment of the gospel works within, increasingly the realization of unity born truly of the Lord will occur.

3

Description

We will now examine some of the Bible's descriptions of the church. Our focus will be on those images that give particular insight into the nature of the church.

I. THE PEOPLE OF GOD

The church as the people of God will be our starting point. This image[1] of the church is basic to whatever else may be said.[2] It provides an extraordinary description of the church, bringing together the witness of both the Old Testament and the New. Let us look first at the Old Testament.

Background: Israel as God's People

In the Old Testament the people of Israel were designated God's people. This first occurred when God spoke to Moses at the burning bush. There God said, "I have seen the affliction of my people . . . and I have come down to deliver them. . . . Come, I will send you to Pharaoh that you may bring forth my people, the sons of Israel, out of Egypt" (Exod. 3:7–8, 10). "My people," hence the people of God, were declared to be the Israelites. Later God said, "I will redeem you with an outstretched arm and with great acts of judgment, and I will take you for my people, and I will be your God; and you shall know that I am the LORD your God" (Exod. 6:6–7). Subsequently the redemption from Egyptian bondage occurred.

Why were the Israelites God's people? The biblical answer is that their selection was wholly due to God's decision. For example, years later Moses declared, "The LORD your God has chosen you to be a people for His own possession out of all the peoples who are on the face of the earth" (Deut. 7:6 NASB). He gave this reason: "Because the LORD loved you and kept the oath which He swore to your forefathers" (v. 8 NASB)—i.e., to Abraham, Isaac, and Jacob—about the future possession of the land of Canaan. Here is both the fact, indeed the mystery, of God's special love for Israel, and His

[1]For a comprehensive presentation of the wide variety of images see Paul S. Minear, *Images of the Church in the New Testament*.

[2]Hans Küng writes, "The idea of the people of God is the oldest and most fundamental concept underlying the self-interpretation of the *ekklēsia*" (*The Church*, 119).

faithfulness to the earlier covenant with Abraham.[3] Accordingly, Israel was God's people not because they decided to call themselves so[4] or because they were a particularly impressive people;[5] rather, it was wholly a matter of God's own doing.

But now an additional fact must be added: Although the Israelites did not choose to be God's people, God's choice laid a definite obligation upon them. Here we turn to the time when God spoke through Moses on Mount Sinai: "You have seen what I did to the Egyptians, and how I bore you on eagles' wings and brought you to myself. Now therefore, if you will obey my voice and keep my covenant, you shall be my own possession among all peoples. . . . You shall be to me a kingdom of priests and a holy nation" (Exod. 19:4–6). This did not mean that God would ever annul a special relationship to Israel; however, obedience to the covenant (particularly the Ten Commandments and the ordinances detailed in chapters 20–23) was required.

The Old Testament picture after these events at Mount Sinai is almost totally one of Israel's failure to obey. Israel remained God's people, though at times God's wrath nearly consumed them. Indeed, while Israel was still at Mount Sinai and Moses was on the mountain receiving instruction for building the tabernacle, Aaron made a golden calf for the Israelites to worship. God declared to Moses, "I have seen this people,[6] and behold, it is a stiffnecked people; now therefore let me alone, that my wrath may burn hot against them and I may consume them; but of you I will make a great nation" (Exod. 32:9–10). Moses interceded, "O LORD, why does thy wrath burn hot against thy people . . . ?" (v. 11); and God relented. Israel continued as God's people despite their frequent acts of rebellion and disobedience. By the eighth century B.C. Israel, through her flagrant idolatry and gross immorality, apparently forfeited any right to be God's people. Indeed, after a certain son was born to Hosea, the Lord said to the prophet, "Call his name Not my people, for you are not my people and I am not your God" (1:9). Thus Israel was declared to be God's people no longer. Immediately God added, however: "In the place where it was said to them, 'You are not my people,' it shall be said to them, 'Sons of the living God' " (v. 10). Thus the hope was held out that Israel would some day fulfill her calling to be God's people.

Finally, we may note the situation of Israel after the Exile. Through the prophet Ezekiel, God gave this promise concerning Judah and Israel: "I will save them from all the backslidings in which they have sinned, and will cleanse them; and they shall be my people, and I will be their God" (Ezek. 37:23). Israel—God's chosen people—will truly become God's people once they have been cleansed of their sinfulness.

This is the climactic Old Testament note about Israel as the people of God. In one sense Israel, chosen by God, remained His people; in another sense Israel, constantly disobeying and finally being sent into captivity, desperately needed a radical change, a full cleansing, a work of salvation ("I will save

---

[3]For more detail on this covenant see *Renewal Theology*, vol. 1, chapter 12.

[4]As, for example, one of the Moslem groups today calls itself "the party of God" (the Hezbollah). This is their self-designation, not something given by God (or Allah).

[5]Deuteronomy 7:7 continues, "It was not because you were more in number than any other people." Also Israel was scarcely more virtuous than other nations!

[6]In calling Israel "this people" rather than "my people,"God seems scarcely to recognize them as His people any longer.

them. . ."). Only then could they become truly the people of God.

A. A Composite People

The church is the composite people of God. One of the most striking features of the New Testament is that it depicts the church as composed of both Jews and Gentiles. The extraordinary fact is that the Gentiles are now included in the Old Testament promises.

Let us look first at Paul's teaching in Romans. At one point the apostle speaks of "us whom he [God] has called, not from the Jews only but also from the Gentiles" (9:24). Then Paul, quoting freely from Hosea, immediately adds in reference to the Gentiles: "As indeed he says in Hosea, 'Those who were not my people I will call 'my people'. . . . And in the very place where it was said to them, 'You are not my people,' they will be called 'sons of the living God' " (vv. 25–26). These words, as we have seen, were spoken by Hosea in regard to Israel; now they are applied to the Gentiles, who formerly were not God's people.[7] Obviously not all Jews or all Gentiles make up God's people, but only those whom God has called "from the Jews" and "from the Gentiles."

In regard to Israel, Paul proceeds to speak of "a remnant" coming to salvation: "Isaiah cries out concerning Israel: 'Though the number of the sons of Israel be as the sand of the sea, only a remnant of them will be saved' " (v. 27).[8] By the calling of the remnant and their coming to faith, God maintains His original covenant with Israel.

It is important to add that God has not rejected the Israelite people. Even though Hosea's words—"not my people"—now refer particularly to the Gentiles, the Jews are still included in God's overall promise. Paul continues to deal with this matter in Romans, beginning with the question, "I ask, then, has God rejected his people [i.e., ethnic Israel]?" He responds vigorously, "By no means!" (11:1). Later Paul speaks again of the remnant: "At the present time there is a remnant, chosen by grace" (v. 5). Thus Israel is not rejected, for through the remnant the promise is maintained. Moreover, as Paul moves on to say, a day is coming when God's promise will be gloriously fulfilled: "all Israel will be saved" (v. 26)! At present, says Paul, "Israel has experienced a hardening in part" and this will continue "until the full number of the Gentiles has come in" (v. 25 NIV). Then Israel will come to salvation.

The people of God—the church—accordingly is now composed of Gentiles and the Jewish remnant. Together both believing Gentiles and Jews constitute the people of God. It is a people no longer based on racial or national lines, but on the calling of God in Christ. Here we return to the significant words of Peter: "You are a chosen race, a royal priesthood, a holy nation, God's own people. . ." (1 Peter 2:9). Although much of this language is borrowed from Old Testament[9] references to ethnic Israel, Peter here applies it to Christian believers in many places.[10] Wherever

---

[7]In Ephesians Paul speaks of Gentiles as formerly "separated from Christ, alienated from the commonwealth of Israel, and strangers to the covenants of promise, having no hope and without God in the world" (2:12). What a change has indeed come about!

[8]Quotation from Isaiah 10:22.

[9]See, for example, Exodus 19:6 and Isaiah 43:20–21.

[10]The word "race" (Gr. *genos*) might seem surprising. However, in the early church Christians were frequently referred to as a "third race" (in addition to Jews and Gentiles considered separately; cf. 1 Cor. 10:32, where Jews, Greeks, and "the church of God" are

they are and whoever they are, Christians corporately are the people of God.

B. A New People

The church is not simply a composite of Jew and Gentile or a collection of people from many nations who now are joined together. It is all of that, but much more. The church is the new people of God. This truth may be viewed from several perspectives.

1. A People Redeemed

One of the most striking New Testament statements in this regard is that by Paul (as quoted earlier): "Our great God and Savior Jesus Christ . . . gave himself for us to redeem us from all iniquity and to purify for himself a people of his own"[11] (Titus 2:13–14). Christ's sacrifice has brought redemption and purification into the lives of those who have received it. They are God's "own," hence the people of God. Here let us observe the words "to redeem us from all iniquity."[12] The new people of God have been redeemed from all iniquity, whatever its size and weight, whatever its perversity and heinousness, whatever its burden and bondage.

The Old Testament people of God, Israel, had likewise experienced a great redemption, namely from bondage in Egypt. In the words of Moses to Israel, "The LORD has brought you out with a mighty hand, and redeemed you from the house of bondage, from the hand of Pharaoh king of Egypt" (Deut. 7:8).[13] This redemption was from physical bondage and served as the immediate background for God's declaration that Israel was to be His special people: "You have seen what I did to the Egyptians. . . . Now, therefore, if you will obey my voice and keep my covenant, you shall be my own possession among all peoples" (Exod. 19:4–5). In a real sense Israel always looked back to God's act of redemption from Egypt—the act that freed them to serve God and to be His people.

The New Testament people of God, Jews and Gentiles alike, have experienced a far greater redemption—from all iniquity. It is a redemption not from physical bondage[14] but from that which is far worse, spiritual bondage, not from the land of Egypt but from the realm of evil, not from the power of Pharaoh but from the dominion of Satan and darkness. Or to change the imagery somewhat, the New Testament people have been delivered by Jesus Christ from their former futile ways and empty lives into newness of life. Peter thus writes, "You were redeemed[15] from the

---

distinguished). Both "race" and "nation" suggest the corporate nature of the Christian community of faith.

[11]The Greek is *laon periousian*, literally, "a people [for] possession." The KJV translation is "a peculiar people."

[12]The Greek word translated "iniquity" is from *anomia*. It is rendered "wickedness" in the NIV.

[13]See also Deuteronomy 9:26; 13:5; 15:15; 24:18.

[14]Later references in the Old Testament speak of redemption in more spiritual terms. For example, Isaiah 44:22 reads, "I have swept away your transgressions like a cloud, and your sins like a mist; return to me, for I have redeemed you." Hence there is also a spiritual dimension in the Old Testament, but in many ways it is anticipatory of what is yet to come. For example, Isaiah 53:5 speaks of One who "*was* wounded for our transgressions . . . *was* bruised for our iniquities." Yet this surely refers to an event in the future. For only in and through Jesus Christ is there full redemption.

[15]Or "ransomed" (RSV). The Greek word *elutrōthēte* may be translated either "redeemed" or "ransomed" (see BAGD).

empty way of life[16] handed down to you by your forefathers . . . with the precious blood of Christ'' (1 Peter 1:18–19 NIV). The lives of the forefathers, whether Jews or Gentiles, whatever their condition, nonetheless represented a condition of emptiness.[17] But for the redeemed people of God, through Jesus Christ, all of life has taken on new meaning and value.

Thus wherever the church assembles, it is a gathering of the redeemed people of God. They may gladly recall God's deliverance of His ancient people Israel from Egypt, or from later captivity;[18] they may even praise God the Redeemer revealed in various places in the Old Testament and yet know that through Jesus Christ full redemption has been received. In the words of Hebrews it is ''an eternal redemption'' (9:12).

Moreover, the redeemed people of God encompass a vast number and range of people. In the Book of Revelation a song sounds forth to Christ the Lamb: ''Worthy art thou to take the scroll and to open its seals, for thou wast slain and by thy blood didst ransom [or 'redeem'][19] men for God from every tribe and tongue and people and nation'' (5:9). Here, indeed, is the new people of God—the church—ransomed, redeemed from all over the world. And it has all happened because of Jesus Christ and His vicarious sacrifice.

2. A Purified People

Redemption also includes purification. To repeat Paul's words: ''Our great God and Savior Jesus Christ . . . gave himself for us to redeem us from all iniquity and to purify for himself a people of his own'' (Titus 2:13–14). Redemption—his deliverance from all sin—is basic, but purification must follow, for God's new people are not only set free from the bondage of sin; they are also a purified and cleansed people.

In the Old Testament, purification followed redemption. For not only was Israel, the people of God, redeemed from Egyptian bondage, but they were also cleansed and purified. Much of this purification was ceremonial—e.g., cleansing rites for dietary and bodily uncleannesses.[20] However, there was also an emphasis on cleansing from sin and transgression, especially as set forth in the Day of Atonement ritual. In Leviticus 16, God declared through Moses to Israel: ''On this day shall atonement be made for you, to cleanse you; from all your sins you shall be clean before the LORD'' (v. 30). This cleansing, despite its significance in marking Israel as God's people, was only a foreshadowing of the deeper and fuller cleansing through Jesus Christ. According to the book of Hebrews, the atonement ritual ''cannot perfect the conscience of the worshiper'' (9:9; cf. also vv. 13–14); indeed, ''it is impossible that the blood of bulls and goats

[16]Or ''futile way'' (NASB).

[17]Regarding Israel, God declared through Jeremiah: ''They went far from Me and walked after emptiness and became empty'' (Jer. 2:5 NASB). In regard to the Gentiles and their idol worship, Paul urges them to ''turn from these vain things to a living God who made the heaven and the earth'' (Acts 14:15).

[18]For example, Jeremiah the prophet, looking to a future deliverance of Israel from Babylonian captivity declares, ''The LORD has ransomed Jacob, and has redeemed him from hands too strong for him'' (Jer. 31:11; cf. 50:33–34).

[19]The KJV reads ''hast redeemed.'' The Greek word *ēgorasas* may also be translated ''purchased'' (as in NIV and NASB).

[20]Leviticus 11–15, for example, contains instructions for purification in regard to unclean animals, a woman's uncleanness after childbirth, uncleanness through contact with leprosy, and uncleanness from bodily secretions.

should take away sins" (10:4). Moreover, the very repetition each year of the Day of Atonement ritual is in itself a demonstration that sins had not been fully cleansed.

The new people of God have received a profound cleansing. It has reached to the inner life, the heart, the conscience. Through the prophet Ezekiel God declared what He would do on a future day: "I will sprinkle clean water upon you, and you shall be clean from all your uncleannesses" (Ezek. 36:25). This word spoken to exiled Israel and pointing to the occasion of their return has been fulfilled in the new people of God. In Hebrews, after reference is made to "the blood of Jesus," the writer speaks about "our hearts sprinkled clean from an evil conscience" (10:19, 22). Thus the new people of God, through the vicarious sacrifice of Jesus, have been purified from every uncleanness.

This has all happened through faith in Christ. In regard to the initial salvation of the Gentiles, the turning of the centurion Cornelius and his household in Caesarea to Christ, Peter declared that God had "cleansed their hearts by faith" (Acts 15:9). Peter had preached the word and baptized these Gentiles, the word and water being the external means of cleansing (see Acts 10:34–48). This recalls the statement of Paul that "Christ loved the church and gave himself up for her, that he might sanctify her, having cleansed her by the washing of water with the word" (Eph. 5:25–26). The church—Jews and Gentiles alike—has been cleansed outwardly by water and the word, even as inwardly there has been a cleansing through faith.[21]

Praise God! The church is the new people of God purified to be His very own!

3. A Changed People

The new people of God are those whose inner lives have been radically changed. Let us now observe several other things.

a. The Law Written on the Heart. Here we turn first to the new covenant as prophesied in Jeremiah 31 and declared as fulfilled in Hebrews 8.[22] The new covenant is first described by Jeremiah with language that seems confined to Israel: "Behold, the days are coming . . . when I will make a new covenant with the house of Israel and the house of Judah" (31:31). The almost identical words are repeated in the Book of Hebrews: "The days will come . . . when I will establish a new covenant with the house of Israel and with the house of Judah" (8:8). However, it is apparent in Hebrews that this new covenant is one mediated by Christ—"the covenant he mediates" (v. 6)[23]—and that this includes *all* who are called to Him.[24] It is no longer a covenant with ethnic Israel (or Israel and Judah), but with all who are called to Christ and believe in Him.[25] The church is this

[21]This of course does not mean that after this initial purification there is no further need of cleansing. Quite the contrary, although the heart has been cleansed, there remains much of the desires of sinful flesh. Hence ongoing purification is always needed. As John writes, "If we say we have no sin, we deceive ourselves, and the truth is not in us." However, "if we confess our sins, he is faithful and just, and will forgive our sins and cleanse us from all unrighteousness" (1 John 1:8–9). The blood of Jesus has cleansed us from all sins and will continue to do so as we humbly make confession.

[22]On "the new covenant" see also *Renewal Theology*, vol. 1, chap. 12.

[23]In Hebrews 9:15 and 12:24 Jesus is described as "the mediator of a new covenant."

[24]Christ as "mediator of a new covenant" relates to "those who are called" (Heb. 9:15).

[25]The church, accordingly, is sometimes called "spiritual Israel" (as over against ethnic

"called" people; and as people of a new covenant, they are a new people of God.

In the new covenant, the first statement refers to the law being written within: "This is the covenant which I will make. . . . I will put my law within them, and I will write it upon their hearts; and I will be their God, and they shall be my people" (Jer. 31:33).[26] The old covenant written on tables of stone (the Ten Commandments) was never truly kept by Israel, because their hearts were not right. As certification of the old covenant Israel practiced circumcision of the flesh, but the real, interior need was for a circumcision of the heart. Moses, who received the tables of stone, knowing where the real problem lay, said to Israel, "Circumcise . . . the foreskin of your heart" (Deut. 10:16). Then in some of his last words he declared, "The LORD your God will circumcise your heart and the heart of your offspring, so that you will love the LORD your God with all your heart and with all your soul, that you may live" (Deut. 30:6). But this never happened under the old covenant: the heart remained "uncircumcised." Thus the new covenant, as spoken through Jeremiah, refers to a future new people of God who will be circumcised in heart:[27] they will have the law cut into, written upon, their inmost being.

So Paul was able to declare that "circumcision is circumcision of the heart, by the Spirit, not by the written code" (Rom. 2:29 NIV). He rejoiced with the Philippians when he said, "It is we who are the circumcision, we who worship by the Spirit of God, who glory in Christ Jesus, and who put no confidence in the flesh" (Phil. 3:3 NIV). This is indeed a spiritual circumcision by which "the foreskin" of the heart of flesh has been removed and the law inscribed by the Holy Spirit on the innermost self.

Hence, one of the distinctives of the new people of God is that God's will is no longer simply an external force that constantly encounters internal resistance;[28] it has now become a positive reality. Paul speaks of how Christ has "condemned sin in the flesh, in order that the requirement of the Law might be fulfilled in us, who do not walk according to the flesh, but according to the Spirit" (Rom. 8:3–4 NASB). As the people of God walk according to the Spirit, they fulfill the law of God.

b. A New Heart. We move on to observe that the promise of the Old Testament is not only the law written upon the hearts of people but also that the people of God will actually have an undivided heart, even a new heart, a new spirit.[29] Shortly after the words in Jeremiah about the new covenant is this declaration of God: "They shall be my people, and I will be their God. I will give them one heart and one way,[30] that they may fear [or 'reverence'] me for

Israel). While such nomenclature is warranted, we must be careful not to exclude ethnic Israel from God's promise. For we must bear in mind that those of ethnic Israel who are "called" likewise, along with Gentiles, belong to "spiritual Israel."

[26]Hebrews 8:10 states, "I will put my laws into their minds, and write them on their hearts, and I will be their God, and they shall be my people."

[27]Before his declaration of the new covenant, Jeremiah, like Moses, had already called out to his people, "Circumcise yourselves to the LORD, remove the foreskin of your hearts" (4:4), and he declared, "All the house of Israel is uncircumcised in heart" (9:26).

[28]The hard resistance of Judah (similarly Israel) is described thus in Jeremiah: "The sin of Judah is written with a pen of iron; with a point of diamond it is engraved on the tablet of their heart" (17:1).

[29]See also *Renewal Theology*, 2:50–52, "A Changed Heart."

[30]The NIV translates this as "singleness of heart and action."

ever, for their own good and the good of their children after them. I will make with them an everlasting covenant"[31] (Jer. 32:38–40). The one heart and one way, in contrast to the former situation of a people with divided hearts and multiple ways, will be fulfilled in the new and everlasting covenant.

Turning next to the prophecy of Ezekiel, we find this promise: "I will give them one heart, and put a new spirit within them; I will take away the stony heart out of their flesh and give them a heart of flesh, that they may walk in my statutes . . . they shall be my people, and I will be their God" (Ezek. 11:19–20).[32] The "one heart" replacing "the stony heart" is likewise fulfilled in the new people of God. Paul writes to the Corinthians that they are "a letter from Christ . . . written not with ink but with the Spirit of the living God, not on tablets of stone but on tablets of human hearts" (2 Cor. 3:3).[33] The "stony heart" has been replaced by the "heart of flesh" through "the Spirit of the living God." Such is the picture of the New Testament people of God.

c. The Spirit Within. Two further passages in Ezekiel go even beyond the one, or new, heart and new spirit. According to Ezekiel 36, God declares, "I will give you a new heart and put a new spirit in you; I will remove from you your heart of stone and give you a heart of flesh. And I will put my Spirit in you and move you to follow my decrees and be careful to keep my laws" (vv. 26–27 NIV).[34] Not only will there be a new heart and a new spirit but God will also place His own Spirit within His people. Again, in Ezekiel, God declares, "I will put my Spirit within you, and you shall live" (37:14).[35]

It is the Spirit of the living God within that is the vital factor of the new people of God. This, of course, goes far beyond the Old Testament people of God, for in the New Testament fulfillment the church composed of Jews and Gentiles alike is indwelt by the Spirit of God. The words of Paul to the Gentile Ephesians are unmistakable: "You also [in addition to believing Jews] are built into it [the household of God, i.e., the church] for a dwelling place of God in the Spirit" (Eph. 2:22). The Spirit has been put within the new people of God.

To summarize: The inner life of the new people of God will be radically

[31]Although the background of these words in Jeremiah 32 is the return of Israel from Babylonian captivity and hence might seem to apply to Israel alone, they are words about "an everlasting covenant" and so correlate with the new covenant of Jeremiah 31. Furthermore, the words above, "they shall be my people, and I will be their God" (v. 38), clearly connect with 31:33, "I will be their God, and they shall be my people." Hence, even as the new covenant promised in Jeremiah 31 is fulfilled in the New Testament people of God, so is the promise of Jeremiah 32.

[32]F. F. Bruce writes, "Although Ezekiel does not use the word 'covenant' here . . . the passage . . . is his counterpart to the 'new covenant' oracle of Jer. 31:31–34, where God undertakes to put his law within his people and write it on their hearts" (*Ezekiel*, IBC, 819).

[33]Paul's words referring back to Ezekiel 11 are another example of what appears to relate only to Israel, for the background is again foreign captivity and the people's return to the homeland (see vv. 16–18). This once more demonstrates how Paul—and the New Testament at large—sees such Old Testament words as fulfilled in the new people of God.

[34]G. R. Beasley-Murray writes, "This passage is Ezekiel's counterpart to the 'new covenant of Jeremiah' " (*Ezekiel*, NBC, rev. ed., 681). Hence, though the reference again in Ezekiel is only to Israel ("the whole house of Israel," v. 10)—as in Jeremiah—the fulfillment will be in the new people of God.

[35]The background for these words is the striking picture of Israel's being like dry and dead bones until they are breathed upon—then "breath came into them, and they lived" (v. 10).

different from that of Israel. The promises in Jeremiah and Ezekiel were that the law would be written upon the heart (circumcision of the heart); there would indeed be a new heart (and spirit) to replace the stony heart; and God's own Spirit would dwell within. But let us change the Old Testament perspective to the present. For the people of God today, what was external has become internal; the law of God is now inscribed on the heart; the heart of stone has been replaced by a new heart and new spirit; and the Spirit of God has come within, bringing new life. Truly this is a new people of God.

C. God Dwelling in and Among His People

Here we reach the climax. We have observed how the new people of God are people whose inner lives have been radically changed by the Spirit of God coming within. Now we view this event from the divine perspective: God Himself is fulfilling His intention to have a people in whom and among whom He can dwell. It is a new mode of God's presence with His people.

Paul uses the imagery of the temple to express this indwelling. He writes, "We are the temple of the living God; as God said, 'I will live in them and move among them, and I will be their God, and they shall be my people' " (2 Cor. 6:16). By these words Paul declares the fulfillment of the Old Testament promise in Leviticus: "I will walk among you, and will be your God, and you shall be my people" (26:12). This Old Testament promise was predicated on the obedience of Israel ("If you walk in my statutes and observe my commandments. . ." [v. 3]), an obedience that Israel never truly fulfilled. There are, to be sure, Old Testament statements such as Exodus 25:8, "Let them make me a sanctuary, that I may dwell in their midst," and Psalm 76:2, "His abode has been established in Salem, his dwelling place in Zion"; and both tabernacle and temple were viewed as places of God's dwelling. However, this was not a direct and personal indwelling of God's people. Moreover, even the indwelling of the temple edifice in later years became a thing of the past when the temple was destroyed and Israel went into exile. Indeed, God promised through Ezekiel that after the Exile Israel and Judah would one day be reunited in their own land and truly be His people: "I will save them from all the backslidings in which they have sinned, and will cleanse them; and they shall be my people, and I will be their God. My servant David shall be king[36] over them. My dwelling place shall be with them . . . my sanctuary is in the midst of them for evermore" (37:23–24, 27–28). The promise concerning God's "servant David" is fulfilled in Jesus Christ—"the Lord God will give to him [Jesus] the throne of his father David" (Luke 1:32)—and the "sanctuary" in the New Testament becomes not an outward building but God's new people, the church. This brings us back to Paul's words "We are the temple of the living God; as God said, 'I will live in them and move among them, and I will be their God, and they shall be my people.' "

The new people of God are uniquely His temple. There is no longer a need or place for an earthly and material sanctuary, no matter how beautiful it may be. Any such sanctuary is greatly limited; for, however close at hand it is, such a temple remains external to God's people. Entrance into it does not include the inmost sanctuary, the Holy of Holies, except for the high priest once a year. Moreover, such a temple at any

[36]Ezekiel 34:23 states, "I will set up over them [Israel] one shepherd, my servant David." Jesus speaks of Himself as "the good shepherd" in John 10:11, 14.

time may be removed or destroyed and God's people left bereft.[37] Now the limitations are totally done away as God lives and moves among His new people.

The church as God's dwelling place is also described by Paul in Ephesians 2. There Paul speaks of the church as "the household of God, built upon the foundation of the apostles and prophets, Christ Jesus himself being the cornerstone . . . in whom you also are built into it for a dwelling place of God in the Spirit" (vv. 19–22).[38] The household of God consists not only of believing Jews but also of Gentiles ("in whom you also"); they together make up the new people of God, the church. The church *is* the dwelling place of God in the Spirit.

Let us for a moment reflect on the amazing fact that God dwells in and among His people. We may here recall the words of Solomon in his prayer at the dedication of the temple in Jerusalem: "Will God indeed dwell on the earth? Behold, heaven and the highest heaven cannot contain thee; how much less this house which I have built!" (1 Kings 8:27).[39] But an extraordinary, almost unbelievable thing has happened. God Himself has come in Jesus Christ, indeed has "tabernacled[40] among us" (John 1:14). Christ was God's new tabernacle, His new temple[41] in a way that no ancient edifice could ever be; thus He was in a unique sense "among us." Now that Christ has returned to heaven, the temple has by no means disappeared. Rather, through His work of redemption and the consequent indwelling of the Holy Spirit, believers—the church—have become the very temple of the living God.

To repeat: it is an amazing fact! Wherever the church, the true believers in Christ, gather, God dwells in their midst. He moves among them. In the Book of Revelation where the seven churches of Asia Minor are depicted as seven golden lampstands, Christ is described as One "who walks among[42] the seven golden lampstands" (2:1) Thus God, who is also Christ, walks in and among His people wherever they are. His presence is there at all times. The God of the whole universe, whom "heaven and the highest heaven"—and surely, then, any earthly temple (be it as magnificent as that of Solomon's)—cannot contain, dwells in and among His people!

Perhaps the most fitting words to close this section are these:

God Himself is with us:
Let us now adore him,
And with awe appear before Him.
God is in His temple,
All within keep silence,
And before Him bow with reverence.
Him alone, God we own;
To our Lord and Saviour
Praises sing forever.[43]

---

[37]One thinks of present-day orthodox Jews who constantly lament the destruction of the Jerusalem temple in A.D. 70. The "wailing wall"—a remnant of the destroyed temple—where Jews gather to weep over the loss of the temple and to pray for its rebuilding is a continuing symbol of their misplaced hope. Would that they knew and believed Paul's words that "we [believers in Christ] are the temple of the living God"!

[38]Recall the brief discussion of Ephesians 2:22 in the previous section.

[39]This is Stephen's same point as he spoke about the temple before the Sanhedrin in Acts 7:48–50.

[40]The Greek word is *eskenōsen*, literally "tabernacled" (see Thayer). The customary English translation is "dwelt" (RSV and others).

[41]On one occasion Jesus declared to the Jews, " 'Destroy this temple, and in three days I will raise it up.'. . . But he spoke of the temple of his body" (John 2:19, 21).

[42]This is the KJV translation of the Greek phrase is *en mesō*, "in the midst of."

[43]From the hymn "God Himself Is With Us," by Gerhardt Tersteegen, 1729.

II. THE BUILDING, BODY, AND BRIDE OF CHRIST

All description of the church centers in Jesus Christ. In order to better apprehend this, we will focus on the church as the building, body, and bride of Christ.

A. The Building of Christ

The first reference in the New Testament to the church is recorded in Matthew 16:18, where Jesus declares, "I will build my church." This statement is similar to words spoken by God through Jeremiah the prophet: "I will bring them [Israel] back to this land. I will build them up, and not tear them down; I will plant them, and not uproot them" (Jer. 24:6).[44] In Matthew the words "I will build" now are spoken by Jesus:[45] He will be the builder.[46] Thus the words of Old Testament prophecy about Israel are fulfilled in Christ.

What, however, is distinctive in Matthew is the phrase "my church." The word *church, ekklēsia*, to be sure, has an Old Testament background: Israel was the assembly of God (the "*ekklēsia* in the wilderness"—Acts 7:38), and there is undoubtedly an important connection between the *ekklēsia* in the Old Testament and the *ekklēsia* in the New Testament. However, Jesus' words are testimony to an *ekklēsia* that will be peculiarly His: "I will build my church." The church in a very special way will be His creation and will belong to Him.

In the previous discussion of the church as "the people of God," we have observed a certain continuity of language. This expression occurs in both Old and New Testaments, even though "the people of God" takes on a broader and deeper meaning in the New. However, the church as the building of Christ ("my church") is language unique to the New Testament and thus points more in the direction of discontinuity, indeed to the new reality that Christ brings about.

1. Foundation

Jesus said, "On this rock I will build my church" (Matt. 16:18). Earlier in Matthew's gospel He had stated that to hear and do His teachings is to build on a rock: "Every one then who hears these words of mine and does them will be like a wise man who built his house upon the rock" (7:24). Hence, one important aspect of the foundation is to hear and do Jesus' words faithfully. But in the context of Jesus' words "on this rock I will build my church," something further is being said. The immediate background is Simon Peter's declaration about Jesus, "You are the Christ, the Son of the living God." Jesus responded, "Blessed are you, Simon Bar-Jona! For flesh and blood has not revealed this to you, but my Father who is in heaven." Then He added, "And I tell you, you are Peter and on this rock[47] I will build my church" (Matt. 16:16–18). The rock was not simply Peter

---

[44]Cf. also Jeremiah 31:4—"Again I will build you, and you shall be built, O virgin Israel!"

[45]Some New Testament scholars have viewed Jesus' words here and in 18:17 (see later) about the church as inauthentic, since they have no parallel in the other Gospels. However, all ancient Greek manuscripts contain these words. Moreover, the text unquestionably expresses a profound truth about Jesus' relation to the church.

[46]Christ is also called a builder in Hebrews 3:2–3: "Moses also was faithful in God's house. Yet Jesus has been counted worthy of as much more glory than Moses as the builder of a house has more honor than the house."

[47]The Greek words are *Petros* and *petra*, an obvious play on words. In the Aramaic, which Jesus spoke, the same form *képhā'* would occur in both places.

himself[48] but his confession that Jesus was the Christ, the Son of the living God.[49] Then Jesus immediately declared, "And the gates of Hades[50] will not overcome[51] it" (v. 18 NIV). No matter what may come against the church—Christ's church—it will endure.

The church is to be founded upon more than hearing and doing Jesus' words, although to do and to hear is to build upon a rock. It must also believe and proclaim that Jesus is the Christ, the Messiah, indeed the very Son of God. A church that is shaky about this foundation or departs from it will be no match for the gates of Hades. If, for example, Jesus is viewed as anyone less than the divine Son of God, or only as one manifestation of God among many, the sure foundation is thereby undermined. It is urgent that this foundation be firm and secure. Paul, writing to the Corinthian church, speaks of them as "God's building" (1 Cor. 3:9). Shortly after that he adds, "No one can lay any foundation other than the one already laid, which is Jesus Christ" (v. 11 NIV). Of Paul—even as of Peter—when he confessed Jesus as the Christ, Jesus could truly say, "On this rock—this foundation—I will build my church."

In regard to this latter point the New Testament also asserts the apostolic foundation of the church. Paul speaks in Ephesians of the church as "the household of God, built upon the foundation of the apostles and prophets" (2:19–20). Here the imagery is somewhat different: rather than portraying Christ as foundation, the picture is that of "apostles and prophets."[52] In one

---

[48]If so, Jesus could have made it much clearer by saying "on you" rather than "on this rock." In this regard see Robert H. Gundry, *Matthew: A Commentary on His Literary and Theological Art*, 334. W. C. Allen on this passage writes, "The Church was to be built on the revealed truth that Jesus was the Messiah, the Divine Son" (*Gospel acc. to St. Matthew*, ICC, 177). Similarly A. H. McNeile declares, "The fact of the Lord's Messiahship was to be the immovable bed-rock on which His 'ecclesia' would stand secure" (*Gospel acc. to St. Matthew*, 241). Various other commentators hold that Peter himself was the rock, e.g., R. T. France, *Matthew*, TNTC, 254–55; D. A. Carson, *Matthew*, EBC, 368–69; H. N. Ridderbos, *Matthew*, BSC, 303. (See next footnote for fuller perspective.)

[49]Peter later fulfills this role as he preaches the gospel of Jesus Christ on the Day of Pentecost. In that sense Peter, as confessing, was the rock. As A. B. Bruce says, "Peter, believing that truth [that Jesus is the Christ] is the foundation, and the building is to be of a piece with the foundation" (EGT, 1:224–25). It is important not to conclude that Peter simply as a man was "this rock."

[50]The KJV reads "gates of hell." However, the Greek word is a form of *hades*, not *gehenna* (the ordinary Greek word for "hell"). Hades is "the underworld as the place of the dead" (BAGD), "the infernal regions" (Thayer). The RSV and NEB translate the word as "powers of death." Whatever the translation, the picture is that the church cannot be overcome by any forces arrayed against it.

[51]The Greek word is *katischusousin*. Both KJV and RSV read "prevail against"; NASB has "overpower." BAGD translates the word in this context "win a victory over." An alternative translation for *katischusousin* as "prove stronger than" (NIV margin) gives a different picture. Rather than "the gates of Hades" being unable to win a victory over the church, the picture is one of "gates" being unable to hold out against the victorious church. This interpretation, despite its basic truthfulness, hardly seems to be Jesus' intent.

[52]"Prophets" most likely refers to Christian prophets who, prior to the formation of the New Testament Scriptures, were an inspired source of Christian truth. That these prophets were not Old Testament prophets seems apparent from further reference to them in Ephesians 3:4 as those who along with apostles had been given "insight into the mystery of Christ," or in Ephesians 4:11, again along with apostles, as gifts of Christ for the building up of the church. Note also that the order each time is apostles and prophets, not prophets and

sense, as we have already observed, the apostle Peter himself as confessing was the rock or the foundation; Paul likewise in Ephesians implies the same about himself and the other apostles. The apostles were the original and foundational witnesses to the truth of Christ as the Son of God, and on their testimony the church is based. Peter was the first to proclaim this truth. Because of that initial testimony, Peter was the rock, the foundational witness at Pentecost and for some time after that event.[53] At Pentecost a complete apostolic witness had already been manifested prior to Paul and other apostles.[54] Thus apostles continued to be foundational in the church of Jesus Christ.[55]

It is worth noting again that "the holy city" in the Book of Revelation is described as having "a great, high wall," and "the wall of the city had twelve foundations, and on them the twelve names of the twelve apostles of the Lamb" (21:12, 14). Since the holy city represents the glorified church ("new Jerusalem, coming down out of heaven from God" [v. 2]), the apostles are depicted as its foundation. This picture again demonstrates the foundational role of the apostles and the apostolic witness.

Let me strongly emphasize the importance of the apostolic foundation of the church. The church must continuously remain under apostolic tutelage as set forth in the New Testament.[56] Whenever there is departure from their authority and teaching, the church forsakes its true foundation. No other writings are on the same level as theirs, no tradition can add anything to them, and no presumed fresh revelation can carry the church beyond their witness.

To conclude this section: It is apparent that no contradiction exists between Christ being laid as a foundation (recall Paul's words in 1 Cor. 3:11) and the apostles being called the foundation. Christ, the Son of God, is the foundational truth and the apostles were those who first declared it. As such, Peter was the primary "rock" or foundation, and the other apostles were additional foundations.

2. *Cornerstone*

Christ Himself is depicted in many Scriptures as the cornerstone of the building. As we will note, the imagery of the cornerstone has an Old Testament background.

Let us first observe the words of Isaiah 28:16: "Behold, I am laying in Zion for a foundation a stone, a tested stone, a precious cornerstone, of a sure foundation: 'He who believes will not be in haste.'" These words, spoken while Israel relied on an alliance with Egypt for protection against Assyrian invasion, depict God laying in Jerusa-

---

apostles. The latter would indeed suggest Old Testament prophets and New Testament apostles. The conclusion follows that Paul is referring to Christian prophets. (On this matter the discussion in EGT [3:299–30] is especially helpful; also see my discussion infra about apostles and prophets in chap. 5, pp. 165–74)

[53]Acts 2 through 12 is largely a record of Peter's early leadership. Paul's missionary ministry begins with Acts 13.

[54]The text reads, "Peter, *standing with the eleven*, lifted up his voice and addressed them [the multitude assembled]" (Acts 2:14). It was a united apostolic witness.

[55]I refer here to their continuing witness as found in Scripture, not to some continuing lineal succession. Recall the previous discussion of one of the attributes of the church as "apostolic" (pp. 35–38).

[56]One of the historic norms of canonicity for any presumed Scripture in the New Testament is that it either be written by apostles or spring directly out of the apostolic circle (see, e.g., F. F. Bruce, *The Canon of Scripture*, "Apostolic Authority," 256–59). This might include Christian prophets also, as noted.

lem a stone, variously described as "tested," "precious," and "sure." Those who believe in this stone will not hastily rely on foreign forces and thus will be secure.[57] On the contrary, those who do not believe will be swept away as by a storm (see v. 17). Earlier, Isaiah had spoken of God Himself as both a sanctuary and a stone: "The LORD Almighty is the one you are to regard as holy . . . and he will be a sanctuary; but for both houses of Israel he will be a stone that causes men to stumble and a rock that makes them fall. . . . Many of them will stumble; they will fall and be broken. . ." (8:13–15 NIV). This extraordinary double picture describes God as a rocklike sanctuary for those who believe (look to the Lord "as holy"); but for Israel who, despite imminent invasion,[58] does not rely on God, He will be a stone on which they will be crushed. A related Old Testament passage is Psalm 118:22–23: "The stone which the builders rejected has become the head of the corner. This is the LORD's doing; it is marvelous in our eyes."[59] This rejection of the stone follows the same pattern as in Isaiah's prophecies. But here, in promise, the rejected stone becomes head of the corner, that is, the cornerstone[60] or capstone[61] of the whole building.

As we move to the New Testament, it is apparent that these Old Testament prophecies are all fulfilled in Jesus Christ. Indeed Jesus himself quotes Psalm 118:22 in the context of His own rejection by Israel. He tells a parable about the owner of a vineyard who, after his servants and finally his own son have been killed by the tenants, puts the tenants to death and rents the vineyard to others. Then Jesus quotes the Psalm: "The very stone which the builders rejected has become the head of the corner; this was the Lord's doing, and it is marvelous in our eyes" (Matt. 21:42; Mark 12:10; cf. Luke 20:17). In the Matthean account Jesus immediately adds, "Therefore I tell you that the kingdom of God will be taken away from you and given to a people who will produce its fruit" (v. 43 NIV). It is clear that this will be a new building for a new people. Christ Himself will be the head cornerstone.

In the Lukan account Jesus interestingly adds words drawn from Isaiah 8:13–15: "Every one who falls on that stone will be broken to pieces; but when it falls on any one it will crush[62] him" (Luke 20:18). Here the picture is that of unbelievers stumbling over the stone, namely, Christ Himself or, even worse, of the day of judgment yet to come when the terrible judgment of Christ will utterly crush them. Hence, while Christ is the chief cornerstone or capstone of the building for believers, the same stone is a cause of breaking, even of crushing, for those who will not believe.

---

[57]As John D. W. Watts puts it, "The believer is affirmed in his patience, as he waits for God to complete his work" (*Isaiah 1–33*, WBC, 370).

[58]In Isaiah 8 the threat was likewise from Assyria (see especially v. 7).

[59]This verse probably refers to the "mountain" of difficulties confronting Zerubbabel in the rebuilding of the temple and the assurance by God that the "top stone" will be put in place: "What are you, O great mountain? Before Zerubbabel you shall become a plain; and he shall bring forward the top stone amid shouts of 'Grace, grace to it' " (Zech. 4:7). However, it is obvious that the words of Psalm 118:22 also reach forward into the New Testament (as will be seen later).

[60]So the NASB translates.

[61]So the NIV translates.

[62]The KJV reads "grind him to powder." The Greek word is *likmēsei*. Thayer translates the word for this verse, "crush to pieces, grind to powder."

The sad and tragic story is that Israel rejected "the stone." In the Book of Acts Peter, after speaking to the Jewish Sanhedrin of "Jesus Christ of Nazareth, whom [they] crucified, whom God raised from the dead," added: "This is the stone that was rejected by you builders, but which has become the head of the corner" (4:10–11). Paul later comments, "They [the Jews] stumbled over the stumbling stone, just as it is written, 'Behold, I lay in Zion a stone of stumbling and a rock of offense, and he who believes in Him will not be disappointed' "[63] (Rom. 9:32–33 NASB).[64] However, for those who believe, there is no disappointment: Christ is the cornerstone in the building of faith.

Peter brings together in one passage all three of the Old Testament references. First, there is the positive word from Isaiah 28: "Behold I lay in Zion a choice stone, a precious corner stone, and he who believes in Him shall not be disappointed" (1 Peter 2:6 NASB). Second, on the negative side, Peter continues the other two passages from Psalm 118 and Isaiah 8 thus: "For those who disbelieve, 'The stone which the builders rejected, this became the very corner stone,' and 'a stone of stumbling and a rock of offense' " (vv. 7–8 NASB). Christ is the cornerstone, precious for believers, but a stumbling block and an offense for unbelievers.

There is one further New Testament passage about Christ as cornerstone, one that relates only to believers, indeed to the church. Writing to the believers in Ephesus, Paul declares, "Ye are no more strangers and foreigners, but fellow citizens with the saints, and of the household of God; and are built upon the foundation of the apostles and prophets, Jesus Christ himself being the chief corner stone"[65] (2:19–20 KJV). We have previously discussed the foundation of apostles and prophets; now we observe that Christ is the chief cornerstone. Paul here seems to be saying that Christ is the cornerstone that brings together both Gentiles and Jews. He had spoken previously of how Christ had "broken down the dividing wall of hostility" (v. 14) that separated Jews and Gentiles. Now with that wall broken down and gone, Christ places Himself in the new building as the chief cornerstone that unites and holds together formerly divided peoples.[66] There is no longer a dividing wall; rather two former walls now meet in Christ and are one in Him.

It is important to realize how far this carries us beyond the Old Testament. There was indeed a dividing wall between Israel and the surrounding world, particularly shown in the sacred pre-

---

[63]Rather than "put to shame" (RSV, NIV, similarly KJV). The Greek word is *kataischunthēsetai* (BAGD in relation to this verse translates it "be disappointed").

[64]Paul actually combines words from the two passages in Isaiah, already noted: 8:13–15 and 28:16. Some slight rewording is also apparent.

[65]The NASB reads "the cornerstone." The Greek word is *akrogōniaiou*, meaning simply "cornerstone" (see Thayer). BAGD has "cornerstone or capstone" (but not "chief" for either). "Chief," however, may suggest the idea of "capstone," a cornerstone that is at the same time above all the other stones. Bruce opts for "top stone": "*Akrogōniaios*, so far as it can be determined, does not mean a cornerstone but a stone which crowns the building, like the 'top stone' of Zerubbabel's temple, the last stone to be put in position" (*Ephesians*, NICNT, 306). "Top stone" or "capstone" would perhaps correspond more with "head of the corner" (see verses previously quoted). "Chief (= 'top') cornerstone" conveys the idea that Christ is both cornerstone and the pinnacle of all the other stones.

[66]Thayer, under *akrogōniaios*, states, "As the corner-stone holds together two walls, so Christ joins together as Christians, into one body dedicated to God, those who were formerly Jews and 'Gentiles.' "

cincts of the temple from which Gentiles were totally excluded.[67] Through Christ's death on the cross those who "once were far off have been brought near in the blood of Christ" (Eph. 2:13). Christ in building His church is Himself the chief cornerstone that binds together and supports all. Just after his words about the chief cornerstone, Paul adds, "in whom [Christ] the whole structure is joined together" (v. 21). Christ as cornerstone unites all in Himself.

Surely this speaks also to any and all divisions of people. Paul writes elsewhere, "There is neither Jew nor Greek, there is neither slave nor free, there is neither male nor female; for you are all one in Christ Jesus" (Gal. 3:28). This obviously does not mean that Jews and Greeks, slaves and free, males and females no longer exist, for they surely do. *But* in Christ—to use again the imagery of cornerstone—they all come together. As *chief* cornerstone He is also "the head of the corner," the top or pinnacle stone,[68] in whom believers, whatever their nationality, social status, or gender, are one.

The church indeed is the building of Christ, with Himself as the cornerstone.

3. *Living Stones*

Finally, the building of Christ is constructed of "living stones." Here we turn primarily to 1 Peter and the relevant words "Coming to Him as to a living stone, rejected by men, but choice and precious in the sight of God, you also, as living stones, are being built up[69] as a spiritual house for a holy priesthood, to offer up spiritual sacrifices acceptable to God through Jesus Christ" (2:4–5 NASB).

It is significant, first, that Christ Himself is addressed by Peter as a living stone. The same Peter, who once had confessed Jesus as "the Christ, the Son of the living God" and thereby was called a rock by Jesus, now calls Jesus a living stone, a living rock![70] It is almost as if Peter were saying, "Whatever might be affirmed about me in regard to a rock, look now to Christ the living One, Son of the living God, for He is the living Rock." Second, among all references to Christ as a rock or stone (head of the corner, cornerstone, etc.) the expression "living stone" exhibits most clearly that He is no inanimate reality holding the building together but is truly alive. Christ Himself is a living stone. Third, this same Christ, while rejected by men, is choice and precious in God's sight, and is the One to whom we are invited to come. This is indeed a beautiful invitation to come to One so highly valued.

Now we arrive at the reality that we too are living stones. Because Christ is a living stone and we are alive through faith in Him, we are also living stones.

---

[67]Posted along the stone balustrade of the temple at regular intervals were stone slabs inscribed in Latin and Greek that forbade Gentiles, on the penalty of death, from entering (see "Inscriptions," ISBE, 2:838, and "Temple," ISBE, 4:772.

[68]It is interesting to note that the NEB in Ephesians 2:20 gives as an alternate translation "keystone." A keystone is a "wedge-shaped piece at the crown of an arch that locks the other pieces in place" (Webster). The imagery is slightly different from a cornerstone, which joins and supports two walls. We may say that Christ as "chief cornerstone" is both "chief," namely a keystone at the top locking and holding other pieces in place, and "corner" uniting and binding all together.

[69]The RSV translates this as an imperative: "Be yourselves built into" (similarly NEB). The indicative above (also in KJV and NIV) is more likely (cf. Eph. 2:22 and Col. 2:7).

[70]"Rock" in Matthew 16:18 is *petra*; here in 1 Peter 2:4 "stone" is *lithon*. However, *petra* is also used for Jesus in 1 Peter 2:8–"a rock [*petra*] of offence" (KJV, likewise Paul in Rom. 9:33). In regard to the word "living," the same Greek word (a form of *zaō*) is used in both accounts.

As such we are not simply stones that are stolid and fixed in place, but we are in the process of being built up in Him "as a spiritual house." Moreover, this means that Christ's building is by no means complete, for although the foundation of apostles and prophets has been laid and the cornerstone of Christ set in place, believers in Him continue to be built as living stones into the edifice. Christ's building is ever alive and growing.

Paul's words in Ephesians, immediately following those about the foundation of apostles and prophets with Christ as chief cornerstone, are relevant here: "in whom [Christ] the whole building, being fitted together is growing into a holy temple in the Lord; in whom you also are being built together into a dwelling of God in the Spirit" (2:21–22 NASB). Although Paul, unlike Peter, does not speak of "living stones," it is apparent that essentially the same thing is being said in speaking of "growing into a holy temple." Growth means life, hence believers are growing, living stones. As such we are "being built together" into a place of God's dwelling.

It is interesting that the architectural language of a building—with foundation, cornerstone, and other stones—shifts into the biological: life and growth. The reason is apparent: whereas the imagery of a building properly structured is basic to an understanding of Christ and His church, the very building must be seen as a living reality. Stones being "fitted together"—the architectural figure—must also be viewed as "growing into"—the biological figure. "Living stones" expresses both figures and makes for a valuable understanding of the place of each member of the church in relation to Christ Himself, who is *the* Living Stone.

A concluding word: Christ the builder, who is Himself also cornerstone and capstone and has already laid the foundation stones of the apostles and prophets, is presently fitting together and building together all the other stones. Christ shapes the stones, knows exactly where each one fits, and sets it in its proper place. Since we are "living stones," there is nothing mechanical about this process. Recall Peter's words: "*Coming to Him* as to a living stone . . . you also, as living stones, are being built up."[71] As we come to Him, we put ourselves at His disposal, and Christ places us properly in His church. He may, and probably will, need to shape us, polish us, and remove rough edges so that He can make precisely the right fitting. So we need to come, and come often, to Him that we may be a vital part of His great building plans.

"I will build my church." His church includes all who truly belong to Him.

B. The Body of Christ

The church is also the body of Christ. This New Testament image is highly significant in setting forth the nature of the church. Although there are suggestions of this imagery elsewhere, it is the apostle Paul who specifically uses it. Let us observe several examples.

Writing to the church at Corinth, Paul says, "Now you are the body of Christ and individually members of it" (1 Cor. 12:27). To the Romans Paul declares, "We, though many, are one body in Christ, and individually members one of another" (12:5). In his letter to the Ephesians Paul states, "Christ is the

[71]In Colossians Paul writes, "As you . . . have received Christ Jesus the Lord, so walk in Him, having been firmly rooted and now being built up in Him" (2:6–7 NASB). Note the challenge to "walk," i.e., live, in Christ, the one in whom we have been firmly rooted. By our so walking, the process of "being built up" continues.

head of the church, his body" (5:23). Paul writes similarly to the Colossian church: "He is the head of the body, the church" (1:18). Other examples could be cited.[72]

Before proceeding further, we should note that there are New Testament references to the body of Christ that are not directly related to the church. They relate to Christ Himself, both physically and figuratively. Physical reference is found in such words as "she saw . . . where the body of Jesus had lain" (John 20:12) and "you have died to the law through the body of Christ" (Rom. 7:4). Figurative usage is to be recognized in the words of Jesus Himself about the bread in the Last Supper, "This is my body" (Matt. 26:26; Mark 14:22; Luke 22:19).[73] The body of Christ, as a description for the church, needs to be viewed separately.

What does it mean, then, to say that the church is the body of Christ?[74] Three observations may now be made as to what this signifies.

1. A Vital Relationship With Christ

Since Christ is the head and the church is His body, the church has no life outside of Jesus Christ. In an organic sense what is a body without a head but a corpse? The church's whole life is vitally connected with Christ, or there is no life whatsoever.

The church, first of all, has been *incorporated* into Christ. The church may be described as "believers incorporate in Christ Jesus" (Eph. 1:1 NEB). Thus as a body of believers we are "in Christ." Paul uses the expression "in Christ" (or "in Him") five times in Ephesians 1:3–13 to express this incorporation. One such statement refers to the fact that God "chose us in him [Christ] before the foundation of the world" (v. 4), making clear that believers corporately have belonged to Christ from eternity. Indeed, there is such a close connection that Paul can later say, "To him [God] be the glory in the church and in Christ Jesus to all generations, for ever and ever. Amen" (Eph. 3:21). To Christ and His body, the church, glory may be attributed.

The church, accordingly, does not consist of individual believers who have collectively formed a body. The body of Christ in this sense preexists any individual or group efforts to form a body. From the moment of salvation we are incorporated with all other believers into Christ and together belong to Him.

The church as the body of Christ, next, is *totally dependent* on Christ. In one of His discourses Jesus uses the figure of vine and branches—"I am the vine, you are the branches." Then He adds, "Apart from me you can do nothing" (John 15:5). Even as the branches totally depend on the vine, so the body totally depends on the head. Paul describes this dependence particularly in relation to the church's growth. He speaks of "holding fast to the Head, from whom the whole body, nourished and knit together through its joints and ligaments, grows with a growth that is

[72]See, in particular, 1 Corinthians 12:12; Ephesians 1:23; 2:16; 3:6; 4:4, 12; 5:30; Colossians 1:24; 2:19.

[73]"Figurative" may not be saying enough about the meaning of Jesus' words (see later discussion in chap. 6, pp. 241–63, "The Lord's Supper"). However, it is apparent that more is meant than just Jesus' speaking of Himself as physical bread.

[74]Two extremes in reference to the church as the body of Christ must be guarded against. One is a literal sense that views the church as Christ's actual body, which has replaced His former physical body. The other extreme is to view the church as Christ's body as only a metaphor to express a gathered body similar, for example, to a political body, "the body politic," etc. The church is neither Christ's literal body nor is it simply a collective body of believers. It is the spiritual body of Christ.

from God" (Col. 2:19). All such growth depends on "holding fast to the Head,"[75] for without union with the Head there can be no life and growth. The church is wholly dependent on Christ the Head.

It is apparent from Paul's words that the church's incorporation into Christ does not mean automatic dependence. The head and body imagery could suggest such a physical and organic relationship that dependence necessarily follows. However, the physical body does not have to be told to "hold fast to the head": it is permanently affixed. But in regard to the body of Christ there is no such physical and organic connection. It is not, so to speak, the torso of which Christ is the head, but the body that He has taken to Himself and that operates freely in relation to Him.

We must therefore avoid any idea of the church as the bodily extension of Christ. It is sometimes said that even as the human head cannot exist without the body, so Christ cannot exist without the church.[76] This is erroneous for many reasons. First, it overlooks the lordship of Christ who is over all things as well as over the church, thus clearly he is not dependent on the church.[77] Second, it confuses the imagery of Christ's spiritual relationship to the church as His body with the fact that even now in heaven He has a glorified body without which He indeed does not exist. Third, the church, despite its spiritual relationship to Christ, is invariably sinful while on this earth.[78] It cannot be ontologically the body of Christ, which as such is pure and sinless. The church is not the bodily extension of Christ; He is both over and beyond it. Hence, the church exists not organically in relation to Christ but in a dynamic relationship of free and glad dependence.

The church as the body of Christ, finally, is *wholly subject* to Jesus Christ. The body is totally subservient to the head, receiving all its direction from it. When the physical head directs, the hand or foot moves. In a well-functioning body every member moves in ready and instant action as the head determines. Paul, speaking about Christ as "head of the church, his body," adds that "the church is subject to Christ" (Eph. 5:23–24).[79] Subjection means to be fully at the service of Christ, doing constantly what He, the Head of the church, wills.

Thus to be "members of his body" (Eph. 5:30) suggests also that even as the physical body has many members, all of which are subject to the head and must move completely at its disposal, so must all members of the spiritual body of Christ. Indeed, there should be

[75]Paul in this passage actually speaks of those "not holding fast to the Head"; however, by implication those who do hold fast will have the bodily growth described.

[76]For example, Hans Küng writes in his book *The Church*, in a chapter entitled "The Church as the Body of Christ," that "Christ does not exist without the Church, the Church does not exist without Christ" (p. 234).

[77]A popular statement declares, "Christ has no hands but our hands . . . no feet but our feet to lead men in the way." While this can be viewed as a challenge to the church to be about Christ's business, this kind of statement surely exaggerates Christ's dependence on the church.

[78]Some day the church will be "a glorious church, not having spot, or wrinkle, or any such thing" (Eph. 5:27 KJV). But this is the future prospect (as the context shows), not the present reality. (For more on this see the section "The Bride of Christ," pp. 72–77.)

[79]These words of Paul are set in the broader context of the subjection, or submission, that wives owe to their husbands. Paul here is shifting from the imagery of an organic relationship of head and body to that of a personal relationship of husband and wife. The latter picture contains more of the idea of a conscious and willing submission than does the former. Submission, or subjection, however, is the key to both images.

instantaneous response of the body to even the slightest direction from the head. If not, only confusion and disorientation will follow.

The church as the body of Christ exists to do the will of the Head. By each member being subject to Christ at every moment and in all things, the church fulfills its highest calling. Christ the Head is truly Christ the Lord!

2. Membership in One Another

Since Christ is the Head and the church His body, this also means that we are members of one another. Paul writes, "We, though many, are one body in Christ, and individually members one of another" (Rom. 12:5). Membership in one another follows from the church's being members of Christ's body.

This signifies, for one thing, an *equality* among all church members. If we are members of one another, no one can be higher than any other. In Ephesians Paul declares that "the Gentiles are fellow heirs and fellow members of the body" (3:6 NASB). Thus, as "fellow members," Gentiles and Jews, indeed all Christians, stand on the same ground. All belong to the same body. There are, to be sure, those who equip others in the body, but no one is higher, no one lower in rank. Indeed in the very passage where Paul speaks of those who give special service to "building up the body of Christ" (Eph. 4:12), he adds that "we [equippers and all others] are to grow up in every way into him who is the head, into Christ, from whom the whole body . . . upbuilds itself in love" (vv. 15–16). Thus no one is superior, no one inferior: all grow together into Christ.

The matter of equality needs to be remembered constantly. The church has far too often departed from this by assigning a higher and more elevated place to some members. There is a diversity of gifts among the membership, but since all are members of one another—indeed since "each member belongs to all the others" (Rom. 12:5 NIV)—equality among all must be recognized. To be sure, some are called to be leaders to whom obedience is due.[80] But leadership is not lordship;[81] it is servanthood: a way of serving others in the body. All Christians, accordingly, are equally brothers and sisters in the body of Christ.

Again, membership in one another signifies *interdependence*. All the members of the body depend on one another. In Paul's words, "The body does not consist of one member but of many" (1 Cor. 12:14). Following this statement Paul writes at some length (vv. 15–25) about the interdependence of hand and foot, of eye and ear, of "our unpresentable" and "presentable parts." For example, the foot should not say, "Because I am not a hand, I do not belong to the body," nor should the eye say to the hand, "I have no need of you." On the contrary each part, each member, fully belongs to the body and fully needs all the others. Indeed, all members are dependent on all the other members and must therefore work together to accomplish anything at all. Further, not only is there interdependence in activity; the same is true in regard to such human experiences as suffering and rejoicing. Therefore Paul adds, "If one member suffers, all the members suffer with it; if one member is honored, all the members rejoice with it" (v. 26 NASB). In this we see the profound interdependence of all members of the body of Christ.

Here I need to speak out strongly

---

[80]E.g., in Hebrews 13:17 is the admonition "Obey your leaders and submit to them."

[81]Peter reminds elders, "Be shepherds of God's flock that is under your care . . . not lording it over those entrusted to you" (1 Peter 5:2–3 NIV).

against the common notion of privatized Christianity. Many acknowledge Christ as their Head, their Lord and Savior, and in that sense are members of Him, but they do not recognize that this also makes them members of one another. *To be a member of Christ's body is to be joined to other believers in the body*. There is no such thing as an isolated Christianity in which the prayer closet or garden[82] is the only vital concern of religious practice. Such individualism actually runs counter to the reality of Christian existence, for to be believers is to belong to Christ as Head and at the same time to belong to one another. Accordingly there is no bona fide Christian existence outside the church.[83]

It is not uncommon today to hear people say or imply: "Jesus, yes; the church, no."[84] This is quite understandable in view of the fact that the church often is, or seems to be, little more than some institutional form that is rather unattractive and even forbidding. However, "Jesus, yes; the church, no" is really an impossible and contradictory statement. There is simply no vertical relationship to Christ that does not also contain the horizontal relation to other Christians. Thus from the moment a person first comes to faith, he is also united to other believers; this is the true church. There is no option whether to join or not to join; a person is already placed in a situation of full interdependence with other believers. We not only need Christ as our Head, but we also need one another.

Let me be quite specific. This means that we must be involved with a local body of believers. It is surely not enough to say that one belongs to the universal church, for though this is true, the universal church must have local embodiment.[85] Any local body of Christians is quite likely to have some negative elements,[86] but if it is at all a church containing "called" people, true believers, we may rightly be a part of it. Staying out of a local church—and by that denying one's God-given relation to and need for other believers—is far worse than being an active member of the church, whatever its supposed or real negative aspects.

"Jesus, yes; church, yes!" How could it be otherwise when the church is a part of His body and every believer a member of it?

Still again, membership in one another makes for *mutual responsibility*. We began this section with these words of Paul: "We, though many, are one body in Christ, and individually members of one another" (Rom. 12:5). Preceding these words Paul points out that "in one body we have many members, and all the members do not have the same function" (v. 4). Although there is differentiation in terms of function

---

[82]"I come to the garden alone. . . . And He walks with me, and He talks with me, And He tells me I am His own" are some words from a familiar hymn. While these words express a personal, even important act of devotion, they may represent for some people a private kind of faith in isolation from the body of Christ. In the church Christ tells us not only that we are "His own" but also that we belong to one another in total interdependence.

[83]I like the words of Claude Welch: "One is never alone in Christ. Membership in him is at the same time membership in one another. There is no purely private Christianity, for to be in Christ is to be in the church and to be in the church is to be in Christ" (*The Reality of the Church*, 165).

[84]See David Watson, *I Believe in the Church*, chapter 1, "Who Believes in the Church?" that begins, "JESUS—YES! CHURCH—NO!" pointing out a typical attitude of many people in our day.

[85]Recall the earlier discussion on the church as local (pp. 38–43).

[86]Recall that of the seven churches addressed in Revelation 2 and 3, five have words of criticism directed to them.

because of the variety of gifts, the ensuing responsibility in the body still remains to exercise these gifts for the benefit of one another. Thus he adds: "Since we have gifts[87] that differ according to the grace given to us, let each exercise them accordingly" (v. 6 NASB).[88] Then Paul lists seven gifts—from prophecy through showing mercy (vv. 6–8)[89]—that are to be exercised in the body. Each member properly functioning in his gift fulfills his responsibility to a fellow believer.

Peter, without specifically using the body imagery, writes, "As each has received a gift, employ it for one another, as good stewards of God's varied grace" (1 Peter 4:10). Since each member has received a gift, each is responsible to exercise it for the benefit of other members in the body. Similarly Paul, writing the Corinthians about "variety of gifts" of the Spirit, declares, "To each is given the manifestation of the Spirit for the common good"[90] (1 Cor. 12:7). "The common good" means "the common advantage," the "profit of others." Peter and Paul, therefore, are both expressing the responsibility of each believer to exercise his or her gifts for the good of other people.

Thus activity in the body is not only essential because each member needs the others (as was earlier discussed), but also because each member has responsibility for the others in the body. The Lord furnishes gifts to members of His body, not primarily for personal blessing, but that each member may be a blessing to others. This further underscores the urgency of local body participation in which we exercise our God-given gifts for the benefit of other believers.

Truly when a body of Christians functions in terms of mutual responsibility, Christ the Head operates through each member to all others and blessings indeed abound.

3. Service to All Mankind

Since Christ is the Head and the church His body, this means finally that the church is to be the servant of all people. If the church is the body of Christ, her form must be that of a servant. Paul writes that Christ "emptied himself, taking the form of a servant, being born in the likeness of men. And being found in human form he humbled himself and became obedient unto death" (Phil. 2:7–8). The "form of a servant" was His form on earth; hence His spiritual body, the church, must now continue to walk the way of sacrificial service.

On one occasion Jesus said to His disciples, "I am among you as one who serves" (Luke 22:27). On another, Jesus declared, "If any one serves me, he must follow me; and where I am, there shall my servant be also" (John 12:26). The servant Lord calls for a servant people. If Christ is the Head of the church and the church His body, then the church is to be a servant church in the world.

Throughout His time on earth Christ ministered to human need: physical, emotional, spiritual. He was the servant, the *diakonos*,[91] of all mankind. At

---

[87]The Greek word is *charismata*. For more on *charismata* see "Excursus on the Word *Charisma*," *Renewal Theology*, 2:345–46 .

[88]"Let each exercise them accordingly" is not in the Greek text. However, such an addition seems clearly implied. The RSV similarly adds, "Let us use them."

[89]For a more detailed discussion of these *charismata* see pages 125–33.

[90]The Greek word translated "the common good" is *sympheron*—"advantage, profit" (Thayer). The KJV reading "to profit withal," though archaic, is on target.

[91]The Greek word means "servant" (also in a more specialized way "deacon"—see infra, pp. 207–10).

the Last Supper Jesus declared about the bread, "This is My body which is given for you" (Luke 22:19 NASB). If Christ's body was "given" for all of us, must not the church, His spiritual body, be given constantly for the sake of the world?

Thus we arrive at the climax of the picture of the church as the body of Christ. The church truly has been incorporated into Christ and is fully dependent on and subject to Him; the members of His body function in total interdependence and mutual responsibility. But also the church as Christ's body must be turned away from itself to be the world's servant. The church is the world's *diakonos*—the world's "deacon"—and, like its "deacon" Lord, must constantly be giving itself for the sake of all mankind.

EPILOGUE: THE CHURCH AS THE FULLNESS OF CHRIST

One of the most remarkable statements about the church as the body of Christ is that found in Ephesians 1:22–23. Paul declares, "He [God] put all things in subjection under His [Christ's] feet, and gave Him as head over all things to the church, which is His body, the fullness of Him who fills all in all" (NASB). The background of these words is God's raising Christ from the dead and placing Him at His right hand far above all rule and authority both in this and the coming age so that all forces are subject to Christ (vv. 20–21). Now note carefully in regard to Christ's headship: He is not described first as head of the church but head over all things. Thus Christ is supreme above every power and authority, and as such a head, He is given by God to the church, His body. This signifies a double sphere of Christ's dominion—world and church—with headship relating to both,[92] but the body relates only to the church. However, the church as His body is the fullness of Christ.

Now let me summarize two of these matters that are particularly relevant to the church. First, it is apparent that the headship of Christ extends far beyond the church to all the powers in the universe. It is not that Christ as head of the church is confronted by alien forces that need yet to be brought under His headship and dominion. No, God has already put them all under Him. This does not mean willing subjection; however, these powers are fully subject to Christ's control. So as head of the church, Christ is already victor over every dominion and power; thus the church, His body, is assured of victory. This calls to mind Jesus' own words about the church: "The gates of Hades shall not overpower it" (Matt. 16:18 NASB). Head of all things to the church (or, "for the church" RSV) means that nothing, absolutely nothing, can prevail against the church, Christ's spiritual body.

Second, it is extraordinary that the church as Christ's body is called "the fullness of Him who fills all in all." Let us first note the latter phrase, "Him who fills all in all" (or, "fills everything in every way" NIV). Christ in His exaltation is not limited to any one sphere. Through the prophet Jeremiah God had already declared, "Do I not fill heaven and earth?" (Jer. 23:24). Now the glorified Christ, as God Himself, fills all things. Paul later refers to the same reality in saying that Christ "ascended far above all the heavens, that he might fill all things" (Eph. 4:10). This adds further weight to the fact that Christ is "head over all things." But there is also the startling expression that the church,

[92]In Colossians this is particularly clear where Paul says in one place that Christ is "the head of the body, the church" (1:18) and another that He is "the head of all rule and authority" (2:10).

Christ's body, is the fullness of Christ. What can this mean?

The amazing answer to this question is that although the exalted Christ is head over all things and fills all things, His fullness, His pleroma,[93] is to be found only in the church. Christ has so associated Himself with the church that, in and through it all, the radiance and glory of deity is manifest. The wonder is not that Christ is related only to the church, for He is head over and fills all things, but that His fullness shines forth in and through the church. This indeed is a spiritual reality seen only by the eyes of faith, but it is present wherever the body of Christ is found.

The church, however, is not perfect, nor has it realized Christ's ultimate intention.[94] The church is not divine either,[95] but it has become the arena in which the fullness of Christ's glory is being manifest. Further, we as Christ's body may more and more be filled with that fullness. Thus Paul later prays for the Ephesians that they "may be filled with all the fullness of God" (3:19). So the glory of God through Christ can be fully experienced in His body, the church.

How fitting as a climax are these words of Paul: "To him be glory in the church and in Christ Jesus to all generations, for ever and ever. Amen" (Eph. 3:21).

C. The Bride of Christ

The church, finally, is the bride of Christ. The central New Testament passage containing this image is Ephesians 5:25–33. The key words are "Christ loved the church and gave himself up for her" (v. 25). These words of Paul are set in the framework of Paul's injunction to husbands to love their wives, "as Christ loved the church. . . ." Christ's love for the church, His bride/wife,[96] was so great that He gave up His life for her. Truly this is the ultimate demonstration of love: sacrifice even unto death.

This description of the church has its Old Testament background in Israel, who is frequently depicted as the wife of the Lord. One of the more dramatic statements is found in Isaiah 54: "Your Maker is your husband, the LORD of hosts is his name" (v. 5). In Jeremiah 2 the picture is drawn of a relationship between Israel and the Lord that goes back to the wilderness days: "I remember the devotion of your youth, how as a bride you loved me and followed me through the desert" (v. 2 NIV). This nuptial imagery is carried still further in Ezekiel 16 where God declares about Israel: "I plighted my troth to you and entered into a covenant with you, says the Lord GOD, and you became mine" (v. 8). The covenant with Israel, accordingly, is depicted as a marriage covenant.

However, the sad matter in the Old Testament is that Israel invariably proved to be a faithless, adulterous wife. For example, shortly after the words quoted from Jeremiah, God de-

---

[93]The Greek word for "fullness," *plērōma*, is sometimes used as an English word. Pleroma may be defined as "the fullness of divine excellencies and powers" (*Webster's Third New International Dictionary*).

[94]"A glorious church, not having spot, or wrinkle" (Eph. 5:27 KJV) is Christ's ultimate purpose for the church.

[95]According to Colossians 2:9, "in him [Christ] the whole fullness of deity dwells bodily." "Bodily" in this case refers not to the church but to Christ's incarnation and present exaltation. Christ continues in heaven in His formerly physical, now glorified, body, which is indeed an aspect of His divinity. This distinction between Christ's glorified body and His spiritual body, the church, must be carefully maintained.

[96]As will be noticed, the New Testament imagery varies between the church as bride and the church as wife.

clares, "As a faithless wife leaves her husband, so you have been faithless to me" (3:20). Ezekiel 16 has a vivid picture of Israel committing repeated acts of harlotry: allying herself to foreign countries, bowing down to foreign idols, constantly turning from the Lord, with the result that God declares He will bring His fury against her. Israel was invariably the unrepentant, adulterous wife. Yet in all of this, God still loved her and promised her a different future. Through the prophet Hosea, God declares, "In that day . . . you will call me, 'My husband,' and no longer will you call me, 'My Baal.'[97]. . . And I will betroth you to me for ever; I will betroth you to me in righteousness and in justice, in steadfast love, and in mercy . . . in faithfulness" (2:16, 19–20). Thus the Old Testament climaxes with the hopeful note of a future God-Israel, husband-wife relationship that will not be broken.

Coming to the New Testament, we observe that all four gospels refer to Jesus as a bridegroom. In the Synoptic Gospels, responding to the question why His disciples did not fast, Jesus replies, "While the bridegroom is with them, the attendants of the bridegroom[98] do not fast, do they?" (Mark 2:19 NASB; cf. Matt. 9:15; Luke 5:34). Jesus thus speaks of Himself as the bridegroom and His disciples as attendants at the wedding. In the Fourth Gospel John the Baptist declares, "He who has the bride is the bridegroom; the friend of the bridegroom, who stands and hears him, rejoices greatly at the bridegroom's voice; therefore this joy of mine is now full" (3:29). Here "the friend of the bridegroom"—the best man—is John himself, who makes preparations for the symbolic marriage between Christ the bridegroom and the bride. The bride is not, as such, designated; however, the implication is that the bride represents the community of disciples around Jesus, which in time will become the church. Drawing together the accounts in the four gospels, we behold Jesus as the bridegroom,[99] the disciples as attendants (and implicitly the bride), and John as the best man. This is an extraordinary picture indeed![100]

The nuptial imagery is carried forward in Jesus' parable about the wedding feast that a king gave for his son (Matt. 22:1–14). Significantly, all the people who first received an invitation declined, so the king invited people from the streets. The king in the parable unmistakably is God the Father, the son is Jesus, and the wedding guests first invited were the Jews who spurned participation in the feast. The street people are the disciples of Jesus who come to join His wedding party. So once again we have a depiction of Christ as the bridegroom and his disciples as a wedding group. While this is not yet the disciples as the bride of Christ,[101] the imagery more closely approximates it.

---

[97]"Baal" refers to any of numerous Canaanite deities that Israel turned to.

[98]"Attendants of the bridegroom" is probably a better translation than "wedding guests" (RSV). The Greek expression literally reads, "sons of the bridal chamber" [the *nymphonons*], which expresses a closer relation to the bridegroom [the *nymphios*] than simply wedding guests. BAGD reads under *νυμφων*, "the bridegroom's attendants."

[99]The Old Testament nowhere depicts the Messiah to come as a bridegroom. In one account, however, God Himself is viewed as a bridegroom: "As the bridegroom rejoices over the bride, so shall your God rejoice over you" (Isa. 62:5).

[100]J. Jeremias puts it vividly: "The days of His earthly ministry were already wedding days for the disciples" (TDNT, 4:1105). I like this very much.

[101]It is interestingly that no bride is mentioned in any of the New Testament accounts

I also briefly mention the further nuptial scene of the bridegroom and the wise and foolish virgins (Matt. 25:1–13). The bridegroom is delayed in returning. However, the wise virgins are ready with oil in their lamps and go in with the bridegroom to the marriage feast; the foolish are not ready and so are shut out. The virgins doubtless represent more than mere bridesmaids or other female participants. Since this is a parable of warning—closing with the words, "Watch therefore, for you know neither the day nor the hour" (v. 13)—it surely is a warning to all who follow Jesus, hence later the church, to be ready.[102]

In the Epistles, Paul further develops the bridal imagery in a letter to the Corinthian church: "I am jealous for you with a godly jealousy; for I betrothed you to one husband, that to Christ I might present you as a pure virgin" (2 Cor. 11:2 NASB). The church here is specifically identified as the bride.[103] Figuratively, Paul depicts himself as best man[104] who has implemented the betrothal between Christ and the Corinthian church. In Ephesians Paul moves beyond the local to the universal church when he says, "Christ loved the church and gave himself up for her" (5:25). No longer does the apostle depict his role in this marriage; the important matter here is Christ's total love for the bride/wife, His church.

The final New Testament pictures of the church as the bride of Christ are in the Book of Revelation. Here we arrive at the consummation in which the marriage feast occurs. A great multitude in heaven cry forth, "Hallelujah! For the Lord our God the Almighty reigns. Let us rejoice and exult and give him the glory, for the marriage of the Lamb has come, and his Bride has made herself ready" (19:6–7). Then an angel commands, "Write this: Blessed are those who are invited to the marriage supper of the Lamb" (v. 9). Later John beholds a new heaven and a new earth, and coming down from heaven "the holy city, new Jerusalem . . . prepared as a bride adorned for her husband" (21:2). Shortly after that an angel speaks: "Come, I will show you the Bride, the wife of the Lamb" (v. 9). The picture then shifts to the holy city "having the glory of God, its radiance like a most rare jewel" (v. 11), the bride adorned becoming one with the holy city bejeweled.[105] The glory of God radiates over all. Finally, as the Book of Revelation draws to a close, there are these memorable words: "The Spirit and the Bride say, 'Come'. . . . And let him who is thirsty . . . take the water of life without price" (22:17).

Now let us reflect on the significance of the church as the bride of Christ. A few points particularly stand out.

1. United in Love

The church as the bride of Christ is united to Him in love. The heart of all

---

above, thus making room for a later equation of the disciples of Christ, the church, as His bride.

[102]It is significant once again that no bride is mentioned; thus there is all the more reason for seeing in the ten virgins a counterpart to the bride. On the ten virgins as the church, see R. H. Gundry: "The virgins represent the church" (*Matthew*, 498) and Jeremias who speaks of them allegorically as "the expectant Christian community" (*The Parables of Jesus*, 51).

[103]So the RSV translates: "a pure bride." The Greek word, *parthenon*, however, is literally "virgin."

[104]Jeremias writes, "Paul compares the community with a bride, Christ with the bridegroom, and himself with the best man who has won the bride, who watches over her virginity, and who will lead her to the bridegroom at the wedding" (TDNT, 4:1104).

[105]See Isaiah 61:10 for interesting Old Testament background: the bride adorned with jewels as a depiction of the event of salvation.

bridal imagery is the relationship of love between the bride and the groom, the wife and the husband. It is an intimate union, intended to be permanent.

From creation man and wife have "become one flesh" (Gen. 2:24).[106] What is extraordinary about the relationship between man and wife is that, as Paul declares it, this unity refers primarily to the church. In the passage where Paul speaks of how "Christ loved the church and gave himself up for her" (Eph. 5:25), he later adds (first quoting freely from Genesis): " 'For this reason a man will leave his father and his mother and be united to his wife, and the two will become one flesh.' This is a profound mystery—but I am talking about Christ and the church" (vv. 31–32 NIV). The close union between Christ and the church is the pattern for the human relationship in marriage. Paul, in a different context, writing that union with a prostitute is to become one with her in body, also quotes from Genesis: " 'The two will become one flesh' " (1 Cor. 6:16 NIV). Then Paul adds, "But he who unites himself with the Lord is one with him in spirit" (v. 17). Projecting this to the church at large (as in Ephesians), we recognize that the essential unity with Christ is not corporeal but spiritual. However, this does not lessen its intensity, or even intimacy, for nothing can exceed the closeness of being united in one spirit with Christ.

The unity is through love. This goes beyond that of an organic unity, of head and body,[107] into that of a relational unity. Christ is still the head as the husband is of the wife. But He is the head in relationship to another in whom the unity is freely given, freely reciprocated. This is covenantal love: a bonded unity of one to the other.

Moreover, this unity of love is grounded in the reality of sacrifice. In one of our hymns we sing: "From heaven He came and sought her to be His holy bride, With His own blood He bought her, and for her life He died."[108] The bride is not only loved as by an earthly husband; she has also been redeemed through the bridegroom's death. *Nothing* can compare with a love written in blood, nor can a greater response come than from those who love because of His incomparable self-giving.

In another context Paul writes, "He died for all, that those who live might live no longer for themselves but for him who for their sake died and was raised" (2 Cor. 5:15). The church, as bride of Christ, can only truly live for the Christ who died for her.

2. *Summoned to Faithfulness and Purity*

The church is summoned by Christ to be a holy and pure bride. Paul says, "Christ loved the church and gave himself for her" and adds, "that he might sanctify her, having cleansed her by the washing of water with the word, that he might present the church to himself in splendor, without spot or wrinkle or any such thing, that she might be holy and without blemish" (Eph. 5:25–27). The church has been cleansed already,[109] but is ever in need of further cleansing and continuing sanctification.

We have observed that in the Old Testament Israel was repeatedly

[106]These words are reaffirmed by Jesus in Matthew 19:5.

[107]As discussed in the previous section.

[108]"The Church's One Foundation," a part of the second stanza.

[109]"By the washing of water with the word" probably refers to "the washing of regeneration" (Titus 3:5), which occurs in connection with the word of the gospel being appropriated.

faithless to God, who as a Husband had taken her as His wife. Spiritual adultery was her way of life. Yet God was always calling her back to purity and devotion to Himself. In the New Testament, Christ as the Bridegroom/ Husband of the church is likewise ever concerned with her faithfulness and purity.

Such faithfulness and purity have several aspects. First, they entail a single-minded devotion to Christ. The church as the bride of Christ must have a devotion to no other husband than Christ. We have noted the words of Paul: "I betrothed you to one husband" (2 Cor. 11:2 NASB). There can be no masters other than Christ, no "Baals," to which the bride gives herself unreservedly. Whenever a church is more committed to a leader, a concern, or to varied causes than to Christ, devotion to Him is diluted and may fade away. Spiritual adultery in relation to Christ is by no means always obvious, but it is ultimately even more destructive than adultery in a human marriage. Christ has to be first of all or not at all: there must be pure and single-minded devotion to Him.

Second, faithfulness and purity involve holding fast to the truth in Christ. Let us continue with the words of Paul in 2 Corinthians: "I betrothed you to one husband, that to Christ I might present you as a pure virgin. But I am afraid, lest as the serpent deceived Eve by his craftiness, your minds should be led astray from the simplicity and purity of devotion to Christ" (11:2–3 NASB). Then Paul speaks about some who come proclaiming "another Jesus," and about the Corinthians receiving a "different spirit . . . or a different gospel," and then he adds, "You submit to it readily enough" (v. 4). By their failure to hold firmly to the truth about Christ, by their openness to other spirits than the Holy Spirit, by their deviation from the gospel, the Corinthian church was slipping away from the purity of truth in Christ, and thereby forsaking Him. According to the Gospel of John, "grace and truth came through Jesus Christ" (1:17). Thus faithfulness to Christ means faithfulness not only to His person but also to the truth He came to bring. Whenever any church begins to depart, for example, from such facts about Christ as His incarnation and His resurrection, it is a departure from Christ. As the bride of Christ, the church is summoned to a continuing faithfulness and purity in the truth.

Third, these qualities involve a walking in holiness and righteousness. Since Christ Himself is holy and righteous, His bride should ever strive to emulate Him. In the Old Testament God declares, "I will betroth you to me in righteousness and in justice" (Hos. 2:19). Even more so, Christ has betrothed Himself to the church so that she might so walk. I have quoted the declaration in the Book of Revelation that "his Bride has made herself ready." Now we note the words that follow: "It was granted her to be clothed with fine linen, bright and pure—for the fine linen is the righteous deeds of the saints" (19:8). The fineness and purity of the bridal clothing at the marriage feast relates to the righteousness of the deeds and actions of the bride in the present life. Thus even as Christ Himself is ever seeking to purify His bride and to remove every spot and wrinkle, so the bride must constantly be devoted to a righteous and holy walk.

3. Living With Expectancy

One of the most significant features about the church as the bride of Christ is that the fulfillment of this relationship is yet to come. In a symbolic but real sense the situation in this present age is that of an absent bridegroom and a bride who ever looks forward to His return. Only at His return will the marriage actually occur and all things be complete.

The church now lives between the times of Jesus' physical absence from His disciples and the future consummation. There is joy even now, for the church is espoused to Christ and rejoices in His spiritual presence. However, all of this is but a small foregleam of the coming day when the heavens will ring with the cry, "Let us rejoice and exult and give him the glory, for the marriage of the Lamb has come" (Rev. 19:7)!

So the church, the bride, even now looks forward with keen expectation to that future glorious day. To be sure, there should be watchfulness in waiting, for we do not know the hour of His coming for the bride. There should also be zeal for a purity worthy of this glorious occasion. But the transcendent note surely must always be that of expectancy. For what is yet to come is the ultimate in joy and blessedness. "Blessed are those"—blessed indeed—"who are invited to the marriage supper of the Lamb" (Rev. 19:9).

Christ will then have His church "in splendor"—and all will be radiant with the glory of God.

III. THE COMMUNITY OF THE HOLY SPIRIT

The church, finally, is depicted in the New Testament as the community of the Holy Spirit.

A. Enlivened by the Holy Spirit

The church owes its very existence to the enlivening action of the Holy Spirit. A people may seem to have life, but there is no spiritual life until the Spirit moves upon them. In the words of Jesus, "It is the Spirit who gives life" (John 6:63 NASB). He spoke these words to a people who could not comprehend spiritual truth about the bread from heaven because of their deadness to things of the Spirit.

For a picture of this let us turn back to the Old Testament to Ezekiel's vision of the valley of dry and dead bones. The prophet was told by God to prophesy to Israel in exile, saying, "Thus says the Lord God to these bones: Behold, I will cause breath[110] to enter you, and you shall live" (Ezek. 37:5). Ezekiel so prophesied, and the bones began to come together and flesh to form, but still there was no life. Again the prophet was told to speak: "Thus says the Lord God: Come from the four winds, O breath, and breathe upon these slain, that they may live" (v. 9). When Ezekiel did so, "the breath came into them, and they lived, and stood upon their feet, an exceedingly great host" (v. 10). Once more God addressed Israel: "I will put my Spirit within you,[111] and you shall live, and I will place you in your own land" (v. 14). Thus Ezekiel prophesied that one day the Spirit of God was to bring new life to the people of God.

Now let us return to the Gospel of John, where a fulfillment of this prophecy is depicted. Jesus, who had spoken about the Spirit giving life, now appears in His resurrection body to the gathered disciples. After Jesus had spoken a few words, He "breathed[112] on them, and said to them, 'Receive the Holy Spirit'" (20:22). This is the primary

---

[110]The Hebrew word is *rûaḥ*; it also means "wind" or "spirit."

[111]Recall the brief discussion of these words on pages 56–57.

[112]The Greek word is *enephysēsen*. In Ezekiel 37:9, quoted above, the Greek word in the Septuagint (LXX) for "breathe" is *emphysēson*, a form of the same word as *enephysēsen*. In Genesis 2:7, which reads, "the Lord God formed man of dust from the ground, and breathed into his nostrils the breath of life; and man became a living being," the LXX for "breathed" has *enephysēsen*. The breath of God, that is, the Spirit of God brings life, whether physically or spiritually.

fulfillment of Ezekiel's prophecy: the risen Lord placed the Holy Spirit within the disciples and they spiritually came alive. Before this they had been like dead people, like Israel, with only a dead Jesus to remember; but now all was radically changed. Truly they were "born anew,"[113] for the Spirit had given them life!

This resurrection event inaugurated the establishment of the church.[114] Fifty days later at Pentecost, it rapidly expanded. But the original breakthrough of the life-giving and transforming Spirit occurred at Easter. Luke, in the opening chapter of Acts, depicts a community of believers prior to Pentecost:[115] first the apostles (1:1–11), next the apostles plus several others (vv. 12–14), then a company of some one hundred and twenty persons (vv. 15–26). That the Holy Spirit was active already is suggested by the fact that the risen Jesus gave "instructions through the Holy Spirit to the apostles" (Acts 1:2 NIV). Thus we see in operation a community of the Holy Spirit between Easter and Pentecost.

At Pentecost the church leaped forward, for "there were added that day about three thousand souls" (Acts 2:41)—"added" to the already existing community of believers. How had this happened? The Spirit had descended upon the community and under that spiritual anointing Peter had proclaimed the gospel. There was such profound conviction of sin that those who heard were "cut to the heart" (v. 37), and they entered into salvation. In John's Gospel Jesus had declared about the Holy Spirit that "He, when He comes, will convict the world concerning sin" (16:8 NASB). The Spirit had now come at Pentecost upon the waiting community of believers, and in His power thousands were convicted of sin and entered into a new life in Jesus Christ.

Thus the church from the beginning has been a community enlivened by the Holy Spirit. The church owes its very life to the breath of the Spirit. If the Spirit has not brought life to the members, what may be called the church is no more than an empty building or a gathering of people functioning on a purely human level. There may even be a multiplicity of activities and much energy expended, but without the Spirit as "the kiss of life,"[116] the church does not really exist.

Paul writes to the Thessalonians that the "gospel came to [them] not only in word, but also in power and in the Holy Spirit and with full conviction" (1 Thess. 1:5). It was the Holy Spirit who wrought the conviction by which the church at Thessalonica was born. Things have not changed since then. Truly the church owes its life, its breath, its existence to the life-giving Spirit.

B. Fellowshipping in the Holy Spirit

One of the most striking features of the church is that it is a fellowship of

---

[113]Along with John 6:63 and 20:22 (which we have noted), Jesus' words in John 3:7, "You must be born anew," are quite relevant. Jesus immediately adds, "The wind blows where it wills, and you hear the sound of it, but you do not know whence it comes or whither it goes; so it is with every one who is born of the Spirit" (v. 8).

[114]John Rea writes: "When the risen Lord Jesus breathed forth the Holy Spirit that first night after His resurrection, His creative work began transforming individual believers into a spiritual community. They became at that moment a new body, His body the church" (*The Holy Spirit in the Bible*, 163).

[115]Hans Küng writes concerning Luke: "For Luke . . . Pentecost is not the moment of the Church's birth: this is Easter, and for Luke too the community of Jesus Christ existed before Pentecost (Acts 1:15)" (*The Church*, 165). This is well said.

[116]David Watson uses this expression regarding the Holy Spirit and the church in his book, *I Believe in the Church*, 170.

the Holy Spirit. At the close of his second letter to the church in Corinth Paul writes, "The grace of the Lord Jesus Christ and the love of God and the fellowship of the Holy Spirit[117] be with you all" (13:14). The Greek word translated "fellowship," *koinōnia*, expresses the idea of close relationship or communion,[118] also a participation or sharing in a profound manner. Such *koinōnia* is made possible through the Holy Spirit.[119]

All that has been said about the church as the people of God and the building/body/bride of Christ is meaningless if the church is not also the fellowship of the Holy Spirit. For through the indwelling Spirit the church is united in a fellowship that transcends anything that is ordinarily known and experienced. Among all people today there is a paramount need for deep and abiding fellowship. Solitariness and loneliness are commonplace. Moreover, even where fellowship is sought, often an uneasy sense of isolation and disharmony still pervades. The only adequate answer to this prevailing situation is the fellowship of the Holy Spirit.

To elaborate further: The church is not a fellowship based on common human interests. It is not a psychical but a pneumatic community. The church is not a community of natural but of spiritual togetherness. It is the only place in the world where true fellowship can be found.

1. Fellowship With God

By the Holy Spirit there is fellowship with God. Paul writes concerning Gentiles and Jews: "Through him [Christ] we both have access to the Father by one Spirit" (Eph. 2:18 NIV). Shortly after that Paul adds, "In him [Christ] you too [Gentiles] are being built together to become a dwelling in which God lives by his Spirit" (v. 22). By the Spirit the church, the household of God, becomes a dwelling in which God lives and fellowships with His people and they with Him. The barrier of sin, which long separated God and man, has been removed through Christ. Now by the indwelling Spirit there can be the ultimate fellowship, namely with God Himself.

Let me amplify this last statement. Man has been so made by God that his deepest need and final fulfillment rests in fellowshipping with his Creator. It is not, first of all, a matter of human fellowship, as important as that is, but of fellowship with God. Ever since man was driven out of Eden, he has been estranged from God. Now through the reconciliation in Christ and the presence of God's Spirit, fellowship has been restored.

John writes in his first letter: "Our fellowship [*koinōnia*] is with the Father and with his Son Jesus Christ" (1:3).

---

[117]The Greek phrase is *hē koinōnia tou hagiou pneumatos*.

[118]The KJV renders *koinōnia* in 2 Corinthians 13:14 as "communion."

[119]I am interpreting "the *koinōnia* of the Spirit" as the fellowship engendered by the Spirit (subjective genitive). The Greek text can also be interpreted as fellowship with the Spirit Himself (objective genitive). Since in this passage both "the grace of the Lord Jesus Christ" and "the love of God" are unmistakably from God and from Christ (subjective genitives), "the fellowship of the Holy Spirit" would more likely be that from the Spirit. Paul, also writing about the *koinōnia pneumatos* in Philippians 2:1, begins, "If there is any fellowship of the Spirit" (NASB, similarly KJV). The RSV reads "any participation in the Spirit"; NIV, "any fellowship with the Spirit" (objective genitives). While these latter translations are possible, I again am inclined to the view that it is a fellowship made possible by, hence from, the Holy Spirit. (This is also strongly suggested by the two preceding clauses in the NIV: "If you have any encouragement from being united with Christ, if any comfort from his love.")

Although John does not directly attribute this to the Holy Spirit,[120] it results from that fellowship made possible by the indwelling Spirit. However, the main point is that we can now have fellowship with God in a beautiful and intimate manner—indeed with Father and Son. *Nothing* can be richer or more meaningful than this! We should note that John, shortly after speaking of our fellowship with Father and Son, adds, "God is light, and in Him there is no darkness at all. If we say that we have fellowship with Him and yet walk in the darkness, we lie and do not practice the truth" (vv. 5–6 NASB). Hence there is no guarantee of continuing fellowship with God if we walk in darkness.

Another striking passage about *koinōnia* is found in Paul's statement to the church in Corinth: "God is faithful, through whom you were called into fellowship with His Son, Jesus Christ our Lord" (1 Cor. 1:9 NASB). If one were to ask how this is possible, as Christ is now in heaven at the right hand of the Father, the answer is that He is with us through the fellowship of the Holy Spirit. This is the presence of Him who said, "Lo, I am with you always, to the close of the age" (Matt. 28:20), and with whom His disciples ever have fellowship. It is a joy to know that God has called us into this fellowship with his own Son and that, especially in the community of the Spirit, it can be an ongoing reality.

This leads me to make two final statements. First, the church is both the actuality of and the occasion for fellowship with God. Because the church is the community of the Spirit, the members must assemble in a proper spirit if there is to be true fellowship with God. For example, in regard to worship Jesus declares, "God is spirit . . . those who worship him must worship in spirit and truth" (John 4:24). Fellowship with God is a reality for those who are prepared to meet with Him. Second, there is no substitute for fellowship with God in the church. To be sure, there is private, personal fellowship with Him also, but since God has determined to have a people and to walk with and among them, the richest fellowship with God is in the community of those who belong to Him.

2. Fellowship With One Another

Through the Holy Spirit's creation of fellowship with Father and Son, He also creates for us a fellowship with one another. It is significant that in the same passage where John speaks about fellowship with God, he also speaks of "fellowship [*koinōnia*] with one another" (1 John 1:7; also v. 3). Through the fellowship of the Spirit this may truly come about.

We do well to recall the situation in the early church. Prior to the coming of the Holy Spirit on the Day of Pentecost (Acts 2), there were already evidences of the disciples' close fellowship. The Gospel of Luke records that after Jesus' ascension the disciples were "continually in the temple blessing God" (24:53). Clearly they were all together. According to the Book of Acts, the apostles, along with a number of women and Jesus' mother Mary and His brothers, "joined together constantly in prayer" (1:14 NIV). Later, the Scripture records that "the company of persons together[121] was in all about a

[120]John later declares, "By this we know that we abide in Him and He in us, because He has given us of His Spirit" (4:13 NASB). Although this statement refers to knowledge ("we know") of an abiding fellowship by virtue of the Holy Spirit rather than the actuality of the fellowship, a close connection with the Holy Spirit is apparent.

[121]I have added the word "together" to the RSV translation above since it is in the Greek text, *epi to auto*. F. F. Bruce translates this phrase as "altogether," adding that it "seems to

hundred and twenty'' (v. 15). So they remained in close fellowship until Pentecost. Then "when the day of Pentecost had come, they were all together[122] in one place'' (2:1) Accordingly, upon such a close knit fellowship of disciples the Holy Spirit was then poured out.

This does not mean that the Holy Spirit was absent prior to Pentecost. As we have noted, before Jesus ascended He gave "instructions through the Holy Spirit to the apostles he had chosen'' (Acts 1:2 NIV). How this was done is by no means apparent; but the words clearly imply the active presence of the Holy Spirit. In that sense even during this transitional period while the risen Jesus was still with them, they were a community of the Spirit. Hence when Jesus says to the apostles (and by implication to the other waiting disciples after that): "Before many days you shall be baptized with the Holy Spirit'' (v. 5), the Holy Spirit was already a known presence. Thus we may say that as a community of the Spirit the disciples received the outpouring of the Holy Spirit at Pentecost.

It is important to stress this matter because of a common misperception that the church did not exist until Pentecost and hence only then became a community of the Spirit. To be sure, the word "church'' is not used in Acts 1, but neither is it used in Acts 2. The Holy Spirit is, however, active in both chapters. Further it is significant to note that the theme of togetherness occurs both before and after Pentecost. In regard to the latter, after some three thousand persons had come to salvation, the Book of Acts records that "all who believed were together''[123] (2:44). Thus they were a close fellowship, a community of the Spirit throughout.

What happened at Pentecost was a deepening of this fellowship.[124] The word *koinōnia* is now used: the new believers "devoted themselves to the apostles' teaching and *fellowship*'' (2:42). Further, the word "together'' (in v. 46) is included in the statement that "all who believed were together and had all things in common'' (v. 44). A number of results followed: selling and sharing possessions for needy persons, daily temple attendance together, breaking bread from house to house, praising God, and enjoying the favor of all people. The climax of this fellowship came as "the Lord added to their number [literally, 'together'][125] day by day those who were being saved'' (v. 47). Thus togetherness, *koinōnia*, was intensified with the outpouring of the Holy Spirit.

The church as the community of the Spirit is the bonding together of people with one another in the Spirit. Believers come together not because of common earthly interests or relationships but because of their union as brothers and sisters in Christ; they are thus united in common spiritual concerns. This fellowship in the Spirit is not, however, invariably operational, for various sins among the members may disrupt the spiritual unity. Here again John has a valuable word: "If we walk in the light as He Himself is in the light, we have fellowship with one another, and the

---

have acquired a semi-technical sense not unlike *εν ἐκκλησίᾳ* ('in church fellowship')'' (*Acts of the Apostles*, 75).

[122]The Greek phrase again is *epi to auto*.

[123]Once again *epi to auto*.

[124]For a fuller presentation of this theme see *Renewal Theology*, 2:314–19, "Deepening of Fellowship.''

[125]"To their number'' is the translation above for *epi to auto*. "Together,'' however, is the basic meaning. Bruce again notes that " 'in church fellowship' makes good sense here'' (*Acts of the Apostles*, 102).

blood of Jesus His Son cleanses us from all sin" (1 John 1:7 NASB). Walking in His light, spurning the things of darkness, makes possible a continuing *koinōnia*; however, if and when the blemish of sin comes in, we may be grateful that Jesus' blood can cleanse completely.

It is this fellowship with one another that makes the church so qualitatively different from all human societies. One aspect of our humanity is the desire and need for fellowship, with its most basic form being the nuclear or the extended family. From the beginning God declared, "It is not good that the man should be alone" (Gen. 2:18). But even the family at its best is interlaced with self-concerns, and therefore needs the correction and supplementation of a deeper spiritual relationship.[126] Going beyond the kinship of the family, people often form associations, clubs, and social groups to accommodate a desire for fellowship on many levels and with many interests. These often prove enriching and valuable indeed. But in the last analysis, only a fellowship in the Spirit can bring people together in a self-transcending unity.

C. The Communion of Saints

I add here a brief section on the phrase "the communion of saints" found in the Apostles' Creed.[127] The final sentence in the Creed begins, "I believe in the Holy Ghost; the holy catholic church; the communion of saints." The last phrase by its placement suggests a connection with both the Holy Spirit and the church. But what does "the communion of saints" mean?

There is no adequate biblical reference to be found. Since the words "communion" and "fellowship" are interchangeable (both are translations of *koinōnia*), perhaps the closest is 2 Corinthian 13:14, "the fellowship [or 'communion' KJV] of the Holy Spirit." If that is the case, the affirmation in the Apostles' Creed refers broadly to believers' (saints') fellowship both with God and with one another.[128] In such a manner the Westminster Confession of Faith interprets the meaning of "the communion of saints":

> All saints that are united to Jesus Christ their head, by his Spirit and by faith have fellowship with him in his graces, sufferings, death, resurrection, and glory; and being united to one another in love, they have communion in each other's gifts and graces, and are obliged to the performance of such duties, public and private, as do conduce to their mutual good, both in the inward and outward man.[129]

This statement affirms a fellowship of believers with Christ of a very profound kind, including fellowship in His sufferings[130] and death, and it affirms a communion of believers with one another in which there is both a receiving from them (their gifts and graces) and a ministry to their total need (both inward and outward).

Another interpretation of "the communion of saints" is that it refers to the

[126]Remember that Jesus Himself reached beyond human family ties to the formulation of a spiritual family: "Whoever does the will of God is my brother, and sister, and mother" (Mark 3:35). The self-concern of Jesus' earthly family may be noted from the preceding verses (31–34).

[127]"The communion of saints" is a later Western addition to the Apostles' Creed. It is included in the statement of the Creed in Roman Catholic and Protestant churches.

[128]As described in the previous section.

[129]Chapter 26, "Of the Communion of Saints," section I.

[130]This calls to mind Paul's intense desire to "know . . . the fellowship [*koinōnia*] of [Christ's] sufferings" (Phil. 3:10 KJV).

unity of believers both living and dead in the total church.[131] This stresses that we are one with those who have passed on into glory and that the church on earth and in heaven is truly one church. The difficulty with such an interpretation, however, is that it may imply that there is an ongoing communication between believers in heaven and believers on earth. Such presumed communication is not biblical, for though the saints above may be aware of what is transpiring on earth,[132] no Scripture suggests that the saints on earth can communicate with them. The misapprehension of this has led to such an unbiblical practice as the invocation of the saints—that is, praying to the saints in heaven.[133]

It seems best to understand "the communion of saints" differently. For although there is a communion of saints that relates to heaven, it is communion with the glorified Christ (what more could one desire?), not with the saints in glory. In this case it is not communion *with* saints, but *of* saints. This communion is also with other saints, i.e., fellow believers, on earth and is of a very rich and meaningful kind. The word "communion" may be better than "fellowship" in both these instances—with Christ and other believers—because it implies intimate communication. Paul speaks of the Lord's Supper as "the *koinōnia* of the blood of Christ" and "the *koinōnia* of the body of Christ" (1 Cor. 10:16 KJV). Whether *koinōnia* is translated "communion" (KJV), "participation in" (RSV and NIV), or "sharing in" (NASB), it means more than fellowship: it is very close communication. Fellowship suggests walking together, perhaps verbally communicating with one another; communion implies a deeper, more intimate relationship that may go beyond the ability of words to express. It is this that characterizes our communion, whether it is communion with Christ or with others who believe in Him.

One further thought about "the communion of saints": It may also refer in a less personal manner to a relationship to believers in all ages, an affirmation of the unity and community of the present church with those who have gone before. We stand together with the saints of the early church, of the Middle Ages, of the Reformation, and of the modern era. While we are not in communication with the saints in heaven, we do recognize within our community those who have preceded us. We draw on their witness of faith (often even to martyrdom), their creedal and confessional formulations, and frequently their hymns and liturgies. In so doing we have communion with the saints of all ages—a communion that also gives strength and encouragement to move ahead. Such a communion of the saints is well expressed in a stanza from the hymn "For All the Saints Who from Their Labors Rest":

> O blest communion, fellowship divine!
> We feebly struggle, they in glory
> shine;
> Yet all are one in Thee,
> For all are Thine.
> Alleluia! Alleluia!

It is a communion that will some day be gloriously fulfilled in heaven.

To conclude: The church is the community of the Holy Spirit. It has been enlivened by the Spirit, knows fellowship in the Spirit, and is the communion of saints. All of this is a given fact of the church's existence and not simply an

[131]Recall the discussion of the transcendent church in chapter 2, pages 41–43.

[132]The Book of Revelation *may* indicate this. The twenty-four elders, possibly representing the heavenly church, frequently express awareness of earthly events.

[133]For a brief summary of this practice see EDT, 568–69.

idealized picture. If the church does not always live up to its true nature (and often it does not), it must always be challenged to become again what God intended it to be. The church functioning truly as a community of the Spirit can be a reality of incalculable significance.

4

Functions

We will now consider the various functions of the church. These will be viewed under the headings of worship, upbuilding, and outreach.

I. WORSHIP

The word *worship* is a modern form of the old English word *weorthscipe*, meaning "worthiness, repute, respect" (Webster).[1] Accordingly, worship as directed to God signifies the activity of attributing to God the worthiness,[2] repute, respect—indeed, the reverence—due Him. The psalmist cries forth, "Ascribe to the Lord the glory due his name. . . . Worship the LORD in holy array" (96:8–9). The glory due God is recognized in the worship of Him.

Background: Worship in Israel

Throughout the Old Testament, worship occupies a highly important place. When, for example, Abraham at God's bidding left the city of Haran and came into the land of Canaan, Genesis records that "the LORD appeared to Abram, and said, 'To your descendants I will give this land.' So he built there an altar to the LORD" (12:7).

Shortly after doing so, Abraham moved to another place in the land of Canaan, and "there he built an altar to the LORD and called on the name of the LORD" (v. 8). Building these altars and calling on the name of the Lord were acts of worship in the earliest days of the sojourn of Abraham in Canaan.[3] Such acts were evidence of the priority this patriarch gave to God throughout his life.

When Moses was commissioned by the Lord at Mount Sinai to bring Israel out of the land of Egypt, God said to him, "You [plural] shall worship[4] God

---

[1]"Worship" is sometimes used, especially in England, in reference to a person of dignity, as, for example, "His Worship the Mayor."

[2]"Thus, the English word 'worship' clearly indicates an essential element in that approach to God; it is the recognition of the absolute worth of God, and it is thus an end in itself" (A. S. Herbert, *Worship in Ancient Israel*, 10).

[3]See also Genesis 13:18, which relates a third time that Abraham built an altar in Canaan. Isaac and Jacob similarly built altars; see Genesis 26:25 (Isaac) and 35:1, 3, 7 (Jacob).

[4]The RSV and KJV read "serve." The Hebrew word *'abad*, while basically meaning "serve," may also signify "worship" (as also NIV translates). "Worship" seems the better

at this mountain'' (Exod. 3:12 NASB). Following the institution of the Passover, "the people bowed their heads and worshiped" (Exod. 12:27). After the crossing of the Red Sea, Moses and all Israel sang forth, "The LORD is my strength and my song . . . this is my God, and I will praise him, my father's God, and I will exalt him" (Exod. 15:2). Many years later, Moses declared to Israel, "He is your praise and He is your God, who has done these great and awesome things for you which your eyes have seen" (Deut. 10:21 NASB). All of these statements, particularly the last, highlight the importance of worship and praise in the life of early Israel.

In the reign of David worship stands out. When the ark of the covenant was brought up to Jerusalem, David "appointed certain of the Levites . . . to invoke, to thank, and to praise the LORD, the God of Israel" (1 Chron. 16:4). Asaph was given the chief position; he and his assistants were "to play harps and lyres . . . to sound the cymbals and . . . to blow trumpets continually" (vv. 5–6). Then, at the appropriate time, Asaph and the other Levites led Israel in singing, "O give thanks to the LORD, call on his name, make known his deeds among the peoples! Sing to him, sing praises to him, tell of all his wonderful works. . . . Worship the LORD in holy array; tremble before him, all the earth" (1 Chron. 16:8–9, 29–30).[5] At the conclusion "all the people said 'Amen!' and praised the LORD" (v. 36). It is also significant that at the close of the singing "David left Asaph and his brethren there before the ark of the covenant of the LORD to minister continually" (v. 37). Thus worship and praise were to be an ongoing expression of the life of Israel.

Another high moment of worship occurred at the dedication of Solomon's temple. After the ark was brought into the temple, and prior to Solomon's address and prayer of dedication, Asaph and his company again led in praise. Then, "when the song was raised, with trumpets and cymbals and other musical instruments, in praise to the LORD . . . the house of the LORD, was filled with a cloud, so that the priests could not stand to minister because of the cloud; for the glory of the LORD filled the house of God" (2 Chron. 5:13–14). Thus the praise of God immediately preceded God's filling the temple with His glory. After Solomon's prayer was ended, "fire came down from heaven and consumed the burnt offerings and sacrifices, and the glory of the LORD [again] filled the temple. . . . When all the children of Israel saw the fire come down and the glory of the LORD upon the temple, they . . . worshiped and gave thanks to the LORD, saying, 'For he is good, for his steadfast love endures for ever' " (7:1, 3). Here worship immediately followed upon God's filling the temple with His glory.

In light of such examples in the reigns of David and Solomon, it is apparent that worship and praise had great significance in the life of Israel. This was the case even though idolatry set in before the end of Solomon's reign[6] and was manifest frequently in the divided kingdoms of Israel and Judah also. When Hezekiah became king in Judah, there was a cleansing and reconsecration of the temple so that "the whole assembly worshiped, and the singers

---

translation in this context. The more common Hebrew term for worship, *shāhâ* (occurring more than one hundred times in Scripture), comes from the primitive root "to bow down."

[5]For the complete song see 1 Chronicles 16:8–36. Verses 8–22 are also contained in Psalm 105:1–15; verses 23–33, in Psalm 96; and verses 34–36, in Psalm 106:1, 47–48.

[6]See 1 Kings 11:1–8.

sang, and the trumpeters sounded . . . the king and all who were present with him bowed themselves and worshiped" (2 Chron. 29:28–29). Similar praise and worship occurred after captivity and exile when the temple was rebuilt and the people again offered "songs of praise and thanksgiving to God" (Neh. 12:46). Unquestionably, worship continued throughout the life and experience of the Old Testament people of God.

The Book of Psalms, covering many centuries of Israel's history, is laden with praise and worship. Note a few examples: "Ascribe to the LORD the glory of his name; worship the LORD in holy array" (29:2); "O come, let us sing to the LORD; let us make a joyful noise to the rock of our salvation!" (95:1); "Extol the LORD our God, and worship at his holy mountain; for the LORD our God is holy!" (99:9); "Let us go to his dwelling place; let us worship at his footstool!" (132:7).

In addition to these psalms relating to Israel's own worship, there are many that look beyond. For example: "All the earth will worship Thee, And will sing praises to Thee; They will sing praises to Thy name"[7] (66:4 NASB); "All nations whom Thou hast made shall come and worship before Thee, O LORD; And they shall glorify Thy name" (86:9 NASB); "Let this be written for a future generation, that a people not yet created may praise the LORD. . . . So the name of the LORD will be declared in Zion and his praise in Jerusalem when the peoples and the kingdoms assemble to worship the LORD" (102:18, 21–22 NIV). The universality of praise is declared in all these verses.

I conclude this background survey with one narrative that emphasizes in a special way the importance of worship in Israel. When Judah under King Jehoshaphat was threatened by an invasion of Moabites and Ammonites, a prophet arose to declare, "Fear not, and be not dismayed . . . for the battle is not yours but God's" (2 Chron. 20:15). The immediate reaction of Israel was to worship: "Jehoshaphat . . . and all Judah and the inhabitants of Jerusalem fell down before the LORD, worshiping the LORD" (v. 18). Early the next morning Jehoshaphat appointed those "who were to sing to the LORD and praise him in holy array, as they went before the army. . . . And when they began to sing and praise, the LORD set an ambush" (vv. 21–22). The result was that the enemy was routed and destroyed. Here the high significance of worship and praise in ancient Israel is clearly set forth.[8]

A. The Primacy of Worship

The primary function of the church is the worship of God: to declare His worth and to offer Him praise. Peter's words are apropos: "You are a chosen race, a royal priesthood, a holy nation, a people for God's own possession, that you may proclaim the excellencies of Him who has called you out of darkness into His marvelous light" (1 Peter 2:9 NASB). The people of God, the church, has been "called out"[9] so as to pro-

[7]The RSV and NIV translate this in the present tense. The RSV reads, "All the earth worships thee; they sing praises to thee, sing praises to thy name." As D. Kidner says, "The tenses allow a present tense but prefer a future one . . . the future also does more justice to the facts: it is a promise which is yet to materialize" (*Psalms 1–72: An Introduction and Commentary*, TOTC, 234).

[8]Summarizing worship in the Old Testament, Herbert says truly: "No one can read the Old Testament without recognizing that worship is the primary obligation upon the people of God" (*Worship in Ancient Israel*, 13).

[9]Recall our earlier discussion of these words on pages 17–18.

claim God's "excellencies."[10] This indeed is the primary function of the church: to worship God.[11]

Let us turn to the account in Acts 2. Immediately after the waiting disciples had been filled with the Holy Spirit, they began to "speak in other tongues" (v. 4), declaring "the wonderful works of God" (v. 11 KJV). These disciples had truly been "called out of darkness into his marvelous light," and as their first community activity they praised God for His "excellencies," indeed His "wonderful works." The record in Acts does not specify the character of these works; however, since the disciples had so recently experienced God's redemption, they were doubtless praising Him for what He had done through the death and resurrection of Jesus Christ.

The point to observe is that before Peter proclaimed the gospel message (2:22–36) through which thousands came to salvation, he and the other disciples had been speaking forth the praises of God. Thus they were first of all a community of worship and praise. Moreover, after the church had been enlarged by some three thousand converts, Acts 2 climactically portrays it as "praising God and having favor with all the people. And the Lord added to their number day by day those who were being saved" (v. 47). Again, the praise of God is mentioned immediately prior to the addition of others to the community.

An emphasis on the priority of worship—prayer and praise—is found scattered throughout Acts. Acts 3 opens with Peter and John going to the temple "at the hour of prayer, the ninth hour" (v. 1). They encountered a lame man at the temple gate and subsequently healed him; nonetheless, the fact that prayer and praise had priority in their ministry is clearly evident. For when the man was healed, he "entered the temple with them, walking and leaping and praising God" (v. 8). Again, the note of praise stands out vividly. Shortly after this, Peter and John, being warned by the Jewish high council to speak no more in the name of Jesus, rejoined the other believers who "lifted their voices together to God and said, 'Sovereign Lord. . .'" (Acts 4:24). They prayed to the Lord as Creator of all things and then asked for boldness to continue proclaiming the gospel (vv. 24–30). As a result of their prayers, "the place in which they were gathered was shaken; and they were all filled with the Holy Spirit and spoke the word of God with boldness" (v. 31). Once again prayer and praise preceded further activity.

Acts 13 records the commissioning of Barnabas and Saul for missionary work by the assembled prophets and teachers: "While they were worshiping[12] the Lord and fasting, the Holy

---

[10]The Greek word is *aretas*, translated "wonderful deeds" in RSV, "praises" in KJV and NIV. "Excellencies" seems most adequate (Thayer defines the word as "excellencies, perfections"). However, "marvelous deeds" may be implied (see infra on Acts 2), and "praises" is possible (in the LXX *aretas* undoubtedly means "praises" in Isa. 42:12; 43:21; 63:7).

[11]The Greek conjunction in the phrase "that you may proclaim" is *hopōs*, which is used here "to indicate purpose" (BAGD). Hence the church is God's people for the purpose of proclaiming His excellencies. Ralph P. Martin puts it well: "The raison d'être of the church's life is to show forth the praises of God who has called the redeemed to himself" (*The Worship of God*, 23).

[12]The Greek word is *leitourgountōn*, translated "ministering [to the Lord]" in NASB (cf. KJV). *Leitourgeō* basically means "to serve" or "to minister" (see Rom. 15:27; Heb. 10:11). However, in this context since the word relates to an activity directed to the Lord and also is

Spirit said, 'Set apart for me Barnabas and Saul for the work to which I have called them.' Then after fasting and praying they laid their hands on them and sent them off" (vv. 2–3). This was the first major missionary activity of the church, and it was undergirded by worshiping the Lord. One further noteworthy account in Acts relates to the conversion of the Philippian jailer. Paul and Silas were in prison at midnight "praying and singing hymns of praise to God" (16:25 NASB). An earthquake suddenly shook the prison's foundations and broke loose the chains holding Paul, Silas, and other prisoners, causing the jailer to awaken and cry out to Paul and Silas, "Sirs, what must I do to be saved?" (v. 30 NASB). In this narrative prayer and praise is depicted as the background for the extraordinary prison events that climaxed in the salvation of the jailer.

The church as portrayed in Acts was primarily a worshiping and praising church. In that spirit the church carried forward all of its other activities. Most of all, it was the praise of God that served as a catalyst to bring many to salvation.

Now let us return to the words of Peter about the church's being "a royal priesthood, a holy nation" (1 Peter 2:9) and note that previously the apostle had declared to his readers (the scattered church): "You also, like living stones, are being built into a spiritual house to be a holy priesthood, offering spiritual sacrifices acceptable to God through Jesus Christ" (v. 5 NIV). The people of God no longer have priests, as in the Old Testament, but they *are* priests—holy priests whose basic function is to offer not animal sacrifices but spiritual sacrifices. These sacrifices doubtless are primarily various acts of worship.[13] A passage in Hebrews echoes this thought: "Through him [Jesus] then let us continually offer up a sacrifice of praise to God, that is, the fruit of lips that acknowledge his name" (13:15). The sacrifice is worship and praise: this is the primary function of the New Testament priesthood, the people of God, the church.

In an extraordinary way the primacy of worship is also highlighted in the Book of Revelation. Before the exalted throne of God are four living creatures who day and night sing forth, "Holy, holy, holy, is the Lord God Almighty" (4:8). As they sing, "the twenty-four elders fall down before him who is seated on the throne and worship him who lives for ever and ever" (v. 10). In the presence of the Lamb myriads of angels proclaim His praise: "Worthy is the Lamb who was slain, to receive power and wealth and wisdom and might and honor and glory and blessing!" (5:12). Every creature in heaven, earth, and sea also cries out, "To him who sits upon the throne and to the Lamb be blessing and honor and glory and might for ever and ever! And the four living creatures said, 'Amen!' and the elders fell down and worshiped" (vv. 13–14).[14] Worship is the central and continuing act of all creatures in heaven and earth. Thus the Book of Revelation depicts the fullness of all that the church represents on earth; for in its worship there is the ongoing

---

connected with fasting, "worshiping" (as also in the NIV, cf. NEB) is preferable. The more common word for "worship" in the New Testament is *proskyneō* (59 times): "to prostrate oneself before," "do obeisance to," "fall down and worship" (see BAGD, Thayer).

[13]"That the 'spiritual sacrifices' are 'acceptable to God through Jesus Christ' supports the view that they are above all acts of worship." So writes J. Ramsey Michaels (*1 Peter*, WBC, 102).

[14]For other references in Revelation to the worship of God see 7:11; 11:1, 16; 14:7; 15:4; 19:4, 10; 22:3, 9.

parallel to, and anticipation of, the continuing worship in heaven.[15] Worship indeed is and remains the primary activity of the living church.

It is apparent that the church's worship, while primary in both the Old and New Testaments, takes on a far deeper significance in the latter. For it is not only worship of God but also of Christ ("God Almighty" and "the Lamb"). It is the worship and praise of Him who has called us "out of darkness into His marvelous light." It is the exultant telling forth of the "wonderful works of God" that center in Jesus Christ, His life, death, and resurrection, and in the redemption wrought through Him.

Worship continues to be the primary function of the church. When, for example, a Christian community gathers together on the first day of the week for a service of worship, that community is fulfilling its basic reason for being. We may ordinarily think of service as an activity related to others; however, the primary service of God is worship. Even so, we speak of the occasion of worship as a "worship service"[16]—the chief service of God being not a matter of doing things for Him but of worshiping and praising His Name.

If it is true that "man's chief end is to glorify God, and to enjoy Him forever,"[17] it surely follows that the glorifying, the worship of God, is the chief end of the church. A church may indeed be much concerned about such matters as education, fellowship,[18] sound teaching, evangelism, and missions. But unless the primary focus is worship, there will be little vitality in whatever else it does.[19] The worshiping church is both fulfilling its highest calling—its chief joy—and providing the dynamism for a significant impact on all other activities.

The worship of God is the highest activity of humankind.[20] The church of the Lord Jesus Christ, knowing the Father, Son, and Holy Spirit, is prepared and privileged as no other people on earth to sing forth the praises of the eternal God.

B. The Character of Worship

We will next consider the character of worship. Our discussion will relate to various elements or components that constitute worship. While what follows will also relate to individual worship, the primary focus will be on the church's worship, with particular atten-

---

[15]Gerhardt Delling speaks of "the heavenly worship" as "a parallel to the earthly" and that "they stand in relation to each other of anticipation and consummation" (*Worship in the New Testament*, 6). What was earlier said about the "transcendent church" (pp. 41–43) may here be viewed as parallel to, and the consummation of, the church's worship on earth.

[16]It is interesting that the Greek noun *latreia* may be translated either "worship" or "service" (see John 16:2; Rom. 9:4; 12:1; Heb. 9:1, 6 in various translations); see likewise the Greek verb *latreuō* (e.g., Luke 2:37; Acts 7:7; 24:14; Phil. 3:3; 2 Tim. 1:3; Heb. 9:9; Rev. 22:3). Also the Greek word *leitourgia* may be translated "service" or "worship" (see Heb. 9:21).

[17]This is the answer given to the first question in the Westminster Shorter Catechism: "What is the chief end of man?"

[18]In regard to fellowship, T. S. Eliot has said it well: "What life have you if you have not life together? There is no life that is not in community, And no community not lived in praise of God" ("Choruses from 'The Rock,' " *The Complete Poems and Plays, 1909–1950*, 101). The praise of God is foundational to genuine fellowship or community.

[19]As E. R. Micklem writes about the church: "Her life depends on her worship" (*Our Approach to God*, 11).

[20]"Christian worship is the most momentous, the most urgent, the most glorious action that can take place in human life" (Karl Barth as quoted by Martin in *The Worship of God*, 1).

tion given to the total character of a service of worship.

1. Reverence and Awe

The true worship of God is suffused with a spirit of reverence and awe. Since God is supremely the Holy One, this spirit must characterize worship throughout. The writer to the Hebrews urges, "Let us offer to God acceptable worship,[21] with reverence and awe; for our God is a consuming fire" (12:28–29). In worship we come spiritually "to Mount Zion and to the city of the living God" (v. 22), the God who is "a consuming fire"; thus we must come before Him with due reverence and awe. The worship of God should begin and continue in a truly reverential atmosphere.

The Old Testament highlights the relation of God's holiness to the human situation. Indeed, the words in Hebrews about God as a consuming fire are quoted from Deuteronomy 4:24; after Moses had warned against idolatry, he declared to Israel, "The LORD your God is a consuming fire" (NIV, NASB). Moses himself, in his initial encounter at Mount Sinai with God, who had come to declare His intention to bring Israel out of Egypt, was first told at the burning bush: "Do not come near; put off your shoes from your feet, for the place on which you are standing is holy ground" (Exod. 3:5).[22] Against this background of His holiness, God told Moses that Israel would later worship Him at the same mountain.[23] Surely one of the most remarkable worship experiences in the Old Testament was that of Isaiah who in the temple beheld the exalted Lord and then immediately heard angelic voices crying, "Holy, holy, holy is the Lord of hosts; the whole earth is full of his glory" (Isa. 6:3). Thrice holy is the Lord God! To worship this God truly calls for reverence and awe. Therefore the psalmists sing forth such words as "Worship the LORD with reverence" (2:11 NASB, NEB);[24] "O come, let us worship and bow down, let us kneel before the LORD, our Maker" (95:6); "You who revere the LORD, bless the LORD" (135:20 NASB). The attitude of reverence, awe, and godly fear is the proper attitude of worship before the holy Lord.

In the New Testament we see this atmosphere of reverence and awe particularly in the Book of Revelation. We have earlier noted the words of the living creatures who constantly cry out, "Holy, holy, holy, is the LORD God Almighty" (4:8), and the response of the elders as they "fall down . . . and worship him" (v. 10). This very prostration signifies reverence and awe in the presence of the holy and mighty God. It is the beginning of true worship. Further on in the book we read that an angel calls to all who dwell on the earth: "Fear God and give him the glory, for the hour of his judgment has come; and worship him who made heaven and earth, the sea and the fountains of water" (14:7). Although these words are not directed to the church, they do express the element of reverence—"fear God and give him the glory"—called for in the worship of God.

The element of reverence and awe is vitally important in the true worship of God. It should never be thought that

---

[21]The Greek word is *latreuōmen*, a verb, hence "let us worship." *Latreuō*, as previously noted, may also be translated "serve" (so KJV; cf. NASB). "Worship" is the better translation here (cf. Heb. 9:9; 10:2).

[22]Cf. also the later words to Joshua in Joshua 5:15.

[23]Recall these words quoted earlier: "You shall worship God at this mountain."

[24]"Serve the LORD with fear" (KJV, RSV, NIV) is a possible translation. "Fear" may, however, too strongly suggest the idea of "being afraid of" rather that "having reverence for." A translation such as "reverential" or "godly" fear might best carry the full idea.

because God is a loving and gracious Father whose arms are ever open to receive His people there is no need for holy awe in His presence. Jesus taught us to pray, "Our Father who art in heaven," thus affirming a warm familial relationship to God as Father, but He immediately added, "Hallowed be thy name" (Matt. 6:9). "Thy name" represents God Himself; so God is the holy Father and is always to be approached, even as Father, with reverence and awe.

Often in our churches we fail to stress the need for an attitude of deep reverence. Indeed, this should be the atmosphere in which we begin: not immediately with praise and thanksgiving but with waiting in silence before Him. The prophet Habakkuk declared: "The LORD is in his holy temple; let all the earth keep silence before him" (2:20). Surely this should be the attitude of that part of the earth, the church, that acknowledges His name. Then when praise and thanksgiving break forth out of silence, they will be all the more meaningful.

Protestant churches especially often lack a spirit of reverence in worship. The main gathering place for worship is frequently viewed as an auditorium (a place to hear) rather than a sanctuary (a holy meeting place). There is little or no room to kneel, and so the psalmist's call "Let us kneel before the LORD our Maker!" (Ps. 95:6) is neither heeded nor practically possible. Moreover, the people often gather to talk first with one another rather than to look expectantly to God. How much many churches need to recover a sense of worship and awe!

The true beginning of worship is beautifully put in these words:

> God Himself is with us: Let us now
> adore Him
> And with awe appear before Him.
> God is in His temple, All within keep
> silence,
> And before Him bow with reverence.
> Him alone, God we own;
> To our God and Saviour
> Praises sing forever.[25]

2. Praise and Thanksgiving

In the worship of God praise and thanksgiving occupy a place of special importance. Of the two, praise is primary because it is the worship of God for Himself. Psalm 150, which climaxes with the words "Let everything that breathes praise the LORD! Praise the LORD!" represents throughout the pure praise of God. In such praise the focus is totally off the self and wholly fixed on God. Because "the LORD is great"—that is, great in Himself—He is "greatly to be praised" (Ps. 96:4 KJV). This is the meaning of praise.

Surely our hearts and mouths should overflow with praise. After a time of reverent quietness, the first words spoken and perhaps sung should be words of praise. Since as Christians we more fully understand God as triune, our worship can be even more elevated than that of the psalmist, for it is the praise of the Lord God who is Father, Son, and Holy Spirit. A hymn such as "Holy, Holy, Holy!" first focuses on God Himself with the words "Lord God Almighty!"; then it climaxes with the words "God in three persons, blessed Trinity." Through such a hymn God may be richly praised.

Praise should continue for a season. One hymn might lead to another, and various choruses of praise can be offered to the Lord. Paul writes to the Ephesians: "Be filled with the Spirit, addressing one another in psalms and hymns and spiritual songs, singing and making melody to the Lord with all your heart" (5:18–19). "Psalms" prob-

[25]The first stanza of a hymn by Joachim Neander, 1680, "God Himself Is with Us."

ably refers to Old Testament psalms; "hymns," to various songs of praise known to all;[26] and "spiritual songs," to Spirit-inspired, spontaneous singing.[27] Such a variety of singing—psalms, hymns, and spiritual songs—with the congregation possibly moving from one expression of praise to another makes for rich and abundant praise. In any event, the congregation should not rush through praise, since this is the foundation and hallmark of true worship.[28]

Closely allied with praise is thanksgiving. The psalmist calls, "Let us come into his presence with thanksgiving; let us make a joyful noise to him with songs of praise!" (95:2). Two lengthy psalms—107 and 136—are expressions of thanksgiving in their entirety. Both begin with the call "O give thanks to the Lord, for he is good; for his steadfast love endures for ever," and then proceed to give thanks for God's great goodness in creation and deliverance. This note of thanksgiving often sounds forth in the Old Testament.

Even more than ancient Israel, the church has reason to thank God. The deliverance for which the Old Testament people of God offered thanks was largely either from personal trials or national enemies.[29] With the New Testament era a far greater deliverance has come, namely from bondage to sin and death; hence there is much more to be thankful for. And it all centers in the gift of God's love in Jesus Christ. So Paul cries out, "Thanks be to God for his inexpressible gift" (2 Cor. 9:15), and in another place he speaks of "abounding in thanksgiving" (Col. 2:7). In connection with worship we have noted the words of Paul in Ephesians about psalms, hymns, and spiritual songs. To these he adds, "always and for everything giving thanks in the name of our Lord Jesus Christ to God the Father" (Eph. 5:20). Here "always" and "for everything" point to thanksgiving in worship that reaches out into the wide range of all the blessings that are ours in Christ.

Thus an occasion of worship should also be a time of joyful thanksgiving. This may of course be included in the expressions of praise, but thanksgiving may also be offered at special moments, perhaps through a congregational litany of thanksgiving or various free utter-

[26]The New Testament itself contains a number of songs, or canticles, of praise such as the *Magnificat* (Luke 1:46–55), the *Benedictus* (Luke 1:68–79), and the *Nunc Dimittis* (Luke 2:29–32) that have been sung through the centuries. Other possible songs, or fragments of songs, may be found, for example, in Ephesians 5:14; Colossians 1:15–20; Philippians 2:6–11; 1 Timothy 1:17; 3:16; 2 Timothy 2:11–13; Revelation 4:11; 5:13; 7:12. "Hymns," or songs of praise, also suggests the many musical expressions both in stately anthems and popular choruses that originated later in the life and worship of the church.

[27]"Spiritual songs"—*ōdais pneumatikais*—probably refers to charismatic singing in the Spirit, or singing in tongues. James Dunn writes that "the word 'spiritual' . . . characterizes the song so described as prompted by the Spirit and manifesting the Spirit," and refers to "spontaneous singing in tongues" (*Jesus and the Spirit*, 238–39). (For more on "spiritual songs" see *Renewal Theology*, 2:218, esp. nn. 40–43.)

[28]Another word frequently used for praise is *adoration*. For example, the church often sings, "O come, let us adore Him, Christ, the Lord." Adoration, like praise, is totally directed away from self to the worship of God. Hence adoration is a possible word to use. It is not, however, a biblical term. The reason may be that adoration suggests a fixed kind of admiration, whereas praise is a more active and outspoken expression of worship. The latter is the basic biblical orientation.

[29]Psalm 107 expresses thanksgiving for deliverance from such personal trials as hunger and thirst, the affliction of prison, sickness and distress, and storms at sea. Psalm 136, after thanksgiving to God for His goodness in creation (vv. 4–9), moves on to gratitude for deliverance from Egypt (vv. 10–22).

ances. One church that I am personally acquainted with often closes the time of morning worship by singing:

Let the peace of Christ
    rule in your heart,
And whatever you do, in word
    or deed
Do it all in the name of the Lord,
Giving thanks, giving thanks to God
    through Christ the Lord.

Thus the congregation is encouraged to move out with thanksgiving in the days ahead. Surely this is the character of Christian thanksgiving.

3. Humility and Contrition

In the prophecy of Isaiah the Lord says, "I dwell in the high and holy place, and also with him who is of a contrite and humble spirit" (57:15). The God who is approached with reverence and awe and who is addressed with praise and thanksgiving does indeed dwell on high, but he also dwells with those who are humble and contrite in spirit. In a similar vein the psalmist declares, "The sacrifice acceptable to God is a broken spirit; a broken and contrite heart, O God, thou wilt not despise" (51:17). "Broken" refers to sorrow for sin, and "contrite" to repentance for sin. Where there is sorrow and repentance, God dwells among His people.

In the true worship of God there is recognition of the need for humility and contrition. For God is a holy God, and the more His awesome presence is realized, the more people sense their own sinfulness and need. The prophet Isaiah, as we noted, heard mighty angels calling out, "Holy, holy, holy is the LORD of hosts; the whole earth is full of his glory." Immediately after that the prophet cried out, "Woe is me! For I am lost; for I am a man of unclean lips, and I dwell in the midst of a people of unclean lips; for my eyes have seen the King, the LORD of hosts!" (Isa. 6:5). This demonstrates that in the vivid presence of the holy God there is a deep sense of personal unholiness and uncleanness. But then something further happened to Isaiah: one of the angels reached down and with a burning coal from the altar touched the prophet's lips, saying, "Your guilt is taken away, and your sin is forgiven" (v. 7). Isaiah, broken and contrite, was fully cleansed and forgiven. In the presence of the holy and merciful God there is also the blessing of forgiveness.

Since no people who assemble for worship are without sin, there is need for contrition and cleansing. The psalmist in another place asks, "Who shall ascend the hill of the LORD? And who shall stand in his holy place?" He then replies, "He who has clean hands and a pure heart" (24:3–4). But we know that none of us who worship—"ascend the hill of the Lord" and "stand in his holy place"—have sinless hands and hearts. Although we have been redeemed by Christ, we do continue to sin and thus need fresh forgiveness. Moreover, as a people we are sinners (as Isaiah came to recognize) and share this common need. In the New Testament a wonderfully reassuring promise to believers is that "if we confess our sins, he is faithful and just, and will forgive our sins and cleanse us from all unrighteousness" (1 John 1:9). Thus if our hearts are truly broken and contrite, and confession of sin is made and forgiveness received, we then are prepared further to worship God.

Therefore in a church worship service an opportunity should be extended for humble confession and receiving the Lord's forgiveness. In some church traditions it may be helpful to use a common prayer of confession, such as the one that begins, "Almighty and most merciful Father, we have erred and strayed from Thy ways like lost sheep; we have followed too much the devices and desires of our own hearts. . . . O Lord, have mercy upon us, miserable offenders"; it closes with the words "and grant, O most merciful Father, for His [Christ's] sake, that we may hereafter live a godly, righteous, and sober life, to the glory of Thy holy Name. Amen." In addition to making such a general confession of sin, the congregation may be given an opportunity in a time of silence and contrition to wait humbly before the Lord, to become more aware of personal shortcomings, and also to make individual confession of sin.[30] Both corporate and individual confession thus have an important place in worship. Following such confession the worship leader may verbally give an assurance of pardon such as, "Hear the good news: in the name of Jesus Christ we are forgiven!"[31] The exact procedure is not too important. Moreover the occasion of confession may be included in some other prayer,[32] or at some other time in the worship service;[33] however, the opportunity for confession and forgiveness is quite important.

A final note in regard to humility and contrition: There are many churches that in worship have a fine season of praise and thanksgiving—everything from psalms and hymns to spiritual songs—but almost totally lack in the matter of confession. This ought not to be. The God who is high and lifted up, indeed "enthroned upon the praises" of His people (Ps. 22:3 NASB), is a holy God, so that the more we become aware of His awesome presence, the more we must also sense a need for humility and contrition, confession and forgiveness. Furthermore, the experience of contrition and forgiveness helps prepare the way for the further expressions of worship (to which we next come). It is important indeed not to minimize the urgent need for humility and contrition.

4. Supplication and Intercession

Paul writes Timothy, "I urge that supplications,[34] prayers, intercessions,[35] and thanksgivings be made for all men, for kings and all who are in high posi-

[30]Outstanding biblical prayers of individual confession are those of Daniel (Dan. 9:3–19) and Nehemiah (Neh. 1:4–11). However, it is significant that these prayers also represent corporate confessions of and for the people.

[31]In churches that have a priestly orientation, this pardon is declared by an officiating priest who, while standing, may say, "The Almighty and merciful Lord grant you absolution and remission of all your sins, true repentance, amendment of life, and the peace and consolation of the Holy Spirit" (as stated in *The Book of Common Prayer*, Episcopal Church, U.S.A.). Interestingly, if a lay person offers such a prayer, he is instructed (in *The Book of Common Prayer*) to remain kneeling and to substitute "us" for "you," and "our" for "your"! In the Roman Catholic church the priest alone may offer absolution, and he does so by saying, "I absolve you from your sins in the name of the Father and Son and Holy Spirit." "Absolution," because it suggests priestly authority, is less commonly used in Protestant churches.

[32]Such as the "pastoral prayer" in many churches. However, since this prayer often comprehends many elements, confession may be little, or not at all, emphasized.

[33]Confession of sin may, for example, occur immediately after a time of reverent silence in which God is sensed in His exaltation and holiness, or immediately following praise and thanksgiving. In the case of Isaiah, as we have noted, the prophet's contrition followed immediately upon his vision of the holy God.

[34]The Greek word is *deēseis*. The KJV likewise reads "supplications"; NIV has "requests"; NASB, "entreaties," NEB, "petitions." All are helpful translations of *deēsis*, which occurs seventeen times in the New Testament.

[35]The Greek word is *enteuxeis*. The KJV and NEB likewise read "intercessions"; NIV has "intercession"; NASB, "petitions." "Intercessions" is probably the best translation. *Enteuxis* and *entygchanō* (the verbal form) occur seven times in the New Testament.

tions'' (1 Tim. 2:1–2). While no sharp distinction can be drawn, ''supplications'' generally refers to a wide range of petitionary prayer, ''intercessions'' to prayers offered on behalf of others. It is Paul's concern that all possible prayers be offered.

Surely such petitionary and intercessory prayers are integral to the church's worship. For example, in the Lord's Prayer, often said in communal worship,[36] there are six basic petitions. The first three relate to God Himself—the hallowing of His name, praying for His kingdom to come, and expressing the desire for His will to be done (Matt. 6:9–10). These petitions regarding God—His holiness, His kingdom, and His will—emphasize that in such prayer the primary matter is not the needs of those praying but the fulfillment of God's glory and purpose. Indeed, such prayer is basically intercessory because it expresses the believers' desire for the coming of God's kingdom (with all that this signifies) and for God's will to be done everywhere on earth. The next three petitions relate to the needs of those praying—for daily bread, forgiveness of debts (sins), and deliverance from evil. Such supplications, while secondary, are likewise important, because God our Father wants His children to make known their needs to Him.

Following the example of the Lord's Prayer,[37] the petitions of the church may be, first, those of intercession for the concerns of God's kingdom. Rather than praying at the outset for the congregation's own needs, the church reaches out in prayer to the whole world. This means praying for the worldwide gospel proclamation, for the church's message in every land and nation, and for those serving in mission fields both at home and far away. It means praying as Jesus did, according to John 17,[38] for the unity of believers everywhere—''that they may all be one'' (v. 21). It means praying for the peoples of all nations that righteousness may prevail and that evil will be cast down. Such intercessions should be primary in the worship of the church.

But surely there is also a place—and an important one—for focusing on the needs of the congregation. The simple words ''Give us this day our daily bread''—however expressed—are an ongoing reminder that even the most elementary of our daily needs[39] depend totally on God's provision and should not therefore be taken for granted. Also, this petition suggests that we may go beyond physical necessities to pray for the many other blessings God has in store for His children. Jesus later says, ''Your Father who is in heaven [will] give good things to those who ask him'' (Matt. 7:11). God our Father delights to give *to those who ask,* and surely the congregational gathering for worship is a significant occasion for us to ask. God's ''good things'' are not limited. Whatever needs exist—healing for sickness, strength for weariness, peace for anxiety, direction for uncertainty,

---

[36]The Lord's Prayer (more strictly, ''the disciples' prayer,'' which the Lord taught them) in Matthew 6:8–13 begins with ''*Our* Father''; hence it relates basically to community worship and prayer.

[37]Jesus prefaced this prayer with the words ''Pray then *like* this''; hence do not simply quote these words (He had just warned: ''do not heap up empty phrases'' [v. 7]), but let them be an example. This needs to be remembered when in some churches the Lord's Prayer recited regularly becomes so many ''empty phrases'' (or ''vain repetitions'' KJV). The other extreme, however, is not to use the prayer at all and thus overlook its basic guidance.

[38]This is literally ''the Lord's prayer''; Jesus Himself was praying to the Father.

[39]Later in Matthew 6 Jesus, in addition to talking about food, talks about clothing and shelter. Hence prayer for daily bread includes all other basic physical necessities.

victory for defeat—God is ready to give. Such prayers may be said for the overall needs of the congregation, but it is important also to pray in particular. Later, Jesus declares, "Even the hairs of your head are all numbered" (Matt. 10:30; Luke 12:7), thus speaking of God the Father's individual concern. Therefore we should pray for particular needs, indeed insofar as possible, even person by person.[40]

The other two petitions in the Lord's Prayer—"Forgive us our debts [or 'sins'],[41] as we also have forgiven our debtors" and "Lead us not into temptation, but deliver us from evil" (vv. 12–13)—express concerns of all believers. The first request is for God to forgive us, since we have forgiven others and do now[42] forgive others.[43] This petition implies that before we seek again the Lord's continuing forgiveness we must forgive anyone who may have done us ill.[44] Thus in worship church members may properly be called upon to consider their own attitude toward others before praying for God's ongoing mercy. The second request is concerned that the heavenly Father not allow us to be led into temptation,[45] but that we be delivered from evil, or the evil one.[46] This

[40]This is obviously difficult in the gathering of a large congregation. However, it may be helpful during the time of petitionary prayer to pray for a few individual needs and thus particularize the prayers. Or there can be a pause in the congregational prayers to divide for a few minutes into smaller groups to offer individual prayers. If the congregation also has home fellowship meetings, these give the members an excellent opportunity for individual prayer ministry to one another.

[41]The parallel passage in Luke reads, "Forgive us our sins" (11:4).

[42]The Lord's Prayer, as recorded in Luke 11, reads at this point: "Forgive us our sins, for we ourselves forgive every one who is indebted to us" (v. 4). Note the present tense.

[43]This petition does not imply that God's forgiveness of us is based on our forgiveness of others; rather, it is a recognition that His forgiveness will be discontinued if we do not forgive others. Jesus clarifies this later in the parable of the unforgiving servant (Matt. 18:23–35) who, though forgiven a huge debt (= sin) by his master, refuses to forgive a paltry amount owed him by a fellow servant and, as a result, the master reinstates the huge debt and throws the unforgiving servant into jail. The parable ends with these sobering words: "So also my heavenly Father will do to every one of you, if you do not forgive your brother from your heart" (v. 35).

[44]It is striking that Jesus, in an earlier statement preceding the Lord's Prayer, declares, "If you are offering your gift at the altar, and there remember that your brother has something against you, leave your gift there before the altar and go; first be reconciled to your brother, and then come and offer your gift" (Matt. 5:23–24). This means that if, while at church (where one brings his gift to "the altar"), you recall that a brother has something against you and you have not yet become reconciled to that brother, you must then go and take care of the matter before proceeding further in worship. This means actually to go, request his forgiveness, and forgive him; then you can pray from the heart, "Forgive me my sins, as I have forgiven one who has sinned against me." This is also in line with Jesus' further words, at the conclusion of the Lord's Prayer, "For if you forgive men their trespasses, your heavenly Father also will forgive you; but if you do not forgive men their trespasses, neither will your Father forgive your trespasses" (Matt. 6:14–15). In regard to saying the Lord's Prayer, it means quite bluntly that before praying the petition about our heavenly Father forgiving us, if we have not personally taken proper care to forgive an unreconciled brother, God will totally disregard our request. I am afraid that too few people realize what a serious matter it is to say the Lord's Prayer.

[45]"Lead us not into temptation" does not mean that God tempts His children. "God . . . tempts no one" (James 1:13).

[46]So NIV and NEB read. The Greek phrase *apo tou ponērou* can be translated "from the evil one," implying Satan. Jesus' words may be reminiscent of His earlier experience of

prayer is much needed by all Christians since temptations abound, and Satan is always seeking to entrap believers. This last of the six petitions in the Lord's Prayer therefore needs to be asked frequently because the church is again and again tempted to succumb to the lures and seductions of the world.

To sum up: The worship activity of the church includes prayers of supplication and intercession. Intercession may be given the priority so that the assembled congregation first prays for others. This is good, because people can easily become so preoccupied with their own needs that they scarcely reach out beyond themselves. Nonetheless, it is entirely proper and indeed necessary that people express their own needs—collectively as well as individually. God is always ready to hear the supplications of His people. So may we as a church be all the more encouraged to offer up continuing intercessions and supplications to the heavenly Father.

5. Consecration and Dedication

Finally, a congregational worship service also offers opportunity for consecration and dedication on the part of all the members.[47] This includes both one's earthly possessions and oneself.

Let us first consider the matter of earthly possessions. In the Old Testament there is particular stress on bringing offerings to the Lord. For example, the psalmist calls out, "Ascribe to the LORD the glory due his name; bring an offering, and come into his courts!" (96:8). In another psalm are these words: "With a freewill offering I will sacrifice to thee; I will give thanks to thy name, O LORD, for it is good" (54:6). There were offerings of many varieties, some voluntary, some required. In the latter category was the tithe, the bringing of one-tenth of a person's property to the Lord.[48] The Old Testament closes with these words of the Lord regarding the tithe: "Bring the full tithes into the storehouse, that there may be food in my house; and thereby put me to the test, says the LORD of hosts, if I will not open the windows of heaven for you and pour down for you an overflowing blessing" (Mal. 3:10). Tithes and offerings of many kinds were regularly presented in the temple worship.

In New Testament worship the stress is almost wholly on voluntary offerings. Jesus Himself praises a poor widow who dropped two copper coins (her whole livelihood) into the temple treasury (Luke 21:1–4), and Paul stresses the value of abundant giving. Paul writes, "He who sows sparingly will also reap sparingly, and he who sows bountifully will also reap bountifully. Each one must do as he has made up his mind, not reluctantly or under compulsion, for God loves a cheerful giver" (2 Cor. 9:6–7).[49]

---

being "led up by the Spirit into the wilderness to be tempted by the devil" (Matt. 4:1). Jesus was not led by the Holy Spirit into temptation but to the place where Satan tempted Him.

[47]This may occur before or after a proclamation of the word or a sacramental celebration. (I am not here including a discussion of either the preaching of the word or the celebration of the sacraments, though of course they both are vital parts of many worship services. See this chapter, pp. 109–17 for a discussion of the Word; chap. 5, pp. 181–96, "Ministry of the Word"; and chap. 6 on the sacraments or ordinances.

[48]According to Deuteronomy 14:22–29, the specified tithe was grain, wine, and oil. On the tithe in the Old Testament see also Genesis 14:17–20; 28:20–22; Lev. 27:30–33; Num. 18:21–32; Deut. 12:5–19; 26:12–15; 2 Chron. 31:4–12; Neh. 10:36–39; 12:44; 13:5, 12; Amos 4:4; Mal. 3:8, 10. There are two or three different tithes mentioned in these passages.

[49]Paul is writing about a special "offering for the saints" (v. 1) in Jerusalem; his words, however, are surely applicable to all Christian giving.

Jesus mentions the tithe twice. First, he does so in connection with a vigorous denunciation of the scribes and Pharisees: "Woe to you, scribes and Pharisees, hypocrites! for you tithe mint and dill and cummin, and have neglected the weightier matters of the law, justice and mercy and faith; these you ought to have done, without neglecting the others" (Matt. 23:23; cf. Luke 11:42). Jesus did not deny the rightness of their tithing[50] but deplored their neglect of justice, mercy, and faith, the weightier, or more important, matters of the law. Jesus' other reference to tithing is in a parable that includes the boastful statement of the Pharisee: "I fast twice a week, I give tithes of all I get" (Luke 18:12). The Pharisee was condemned by Jesus not for his fasting and tithing but for his pride: "Every one who exalts himself will be humbled" (v. 14). The only other New Testament reference to tithing is in Hebrews 7 where the writer relates that Abraham gave Melchizedek tithes and that the Levites according to the law took tithes from their brethren (vv. 4–10). There is no reference, however, in Hebrews to Christians continuing this practice. Paul never refers to tithing in any of his letters. Thus tithing in the New Testament occupies a very marginal place. Even Jesus, who does not deny the validity of tithing, never gives positive instruction to His disciples in this regard.

Jesus does, however, without referring to any particular amount, speak quite positively of giving alms: "When you give alms . . ." (Matt. 6:2). Here He warns His disciples against the hypocrisy of those who make a public show of their giving. Then Jesus adds, "But when you give alms, do not let your left hand know what your right hand is doing, so that your alms may be in secret; and your Father who sees in secret will reward you" (vv. 3–4). The important matter is not giving a specific amount (e.g., a tithe), but giving quietly and secretly. In regard to the amount, there is no limit (recall the widow who gave all she had). Later Jesus instructs a rich young ruler: "Sell all that you have and distribute to the poor, and you will have treasure in heaven" (Luke 18:22).[51] The stress by Jesus in another place is on open-hearted giving: "Give, and it will be given to you; good measure, pressed down, shaken together, running over, will be put[52] into your lap" (Luke 6:38). This does not mean giving in order to receive—a kind of calculated giving. But when one freely gives without seeking a return, abundant blessings will surely come in.

What does all of this say concerning church giving today? By New Testament principles, the emphasis should be on voluntary and joyous giving. If tithing is mentioned, it should be understood not as a New Testament command but as a minimal amount to give (should the Christian do less than the Old Testament Jew?) in the context of

[50]The scribes and Pharisees, however, went beyond the Old Testament requirements in tithing. They added to grain, wine, and oil all kinds of spices, even the most insignificant such as mint, dill, and cummin. In Luke 11:42 the words of Jesus include "every herb" ("all manner of herbs" KJV).

[51]Neither the widow's giving all nor Jesus' injunction to the rich young ruler to do the same is a necessary example or command for Jesus' disciples. The widow was commended in contrast to the rich who gave to the treasury out of their abundance much more than she did, and the rich young ruler was allowing his riches to block the way to eternal life. Although Jesus did not command his disciples to give all, limitless giving surely has His blessing.

[52]Literally, "they will put," or "give" (*dōsousin*). Hence the reference in this case is to abounding blessings coming from one's fellow man.

the larger call for free and voluntary giving. It is questionable to quote such an Old Testament command as "Bring the full tithes into the storehouse" when the New Testament places almost total emphasis on voluntary giving. Also, there is need to stress thoughtfulness in giving—each person "to do as he has made up his mind"—in order to particularize giving in light of one's own available resources. This calls for stewardship, namely, to make the best possible use of the means God has provided. Anonymity in giving is also important: there should be no broadcasting or announcing of one's giving either by the church or by the individual who gives. The blessings of voluntary giving may properly be stressed: the Father will reward, and good measure, even "running over," will be returned. Giving is not done in order to receive a reward from God or man; however, those who give abundantly will be abundantly blessed.

Finally, for the church the main stress in giving should be against the background of God's own total giving of His Son: "God so loved the world, that he gave his only begotten Son" (John 3:16 KJV). The ultimate question for the recipients of God's gift is not How much should we give? but How much can we hold back in light of what God has done for us?

This leads to the other emphasis in giving—the dedication of the self. A worship service affords opportunity for the giving of material possessions; it also, and climactically, should lead to a further consecration of the worshipers themselves.

Here let us note two passages in Scripture, the first in Isaiah 6. We have already recalled that Isaiah's experience in the temple of the thrice-holy God resulted in the prophet's profound confession of sin and his being forgiven by God. Following this, we now note, Isaiah heard the Lord saying, "Whom shall I send, and who will go for us?" and thereupon Isaiah replied, "Here I am! Send me" (v. 8). He neither asked where he would be sent nor what he would be doing. It was simply an act of total self-dedication.

The second passage is in Romans 12. The chapter begins with these stirring words of Paul: "Therefore, I urge you, brothers, in view of God's mercy, to offer your bodies as living sacrifices, holy and pleasing to God—this is your spiritual act of worship"[53] (v. 1 NIV). Against the background of what God has done in Christ—"God's mercy"—we are urged to present our bodies, our selves,[54] as living sacrifices. Paul's words of course apply to more than a particular worship service, because we are called upon to be "living sacrifices" daily throughout life. However, it is also fitting that this "spiritual act of worship"—total self-dedication—oc-

[53]"Spiritual act of worship" in the Greek text is *logikēn latreian*. The KJV reads "reasonable service." This is a possible translation, since *logikēn* can also mean "rational," and *latreian* can mean "service." However, *latreian* is a cultic term and refers to the "service or worship of God" (BAGD); hence there is less ambiguity in translating the word here as "worship" (also as in Rom. 9:4; cf. Heb. 9:1, 6). Paul's thought is that the presentation of ourselves as living sacrifices is a reasonable/spiritual act of worship. Based on the great sweep of God's atoning work in Christ (propounded variously in Romans 1–11), it is both rational and spiritual to respond in this fashion.

[54]By his reference to "bodies" Paul is contrasting animal bodies, which are given up to death in sacrifices, with human bodies, which are to be "living sacrifices." Since Paul is not speaking of the human body separate from the spirit or soul, but of the body as our way of earthly existence, "selves" can well convey the meaning. (See also Romans 6:13 where Paul shifts from the "members" [of the body] to "yourselves," thus demonstrating the identity of the two.)

cur at the close of a community gathering for worship. Such an act of dedication carries the members of the church out into the world to be continual living sacrifices.

The final dedication may be in the form of a hymn such as "Take My Life and Let It Be Consecrated, Lord, to Thee" and/or a prayer. The opportunity may also be given for people to come forward and kneel in self-offering to the Lord. The important thing, however, is not the exact method but the act of renewed commitment to serve the Lord faithfully in the days ahead.

C. The Way of Worship

Now that we have considered the character of worship in terms of its various components, let us reflect briefly on the way of worship.

1. Trinitarian

Christian worship is essentially Trinitarian: it involves the worship of the one God as Father, Son, and Holy Spirit.[55]

a. One God. The worship of *one* God is basic to the witness of both the Old Testament and the New. Israel, in the midst of surrounding nations that worshiped many gods, was a people called to faith in and worship of one God. In the Ten Commandments we find these words: "You shall have no other gods before me. . . . You shall not bow down to them or worship them" (Deut. 5:7–9 NIV).[56] Shortly after that Moses calls to Israel, "Hear, O Israel: The Lord our God, the Lord is one" (Deut. 6:4 NIV). The one and only Lord God was to be worshiped by the people of Israel. Likewise in the New Testament Jesus Himself reaffirmed the oneness of God by quoting the words "Hear, O Israel, the Lord our God, the Lord is one" (Mark 12:29). Paul does the same in such words as "God is one" (Gal. 3:20) and in an ascription of worship: "To the King of ages, immortal, invisible, the only God, be honor and glory for ever and ever. Amen" (1 Tim. 1:17). Israel and the church, Jewish faith and Christian faith, affirm the oneness of God and the worship of no other gods.

Christian worship, it is important to emphasize, centers in the one and only God. Whatever is said about the worship of God as Father, Son, and Holy Spirit must not in any sense derogate from the focus of worship on the one God. If Father, Son, and Holy Spirit are worshiped, it is not as if three deities are being recognized, for each person is wholly God. For example, in the Book of Revelation, although there is the heavenly worship of "the Lord God Almighty" on the throne in chapter 4 and of "the Lamb" standing near Him in chapter 5 and of the two in conjunction in 5:13—"To him who sits upon the throne and to the Lamb be blessing and honor and glory and might for ever and ever!"—there is still only one God being worshiped. For Christ the Lamb of God also occupies the throne—"I myself conquered and sat down with my Father on his throne" (Rev. 3:21), and both use the same language of "Alpha and Omega"[57] in referring to themselves. In Revelation 1:8 the words are " 'I am the Alpha and the Omega,' says the Lord God, who is and who was and who is to come, the Almighty"; in Revelation 22:12–13 the text reads, "Behold, I [Christ] am coming soon. . . . I am the Alpha and the Omega, the first and the last, the begin-

---

[55]For more detailed background on the one God in three persons, see *Renewal Theology*, 1:83–94 (chap. 4, "The Holy Trinity").

[56]The same words are found in Exodus 20:3–4.

[57]The first and last letters of the Greek alphabet, hence, symbolically, "the beginning and the end."

ning and the end."[58] There is only one throne of God, only one Alpha and Omega—even if there are two persons—and thus the Lord God Almighty and the Lamb are to be worshiped as the one and only true God.

Accordingly, the church in its worship is centrally fixed upon the one God. If the Son is worshiped, it is not a worship of one other than God, less than God, or second to God: it is a worship of God in His entirety. Thus in worship there is no need to feel that by lifting our praise to Christ we are focusing on less than the holy God, or that perhaps we need to balance our worship of Christ by turning to the Father. Whenever the Son or the Father is worshiped, God is being extolled in His totality.

Quite often in worship, the church uses the Old Testament psalms as readily as did Israel, or as Jews do to the present day. In so doing we praise the one God with no less intensity than Israel did. The church has no hesitation in affirming the first commandment about "no other gods," or saying, "the Lord our God, the Lord is one." The church in its worship is as vigorously opposed to polytheism as was Israel.[59] Among the people of many religions that claim multiple deities we worship the one Lord God.

b. Three Persons. In Christian faith the worship of God also involves three persons: Father, Son, and Holy Spirit. Here we definitely go beyond Israel by declaring that in the one God there is a unity of persons. These three persons are not separate beings (as in polytheism) nor merely attributes of the one God: they are each fully the one God yet each a distinct person.[60]

This means, first, that each person may be worshiped separately.[61] In regard to God as Father, Jesus declares, "The hour is coming, and now is, when the true worshipers will worship the Father in spirit and truth, for such the Father seeks to worship him" (John 4:23). God the Father is to be worshiped. Jesus Himself also received worship while on earth; for example, the wise men "fell down and worshiped him" (Matt. 2:11); "those in the boat worshiped him" (Matt. 14:33); "they [the women at the tomb] . . . took hold of his feet and worshiped him" (Matt. 28:9). In heaven, as we have noted, both God (the Father) and the Lamb (the Son) are praised—"to him who sits upon the throne and to the Lamb"—and the scene climaxes with the statement that "the elders fell down and worshiped" (Rev. 5:14). Father and Son are equally worshiped. There seems to be no direct biblical reference to the Holy Spirit being worshiped;[62] however, His activity in worship may be suggested by Paul's words when he said, "It is we who are the [true][63] circumcision, we who worship by the

[58]Other texts in Revelation show the language of Alpha and Omega, or of "first and last," being applied both to God (the Father) in 21:6 and to Christ in 1:17 and 2:8.

[59]The same may also be said about Islam. The beginning of the Muslim daily watchword, "There is no God but Allah," is likewise a declaration of the oneness of God. Whatever the great differences about the Trinity, Jews, Muslims, and Christians are united in affirming the worship of only one God.

[60]See *Renewal Theology*, 1:84–90, the section entitled "In Three Persons," for further discussion how "each is a person" and "each person is God."

[61]Yet in so worshiping the Trinity of persons we recognize God's essential unity. In the words of the Athanasian Creed (c. A.D. 400), "We worship one God in Trinity, and Trinity in Unity."

[62]But see also note 64 below.

[63]"True" (RSV, NASB), over against Jewish circumcision in the flesh, is implied.

Spirit of God"[64] (Phil. 3:3 NIV). However, since the Holy Spirit is fully God, there is ample reason for worshiping Him even as we worship the Father and the Son.[65] We do this in many of our prayers and hymns.[66]

Second, each person may also fill a distinct role in worship. In Ephesians 5 Paul writes, "Be filled with the Spirit . . . always and for everything giving thanks in the name of our Lord Jesus Christ to God the Father" (vv. 18, 20). In these words referring to all persons in the Trinity, Paul is declaring a worship procedure. God the Father is the ultimate person to whom thanks (hence worship) is directed, but it is to be done in the name of the Lord Jesus Christ, the second person, and by the filling of the Holy Spirit, the third person of the Trinity. Although all the persons are God, the procedure outlined is from third to second to first.

Being "filled with the Spirit" is the basis and ground for rich worship of God. This is similar to Paul's words cited regarding worship "by the Spirit of God." This is distinctive of Christian worship (beyond that of Jewish), namely, that the Holy Spirit inspires the worship,[67] and the more that inspiration is present, the more fully God is glorified. Thus it is by no means only that our human spirits are raised in worship to God; rather, we are lifted by the Holy Spirit into the heights of praise and worship.

By "giving thanks in the name of our Lord Jesus Christ," we worship God the Father through the medium of the Son who has opened up for us the way to the Father. Jesus Himself declares, "No one comes to the Father except through me" (John 14:6 NIV). According to Hebrews, "we have confidence to enter the sanctuary [hence to worship] by the blood of Jesus, by the new and living way which he opened for us through the curtain, that is, through his flesh" (10:19–20). Because of what Christ has done in the Atonement, there is "the new and living way." Since "we have a great priest over the house of God" (v. 21), we can now "draw near with a true heart in full assurance of faith" (v. 22). So again Christian worship goes beyond Old Testament possibilities because of the atoning blood of Jesus Christ and His continuing priestly ministry. Thus we have total assurance of entering into the very presence of God.

To summarize, although each person of the Trinity may be worshiped separately, they also have distinctive roles. In this latter case, we come to God the Father through Jesus Christ the Son by

[64]Another grammatical possibility is "who worship the Spirit of God." The Greek phrase is *pneumati theou latreuontes*. If this is the proper translation, here would be a specific reference to worshiping the Holy Spirit. However, it is probably best to follow the NIV reading "by the Spirit" and view the *pneumati* as a dative of agency (as in Rom. 8:14 and Gal. 5:18).

[65]The Nicene Creed (A.D. 325) contains this statement: "And [we believe] in the Holy Spirit, the Lord and Giver of Life, who proceedeth from the Father [and the Son], who with the Father and the Son together is worshiped and glorified." This ancient creed, affirmed today across a wide spectrum of the Christian church, rightly confesses the propriety of the worship of the Holy Spirit.

[66]E.g., in the Doxology we sing, "Praise God from whom all blessings flow; Praise Him, all creatures here below; Praise Him above, ye heavenly host; Praise Father, Son, and Holy Ghost." The church joyously praises, therefore worships, along with Father and Son, the Holy Spirit.

[67]Peter Brunner writes, "It is *the Spirit Himself who performs the [worship] service in the presence of God*" (*Worship in the Name of Jesus*, 21, italics his).

the activity of the Holy Spirit.[68] This is uniquely Christian worship. We may not in every act of worship mention the name of Jesus (for example, when we pray the words of the Lord's Prayer: "Our Father . . .") or be consciously aware of the Holy Spirit's activity. However, in true Christian worship there is always the sense that we come not in our own name (which is far too inadequate) or in our own power (which is far too impotent), but we come through the name (i.e., the person) of Jesus and by the presence and power of the Holy Spirit.

2. Freedom and Order

The worship of God involves freedom and order. Spontaneity and orderliness should characterize all that is done.

a. Freedom. Paul writes that "where the Spirit of the Lord is, there is freedom" (2 Cor. 3:17). Hence, if the Holy Spirit is active in worship, genuine freedom is present. This means that freedom, liberty, and spontaneity should mark the spiritual worship of God. We have previously noted Paul's words about "psalms and hymns and spiritual songs, singing and making melody to the Lord with all [our] heart" (Eph. 5:19). These "spiritual songs" are songs inspired by the Holy Spirit, that is, spontaneous songs in which both the melody and the words are given by the Spirit.[69] Such spiritual singing may well follow the singing of various psalms and hymns and thus be the overflowing occasion of "making melody to the Lord with all [our] heart." This, however, is an act of free and spontaneous worship that cannot be programed ahead of time, nor can its contents be previously known.

There should be newness in worship. In the Old Testament the psalmist declares, "He put a new song in my mouth, a song of praise to our God" (40:3), and, again, "O sing to the Lord a new song, for he has done marvelous things!" (98:1).[70] God has done so much for us, both past and present, that only a new song can declare it. Unfortunately, the church has often—and totally contrary to the psalmist's intention—simply repeated again and again the psalmist's words, so that they become an old, old song. But if the Lord has done marvelous things, even new things in the present, should we not sing them forth spontaneously and freely? Sometimes in our churches we sing the Magnificat, the song of Mary, that begins, "My soul magnifies the Lord, and my spirit rejoices in God my Savior" (Luke 1:46–47). This is a beautiful song and well worth repeating, but we render the Lord a disservice if we simply continue to repeat what was for Mary a new song. Rather, as we likewise magnify the Lord, we should sing our own new and spontaneous expressions. One further word on "a new song": heaven, not just earth, is a place where new songs are heard! According to Revelation 5, the elders "sang a new song" (v. 9) about the Lamb, and in Revelation 14 the multitude of redeemed saints "sing a new song before the throne" (v. 3). Surely this suggests that similar new songs should be a part of our worship on earth.

How can this occur in the church at worship? If someone has a new song,

[68]"By" may also be used in regard to Jesus, as in Hebrews 10, "by the blood of Jesus"; however, the basic idea is instrumentality ("*through* me"), not agency (expressed in the language of "*by* the Holy Spirit").

[69]The Jerusalem Bible, in a note on the comparable passage in Colossians 3:16, says that "these 'inspired songs' could be charismatic improvisations suggested by the Spirit during liturgical assembly." (See also previous note 27.)

[70]See also Psalms 33:3; 96:1; 149:1; Isaiah 42:10.

he or she should be offered the opportunity to sing it. This could mean loosening up the regular order of worship to make room for free expressions. Also the "spiritual songs," earlier referred to, can be congregation-wide singing in the Spirit in which praise and blessing are offered to Almighty God. Through such singing the Holy Spirit weaves together the melodies in the hearts of God's people into a beautiful and harmonious offering of praise and thanksgiving.

This freedom in the Spirit should mark all aspects of worship. I have previously listed various components of worship from opening reverence and awe to a concluding time of consecration and dedication. What is important is the components of worship, not necessarily the order. The Holy Spirit, for example, may lead to an early expression of humility and contrition or a later one of praise and thanksgiving. The urgent matter is that we be flexible in the Lord, who is beyond all rigid programing and thus free to move through worship as He wills.

A final word on freedom in worship: This must always be safeguarded because of the human tendency to lapse into form and ritual. This began to happen early in the history of the church when, along with the diminution of vital faith in many quarters, formalism and ritualism set in. When Christianity became the official religion of the Roman Empire early in the fourth century, form and ceremony became all the more dominant. Despite the sixteenth-century reformation in doctrine, there was—and still is—a lack of emphasis on freedom in worship in the historic churches. We may be grateful indeed for the "free" churches that have sought to break the gridlock on worship, and particularly for the charismatic renewal that has brought fresh emphasis on neglected elements in vital worship. However, the renewal itself is by no means free of form and ritual, for many participating churches and fellowships slip into patterns of ritual and repetition.

"For freedom Christ has set us free," Paul writes in Galatians 5:1. Surely this great act of emancipation not only relates to the bondage of sin but also to the bondage of forms and traditions in worship. Let us therefore worship in freedom!

b. Order. There should also be orderliness in worship. Freedom is basic, but there is also need for order. At the close of a lengthy discussion of worship practices relating to the operation of spiritual gifts in the church at Corinth (1 Cor. 12–14), Paul declares, "But let all things be done properly[71] and in an orderly manner"[72] (1 Cor. 14:40 NASB). These words conclude Paul's discussion that begins, "When you assemble, each one has a psalm, has a teaching, has a revelation, has a tongue, has an interpretation. Let all things be done for edification" (v. 26 NASB).[73] It is apparent from Paul's further presentation that the Corinthians were especially disorderly in their practice of speaking in tongues and prophesying, and thereby provoked a rebuke from the apostle: "God is not a God of disorder[74] but of peace" (v. 33 NIV). Freedom in worship should not degenerate into confusion and disorderliness.

Let us reflect for a moment on the fact that God is not a God of disorder. God is surely a God of freedom, but in

---

[71]The Greek word is *euschēmonous*—"decently" (KJV, RSV, NEB), "in a fitting way" (NIV).

[72]The Greek phrase is *kata taxin*—"in order" (KJV, RSV, NEB), "in an orderly way" (NIV).

[73]For further discussion on this verse see the next section, "Total Participation."

[74]The Greek word is *akatastasias*; KJV, RSV, and NASB translate it as "confusion."

His own being He Himself is a God of order: the Father, the Son, and the Holy Spirit (in that order); and the universe, including man, while evidencing a definite freedom and spontaneity, represents structure and order. Cosmos, not chaos, is the reality in which we exist, and so it should be in our worship. God Himself as the ground of all things is also both Word (structure) and Spirit (freedom), so that in Himself, in the universe and man He has made, and in our worship there should be the reflection of both structure and freedom.[75] Freedom must not be at the expense of order.

This is why a certain order in worship is essential. Accordingly, in a previous section we have discussed certain elements in worship that also generally make up a worship sequence. Some such order, if not so binding as to eliminate spontaneity and freedom, is valuable because we are creatures who must have order in our daily lives—eating, sleeping, working, and so on—if we are to function properly. So when we gather together, some order is needed whereby we worship and glorify God.

Thus liturgy, to some degree, is invaluable. A printed outline of worship, a book of common prayers, the use of such confessions of faith as the Apostles' Creed and the Nicene Creed—and other traditional forms[76]—help to bring order into the service of worship. Some prescribed forms for such rites as baptism, confirmation, and the Lord's Supper are also helpful. Great hymns of the church have a proper place and should not be neglected. Recall again that Paul speaks of "psalms and hymns" along with "Spirit-inspired songs." Liturgy is important in worshiping the God of order Himself.

The danger, I must quickly add, is that order and structure will stifle freedom and spontaneity. Thus room must be made for both order and freedom. It is a false polarization that sets liberty against liturgy, freedom against order. True worship of God, who Himself is the God of both liberty and order, contains both elements.

In regard to the true worship of God we may now refer again to the words of Jesus in the Fourth Gospel: "The hour is coming, and now is, when the true worshipers will worship the Father in spirit and truth, for such the Father seeks to worship him" (John 4:23). Then Jesus adds, "God is spirit,[77] and those who worship him must worship in spirit and truth" (v. 24). Jesus is teaching two important things about worship.

First, His statements are against the background of the question about where people should worship and Jesus' reply that "the hour is coming when neither on this mountain nor in Jerusalem will you worship the Father" (v. 21). Since God is spirit, and thus everywhere present, worship will be no longer fixed to a certain location or building, but can occur anywhere. Jesus' words, accordingly, are a strong reminder to the church that the worship of God's people is by no means tied to a presumed holy place or sanctuary. The very idea of a special consecrated building, where alone God can be truly worshiped, is foreign to the essence of Christian faith. True worship may be in a home, a storefront, a stadium, anywhere; for God as spirit is present wherever His people worship Him. Sec-

[75]On Logos and structure see *Renewal Theology*, 1:103–4. We have already noted the words relating the Spirit to freedom in 2 Corinthians 3:17.

[76]Including perhaps congregational prayers of thanksgiving and confession.

[77]Rather than "a Spirit" (KJV). Such a translation suggests that God as "a Spirit" is one spirit among many.

ond, true worship is "in spirit[78] and in truth." "In spirit" means that genuine worship is a matter deeply of the human spirit, the inmost essence of a person, reaching out to God. True worship is more than words repeated or mental exercises; it is profoundly spiritual whether offered in free expression or traditional form. "In truth" means that our worship must in every way reflect the truth about God in His self-revelation, particularly in regard to Christ Himself, who is "the way, and the truth, and the life" (John 14:6). The church is properly concerned about doctrinal truth; an equal or greater concern needs to be expressed about truth in worship—hymns, prayers, sermon, sacraments, and whatever else;[79] for in worship God is not being talked about (as in theology or doctrine), He is being talked to. To worship in spirit and truth is the nature of genuine worship—and indeed, as Jesus declares, those who so worship, "the Father seeks to worship him." If that is what God seeks, namely a people who worship from the depths of their being and in the truth that He has given, should not God's desire be all the more ours?

3. *Total Participation*

Finally, there should be total participation in worship. All should fully share in worship, and we should worship with all our being.

a. All Participating. In the Old Testament there is a frequent call for all creation to worship and praise the Lord. For example, "Praise the LORD! . . . Praise him, all his angels, praise him, all his host! Praise him, sun and moon, praise him, all you shining stars . . . kings of the earth and all peoples. . . . Let them praise the name of the Lord" (Ps. 148:1–3, 11, 13). All of God's people likewise are called upon to praise the Lord: "Let all the people [in Israel] say, 'Amen!' Praise the LORD!" (Ps. 106:48). In the book of Revelation, a voice from the throne cries forth, "Praise our God, all you his servants, you who fear him" (19:5). All creation, all people, all God's servants are summoned to praise and worship God.

Hence when the people of God gather for worship and praise it is quite important that everyone takes part. This should be the case, as much as possible, in all aspects of the worship service. People who gather for worship are not an audience simply to listen but a congregation to participate. For example, it is far better for those worshiping to share in prayers of thanksgiving and confession and supplication than to have a prayer said for the whole congregation. Occasionally it may be better, rather than having a worship leader announce songs and lead in the singing, to allow the congregation to break forth into singing spontaneously (remember again Paul's words "addressing one another in psalms, hymns, and spiritual songs"). It is even possible to forgo the sermon at times, if the Holy Spirit should so lead, in order that teachings and testimonies may take place. I am not suggesting disorder—surely such must be guarded against—but fuller participation by all the church in the service of worship.

We may also use the word *each*: not only all participating but each one taking his part. I earlier quoted these

[78]Not here "in the Holy Spirit" (though the Holy Spirit does operate through the human spirit).

[79]Much needs to be explored here because often foreign elements come in; for example, superficiality in some of our hymns and choruses, prayers that are either "vain repetitions" or careless utterances, sermons that forsake the truth of God's Word, and sacramental practices that distort Christ's intention. Truth *must* be sought in every area of worship.

words of Paul: "When you assemble, each one has a psalm, has a teaching, has a revelation, has a tongue, has an interpretation"[80] (1 Cor. 14:26 NASB). This clearly states that each person who gathers in worship has something to offer; it does not necessarily mean that all will do so. Obviously, even in a fairly small congregation, there would not be time and opportunity for each person to contribute. But the point is that each person has something to give, and should be prepared to make his particular contribution.[81] Paul's words to the church in Corinth may seem to be a far distance from where most of our churches are; perhaps we are not even sure of their relevance for today. I would, however, urge that we examine Paul's words afresh with an openness to practice more of what he prescribes by way of individual participation in the service of worship.[82]

The basic point is that there should be full participation of God's people in the act of worship. Let all God's people praise and magnify His holy name!

b. All Our Being. Another cry from the psalmist rings forth: "Bless the Lord, O my soul; and all that is within me, bless his holy name!" (103:1). God's people are called upon to worship Him with their whole inner being: all that is within. Quoting the "great and first commandment," Jesus declares, "You shall love the Lord your God with all your heart, and with all your soul, and with all your mind" (Matt. 22:37). Such total love calls for total worship with all our inner spiritual being: the heart, the soul, and the mind. True worship includes all our faculties uplifted in the praise and glorifying of God. The heart feels deeply, the soul is stirred up, and the mind reaches out in worship to ponder and meditate on the things of God. It should be the yearning of all who worship God to do so with their total selves.

As an act of the whole person, worship also includes outward expression. We have talked about singing in various ways—and indeed this singing should be with all one's being through psalms, hymns, and spiritual songs. In addition to using the voice, there is an important place for other bodily activities, such as clapping and dancing. The psalmist cries out, "Clap your hands, all peoples! Shout to God with loud songs of joy!" (47:1). We often clap, for example, upon hearing an outstanding speaker or a fine musical performance. How much more should God's people clap in honor of Him; yes, even shout to the Lord! We do not hesitate to shout loudly at a sports event where the players perform well; how much more should God's people shout out their acclaim for Him and His far more wonderful deeds. Clapping, shouting—but also dancing. The psalmist exhorts the people of Israel: "Let them praise his name with dancing and make music to him with tambourine and harp" (149:3 NIV). In the final psalm the call rings out: "Praise God in the sanctuary . . . praise him with tambourine and dancing. . . . Let everything that has breath praise the LORD" (150:1, 4, 6 NIV). It is a sad commentary on our contemporary situation that dancing is so largely a secular activity and so little occurs in the worship of the church. Thankfully, dancing to the Lord is being

[80]I referred to these words in a discussion about how the Corinthians were not functioning in such matters in an orderly manner. However, Paul is by no means discounting the place and importance of any of these worship activities.

[81]In this regard smaller meetings ("house church," prayer cells, etc.) are valuable in affording greater opportunity for all to participate.

[82]See my fuller discussion of 1 Corinthians 14:26 on individual participation in *Renewal Theology*, 2:336–38.

restored in many churches, even if it is largely performed by a select group (usually of women). However, as with other worship activities, such as singing and praying, we may hope for the day when all God's people generally will join in dancing before the Lord.[83]

The worship of God with our entire being—heart, soul, mind, and strength—is the worship that truly honors the Lord. Let us offer Him our total selves!

II. UPBUILDING

The second function of the church is *upbuilding*, or edification. The church is not only a worshiping community; it is also a people who are growing in faith and love. The church that truly exists under the leadership of Christ is a growing, maturing church; hence, its central function is that of enabling its members to be built up in their faith and Christian walk.

Let us look into some words of Paul in Ephesians. Following his designation of various gifts of Christ to the church—namely apostles, prophets, evangelists, pastors and teachers (4:11)—he adds that these gifts are "for the equipping of the saints for the work of service, to the building up of the body of Christ; until we all attain to the unity of the faith, and of the knowledge[84] of the Son of God, to a mature man, to the measure of the stature which belongs to the fullness of Christ" (4:12–13 NASB). The goal, in addition to equipping, is to build up the body so that it may attain unity in faith and fuller knowledge of Jesus Christ. This is the way to maturity ("a mature man")—even a growing up into Christ. This means further that in this process of growing up, we will no longer be children "tossed to and fro and carried about with every wind of doctrine" (v. 14); "rather, speaking the truth in love," we will "grow up in every way into him who is the head, into Christ" (v. 15). To speak the truth in love is the mark of Christian maturity. Knowing the truth and acting in love produces proper body functioning and a continuing growth and upbuilding of one another.

We may make this concrete by viewing upbuilding in terms of *word* and *deed*.

A. Word

The central function of the church from its earliest days has been that of building up by the word. Here we focus on the word in teaching. In the Great Commission Jesus told His disciples, "Go . . . and make disciples of all nations, baptizing them in the name of the Father and of the Son and of the Holy Spirit, teaching them to observe all that I have commanded you. . ." (Matt. 28:19–20).[85] Teaching was to be an integral part of the evangelistic commission: evangelize, baptize, then teach!

On the Day of Pentecost this happened precisely. Following Peter's gospel message, some three thousand persons were baptized, and "they devoted themselves to the apostles' teaching" (Acts 2:42). The apostles, accordingly, made teaching the first priority of the

---

[83]The Old Testament version of the great commandment contains "might" (or "strength"): "You shall love the LORD your God with all your heart, and with all your soul, and with all your might" (Deut. 6:5). "Might" or "strength" doubtless includes such bodily activities as singing, playing instruments, clapping, shouting, even dancing. It was said of King David that he "danced before the LORD with all his might" (2 Sam. 6:14). Dancing surely involves the most strength of all worship activities!

[84]The Greek words is *epignoseōs*. According to Thayer, this is "precise and correct knowledge."

[85]For more on the Great Commission see Section III, infra.

newly founded church in Jerusalem. Moreover, the word "devoted" here strongly suggests that this teaching was an ongoing matter. If the apostles were to fulfill Jesus' commission to teach "all" He had commanded them, this would surely take much time and effort. In this way the early Christians were built up in their faith.

Throughout the Book of Acts the preaching and teaching of the word is shown. For example, "every day in the temple and at home they [the apostles] did not cease teaching and preaching Jesus as the Christ" (5:42). Again, "Paul and Barnabas remained in Antioch, teaching and preaching the word of the Lord" (15:35). Later in Corinth Paul "stayed a year and six months, teaching the word of God among them" (18:11). After that Paul went on to Ephesus, where, with his disciples present, he had daily discussions "for two years, so that all the Jews and the Greeks who lived in the province of Asia heard the word of the Lord" (19:10 NIV). Having developed a strong church in Ephesus, Paul later summoned the elders of the church and said to them, "I did not shrink from declaring to you anything that was profitable, and teaching you in public and from house to house. . . . I did not shrink from declaring to you the whole counsel of God" (20:20, 27). The Book of Acts ends with Paul in Rome for "two whole years . . . preaching the kingdom of God and teaching about the Lord Jesus Christ quite openly and unhindered" (28:30–31).

The critical point is that the word has power to build up. Paul, in his message to the Ephesian elders, also declared, "I commend you to God and to the word of his grace, which is able to build you up and to give you the inheritance among all those who are sanctified" (Acts 20:32). "The word of his grace" is particularly the message about Jesus, but surely includes all things related to the grace of God. It is the word of grace that builds up believers in their faith. Further, this word that edifies includes, in Paul's language, "the whole counsel of God," hence the full range of God's revealed truth. This indeed is the word that fully builds up.

If Paul's letter to the Ephesians is the essence of what he taught in Ephesus for two years, particularly to the Ephesian elders, we have in that letter a vivid portrayal of something of "the whole counsel of God." Ephesians 1:3–14, for example, magnificently sets forth God's activity in election "before the foundation of the world" (v. 4), redemption in time through the blood of Christ (v. 7), and sealing for the world to come (v. 14).[86] Paul's other letters also express many aspects of this "whole counsel."

The importance Paul attached to teaching is especially shown in his letters to Timothy and Titus. For example, he wrote to Timothy, "Until I come, give attention to the public reading of Scripture, to exhortation and teaching. . . . Pay close attention to yourself and to your teaching" (1 Tim. 4:13, 16 NASB). Again, "What you have heard from me before many witnesses entrust to faithful men who will be able to teach others also" (2 Tim. 2:2). Still again, "Be unfailing in patience and in teaching. For the time is coming when people will not endure sound teaching" (2 Tim. 4:2–3). To Titus he wrote, "As for you, teach what befits sound doctrine" (2:1).[87] Sound teaching is essen-

---

[86]In this same passage Paul speaks of God as one "who accomplishes all things according to the counsel [*boulēn*] of his will" (v. 11). The same Greek word (*boulēn*, from *boulē*) is used in both Acts and Ephesians.

[87]See also 1 Timothy 1:10; 6:3; Titus 1:9.

tial to the life and upbuilding of the church.

Now let us pause to reflect on this in light of the church's ongoing teaching function. The church must continually be involved in teaching the Word of God to build up its membership. Of course, we cannot share the apostles' experience of personally hearing what Christ commanded, nor do we have the apostles actually present to instruct us, but we do have apostolic teaching in the New Testament. Beyond Jesus Himself and His teachings set forth in the four gospels are the writings not only of Paul but also of Peter, John, James, and Jude.[88] The church recognizes those writings as having apostolic authority,[89] and thus establishes them along with the Gospels as the source of all true doctrine.

A further word needs to be added about the whole of Scripture being the source of doctrine. Paul explained to Timothy, "All Scripture is inspired by God and profitable for teaching, for reproof, for correction, and for training in righteousness, that the man of God may be complete, equipped for every good work" (2 Tim. 3:16–17). Thus the Old Testament Scriptures are definitely included,[90] and by extension Paul's words refer to the New Testament canon, which at that time was still growing.[91] The Scriptures of the Old and New Testaments are God's inspired Word and are the ongoing revelation of God's truth that "the man of God"—and here we may substitute the word "Christian"—"may be complete."

Having said all this, I must now emphasize the necessity of the church's always keeping as its central function the teaching of the Word of God. This means scripture by scripture, book by book, Old Testament and New Testament; indeed, in Paul's terminology to teach "the whole counsel of God."[92] Among Christ's gifts to the church, as we have noted, the last listed are those of "pastors and teachers"[93]—those who may be said particularly to serve "that we may no longer be children, tossed to and fro and carried about with every wind of doctrine [or 'teaching']." This means that pastors and teachers must themselves be thoroughly grounded in the whole of Scripture and able to impart God's truth to others also.[94] *This must be their primary task: to impart the truths of God's Word.*

The goal in the church's teaching is maturation, hence the maturity of Christian believers. Believers, of neces-

---

[88]The authorship of Hebrews is uncertain.

[89]Apostolic authority does not necessarily mean apostolic authorship (recall p. 61, n.56).

[90]The preceding verse makes this clear: "From infancy you have known the holy Scriptures, which are able to make you wise for salvation through faith in Christ Jesus" (v. 15 NIV). Timothy, of course, had only the Old Testament Scriptures.

[91]Paul himself speaks at one place of his own written words as not his own but the word of God: "We also thank God . . . that when you received the word of God which you heard from us, you accepted it not as the word of men but as what it really is, the word of God" (1 Thess. 2:13). Peter refers to Paul's letters as Scripture: "His letters contain some things that are hard to understand, which ignorant and unstable people distort, as they do the other Scriptures, to their own destruction" (2 Peter 3:16 NIV).

[92]This study needs to be done with due regard for progressive revelation. The Scriptures contain a gradual unfolding of God's truth with the climax being in the New Testament. On progressive revelation see also note 112 infra.

[93]Later we will be discussing "pastors and teachers" as one basic equipping ministry with a twofold responsibility (chap. 5, pp. 178–81). Here our focus will be on the teaching area.

[94]One of the requirements for one who holds the office of elder is that he be "an apt teacher" (1 Tim. 3:2; cf. Titus 1:9). Later we will observe the New Testament identification of pastor with "teaching elder." See infra chap. 5.

sity, begin as babes in Christ who need to mature. In this connection Peter addresses his readers, saying, "Like newborn babes, long for the pure spiritual milk,[95] that by it you may grow up to salvation" (1 Peter 2:2). What, then, if pastors and teachers do not supply the "pure spiritual milk" that believers must have to grow? The sad truth is that many people come to church hungry but receive either no milk at all or impure milk, that is, milk adulterated by false, impure, human-biased ingredients. The pure milk, the "sincere milk,"[96] must be wholly drawn from Scripture and everything said and taught in consonance with it. Milk, of course, is not enough; believers need to go on to solid food, in which the deeper things of faith are imparted and digested. It is not enough to continue to teach and learn only the bare essentials of faith. People need to move on to maturity[97] and experience the excitement and joy of fuller understanding.

If there is a failure to mature in understanding, the fault may not always lie with the teachers. Paul himself, teacher par excellence, once referred to the Corinthians as continuing to be "babes in Christ": "I, brethren, could not address you as spiritual men, but as men of the flesh, as babes in Christ. I fed you with milk, not solid food; for you were not ready for it; and even yet you are not ready, for you are still of the flesh. For while there is jealousy and strife among you, are you not of the flesh?" (1 Cor. 3:1–3). Significantly, the problem in Corinth was not intellectual but moral—jealousy and strife, which inhibited their ability to receive "solid food." A similar situation is presented by the author of Hebrews: "About this[98] we have much to say which is hard to explain, since you have become dull of hearing. For though by this time you ought to be teachers, you need some one to teach you again the first principles of God's word. You need milk, not solid food" (5:11–12.) A little later he adds, "Solid food is for the mature, for those who have their faculties trained by practice to distinguish good from evil" (v. 14). It is the mature in moral discernment who are able to receive solid food, i.e., the weightier matters in God's Word.

This emphasizes an important point in Christian knowledge. It is possible that the chief block to receiving further enlightenment from God's Word lies with impediments in the hearers. As just illustrated, a congregation laden with strife and division and demonstrating little moral principle is not really capable of receiving deeper knowledge of the things of God. The teaching may be good (even apostolic!), but in such hearers there can be little or no reception.

This may be further illustrated from Jesus Himself. In one of His parables Jesus speaks of the sower who sows seed, some of which falls on shallow, some on rocky, some on thorny, and some on good soil. Only with the last, the good soil, is an abundance of grain produced. The sower did his job, the seed was good seed, but the nature of the soil—its receptivity—made the crucial difference. Accordingly, even

---

[95]The Greek phrase is *to logikon adolan gala*. The word *logikon* means either "rational" or "spiritual" (see BAGD). The root is *logos*, "word," hence "the pure spiritual milk" is doubtless the Word of God. This also may be seen from Peter's reference to the "word" in 1 Peter 1:23–25.

[96]The KJV translation.

[97]Even to some of the "things that are hard to understand" (Peter's words in 2 Peter 3:16) in Paul's letters!

[98]The writer had just begun to discuss Jesus as "high priest after the order of Melchizedek" (v. 10).

with the best of teaching (and what could be superior to that of Jesus Himself?), there may be little receptivity, little growth, little maturity because of impediments and obstacles on the side of those hearing.

If similar situations exist in a given church—and often they do—it is very difficult for people to mature in their understanding of God's Word. Pastors and teachers (and others in leadership) may need to deal with schismatic and/or moral breaches that hinder further Christian growth.[99]

Before proceeding further we should note that the task of teaching the Word should not be limited to official pastors and teachers. While it is true that congregational leaders have the basic responsibility, others should share in it. In this connection we may first recall what Paul says to the Colossians: "Let the word of Christ dwell in you richly, as you teach and admonish one another in all wisdom. . ." (3:16). Notice that the emphasis is on teaching one another[100]—mutual teaching. But first the background is essential: the rich indwelling of Christ's word. This portrays a church maturing (beyond the "milk" stage) in the word of Christ[101] by its rich presence in their lives. Because of this, the Colossians were able to teach one another.[102] Second, John declares to his readers, "You have been anointed by the Holy One, and you all know[103]. . . . You have no need that any one should teach you . . . his anointing teaches you about everything" (1 John 2:20, 27). Here the emphasis lies on the anointing of the Holy Spirit—the Spirit whom Jesus had said "will teach you all things" (John 14:26)—who is *the* basic teacher. By implication anointed believers can teach one another.[104] When we view the words of Paul and John together, it is apparent that both the rich indwelling of Christ's word and the anointing of the Holy Spirit make a fellowship of believers into a community of those who can truly teach one another.

This means that the more a congregation matures through Word and Spirit, the better qualified its members are for mutual teaching. Consequently, increased opportunities should be made available for such teaching to occur. The importance of small groups is apparent. In the large congregational gath-

---

[99]Paul does this many times in his Corinthian correspondence (even to the point of calling for excommunication of one especially immoral person [1 Cor. 5:1–5]). The writer of Hebrews, after speaking of his readers' immaturity (recall: "you need milk not solid food"), proceeds to say, "Let us leave the elementary doctrines of Christ and go on to maturity" (6:1). Nonetheless the author first feels constrained to name these doctrines (vv. 1–2), and then (surprisingly perhaps), rather than moving on to more comprehensive teaching, he interjects an urgent warning against apostasy (vv. 4–8). Only later (beginning with v. 13) does he discuss matters that belong to Christian maturity.

[100]See infra on the matter of admonition (pp. 120–23).

[101]Paul had earlier spoken to the Colossians of "Christ in you, the hope of glory." Then he added, "And we proclaim Him, admonishing every man and teaching every man with all wisdom, that we may present every man complete [or 'mature'] in Christ" (Col. 1:27–29 NASB). Because—we may assume—the Colossians had faithfully received Paul's wise admonition and teaching, they could now "teach and admonish one another in all wisdom."

[102]This is just the opposite of the situation in Hebrews. Recall the words "By this time you ought to be teachers." They still needed "milk."

[103]Or "ye know all things" (KJV). See comments on this verse in *Renewal Theology*, 2:239, n.15.

[104]This of course does not rule out the need for pastors and teachers (John himself is teaching in this letter!). But it does say that the Spirit's anointing makes for *essential* understanding.

ering (the regular worship service) official pastors and teachers properly function; mutual teaching is inappropriate and impractical. This may be true also in the usual Sunday school classes where ordinarily one person occupies the significant role of teaching all the others. Capable pastors and Sunday school teachers are urgently needed to deliver sermons and lessons—let me first emphasize that fact. But it is only as a congregation moves into smaller fellowships in which mutual teaching can occur that it exercises its fullest opportunity to know and understand God's Word.[105]

Now we move on to observe the critical point about knowing and teaching the Word: the focus must be on Jesus Christ, *the Word*. I have previously referred to Paul's injunction about "the word of Christ" richly indwelling. The word of Christ—both from Him and about Him—should be at the center of the church's teaching. All Scripture is God's inspired Word—and thus should be studied in its entirety—but particularly those Scriptures that relate to Christ.

This does not mean the New Testament only, for, as Jesus Himself said about the Scriptures of the Old Testament, "It is they that bear witness to me" (John 5:39). In the account of the risen Christ speaking to two disciples on the road to Emmaus, "Beginning with Moses and with all the prophets, He explained to them the things concerning Himself in all the Scriptures" (Luke 24:27 NASB). Later in talking to the larger gathering of disciples, Jesus declared, "All things which are written about Me in the Law of Moses and the Prophets and the Psalms must be fulfilled" (v. 44 NASB). In the early church, Philip the evangelist proclaimed the word about Christ to the Ethiopian eunuch who was reading Isaiah 53:7–8: "Beginning from this Scripture he preached Jesus to him" (Acts 8:35 NASB). Hence we may properly, indeed needfully, recognize and study the Old Testament witness to Christ.

In regard to the New Testament, the word of Christ is not found in the Gospels only, for Acts, the Epistles, and the Book of Revelation all relate to Him.[106] They are all words about Christ or (in the case of Revelation) words from Him: in both cases, the word of Christ. The more the church studies these books and understands them in their multifaceted truth, the more fully the church grows and matures.

The Gospels, of course, must be the center of all study. For in them is the record of Jesus Christ Himself who is the Word of God. As the Fourth Gospel declares, "The Word became flesh and dwelt among us" (1:14). Since Christ Himself is the living Word to whom the written Word bears recurring testimony, what He says and does as recorded in the four gospels affords the most direct knowledge of the word of truth. Paul's words in Ephesians about the gifts of Christian leaders "for building up the body of Christ" refer particularly to the goal of "the knowledge of the Son of God"[107] (4:13). This knowledge is more than intellectual: it contains a deeply personal commitment;

[105]We will reserve for later study (p. 129) two further relevant matters: first, the gift (or charisma) of teaching (as specifically mentioned by Paul in Rom. 12:7) and the way this relates to both the office and congregational practice of teaching; second, the admonition of James, "Let not many of you become teachers, my brethren" (3:1) and how this relates to the emphasis (above) on the importance of mutual teaching.

[106]Note, for example, the name of Jesus in the opening verses of Acts, Romans, and Revelation.

[107]This precedes Paul's reference to not being "carried about with every wind of doctrine" (v. 14).

and this must be the essence of all teaching. Paul states this vividly to the Colossians: "As . . . you received Christ Jesus the Lord, so live in him, rooted and built up in him and established in the faith, just as you were taught" (2:6–7). True teaching makes for a life rooted in Christ—a life that is constantly being built up and established in Him.

All in all, it is the word about the grace of God in Christ Jesus that most builds people up. In this connection Paul's final words to the Ephesian elders are memorable: "I commend you to God and to the word of his grace, which is able to build you up and to give you the inheritance among all those who are sanctified" (Acts 20:32). The more truly and fully that word of grace is made known and received, the more fully people are built up in the Lord.

I will now add a few matters of practical importance. First, there needs to be a program of total teaching in which the Word of God is central. This includes both children and adults. The "lambs" need feeding and nurturing as well as the "sheep."[108] Of course, there may be adjustments for various age levels, but the "food" is the same: the Word of God. There may be more emphasis on Bible stories for children than for adults. Such stories need to be truly taught, but with a minimum of imaginative embellishments. Portraying biblical narratives through visual means[109] or through dramatic forms[110] can also prove pedagogically valuable for both children and adults—if again there is faithfulness to the Scriptures.

Second, it is important that the church membership be taught how best to study and know the Bible. This means at first the use of various translations (the teacher explaining how they range from paraphrase to literal rendering of the original languages); the relevance of historical and cultural setting; the recognition of literary forms such as history, poetry, parable, and apocalypse; the intention of a given book;[111] and the significance of progressive revelation.[112] Also—even as fundamental in importance—there is the need for Spirit-guided reading and study. The Bible is inspired as no other book is—it is "God-breathed"[113] or "God-Spirited"—and thus can be adequately understood only through the illumination of the Word by that same Spirit of God. This means that both the teaching of the Word and its reading must be under the guidance of the Holy Spirit.

Third, the church needs to work closely with the home. This is true first of all in regard to children, for whom

[108]Peter is commanded by the risen Christ: "Feed my lambs" and "Feed my sheep" (John 21:15, 17). These commands of Jesus surely devolve upon the whole church.

[109]Through pictures, video presentations, and the like.

[110]Through acted parables, passion plays, and the like.

[111]As, for example, Luke 1:3, where the author states his intention to "write an orderly account" of gospel events; John 20:31 where the author, looking back on the many miraculous signs of Jesus, says, "These [words] are written that you may believe that Jesus is the Christ, the Son of God, and that believing you may have life in his name." In most cases, however, the intention of a book can be gained only from its internal content.

[112]That is, the recognition that the New Testament fulfills the Old so that not everything said in the Old Testament is God's final word. E.g., we cannot take as a final word the Old Testament command "eye for eye, tooth for tooth" (Exod. 21:24; Lev. 24:20; Deut. 19:21) because of Jesus' words, "You have heard that it was said, 'An eye for an eye and a tooth for a tooth.' But I say to you, Do not resist one who is evil" (Matt. 5:38–39). The New does not abolish the Old but fulfills it.

[113]The literal rendering of "inspired" in 2 Timothy 3:16. "All Scripture is God-breathed" (NIV).

the home is the basic place of nurture. In the New Testament, Timothy is an outstanding example of a young man who came from a Christian home. Paul speaks of Timothy's "sincere faith" and then adds, ". . . a faith that dwelt first in your grandmother Lois and your mother Eunice and now, I am sure, dwells in you" (2 Tim. 1:5). Later Paul adds, "From infancy[114] you have known the holy Scriptures, which are able to make you wise for salvation through faith in Christ Jesus" (3:15 NIV). Children who are raised in godly homes and from their earliest days are trained in the faith find their later church experience all the more meaningful. Christian parents, not church pastors and teachers, have the primary responsibility. Another word from Paul, directed to fathers, is quite relevant: "Fathers, do not exasperate[115] your children; instead, bring them up in the training and instruction of the Lord" (Eph. 6:4 NIV). Here is laid upon fathers the primary responsibility for home training and instruction. This needs emphasis today, for although both parents are important for child nurture, it is the father who should give the leadership.[116] How can a child truly learn about God as heavenly Father if his own father fails to demonstrate Him? All in all, the home must be the primary center of Christian nurture and teaching. When that is the case, the church through its various programs of Christian education can build more effectively on a solid and continuing foundation.

In conclusion, I will mention three reasons why it is so important for the church to build up people in the Word of God.

First, the Word of God alone can satisfy deep spiritual hunger. On one occasion Jesus said, "Man shall not live by bread alone, but by every word that proceeds from the mouth of God" (Matt. 4:4, quoting from Deut. 8:3). Material bread is necessary to physical life, but it is only the Word of God that can feed and sustain the life of faith.[117] The church's function to provide the teaching and hearing of the Word cannot be overestimated. The sad thing is that in many churches largely current events are discussed from the pulpit, classroom teaching is not biblically based, and groups meet only to discuss secular matters. Thus because the Word of God is not the main source and staple of the people's lives the church suffers malnutrition. The hungry "sheep" and "lambs" are simply not fed, and the result is bleak indeed.

Second, the Word of God is needed to offset and counteract false doctrines.

---

[114]Or "early childhood" (NEB). The Greek word is *brephous*.

[115]The Greek word is *parorgizete*—"to rouse to wrath, to provoke, exasperate, anger" (Thayer). F. F. Bruce writes that in this text (as well as Col. 3:21) "fathers (or parents) are urged not to assert their authority over children in a manner more calculated to provoke resentment than ready obedience" (*The Epistle to the Ephesians*, NICNT, 398).

[116]Timothy's father was a nonbelieving Greek (this is implied in Acts 16:1). The responsibility perforce fell upon his mother Eunice, a Jewish believer (with obvious encouragement from Timothy's grandmother Lois). Often it is the case today that the father is not a believer; thus the responsibility for training in faith must fall upon the mother. A Christian father, however, should not relegate this basic paternal responsibility to his wife. (Of course, if there has been divorce, or one parent is deceased, the religious responsibility must fall upon the other parent. This, to be sure, is not an easy situation: it takes all the more reliance upon God's strength and direction.)

[117]There is no worse famine than that of a lack of the Word of God. In the prophecy of Amos, God declares, "Behold, the days are coming . . . when I will send a famine on the land; not a famine of bread, nor a thirst for water, but of hearing the words of the LORD" (8:11). Such a famine in the church is a tragic situation.

Unfortunately false teaching often comes into the church. Jesus Himself spoke of "false prophets" who would arise (Matt. 24:24); Paul, of "false apostles . . . disguising themselves as apostles of Christ" (2 Cor. 11:13); Peter, of "false teachers . . . who will secretly bring in destructive heresies" (2 Peter 2:1). Unless a congregation is maturing in the Word of God, it can be torn and divided in many directions. This doubtless is why Paul speaks of "mature manhood" in terms of not being "children, tossed to and fro and carried about with every wind of doctrine, by the cunning of men, by their craftiness in deceitful wiles" (Eph. 4:13–14). The surest way to prevent falsity and deceit from coming into a church is to have a congregation growing and maturing in the truth of God's Word. They will perceive the untruth and expel it from their midst.

Third, the Word of God is essential as a guide to daily living. The psalmist declared, "Thy word is a lamp to my feet and a light to my path" (119:105). This is all the more true now that we have the additional word of the New Testament: the "lamp" and "light" shine even more brightly. Truly, Christian believers need to live and walk by God's holy Word.

B. Deed

The church is also built up by deeds. As believers do for one another the things they have been taught in the Word, they are together built up. This means primarily an upbuilding through love. The climactic words in Paul's picture of Christ's giving gifts for the church (apostles, prophets, etc.) is that in this way the church "upbuilds itself in love" (Eph. 4:16). Love in this connection refers to the Christians' walk in love for one another.[118] By such a walk the body of Christ is built up. Now let us examine some of the particular deeds by which this upbuilding occurs.

1. Seeking to Maintain Unity

Paul urges the Ephesians to be "eager to maintain the unity of the Spirit in the bond of peace" (Eph. 4:3). There should always be an eagerness in the church to maintain[119] the unity of the Holy Spirit. The Holy Spirit, by uniting us to Christ, has also bonded us in love to one another; so we should be eager to maintain that unity.

The Christian community is described early in Acts thus: "Now the company of those who believed were of one heart and soul" (4:32). Later when this unity was threatened by murmurings about some neglect of widows in the daily distribution of food, the apostles quickly arranged for the selection of seven men to handle this problem (6:1–6). Thus the unity of the Spirit was maintained, "and the word of God increased; and the number of disciples multiplied greatly" (v. 7). A united body of believers has great internal strength and also makes a strong impact on the surrounding world.

The chief problem that Paul had with the Corinthian church was divisiveness. Paul appealed to the people to put aside dissensions and be "united in the same mind and the same judgment" (1 Cor. 1:10). The Corinthians were dividing along party lines: "I belong to Paul" . . . "I belong to Apollos" . . . "I belong to Cephas [Peter]" . . . "I belong to Christ" (v. 12), so that schism was about to occur. Paul later speaks of that church's inner "jealousy and strife" (3:3) as the root of the problem. Thus the Corinthians were not really

[118]In Ephesians 4:2 Paul speaks about "forbearing one another in love"; similarly he writes about believers' concern for one another in 4:16.

[119]The NIV reads "keep"; NASB, "preserve." The Greek word is *tērein*.

"spiritual" (the Spirit makes for unity); they were "behaving like ordinary men" (vv. 1 and 3). The church, given birth by the Holy Spirit, must find ways to overcome all dissension and be built up in love.

"The bond of peace" needs to be recognized and maintained by all believers. We are bound together by the Holy Spirit in Christ and must not be separated from one another. As Paul says elsewhere, "Let us . . . pursue what makes for peace and for mutual upbuilding" (Rom. 14:19). To "pursue" peace means more than to contemplate or talk about it; it means doing everything possible to preserve the bond of peace.

Since in any body of believers problems will arise, one way to maintain unity is through *forbearance*. Immediately before Paul mentions the bond of peace, he speaks of "forbearing one another in love" (Eph. 4:2). To forbear means to endure, bear with, or put up with[120]—and sometimes a Christian community needs all of these aspects of forbearance! Disagreements on various matters, differences of opinion, and even diverse ways of doing things often occur. Some of these may lead to serious division and disruption in the body. Forbearance is much needed to maintain unity—and it can happen only when the members have genuine love for one another.

The situation in a church at a given time may call for a further step, namely, *forgiveness*. Paul later in Ephesians 4 enjoins, "Be kind to one another, tenderhearted, forgiving one another" (v. 32). Although it is not easy to forbear, forbearance is a relatively simple matter compared with forgiveness. Forgiveness pertains to something beyond outward disagreements; it relates deeply to personal matters in which a member or members in the community have been wrongly dealt with, and there is every natural reason to retaliate. If such a wrong occurs, unity is seriously jeopardized. Hence forgiveness is urgent, even in the midst of bitter attacks. But is forgiveness really possible? The answer: only if we bear in mind Paul's further words in Ephesians 4:32 . . . "as God in Christ forgave you." God in Christ has forgiven *all* our sins, *all* our wrongdoing, *all* our offenses against Him. Knowing that, and letting it freshly grip our hearts, we can forgive one another.

Unity means dwelling together in *harmony*. Through harmony the community of believers is steadily built up and together can glorify God. Paul's prayer for this is beautifully spoken to the Romans: "May the God of steadfastness and encouragement grant you to live in such harmony with one another, in accord with Christ Jesus, that together you may with one voice glorify the God and Father of our Lord Jesus Christ" (15:5–6). Amen indeed!

2. *Showing Brotherly Love*

Paul enjoins the Romans to "be devoted to one another in brotherly love"[121] (12:10 NIV, NASB). The thought in this admonition is that of reciprocal affection.[122] There should be a responsive love of brothers and sisters to one another. By such mutuality the community is built up together. Let us note a number of ways this can be expressed.

First, we may mention *hospitality*. Paul continues in Romans 12 by saying, "Practice hospitality"[123] (v. 13). Peter makes a similar statement in a slightly different context: "Above all hold un-

---

[120]The Greek word is *anechomenoi*. See BAGD.
[121]The Greek word is *philadelphia*.
[122]The NEB reads, "Let love for our brotherhood breed warmth of mutual affection."
[123]The Greek phrase is *tēn philoxenian diakontes*, literally, "pursuing hospitality."

failing your love for one another . . . practice hospitality ungrudgingly to one another" (1 Peter 4:8–9). Hospitality is a clear mark of brotherly affection and love. Indeed, in Hebrews 13 just after the statement "Let brotherly love continue" (v. 1), the text reads, "Do not neglect to show hospitality to strangers,[124] for thereby some have entertained angels unawares" (v. 2). Hospitality—glad, ungrudging, warm—is a sign of brotherly love and surely makes for upbuilding the community of faith.

Second, *encouragement* is important for upbuilding. Paul writes to the Thessalonians, "Encourage one another and build one another up, just as you are doing"[125] (1 Thess. 5:11). Mutual encouragement builds up believers in their life and faith. Three verses later Paul adds, "Encourage the fainthearted"[126] (v. 14). Often there are the fainthearted in the Christian fellowship who need encouragement, perhaps by merely a word or a smile.

Paul writes also to the Romans about mutual encouragement: "For I long to see you, that I may impart to you some spiritual gift to strengthen you, that is, that we may be mutually encouraged by each other's faith, both yours and mine" (1:11–12). It is quite significant that the great apostle senses the need not only for encouragement of the believers in Rome but also for his own encouragement through them. This need exists today also; for example, pastors who devote much time to encouraging their parishioners may often be in real need of encouragement themselves.

There are many other New Testament statements about encouragement;[127] however, I will quote only one more that may be particularly relevant to our time: "Let us hold fast the confession of our hope without wavering . . . and let us consider how to stir up one another to love and good works, not neglecting to meet together, as is the habit of some, but encouraging one another, and all the more as you see the Day drawing near" (Heb. 10:23–25). As the day of Christ's coming approaches, we all the more need to meet together, to stir up one another to love and good works, and to encourage one another in every possible way.

Third, brotherly love includes *compassion*. Peter writes, "Finally, all of you, live in harmony with one another; be sympathetic, love as brothers, be compassionate and humble" (1 Peter 3:8 NIV). Sympathy and compassion are closely related,[128] both suggesting deep feeling and concern. In regard to compassion, some other words of Paul stand out: "As those who have been chosen of God, holy and beloved, put on a heart of compassion, kindness, humility, gentleness and patience" (Col. 3:12 NASB). A heart of compassion is a heart that reaches out to the deepest need and situation of someone else.

---

[124]"Strangers" probably does not refer to non-Christians but to believers visiting a local fellowship. Incidentally, the wording about "angels unawares" is reminiscent of the Old Testament narrative about Abraham's hospitality to those strangers who (at least two of them) later turned out to be angels (see Gen. 18–19).

[125]This is said by Paul in the context of teaching "that the day of the Lord will come like a thief in the night" (v. 2).

[126]The KJV reads "comfort the feebleminded" (!). Obviously a contemporary, and better, translation is much needed!

[127]See, e.g., Acts 4:36 (re: Barnabas, "Son of encouragement"); 15:32; 16:40; 18:27; Romans 12:8; 15:5; Ephesians 6:22; Philippians 2:19; Colossians 2:2; 4:8; 4:11; 1 Thessalonians 2:11; 3:2; Hebrews 3:13. In some cases the English translation may be "exhort" or "comfort."

[128]The Greek words are *sympatheis* and *eusplangchoi*.

Such compassion goes far beyond superficial human relationships and shares the burden and the pain that weigh heavily. Surely, this is an aspect of brotherly love that is much needed in every Christian community.

Still another of Paul's exhortations comes to mind: "Rejoice with those who rejoice, weep with those who weep" (Rom. 12:15). This means that we must have a vital empathy with other persons, identifying with their joys as well as their sorrows. When we do so, joys are multiplied and sorrows diminished—and the fellowship of believers is truly edified.

This leads to a further injunction of Paul that calls for compassion: "Bear one another's burdens, and so fulfill the law of Christ" (Gal. 6:2). Family members often are called upon to bear the burden of another member because of a family situation; even more so is this the case for those who belong to the body of Christ as spiritual family. Christ Himself is the great burden-bearer who has borne our sins and transgressions and to whom we may turn at any time—"Come to me, all who labor and are heavy laden, and I will give you rest" (Matt. 11:28). However, there are times when believers also need fellow believers who in compassion will spiritually enter in and vicariously bear their burdens. To do this is to "fulfill the law of Christ," which is none other than the law of love.[129] Incidentally, to bear one another's burdens is not to add to any one person's load (it might seem that way), but it is to live in a situation of mutual burden sharing and bearing. In a true community of brotherly love, believers gladly and freely participate in and bear the burdens of one another.

3. *Exercising Discipline*

According to the words of Jesus in Matthew 18:15–17, the church has an important role in hearing the case of one brother who sins against another, and in possibly exercising discipline. The case cited by Jesus comes before the church only if the sinning brother has not admitted his fault when personally confronted first by the other brother and after that by additional witnesses. In regard to the latter, Jesus says, "If he refuses to listen to them, tell it to the church; and if he refuses to listen even to the church, let him be to you[130] as a Gentile and a tax collector." From what is said in this passage, the church has a critical role in a situation where one brother so adamantly refuses to admit his fault to another and to witnesses that he must be personally ostracized. Then Jesus adds the striking words addressed to the church: "Truly, I say to you,[131] whatever you bind on earth shall be bound[132] in heaven, and whatever you loose on earth shall be loosed[133] in heaven" (v. 18). To bind and loose most likely refers to the church's given authority to exclude as well as to reinstate[134]—or to impose (bind) and remove (loose) the ban.[135] Thus the church in this case stands behind the member who has been

---

[129]John 13:34—"A new commandment I give to you, that you love one another; even as I have loved you, that you also love one another." Paul had earlier in Galatians declared that "the whole law is fulfilled in one word, 'You shall love your neighbor as yourself' " (5:14). On the "new commandment" see infra (sec. 5, pp. 124–25).

[130]"You" is singular in the Greek: *soi*.

[131]"You" is plural in the Greek: *hymin*.

[132]Literally, "shall have been bound."

[133]Literally, "shall have been loosed." The action of the church in both loosing and binding is auxiliary to what has already happened in heaven.

[134]See article "Binding and Loosing" in EDT, 152.

[135]See article on *deō*, "bind," in TDNT, 2:60–61.

forced to ostracize his unrepentant brother. However, there is the additional picture of a possible reinstatement through unbinding the offender in the community of believers.

All of this is important for the upbuilding of the church. While the community of believers is a place of unity and brotherly love, that very setting can be seriously damaged by a member (or members) who is recalcitrant and unrepentant. The church is *not* a place where "anything goes." Rather, at times severe action must be taken internally to preserve the peace and unity of the body. Even exclusion may be called for. However, the goal is not negative but positive, that is, ultimately to bring about restoration.

Discipline, therefore, is necessary to the edification of the body of believers. We have earlier discussed the importance of the church's being a forgiving community, but forgiveness does not mean toleration of sin. Forgiveness, as loosing the sinner, is always the goal of discipline, but it cannot come about until repentance has occurred. If there has to be a ban from the community, the hope is that the unrepentant one will come to realize his isolated condition and the gravity of his sin and in penitence seek restoration.

Looking briefly beyond Matthew 18, we note that Paul on occasion speaks about *admonition* among believers. For example, he writes to the Colossians, "Let the word of Christ dwell in you richly, as you teach and admonish[136] one another in all wisdom" (3:16). In addition to mutual teaching of the Word, which builds up the body,[137] mutual admonition is also a part of the community life. Warnings about the dangers of sin and evil should especially occur within the fellowship of believers. Friendly admonition, although ordinarily not easy to give or to receive, is an essential deterrent against evil disrupting the church.

Earlier we observed that Paul said to the Thessalonians, "Encourage the fainthearted." However, just prior to this are the words "We exhort you, brethren, admonish the unruly"[138] (1 Thess. 5:14 NASB), the disorderly. Admonition, a mild form of rebuke, may be essential to prevent serious problems from breaking out.

Admonition may also call for *avoidance*. In his second letter to the Thessalonians Paul writes, "Now we command you, brethren, in the name of our Lord Jesus Christ, that you keep aloof from every brother who leads an unruly life" (3:6 NASB). Paul later adds, "If anyone does not obey our instruction in this letter, take special note of that man and do not associate with him, so that he may be put to shame" (v. 14 NASB). This avoidance of a brother by the church, while seemingly harsh, is meant to bring him to shame and repentance. However, the unruly person does not cease to be a brother, for Paul says, "And yet do not regard him as an enemy, but admonish him as a brother" (v. 15 NASB). This is the delicate balance the church must maintain: admonish, even avoid, but do not view an unruly brother as an enemy. So brotherly love—even in this adverse situation—may continue.

However, there is a third stage, be-

---

[136]The Greek word is a form of *noutheteō*—"admonish," "warn," "instruct" (BAGD). "Admonish" and "warn" are the preferred meanings in this context.

[137]Recall our earlier discussion of upbuilding by the teaching of the Word.

[138]The Greek word is *ataktous*—"disorderly" (Thayer). The RSV and NIV translation, "idle," is also possible. Bruce translates it "disorderly" and adds that the *ataktoi* "are those who are undisciplined, not maintaining proper order (*taxis*) but playing the truant; more particularly in this context they are the 'loafers' (Moffatt) who neglect their daily duty and live in idleness, at the expense of others" (*1 & 2 Thessalonians*, WBC, 122).

yond admonition and avoidance, namely, *exclusion*. We have discovered this matter already in connection with Matthew 18. Now we turn to the church in Corinth where, concerning the very serious situation of incest, Paul urges both avoidance and exclusion. The Corinthians were arrogantly disregarding the evil of a brother in their midst. Paul writes, "Shouldn't you rather have been filled with grief and have put out of your fellowship the man who did this?" (1 Cor. 5:2 NIV). Indeed, says Paul in strong language, "You are to deliver this man to Satan for the destruction of the flesh, that his spirit may be saved in the day of the Lord Jesus" (v. 5). This implies an act of total exclusion whereby the church was to deliver the gross sinner to Satan[139] for his bodily destruction.[140] The purpose, however, was not the believer's damnation but, beyond the penalty of bodily destruction, his ultimate salvation.

Throughout this chapter Paul is much concerned about evil being allowed to continue and thus permeate the church. He asks, "Do you not know that a little leaven leavens the whole lump?" Then he adds, "Cleanse out the old leaven that you may be a new lump, as you really are unleavened" (1 Cor. 5:6–7). A little later he urges the Corinthians "not to associate with any one who bears the name of brother if he is guilty of [sexual] immorality or greed, or is an idolater, reviler, drunkard, or robber—not even to eat with such a one" (v. 11). In these words Paul again (as in 2 Thessalonians) calls the church to avoid all internal church association[141] with perpetrators of evil. This is not a call to a "holier than thou" attitude in the church, nor is it a call to try to remove each obvious sinner, but it is a summons to be what "you really are" in Christ, an "unleavened" people.

To conclude: When a sin is as heinous as incest, not only should there be dissociation but also expulsion. Paul's final word in 1 Corinthians 5 is "Expel the wicked man from among you" (v. 13 NIV).

All of this may seem somewhat strange to the church in our time. Admonition—perhaps. Avoidance—not so sure; isn't that judging other people? Exclusion—ought the church really to go that far? This process may seem hardly like upbuilding, unity, and brotherly love (already discussed). Yet—and this is the basic point—there can be no solid upbuilding if there is rot that is allowed to remain and grow. It is necessary for every church to "cleanse out the old rot" (to change the figure slightly) if there is to be healthy growth and upbuilding in the Lord.

The goal, however, of the whole

[139]Satan is described by Paul in 2 Corinthians as "the god of this world" (4:4).

[140]Some commentators interpret "the destruction of the flesh" as referring to carnal flesh, i.e., man's sinful nature; however, it is hard to see how Satan would destroy what he delights in! It is preferable to understand Paul as referring to physical flesh, its harassment and destruction. (E.g., as illustration of a similar penal sentence in the physical sphere, see Acts 5:1–10 where Ananias and Sapphira committed an even worse sin than that of the incestuous man: they, although believers, "lie to the Holy Spirit" [v. 3] and "tempt the Spirit of the Lord" [v. 9]; they were consequently struck dead. "Satan" had "filled" [v. 3] Ananias's heart [and presumably Sapphira's also]. Peter, who uncovered the lie, delivered them both over to physical death, for which Satan was accountable.) Possibly the harassment and destruction that Paul spoke of would occur over a period of time, e.g., like the destruction by cancer that is sure but often lengthy. The sexual perversion would lead to increasing deterioration of the body until Satan had completed the destruction.

[141]Paul earlier made it clear that he is not referring to external association with the immoral of the world "since then you would need to go out of the world" (v. 10)—a practical impossibility!

process is not negative but positive: even exclusion points to final salvation. When sins are less heinous and call for admonition and avoidance (not final exclusion), then the church should be deeply concerned about the reclamation of the sinner. In Galatians Paul writes, "Brothers, if someone is caught in a sin,[142] you who are spiritual should restore him gently" (6:1 NIV). Surely there must be repentance on the part of the sinner, but the deep concern of Christians must always be the forgiveness and restoration of the sinning person. In so doing the church is being built up as a fully functioning body of Christ.

4. Serving One Another

The upbuilding of the church also happens as its members truly serve one another. Paul writes to the Galatians, "Through love serve one another" (5:13 NASB). Jesus had stressed the servant role in His own ministry: "I am among you as one who serves" (Luke 22:27), and accordingly He calls all His disciples to a similar servanthood. Let us observe how serving relates to the community of faith.

We may begin with the challenge of *helping one another*. Since the Holy Spirit is "the Helper,"[143] and He is at work in the believing community, then our helping—sharing, giving—truly makes for the upbuilding of the church.

In the earliest gatherings believers were continually helping and sharing with one another. The believers "sold their possessions and goods and distributed them to all, as any had need" (Acts 2:45). Again, the record reads, "Great grace was upon them all. There was not a needy person among them. . . . Distribution was made to each as any had need" (4:33–35). Later the first "deacons"[144] were elected for the given purpose of helping widows who were neglected in "the daily distribution" of food (6:1–6). Paul in his letters similarly stresses this; he writes, for example, "Contribute to the needs of the saints" (Rom. 12:13). Moreover Paul, along with his busy missionary activity, was much concerned that the churches contribute financially to the impoverished Christians in Jerusalem,[145] and on occasion he carried the offerings himself to that city.

The church is built up when its members help those who are in need. Paul writes to the Thessalonians, just after his injunction about encouraging the fainthearted: "Help the weak" (1 Thess. 5:14). This probably refers to those who are weak in faith (see Rom. 14:1), members who need the encouragement and support of stronger, more mature believers.[146] Such spiritual help is surely the primary need. However, the material needs of the saints must not be overlooked. James writes, "If a brother or sister is ill-clad and in lack of daily food, and one of you says to them, 'Go in peace, be warmed and filled,' without giving them the things needed for the body, what does it profit?"

---

[142]The Greek word is *paraptōmati*—"fault" (KJV), "trespass" (RSV, NASB). According to Thayer, it is "a lapse or deviation from truth and righteousness." Such a deviation would not, for example, be as severe as that of incest.

[143]Jesus spoke of the Holy Spirit as the *paraklētos*, which may be translated "the Helper" (so the NASB in John 14:26; 15:26; 16:7).

[144]Certain men were elected "to serve [*diakonein*] tables" (Acts 6:2).

[145]See especially 2 Corinthians 8 and 9, where Paul appeals to the church in Corinth to join other churches in the relief of the saints.

[146]In Romans 15:1 Paul writes, "We who are strong ought to bear with the failings of the weak, and not to please ourselves."

(2:15–16).[147] The answer surely is that it profits nothing; indeed it damages the Christian community if material help is not provided.

Let me add a further word about helping. Earlier I wrote about the sacrifice of praise to God—"the fruit of lips that acknowledge his name" (Heb. 13:15). It is now important to note the next words: "Do not neglect to do good and to share what you have, for such sacrifices are pleasing to God" (v. 16). Helping and sharing, in addition to praise, are pleasing sacrifices to God.

Next, serving one another means always seeking the best interests of others. This means, on the negative side, doing no harm to a brother. For example, the church is being built up when no stumbling blocks are put in the way of a neighbor. Paul declares in Romans 14: "It is right not to eat meat[148] or drink wine or do anything that makes your brother stumble" (v. 21). Eating meat and drinking wine may in principle be all right, but to do such things in the presence of those who cannot conscientiously partake may cause serious injury to a brother. Earlier Paul wrote, "If your brother is being injured by what you eat [or 'drink'], you are no longer walking in love. Do not let what you eat cause the ruin of one for whom Christ died" (v. 15). Therefore, one should try to avoid all possible harm to fellow believers.

This means, on the positive side, that believers are to give priority to the best interests of others. Paul continues in Romans 15: "Let each of us please his neighbor for his good, to edify him. For Christ did not please himself" (vv. 2–3). This is not a call to be "men-pleasers"—for one's own ends,[149] but to please the neighbor, the fellow believer, for his own edification. It means always to seek the best for him, even to put his best interest before one's own.

This leads to a recognition of the importance of humility in serving one another. Paul writes to the Philippians: "Do nothing out of selfish ambition or vain conceit, but in humility consider others better than[150] yourselves" (2:3 NIV).[151] This statement undoubtedly strikes against all our natural inclinations to self-centered orientation. It also runs counter to the possible objection that what people need basically is to build their own self-esteem rather than esteeming others as superior to themselves. However, all such natural (indeed sinful) thinking is reversed in the community of believers. We are called upon always, and in a humble attitude, to regard our neighbor, even the most lowly, as better and more important than ourselves. When this is done and natural egos are transcended, the community truly is greatly blessed and edified!

5. *Loving With the Love of Christ*

We now arrive at the climax in the upbuilding of the church: It happens

[147]James is discussing this matter in the context of faith and works. Immediately following that, he writes, "So faith by itself, if it has no works, is dead" (v. 17). (For a statement similar to James 2:15–16, see 1 John 3:17–18).

[148]This refers in the larger context possibly to three groups: vegetarians (Rom. 14:2), Jewish believers who would still have trouble eating some formerly "unclean" foods (14:14), and meat offered in sacrifice to idols (see 1 Cor. 8).

[149]Paul speaks frequently against self-oriented men-pleasing: see Galatians 1:10; Ephesians 6:6; Colossians 3:22; 1 Thessalonians 2:4.

[150]Or "more important than" (NASB). The Greek word *hyperechontas* literally means "surpassing."

[151]Note also Peter's words: "Clothe yourselves, all of you, with humility toward one another" (1 Peter 5:5).

supremely when its members love as Christ loved. Jesus Himself declares, "A new commandment I give to you, that you love one another; even as I have loved you, that you also love one another" (John 13:34). The new commandment is not just to love one another; that had long been declared in the command "You shall love your neighbor as yourself."[152] It is rather for the followers of Christ, now the church, to love one another with the same love Christ showed His disciples. This love was vividly demonstrated shortly before Jesus gave the "new commandment" when He washed His own disciples' feet. The record of Christ's action is prefaced by the statement "Having loved his own who were in the world, he loved them to the end" (John 13:1). Thus the church that belongs to Christ is one in which the members willingly serve one another even in the most menial of tasks and never weary of doing so. Moreover, for Jesus, "to the end" meant loving even to death. Later, after saying similarly, "This is my commandment that you love one another just as I have loved you," Jesus adds, "Greater love has no man than this, that one lay down his life for his friends" (John 15:13 NASB). Correspondingly, the Christian community that truly emulates its Lord will always be willing to pay the utmost price, even the sacrifice of life itself.[153] As John himself later wrote, "By this we know love, that he laid down his life for us; and we ought to lay down our lives for the brethren" (1 John 3:16). This is the ultimate test of a community of believers.

However, whether or not a situation occurs that calls for the ultimate in self-sacrifice, there continues to be the new commandment of Christ: to love one another even as He loved. This love always contains the element of sacrifice, namely reaching beyond oneself—for example, in the self-giving of time, energy, and means. Such commodities as these are precious: a person has only so much time, so much energy and strength, and so much in worldly possessions. Hence, to reach out in love in any of these ways can be a personal sacrifice. But this was the way of Christ—and it must be the way of those who truly follow Him.

Our final point is that all such sacrificial love is the ultimate in the upbuilding of the church. For through such love Christ Himself is spiritually present among His people. Christ declared, "I will build my church" (Matt. 16:18)—and there is no surer way of building than the way of His own sacrificial love.

C. Word and Deed

In this closing section we focus on the *gifts* of word and deed. The whole church is involved, with each member of the congregation having special gifts for ministering to others in the body of Christ.

Peter writes, "As each has received a gift,[154] employ it for one another, as good stewards of God's varied grace; whoever speaks, as one who utters oracles of God; whoever renders service, as one who renders it by the strength which God supplies; in order that in everything God may be glorified through Jesus Christ" (1 Peter 4:10–11). Each believer, then, has a special gift of God's grace to be used not for himself or herself but for others. These

[152]See Leviticus 19:18; cf. Matthew 19:19; Mark 12:31.

[153]The church father Tertullian, writing about a century later, reported that the pagans of his day marveled at the Christian community: "See how they love one another! . . . how ready are they to die for one another!" (*Apology* 39.7). May this continue to be true!

[154]The Greek word is *charisma*. A *charisma* is a particular gift of God's grace.

can be called gifts of word and deed, or, in Peter's language, gifts of speech and service. All those so gifted by God's grace must be good stewards of their gifts, both to build up one another and to glorify God. Further, these gifts of word and deed should be so much from God's grace that the words will be as if they are the oracles, the very utterances, of God, and the deeds as wholly performed by God's strength.

What the apostle Peter says underscores the particularization of God's grace. Because each member has received a special gift, he or she is called upon to be a good steward and to exercise that gift faithfully for the benefit of other members of the fellowship. Thus, although all members should say and do whatever is needed in a given situation, for example, a word of instruction or a deed of love,[155] there are also those members who by God's grace and gift have particular abilities to speak and act—thus, in the example mentioned, to teach and show mercy.

Paul spells this out in more detail in Romans 12: "Since we have gifts[156] that differ according to the grace given to us, let each exercise them accordingly: if prophecy, according to the proportion of his faith; if service, in his serving; or he who teaches, in his teaching; or he who exhorts, in his exhortation;[157] he who gives, with liberality; he who leads, with diligence; he who shows mercy, with cheerfulness." (vv. 6–8 NASB). This list of seven gifts of grace covers both speaking and serving (the two gifts to which Peter refers), that is, word and deed. The gifts may be divided thus: word—prophecy, teaching, and exhorting; deed—serving, giving, leading, showing mercy.[158]

Before examining these gifts let us note several matters. First, since these are all gifts of God's grace (according to both Peter and Paul), *they are not natural talents or achieved abilities*. A person may of course have certain proclivities or training in a given area such as teaching or leading, and God may surely use such; however, basically these are divine gifts, not human achievements.[159] Thus Peter said we should use our gifts in such way "that in everything God [not we ourselves] may be glorified through Jesus Christ" (1 Peter 4:11). Second, these are all *functional* gifts. Prior to Paul's listing these seven gifts, he writes, "For as in one body we have many members, and all the members do not have the same

---

[155]Recall our prior discussion in sections A and B (pp. 109–25).

[156]The Greek word is *charismata*.

[157]Or "he who encourages, in his encouragement." The Greek words used are forms of *parakaleō* and *paraklēsis*, both with a wide range of meanings. The NIV translates, "if it is encouraging, let him encourage."

[158]In *Renewal Theology*, 2:347–409, I discussed the *manifestation* gifts of 1 Corinthians 12: 7–10. I will be treating the *equipping* gifts of Ephesians 4:11–12 in the next chapter. The manifestation gifts—or the gifts of the Holy Spirit—are similar to the gifts of Romans 12 in that they are likewise called *charismata* (see 1 Cor. 12:4) and operate through all the church membership. The equipping gifts—or the gifts of the exalted Christ—are called *domata* (Eph. 4:8) and are limited to certain persons.

[159]E. F. Harrison writes, "Paul is not referring to gifts in the natural realm, but to those functions made possible by a specific enablement of the Holy Spirit granted to believers. The gift does not contradict what God has bestowed in the natural order and, though it may even build on the natural gift, it must not be confused with the latter. . . . These new capacities for service are not native to those who exercise them but come from divine grace" (EBC, 10:130). This is well said.

function,[160] so we, though many, are one body in Christ, and individually members one of another" (Rom. 12:4–5). As each member of the human body has a particular function to fulfill, so it is with each member of the body of Christ. Third, these are gifts that need *appropriate expression*: prophecy according to the proportion of faith; serving, teaching, and exhortation in their corresponding activity; and giving, leading, and showing mercy with particular attitudes of liberality, diligence, and cheerfulness. It is not so much a matter of what gift a person possesses, but of its adequate and appropriate expression.

A further word may be said on this last point. Since the seven gifts listed by Paul are quite concrete—from prophecy to showing mercy—and are important to the full functioning of the body of Christ, we may ask, How are we to recognize and identify these gifts? Paul, however, does not make a point that members should seek to know what their gifts are. He simply mentions them one by one and urges the person who possesses a particular gift to make use of it. The important matter is that a gift of grace becomes concrete only in the doing, whether in terms of a spoken word or a performed deed. The issue, then, is not so much what your gift is but how you are functioning in using and expressing it. *The gift is seen in the action.*[161]

Many of the gifts listed by Paul in Romans 12 have already been discussed as general functions of the whole congregation. Teaching, for example, as we have observed, may be done by all ("as you teach and admonish one another in all wisdom"); but there is also a special grace gift of teaching that a particular individual should practice. How then does one know if he has the special gift of teaching? The answer may best be found in the use of the gift; that is, when one who has the gift does teach, God brings results. The individual knows, and others know, that the gift of teaching is present and in operation.

We will now look briefly at the seven functional gifts. Definition will scarcely be needed in some cases because of our previous discussions.

1. Prophecy—"if prophecy, according to the proportion of his faith"

Prophecy is that gift of grace through which God speaks directly to His people. It is referred to also among the spiritual gifts of 1 Corinthians 12:10, "to another prophecy," and is given a place of special prominence: "Earnestly desire the spiritual gifts, especially that you may prophesy" (14:1). In Romans 12 Paul gives prophecy prominence by speaking of it first among the functional gifts. Why is this gift so important? The answer is found in 1 Corinthians 14:3: "He who prophesies speaks to men for their upbuilding and encouragement and consolation." Prophecy, I should add, is not words spoken through a person's natural capacities but those spoken through a supernatural activity of God's Spirit of grace.[162]

In Romans Paul says that one should prophesy "according to the proportion

[160]The Greek word is *praxin*, a form of *praxis* ("acting, activity, function"—BAGD). Compare our English word *praxis*. The KJV translation "office" is less adequate than "function" or "activity."

[161]In this sense there is gift recognition both by the person functioning in the gift and by others in the body. Furthermore, there may also be encouragement to continue more fully in the exercise of the gift. Such recognition and encouragement can be valuable aids in the functioning of a particular gift.

[162]For more detail on prophecy see *Renewal Theology*, 2:380–88.

of his faith" (Rom. 12:6 NASB). Earlier Paul said, "God has allotted to each a measure of faith" (v. 3 NASB); thus out of such measure—not to exceed or fall below—one who has the gift of prophecy is to speak.[163] It is interesting to note that this corresponds to Paul's listing of the gift of faith prior to that of prophecy in 1 Corinthians 12:10[164]—though there the gift of faith may be given to a person other than the one prophesying. In any event, faith and prophesying have a vital connection with each other.

How does someone know if he or she has the gift of prophecy? Certainly it cannot be known by even the closest examination of one's natural abilities and tendencies, or even one's spiritual inclinations,[165] but only by the exercise of prophesying itself.

Further, the gift of prophecy is not to be identified with the ministry of a prophet.[166] All prophets, by definition, prophesy, but not all who prophesy are prophets. Prophesying occurred on the Day of Pentecost (in fulfillment of the words of Joel that "in the last days . . . your sons and your daughters shall prophesy" [Acts 2:17]); the Ephesians "spoke with tongues and prophesied" (Acts 19:6); and there were the daughters of Philip the evangelist "who prophesied"[167] (Acts 21:9).[168] All such activity represents the gift of prophecy.

2. Service—"if service, in his serving"

All Christians are called upon to be servants of Jesus Christ and of one another. I have previously discussed at some length[169] what is involved in serving one another—a service to which all believers are called. What Paul is saying here is that some persons may have a special gift of service that is concretized in the very activity of service. This is why Paul says "if service, *in* his serving." How does one know if he or she has the functional gift of service? Again, the answer is found in the action[170]—by the very quality and effectiveness of the deeds of service.

It is possible that Paul has in mind the particular service associated with the office of deacon. The Greek word *diakonos* (broadly, "servant") is the corresponding term to *diakonia* ("service").

---

[163]Some commentators refer to "the proportion of faith" (there is no "his" here or throughout this passage in the Greek text) as a kind of external norm of the truth of the gospel as found in "liturgical and . . . catechetical instruction" (E. Käsemann, *Commentary on Romans*, 341). However, I agree with James Dunn that "the faith is the faith exercised by the one who prophesies" (*Romans 9–16*, WBC, 728). Similarly, TDNT 1:347–48.

[164]Actually the gift of faith there is listed prior to gifts of healing, working of miracles, and prophecy—in that order.

[165]I have recently read a listing of five characteristics of one who may have the function gift of prophesying: (1) urgency to speak plainly and persuasively; (2) ability to discern people's character and motives; (3) capacity to identify, define, and hate evil; (4) willingness to experience and prompt brokenness; and (5) dependence on scriptural truth and authority. My response is that one may score high on all these points and yet by no means be any closer to the function of prophesying. I repeat: the only way to know that one has this particular gift, or any other, is by *experiencing* its occurrence and *knowing* that it is totally a gift of grace.

[166]On the ministry of a prophet, see pages 170–74.

[167]The NASB errs in translating "who were prophetesses." The Greek word is *prophēteuousai*, literally "prophesying."

[168]Also see especially 1 Corinthians 11:4–5, and 1 Thessalonians 5:20.

[169]On pages 123–24.

[170]As Dunn puts it, "The focus is wholly on the act and not on the actor" (*Romans 9–16*, WBC, 729).

But *diakonos* has also the more limited meaning of *deacon*,[171] and thus there could be reference to the diaconate.[172] However, I think it more likely that Paul is referring to a particular gift of serving by one who may or may not be a designated "deacon." Such gifted actions could surely prepare the way for official service as a deacon. But here, I believe, it is more accurate to understand the gift in Romans as functional rather than official, and to view it as any kind of service, including the most menial, to which a person may be called.

3. Teaching—"he who teaches, in his teaching"

I have already discussed how teaching is both an official activity of pastors and teachers and a mutual responsibility of all members of the church. But in Romans 12 Paul is referring to a particular gift of teaching that operates through some in the congregation, a gift that will be demonstrated in the very act of teaching. Such teaching represents a kind of intermediate level between official teaching and congregation-wide mutual sharing in the Word.

Paul is likely referring to such teaching in this statement to the Corinthians: "When you assemble each one has a psalm, has a teaching, has a revelation, has a tongue, has an interpretation" (1 Cor. 14:26 NASB). "Has a teaching" hardly seems to refer to an official teacher; it also implies more than congregational mutual instruction.[173] The teaching here may well be by gifted (i.e., charismatic) teachers.[174]

In a practical way this says to a congregation that by God's grace there may be some who will amply demonstrate this in their teaching. They are not necessarily trained as teachers (although they may be), but they are supernaturally gifted with knowledge and insight into the word of truth and have a way of getting this truth across to people.[175] Such people should be encouraged to teach often in the church's educational program. For by their teaching—"in" their teaching—they have demonstrated that by God's grace they possess the gift that can bless many.

---

[171]As in 1 Timothy 3:8–13.

[172]Käsemann writes, "Something like a definite 'office' has emerged at this point" (*Commentary on Romans*, 342). John Murray, after weighing various alternatives, says, "There does not . . . appear to be any conclusive reason for rejecting the view that this reference is to the diaconate" (*Epistle to the Romans*, NICNT, 124). To the contrary, Leon Morris writes that "this is surely to make too specific a very general word [namely, 'serving']" (Epistle to the Romans, 441). Similarly, Dunn (*Romans 9–16*, 728–29). I concur with Morris and Dunn.

[173]Recall also these words in Hebrews 5:12: "By this time you ought to be teachers." James writes, "Let not many of you become teachers . . . for you know that we who teach shall be judged with greater strictness" (3:1). Both of these statements suggest an intermediate level of instruction.

[174]Dunn writes about 1 Corinthians 14:26: "*Teaching was not limited to the group of teachers* [italics his] . . . any member might be given a charismatic interpretation for the benefit of the whole assembly" (*Jesus and the Spirit*, 284).

[175]This is where "the word [or utterance] of knowledge" (1 Cor. 12:8) and the gift of "teaching" largely coincide. If the word of knowledge may be described as "an inspired word of teaching" and "a special impartation of teaching that is given by the Holy Spirit through a particular person" (*Renewal Theology*, 2:356), then the parallel is close. The only difference may lie in the intensity of the anointing of the one teaching.

4. *Exhortation—"he who exhorts, in his exhortation"*

This may also be translated "he who encourages, in his encouragement."[176] Whatever the translation, Paul is stating that by the grace of God some are so gifted.

Paul himself was surely an exhorter, for the opening words of Romans 12 read, "I urge[177] you therefore, brethren, by the mercies of God, to present your bodies a living and holy sacrifice" (NASB). Hence, Paul is likely saying later (in v. 18) that one of the gifts of grace is experienced by those who similarly urge or exhort in regard to a particular matter. In a letter to Timothy Paul combines teaching and exhorting: "These things teach and exhort" (1 Tim. 6:2 KJV).[178] He also writes to Titus, "These things speak and exhort and reprove" (Titus 2:15 NASB).[179] "Exhort" contains the idea of urging strongly and thus goes beyond teaching. Whereas teaching is directed to the mind primarily, exhortation is to the heart and will. In a local congregation the gift of exhortation operates through one who is granted by God's grace the special ability to urge people to action.

If the basic idea is encouragement, Paul surely also stresses this. He refers early in Romans to mutual encouragement—"that we may be mutually encouraged by each other's faith" (1:12)—and later speaks of God as "the God of steadfastness and encouragement" (15:5). We have previously observed many references to encouragement as an activity of the whole body.[180] However, particular persons may also have this gift. In the New Testament Barnabas is called "the Son of encouragement" (Acts 4:36) and on many occasions demonstrated that gift.[181] Paul writes the Ephesians about Tychicus "the beloved brother and faithful minister in the Lord": "I have sent him to you . . . that he may encourage your hearts" (6:21–22).[182] Correspondingly, by the grace of God there continues to be the special gift of encouragement for some "Barnabases" and "Tychichuses" in the Christian body through whom many will be blessed.

Whether it is called exhortation or encouragement, it is a valuable gift to be recognized and activated in the body of Christ. The same persons may very well be both exhorters and encouragers. In any event, a congregation is surely enriched by those who function in this gift of grace.

We move now to consider various gifts that Paul describes with an accompanying disposition of heart and will—"with liberality," "with diligence," "with cheerfulness."

5. *Giving—"he who gives,[183] with liberality"[184]*

In regard to giving, Paul has much to say in 2 Corinthians 8 and 9 about

[176]The NIV translates, "if it is encouraging, let him encourage."

[177]The Greek word is *parakalō*.

[178]Cf. 1 Timothy 4:13.

[179]Cf. Titus 1:9.

[180]In the section "Showing Brotherly Love," pages 118–20.

[181]See Acts 9:27; 11:22–23; 15:37.

[182]Cf. Colossians 4:7-8.

[183]Or "shares." The Greek word is *metadidous*, a form of *metadidōmi*. See, e.g., Luke 3:11 and 1 Thessalonians 2:8 where "share" seems the likely translation; however, in Romans 1:11 and Ephesians 4:28, "give" or "impart" seems better. Dunn writes that *metadidous* "means not just 'giving,' but giving a share of, sharing" (*Romans 9–16*, 730). BAGD translates this word as "gives" in our passage.

[184]Or "simplicity" (KJV). The Greek word is *haplotēti*, a form of *haplotēs*. *Haplotēs* is best translated "simplicity" in 2 Corinthians 11:3—"simplicity and purity of devotion to Christ"

liberality and generosity on the part of the whole congregation. He states, for example, that he who "sows bountifully" will "reap bountifully" (2 Cor. 9:6). Surely all churches do well to heed Paul's words about generosity of giving on the part of everyone.

However, in addition, a special *charisma* of God's grace is that of giving or sharing. Moreover, this reference in Romans 12 does not imply that because it is to be done "with liberality" this gift is possible only for the wealthy. Probably the most liberal act of giving in the Bible was that of the poor widow who put two coins into the temple treasury. Jesus declared, "This poor widow has put in more than all those who are contributing to the treasury. For they all contributed out of their abundance; but she out of her poverty has put in everything she had, her whole living" (Mark 12:43–44). Out of abundance many gave, some probably large amounts, but this was little as compared with the widow's total gift. Thus it is apparent that one who gives may be materially poor but still give with great liberality.[185] But whether poor or rich, what counts is the spirit of the giving. This is to "give with all your heart."[186]

Paul's point in the statement "he who gives, with liberality" is that this is a special gift of God's grace. Whereas all believers are called upon to be liberal in their giving, a particular person or persons may be so graced with liberality that they find generous giving to be their main function in the community. Blessed indeed is the church that has people functioning in this gift!

6. Leading—"he who leads,[187] with diligence"[188] (NASB)

Another of the gifts of grace is leading, and doing so with diligence. Paul writes to the Thessalonians, "We beseech you, brethren, to respect those who labor among you and are over you [literally, "taking the lead"][189] in the Lord and admonish you, and to esteem them very highly in love because of their work" (1 Thess. 5:12–13). Also, Paul speaks of a bishop (or overseer) as one who must be able "to manage[190] his own household" (1 Tim. 3:1, 5), and of deacons as being able to do the same: to

---

(NASB); as "singleness" in Ephesians 6:5 and Colossians 3:22—"singleness of heart." However, in other passages that have to do with giving, "liberality" or "generosity" is the better translation: 2 Corinthians 8:2—"a wealth of liberality"; 9:11—"great generosity"; 9:13—"generosity." The cognate adverb *haplōs* is rendered "generously" in James 1:5—"God, who gives to all men generously."

[185]A parallel to the poor widow's giving was that of the churches in Macedonia. Paul writes that "in a severe test of affliction, their abundance of joy and their extreme poverty have overflowed in a wealth of liberality on their part" (2 Cor. 8:1–2). Note: "extreme poverty" but "wealth of liberality."

[186]The NEB translation of Romans 12:8.

[187]The Greek word is *proistamenos*, a participial form of *proistēmi*. The KJV translates it "he that ruleth"; NIV, "if it is leadership"; NEB, "if you are a leader"; RSV, "he who gives aid." This last translation is possible in light of the use of a form of *proistēmi* in Titus 3:8—speaking of believers as being "careful to apply [*proistasthai*] themselves to good deeds" (also see Titus 3:14). However, "leading" is probably a better translation in Romans 12:8 (incidentally the NRSV translates this word as "the leader" [instead of "he who gives aid"]) in light of other passages that will be noted in the first paragraph below. "Managing" or "taking care" is another possible translation.

[188]Or "zeal"—"zeal in matters of religion" (BAGD). "What is meant is the 'holy zeal' which demands full dedication to serving the community" (TDNT 7:566).

[189]The Greek word is *proistamenous*.

[190]The Greek word is *prostēnai*.

"manage[191] their children and their households well" (v. 12). Thus leaders in the church are to be both highly regarded and able to lead or manage their own households.

In the next chapter we will consider the important roles of overseers and deacons. However, it is not likely that in Romans 12 Paul is referring to any official position in the church; rather, he refers to those who are granted by God gifts of grace to exercise leadership in various ways. There is probably a close parallel to what Paul in 1 Corinthians 12 calls "administrations"[192] (v. 28 NASB), which could refer to those in less than the higher official positions. Those with the grace of leadership may serve well in the administration of the affairs of the church.

Once again, however, this role of leadership is not a position stemming from natural capacities or training but is a gift of God's grace. It is of course possible that leadership ability in other fields may be used by God in the church; however, as with all the other gifts of grace, Paul is referring to a supernatural gift. Some leaders and administrators, known for their secular abilities, may not do so well in the church because of the very nature of the church and God's way of working spiritually. A church in some sense is a business and surely accountable to the community at large and its own membership for proper procedures. But it must have a style of leadership that is very different from that of worldly authority. Jesus declared, "Let the greatest among you become as the youngest, and the leader as one who serves" (Luke 22:26). Christian leadership—church leadership—is the leadership of those who seek nothing for themselves and are willing to be the servants of all others.

7. Showing mercy—"he who shows mercy,[193] with cheerfulness"

This final gift of God's grace is also the climactic one. For God Himself is a God of mercy;[194] thus, showing mercy is a God-given grace. In this verse Paul is referring to acts of mercy,[195] most likely in regard to the physical and material needs of people.

Two New Testament examples may be mentioned. The first is that of the Good Samaritan (Luke 10:29–37), who, unlike the priest and Levite, bound up the wounds of a man who had been stripped and beaten by robbers. Then the Samaritan placed the battered man in an inn and provided means for his care. In reply to Jesus' question as to who proved to be neighbor, the proper answer was given: "The one who showed mercy on him." Then Jesus added, "Go and do likewise" (v. 37). One who "shows mercy" is one who acts like the Good Samaritan.

Another example is that of Dorcas (Tabitha, in Aramaic). She is described in the Book of Acts as a woman "full of

---

[191]The Greek word is *proistamenoi*.

[192]The Greek word is *kybernēseis*—"administrators" (RSV), "gifts of administration" (NIV), "governments" (KJV).

[193]The Greek word is *eleōn*, "showing mercy," from the verb *eleeō*.

[194]This is shown throughout the Scriptures. For example, "The LORD your God is a merciful God" (Deut. 4:31); "The LORD is merciful and gracious" (Ps. 103:8); "God, who is rich in mercy" (Eph. 2:4); "By his great mercy we have been born anew" (1 Peter 1:3). Shortly before our passage in Romans 12, Paul had spoken of God as having "mercy upon all" (Rom. 11:32).

[195]The RSV translates the words in Romans 12:8 as "he who does acts of mercy." This conveys the dynamic sense of *doing* merciful deeds.

good works and acts of charity"[196] (9:36). Dorcas became sick and died. Peter was summoned and went to the room where widows whom she had helped were weeping and "showing coats and garments which Dorcas made while she was with them" (v. 39). Shortly thereafter God in mercy through Peter raised Dorcas from the dead. She had already, through her sewing, shown mercy to widows in need.

Now to return to Romans 12: Paul is here saying that the showing of mercy, the act of mercy (Samaritanlike or Dorcaslike), is a particular gift of God's grace. All Christians should show mercy to those who are needy and afflicted, but now and again God especially gives some people the *charisma* of mercy. It is more than mercy in general or even acts of mercy; it is a supernatural gift enabling one to perform certain acts in relation to specific persons in need.

Then Paul adds the crowning touch—"with cheerfulness."[197] Showing mercy ought not to be a grim duty but a joyful one. Paul declares elsewhere that "God loves a cheerful giver" (2 Cor. 9:7)—one who gives "not reluctantly or under compulsion." If that is true about monetary giving, which can be impersonal,[198] it is surely also true that God loves the one who shows mercy cheerfully to particular persons—those afflicted, disabled, aged, or poor (whatever the situation). Furthermore, an act of mercy cheerfully done can bring added pleasure to the one who receives it. Showing mercy in a cheerful and joyful[199] manner is a delight to both God and man.

It is likely that the note of cheerfulness in showing mercy is the clearest identifiable mark of a person who has this special God-given *charisma*.[200] Accordingly, the church does not need to seek out this gift or to ask its members to check their own characteristics to see if they qualify. Rather, the important thing for the church is to recognize and perhaps encourage those who are already using the gift. And one of the surest evidences of the presence of the gift is the spirit of cheerfulness that surrounds a person who does acts of mercy. May the Lord grant us more people like that!

III. OUTREACH

The church is also the community for the world. It exists not only for the worship and glorifying of God and for the upbuilding of its membership in faith and love, but also for communicating the gospel to the whole world. Indeed, the function of outreach is essential to the life and vitality of the church.

A. The Great Commission

The church stands constantly under the Great Commission of the risen Christ, who declared, "All authority in heaven and on earth has been given to

---

[196]The Greek word for "acts of charity" is *eleēmosunon*, from the same root as *eleeō*, to "show mercy." (Note our English word *eleemosynary*, which refers to charity or charitable deeds [such as "a person given to eleemosynary activities"].) Mercy and charity are closely related.

[197]The Greek word is *hilarotēti*, from *hilarotēs*. This is the origin of our English word "hilarity."

[198]Paul, in 2 Corinthians, is referring to an offering he was taking for the believers in Jerusalem who were not likely known by the people in Corinth.

[199]Even *hilarious*!

[200]C. E. B. Cranfield writes that "a particularly cheerful and agreeable disposition may well be evidence of the special gift that marks a person out for this particular service" (*Romans: A Shorter Commentary*, 307).

me. Go therefore and make disciples of all nations, baptizing them in the name of the Father and of the Son and of the Holy Spirit, teaching them to observe all that I have commanded you; and lo, I am with you always, to the close of the age'' (Matt. 28:18–20). This commission concludes the Gospel of Matthew.

The Great Commission is variously stated in the other three gospels. In Mark 16 the words of Jesus were ''Go into all the world and preach the gospel to the whole creation. He who believes and is baptized will be saved'' (vv. 15–16).[201] In Luke 24, Jesus' words read: ''Thus it is written, that the Christ should suffer and on the third day rise from the dead, and that repentance and forgiveness of sins should be preached in his name to all nations, beginning from Jerusalem'' (vv. 46–47). According to John, the risen Jesus declared, ''Peace be with you. As the Father has sent me, even so I send you. . . . If you forgive the sins of any, they are forgiven; if you retain the sins of any, they are retained'' (20:21, 23).

In all four gospels those addressed were primarily His eleven disciples,[202] who now represent the incipient church.[203] Thus the Great Commission was given by Christ not only to the original eleven apostles, but also by implication to all who follow Him.[204]

Now let us examine more closely some of the components of the Great Commission in its various formulations.

1. Christ the Commissioner

The One who commissions is the risen Christ, to whom ''all authority in heaven and on earth'' has been given. It is He who suffered death on the cross, rose triumphant on the third day, and is now invested with total authority. Thus the Great Commission is from the victorious Christ who has defeated the forces of sin and evil and therefore now has all power and authority.

The Commissioner is both Savior and Lord. He speaks to those who have received His peace—''Peace be with you''—and now sends them forth to proclaim His salvation to all mankind. He speaks as Lord of their lives and does so with authority both in heaven and on earth.

Surely no other commission has ever been given that is invested with such total power and authority.

2. The Commission

The disciples were told, ''Go therefore.'' ''Therefore'' stresses the authority that lies behind the Commission;

[201]This form of the Great Commission in Mark 16 occurs in the so-called long ending, verses 9–20. These verses are not found in a number of ancient New Testament manuscripts, hence often are relegated to marginal status (see RSV, NIV, NASB). This, however, should not be thought to deny their being valid Scripture. As Stephen S. Short puts it, ''From the fact that verses 9–20 are relegated . . . to the margin, it is not to be deduced that they are no part of the inspired word of God. The reason for their being relegated to the margin is that it is unlikely that they were written by Mark himself . . . '' (IBC, 1180). (See *Renewal Theology* 2:150, n.36, 388, n.18.)

[202]Matthew refers to ''the eleven disciples'' (28:16); Mark, ''the eleven'' (16:14); Luke, ''the eleven . . . and those who were with them'' (24:33); John simply, ''the disciples'' (20:19). Thus the Great Commission, while addressed first to the eleven apostles, extends to the larger group of disciples.

[203]The word *church* is not used here nor for that matter later in Acts 2 at Pentecost. However, as those who now know the risen Christ, they are His new spiritual community.

[204]It would be a mistake therefore to limit the Great Commission to the original apostles. That such is incorrect is apparent from the stress upon the worldwide extension of the Commission—''all nations,'' ''into all the world,'' ''to all nations.''

"Go"[205] signifies that they were to move out beyond their own group. The disciples, and therefore the church, could not simply remain in their own experience of Christ's blessings.

The going is also a sending. As was noted, according to the Fourth Gospel, Jesus said, "As the Father has sent me, even so I send you" (John 20:21).[206] The church is a "sent" people—"into all the world" (Mark 16) and "to all nations" (Matt. 28 and Luke 24). There is no limit to the Great Commission: it encompasses the whole earth.

3. *Content of the Commission*

Now let us examine the content of the Commission in detail.[207]

a. Make Disciples[208]*—"Go therefore and make disciples of all nations."* The making of disciples implies such a proclamation of the gospel that people receive it and thereby become disciples. The means of making disciples of all nations is to "preach the gospel to the whole creation" (Mark 16). This occurs through proclaiming "repentance and forgiveness of sins . . . to all nations" (Luke 24). By this proclamation of the Good News, peoples and nations may turn to Christ and become His disciples.

It is important to recognize that the purpose of the Great Commission is to "make disciples." The church from its beginning has stood under the command of the risen Christ to proclaim the Good News of repentance and forgiveness, the message of salvation. The Commission totally applies to the desperate plight of the world—nations, peoples—dominated by evil and on the way to destruction, and it declares that there is a glorious redemption through Jesus Christ. Thus anything else the church may do in relation to the world—for example, in terms of bodily needs and social ills—is secondary to the Great Commission, which focuses on the spiritual plight of mankind.

A further word of clarification may be in order. True disciples of Christ should be concerned, as was their Master, with the whole human condition.[209] Jesus ministered to the poor, the hungry, the sick, the outcast, and the demon-possessed; so must the church. However, His fundamental task was the preaching of the gospel: "Jesus came . . . preaching the gospel of God . . . repent, and believe in the gospel" (Mark 1:14–15). This was His basic commission; so it must be for the church that stands under the Great Commission. Indeed, shortly after the events quoted from Mark 1, Jesus called out to the fishermen Simon (Peter) and Andrew: "Follow me and I will make you become fishers of men" (v. 17). Fishing for people: to bring them out of the sea of darkness and death and into the presence of God's light and love is *the* concern of the Great Commission.

There is surely no other challenge of like importance. Since all people outside of Christ are forever lost, the only ultimate imperative for the church, the community of born-again believers, is the proclamation of the gospel, the way of salvation. Incidentally, a few ancient New Testament manuscripts end the Gospel of Mark with these words: "And . . . Jesus himself sent out by means of them [His disciples], from east to west, the sacred and imperishable proclamation of eternal salvation." Al-

---

[205]The Greek word translated "go" in both Matthew 28 and Mark 16 is literally "going," *poreuthentes*.

[206]Jesus had earlier said in prayer to the Father: "As thou didst send me into the world, so I have sent them into the world" (John 17:18).

[207]I will follow the wording in Matthew 28 but also note further details in the other gospels.

[208]Or "disciple" (as a verb). The Greek word is an imperative verb: *matheteusate*.

[209]For more on this see section C, "The Whole Human Condition," pages 151–53.

though the authenticity of these words is questionable, they nonetheless do express the purpose of the Great Commission: the universal proclamation of eternal salvation. This remains the church's high challenge and task.

What is urgently important is, as Jesus said at the beginning of His ministry, that people "repent and believe in the gospel." This is why Jesus also told the disciples in some of His final words that "repentance and forgiveness of sins should be preached in his name to all nations." By such repentance and faith there is forgiveness of sins, and its result: eternal salvation.

b. Baptizing—"baptizing them in the name of the Father and of the Son and of the Holy Spirit." Following the Commission in Mark 16, the text reads, "He who believes and is baptized will be saved; but he who does not believe will be condemned." Thus baptism in both Matthew and Mark is found in close conjunction with making disciples and preaching the gospel. Now a number of comments.

First, baptism is a vital part of the Great Commission. It is just as much a part of it as are both the preceding "Go . . . and make disciples of all nations" and the ensuing "teaching them to observe all that I have commanded you." Thus on the Day of Pentecost "those who received his [Peter's] word were baptized, and there were added that day about three thousand souls" (Acts 2:41). Throughout the Book of Acts, baptism regularly followed receiving the word (i.e., through faith and repentance).[210]

Second, baptism relates primarily to the forgiveness of sins. As was noted, the Commission in Luke speaks of "repentance and forgiveness of sins"; hence subsequent baptism is in connection with these realities. So also Peter at Pentecost proclaimed, "Repent, and be baptized every one of you . . . for the forgiveness of your sins" (Acts 2:38). The word "for" here does not mean to obtain forgiveness but to serve as channel or medium through which forgiveness is received.[211] Thus there is a close connection between baptism and forgiveness of sins. Through repentance and forgiveness the heart—the inner person—is cleansed from sin; and, in connection with this, by baptism in water, the body—the outer person—is symbolically cleansed.

Salvation, which stems from repentance and forgiveness and thus is essentially of the soul, relates also to the body. Therefore the making of disciples includes their being baptized.[212] The shortened form of Mark 16 states simply, "He who believes and is baptized will be saved." Baptism obviously is not the cause of salvation, for without faith baptism is ineffectual. Indeed, the basic stress must remain on faith. The subsequent words in Mark 16 are "He who does not believe will be condemned"—and no mention is made of baptism. It is unbelief that condemns, not a lack of baptism. Still baptism remains important as the ordinary outward means of the receiving of forgiveness and of salvation.[213] Thus the Great

---

[210]See also Acts 8:12, 38; 9:18; 10:48; 16:15, 33; 18:8; 19:5.

[211]See *Renewal Theology*, 2:283–85 for a fuller presentation of the relation of water baptism to forgiveness of sins. Also there will be further discussion later, in chapter 6.

[212]This of course does not mean "baptismal regeneration." Water can serve as a channel of forgiveness, of cleansing from sin, but it is not the cause.

[213]It would be too much to say that baptism is the necessary means of salvation. It is significant that in Peter's second proclamation of the gospel he declared, "Repent therefore, and turn again, that your sins may be blotted out, that times of refreshing may come from the

Commission contains a close connection between making disciples and baptism.

Third, baptism as portrayed in the Great Commission is vitally related to the name of Father, Son, and Holy Spirit. This wording "in the name" suggests that baptism is related to the triune God, and that in His triune name people are to be baptized. That this is not an absolute baptismal formula is shown by the fact that in the Book of Acts baptism is stated as being done only in the name of Jesus.[214] For example, Peter's first sermon climaxed with these words: "Repent, and be baptized . . . in the name of Jesus Christ for the forgiveness of your sins." However, Peter does also refer to the Holy Spirit by adding, "and you shall receive the gift of the Holy Spirit" (2:38). How then are we to understand the wording in the Great Commission?

To answer: the comprehensive triune formula depicts the nature of full discipleship. While at the heart of this is Jesus Christ, and therefore the forgiveness of sins in His name, there is also the role of the Father and the Holy Spirit. This suggests two things. First, the triune God—not Jesus Christ alone—is involved in salvation. The Father is the source, the Son the mediator, the Holy Spirit the enabler of salvation. Hence baptism, while done in the name of Jesus Christ (as Acts depicts it), is actually in the name of all three persons in the Godhead.

Second, full discipleship is a baptism *into*[215] the reality of the Father, the Son, and the Holy Spirit, which includes (as Acts depicts it) not only forgiveness of sins in the name of Jesus Christ but also the gift of the Holy Spirit. Although no triune baptism is depicted in Acts on the Day of Pentecost, there is (as noted) immediate mention of the gift of the Holy Spirit pursuant to the forgiveness of sins. Moreover, on two occasions, following baptism in the name of Jesus, those who were baptized received the Holy Spirit. The Samaritans were baptized by Philip (Acts 8:12), and later through the ministry of Peter and John "they received the Holy Spirit" (v. 17). The Ephesians were baptized by Paul (Acts 19:5), and afterward through the laying on of Paul's hands the Holy Spirit "came on them" (v. 6). Thus—it is possible to say—their Christian initiation was complete: they had become full disciples.

Now we may see more clearly that "making disciples" includes a vital relationship with the triune God. At the heart of this relationship is forgiveness of sins through the Son, and therein is salvation. The background is God the Father, the Creator, whom Christ reveals totally; the foreground is God the Holy Spirit, whom Christ promises. Immediately after saying, "Repent, and be baptized every one of you in the name of Jesus Christ for the forgiveness of your sins; and you shall receive the gift of the Holy Spirit," Peter added, "For the promise[216] is to you and to

---

presence of the Lord" (Acts 3:19). He made no reference to baptism, for the crux of salvation is repentance and faith. However, baptism surely would have followed. Cf. Acts 10:43–48 where Peter preached faith in Christ for forgiveness of sins (v. 43), simultaneously the Holy Spirit fell on his audience (v. 44)—a sure sign of their salvation, and after that they were baptized (vv. 47–48).

[214]For more on the baptismal formula see *Renewal Theology*, 2:286–87, and chapter 6 infra, pages 222–23.

[215]The Greek word usually translated "in" ("in the name of") is *eis*, ordinarily meaning "into."

[216]"The promise" relates only to the gift of the Spirit. Note also Acts 1:4–5 and 2:33. Cf. Luke 24:49.

your children and to all that are far off, every one whom the Lord our God calls to him'' (Acts 2:39). It is only when the promise of the Spirit is received that discipleship is fully entered into.

Thus the Great Commission to "go and make disciples," while centrally relating to the forgiveness of sins, also includes the gift of the Holy Spirit. Since the primary purpose of the gift of the Holy Spirit is to enable believers to minister effectively for Christ,[217] fully equipped disciples are those who have received both salvation and the enabling power of the Holy Spirit. Thus when Peter and John and Paul led people into the forgiveness of their sins and the reception of the Holy Spirit, they were leading them into full discipleship and thereby fulfilling Christ's command in the Great Commission.

When this more comprehensive picture of the Great Commission is realized, the church today should likewise follow their example. The task of evangelizing is of course central, for until people have received forgiveness of their sins there can be no gift of the Spirit. But the church ought not to stop with the message and reality of salvation; it should also proclaim the promise and reality of the gift of the Holy Spirit. For only when this gift is received is there a complete entrance into Christian discipleship. In this area the church often fails in the making of disciples. Actually the last phrase in the triune baptismal formula—"of the Holy Spirit"—underscores this further ministry, but too often this additional experience to which triune baptism points is overlooked. The church needs to act again as Peter and John and Paul did in enabling converts to complete their baptism in the name of the Holy Spirit.

I must say something further about baptismal formulas. There is basically no difference between Christ's triune baptismal command in Matthew 28 and the early church's practice in Acts of baptizing only in the name of Jesus, because after baptizing with water they proceeded to minister the gift (or baptism) of the Holy Spirit. What Acts dramatizes is that triune baptism is more than a formula, more even than an aspect of salvation: it also includes the gift of the Holy Spirit for ministry and mission. Thus in seeming contradiction to Jesus' words in Matthew 28, the triune formula in Acts becomes singular—Jesus only—but not without recognition of the additional dimension of Holy Spirit empowerment. Hence what is signified in the triune formula is acted out in the Book of Acts![218]

What baptismal formula should be used today—that in Matthew or in Acts? Traditionally the church has utilized the triune formula as stated in the Great Commission. Since this is declared in Matthew to be an utterance of Christ, the church is surely acting properly in this regard. Since, as stated, triune baptism points to entrance into full discipleship, such baptism is wholly in order. However, because the early church in Acts practiced baptism only

---

[217]See the next section: "The Enabling of the Spirit." (Also for a more comprehensive study see *Renewal Theology*, 2:243–63, "Power for Ministry.")

[218]The first part of the formula—"in the name of the Father"—might, however, seem to be experientially missing. The apostles outwardly seemed to be concerned only about the Son (baptism in His name) and the Holy Spirit (the gift of the Holy Spirit). However, one should recognize that much of their preaching presupposed some recognition of God the Father as the background for their ministry. For example, the centurion Cornelius, who was later to receive forgiveness of sins (Acts 10:43) and the gift of the Holy Spirit (v. 45), was earlier described as "a devout man who feared God with all his household . . . and prayed constantly to God" (v. 2). Already a "God-fearing" Gentile, he needed only to receive forgiveness in Christ and the gift of the Holy Spirit.

in the name of Jesus Christ, this can hardly be ruled out. Indeed, since Peter and John were surely among those who heard the Great Commission but obviously did not feel obligated to practice triune baptism, neither should the church today. In fact, by the apostles' very practice of baptism in Jesus' name *and* the additional emphasis on the ministry of the gift of the Holy Spirit, they may be calling us afresh to a fuller realization of what discipleship is all about. One could say that the apostles were following out the practical implications of the trinitarian formula (by no means foregoing it), and being sure that the dimension of the Holy Spirit was fully recognized. Hence, there might be a significant gain in the ministry of the church today if, like the early church in Acts, we were to practice both baptism in the single name of Jesus[219] and the laying on of hands for the reception of the Holy Spirit. However, even with retention of the triune baptismal formula—as practiced in most churches—there could still be an additional occasion and opportunity for ministering the Holy Spirit.[220]

This all basically relates to Christian initiation or to Christian beginnings. Whether viewed from the aspect of the Gospel of Matthew or the Book of Acts, what is at stake is the proper undergirding of Christian life and ministry. Moreover, the gift of the Holy Spirit is not some further or higher step beyond the forgiveness of sins but is the implementation of Christ's ministry in and through believers. Christian initiation into full discipleship includes both baptism and the imparting of the gift of the Holy Spirit as belonging to the beginnings of the Christian walk.

c. Teaching—"teaching them to observe all that I have commanded you." The climax in making disciples is teaching those who have come to faith and been baptized to observe all—literally, "all things whatever"[221]—that Christ has commanded. Thus, although discipleship has been entered into (initiation has been completed), "making disciples" includes teaching believers to observe—keep, obey[222]—all that Christ commanded His original disciples.

The apostles who received the Great Commission from Jesus were soon to begin teaching the new converts at Pentecost. For after the apostles baptized some three thousand people, these new believers "devoted themselves to the apostles' teaching" (Acts 2:42). This teaching was surely none other than what Christ had given the apostles. Now they were passing it on in the making of other disciples.

It is apparent from what Jesus said that making disciples also includes teaching all His commandments as well as calling for their observance. It is not a matter of *some* of His commandments but *all*, indeed "all things whatever"

---

[219]This is done by "oneness" or "Jesus only" Pentecostals, such as the United Pentecostal Church. However, these Pentecostals unfortunately deny the triune basis of Christian faith by viewing the triune statement of Matthew 28 as referring to Jesus only, the terms "Father" and "Holy Spirit" being understood as various aspects of Christ's nature. This is a modern form of unitarianism focusing on the second person of the Trinity. (See *Renewal Theology*, 1:92.)

[220]In some sense this is done in the Roman Catholic Church, which practices both triune baptism and confirmation through the laying on of hands. However, both the acts of baptism and confirmation are viewed as in themselves (*ex opere operato*) conferring grace. (For more on confirmation see *Renewal Theology*, 2:289, esp. n.58.) What is needed is to lead people into the experiences to which these two practices point.

[221]The Greek phrase is *panta hosa eneteilamēn*. The KJV well translates it as "all things whatsoever."

[222]The Greek word is *tērein*. The NIV translates it "obey."

Jesus had commanded. The church today must likewise carefully and thoroughly teach every word of Christ as contained in the Scriptures so that those being discipled can observe and do what He commanded.

Such teaching should include as a minimum Jesus' Sermon on the Mount (Matthew 5–7).[223] Because the Gospel of Matthew closes with the Great Commission's emphasis on Jesus' teaching, and because the Sermon on the Mount is an early summary of that teaching, attention may first be focused there. We must heed not just some commands but all of them; again, it is a matter of "all things whatever." Hence when Jesus gives commandments about such things as anger, lust, divorce, swearing, resisting evil, loving one's enemies (chap. 5), almsgiving, prayer, fasting, mammon, anxiety (chap. 6), judging others, throwing pearls before swine, the Golden Rule, the narrow gate, and fruitbearing (chap. 7), the church needs to teach both substantively and in detail what Jesus commanded. Indeed, the climax of the Sermon on the Mount goes beyond learning what Jesus commanded. It also includes practicing: "Every one . . . who hears these words of mine and does them will be like a wise man who built his house upon the rock" (7:24; see also vv. 25–27). Those who practice Jesus' commands are truly His disciples.

The church in its outreach, accordingly, has the great responsibility not only to initiate people into the Christian life and ministry but also immediately and continuously to instruct them in all the matters that Christ commanded. Since such persons have entered into a new life through forgiveness in Christ, it is not as if His commandments are foreign to their new nature. However, instruction is much needed so that they may see more clearly the way of Christ and walk in it.

Thus Christian discipleship clearly involves specific obedience to Jesus' commands. The believer whose burden of sins and guilt has been lifted through the marvel of divine forgiveness is not left on his own in regard to basic steps in living. To be sure, in and through Christ a person is free of his sinful past, but this does not mean that henceforth he should pursue his own will and purpose. No, he is free at last to do the things Christ commanded! For the person outside of Christ, the Sermon on the Mount is an impossible set of commands contrary to sinful human nature, but for one in Christ that same Sermon becomes the guidepost of a new way of living.

Further, Jesus also teaches, especially in the Fourth Gospel, that our duty to obey all His commands should flow out of our love for Him: "If you love me, you will keep my commandments" (John 14:15). Christ is no stern commander who simply, even coldly, lays down laws, and to whom we must, perhaps out of fear, give obedience. Rather, it is He who has first loved us, and out of our responsive love and gratitude to Him we should gladly seek to fulfill His every command.

One additional word: Doing whatever Christ has commanded, whether in the Sermon on the Mount or elsewhere, is not necessarily easy or simple. Thus the church must continuously instruct people in the ways and commandments of Christ, interpreting their meaning, their relevance for the present-day situation, and the way they are to be fulfilled. The challenge is great indeed!

Finally, we note the climax of Jesus' words in the Great Commission: "Lo, I am with you always, to the close of the

[223]I said "as a minimum" because there is much else of Jesus' teachings in Matthew as well as in the other gospels. However, Matthew 5–7 in itself is quite comprehensive.

age." These words are addressed to those who are actively carrying forward Christ's Commission. Two things stand out.

First, the church is not on her own. The Great Commission was not given by One who spoke and then left His disciples alone to fulfill His commands. Rather, as the church seeks to carry out the Great Commission, Christ's presence will accompany His people—"I am with you." What a huge difference that makes!

Second, Christ will be with His church through all the years ahead. Since making disciples of all nations will surely take much time, it is a further joy to know that Christ will be with His people "always," even "to the close of the age." Such an assurance can sustain the church in times of darkness—persecution, seeming defeat—as well as in times of great success. It is Christ with His people all the way!

B. The Enabling of the Holy Spirit

The church can carry forward its outreach only through the enabling of the Holy Spirit.[224] Jesus closed the Great Commission with the promise that He would always be with the church. Now we find this spelled out in reference to the Holy Spirit. In the Fourth Gospel Jesus declares, "If you love me, you will keep my commandments. And I will pray the Father, and he will give you another Counselor, [the Holy Spirit] to be with you for ever" (14:15–16). The Holy Spirit, the Spirit of Christ, will be with God's people to the end of the age—"for ever." He will be the enabler of the church's mission to carry the gospel to its final goal.

Let us now examine this enabling of the Holy Spirit in three aspects: power, direction, and supernatural manifestations.

1. Power

According to Luke 24, immediately following Jesus' words to His disciples about repentance and forgiveness of sins being "preached in his name to all nations, beginning from Jerusalem," He added, "You are witnesses of these things. And behold, I send the promise of my Father upon you; but stay in the city, until you are clothed with power from on high" (vv. 48–49). That this "power from on high" is the power of the Holy Spirit is apparent from Jesus' words in Acts 1:8: "You shall receive power when the Holy Spirit has come upon you; and you shall be my witnesses in Jerusalem and in all Judea and Samaria and to the end[225] of the earth." The enabling power of the Holy Spirit is essential to the witness of Jesus and the outreach of the church.

In the Great Commission Jesus referred to the Holy Spirit in connection with Father and Son. But this reference was to the ongoing activity of the church in making disciples—"baptizing them in the name of the Father and of the Son and of the Holy Spirit." The words of Jesus in Luke 24 and Acts 1 relate rather to what is prior, namely, the necessity that those who carry forward the Commission do so in the power of the Holy Spirit. This is highly important since there was, and is, no way that the Commission can be fulfilled through human strength and power.

The apostles were to begin in Jerusalem. It would be hard to imagine a more difficult place to bear witness to Jesus. Only a few weeks earlier Jesus had been crucified by the combined forces of Romans and Jews in Jerusalem.

[224]See also *Renewal Theology*, 2:177–79, 243–63.

[225]The Greek word is *eschatou*—"remotest part" (NASB), "ends" (NIV and NEB), "uttermost part" (KJV).

Hatred and antagonism against Him had run very deep. Now His disciples were to begin preaching and witnessing in that same city. Humanly speaking, the task would be impossible. They would need all possible "power from on high."

Further, the apostles knew by now how utterly incapable they were of accomplishing anything in their own strength. At Christ's recent crucifixion they had all lacked courage and deserted Him out of fear for their own safety. Peter had boasted, "'If I must die with you, I will not deny you.' And they all said the same" (Mark 14:31). But they had all deserted Him and fled. Surely they needed much spiritual reinforcement.

But even more, the apostles had been commissioned by Jesus to proclaim the gospel with such effectiveness that it would bring about life-transforming repentance and faith. The words they spoke would need to probe deeper than had any human words that had ever been spoken before; indeed they had to go to the very hearts of people and bring about a real life-change. Since the fall of the human race, human hearts had been hardened to the things of God. Even Israel, God's ancient covenant people, proved to be people "uncircumcised in heart" (Jer. 9:26). No word of Old Testament prophets had ever been able to cut deep enough to bring about radical repentance and faith. Now at last through the redemption wrought by Christ and the promised enabling power of the Holy Spirit it could take place! There was utterly no way the apostles could have proceeded without this spiritual investment of power.

Then on the Day of Pentecost it first happened: "They were all filled with the Holy Spirit" (Acts 2:4). The Spirit came "like the rush of a mighty wind" and like "tongues as of fire, distributed and resting on each one of them" (vv. 2–3). Immediately by this transcendent power they did the hitherto unimaginable—"they . . . began to speak in other tongues" (v. 4) through the Spirit's enabling. A multitude of "Jews, devout men from every nation under heaven" (v. 5), came together at this sound, and to their utter amazement "each one heard them speaking in his own language" (v. 6). Not long after that Peter stood with the other apostles ("Peter, standing with the eleven," v. 14) and proclaimed the gospel with such power that some three thousand of these Jews were "cut to the heart" (v. 37) and came to salvation (v. 41). These were Jews who had crucified Christ (Peter's words in v. 36: "this Jesus whom you crucified"), so it would be hard to imagine an audience more hardened against anything that had to do with Jesus Christ. But when the power of the Holy Spirit broke through their animosity and hatred, they repented, believed, and were baptized.

The point for today is unmistakable: the church in its outreach to the world—including countless adherents of Judaism, Islam, and other religions—can still break down the barriers of prejudice and antagonism against the gospel of Christ only by the power "from on high," the anointing of the Holy Spirit. That power is still available. It did not simply come at Pentecost once and for all so that the church can presume that somehow she possesses it already. No, the power of the Holy Spirit is a gift from God—"the gift of the Holy Spirit"—and is an ongoing promise to believers of all generations. We recall again Peter's words regarding the gift of the Holy Spirit: "For the promise [of the Spirit] is to you and to your children and to all that are far off, every one whom the Lord our God calls to him" (Acts 2:38–39). The promise is to all believers—those "called to him"—down through the ages. It remains valid for the church in every day and generation.

Now we come to the truly critical point. The promised gift of the Holy Spirit must be received if the church is to move with maximum effectiveness in the power of that same Spirit. The fact that the true church is composed of people who have come to salvation is no guarantee of the reception of the gift of the Holy Spirit and its transcendent power for outreach to all nations. This does not mean that the church is without the Holy Spirit, for truly He dwells in all believers; nor does it mean that no outreach is possible, for His very inner presence can have far-reaching effects. However, there is the further Pentecostal gift of the Holy Spirit. This outpouring of the Spirit, which is possible for all believers, can endow the church with additional supernatural power. The urgent question remains: Has the church—in general and in particular—as it seeks to reach the world with the gospel received that power?

Returning to Acts, we need to recognize afresh that the outreach of the church was carried forward by Spirit-empowered people. A short time after Pentecost, following Jewish threats against Peter and John, the believers prayed, "Grant to thy servants to speak thy word with all boldness. . . . When they had prayed, the place in which they were gathered together was shaken; and they were all filled with the Holy Spirit and spoke the word of God with boldness" (Acts 4:29, 31). Thus the church at large received a powerful anointing of the Spirit for its witness. A little later we read, "With great power the apostles gave their testimony to the resurrection of the Lord Jesus" (v. 33). Thus the apostles continued in the power they had received at Pentecost for their testimony to Christ. The next two outstanding witnesses were Stephen (Acts 6 and 7) and Philip (Acts 8)—neither of them apostles. Both men were "full of the Spirit" (Acts 6:3, 5) and proclaimed the gospel mightily. The next, and most outstanding of all, was Saul of Tarsus (Paul). He was called by Christ—"he is a chosen instrument of mine to carry my name before the Gentiles and kings and the sons of Israel"—and for that purpose was "filled with the Holy Spirit" (Acts 9:15, 17). Thus, to repeat, the total missionary thrust of the church in the Book of Acts was carried forward by Spirit-endowed people.

Moreover, as was discussed in the previous section on the Great Commission, Peter, John, and Paul were particularly concerned that newly formed bodies of believers receive the same endowment of the Holy Spirit. Accordingly, the church—whether in Jerusalem, Samaria, Ephesus, or elsewhere—was endowed with power for the outreach of the gospel to the surrounding world.

So we return again to the essential and urgent question for the church in our time: Are we endowed with the missionary power that alone can mightily energize the church—any body of true believers—for the vital task ahead? Paul later asked some disciples at Ephesus, "Did you receive the Holy Spirit when you believed?" (Acts 19:2). Only if that question is answered affirmatively is it possible to make a powerful witness to the world.

Thus we come back to foundational matters. Whether the outreach of the church is local or far away, the all-essential matter is the endowment of the Holy Spirit. This was true for Jesus Himself, some years prior to His commissioning of the church, when at the Jordan River the Holy Spirit came upon Him and He then "returned in the power of the Spirit" (Luke 4:14) to preach the gospel. Incidentally, Peter made reference to this in his sermon to the Gentiles in Caesarea—"God anointed Jesus of Nazareth with the Holy Spirit and with power" (Acts 10:38). Jesus was anointed with the power of the Spirit; the early church in Acts was likewise so anointed. Can there be any less the need for this power in our own day?

As we face the near future hoping to carry the gospel to all the peoples of earth—a truly noble desire—we must reassess our own potential. It will not be enough to muster forces and dedicate full energy for the task: there must be, in addition, a baptism of the Holy Spirit from on high. Those who go forth must go as Spirit-empowered people; if they are not Spirit-empowered, they should receive the Spirit's anointing before any further endeavor occurs.[226] This must be the primary concern for the outreach of the church in these critical days.

2. Direction

By the enabling of the Holy Spirit the church is also given direction. In the Book of Acts the direction came from either the Holy Spirit or an angel of God; in either event the church experienced supernatural direction. At a number of critical points this direction was given. Let us note some of these instances.

In the early days the apostles were arrested and imprisoned. During the night, however, an angel of the Lord set them free, saying, "Go and stand in the temple and speak to the people all the words of this Life" (Acts 5:20). Following this direction, "they entered the temple at daybreak and taught" (v. 21). On another occasion an angel of the Lord said to Philip, "Rise and go toward the south to the road that goes down from Jerusalem to Gaza" (8:26). Philip obeyed, and when he arrived at the road, there was an Ethiopian eunuch seated in his chariot. Then "the Spirit said to Philip, 'Go up and join this chariot' " (v. 29). After he did so, the conversion and baptism of the Ethiopian occurred. Peter later was guided by the Holy Spirit to carry the gospel to the Gentiles in Caesarea. After Peter received a vision of a sheet from heaven containing unclean food, a voice spoke to him: "Rise, Peter; kill and eat" (10:13). While Peter was still pondering the vision, "the Spirit said to him . . . 'Rise and go down and accompany them' " to Caesarea (vv. 19–20). Peter would never have gone to "unclean" Gentiles of his own volition, but at the Spirit's command he went. As Peter later said, "The Spirit told me to go . . . making no distinction" (11:12).

At a gathering of prophets and teachers in the church at Antioch, "the Holy Spirit said, 'Set apart for me Barnabas and Saul for the work to which I have called them' " (13:2). Immediately after that they were "sent out by the Holy Spirit" (v. 4), and Paul's first missionary journey began. Significantly, in his second missionary tour, Paul and his companions "went through the region of Phrygia and Galatia, having been forbidden by the Holy Spirit to speak the word in Asia" (16:6). They obviously had planned to go into the province of Asia, but the Holy Spirit said no and set them on a different path. This occurred again when they made plans to go into Bithynia. Arriving at Mysia, "they attempted to go into Bithynia, but the Spirit of Jesus did not allow them; so, passing by Mysia, they went down to Troas" (vv. 7–8). After the Holy Spirit twice changed his itinerary,[227] Paul finally arrived at Troas and

[226]See *Renewal Theology*, 2:271–306, chapter 11, entitled "The Reception of the Holy Spirit" for a discussion of how this reception occurs. Especially note pages 293–306, section III, "Context," for particular details.

[227]The Scripture does not say *how* the Holy Spirit prevented Paul and Barnabas from

had a vision of a man from Macedonia crying out, "Come over to Macedonia and help us" (v. 9). As a result of this vision, Paul sailed across the Aegean Sea into what is now Europe and carried forward his missionary outreach.

This brief review of certain events in Acts should amply demonstrate the supernatural direction of outreach activity.[228] Whether the direction is designated as coming from an angel of God or the Holy Spirit (or the Spirit of Jesus), it is all of a piece: the Lord was in charge of the outreach of His church, and at one critical juncture after another, He specified the direction. Moreover, the Lord Himself had laid out a broad plan at the outset. Let us recall Acts 1:8: "You shall be my witnesses in Jerusalem and in all Judea and Samaria and to the end of the earth." And surely this general plan did unfold as the church first reached out into Jerusalem (Acts 1–7), Judea and Samaria (Acts 8–12, including Antioch of Syria), and then throughout the Roman Empire (Acts 13–28). However, the particulars—as we have noted—were directed by His Holy Spirit.

How much, then, did human planning affect the outreach of the church? Perhaps the best way of answering this is to look briefly at the apostles and elders in the Jerusalem church (Acts 15) when they discussed the issue of whether Gentile converts had to be circumcised if they were to receive salvation. There was "much debate" (v. 7) by the apostles and elders. Afterward Peter testified how uncircumcised Gentiles in Caesarea had received the gospel (vv. 7–11), and then Barnabas and Paul, making no reference to circumcision, spoke of their missionary work among the Gentiles (v. 12). James, the moderator of the meeting, then gave his judgment that circumcision should not be required of the Gentiles; rather, they should abstain from certain pagan activities. To this all the other apostles and elders agreed. They then chose certain leading men to take a letter to the Gentiles. The letter began, "It has seemed good to the Holy Spirit and to us. . ." (v. 28). Thus there was debate, testimony, decision making—all quite legitimate and important—but in the final analysis it was not they but the Holy Spirit who provided the basic answer and the direction. It was *not* "to us and the Holy Spirit" but "to the Holy Spirit and to us."

Although the event just described does not relate specifically to the outreach of the church (it dealt more with handling a critical problem within the Gentile churches), it demonstrates that being directed by the Holy Spirit does not exclude human discussion and decision making. Indeed, these are valuable in developing missionary strategy, in seeking to work together with other churches, in planning for the planting of churches among unreached people, in recognizing and seeking to deal with cross-cultural differences, and so on. It is exciting that there is an unparalleled

going into the province of Asia and into Bithynia. Perhaps it was by a prophetic utterance, as was likely the case earlier in Antioch. On a later occasion Paul declared that "the Holy Spirit solemnly testifies to me" (Acts 20:23 NASB). This could have been in a time of personal prayer, such as on a still later occasion when "the following night the Lord stood by him" (Acts 23:11) and gave encouragement and direction. However these occasions occurred, Paul was obviously very sensitive to the Spirit of the Lord.

[228]We could continue with Paul's intended journey to Rome and the frequent direction and intervention of the Holy Spirit (e.g., Acts 19:21; 20:22–23; 21:4, 11). It is not fully clear in these passages how much the Holy Spirit was determining all of Paul's actions; however, it is certain that Paul sought to rely on supernatural directions. In any event Paul was assured finally by an angel of the Lord: "You must stand before Caesar" (Acts 27:24).

effort today by many churches, missionary organizations, and parachurch bodies to carry the gospel "to the end of the earth." However, in the midst of all planning and action, it is urgent that the Holy Spirit be continually relied on for direction of the whole missionary enterprise. Whether it be leaders of the church at large or of a local body of Christians, they must constantly look to the Holy Spirit so that when decisions are made, those involved can say truly, "It seemed good to the Holy Spirit and to us. . . ." The Holy Spirit is the director of genuine missionary enterprises. Much time must be spent in listening to Him; and as we concur with His direction, the way ahead becomes increasingly clear.

There should always be a certain spontaneity about acting under the direction of the Spirit. We must never forget that even our best-laid missionary plans can be radically altered by the Holy Spirit. Remember that Paul and his company were prevented by the Holy Spirit from preaching in the province of Asia. Paul doubtless had planned to go there next to evangelize this important area with its large city of Ephesus. Strategically this made much sense, for after Ephesus on the coast of Asia had been evangelized, Paul could from there launch a missionary effort across the Aegean Sea into Greece. But the Holy Spirit said no—for *His* plan, contrary to the best human strategizing, was to reach Europe first with the gospel, then Ephesus and the province of Asia. So indeed it did work out. Paul returned from Greece by way of Ephesus, and still later in Ephesus he preached for two years "so that all the residents of Asia heard the word of the Lord, both Jews and Greeks" (Acts 19:10). The Holy Spirit had His own strategy, and by Paul's readiness to hear and act with spontaneous obedience, the cause of Christ went forward mightily.

The critically important matter for the church is to be so sensitive to the presence of the Holy Spirit that His guidance will be constantly recognized. This by no means derogates from our planning—indeed, we will give even more assiduous effort in that connection. But all that we do must be under the immediate direction of the Holy Spirit. He alone knows what steps should next be taken, how the many unreached peoples are to be reached, and when the task of evangelization will be completed. Let us then look with renewed zeal to the leading of the Spirit of the Lord.

3. *Supernatural Manifestations*

The outreach of the church should be accompanied by spiritual manifestations: miracles, signs, wonders. These manifestations are attestations to the validity of the gospel proclamation. They often awaken interest and make for receptiveness to the gospel.[229]

This was doubtless the case on the Day of Pentecost. Among the extraordinary signs was the activity of one hundred and twenty persons speaking in other tongues. Before Peter preached the message that resulted in the salvation of three thousand people, the multitude had assembled as a result of this strange phenomenon: "At this sound the multitude came together, and they were bewildered, because each one heard them speaking in his own language" (Acts 2:6). They heard the disciples declaring in their own tongues "the mighty works of God" (v. 11). This then prepared the way for Peter's proclamation of the gospel and for the coming of many to salvation. So it was that the phenomenon of tongues gave supernatural attestation to the validity of what was to take place after that.

[229]For what follows see also *Renewal Theology*, 2:250–63.

It is also significant that Peter, after explaining the miracle of tongues as the fulfillment of a prophecy by Joel, spoke immediately of Jesus: "Jesus of Nazareth, a man attested[230] to you by God with mighty works [i.e., miracles] and wonders and signs which God did through him in your midst, as you yourselves know. . ." (Acts 2:22). The attestation, the accreditation, of Jesus was His miracles. Many refused to believe in spite of His miraculous signs; however, many others were led by them to a vital faith. So it was with the miracle of tongues on the Day of Pentecost: the way was prepared for the good news of salvation.

The next recorded event in Acts was the healing through Peter and John of a man born lame. The lame man was known by people because he was daily carried to the Beautiful Gate of the temple to beg alms. The healing was unmistakably a miracle, so that people "were filled with wonder and amazement" (Acts 3:10). A large audience gathered around Peter and John, and the healed man who clung to them. After declaring that Jesus had performed this miracle, Peter again preached the gospel; "Repent therefore," he urged them, "and turn again, that your sins may be blotted out" (v. 19). The result was that "many of those who heard the word believed; and the number of men came to about five thousand" (4:4). A miracle of supernatural healing had made way for the hearing and believing of the gospel!

But it was not only apostles who were used by the Lord in supernatural manifestations. After Peter and John had been threatened by the Sanhedrin and ordered to desist from preaching, the company of disciples prayed, "Lord, look upon their threats, and grant to thy servants to speak thy word with all boldness, while thou stretchest out thy hand to heal, and signs and wonders are performed through the name of thy holy servant Jesus" (Acts 4:29–30). Their prayer was indeed heard, for "they were all filled with the Holy Spirit and spoke the word of God with boldness" (v. 31), and signs and wonders were performed through the apostles (5:12) and various other members of the church.

This latter point becomes apparent in the later narratives about Stephen and Philip. Stephen was soon preaching the gospel and, "full of grace and power, did great wonders and signs among the people" (Acts 6:8). Philip—later called "the evangelist" (Acts 21:8)—went to a city in Samaria and proclaimed Christ. But first Philip got a hearing through his preaching and working of miracles: "The multitudes with one accord gave heed to what was said by Philip, when they heard him and saw the signs which he did. For unclean spirits came out of many . . . and many who were paralyzed or lame were healed" (Acts 8:6–7). Many of these Samaritans came to believe and were baptized (v. 12). Thus two "table servers" (!)—definitely not apostles—likewise proclaimed the gospel with accompanying spiritual manifestations.[231]

So it is that all Christians—apostles and others alike—are called to proclaim the gospel in the context of supernatural manifestations. According to Mark 16—as earlier noted in part—Jesus had commanded His disciples to preach the gospel. Then He added, "And these signs will accompany those who believe: in my name they will cast out demons; they will speak in new

---

[230]"Accredited" (NIV). The Greek word is *apodedeigmenon*.

[231]The result of Stephen's preaching, unlike that of Philip, was *not* that a multitude received the gospel; rather, Stephen was stoned to death by the Jewish high council. Nonetheless his miracles prepared the way for the preaching of Christ.

tongues; they will pick up serpents, and if they drink any deadly thing, it will not hurt them;[232] they will lay their hands on the sick, and they will recover" (vv. 17–18). Then the climax: "And they went forth and preached everywhere, while the Lord worked with them and confirmed the message by the signs that attended it" (v. 20). The supernatural manifestations were—and are—confirmations of and attestations to the validity of the gospel message.

We should note one further passage in Acts relating to this matter. Paul and Barnabas preached in Iconium with the result that many Jews and Greeks came to the Lord (Acts 14:1). Later the Scripture reads, "So they [Paul and Barnabas] remained for a long time, speaking boldly for the Lord, who bore witness to the word of his grace, granting signs and wonders to be done by their hands" (v. 3). The Lord Himself "bore witness"—confirmed, attested—the message of saving grace by supernatural manifestations.

All that has been said above about supernatural manifestations has vital relevance for the ongoing church. Too often one hears it said that miracles—signs and wonders—belonged only to the ministry of the apostles, that miracles were apostolic credentials, so that with the passing of the apostles signs and wonders also passed away. In this connection Paul's words in 2 Corinthians 12:12 are sometimes quoted: "The signs of a true apostle were performed among you in all patience, with signs and wonders and mighty works." However, Paul is not here saying that only an apostle can perform miracles; it is rather that in comparison with certain "super-apostles"[233] (v. 11 NIV), probably false apostles,[234] the miracles performed were validations of his genuine apostleship. Indeed, Paul could not possibly have meant that only an apostle could perform miracles, for in 1 Corinthians he had earlier spoken of miracles as being one of the gifts of the Holy Spirit that any member of the body might manifest: "to another [person] the working of miracles" (12:10). In his letter to the Galatians Paul also refers to Christ as "he who supplies the Spirit to you and works miracles among you" (3:5). So the working of miracles surely occurred beyond the apostolic period.[235] We have earlier observed in the brief survey of supernatural manifestations in Acts that Stephen and Philip worked miracles and that indeed members of the whole church prayed for miracles to be wrought through themselves. We also have recalled the words in Mark 16 that refer to believers in general (not just apostles) as working miracles and that wherever they went in proclaiming the gospel, signs and wonders attended the proclamation.

So let us again emphasize (it would be hard to do so too strongly) that we

[232]In regard to picking up serpents and drinking something deadly: this does *not* mean that believers should actively seek to do such things to prove the validity of the gospel. These are *protectional* statements, e.g., in the case of Paul who accidentally picked up a serpent but was not harmed by it (Acts 28:1–6). (For a fuller comment see *Renewal Theology*, 2:377, n. 142.)

[233]Paul is using irony in speaking about others who arrogantly regarded themselves as apostles.

[234]Note also 2 Corinthians 11:5 and 13, where Paul may be drawing a connection between "super-apostles" and "false apostles." On this matter see Philip E. Hughes, *The Second Epistle to the Corinthians*, NICNT, 378–80, 454–56.

[235]Another argument, sometimes heard, is that, in addition to the apostles themselves, only those on whom they laid hands, the so-called apostolic circle, could perform miracles. This argument cannot stand up in light of 1 Corinthians 12 and Galatians 3. (For further discussion of this matter see *Renewal Theology*, 1:162–68.)

should expect supernatural manifestations still to accompany the proclamation of the gospel. This is not to say that people are unable to hear and believe without such manifestations, for surely countless numbers have come to Christ by the preaching of the Word (the Spirit applying the message) without any outward evidence of signs and wonders. However, the quite visible fact, for example, of a supernatural healing lends concrete credibility to the message, namely, that even as the body has been healed, so likewise the spirit can be or has been.[236] Surely the same Lord who has healed a diseased body can save a sin-sick soul.

Why, we may ask, is the church so often lacking in the realm of signs and wonders? For one thing, it may be that the church is first of all lacking in the power of the Spirit. This power was discussed earlier in this section. If the enabling power is minimal or not present, we can hardly expect that the message will be accompanied by signs and wonders. In this connection a statement of Paul about his worldwide ministry is relevant. He says to the Christians in Rome: "Christ has wrought through me to win obedience from the Gentiles, by word and deed, by the power of signs and wonders, by the power of the Holy Spirit,[237] so that from Jerusalem and as far round as Illyricum I have fully preached the gospel of Christ" (Rom. 15:18–19). "The power of signs and wonders" is set next to "the power of the Holy Spirit," for surely there is a vital connection. If the church truly operates in the power of the Spirit, there should be supernatural manifestations.

As we have just noted, Paul speaks about winning "obedience from the Gentiles"—and this in part by "the power of signs and wonders." Surely it is no less true today that the secular world needs not only to hear the word of the gospel but also to see its supernatural manifestations. It is often said that if the proclamation of the church is to be truly heard, the church should do a better job of accompanying the word by deeds of love and concern for the poor, the downtrodden, the alienated in society. However true it is that the world needs to see the church active in word and deed (and who can deny the importance of both?), the gospel is fully evidenced only when also accompanied by "signs and wonders." There are many humanitarian agencies that can serve the physical, economic, and social needs of people, but *none outside the church* that can accompany word and deed with signs and wonders. If, and when, that happens—a supernatural healing, a demon cast out, even a raising of someone from the dead (all of which occurred in the New Testament church)—people are bound to take notice. When they begin to ask, How did this happen? it is a quick step to proclaim the living Christ, and as a result many come to faith in Him.[238]

[236]Supernatural manifestations may precede or follow a spiritual conversion. In the former case the way is prepared for the reception of salvation; in the latter, salvation is visibly confirmed.

[237]There seems to be a crescendo here: Paul moves from word and deed to signs and wonders and then to the power of the Holy Spirit.

[238]It is sometimes said that a faith based on miracles is superficial faith. E.g., in the Gospel of John we read that "many believed in his [Christ's] name when they saw the signs which he did; but Jesus did not trust himself to them . . . for he himself knew what was in man" (2:23–25). However, this same Gospel includes many miracles, and near the end the author writes, "Jesus did many other signs in the presence of the disciples . . . but these are written that you may believe that Jesus is the Christ, the Son of God, and that believing you may

As we contemplate the yet uncompleted missionary task of the church, the importance of signs and wonders looms increasingly large. For example, in reaching out to the Muslim world that is adamantly opposed to any proclamation of the Christian gospel, there can be no surer way to break through hostility and opposition than for a miracle of healing, or some other, to occur in the name of Jesus. In many animistic cultures where shamans and witch doctors often demonstrate demonic magical powers, our Christian witness must go beyond words of faith and deeds of love into the power dimension of the Holy Spirit who alone can offset demonic forces and demonstrate the validity of Christ and the Christian faith. In our own secular society, people need to see churches whose proclamation of Christ is in "demonstration of the Spirit's power,"[239] so that by this very demonstration in "signs and wonders" they will be aware that something more than pious words and deeds is taking place. Thus there is critical need today for "power evangelism"[240] whether at home or abroad.

Let me conclude by commenting on three matters. First, signs and wonders are not only visible attestations of the validity of the gospel proclamation, but they are also vitally connected with the gospel itself. For example, Jesus came both proclaiming the good news of the kingdom and healing the sick: "He went about all Galilee . . . preaching the gospel of the kingdom[241] and healing every disease and every infirmity among the people" (Matt. 4:23). The conjunction "and" is quite important, for it signifies that Jesus' ministry included both preaching and healing. Both are aspects of God's love and concern.[242] Hence true evangelism (gospel preaching) that results in the salvation of people should be accompanied by healings wherever needed. It is surely not enough (Jesus being our example) to bring a person to salvation and leave him or her in bodily misery.[243]

have life in his name" (20:30–31). If such signs continue today (and Jesus promised they would), then the world has the living demonstration of the reality of Jesus Christ. We may proclaim the biblical miracles of Jesus, and many indeed will believe; but even more compelling to faith is the occurrence of miracles in our own time.

[239]Paul's words in 1 Corinthians 2:4: "My message and my preaching were not with wise and persuasive words, but with a demonstration of the Spirit's power" (NIV). The Greek word for "demonstration," *apodeixis*, may also be translated "proof" (see BAGD). Gordon Fee writes that "the 'proof' lies not in compelling rhetoric, but in the accompanying visible ἀποδείξει of the Spirit's power" (*First Epistle to the Corinthians*, NICNT, 95, n.28). The visible "demonstration" or "proof" suggests Paul's reference in Romans 15 to "signs and wonders."

[240]John Wimber writes, "Most evangelism practiced in the West lacks the power seen in New Testament evangelism" (*Power Evangelism*, 38–39). See also "Appendix B: Signs and Wonders in the Twentieth Century."

[241]This gospel relates to salvation through repentance and faith. According to the Gospel of Mark, "Jesus came into Galilee, preaching the gospel of God [= the kingdom], and saying, 'The time is fulfilled, and the kingdom of God is at hand; repent, and believe in the gospel' " (1:14–15).

[242]In a later place in the gospel of Matthew, just after the same statement about preaching the gospel and healing every disease, the text reads, "When he [Jesus] saw the crowds, he had compassion for them, because they were harassed and helpless, like sheep without a shepherd" (9:36). Jesus' compassion for these "harassed and helpless" ones was for their distress of both soul and body.

[243]We may recall the incident in Jesus' ministry when he first forgave a person, saying,

Thus while "signs and wonders" are not the gospel itself, true evangelism should lead directly to a ministry to people's needs occurring through supernatural acts of healing, deliverance, and the like.

Second, signs and wonders are essential in the warfare against Satan and his powers. I have earlier mentioned animistic cultures where demonic powers operate; however, these powers are by no means limited to certain "dark" parts of the world: they are everywhere present. Occult practices, magic rituals, satanic activities—many of which include supernatural manifestations—seem to be increasingly prevalent. Indeed, such manifestations could be preparing the way for "the man of lawlessness,"[244] whose coming will be "in accordance with the work of Satan displayed in all kinds of counterfeit miracles, signs and wonders" (2 Thess. 2:9 NIV). "Counterfeit miracles," literally "miracles of a lie,"[245] do occur through Satan and can be counteracted only by genuine miracles that come from God through the Holy Spirit. Only the *Holy* Spirit can overcome *unholy* spirits, and bring genuine—not counterfeit—healing and deliverance to people in bondage. Signs and wonders, representing the power of God, will surely be more and more needed in the end times to stand against Satan and his demonic forces.

Third, signs and wonders are also signs of the coming age. Every time a body is healed, a demon cast out, or another miracle wrought, this is a pointer to the coming age when bodies are perfected, demons totally abolished, and God's power everywhere manifested. Miracles may be described as "powers of the age to come" (Heb. 6:5), which break in on our present age and signify the totality and perfection of what is yet to come. As that future age draws nearer and nearer, we may by God's power and grace see a multiplying of signs and wonders. It will not be our doing but God's as He works through His people, the church, moving mightily to consummate His kingdom. To God be the glory!

C. The Whole Human Condition

Thus far in relation to outreach we have concentrated on the Great Commission and its fulfillment through the enabling of the Holy Spirit. The focus has been on the human spiritual condition to which the gospel is primarily addressed. Finally, we need to recognize that the outreach of the church should also include other aspects of life: the whole human condition.

A key statement in this regard is found in Peter's words about Jesus in Acts 10:38: "He went about doing good." The primary matter for Jesus was the proclamation of the gospel, the good news of salvation, but He also reached out to all human need. "Doing good" often included supernatural acts of healing[246] and other miracles. However, He ministered to the whole human condition: to the spiritual primarily but also to the physical and emotional needs of people. So it should be with those who belong to Christ: not only proclaiming the gospel in the power of His miracle-working Spirit but also doing good, in His name, to all in need.

God Himself is One who does good to all people. At one time Paul addressed a Gentile audience, saying, "He [God] did good and gave you from

---

"Man, your sins are forgiven you" and then healed his physical paralysis, saying, "Rise, take up your bed and go home" (Luke 5:20, 24).

[244]For more on "the man of lawlessness [or 'sin']" see pages 334–39.

[245]The Greek phrase is *terasin pseudous*.

[246]Peter continues by adding, "and healing all who were oppressed by the devil."

heaven rains and fruitful seasons, satisfying your hearts with food and gladness'' (Acts 14:17). This recalls Jesus' words about the Father in heaven: ''He makes his sun rise on the evil and the good, and sends rain on the just and the unjust'' (Matt. 5:45). It follows that if God our Father does good to Gentile unbelievers and to both evil and good, just and unjust people, then the people of God, the church, should do the same. Jesus went about doing good; the Father constantly does good. Can Christians act otherwise?

The theme of doing good, or good deeds, is frequently found in the New Testament. For example, Paul writes to the church in Corinth: ''Nobody should seek his own good, but the good of others'' (1 Cor. 10:24 NIV). To the Thessalonians Paul says, ''See that none of you repays evil for evil, but always seek to do good to one another and to all [people]'' (1 Thess. 5:15). Paul tells Titus ''to be ready to do whatever is good'' so that ''those who have trusted in God may be careful to devote themselves to doing what is good. These things are excellent and profitable for everyone'' (3:1, 8 NIV). In his first letter Peter urges his readers, ''Live such good lives among the pagans that, though they accuse you of doing wrong, they may see your good deeds and glorify God'' (2:12 NIV).[247] In summary, instead of seeking one's own good, or repaying evil for evil, always strive to do good to others; for good deeds are profitable to people. Even unbelievers, often critical of Christians, when they see their deeds, will glorify God.

Good deeds thus represent an important outreach of the church. Even if such deeds are not aimed directly at fulfilling the Great Commission, they are an expression of the goodness of God the Father and Christ the Son in relation to all mankind. Hence, there is *no* human need that should be outside the concern of the church.

This last statement may call for further clarification. I do not mean that the church should become a humanitarian agency whose focus is on bodily needs and social ills. Always its priority must remain with the far deeper spiritual problems of people. However, even as human beings are corporeal entities set within a social context, the church must also be concerned for people in their total human condition. Doing good, then, means to reach out beyond ministering the gospel of salvation to all aspects of human life.

Here we may recall Jesus' own concern for doing good as set forth in His words about the Day of Judgment: ''The King [Christ] will say to those at his right hand 'Come, O blessed of my Father, inherit the kingdom prepared for you from the foundation of the world; for I was hungry and you gave me food, I was thirsty and you gave me drink, I was a stranger and you welcomed me, I was naked and you clothed me, I was sick and you visited me, I was in prison and you came to me' '' (Matt. 25:34–36). Then remember also His further words: '' 'Truly, I say to you, as you did it to one of the least of these my brethren, you did it to me' '' (v. 40). ''Brethren'' may refer to other disciples of Christ, hence believers, or, by extension, to any who are in need: the starving, the outcasts of society, the destitute and the miserable, the sick and abandoned, those isolated in prison.[248]

---

[247]For other scriptures on doing good, or good deeds, see especially Romans 12:21; Galatians 6:10; 2 Thessalonians 2:17; 1 Timothy 2:10; 5:10; Titus 2:7, 14; 3:14; Hebrews 10:24; 13:16.

[248]According to EGT, ''The brethren are the Christian poor and needy and suffering, in

The importance of doing good could hardly be more highlighted than in this Judgment-Day scene; for every such good activity is actually directed to Christ Himself. Further, those who do such good are "the righteous" who will "go away into eternal life"[249] (v. 46). This last statement adds a note of ultimate urgency to the importance of doing good.

Thus there can be no excuse for the church to minimize or overlook the need for doing good deeds. However true that the primary outreach of the church must always be evangelistic, it cannot, dare not, neglect doing good to all people, whatever their situation of need. Such neglect cannot be found in a church that truly follows the example of Jesus both in His ministry and His teaching.

The church is always in danger of going to one extreme or another—evangelism *or* social action. Some so-called evangelical churches have so emphasized the call to salvation as to play down, or perhaps be antagonistic to, any stress on other human needs. Even the emphasis on evangelism with miraculous signs accompanying[250] *can* be an evasion of helping to alleviate broader human needs.[251] Other so-called liberal churches have tilted so strongly in the direction of humanitarian concerns as practically to identify the gospel with ministry to the poor and neglected. Thereby they leave out, even forsake, the primary need of all people for salvation. *The church must maintain both.* This does not mean an equality between the gospel of salvation and the "social gospel,"[252] for the gospel *is* the message of salvation and must have priority. However, the meeting of other human, social needs must not be neglected.[253]

The proper concern of the church for human needs does not mean that it is to act as a political force to secure the meeting of these needs. The civil gov-

---

the first place, but ultimately and inferentially any suffering people anywhere . . . the brethren of the Son of man are the insignificant of mankind, those likely to be overlooked, despised, neglected" (1:306).

[249]This does not mean salvation by works; it is rather that the righteous (the *dikaioi*) give evidence of their righteousness (or salvation) by the good works they perform. This is in line with what Jesus had said earlier: "The tree is known by its fruit" (Matt. 12:33). Paul later declared that God "will render to every man according to his deeds, to those who by perseverance in doing good seek for glory and honor and immortality, eternal life" (Rom. 2:6–7 NASB).

[250]Recall the previous discussion of "Supernatural Manifestations" regarding miraculous signs.

[251]In the discussion of supernatural signs, I talked about many miracles that relate to human needs. However, the main point there was the attestation of such supernatural manifestations to the validity of the gospel. Now I am concerned to emphasize the importance of reaching out to all human needs.

[252]The "social gospel" is a term often applied to a movement in theologically liberal Protestant thought of the late nineteenth and early twentieth century that tended to replace the gospel of salvation with concern for the transformation of society. A leading exponent of this movement was Walter Rauschenbusch. See especially his books *Christianity and the Social Crisis* (1907) and *A Theology for the Social Gospel* (1917).

[253]The "Manila Manifesto" of 1989, a statement of evangelicals from some 170 countries, declares, "Evangelism is primary because our chief concern is with the gospel, that all people may have the opportunity to accept Jesus Christ as Lord and Savior. . . . In a spirit of humility we are to preach and teach, minister to the sick, feed the hungry, care for prisoners, help the disadvantaged and handicapped, and deliver the oppressed . . . good news and good works are inseparable" (from the section entitled "The Gospel and Social Responsibility").

ernment, not the church, exists for the express purpose of securing and enforcing justice for all people.[254] The church may, and should, speak out against societal evil;[255] however, the church's role is best fulfilled when it operates in a positive and personal manner to help the needy and distressed.

The church is to *do* good. Thereby it will follow the example of God in Christ and be a blessing to all people.

EXCURSUS: THE SALT OF THE EARTH

In the Sermon on the Mount Jesus declared to His disciples: "You are the salt of the earth" (Matt. 5:13). By such words Jesus propounds a vital aspect of outreach: those who follow Him, thus the church, are to be salt to the world.[256]

Preceding these words are the Beatitudes (Matt. 5:3–12), in which Jesus speaks a number of blessings on His disciples. Those blessed are the poor in spirit, those who mourn, the meek (or gentle), those who hunger and thirst after righteousness, the merciful, the pure in heart, the peacemakers, and those who are persecuted for righteousness' sake. Next Jesus declares that those who are so blessed are the salt of the earth. In saying this, Jesus is not referring to the evangelization of the world (as later in the Great Commission) but to the positive effect that His disciples who are poor in spirit, mourn, etc., have on other people. Embodying such characteristics, Jesus' disciples are the salt of the earth.

The use of the word "salt" suggests three things. First, salt is a *seasoning* agent. In the Old Testament salt was used to season incense[257] and other offerings.[258] Salt is also valuable for the taste of food: "Can that which is tasteless be eaten without salt?" (Job 6:6). In the New Testament Paul writes believers, "Conduct yourselves with wisdom toward outsiders, making the most of the opportunity. Let your speech always be with grace, seasoned, as it were, with salt, so that you may know how you should respond to each person" (Col. 4:5–6 NASB). Salt is not depicted here as material salt but as a special flavor of gracious speech to "outsiders," that is, to unbelievers.

In reaching out to those who are not Christians, much wisdom is needed not only in what one says but also in how one says it. Unbelievers may have questions, perhaps objections, even angry opposition. This, however, is an open opportunity for wise and gracious speech. Jesus Himself said to His disciples, "I will give you a mouth and wisdom, which none of your adversaries will be able to withstand or contradict" (Luke 21:15). Such inspired wisdom is all the more enhanced when it is spoken "with grace . . . seasoned with salt." This suggests speech that is flavored with graciousness, pleasantness,[259] even winsomeness.[260] Such

---

[254]See infra chapter 7, "The Church and Civil Government."

[255]Such evils as racial discrimination, sexual immorality, drug abuse, abortion, and violence.

[256]The NEB reads "salt to the world." The Greek text has *halas tēs gēs*, literally "salt of the earth"; however, the meaning of the phrase is well captured by the NEB translation.

[257]Exodus 30:34–35—"The LORD said to Moses . . . make an incense blended as by the perfumer, seasoned with salt."

[258]Leviticus 2:13—"You shall season all your cereal [or 'grain'] offerings with salt . . . with all your offerings you shall offer salt." For the salting of bloody offerings, see Ezekiel 43:23–24.

[259]The NEB translates: "Let your conversation be always gracious, and never insipid"! Insipid speech is never very engaging.

speech is not easy, for the temptation to respond irascibly and unpleasantly is always at hand. Peter, incidentally, adds the note of gentleness and respect: "Always be prepared to give an answer to everyone who asks you to give the reason for the hope that you have. But do this with gentleness and respect" (1 Peter 3:15 NIV). Speech, both pleasant and gentle, is sure to be effective.

"You are the salt of the earth" refers, in part at least, to the fact that Jesus' disciples in their speech and behavior are to add flavor to a world that is rather bland and often dull. Sophisticated and witty speech is presumably a mark of the highly civilized, but such speech cannot compare with that of a Christian whose conversation is gracious and pleasant and wholly directed to bless others. In regard to manner of life, there is nothing in the world, or in worldly ways, that can withstand one who embodies such Beatitudes as humility, gentleness, peaceableness, and mercy. Without those who salt the earth with such manner of speech and life, the earth can be a barren and insipid place in which to live.

Second, salt also suggests *preservation*. The preservative character of salt has long been recognized. Indeed in biblical times, and until recently, salt was an absolute necessity for preserving food. In the Old Testament apocryphal book of Ecclesiasticus is this statement: "Basic to all the needs of man's life are water and fire and iron and salt" (39:26). Salt alone could keep food from putrefying, and so it was essential to life itself.

It is interesting that there is also reference in the Old Testament to a "covenant of salt." This is spoken of in relation to God's continuing covenant with Israel[261] and in regard to the house of Aaron[262] and to David's kingship.[263] The enduring character of these various covenants was confirmed by the sprinkling and mixing of salt.[264] Salt thus symbolized preservation of the covenant through all the years ahead.

Now we return to Jesus' words "You are the salt of the earth." This statement suggests salt not only as a seasoning (previously discussed) but also as a preservative. The disciples of Jesus are to be a preserving force throughout the earth. They are not to withdraw into an ascetic lifestyle (what good is salt in an isolated pile?) but are to act as salt in the preservation of the world from putrefaction and corruption. Such preservation can occur only as Christian believers, the people of God, mix in with the surrounding world and by their moral and spiritual vigor counteract evil and strengthen the good.

In another statement Jesus says, "Have salt in yourselves, and be at peace with one another" (Mark 9:50). Here, then, is a connection between salt and peace that, by implication, may refer to the preservation of peace (cf. "Blessed are the peacemakers") and stability in the world around. Christians by being salt are an essential preserva-

[260]The saying "Christianity to win must be winsome" carries much truth.

[261]Leviticus 2:13: "the salt of the covenant with your God."

[262]Numbers 18:19: God said to Aaron, "It is a covenant of salt for ever before the LORD for you and for your offspring with you." (This was in reference to the "holy offerings" given to Aaron's house "as a perpetual due.")

[263]2 Chronicles 13:5—"Ought you not to know that the LORD God of Israel gave the kingship over Israel for ever to David and his sons by a covenant of salt?"

[264]Possibly in a special covenantal ceremony of shared food.

tive force in an earth always tending to degenerate and disintegrate.[265]

Third, salt also serves for *purification*. Here we may note the Old Testament account of the prophet Elisha and the men of Jericho who complained about the bad water there. Elisha said to them, "Bring me a new bowl, and put salt in it" (2 Kings 2:20). After they brought it to him, Elisha threw salt into the city's polluted spring, with the result that, as the writer puts it, "the water has been wholesome to this day" (v. 22). There are also the words in Ezekiel relating to a newborn infant being "rubbed with salt" (16:4), probably referring to the medicinal and antiseptic properties of salt.

Again, we hear the words of Jesus to His disciples when He said, "You are the salt of the earth." His followers are to be a kind of moral disinfectant in a dirty and polluted world. Two of the Beatitudes are particularly relevant in this regard: "Blessed are those who hunger and thirst for righteousness" and "Blessed are the pure in heart." Believers who truly hunger and thirst for righteousness and whose hearts are pure will have a pervasive influence on an unrighteous and impure world. They are like salt that is totally unlike the medium into which it is put, but which serves to cleanse and purify by its very presence.

All of this means that Christians whose lives evidence cleanness and purity have a salutary effect on the surrounding world. Without their salt sprinkled on an evil world, things can only become worse. Christians as the people of God have a great responsibility by their manner of speech and life to bring some measure of purity and wholesomeness across the face of the earth.

Unfortunately we cannot stop at this point with all the favorable things said about Christians being the salt of the earth. It is surely true that as salt they serve to season, preserve, and purify the earth. But what if believers lose their saltiness? Here we must listen to Jesus' further words. After He said, "You are the salt of the earth," He added, "But if the salt loses its saltiness,[266] how can it be made salty again? It is no longer good for anything, except to be thrown out and trampled by men" (Matt. 5:13 NIV). The parallel words in Luke read, "Salt is good, but if it loses its saltiness, how can it be made salty again? It is fit neither for the soil nor for the manure pile;[267] it is thrown out" (14:34–35 NIV). In the Markan account, after asking, "How can you make it salty again?" Jesus adds, "Have salt in yourselves" (9:50 NIV). This stresses the urgency of believers' having and therefore keeping salt in their lives.

Jesus' words point up two things. First, there is the real danger of Christians losing their saltiness. There is no automatic continuance in such virtues

[265]In connection with Mark 9:50 Alan Cole writes, "Christians are to be the moral preservative of the world; they are to savour life, to season it, and also to stop it from becoming utterly corrupt" (*The Gospel According to St. Mark*, TNTC, 154).

[266]Is this literally possible, since salt, sodium chloride, is a stable compound? R. T. France makes a helpful comment: "Strictly, pure salt cannot lose its salinity, but the impure 'salt' dug from the shores of the Dead Sea could gradually become unsalty as the active sodium chloride dissolved" (*Matthew*, TNTC, 112). France wisely adds, "In any case Jesus was not teaching chemistry, but using a powerful biblical image."

[267]Thus useless as a fertilizer: "Tasteless salt has no immediate or future use as a fertilizer" (S. M. Gilmour, *Luke*, IB, 263). Hence Jesus' words may mean that "it is useless to put it [salt] on the land forthwith or to keep it on the manure-heap for future use" (N. Geldenhuys, *The Gospel of Luke*, NICNT, 400).

as humility, gentleness, hunger for righteousness, mercifulness, purity of heart, and peacemaking; these can be lost amid the pressures of life in the world. Pride, harshness, materialism, an unforgiving spirit, impure desires, quarrelsomeness, and the like may gradually set in. No longer do such believers know personal beatitude, but, even worse, they are no more a blessing to others. In this way the salt has lost its savor, and the earth is missing its vital seasoning, preserving, and purifying properties. What a loss to the earth when this happens! Second, not only may Christians lose their salt, but also—and this is a very sobering fact—since they are no longer a blessing to others, the opposite may occur. They may be "thrown out and trampled," that is, disregarded and trodden underfoot by the people of earth. They are "no longer good for anything" in terms of being a blessing to the world and thus deserve only to be cast aside.

Little wonder that Jesus said, "Have salt in yourselves." Thus, do not lose your saltiness, but constantly serve to season, preserve, and purify the earth. Remember too—and finally—salt is of no use by itself; its only worth is that of being spread abroad. When believers truly salt the earth, the earth is a far better place in which to live.[268]

[268]At this point there could be another excursus on Jesus' next words beginning, "You are the light of the world" (Matt. 5:14). Even as God's people ought not to lose their saltiness, so they should not hide their light "under a bushel" (v. 15). Moreover, even as salt is a blessing, so is the light shining: people will "see your good works and give glory to your Father who is in heaven" (v. 16). However, I am not continuing with a discussion of these equally compelling words of Jesus because I have dealt with Christians as light in *Renewal Theology*, 2:420–27.

5

Ministry

We come now to a study of the ministry of the church. Our concern will be with those who carry forward the purposes of worship, upbuilding, and outreach. Let us proceed by considering ministry in terms of the whole church, various equipping ministries, and church government.

I. THE WHOLE CHURCH

A. All Christians Are Ministers

It is important at the outset to stress the common ministry of the church. Jesus declared about Himself: "The Son of man came not to be ministered unto, but to minister" (Mark 10:45 KJV). To minister is to serve.[1] Hence all who follow Jesus in His church are called upon to serve, to minister in His name.

Thus whatever the particular place people occupy in the church of Jesus Christ, all are called upon to be ministers. The apostle Paul speaks of himself as "a minister": "the gospel . . . of which I, Paul, became a minister"[2] (Col. 1:23). But he also speaks of "the work of ministry"[3] (Eph. 4:12) as that in which all believers are involved.[4] We are all called to be ministers of Jesus Christ.

Further, whatever may be said about church leaders as occupying seemingly higher or more important positions, all are ministers, that is, servants. Paul writes about Apollos and himself: "What then is Apollos? What is Paul?

---

[1]The Greek word translated in the KJV above as "minister" is a form of *diakoneō*. "Serve" is now the more common translation.

[2]The Greek word is *diakonos*.

[3]The Greek word is *diakonias*.

[4]We will shortly consider the various roles of apostles, prophets, evangelists, and pastors and teachers who "equip the saints for the work of ministry" (NRSV). Accordingly, while Paul an apostle is "a minister," so likewise are "the saints" (believers), who are equipped by the apostles and others. Incidentally, the RSV translation (similarly KJV) of Ephesians 4:12—"for the equipment of the saints, for the work of ministry"—is misleading. When a comma is used (it is not found in NRSV, NASB, NIV, or NEB), the statement suggests that the equipping of saints is one thing, and the work of ministry ("the ministry" KJV) is another; therefore, ministry relates only to certain persons. No, *all*, whatever their position, are involved in ministry.

Servants[5] through whom you believed" (1 Cor. 3:5). Servants—by no means masters or lords! Indeed, Paul goes so far as to call himself a "bond-servant" or "slave" in regard to the Corinthians: "We do not preach ourselves but Christ Jesus as Lord, and ourselves as your bond-servants [or 'slaves'][6] for Jesus' sake" (2 Cor. 4:5 NASB). Christ is the only Lord, so that Christians in high positions are still servants, even slaves, of all others. They, like all believers, are ministers of Christ.

Accordingly, it is a mistake to regard only certain persons in the church as ministers. In some churches the pastor is frequently referred to as "the minister," implying that other persons do not minister at all. It is significant historically that whereas the Reformation stressed the priesthood of all believers,[7] there was not the same emphasis on the ministry of all believers. The Second Helvetic Confession (1566), for example, declared: "The ministry . . . and the priesthood are things far different one from the other. For the priesthood is common to all Christians; not so is the ministry."[8] Surely there is a difference between the ordained ministry of the word[9] and other forms of ministry; however, "the ministry" *is* common to all Christians.

It is important to recognize this common ministry. When we realize afresh that all Christians are ministers, it helps to close the gap between those who think too highly of their ministry ("I am *the minister*") and those who think too lowly ("I am *no minister* at all"). We need to emphasize that all Christians by their very identification with Christ are ministers. *Together* we are ministers, that is, servants of Him who "came to minister." Ministry through servanthood must be the way of all who truly belong to Jesus Christ.

B. All Christians Are Priests

We must also emphasize that all Christians are priests by virtue of what is commonly known as "the priesthood of all believers."

Peter in his first letter writes, "You are a chosen race, a royal priesthood. . ." (2:9). He is addressing "the exiles of the Dispersion" (1:1), scattered Christians who compose a priesthood. In the Old Testament covenant with Israel God said, "If you will obey my voice and keep my covenant . . . you shall be to me a kingdom of priests" (Exod. 19:5–6). Because of Israel's failure to keep the covenant, the new people of God—the church—through the sacrifice of Christ, have inherited the blessing of being "a kingdom of priests," "a royal priesthood."

This means that all Christians are priests. In the Old Testament the promised priesthood was limited to the tribe of Levi, with Aaron as its first priest. Accordingly, the priesthood, which was given the primary responsibility of offering sacrifices, was the province of a few. But now since Christ has come as the "great high priest" (Heb. 4:14) and offered Himself as the supreme sacrifice, He has made unnecessary the offering of further sacrifice, annulled any special order of priesthood, and made all believers into priests able to offer spiritual sacrifices to God. Earlier in his letter Peter puts it like this: "You . . . are being built up as a spiritual house for a holy priesthood, to offer up spiritual sacrifices acceptable to God

---

[5]Or "ministers" (as in KJV). The Greek word is *diakonoi*.

[6]The Greek word is *doulous*, literally "slaves" (as in NRSV).

[7]See the next section.

[8]Chapter 18—"Of the Ministers of the Church, Their Institution and Offices."

[9]See "Ministry of the Word" infra, pages 181–96.

through Jesus Christ" (1 Peter 2:5 NASB).

All Christians together form a new order of priesthood. They do not look to priests to offer up material sacrifices on their behalf; rather, they themselves offer up spiritual sacrifices. What are those sacrifices? The best answer is found in Hebrews 13:15–16: "Through Jesus . . . let us continually offer to God a sacrifice of praise—the fruit of lips that confess his name. And do not forget to do good and to share with others, for with such sacrifices God is pleased" (NIV). The sacrifices of course are not for sin but are offerings of the self in praise to God[10] through doing good and sharing with other people.

Since all Christians are priests, the word *priest* is never applied in the New Testament to any individual believer or group of believers. The word is used many times in relation to the Jews—their priests, the high priest, etc.—but *never* in regard to a Christian believer. Moreover, in the list of Christ's gifts to the church—apostles, prophets, evangelists, pastors and teachers (Eph. 4:11)—and God's appointments—apostles, prophets, teachers, workers of miracles, healers, helpers, administrators, speakers in tongues (1 Cor. 12:28)—there is absolutely no mention of priests. There is also reference to bishops (or overseers) and deacons (Phil. 1:1), elders that rule and teach (1 Tim. 5:17), the ministry of the word (Acts 6:4)—but again no mention of priests. Priesthood now belongs to *all* the people of God.

Hence, there is serious irregularity in any church that has a separate order of priests. If the New Testament never speaks of priests in this distinctive sense, even more if Christ as "great high priest" has abolished and fulfilled the Old Testament Levitical priesthood, how can a continuing office of priests be justified?[11] Unfortunately, in some churches the office of priest is considered essential because of the view that the sacrifice of Christ needs continual offering, and that only one who is ordained as a priest is qualified to offer it.[12] Also he alone is qualified to remit sins.[13] Such a view is grievously in error, for it detracts from the singular priestly role of Christ, gives to men unwarranted authority, and effectively denies the priesthood of all believers.

It is urgent that we fully understand all Christians to be "a royal priesthood." Thus as the congregation gathers for worship and the praises of God sound forth, the people of God are acting as priests: they are offering up to

[10]Peter says basically the same thing shortly after his words about royal priesthood by declaring the purpose of this priesthood: "that you may proclaim the excellencies [or 'praises'] of Him who has called you out of darkness into His marvelous light" (1 Peter 2:9 NASB).

[11]David Watson has written, "The perfect priesthood of Christ means that there is therefore no need, and no room, for any priestly office within the church" (*I Believe in the Church*, 248). It is striking that Watson was an Anglican priest! Michael Harper, likewise an Anglican priest, says bluntly: "We need to drop the word 'priest' from our vocabulary and restore the ministry of the presbyterate to its rightful and scriptural position" (*Let My People Grow*, 38). If Anglican priests are saying such things, there is at least hope for some important changes!

[12]According to the Roman Catholic Council of Trent, Christ "instituted a new Passover, namely, Himself, to be immolated [offered in sacrifice] under visible signs by the Church through the priests" (*Doctrine Concerning the Sacrifice of the Mass*: chap. 1). Priests thus are viewed as necessary to perform this continuing sacrifice of Christ.

[13]The Vatican II Council speaks of "the sacred power of their [priests'] order to offer sacrifice and to remit sin" (*Degree on the Ministry and Life of Priests*: chap. 1). Accordingly, a distinct order of priests is totally essential to the life of the church.

God "a sacrifice of praise." The congregation (not some persons who may be ministering at the altar) is therefore "a holy priesthood." The people of Christ are offering up sacrifices, not *of* Christ, but spiritual sacrifices *through* Christ. Further, no priestly absolution of sin is required, because in Christ's name his holy priests, the people of God, can together receive afresh His forgiveness of sins. Moreover, as the people of God go forth to minister as living sacrifices,[14] they continue their function as the priests of God.

I will close this section with two further quotations, one in prediction, one in fulfillment: "You shall be called the priests of the LORD, men shall speak of you as the ministers of our God" (Isa. 61:6), and "To Him who loves us and has freed us from our sins by his blood and made us a kingdom, priests to his God and Father, to him be glory and dominion for ever and ever" (Rev. 1:5–6). Priests of the Lord, priests to God the Father—all of God's people. What a high, even amazing, calling!

C. All Christians Are Clergy

If it sounds strange to say that all Christians are clergy, it is doubtless because of the clergy/laity distinction that is prevalent in many churches. However, such a distinction is quite artificial and unbiblical.

First, the word *clergy*, or *clergyman*, as understood today is not found in the New Testament. "Clergy" derives originally from the Greek word *klēros*, which may be translated "lot," "portion," "share," or "inheritance."[15] Paul quotes Jesus as commissioning him to serve and bear witness so that people "may receive forgiveness of sins and an inheritance [*klēron*] among those who have been sanctified by faith in [Him]" (Acts 26:18 NASB). In one of his letters Paul speaks of "giving thanks to the Father, who has qualified us to share in the inheritance [*klērou*] of the saints in light" (Col. 1:12). Since all Christians have received and thereby share in this inheritance, to them all belongs the *klēros* of God. Peter exhorts "the elders" that they should not be "lords over God's heritage[16] [*klēron*], but . . . examples to the flock" (1 Peter 5:1, 3 KJV). The people for whom the elders are responsible are God's heritage, God's *klēroi*,[17] even God's "clergy." This statement of Peter reverses the customary idea of clergy being the ones over the flock, because the flock are here called "clergy"!

Second, the word *laity* refers likewise to all Christians. "Laity" derives from *laos*, which means simply "people." In the same statement about "a royal priesthood" Peter writes, "You are . . . God's own people [*laos*]. . . . Once you were no people [*laos*] but now you are God's people [*laos*]" (1 Peter 2:9–10). Thus all Christians, the church, compose the laity of God.

Historically, a distinction between clergy and laity appeared at a very early date. In regard to laity, already in 1 Clement (ca. A.D. 96) we find these words: "The layman is bound by the

[14]Paul writes to the Romans, "I urge you . . . in view of God's mercy, to offer your bodies as living sacrifices, holy and pleasing to God" (12:1 NIV). This is a priestly offering that may be made by all believers.

[15]*Klēros* may refer to "lot" in the sense of "casting a lot." Acts 1:26: "They cast lots [*klērous*] . . . and the lot [*klēros*] fell on Matthias." This meaning broadens to include the lot apportioned to someone, hence portion, share, inheritance.

[16]"Those allotted to your charge" (NASB). Note the idea of "lot" in "allotted."

[17]According to BAGD, under *klēros*, "[in] 1 Pt 5:3 the κλῆροι seem to denote the 'flock' as a whole, i.e., the various parts of the people of God which have been assigned as 'portions' to the individual presbyters ['elders'] or shepherds."

layman's rules. Let each of you, brothers, in his proper order [or 'rank'] give thanks to God . . . not overstepping the designated rule of his ministry" (40:5; 41:1).[18] After this, Clement discusses the role of apostles, bishops, and deacons (42). The laity should not overstep their bounds. From about A.D. 200, "laity" became the common term to designate nonclergy. They were viewed as having little more to do in ministry than to hear and obey those above them. "Clergy," on the other hand, became increasingly the privileged class in the church with numerous benefits and often increasing titles to designate their high position.[19]

To say that all Christians are clergy is definitely to run counter to most popular and ecclesiastical understanding. It is far easier, in Protestant circles at least, to speak of all Christians being priests than all being clergy. However, if we can say that all the church is a royal priesthood as it offers up spiritual sacrifices, it is also true that all God's people are His inheritance, His *klēroi*, His "clergy." Of course, the important thing is not to have God's people called either priests or clergy (neither is likely to happen), but to recognize that all Christians, whatever their position, are alike servants of Jesus Christ. In Him we are all brothers and sisters of one another.

When we reflect on this matter, we become all the more aware of the fact that the church is essentially people worshiping together, building up one another, and unitedly reaching out to the world. Whatever our position in the church, in these various ways we are servants of Jesus Christ.

Now this does not mean that all Christians do the same thing. For not only is the whole church a ministering body; there are also individual ministries. Previously I have discussed ministry in the church through the gifts of the Holy Spirit by which various persons fulfill distinctive roles,[20] and I have also pointed out the several gifts of God's grace whereby believers exercise a number of functions[21] in the body. Hence, it is appropriate to say both that *the church is ministry* and that *the church has ministries*. Each person fulfilling his own ministry in the context of overall ministry is the way whereby

---

[18]This is a somewhat ambiguous statement. Clement had just been talking about the high priest, priests, and Levites and their "proper ministries" (40:5). So it could be argued that Clement is not applying this to the church. However, since immediately following his statement about the layman, Clement adds, "Let each of you, brothers, in his proper order . . . ," this shows at least a strong inclination to viewing a separate order for Christian laymen.

[19]One can only deplore the many titles assumed today by "the clergy" such as "Reverend," "the Right Reverend," "the Most Reverend," all the way up to "His Eminence" and "His Holiness." Incidentally, any use of "reverend" is inappropriate, for it means basically "worthy of reverence" (Webster), and God alone is of such worth (so Psalm 111:9: "holy and reverend is *his* name" [KJV]). Jesus, after talking about how the scribes and Pharisees loved to be called Rabbi, declared to his disciples: "But do not be called Rabbi; for One is your Teacher, and you are all brothers" (Matt. 23:8 NASB). How would Jesus react to the far more splendiferous titles "the clergy" delight to go by? Why not simply say "brothers," or "brother," as Jesus instructed us? This was surely the language of Jesus' followers in the New Testament (e.g., Peter addresses the apostles and elders in Jerusalem as "brothers" [Acts 15:7 NIV], and refers to Paul as "our beloved brother Paul" [2 Peter 3:15]; Paul refers to "our brother Apollos" [1 Cor. 16:12] and "our sister Phoebe" [Rom. 16:1], etc.). Using "brother(s)" and "sister(s)" as titles for *everybody* might even promote a little more humility, and perhaps help to close the chasm separating God's people.

[20]See *Renewal Theology*, 2:335–39, "Ministry in the Community."

[21]See preceding chapter 4, pages 127–33.

the church is truly the church of Jesus Christ.

Moreover, there are some ministries that serve to equip others for ministry. By no means are all believers adequately prepared for their ministry. There is continuing need for the equipping of believers. How equipping takes place will be considered in the pages that follow.

II. EQUIPPING MINISTRIES

We now turn to the various *equipping* ministries. Paul writes of Christ, "'When He ascended on high, he led captive a host of captives, and He gave gifts [*domata*] to men'. . . .[22] And He gave some as apostles, and some as prophets, and some as evangelists, and some as pastors and teachers, for the equipping[23] of the saints[24] for the work of service [or 'ministry']" (Eph. 4:8, 11–12 NASB). Thus apostles, prophets, evangelists, pastors and teachers are equipping ministries for the body of Christ.

We should note several things. First, these ministries are *sovereign grants* from the ascended and reigning Christ for the equipping of His church. They are not the result of individual choices but come about through divine action.[25] Second, the gifts are *persons*—apostles, prophets, etc. (and not activities such as prophesying, evangelizing, teaching)—who are given by Christ to the church for the equipping of the body of believers. The personal, exalted Christ provides persons for this critical task. Third, these gifts are *limited in number*: not every Christian shares in them. Unlike *charismata* gifts, in which all believers participate,[26] these *domata* gifts are of the few (note the recurring word "some"). Fourth, these equipping ministries are *necessary to the continuing life of the church*. The fact that Christ "gave" cannot refer only to the past, because the gifts are for the ongoing work of equipping the saints of all times and places for their work of ministry. Fifth, pastors and teachers are *more closely linked* than the other gifts. "Some" each time precedes apostles, prophets, and evangelists, but does not do so in regard to teachers: "some pastors and teachers." It is likely that Paul is describing basically a single equipping ministry;[27] however, the fact

---

[22]Paul's quotation is a paraphrase of Psalm 68:18. It is interesting that the psalm reads "received gifts" rather than "gave gifts." "Gave" is found in neither the MT nor LXX of Psalm 68:18. F. F. Bruce (*The Epistles to the Colossians, to Philemon, and to the Ephesians*, 342–43) speaks of Paul's wording as "a targumic rendering" (see Bruce on this expression). In any event Paul is expressing the important point that the ascended and victorious Christ bestows gifts for the equipping of His church.

[23]The Greek word is *katartismon*. The KJV reads "perfecting"; NIV, "to prepare"; NEB, "to equip." "Equipping" (or "equipment" RSV) is the best translation (see BAGD) here.

[24]The RSV places a comma here. Recall my earlier comment (n.4) that this is misleading.

[25]Paul writes in 1 Corinthians 12:28: "God has appointed in the church first apostles, second prophets, third teachers. . . ." There is no direct reference here to evangelists and pastors; however, apostles, prophets, and teachers are in the same sequence as Ephesians 4:11. The point of immediate relevance is that in both texts, whether they are called gifts of Christ or God's appointments, the action is wholly from the divine side.

[26]In the previous chapter I discussed the "functional" gifts of Romans 12:6–8, which are the exercise of *charismata*, gifts of grace. Such gifts are found throughout the body of Christ. The same is true of the "manifestation gifts" (also called *charismata*) of 1 Corinthians 12:8–10: all may share in them (see *Renewal Theology*, vol. 2, chaps. 13, "The Gifts of the Holy Spirit," and 14, "The Ninefold Manifestation").

[27]This would follow also from Paul's list in 1 Corinthians 12:28, where no mention is made of pastors; thus Paul may be viewing "teachers" as pastors.

that he lists in Ephesians both pastors and teachers suggests that this ministry is composed of two closely related functions.[28]

Now let us turn to a consideration of each of the equippers in Ephesians 4.

A. Apostles—"some as apostles"

We begin with *apostles* as the first of the equipping ministries. Not only are apostles mentioned first; they are also specified as first of the divine appointments in 1 Corinthians 12:28—"God has appointed ['set' KJV] in the church first apostles." Even as Jesus in His earthly ministry early chose apostles to be associated with Him, so from heaven the exalted Lord continues that ministry first of all through apostolic activity. Whether the language is "some as apostles" or "first apostles," the truth is the same: the apostles occupy the primary place among the equipping ministries.

One further preliminary word: Christ Himself is the supreme apostle. In Hebrews He is called "the apostle and high priest of our confession" (3:1). Since Jesus is "*the* apostle," all others who are called apostles derive their position and authority from Him.

Now we observe that the word "apostles" in the New Testament has a twofold usage. It refers, first, and primarily, to the original twelve apostles[29] plus Paul, and, second, to a larger group of apostles, both named and unnamed. So before dealing further with Ephesians 4, let us briefly examine this twofold usage.

1. The Twelve Plus Paul

We recognize first that the word "apostles" refers most often to the Twelve whom Jesus chose out of all His disciples. The Gospel of Luke records, "He called his disciples, and chose from them twelve, whom he named apostles" (6:13).[30] After Judas's defection and after Jesus had returned to heaven, the disciples prayed for the Lord to choose another. They set forward two men and prayed, "Lord, who knowest the hearts of all men, show which one of these two thou hast chosen to take the place in this ministry and apostleship[31]. . . . And they cast lots for them, and the lot fell on Matthias; and he was enrolled with the eleven apostles" (Acts 1:24–26). Thus the number of apostles chosen by Jesus was again complete. The Book of Acts has many other references to the apostles, understood with one exception to be the Twelve.[32] "The Twelve" is also Paul's language in 1 Corinthians 15:5.

In regard to the Twelve, two things stand out. First, they were all specially chosen by Jesus. As we have noted, even Matthias, whom Jesus had not chosen during His ministry on earth, was chosen later by Him from heaven. Second, they had all been with Jesus from the beginning of His ministry and had seen Him in His resurrection. This

[28]For this twofold function see pages 178–81.

[29]The "original twelve apostles" actually included Judas. However, Matthias later replaced him (see next paragraph) and so fills out the original group.

[30]Cf. Matthew 10:1–2 and Mark 6:30. All other references (twelve) to "the apostles" in the Gospels are found in Luke. "The Twelve" is a frequent expression (twenty-one times) in all four Gospels.

[31]The Greek word is *apostolēs*, a form of *apostolē*. Significantly, "ministry" (*diakonia*) and "apostleship" are joined together. Thus (as I have commented earlier) "ministry" is the basic purpose. Apostleship accordingly is a ministering office.

[32]"The apostles," referring to the Twelve, occurs twenty-eight times in Acts; in one instance, however, they are simply called "the twelve" (Acts 6:2). The one exception is Acts 14:14, which refers to "the apostles Barnabas and Paul." Incidentally, in both the Gospels and Acts the plural is always used—"apostles."

is illustrated by the fact that when the time came to replace Judas, Peter declared that only one who had been with them "from the baptism of John until the day when he was taken up from us . . . must become with us a witness to his resurrection" (Acts 1:22). Matthias was one who fulfilled both requirements and became the new twelfth apostle.

It is apparent, from their having been chosen by Jesus and having lived together with Him throughout His ministry, that these twelve apostles occupied a uniquely important position of authority. They had known Jesus intimately, they had been under His immediate direction as they ministered in His name, they had heard all His teaching and had been given private explanations of matters hidden to others, and they had seen Him in His resurrection. Thus they were fully prepared to proclaim the gospel, establish the church, and pass on His truth to all generations to come. The twelve apostles accordingly had a unique, indispensable, and unrepeatable place in the body of Jesus Christ.

But what of Paul? He was the one who, more than any other, carried the gospel to many peoples. Moreover, he wrote more of the New Testament than any of the Twelve. How does he meet apostolic qualifications? The answer is that he was likewise chosen by Jesus and by special revelation had seen Jesus and was given the gospel to write down. First, Paul over and over again declares himself to be an apostle by Jesus' call. For example, he begins Galatians by saying, "Paul an apostle—not from man nor through man, but through Jesus Christ and God the Father" (1:1).[33] Indeed, at the time of Paul's conversion Jesus had declared through Ananias: "He is a chosen instrument of mine to carry my name before the Gentiles and kings and sons of Israel" (Acts 9:15). Second, in addition to being specially chosen, as were the Twelve, Paul had also seen Jesus. Paul writes, "Am I not an apostle? Have I not seen Jesus our Lord?" (1 Cor. 9:1). The answer is yes, for Paul later explains, "As to one untimely born, he appeared also to me" (1 Cor. 15:8). This appearance, Paul insists, was not just a vision but as much a real encounter with the risen Jesus as any of the Twelve had experienced. Elsewhere Paul says simply, "[God] was pleased to reveal his Son to me" (Gal. 1:16). Thus Paul qualified with the Twelve both as being specially chosen by Jesus and as a witness to His resurrection. But what about the gospel the Twelve had learned from Jesus during their years with Him? Again, and in the third place, Paul was in no way inferior to the original Twelve, for he also declares, "The gospel which was preached by me is not man's gospel. For I did not receive it from man, nor was I taught it, but it came through a revelation of Jesus Christ" (Gal. 1:11–12). Paul in an extraordinary manner received from the exalted Lord what the Twelve had received during Christ's earthly ministry!

It is clear, then, that Paul, even though he spoke of himself as "the least of the apostles, unfit to be called an apostle, because [he] persecuted the church of God" (1 Cor. 15:9), has equal standing with the Twelve. It follows that what he has written in the New Testament is truly God's Word, and is authoritative for the church through the ages.

Thus the Twelve plus Paul are apostles who occupy a unique and authoritative place in the life and history of the church.

Here the word *apostleship* may appropriately be used: it refers to this

[33]See also Romans 1:1; 1 Corinthians 1:1; 2 Corinthians 1:1; Ephesians 1:1; Colossians 1:1; 1 Timothy 1:1; 2 Timothy 1:1; Titus 1:1.

original group. We have observed how Peter in Acts 1:24–25 used the word apostleship in reference to the position Judas had vacated and now needed to be filled: "Lord . . . show which one of these two thou hast chosen to take the place in this ministry and apostleship." Paul speaks of how God "effectually worked for Peter in his apostleship to the circumcised" (Gal. 2:8 NASB). Paul twice speaks of his own apostleship: "Jesus Christ . . . through whom we have received grace and apostleship" (Rom. 1:4–5), and "you [Corinthians] are the seal of my apostleship in the Lord" (1 Cor. 9:2). These are all the uses of this word in the New Testament, and they apply only to the Twelve plus Paul.

This means that there can be neither succession nor restoration of the apostleship. Succession is out of the question[34] not only because these apostles appointed no successors[35] but also because of the unique and unrepeatable character of their apostleship. Restoration is likewise impossible[36] because these apostles fulfilled their role, and continue their ministry through the apostolic writings of the New Testament. Any idea of perpetuating or restoring apostleship as an official office is totally foreign to the New Testament and to Christ's intention for His church.

2. *Others Called Apostles*

Now we proceed to observe that in addition to the twelve apostles and Paul, a number of others are mentioned as apostles in the New Testament. First, we may note Barnabas who often traveled with Paul. In Acts 14:14 the two are called "the apostles Barnabas and Paul." It is interesting that Barnabas's original name was Joseph, but because of his ways he was early "surnamed by the apostles [the Twelve] Barnabas (which means, Son of encouragement)" (Acts 4:36). Second, there was James, the brother of Jesus, who presided at the council in Jerusalem (Acts 15). In Acts he is not called an apostle; however, in Galatians Paul so designates James: "I went up to Jerusalem to visit Cephas [Peter]. . . . But I saw none of the other apostles except[37] James the Lord's brother" (1:18–19). Third, Paul, in his letter to the Romans, refers to Andronicus and Junias as apostles: "Greet Andronicus and Junias,[38] my relatives who have been in prison with me. They are outstanding[39] among the apostles, and they were in Christ before I was" (16:7 NIV). Nothing

---

[34]See a discussion of the theory of "apostolic succession" in chapter 2, pages 35–38.

[35]Matthias was chosen to be an apostle *not as a successor* to Judas but as a *replacement*: the apostleship (except for Paul) was then complete. This completeness is all the more confirmed by the fact that when James, one of the Twelve, was put to death by Herod (Acts 12:1–2), no successor was appointed.

[36]In church history there have been various restorationist attempts. For example, the Catholic Apostolic Church, founded by Edward Irving in the nineteenth century, claiming that God was restoring this foundational office of apostle in the church, established "the Restored Apostolate."

[37]There is some ambiguity here. "Except"—Greek *ei mē*—may also be translated "only" (NIV). Such a translation obviously *excludes* James from being an apostle. However, the more natural reading is "except" (so BAGD) as found in RSV, NASB, and NEB (KJV has "save," meaning the same thing as "except").

[38]The Greek word is *Iounian*. The KJV reads as "Junia," hence feminine. *Iounian* can be read as the accusative of the feminine *Iounia* or as a contraction of the masculine *Iounianus*. BAGD prefers *Iounianus* or Junias: "Junias . . . probably short form of the common Junianus." This is more likely.

[39]The Greek word is *episēmoi*. The KJV reads "of note"; RSV, "men of note"; NEB, "eminent." The NASB (like NIV above) translates the word as "outstanding."

more is known about Andronicus and Junias. Fourth, Paul seems to include Silas and Timothy with himself as apostles in 1 Thessalonians. The letter begins, "Paul, Silvanus [Silas], and Timothy, to the church of the Thessalonians" (1:1).[40] Later Paul says, "We might have made demands [upon you] as apostles[41] of Christ" (2:6). Fifth, and quite strikingly, in 1 Corinthians 15, Paul speaks of Christ's appearances to "the twelve" and thereafter to "all the apostles." The text reads, "He appeared to Cephas, then to the twelve. Then he appeared to more than five hundred brethren at one time. . . . Then he appeared to James, then to all the apostles. Last of all, as to one untimely born, he appeared also to me" (vv. 5–8). By this statement, "all the apostles" goes beyond "the twelve."

There are two other references in Paul's letters to "apostles," although there the word is usually translated "messengers" or "messenger." He refers, in one case, to two unnamed brothers (2 Cor. 8:18 and 22) whom he speaks of as "messengers[42] [*apostoloi*] of the churches" (v. 23). Both brothers were being sent[43] by Paul and Titus to the church in Corinth to help collect an offering for the poor Christians in Jerusalem. The first brother was said to be "famous among all the churches for his preaching of the gospel" and, Paul writes, "He has been appointed by the churches to travel with us in this gracious work" (vv. 18–19); Paul describes the second as "our brother whom we have often tested and found earnest in many matters" (v. 22). The other case is that of Epaphroditus, who had been very ill and nearly died in bringing gifts from Corinth to Paul during his imprisonment (Phil. 2:25–30). Paul planned to send[44] Epaphroditus back to Philippi; he describes him as "my brother and fellow worker and fellow soldier, and your messenger [*apostolon*] and minister to my need" (v. 25). In both instances, the unnamed brothers and Epaphroditus are "apostles" of the churches sent by Paul and by the churches to fulfill particular needs. The word *apostolos* thus is used broadly to refer to a messenger, or perhaps a delegate or envoy, from particular churches to serve a larger need.[45]

From the broadest perspective apostles in the New Testament are those *sent* by God for whatever mission is required of them. *Apostolos* is derived from the word *apostellō*, which means to "send" or "send out." Jesus Himself is *the* apostle because He was the one sent by God the Father[46] to perform His mission on earth. Incidentally, the

[40]Silas, however, is called a prophet in Acts 15:32. Timothy is perhaps more of an assistant to Paul, and in the case of the church in Ephesus (see 1 Tim. 1:3) both an apostolic delegate and a teacher. Still in a broad sense (as will be discussed later) both Silas and Timothy were apostles.

[41]The NEB reads "envoys"; the Greek word, however, is *apostoloi*. F. F. Bruce in his commentary translates it "messengers" (which is possible, see the following discussion), stating that the "apostles . . . can scarcely be stretched to include Timothy, his own 'son in the faith' (1 Tim. 1:2), whatever may be said of Silvanus" (*1 & 2 Thessalonians*, WBC, 31). "Messengers," however, seems too weak a translation to fit the context. Messengers, unlike apostles, could hardly make "demands."

[42]This is also the translation in KJV and NASB. The NIV reads "representatives."

[43]"We are sending"—vv. 18 and 22.

[44]"I have thought it necessary to send"—v. 25.

[45]According to BAGD, *apostolos* "can also mean delegate, envoy, messenger . . . perhaps missionary."

[46]Many times, particularly in the Gospel of John, the word *apostellō* is used in regard to

single use of the word *apostolos* in the Gospel of John is found in this statement of Jesus: "Truly, truly, I say to you, a servant is not greater than his master; nor is he who is sent[47] [*apostolos*] greater than he who sent him" (13:16). The apostle, whatever his identity, is one sent by the Lord to carry forward His mission.

To summarize thus far: In the New Testament there is both a narrow and a broad use of the word "apostles." The narrow relates to the Twelve plus Paul; the broad, to many other disciples both named and unnamed. All who are called apostles have been sent out in the cause of the gospel.

Now in returning to Ephesians 4 we observe that the gift of apostles—"He gave some as apostles"—refers to the exalted Lord's donation: "When he ascended on high . . . he gave gifts." Hence, this goes beyond the original apostles and reaches out to encompass others.[48] Paul earlier in Ephesians does refer twice to apostles, along with prophets, "apostles and prophets" (2:20 and 3:5), in the more restricted sense;[49] however, here apostles needs to be understood in a broader way as Christ's *continuing* gift to His church.

Our earlier review of the New Testament clearly shows that beyond the Twelve and Paul, who were uniquely apostles, many others were designated as apostles. They did not have the authority of the Twelve or of Paul but often functioned in relation to them. Barnabas worked hand in hand with Paul on missionary travels; so did Timothy and Silas. Andronicus and Junias at some time were imprisoned with Paul. Epaphroditus was Paul's fellow worker and an *apostolos* sent out from the Philippian church. One of the unnamed *apostolos* brothers was, as noted, "famous among all the churches for his preaching of the gospel" and had been appointed by the churches to accompany Paul. There were many in the New Testament church who preached widely, functioned as missionaries, and represented the churches in different ways. These were also apostles—and leaders like these are surely needed at all times in the life of the church.

A distinction may be made between the foundational ministry of apostle, that is, the apostleship, and the ongoing ministry[50] of others who are called

Jesus' being sent by God: John 1:6, 3:17, 34; 4:38; 5:36, 38; 6:57; 7:29; 8:42; 10:36; 11:42; 17:3, 8, 21, 23, 25; 20:21. See also Matthew 10:40; Mark 9:37; Luke 4:18, 43; 9:48.

[47]The NIV translates this as "messenger" (instead of "he who is sent"). Since *apostolos* in this text is a noun, "messenger" might seem preferable. However, it fails to carry the relation between one sent and the one sending him.

[48]According to EGT: "As they are the gifts of the exalted Christ, it is plain that the ἀποστόλους are not to be restricted to the original Twelve, but are to be taken in the wider sense, including not only Paul but Barnabas . . . probably James . . . Silvanus . . . perhaps also Andronicus and Titus" (3:329). I would add that there is no reason to stop with these New Testament names, for the gift is doubtless a continuing one.

[49]In Ephesians 2:20 the apostles and prophets mentioned are *foundational*—"the household of God, built upon the foundation of the apostles and the prophets"; in 3:5 they are *recipients* of "the mystery of Christ . . . as it has now been revealed to his holy apostles and prophets by the Spirit." "Apostles" (as well as "prophets") obviously refers in these verses only to original apostles.

[50]Gordon Fee distinguishes between the "functional" (ongoing ministry) and "positional/official" use of the term (*First Epistle to the Corinthians*, 620). Fee earlier speaks of the

apostles. In this broader sense an apostle is one *sent, commissioned*, and therefore is not affixed to a particular location or church. He does not have the authority of a foundational apostle nor are his words equally inspired. Such an apostle operates in translocal manner, but does not operate independently. He is church-based, representing a particular church, but ministering largely in a field beyond.[51] *Such apostles are always essential to the life of a church that realizes its call to reach out beyond itself in the mission of the gospel.*

Finally, in addition to the words in Ephesians 4 about Christ's gift of apostles, we recall that when Paul speaks of God's appointments in 1 Corinthians 12, he mentions the appointment of apostles as being first of all: "God has appointed in the church first apostles. . ." (v. 28). Such appointment must refer to more than an act or acts of past history—especially since Paul continues with other appointments that indicate an ongoing occurrence.[52] Hence, whether apostles are spoken of as Christ's gift or God's appointment, they do have vital significance for the life of the church at all times in history.

B. Prophets—"some as prophets"

The second of the equipping ministries is that of *prophets*. For immediately following the words "He [Christ] gave some as apostles," Paul adds, "and some as prophets." This is the same pattern as in 1 Corinthians 12:28: "God has appointed in the church first apostles, second prophets." Prophets are Christ's gift, God's appointment, and second only to apostles.

It should be clear at the outset that Paul is *not* referring to Old Testament prophets. Because Paul speaks earlier of the church as "built upon the foundation of the apostles and prophets," one might think this refers to the Old Testament prophets and to New Testament apostles. However, such an idea is out of the question. First, both apostles and prophets are called gifts of the exalted Christ; second, prophets in all three cases where they are mentioned in Ephesians *follow* apostles;[53] and, third, they together with apostles have received special revelation concerning "the mystery of Christ, which was not made known . . . in other generations as it has now been revealed to his holy apostles and prophets by the Spirit" (Eph. 3:4–5). "Prophets" in this context thus refers only to the New Testament period.

Before proceeding further, we must recognize Jesus Himself as "*the* prophet" (even as He is "*the* apostle"). According to Deuteronomy 18:15, Moses had declared, "The LORD your God will raise up for you a prophet like me from among you, from your brethren—him you shall heed." When John the Baptist appeared on the scene, he was asked by many, "Are you the prophet?" to which John answered,

"functional" as having "its modern counterparts in those who found and lead churches in unevangelized areas" (p. 397).

[51]Recall that Barnabas was sent out with Paul from the church at Antioch. Epaphroditus and the unnamed brothers who served widely were appointed by particular churches. Andronicus and Junias, greeted by Paul as apostles in Rome, possibly came there as missionaries from an earlier established church. According to E. Käsemann, they "probably . . . were delegates of Antioch, as Paul and Barnabas were" (*Commentary on Romans*, 414). In any event, they were Jewish Christians who, as missionaries of the faith, had been fellow prisoners of their kinsman Paul.

[52]Paul adds, "second prophets, third teachers, then workers of miracles, then healers, helpers, administrators, speakers in various kinds of tongues" (same verse).

[53]Ephesians 2:20; 3:5; 4:11. Also recall 1 Corinthians 12:28.

"No!" (John 1:21). Later the people declared about Jesus, "This is indeed the prophet who is to come into the world!" (John 6:14).[54] In the Book of Acts both Peter and Stephen interpret the words of Moses as referring to Christ (see Acts 3:22; 7:37). Jesus of course was more than a prophet; but that he was a prophet[55] and, beyond all others, *the* prophet is the New Testament witness.

Now let us turn to a consideration of Christian[56] prophets. Here we look primarily to the record in Acts. The first reference reads, "Now in these days prophets came down from Jerusalem to Antioch. And one of them named Agabus stood up and foretold by the Spirit that there would be a great famine over all the world; and this took place in the days of Claudius" (11:27–28). Antioch was again the locale for later prophetic activity, this time in the church: "Now in the church at Antioch there were prophets and teachers. . . . While they were worshiping the Lord and fasting, the Holy Spirit said, 'Set apart for me Barnabas and Saul for the work to which I have called them' " (13:1–2). The statement that "the Holy Spirit said" probably occurred through one of the prophets. Following the decision of the church in Jerusalem about the circumcision issue, a letter was sent to the Gentile churches, including Antioch, by the hands of Judas Barsabbas and Silas (15:22), who were called prophets: "Judas and Silas, who themselves were prophets, said much to encourage and strengthen the brothers" (v. 32 NIV). Finally, Agabus appeared once more, this time to inform Paul in Caesarea of what would happen to him in Jerusalem: "Agabus came down from Judea. . . . He took Paul's belt, tied his own hands and feet with it, and said, 'The Holy Spirit says, "In this way the Jews of Jerusalem will bind the owner of this belt and will hand him over to the Gentiles" ' " (21:10–11 NIV). Thus the prophets mentioned in Acts consisted of Agabus, the prophets in the church at Antioch, and Judas Barsabbas and Silas.

From the record in Acts several things regarding prophets are noteworthy. First, foretelling occurred through Christian prophets. Agabus twice foretold events to come—in the second incident his prophecy was accompanied by acted symbolism using Paul's belt. In both instances the Holy Spirit was directly involved: Agabus "foretold by the Spirit" and declared, "Thus says the Holy Spirit." Second, the choosing of Barnabas and Saul for missionary work stemmed from a gathering of prophets and teachers and doubtless occurred through prophetic utterance. Again, "the Holy Spirit said. . . ." Third, Judas and Silas as prophets fulfilled the important spiritual role of encouraging and strengthening[57] the people of the church in Antioch. Fourth, these prophets functioned in both a translocal and a local manner.

---

[54]See also Matthew 21:11: "This is the prophet Jesus from Nazareth."

[55]Jesus also spoke of Himself indirectly as a prophet. See Matthew 13:57: "A prophet is not without honor except in his own country and in his own house" (cf. Mark 6:4; Luke 4:24; John 4:44); Luke 13:33: "It cannot be that a prophet should perish away from Jerusalem."

[56]I say "Christian" rather than "New Testament." This means excluding John the Baptist, whom Jesus extolled as "a prophet . . . and more than a prophet" (Matt. 11:9; Luke 7:26). As the immediate forerunner of Jesus, John occupied the climactic place in a long line of precursors of Christ. Still, John was not a Christian prophet.

[57]Paul declares in 1 Corinthians 14:3 that one "who prophesies speaks to men for their upbuilding [= 'strengthening'] and encouragement and consolation." Judas and Silas were surely fulfilling this task.

Agabus, Judas, and Silas came from Jerusalem (or Judea) to carry out their prophetic ministry, whereas it was local prophets at the church in Antioch through whom the Holy Spirit spoke. Fifth, Silas may be viewed as both an apostle[58] and a prophet. Hence there seems to be some overlap between the two roles.

We look next to the Book of Revelation. It is declared to be a book of prophecy—"Blessed is he who reads aloud the words of the prophecy" (1:3). Moreover, the author John himself is included among the prophets by an angel: "you and your brethren the prophets" (22:9). Within the Book of Revelation is the statement that "the mystery of God will be accomplished, just as he announced to his servants the prophets" (10:7 NIV). In another place, as Babylon is being destroyed, the cry goes forth, "Rejoice over her, O heaven, O saints and apostles and prophets,[59] for God has given judgment for you against her!" (18:20). Several times John is said to be "in the Spirit,"[60] and the Lord is said to be "the God of the spirits of the prophets" (22:6).

Several comments may be made. First, in the Book of Revelation prophecy contains much foretelling. John is told, "Write, therefore, what you have seen, what is now and what will take place later" (1:19 NIV). The "later" events and visions occupy most of the book. Second, the prophets speak out concerning "the mystery of God" in relation to the consummation of all things. God announces this to "his servants the prophets." Thus they bear a close relation to the apostles.[61] Third, many of the revelations come to the prophet while he is "in the Spirit." He sees supernaturally with spiritual vision.

What has been said about the prophets in Acts and Revelation enables us to perceive their role. In the early life of the church, prophets clearly were special persons, second only to the apostles. However, although second, they shared a foundational role in the formation of the church. As we have observed, Paul speaks of "the foundation of the apostles and prophets" (Eph. 2:20) and associates them with the apostles in receiving the revelation of "the mystery of Christ" (3:5). They were involved in laying the original foundations of the church and often spoke with the special revelation that was given them by the Holy Spirit. In that respect such prophets have fulfilled their task—even as have the original apostles—and no longer continue as persons in the life of the church.

Now let us return to Ephesians 4 and consider the phrase "some as prophets." Here, as in the case of "some as apostles," reference is made to those who have this ministry *in and beyond the New Testament record*. This is apparent from the fact, first of all, that they are depicted along with apostles, evangelists, pastors and teachers as being given by the exalted Christ for the equipping of believers. There is no suggestion that the church at any time needs only certain ones of these ministries for such equipping to occur. The same is true in 1 Corinthians 12 where Paul speaks of God's

[58]Recall the previous discussion about Silas and Timothy as possible apostles.

[59]For the linkage of saints and prophets also see Rev. 11:18; 16:6; and 18:24.

[60]Revelation 1:10; 4:2; 17:3; 21:10.

[61]We recall that Paul speaks of "the mystery of Christ . . . revealed to his holy apostles and prophets by the Spirit." In the Book of Revelation the focus is on the prophets. However, as quoted, "apostles and prophets" (with "saints") are mentioned together in Revelation 18:20.

having appointed in the church prophets along with apostles, teachers, workers of miracles, healers, helpers, administrators, and speakers in tongues (v. 28). Surely we cannot declare that some (or all) of these appointments are for today and then say that prophets (and apostles) belong only to past history. We must rather affirm vigorously that prophets represent important continuing gifts, or appointments, in the church.

It is important, however, as in the case of apostles, to differentiate between original and continuing prophets. Even as there is a foundational and a continuing apostolic ministry, so there is a foundational and a continuing prophetic ministry. Such continuing ministry likewise is a gift of Christ that serves for the equipping of the church.

The question may now be put: How does the ministry of a prophet relate to the activity of prophesying? In regard to activity, we recall that Paul speaks in Romans 12:4–8 of prophecy as one among several functional gifts for the upbuilding of the body of Christ, and in 1 Corinthians 12:7–10 of prophecy as a manifestation gift to serve the common good.[62] Persons who so prophesy are not necessarily prophets in the sense of having a prophetic ministry. Nonetheless, quite possibly some are fulfilling a prophetic calling. If so, while their messages may not differ essentially from others who prophesy, upon them a prophetic mantle will be increasingly apparent. They not only prophesy: they have a prophetic ministry. Furthermore, because of this special ministry, these special prophets may serve the church at large.[63]

The purpose of prophetic ministry may be defined by Paul's words in 1 Corinthians 14:3—"He who prophesies speaks to men for their upbuilding and encouragement and consolation."[64] This sounds, incidentally, much like what the prophets Judas and Silas did "to encourage and strengthen the brothers" (Acts 15:22, 27, 32). Prophets who fulfill such a role can be a blessing to both the local and the larger church.

Prophets likewise are persons who speak particular words regarding what God is saying to His people in any given situation. Their messages may speak significantly to the church and afford special insight into God's present way and purpose. Such prophetic utterances may also relate to the future and thus enable the people of God to move ahead with more assurance and direction. The chief burden of the continuing prophets, however, is the present; further, their words may relate both to individuals as well as to the church at large. Prophets uniquely speak for God to God's people.[65]

But now, immediately, we need to recognize one major and critical differ-

---

[62]See the prior discussion of prophecy as a functional gift on pages 127–28 and as a manifestation gift in *Renewal Theology*, 2:380–88.

[63]Reference may here be made to the contemporary "prophetic movement." A number of persons viewed as prophets travel widely for ministry to churches and individuals, conduct seminars on prophecy, and the like. (See, for example, *Prophets and the Prophetic Movement*, by Bill Hamon; also the magazine *Ministries Today*, January/February, 1992, for several relevant articles.) I believe that such a movement has significant bearing on the role of prophetic ministry in our time.

[64]Although these words apply to prophesying in general, they surely also relate to the activity of one who is a prophet.

[65]Michael Harper writes: "How desperately the Church needs people who are prophets . . . able to speak clearly and practically God's word for the hour; able to foretell the future and so warn the Church of dangers and changes so that it can steer a safe course; able to discern the secrets of men's hearts and so deliver discussion and counselling from unreality" (*Let My People Grow*, 53–54). I can only say "Amen" to this!

ence between prophets today and the original New Testament prophets. Those original prophets, along with the original apostles, received the special revelation of "the mystery of Christ" (recall Eph. 3:4–5; cf. also John in the Book of Revelation)). Continuing prophets, while speaking out of revelation,[66] do not receive special or new revelation. If they did receive and speak that type of prophecy, their words would be equivalent to Holy Scripture. The church, accordingly, must always be on guard against presumed prophetic messages that claim equal or superior authority to God's written words in Scripture. True prophecy is thoroughly grounded in Scripture and, based upon it, speaks forth God's particular word for the contemporary scene.

A final word on "some as apostles, and some as prophets." We have observed that the original apostles and prophets were foundational to the life of the church. They received special revelation from God, and they have completed their ministry. However, apostles and prophets, along with evangelists, pastors, and teachers, are gifts of the exalted Christ and continue to be available to the church through all ages.[67] Doubtless we need today to give fresh recognition to these ministries that are essential to the life of the church.

C. Evangelists—"some as evangelists"

We arrive at a consideration of the third of the equipping ministries, namely, that of *evangelists*. The exalted Lord has also given evangelists to equip the saints for the work of ministry.

Evangelists are those who proclaim the gospel. The gospel is the *evangellion*—"the good news," to preach good news is *evangelizō*—"to evangelize," and the evangelist is the *evangelistēs*—the proclaimer or preacher of the good news.

Jesus Himself, accordingly, is *the* evangelist.[68] The Gospel of Mark opens with the declaration that "Jesus came into Galilee, preaching the gospel of God" (1:14). Jesus thus was an evangelist from the beginning of His ministry. In His hometown of Nazareth Jesus, quoting from Isaiah, declared, "The Spirit of the Lord is upon me, because he has anointed me to preach good news to the poor" (Luke 4:18). A short time later in Capernaum, when the people tried to keep Him from leaving them, Jesus replied, "I must preach the good news of the kingdom of God to the other cities also; for I was sent for this purpose" (Luke 4:43). Jesus had a strong and compelling sense that He had been sent for the great purpose of proclaiming the gospel. As such, Jesus was the original evangelist and the example for all who share the same compulsion and dedication. This is particularly true for those whom the Lord especially calls to this ministry. It is they that receive this gift from the exalted Lord: He "gave . . . some as evangelists."

Before considering this statement, two preliminary remarks are in order.

[66]All genuine prophecy stems from revelation. See 1 Corinthians 14:30—"if a revelation is made to another [prophet] sitting by. . . ." This statement implies that all prophecy occurs through revelation.

[67]Marcus Barth writes in regard to all these ministries: "Eph 4 does not contain the faintest hint that the charismatic [or gift] character of all church ministries was restricted to a certain period of church history and was later to die out" (*Ephesians 4–6*, AB, 437). In regard to apostles and prophets Barth adds, "Ephesians distinctly presupposes that living apostles and prophets are essential to the church's life" (p. 437, n.72). I fully agree with Barth on these matters.

[68]Even as He is "*the* apostle" and "*the* prophet."

First, there is a real sense in which all Christians are called to be evangelists. To proclaim the word in every way possible is not some addition to Christian faith; this belongs to its essence. In the Book of Acts it is apparent that members of the early church were strongly aware of this. For example, on one occasion the whole community prayed, "Lord . . . grant to thy servants to speak thy word with all boldness" (4:29). As a result, "they were all filled with the Holy Spirit and spoke the word of God with boldness" (v. 31). On a later occasion when great persecution broke out against the church in Jerusalem and all the believers except the twelve apostles were scattered abroad, Luke records, "Those who had been scattered preached the word wherever they went" (8:4 NIV). Thus in a broad sense all the believers were evangelists.

Second, the apostles themselves were also proclaimers of the good news. One verse in Acts stands out: "Day after day, in the temple courts and from house to house, they [the apostles] never stopped teaching and proclaiming the good news that Jesus is the Christ" (5:42 NIV). Paul and Barnabas "preached the gospel" (14:7, 21) in various cities; and Luke writes about what occurred after Paul had received a vision calling them over to Macedonia: "Immediately we sought to go on into Macedonia, concluding that God had called us to preach the gospel to them" (16:10). Many times in his letters Paul speaks of his call to preach the gospel.[69] Peter writes, "That word is the good news which was preached to you" (1 Peter 1:25). Thus, to sum up, proclaiming the gospel, evangelizing, belongs to the ongoing life and mission of the whole church.

But also some persons have a special calling to be evangelists—"some as evangelists." The clearest New Testament illustration of this is Philip, not Philip the apostle, but "Philip the evangelist."[70] Luke writes "We . . . came to Caesarea; and we entered the house of Philip the evangelist, who was one of the seven" (Acts 21:8). "One of the seven" refers to earlier days when Philip, along with six others, was selected to handle the distribution of food in the community of believers (6:1–6). Some time later, after the persecution and scattering of believers, "Philip went down to a city of Samaria, and proclaimed[71] to them the Christ" (8:5). Later after Philip had also done many signs—"unclean spirits came out of many . . . and many who were paralyzed or lame were healed" (v. 7)—"they believed Philip as he preached good news about the kingdom of God and the name of Jesus Christ" (v. 12). Philip then baptized those who believed. Thus he did the work of an evangelist: he not only preached the good news but also through his proclamation the Samaritans came to faith and baptism.

Philip the evangelist is next seen on a desert road between Jerusalem and Gaza ministering to an Ethiopian eunuch, a highly placed court official. Philip "preached Jesus to him" (8:35 NASB). Then after the Ethiopian came to faith and was baptized, "the Spirit of the Lord caught up Philip" (v. 39). After that "Philip was found at Azotus, and passing on he preached the gospel

[69]E.g., Romans 1:15; 1 Corinthians 1:17; 2 Corinthians 2:12; Galatians 1:11; Ephesians 6:19; 1 Thessalonians 2:9.

[70]All apostles (as we have seen) are evangelists (this includes Philip the apostle), but not all evangelists are apostles (as in the case of Philip the evangelist).

[71]The Greek word is *ekēryssen* from *keryssō*—"the declaration of an event" (TDNT, 3:703). The noun *kērygma* refers to "preaching by a herald sent from God" (BAGD).

to all the towns till he came to Caesarea" (v. 40)[72]. Truly he was "Philip the evangelist."

Evangelism, as Philip demonstrated it, involves both proclaiming the gospel and bringing people to a saving faith. When Jesus called Peter and Andrew, He said, "I will make you fishers of men" (Matt. 4:19; cf. Mark 1:17)—and fishing means not only casting the net but also bringing in the fish. Philip the evangelist preached the gospel and brought people in—into the kingdom.

This brings us to Paul's charge to Timothy: "Do the work of an evangelist" (2 Tim. 4:5). This is in the context of Paul's fuller statement "Always be steady, endure suffering, do the work of an evangelist, fulfill your ministry." Unlike Philip, Timothy is not called an evangelist; rather, Paul seems to be speaking of evangelism as one aspect of Timothy's total ministry. Timothy of course had preached the gospel with Paul in numerous places;[73] thus he had engaged in evangelistic work; but Timothy's main calling was probably elsewhere.[74] However, the fact that Paul links Timothy's doing the work of an evangelist with fulfilling his ministry suggests that evangelism is an essential part of a complete ministry.

Now a word concerning the relevance of Paul's injunction for today. Sometimes one hears pastors[75] say that since their calling is to shepherd the flock, to build up a congregation by word and deed, they cannot also do the work of an evangelist. In response, let me say that pastors may not be called to be evangelists, but they can scarcely avoid doing the work of an evangelist since any congregation (unless it is totally sealed off from the world) will also include unbelievers who need to hear and believe the gospel. Moreover, there should be times and occasions for preaching and witnessing outside the confines of the local congregation. Thus to be an evangelist may not be a pastor's gift but, in line with Paul's word, evangelism surely has a vital place in fulfilling pastoral ministry.

Now let us return to Philip the evangelist and summarize some points that may have particular relevance for those likewise gifted by Christ for this task.

1. He was a man "full of the Spirit" (see Acts 6:3, 5) and moved under the direction of the Holy Spirit. In regard to the Ethiopian eunuch, "the Spirit said to Philip, 'Go up and join this chariot' " (8:29). After his experience with the Ethiopian, as we have noted, "the Spirit of the Lord caught up Philip . . . [and] Philip was found at Azotus." Fullness of the Spirit, direction by the Spirit, even being transported by the Spirit: what a divine enablement for the task of evangelism!

2. As Philip proclaimed Christ, he also performed "miraculous signs" (Acts 8:6 NIV) such as casting out evil spirits and healing the lame and paralyzed. By such miracles not only were many people blessed, but also by experiencing and seeing the power of God in action they were all the more ready to

[72]From Azotus (the Greek name for Ashdod), a town twenty miles north of Gaza, to Caesarea there were such towns as Lydda and Joppa where Philip doubtless preached. Acts 9 first tells of "saints that lived at Lydda" (v. 32), and then reports that "at Joppa [there was] a disciple named Tabitha" (v. 36). It is possible that all of these believers came to faith through Philip's preaching the gospel. As a side note it is interesting that Philip later made Caesarea his home (see earlier quotation from Acts 21:8).

[73]For example, Paul writes to the Philippians, "As a son with his father he [Timothy] has served with me in the work of the gospel" (2:22 NIV).

[74]Paul had just urged Timothy to be "unfailing in patience and in teaching" (2 Tim. 4:2). (On Timothy as teacher, as "minister of the word," see infra, pages 181–96).

[75]Or pastors and teachers (so throughout this paragraph).

receive the good news of salvation. Surely today there is need for power evangelism that heals body, soul, and spirit.

3. Philip made effective use of the Scriptures. The Ethiopian eunuch was reading Isaiah 53:7–8 when Philip joined his chariot, and "beginning from this Scripture he [Philip] preached Jesus to him" (Acts 8:35 NASB). What the miraculous signs had been to the Samaritans, the opening up of Scripture was to the eunuch. Philip knew the Scriptures thoroughly—and so must one who today is to be a truly effective evangelist.

4. Philip's words and actions brought about decision and commitment. The Samaritans and the Ethiopian eunuch believed and were immediately baptized. It continues to be urgent that faith and baptism—the inward belief and outward confirmation—be closely joined.

5. Philip's work of evangelism also prepared the way for the reception of the Holy Spirit. Some days after the Samaritans had believed and been baptized, Peter and John came from Jerusalem and enabled the Samaritans to receive the gift of the Holy Spirit: "They [Peter and John] laid their hands on them and they received the Holy Spirit" (Acts 8:17). This suggests that, although the evangelist's work may not always include the converts' receiving the Holy Spirit, his bringing people to salvation is essential background for this reception to occur. In regard to the Ethiopian eunuch, the text ordinarily used in Acts says nothing about such a reception of the Spirit on his part; however, some versions of Acts 8:39 read immediately following the report of the Ethiopian's baptism: "The Holy Spirit fell upon the eunuch."[76] Whether or not this belongs in the original text, the later words, "the eunuch . . . went on his way rejoicing" (v. 39), may imply as much.[77] In any event, the evangelist's work should prepare the way for those who believe to receive the Holy Spirit. This matter needs much emphasis in our time lest the evangelist fail to recognize God's intention that people both believe in Christ and receive the Holy Spirit.

To conclude on "some as evangelists": This is unquestionably a ministry both in the New Testament and throughout the history of the church. In regard to "apostles and prophets," if there is any question about their continuation, there can surely be none about evangelists. For the preaching of the gospel is at the heart of the church's life and mission.

Christ still gives "some as evangelists." Indeed, today we need to see more and more evangelists raised up by the Lord who are full of the Holy Spirit, know the Scriptures thoroughly, move in "signs and wonders," bring about life-changing faith and commitment, and prepare people for receiving the gift of the Holy Spirit. May the gracious Lord give many such evangelists to proclaim the gospel in our time!

D. Pastors and Teachers—"some as pastors and teachers"

As we begin this study, we will be viewing pastors and teachers as those who are called to an equipping ministry basically for the local church. Let us

[76]This longer reading, belonging to the Western text, is less well attested than the rendering earlier quoted: "The Spirit of the Lord caught up Philip." However, it is quoted by such church fathers as Jerome, Augustine, and Cyril of Jerusalem. Bruce writes that the "important effect of the longer reading is to make it clear that the Ethiopian's baptism was followed by the gift of the Spirit" (*The Book of Acts*, rev. ed., NICNT, 178).

[77]E.g., in Acts 13:52, there is this statement: "The disciples were filled with joy and with the Holy Spirit." The connection between the filling of the Holy Spirit and joy is apparent.

consider this ministry in its twofold function.[78]

1. The Twofold Function

a. Shepherding. In regard to the word "pastors," it is important to recognize that this is simply another word for "shepherds."[79] The basic responsibility of pastors is to tend their congregation, the "sheep" God has committed to their care.

First of all, we observe that Christ Himself is *the* shepherd. Even as Christ is *the* apostle, *the* prophet, and *the* evangelist, He is also *the* pastor or shepherd. He is the *good* shepherd. In the Gospel of John, Jesus declares, "I am the good shepherd. The good shepherd lays down his life for the sheep" (10:11); again, "I am the good shepherd; I know my own and my own know me" (v. 14). He is the *great* shepherd. The writer to the Hebrews speaks of "the God of peace who brought again from the dead our Lord Jesus, the great shepherd of the sheep" (13:20). He is the *chief* shepherd. Peter first refers to Christ as "the Shepherd and Overseer of your souls" (1 Pet. 2:25 NIV) and later speaks of the day "when the Chief Shepherd appears" (5:4 NIV). Truly, as good, great, and chief, Christ is *the* shepherd.[80]

The gift of the exalted Christ in giving "some as pastors" accordingly means that He gives gifts to certain ones to share in His shepherding ministry. Significantly, the primary reference to this is in the Gospel of John. The One who calls Himself "the good shepherd" summoned His first apostle, Peter, to fulfill a shepherding role. Three times Jesus asked about Peter's love for Him, and after Peter's threefold affirmative reply, Jesus said in sequence: "Feed my lambs" (21:15); "Tend[81] my sheep" (v. 16); and "Feed my sheep" (v. 17). Jesus was therefore saying something like this: "Peter, you will demonstrate your love for Me as you take care of the flock that belongs to Me. I have laid down My life for the sheep; now it is up to you to take care of those for whom I died. Feed My lambs, My little ones. Guard My sheep, My grown ones. Feed them too, that they may truly live." Simon Peter was commanded by Christ the Good Shepherd to shepherd His total flock.

Peter was by no means the only one so commanded, for Christ gave "some as pastors." The task of shepherding is

---

[78]Unlike the previous equipping ministries, there is no "some as" before "teachers." Hence pastors and teachers are best understood, not as distinct orders but as separate functions. EGT—"not two distinct offices but designations of the same men . . . in different functions, the former defining them according to their office of oversight, the latter according to their office of instruction and guidance" (3:330). See also F. F. Bruce, *The Epistles to the Ephesians*, NICNT, 348; Marcus Barth, *Ephesians 4–6*, AB, 438–39. Calvin writes that "Paul speaks indiscriminately of pastors and teachers as belonging to one and the same class," but then he adds, "But this does not appear to me a sufficient reason why the two offices . . . should be compounded" (*Commentary on Ephesians*, in loco, Beveridge trans.). It seems best to speak of one basic ministry with a twofold function.

[79]The Greek word in Ephesians 4 is *poimenas*, a form of *poimēn*. *Poimēn* (whether singular or plural) is regularly translated "shepherd" elsewhere in the New Testament.

[80]There are other indirect references to Christ as shepherd in the Gospels. See Matthew 26:31: " 'I will strike the shepherd, and the sheep of the flock will be scattered' " (an OT quotation that Jesus applied to Himself and His disciples); Mark 6:34: "He had compassion on them, because they were like sheep without a shepherd"; Luke 12:32: "Fear not, little flock, for it is your Father's good pleasure to give you the kingdom"; 15:3–7, the parable about the lost and found sheep: "Rejoice with me, for I have found my sheep which was lost."

[81]Literally, "shepherd" (as in NASB). The Greek word is *poimaine*.

also given to others. Peter himself makes this clear in his first letter when he writes to the elders, "I exhort the elders among you, as your fellow elder . . . shepherd[82] the flock of God among you, exercising oversight. . ." (5:1–2 NASB). Then Peter adds three sets of contrasts: "not under compulsion, but voluntarily . . . not for sordid gain, but with eagerness; nor yet as lording it over those allotted to your charge, but proving to be examples to the flock" (vv. 2–3 NASB). And then he gives this glorious promise: "And when the Chief Shepherd appears, you will receive the unfading crown of glory" (v. 4 NASB).

It is noteworthy that the elders are immediately told to shepherd. They are not as such called pastors or shepherds (as in Ephesians 4), but in the discharge of their responsibility they are enjoined to shepherd or pastor God's flock. The elders in that sense are shepherds.[83]

This brings us to some words of Paul likewise addressed to elders. Paul sent to Ephesus for "the elders of the church" (Acts 20:17), and in his farewell address to them he said, "Be on guard for yourselves and for all the flock, among which the Holy Spirit has made you overseers, to shepherd[84] the church of God which He purchased with His own blood" (v. 28 NASB). Hence Paul, even as Peter did, enjoins the elders to shepherd the flock, the people of the church. Thus the elders fulfill a pastoral function.

The pastoral role, according to both Peter and Paul, is first of all one of *oversight*. Pastors are to oversee the activities of the flock. They are to perform this function willingly and freely—not because it is required of their position, or because anyone is forcing them. They are to serve as pastors with eagerness and enthusiasm, not for monetary gain. Moreover, they are to be examples of humble service to the flock, not domineering or lording it over those committed to their care.[85] If pastors thus serve willingly and eagerly, with no desire for "sordid gain," and do not use their positions to domineer their flock, but walk humbly among those in their charge, they will be good pastors. When the Chief Shepherd appears, they will receive an "unfading crown of glory." The Chief Shepherd will gloriously reward His faithful undershepherds.

Beyond overseeing the activities of the flock, pastors have a particular concern for the spiritual lives of their people. As we noted, Peter says that Christ is "the Shepherd and Overseer of [our] souls." Pastors are given by Christ to exercise special oversight of the souls of those He has redeemed and who thereafter need to be nourished so as to grow more and more like Him. This is indeed a high and grave responsibility that pastors have—to be overseers of souls!

Further, recall the example of Christ Himself as "the good shepherd." Good pastors know their sheep, and their sheep know them; hence there is a close personal relationship between them. Good pastors reach out to their sheep at any point of need, and the sheep in return trust them. Indeed, good pastors are ready and willing to give themselves totally and sacrificially for the sake of their flock. Christ laid down His life for His sheep: this is the ultimate test of pastoral devotion.

The pastoral role is also that of *guarding*. Paul refers to this in his

[82]The Greek word is *poimanate*.

[83]We will discuss this in more detail later under nomenclature of elders, pages 202–3.

[84]The Greek word is *poimainein*.

[85]Recall the words of Paul to the Ephesian elders about "the flock, *among* [or "in"—*not* "over" as in KJV—the Greek word is *en*] which the Holy Spirit has made you overseers."

words to the elders from Ephesus: "Be on guard[86] for yourselves and for all the flock." The brunt of Paul's words is related to dangers both from without and within, for shortly following his injunction to the elders, Paul says, "I know that after my departure fierce wolves will come in among you, not sparing the flock; and from among your own selves will arise men speaking perverse things, to draw away the disciples after them" (Acts 20:29–30). Even as shepherds must always be on guard against fierce wolves that would ravage and devour the flock, so must pastors constantly guard against those who bring in false and destructive teaching. Such teaching may arise even from within the church; it may seem true but actually be deceptive. By this means people are led away from others in the flock. Pastors must always be on guard, for the souls of their people are at stake.

Here we may return to Ephesians and recall Paul's statement that one of the purposes of the equipping ministries is "that we may no longer be children, tossed to and fro and carried about with every wind of doctrine, by the cunning of men, by their craftiness in deceitful wiles" (4:14). The "cunning of men" may well refer to those both outside and inside the church who cause havoc to believers. "Pastors and teachers," whose work is the climax of the equipping ministries, occupy an urgent and important role in constantly guarding against such disturbances.

One thing for which pastors must be on the alert is any teaching that does not center in Christ as the only way of salvation. In regard to this, Jesus not only speaks of Himself as "the good shepherd" but also as "the door" of the sheep (John 10:9). Earlier He referred to "thieves and robbers," who seek to come in some other way than through the door (see vv. 1, 8); then He adds, "I am the door; if any one enters by me, he will be saved, and will go in and out and find pasture" (v. 9). There is no other way to salvation but through Christ, who is "the way, and the truth, and the life" (John 14:6). Thus any teaching from without or within that would weaken or distort this fact must be guarded against by vigilant shepherds.

b. Teaching. This brings us to a more direct consideration of the importance of the teaching function: "some as pastors and *teachers*."

Before examining this further, let us remember that Jesus was not only *the* pastor or shepherd, but He was *the* teacher (even as He was *the* apostle, *the* prophet, and *the* evangelist). Throughout the Gospels Jesus is many times addressed as "Teacher,"[87] and He also refers to Himself as "the Teacher." For example, "the Teacher says to you, Where is the guest room, where I am to eat the passover with my disciples?" (Luke 22:11; cf. Matt. 26:18; Mark 14:14). In the Fourth Gospel Jesus says, "You call me Teacher and Lord; and you are right, for so I am" (13:13). As the Teacher, "Jesus went about all the cities and villages, teaching in their synagogues" (Matt. 9:35); He "taught the people from the boat" (Luke 5:3); in "the region of Judea and beyond the Jordan . . . as his custom was, he taught them" (Mark 10:1); He "taught in the temple" (John 7:28)—on and on. His teaching was the life-giving word of God. Early in His ministry, in response to a temptation by Satan, Jesus declared, "Man shall not live by bread alone, but by every word that proceeds from the mouth of God"

[86]The Greek word is *prosechete*, "take heed" (KJV, RSV), "keep watch over" (NIV, NEB).

[87]The Greek word is *didaskolos*, and is used some forty times as a title for Jesus. Thirteen times Jesus is addressed as "Rabbi," a common title for a public teacher.

(Matt. 4:4).[88] Hence, His teaching of the word of God brought life—"the words that I have spoken to you are spirit and life" (John 6:63).

Thus the primary purpose of all Christian teaching is to feed people with the same life-giving word. I have spoken of the role of pastors in overseeing and guarding the sheep; now let us view this from the aspect of *feeding* and *nourishing* the sheep. Recall that Peter was commanded by Jesus not only to tend His sheep—referring essentially to overseeing and guarding—but also to feed His lambs and feed His sheep. This feeding can occur only through "every word that proceeds from the mouth of God"—and it is the teacher's responsibility to enable people to understand and receive this word.[89]

2. Ministry of the Word

We come now to a consideration of the role of those whose primary task is the ministry of the word. In doing so we will note Paul's instructions to Timothy in relation to the church in Ephesus.[90] I will also refer to Paul's words to Titus in Crete.[91] Let us observe some of the directions Paul gave Timothy and Titus, especially in regard to preaching and teaching,[92] that is, the ministry of the word. We will be concerned also to observe the relevance of this for the local church today.

We note first that preaching and teaching stand in close connection. Paul tells Timothy, "[Give] attention to the public reading[93] of scripture, to preaching,[94] to teaching" (1 Tim. 4:13). Paul's references to both preaching and teaching relate to the public function of speaking to the local congregation. Preaching, or exhortation, is speech that appeals basically to heart and will; teaching is directed more to the mind. In a certain sense the two are inseparable, because preaching also speaks to the mind and teaching to the heart and will. However, there are times and occasions when preaching or teaching is the principal thrust and may occur on separate occasions.[95] Together the two

---

[88]Jesus quoted these words from Deuteronomy 8:3.

[89]I will not elaborate further at this point on the teaching function since in the next section, "Ministry of the Word," much of that function will be discussed.

[90]Paul, when he was "going to Macedonia," urged Timothy to "remain at Ephesus" (1 Tim. 1:3). Timothy did remain there for several years (2 Timothy dates from Paul's final imprisonment).

[91]See Titus 1:5: "I left you in Crete." Timothy and Titus may be spoken of "as Paul's apostolic delegates" (Gordon Fee, *1 and 2 Timothy, Titus*, NIBC, 21). However, they both performed preaching and teaching functions while in Ephesus and Crete.

[92]The focus will be more on Timothy to whom Paul wrote in fuller detail.

[93]The Greek word is *anagnōsei*. The KJV has "reading," which might suggest private reading. However, *anagnōsis* was a word used for "the reading of law and prophets in the synagogue" (BAGD)—see, e.g., Acts 13:15—and carries over into the church. ("Of scripture" is not as such in the Greek text but is implied; it is added also in NIV, NASB, and NEB).

[94]Or "exhortation" (*paraklēsai*). Recall the earlier discussion of exhortation in chapter 4. Preaching or exhorting is speaking with urgency. See also 1 Timothy 6:2: "Teach and urge [*parakalei*—'preach' in NASB] these things." "Preaching" in these passages does not refer to evangelism, as in "preaching the good news," which equals evangelism (see previous discussion under "Evangelists") and is thus to nonbelievers. It refers rather to the exhortation of believers in the congregation.

[95]The relationship between the two is somewhat analogous to that of pulpit and lectern. One ordinarily thinks of the pulpit for preaching and the lectern for teaching. However,

may be called "the ministry of the word."[96]

The background for such a ministry of preaching and teaching, Paul enjoins, is the public reading of Scripture. This continues to be of signal importance in regard to all who speak officially because it is their responsibility to ground all that is said in the revealed Word of God. Reading the Scriptures aloud is important because the Bible is more than a silent document; it is God speaking to people, and therefore is best received if people hear the spoken word.[97] The Book of Revelation states, "Blessed is he who reads aloud[98] the words of the prophecy, and blessed are those who hear" (1:3). Public reading, or reading aloud, is important background for preaching and teaching the word.

As we examine Paul's words to Timothy, we now observe that Paul emphasizes the need to "give attention."[99] To "give attention" is far more than a casual thing; it calls for devotion to these matters. "Devote yourself to"[100] (NIV) is what Paul is urging Timothy. The public reading of Scripture, preaching, and teaching must be a matter of applying oneself in a total kind of way.

a. Soundness of Doctrine. The minister of the word is called upon to teach sound doctrine. Throughout his letters to Timothy Paul emphasizes sound words, teaching, or doctrine. For example, he speaks of "the sound[101] words of our Lord Jesus Christ" (1 Tim. 6:3); and "the sound words which you have heard from me" (2 Tim. 1:13). He also urges Titus to "teach what befits sound doctrine" (Titus 2:1). Soundness of doctrine must be the primary concern of the teacher of the word.

The importance and urgency of sound teaching was accentuated by the fact that much was being taught and practiced "contrary to sound doctrine" (1 Tim. 1:10). But also, says Paul, "the time is coming when people will not endure sound teaching, but having itching ears will accumulate for themselves teachers to suit their own likings" (2 Tim. 4:3). The responsibility of the minister of the word is great: he must find ways of bringing people back to the truths of Christian faith.

Sound doctrine was Paul's primary

some pulpits are used more for teaching and some lecterns are even used for preaching! Still, within an overarching unity there remains some difference between the two.

[96]This expression, found in Acts 6:4, is from a statement by the twelve apostles: "We will devote ourselves to prayer and to the ministry of the word." The "ministry of the word" refers particularly to the activity of the apostles in exhorting and teaching the rapidly growing community of believers.

[97]For example, the Ten Commandments were first spoken by God: "And God spoke all these words, saying. . ." (Exod. 20:1). Jesus many times in His teaching ministry emphasized hearing; e.g., "He who has ears to hear, let him hear" (Matt. 11:15; Mark 4:9; Luke 8:8; cf. Matt 13:9, 43; Mark 4:23; 7:16; Luke 14:35).

[98]The Greek word is *anaginōskōn* (similar to *anagnōsei* in 1 Tim. 4:13). The KJV, NIV, NASB, and NEB do not have "aloud." The RSV "reads aloud," I believe, better expresses the fact that the reading is preparatory to the hearing. (Similarly in regard to *anaginōskō*, see Luke 4:16 and Col. 4:16.)

[99]The Greek word is *proseche*, a present imperative derived from *prosechō*.

[100]According to Thayer, *prosechō* in 1 Timothy 4:13 means "to devote thought and effort to."

[101]The Greek word is *hygiainousin* (from *hygiaianō*), "healthy" or "sound." This may refer to physical health or soundness as in Luke 5:31 (NIV): "It is not the healthy [*hygiainontes*] who need a doctor, but the sick" (cf. Luke 7:10; 15:27). In the Pastoral Epistles *hygiaianō* invariably refers to words, teaching, doctrine. (*Hygiainounō* is the origin of our word "hygienic.")

concern. This clearly emerges from the exhortation after his opening salutation in 1 Timothy: "I urged you . . . [to] remain at Ephesus that you may charge certain persons not to teach any different doctrine"[102] (1:3). Then Paul mentions "myths and endless genealogies which promote speculations" (v. 4) and thus lead many from the truth. Later, after speaking of "good doctrine" (1 Tim. 4:6), Paul urges Timothy to "have nothing to do with godless and silly[103] myths" (v. 7). In his letter to Titus, Paul speaks of those "giving heed to Jewish myths" (Tit. 1:14), and tells Titus to "rebuke them sharply" (v. 13).[104] Sound doctrine has no place for godless myths and speculations that pervert faith. If rebuke is called for, it must be given.

In addition, Paul speaks of those who, totally contrary to sound doctrine, teach that "the resurrection has already taken place" and thereby "destroy the faith of some" (2 Tim. 2:18 NIV). In this case—even more than speculation about myths and genealogies—both sound doctrine and action[105] are needed. The true minister of the word must on every possible occasion stand firm on such pivotal doctrines as the resurrection and firmly resist any contrary teaching lest the faith of people be destroyed.

In regard to the future, Paul also says[106] that "in later times some will abandon[107] the faith and follow deceiving spirits and things taught by demons" (1 Tim. 4:1 NIV). He adds, "Such teachings come through hypocritical liars" (v. 2 NIV). As evidence of this, he says, "they forbid people to marry and order them to abstain from certain foods" (v. 3 NIV). Although these may not at first sound like the worst things that could be taught, they are demonically inspired. For such teachers actually deny God's good creation, including marriage as His blessed ordinance (Gen. 2:22–24) and food of all kinds as His gracious provision (Gen. 1:12, 29–30). So Paul adds, "Everything created by God is good" (1 Tim. 4:4). Thus the teaching about forbidding marriage and abstaining from certain foods—which might seem only to emphasize bodily rigor and asceticism—is actually extremely dangerous because it is an outright denial of God's Word and God's good creation. The tragedy is that one who embraces such a doctrine is on the slippery slope that leads to destruction. Paul adds truly: "If you [Timothy] point these things out to the brothers, you will be a good minister of Christ Jesus" (v. 6 NIV).

Pointing such things out remains the task of the true minister of the word. Indeed, if it is true that we live "in later times," we must expect an even greater increase in teachings that are inspired by demonic spirits. So again sound

---

[102]The Greek word is *heterodidaskalein*—"strange doctrines" (NASB), "false doctrines" (NIV).

[103]Or "old wives" (KJV, NIV). The Greek word is *graōdeis*—"a sarcastic epithet which . . . conveys the idea of limitless credulity" (Kelly, *The Pastoral Epistles*, HNTC, 99).

[104]It is not altogether clear what the "myths" (referred to three times above) were. Walter Lock, in reference to the "myths and genealogies," says that they were "probably . . . legends and stories centering around the pedigree of the patriarchs and O.T. history, which were handed down in tradition" (*The Pastoral Epistles*, ICC, 8).

[105]One of the two promoting this teaching was Hymenaeus (2 Tim. 2:17). In 1 Timothy Paul declares concerning Hymenaeus (as one of two): "I have delivered [him] to Satan that [he] may learn not to blaspheme" (1:20). This doubtless meant excommunication but with hope of final restoration.

[106]Recall Paul's words about the future in 2 Timothy 4:3.

[107]Or "fall away from" (NASB). The Greek word is *apostesontai*, literally "commit apostasy."

doctrine and teaching are desperately needed lest people abandon the faith and be spiritually destroyed. How important is Paul's word: "Teach (and keep on teaching) what befits sound doctrine!"

b. The Importance of Scripture. I earlier referred to the public reading of Scripture as the background for the ministry of the word. Now I comment on Scripture as the *basis* for everything the minister of the word says. Public reading is valuable, but even more important is the continued reliance on it in the speaking of God's truth. To read Scripture aloud and then to pass on to other unrelated things in preaching and teaching is not to be a true minister of the word. Scripture is background, but also, and primarily, it is the substance and norm of what is to be said. Scripture alone contains the basic truth to be set forth.

Let us note several things Paul said to Timothy about the truth of God's Word. First, Paul says, "Retain the standard[108] of sound words which you have heard from me. . . . Guard, through the Holy Spirit who dwells in us, the treasure[109] which has been entrusted to you" (2 Tim. 1:13–14 NASB). Of course, there were no New Testament Scriptures when Paul wrote Timothy, but Timothy had been taught the "sound words" of the apostle Paul. These were to be the standard of Timothy's teaching and a treasure to be carefully guarded. "O Timothy," Paul cries in another place, "guard what has been entrusted to you" (1 Tim. 6:20). Since Timothy's time, the church has been blessed to have Paul's words and other apostolic writings in the New Testament. They are the standard, the norm of all teaching, and must be carefully guarded as a treasure. "O church, O teacher, guard what has been entrusted to you!" Paul's words are words of truth so that Timothy, the church, and all teachers of the word must be careful to guard and explicate faithfully the apostolic teaching.

It is significant that Paul also stresses the importance of the indwelling Holy Spirit for guarding the entrusted treasure. This counsel to guard implies that there will be persons who treat the treasure lightly, perhaps some will even disregard or distort it. Their standard will no longer be scripturally sound words but their own judgments and reflections. Whatever the case, it is urgent that ministers of the word rely on the Holy Spirit who dwells within to guard and protect this holy treasure of God's truth.

Since the Holy Spirit is the final Author of Scripture, and every true believer has the Spirit dwelling in him, there is strong inner resistance to any abuse of God's word. Only by the indwelling Spirit's wisdom and power can the teacher stand firm in protection and explication of the treasure of Holy Scripture.

Second, Paul says to Timothy, "Be diligent to present yourself approved to God as a workman who does not need to be ashamed, handling accurately[110]

---

[108]The Greek word is *hypotypōsin*. The RSV and NIV read "pattern"; KJV, "form." BAGD has "model, example . . . in the sense of standard." "Standard" is probably the best translation.

[109]Literally, "the good deposit" (*tēn kalēn parathēken*) as in NIV. According to Thayer, the term *parathēke* refers to "a deposit, a trust or thing consigned to one's faithful keeping . . . [and is] used of the correct knowledge and pure doctrine of the gospel, to be held firmly and faithfully, and to be conscientiously delivered unto others."

[110]The Greek is *orthotomounta*. The KJV reads "rightly dividing"; RSV, "rightly handling"; NIV, "correctly handles." The word *orthotomeō* is not found elsewhere in the

the word of truth" (2 Tim. 2:15 NASB). It is one thing to have the treasure of God's word in Scripture; it is another to handle accurately and rightly that word of truth. This does not come easily. There is the call for diligence—"be diligent"—in study,[111] so that the one who ministers the word is first of all taught by God's Word. A teacher is a workman, and, like any other good workman, he must come forth with a good and approved product. In the case of the teacher, the approval is not from men but from God, the One whose Word is being studied and will be expounded. The accountability is *extremely* high.

Thus the minister of the word must accurately handle the word of God's truth. This means to avoid wrangling and quibbling about words,[112] disputing their truth. As one illustration of this, Paul later cites those who have "wandered away from the truth" by saying that "the resurrection has already taken place" (2 Tim. 2:18 NIV).[113] God's Word clearly teaches a future resurrection,[114] and those who quibble and argue about it can be destructive of people's faith. "Godless chatter"—which is what this amounts to—"will eat its way like gangrene" (vv. 16–17). This is the fatal damage wrought by godless teaching.

What is called for is *not* wrangling or disputing about words but rightly and accurately setting forth God's truth. This means careful study of each word in a given text of Scripture, recognizing the words in their larger context and being aware of the broader range of Scriptures that will help clarify the meaning of a given passage.[115] Then—and surely with the help of the indwelling Spirit—the minister of the word will set forth the truth of Scripture in such a way that listeners will be strengthened and blessed.

Third, Paul writes Timothy, "All scripture is inspired by God[116] and profitable for teaching, for reproof, for correction, and for training in righteousness, that the man of God may be complete, equipped for every good work" (2 Tim. 3:16–17). Prior to these words, Paul reminded Timothy that from childhood he had been acquainted with "the sacred writings" (v. 15), that is, the Old Testament Scriptures. Then Paul adds the emphasis that all Scripture is inspired by God: it is basically not man's word but God's Word. "All scripture" now goes beyond the Old

---

New Testament. In the LXX it occurs in Proverbs 3:6: "In all your ways acknowledge him, and he will make straight [*orthotomē*] your paths." BAGD suggests (in line with Prov. 3:6) that perhaps the meaning of Paul's statement is "to guide the word of truth along a straight path."

[111]The KJV reads, "*Study* to show thyself approved."

[112]In regard to some teachers, Paul had just urged Timothy, "Solemnly charge them . . . not to wrangle about words" (v. 14 NASB). The Greek for "to wrangle about words" is *logomachein* (so our English word "logomachy"—a dispute about words).

[113]Recall my comments in the previous section on the contention that "the resurrection has already taken place."

[114]As in 1 Corinthians 15:12–57. Belief in the future bodily resurrection is an essential truth in Christian faith. "If there is no [future] resurrection of the dead, then Christ has not been raised. If Christ has not been raised . . . you are still in your sins" (vv. 13, 17).

[115]This is sometimes called "the analogy of Scripture," namely, that since Scripture is an overall unity, the meaning of a particular passage can be illuminated by a study of other passages.

[116]Or "God-breathed" (NIV). The Greek word *theopneustos* used here does not mean "God-dictated." Words of Scripture are breathed by God through human words and human ways of speech, so that man is fully active in setting God's truth in writing. (See *Renewal Theology*, 1:22, nn.17, 18.)

Testament. Paul himself speaks elsewhere of accepting his message "not as the word of men but as . . . the word of God" (1 Thess. 2:13), and Peter refers to Paul's letters as Scripture.[117] The Gospels, the Epistles, and the Book of Revelation are recognized to be the New Testament canon, and thus, along with the Old Testament, constitute "all scripture" that is divinely inspired.

Since all Scripture is given by divine inspiration, it is therefore "profitable[118] for teaching." The minister of the word may fully depend on Scripture for everything that Paul next mentions—reproof, correction, and training in righteousness. Scripture thus makes him, as "a man of God,"[119] one who is "complete,[120] equipped for every good work." The complete teacher has his life and teaching thoroughly grounded in the inspired Word of God. Further, such a teacher has no need for other sources than the Scriptures:[121] by the Scriptures alone he is "complete" and thus "equipped for every good work."

c. Quality of Life. Next we consider the quality of life expected of one who is a minister of the word. Paul speaks at one point of Timothy being "a good minister[122] of Christ Jesus" (1 Tim. 4:6). Let us observe some qualifications.

1. *Sincere faith.* Paul says to Timothy, "The aim of our charge is love that issues from a pure heart and a good conscience and sincere faith" (1 Tim. 1:5). This is Paul's aim in all his teaching, and he charges Timothy to keep this same goal before him as he instructs others.[123] If the teacher is to inculcate this in others, he must likewise embody what he is teaching.

We look first at "sincere faith." Paul speaks highly of this quality in Timothy: "I am reminded of your sincere[124] faith, a faith that dwelt first in your grandmother Lois and your mother Eunice and now, I am sure, dwells in you" (2 Tim. 1:5). Timothy had a genuine faith. He had been blessed by both a mother and a grandmother of faith. Indeed, as we have previously noted, Paul later refers to the fact that Timothy "from childhood" had been acquainted with "the sacred writings" of the Old

[117]Peter says about Paul's letters that "there are some things in them hard to understand, which the ignorant and unstable twist to their own destruction, as they do the other scriptures" (2 Peter 3:16). The "other scriptures" clearly implies Paul's letters to be Scripture. (See also p. 111, n.91.)

[118]The Greek word is *ōphelimos*—"useful, beneficial, advantageous" (BAGD). It might also be translated "valuable," as in 1 Timothy 4:8 where Paul says that "godliness is of value [*ōphelimos*] in every way."

[119]"The man of God" is the teacher, not the one taught. Timothy was addressed earlier by Paul as a "man of God" (1 Tim. 6:11).

[120]The Greek word is *artios*, "perfect" (KJV), "adequate" (NASB), "efficient" (NEB). "Complete" is probably best. BAGD has "complete, capable, proficient = able to meet all demands."

[121]I do not mean by this that the teacher should not draw on biblical helps such as lexicons, commentaries, and the like (but even then the focus must remain on the Scriptures themselves). My point is that other sources—such as philosophy, science, and psychology—add nothing essential to the Christian teacher's understanding. Such sources may, on occasion, be utilized as points of contact and as media for biblical truth (as Paul, e.g., quotes Stoic philosophy and uses it to express truth about God—see Acts 17:27–29). Natural understanding cannot, however, be the source of Christian truth.

[122]Or "servant" (NASB, NEB). The Greek word is *diakonos*.

[123]The charge relates to the life of the church as a whole. However, it refers in a special way to the teacher. Note the words that follow in verses 6 and 7.

[124]The KJV has "unfeigned." The Greek word is *anypokritou*—literally, "without hypocrisy."

Testament. Faith dwelt in those who instructed young Timothy, and now the faith was likewise *in* him.[125] Thus when it came to teaching about Christian faith, Timothy could speak as one who deeply and sincerely believed: faith was in him.

Paul also mentions "the faith" a number of times. He speaks of Timothy's being "constantly nourished on the words of the faith and of the sound doctrine" (1 Tim. 4:6 NASB). Faith refers here not so much to believing as it does to the body of faith of Christian truth (analogous to "the sound doctrine"). This is important also: not only to have faith dwelling within but also to be nourished constantly by the words, the truths of faith. By them one who teaches the faith will himself continue to grow and be strengthened.

The priority, however, lies with the minister of the word being himself a person of sincere, genuine faith. It is a faith in Christ, not simply of the mind but of the heart, a faith that comes from Christ Himself and is the inner reality of one's life. Without such an inward anchor of heart and soul, there is a lack of sincerity and genuineness in one who ministers the word of God. He may mouth the words of faith, but they have no life-giving quality.

2. *A good conscience*. I have already quoted Paul's words about "a good conscience and sincere faith" (1 Tim. 1:5). He again links these two in a charge to Timothy about waging "the good warfare, holding faith and a good conscience"[126] (1 Tim. 1:18–19). Faith is primary, but there is also the importance of a good conscience.

Paul spoke of himself as having a clear conscience: "I thank God whom I serve with a clear conscience" (2 Tim. 1:3). In his trial before the governor Felix, Paul declared, "I strive always to keep my conscience clear before God and man" (Act 24:16 NIV). Thus Paul speaks of what he personally knows by emphasizing to Timothy the importance of a clear, or good, conscience. It is interesting that Peter similarly writes, "Keep your conscience clear, so that, when you are abused, those who revile your good behavior in Christ may be put to shame" (1 Peter 3:16). A good conscience and good behavior are closely associated.

Conscience, according to Paul, exists in all people as an inward moral sense of right and wrong. Paul says elsewhere that the Gentiles have "the requirements of the law . . . written on their hearts, their consciences also bearing witness, and their thoughts now accusing, now even defending them" (Rom. 2:15 NIV). Hence conscience is a kind of inner monitor, bearing witness to the rightfulness or wrongfulness of any action. The writer to the Hebrews says, "Let us draw near . . . with our hearts sprinkled clean from an evil conscience" (10:22). This has happened through "the blood of Jesus" (v. 19). Now the critical matter is to keep the conscience clear—that monitor of right and wrong—by walking in all good conscience.

It is urgent that one who teaches others maintain a good and clear conscience. This does not mean that the minister of the word will never do wrong (there is no complete sanctification in this life), but it does mean that he will be constantly striving to turn from evil and walk in the truth. If this is his continuing concern, even if there are failures now and then, the teacher will maintain a good conscience.

There is always the danger that min-

[125]A rich heritage of faith is a special blessing for one who is to be a teacher of God's word.

[126]The Greek word for "conscience" is *syneidēsin*, a form of *syneidēsis*.

isters of the word will become involved in acts of moral turpitude that harm their ministry. Paul warns Timothy about the teachings of "hypocritical liars, whose consciences have been seared as with a hot iron" (1 Tim. 4:2 NIV). Such people hardly recognize their own wrongdoing and can only mislead those they teach. A teacher's conscience may not have been that severely "seared," but his moral actions may constantly belie the truth of what he says.

Paul also speaks of some who have actually gone so far as to *reject* conscience. Immediately following his words about "holding faith and a good conscience," Paul adds, "By rejecting conscience, certain persons have made shipwreck of their faith" (1 Tim. 1:19). Among them are Hymenaeus and Alexander (v. 20), the former being one who caused much trouble by teaching a past resurrection only.[127] It is significant that as the call of conscience was rejected, false teaching made its headway. Indeed, false teaching is frequently more the result of rejecting the call of conscience than of simply erring intellectually.

We much need to hear Paul today on the importance of a good and clear conscience. Far too many who are involved in preaching and teaching the word are walking in immorality. Sexual promiscuity needs particularly to be warned against, for many slip into it even though God's Word and their consciences testify against it. Before long their consciences are "seared," and gradually they "shipwreck" their own faith. Whatever the words they may continue to speak—however fervently, even sanctimoniously—they are bearers of death, not of life. If the ministers of the word do not keep a good conscience, there is little hope for them or for their people.

3. *Godliness*. What has been said about a good conscience leads to the importance of godliness in the teacher's life. Paul speaks of "the teaching which accords with godliness"[128] (1 Tim. 6:3), or "godly teaching" (NIV). It is teaching that springs from and promotes godly living.

Godliness is much to be desired. Paul speaks of it first in terms of all believers. He urges that prayer be offered for governing authorities "that we may live peaceful and quiet lives in all godliness and holiness" (1 Tim. 2:2 NIV). Paul next declares that "the mystery of godliness[129] is great" (1 Tim. 3:16 NIV), and then proceeds to outline a statement about the Incarnation: "He was manifested in the flesh . . . taken up in glory" (v. 16). Again, Paul says, "There is great gain in godliness with contentment" (6:6). In writing to Titus, Paul enjoins that believers "say 'No' to ungodliness and worldly passions, and . . . live self-controlled, upright and godly lives in this present age" (Titus 2:12 NIV). Godliness is of signal importance for all Christians.

Now focusing on teaching, we observe Paul's emphasis that it be godly, hence coming from one who is living a godly life. This, however, does not come easily: it calls for exercise and training. Paul writes to Timothy, "Train[130] yourself in godliness" (1 Tim. 4:7). Then he adds, "While bodily training is of some value, godliness is of

[127]Recall the earlier quotation from 2 Timothy 2:18: "holding that the resurrection is past already."

[128]The Greek word is *eusebeian*, "piety toward God, godliness" (Thayer).

[129]The RSV and NEB translate this phrase as "the mystery of our religion." This is also possible. For *eusebeia* BAGD gives "piety, godliness, religion."

[130]Or "exercise" (KJV). The Greek word is *gymnaze* (hence our English words "gymnastic" and "gymnasium").

value in every way, as it holds promise for the present life and also for the life to come" (v. 8). Paul does not discount bodily exercise and training. It is "of some value,"[131] but what is really important is training in godliness. Paul later adds, "To this end we toil and strive" (v. 10).

Paul does not elaborate much on what this training is. However, after he speaks of "godliness with contentment," Paul talks about "hurtful desires that plunge men into ruin and destruction" (1 Tim. 6:9), immediately adding, "For the love of money is a root of all sorts of evil,[132] and some by longing for it have wandered away from the faith, and pierced themselves with many a pang" (v. 10 NASB). Although Paul includes all people in declaring that evil and ruin can follow from the love of money, it is particularly true of the minister of the word. Such craving for money may lead not only to his own destruction but also to that of many who sit under his instruction. Paul's statement to Titus (previously quoted) in this context is now quite relevant: "Say 'No' to ungodliness and worldly passions." Training in godliness demands a constant turning away from the worldly yearning for money and all other ungodly passions.

Paul also warns against spurious godliness. He speaks of false teachers "who are depraved in mind and bereft of the truth, imagining that godliness is a means of gain" (1 Tim. 6:5). This is not a true godliness but an affected one, a kind of public piety that serves only to mask another end: personal gain. Paul also speaks about people "holding to a form of godliness, although they have denied its power" (2 Tim. 3:5 NASB). The form remains—a shell of godliness—but the power is far gone.

It is urgent that those who minister God's word manifest a genuine godliness. This is not easy: the teacher, like an athlete, should be in daily training for strengthening and development. There will be difficulties, including attacks, from many. "Indeed," says Paul, "all who desire to live a godly life in Christ Jesus will be persecuted" (2 Tim. 3:12). Still, it is abundantly worth all effort, for in so living both the teacher and those who are taught by him will be richly blessed.

4. *Purity*. I have earlier quoted this statement of Paul: "The aim of our charge is love that issues from a pure heart and a good conscience and sincere faith" (1 Tim. 1:5). Let us now give consideration to Paul's stress on purity.[133]

Shortly after talking about training in godliness, Paul says to Timothy, "Let no one despise your youth, but set the believers an example in speech and conduct, in love, in faith, in purity"[134] (1 Tim. 4:12). In regard to purity, Paul later speaks of this concerning younger women: "Treat . . . younger women

[131]The KJV rendering, "bodily exercise profiteth little," implies that it has almost no value.

[132]The RSV translates, "The love of money is the root of all evil." "A root" is more accurate (there is no article in the Greek text), and "all sorts of evil" is better, lest the translation suggest that "all evil" stems from the love of money. As C. K. Barrett says, "It is extravagant to assert that love of money is the root cause of all sins" (*The Pastoral Letters*, HNTC, 138). I hardly need to add that the statement one frequently hears that "money is the root of all evil" is even farther from Paul's teaching.

[133]I have already discussed "good conscience" and "sincere faith," and, in a sense, under "godliness" have considered "purity" since the latter two are in many ways similar. However, although I recognize some overlap between godliness and purity, it is helpful to separate the two because Paul often speaks of them separately; moreover, both are vital descriptions of the teacher's quality of life.

[134]The Greek word for "purity" is *hagneia*.

like sisters, in all purity" (1 Tim. 5:2). Both of these injunctions of Paul are addressed to Timothy as a young man, but they surely apply to all who lead and teach others. Exemplary speech and behavior, as well as total purity in relation to the opposite sex, are imperative for the minister of the word.

Next, in regard to purity, Paul charges Timothy, "Do not . . . participate in another man's sins; keep yourself pure" (1 Tim. 5:22). There is always the danger of sharing in, and thus giving consent to, another person's sinful actions, and thus forsaking personal purity. The minister of the word perhaps would not himself commit the sinful deed, but he feels less guilty if he simply goes along with another's action. Paul's charge: Don't do it. Keep yourself pure!

In 2 Timothy, Paul speaks of purifying oneself. "If any one purifies[135] himself from what is ignoble, then he will be a vessel for noble use, consecrated and useful to the master of the house, ready for any good work. So shun [or 'flee from' NASB] youthful passions and aim at righteousness, faith, love, and peace, along with those who call upon the Lord from a pure heart" (2:21–22). Timothy, a man of God, is called upon to purify himself so that he will be ready for any good work that the Master of the house may assign him. Then Timothy with others can call upon the Lord with a pure heart and aim at, or pursue, righteousness, faith, love, and peace. Shun, flee from, youthful passions! Once again, although Paul is addressing Timothy as a young man, his words are applicable to all who minister the word. There is always the need to purify oneself, to flee every evil passion, and thus to be a consecrated and holy vessel for the Lord's use.

It remains critically important that the minister of the word represent in himself a life that shows faith, purity of heart, and righteousness of action. The teacher must be an example before those whom he teaches. To be sure, like all believers, he will make mistakes at times, but this does not relieve him of the necessity of being a role model for others. The teacher must be truly a man of God.

5. *Love*. Now we arrive at the climax: love. Recall that Paul said, "The aim[136] of our charge is love that issues from a pure heart and a good conscience and sincere faith." We have already discussed, in reverse order, sincere faith, a good conscience, and purity. If those virtues, along with godliness, are present in the minister of the word, genuine love can then issue forth.

Faith and love are closely connected. Paul says that, even though he had blasphemed and persecuted Christ, he received mercy: "The grace of our Lord overflowed for me with the faith and love that are in Christ Jesus" (1 Tim. 1:14). The grace and mercy of Christ brought about in Paul both faith and love rooted in Christ. In 2 Timothy, Paul again refers to faith and love: "Follow the pattern of the sound words which you have heard from me, in the faith and love which are in Christ Jesus" (1:13). Faith in Christ is primary, and out of the continuing realization of His mercy and grace, love for others should flow.

Love is the constant goal. Sincere faith, a good conscience, godliness of life, and purity of heart are all important attributes in the minister of the word. But the aim, the goal, must always be love. Indeed, without love the other qualities of life avail little. They come

---

[135]The Greek word here is *ekkatharē*, from *ekkathairō*—"to cleanse out, clean thoroughly" (Thayer). (Note our derivative English word "catharsis.")

[136]Or "end"—the Greek word is *telos*.

to fruition only in the expression of love.

This needs to be emphasized because there are some fine ministers of the word who exemplify the virtues mentioned, but have a certain coldness, even aloofness, in their teaching. They are godly and moral persons, but there is not a genuine outreach in love to other people. Perhaps they need to reflect again and again, as Paul did, upon "the grace of our Lord" that "overflowed" for them also and yearn to express something of that love to those they teach.

The end of our charge is love; it can never be anything else.

d. Ordination. Ordination means appointing and setting apart for a special ministry. In the New Testament Jesus Himself is described as "appointed" by God: "He [Jesus] was faithful to him who appointed him" (Heb. 3:2). In turn, Jesus appointed, or ordained, twelve disciples: "He appointed ['ordained' KJV) twelve, to be with him, and to be sent out to preach and have authority to cast out demons" (Mark 3:14–15). Later "the Lord appointed seventy others, and sent them on ahead of him" (Luke 10:1). Toward the end of His ministry Jesus said to His apostles, "You did not choose me, but I chose you and appointed ['ordained' KJV] you that you should go and bear fruit" (John 15:16). In all of these cases the appointment (or ordination) was both the setting apart and giving authority to perform some special ministry.

Paul speaks of himself as appointed by Christ. In one of his conversion accounts, Paul quotes Jesus as saying, "I have appeared to you . . . to appoint you to serve and bear witness" (Acts 26:16). Similarly Paul writes to Timothy, "I was appointed ['ordained' KJV] a preacher and apostle . . . a teacher of the Gentiles in faith and truth" (1 Tim. 2:7). Paul's appointment, or ordination, was mediated through the laying on of hands by Ananias, who was told by the Lord in a vision to go to Paul ("Saul" at the time), "for he is a chosen instrument of mine" (Acts 9:15). After Ananias laid his hands on him (v. 17), Paul was as surely ordained for his ministry as any of the other apostles.[137]

Next we observe that Paul and Barnabas appointed elders in the churches where they had been ministering: "They . . . appointed ['ordained' KJV] elders for them in every church, with prayer and fasting" (Acts 14:23). Titus was asked by Paul to do the same thing in Crete. In his letter to Titus, Paul says, "The reason I left you in Crete was that you might straighten out what was left unfinished and appoint ['ordain' KJV] elders in every town, as I directed you" (1:5 NIV). It is clear, then, that elders were also ordained for their particular service in the church.[138]

Now we come to Timothy and his ordination. This is particularly important because of his teaching office; it therefore has vital relevance for the practice of such ordination in church history as well as today.

The clearest reference to Timothy's ordination is in 1 Timothy 4:14, where Paul says, "Do not neglect your gift,[139] which was given you[140] through a prophetic message when the body of el-

---

[137]There is no reference to Jesus' laying on hands in appointing the Twelve or the seventy. Of course, Jesus was personally present when He appointed those men. Now that He is in heaven, the laying on of hands is a way of personalizing His appointment for special ministry.

[138]For more on elders, see the next section, "Eldership."

[139]The Greek word for "gift" is *charismatos*, a form of *charisma*.

[140]Literally, "within you," *en soi*.

ders[141] laid hands on you" (NIV). Although the word "appointed" or "ordained" is not used regarding Timothy here, this seems clearly to be his "ordination."[142] Let us observe several points.

First, there was the impartation of a "special gift," or *charisma*. A *charisma* is a gift of grace,[143] not a natural talent or achievement. Such a gift therefore had been received by Timothy. What then was its nature? The answer seems clearly to be the gift of preaching and teaching. For immediately prior to the admonition "Do not neglect your gift," Paul had said, "Attend to the public reading of scripture, to preaching, to teaching" (1 Tim. 4:13). Also a little after that Paul writes, "Take heed to yourself and to your teaching" (v. 16). Thus, the gift bestowed was the ministry of the word.[144]

Accordingly, there is some parallel to the gift Timothy received in his ordination with the gifts or *charismata* of teaching and exhortation in Romans 12:7–8. Those gifts are linked even as preaching and teaching are in 1 Timothy. Actually "exhortation" and "preaching" are both translations of the same Greek word *paraklēsis*; thus Timothy's gift might also be translated "exhortation and teaching." Therefore, what Timothy received in his ordination was the combination of two gifts of grace, which are also one, the gift of preaching/teaching, that is, the ministry of the word.

Now looking again at Timothy's ordination, we observe that the first and altogether essential point is that the office of ministry of the word, indeed the whole preaching/teaching office, is *a gift of God's grace*. A person may surely prepare for it—indeed there could be years of preparation—but ultimately the office comes as a gift of grace. This means that there can be no claim to have earned it or merited it: it is wholly the gracious gift of God.

Second, the gift was bestowed on Timothy through *prophetic utterance*. Such utterance was doubtless inspired by the Holy Spirit and occurred while Timothy was being ordained.

A significant parallel to this event may be found in the commissioning of Paul and Barnabas[145] for missionary work. According to Acts 13, in the church at Antioch "there were prophets and teachers" (v. 1), including Paul and Barnabas, and "while they were worshiping the Lord and fasting, the Holy Spirit said, 'Set apart for me

[141]Or "presbytery" (KJV, NASB). The Greek word is *presbyteriou*.

[142]There is some hesitation in calling this an ordination. E.g., E. Schweizer writes, "It is not certain that it is a matter of ordination here at all, but . . . it most probably is" (*Church Order in the New Testament*, 209). Gordon Fee says, "It is probably an anachronism to refer to this event as an 'ordination' " (*1 and 2 Timothy, Titus*, NIBC, 108). However, J. N. D. Kelly does not hesitate to speak of the passage as referring to "the occasion of his [Timothy's] ordination or consecration to his office" (*The Pastoral Epistles*, HNTC, 106). Similarly TDNT speaks of the "ordination of Timothy by the laying on of hands" (6:666), also J. D. G. Dunn refers to it as "an act of ordination" (*Jesus and the Spirit*, 348). Perhaps the hesitancy of some to call this an ordination is due to later accretions in the history of the church wherein ordination takes on more sacramental significance (see p. 222, n.3). However, I would urge that 1 Timothy 4:14 be understood as a definitive picture of ministerial ordination in light of which later ordination practices may be evaluated.

[143]Recall the discussion of this in chapter 4, pages 125–33.

[144]Fee speaks of Timothy's gift as "the calling and gift for ministry as a preacher/teacher of the word" (*1 and 2 Timothy, Titus*, NIBC, 108).

[145]I say "commissioning" because this was not the beginning of Paul and Barnabas's ministry. (For their earlier association and work together see Acts 9:26–27; 11:22–26, 29–30; 12:25.)

Barnabas and Saul for the work to which I have called them' " (v. 2). After further fasting and praying, "they laid their hands on them and sent them off" (v. 3). What "the Holy Spirit said" was probably an utterance by one of the prophets present, and as such it clearly stated that the Holy Spirit was calling Paul and Barnabas to be set apart for missionary activity. It was not that Paul and Barnabas were unaware of this call on their lives, but this was the moment when through prophecy the Holy Spirit commissioned them for their upcoming work. In a similar manner the Holy Spirit undoubtedly spoke through prophecy concerning the work to which Timothy was being called.

Actually there seems to have been more than one prophecy in Timothy's case. Earlier in his letter to Timothy, Paul writes, "This command [or 'charge'] I entrust to you, Timothy, my son, in accordance with the prophecies previously made concerning you, that by them you may fight the good fight, keeping faith and a good conscience" (1 Tim. 1:18–19 NASB). These prophecies in all likelihood refer to the occasion of Timothy's ordination when there was prophetic utterance. Moreover, the prophecies at that time were of such significance that Paul could call them to Timothy's remembrance as background for the charge he was delivering to him.

Now let us try to view more clearly the scene at Timothy's ordination. Probably, as in the commissioning of Paul and Barnabas, there was worshiping and fasting. If so, this could have meant some extended time of preparation by both Timothy and those who were to ordain him. Then when the moment came for the "setting apart" to occur, various prophecies came forth. They may have included words relating to the responsibilities in Ephesus that Paul was later to assign him. Those prophesying may even have said something like this, in Paul's own words: "Fight the good fight" (1 Tim. 6:12); thus, be bold and courageous. In his second letter to Timothy, just after speaking again about "the gift [*charisma*] of God" that was within Timothy, Paul adds, "God did not give us a spirit of timidity but a spirit of power and love and self-control" (1:6–7). Perhaps, therefore, prophetic utterance reminded Timothy at his ordination that, whatever his natural inclinations,[146] God's *charisma* would be manifest in these various graces of the Holy Spirit: power, love, and self-control. Such prophecies as these would have so much significance that, as we have observed, Paul later refers to them in his own words to Timothy.

All of this has much relevance for us today. At the ordination of a minister of the word there should be opportunity for prophetic utterance. There may be preparation through prayer and fasting, perhaps also a solemn charge to the candidate; but when the actual moment of ordination is at hand, prophecies may be freely given. For it is through prophecy that God speaks directly in human words. For the one being ordained such words can have memorable significance for years to come. Unfortunately, many churches have almost totally overlooked, or looked down upon,[147] prophesying, and have allowed other ordination procedures to take its place.

---

[146]Timothy seems to have been a person of natural timidity. Paul added, immediately after the words quoted above, "Do not be ashamed then of testifying to our Lord, nor of me his prisoner" (v. 8). Again, "Be strong in the grace that is in Christ Jesus" (2 Tim. 2:1).

[147]Paul in one place writes, "Do not despise prophesying" (1 Thess. 5:20). Looking down upon or despising prophesying may be the real problem in many churches. Prophesying will hardly be expected at an ordination when it is really not desired at any time.

How much we need to recover the vital significance of prophetic utterance that Paul and Timothy knew and experienced!

Third, the climactic moment in ordination was the *laying on of hands by the body of elders*. The body of elders, or the presbytery,[148] acted as a unit.

Paul apparently functioned alongside the elders in laying hands on Timothy, for he says in 2 Timothy 1:6: "I remind you to rekindle the gift [*charisma*] of God that is within you through[149] the laying on of my hands." There was surely only one occasion of laying hands on Timothy, and the same word *charisma* is used in both 1 Timothy 4:14 and 2 Timothy 1:6. Hence it must have been Paul *with* the elders[150]—in Peter's language as a "fellow elder" (recall the phrase in 1 Peter 5:1)—although in 2 Timothy 1:6 Paul mentions only himself.[151] Paul by no means suggests that Timothy's ordination required his apostolic authority and presence, because he makes no reference to himself in 1 Timothy 4:14. It was the local body of elders who did the ordaining. Timothy was ordained "when the body of elders laid their hands on [him]" (NIV). To sum up: his ordination occurred *through* and *with* the laying on of hands.

Next we need to recognize the importance of the laying on of hands. In both accounts of Timothy's ordination, the laying on, or imposition, of hands is stated. Prophecy is not mentioned by Paul in referring to his own participation, as if to say that while prophecies are indeed valuable, the critical action is the imposition of hands. Prophetic utterance assured Timothy of his call to the ministry of the word, but it was by the laying on of hands that Timothy was placed in office.

We may ask, Did the laying on of hands automatically convey the gift of ministerial office to Timothy? The answer must be no. Three other factors need to be borne in mind. The first is *faith*. Timothy was a man of genuine faith. Immediately before Paul wrote to Timothy about rekindling the gift of God that was in him through the laying on of Paul's hands, he wrote the words earlier quoted, "I am reminded of your sincere faith, a faith that dwelt first in your grandmother Lois and your mother Eunice and now, I am sure, dwells in you" (2 Tim. 1:5). A sincere faith dwelling in Timothy was the human context for the *charisma* of special ministry to be received. Recall that the statements in both 1 Timothy 4:14 and 2 Timothy 1:6 speak of the charismatic gift as being within Timothy. Because Timothy was a man of sincere inward faith, the gift could likewise be received within. Second, there was the activity of a *valid ordaining body*, namely the elders of the church. The elders themselves had been ordained to office,[152] and because of this they could convey the gift of special ministry to others. This does not mean that other members

[148]The Greek word *presbyterion* refers in 1 Timothy 4:14 to the local body of elders: "the elders of any body (church) of Christians" (Thayer); "the presbyters [elders] in a local church" (EGT). *Presbyterion* is also used in reference to the high council of Jewish elders—"the assembly of the elders" (Luke 22:66), "the council of elders" (Acts 22:5). The one occurrence of *presbyterion* in regard to the Christian church is in 1 Timothy 4:14 and refers to no higher body than the local church. There was no presbytery representing several churches or with authority beyond the local church.

[149]The Greek preposition is *dia*.

[150]The Greek preposition is *meta*.

[151]Fee writes, "Here where the interest is almost totally personal, the focus is on Paul's part . . . thus appealing to their personal ties" (*1 and 2 Timothy, Titus*, NIBC, 226).

[152]For more on this see the next section, "Eldership."

of the congregation were not present for the ordination—indeed, some of the nonelders may have been the very ones who spoke prophecies—but the ordination itself occurred only through previously ordained elders. Third, there was the all-important *operation of the Holy Spirit*. That prophetic utterance occurred was in itself evidence of the Spirit's presence, for prophecy is one of the manifestations of the Holy Spirit.[153] Remember that in the commissioning of Paul and Barnabas the Holy Spirit spoke through prophecy; doubtless the same thing occurred in Timothy's ordination. But the critical matter was not so much prophetic utterance itself but what this utterance implied, namely, that the Holy Spirit, the inspirer of prophecy, was Himself actively on the scene. The ultimate validation of Timothy's ordination was the presence and power of the Holy Spirit.

Let us briefly reflect on the three matters just mentioned. For a valid ordination to occur the candidate must be an individual of sincere faith. Without such faith the whole procedure is null and void. One might speak of objective efficacy (through hands and the Spirit), but there could be no subjective appropriation. It would be ordination in name and rite only. Again, there must be the proper ordaining authority, namely, the body of elders, the presbytery. Whereas the presence of the congregation is important because it is the members whom the ordinand will serve, they do not participate in the laying on of hands. It is the body of elders[154] that has this particular responsibility. Finally, the action of the Holy Spirit is essential. While prayer and fasting may be needed for requesting God's grace in the Holy Spirit to be manifest,[155] we must recognize throughout that the Holy Spirit alone can confer the spiritual gift that makes ordination a valid and living experience. Come, Holy Spirit!

Let us note three additional points. First, while ordination occurs within the setting of a local church, and the one being ordained is usually installed there as minister of the word, the ordination is at the same time an action of and for the whole church of Jesus Christ. Thus he becomes an ordained minister of the word to serve the whole body of Jesus Christ. Timothy himself may have been ordained earlier in his home church at Lystra (see Acts 16:1),[156] but he is called by Paul later to serve the church in Ephesus. Second, in ordination a real conferring of grace occurs: there is a definite impartation of a gift, a *charisma*. It is a "gift . . . given" (1 Tim. 4:14), namely, a gift for teaching, or ministering the word. Third, there is no need for further ordination. If it has been a valid ordina-

[153]See *Renewal Theology*, 2:380–88.

[154]In some churches a bishop or presbytery above the local congregation is assumed to have this authority; in other churches the authority is viewed as resting in the whole congregation. Since ordination is an action of the church, neither viewpoint is so extreme as to render invalid its ordination practice. However, the ideal is to follow the New Testament procedure.

[155]In regard to ordination Calvin asks, "Was grace given by the outward sign [i.e., the laying on of hands]?" He replies, "Whenever ministers were ordained, they were recommended to God by the prayers of the whole church, and in this manner *grace from God was obtained for them by prayer*, and was not given to them by virtue of the sign, although the sign was not uselessly or unprofitably employed, but was a sure pledge of that grace which they received from God's own hand [italics added]" (*Calvin's Commentaries, Pastoral Epistles*, 190, Beveridge trans.).

[156]William Hendriksen writes that "in all probability this . . . happened at Lystra on Paul's second missionary journey" (*I & II Timothy and Titus*, NTC, 159).

tion,[157] repetition is unwarranted and unnecessary. Ordination is for one's whole future ministry in the church.

On this last point, there is, however, the possibility of *neglecting* this gift of ministry. Paul writes, as we have noted, "Do not neglect your gift." Then he adds, "Be diligent in these matters; give yourself wholly to them" (1 Tim. 4:15 NIV). The ministerial office, while a definite *charisma* from God, is no guarantee of automatic success. Rather it is an office of high and sober responsibility that needs constant diligence and unremitting devotion. Neglect can—and often unfortunately does—happen, to the great detriment of both the minister of the gospel and his people.[158]

One further word: a *rekindling* of the gift may be needed. Even to Timothy, a man with rich indwelling faith, Paul felt constrained to write (as we have noted), "I remind you to rekindle[159] the gift of God that is within you through the laying on of my hands" (2 Tim. 1:6). Timothy had received the gift several years before,[160] but now it needed to be freshly stirred up and fanned into flame. The gift was not gone, but it was like embers burning low that needed to be rekindled into a fresh flame of ardor and zeal for his high calling. Paul's words are surely relevant to many ordained ministers today, who may feel that they are accomplishing little for the kingdom and wonder if their ordination means anything. Paul's word is very timely: "The gift, the *charisma*, is within you"; you need only to "rekindle the gift," the charismatic fire. Truly, the challenge of ordained ministry of the gospel can shine with renewed brightness and zeal.

3. Eldership

We move now to a consideration of the role of elders in the ministry of the church. The main scriptural references are 1 Timothy 3:1–7 and Titus 1:5–9.

a. Background. 1. *Old Testament elders.* Elders are referred to over a hundred times in the Old Testament. In almost every instance the term "elders" is used in regard to Israel,[161] such as "the elders of Israel," the "elders of the people," the "elders of the city."[162] The elders were representatives of the people. Moses frequently called the elders together to hear God's word so that they could pass it on to their fellow Israelites.[163] On one occasion Moses gathered seventy of Israel's elders to share the burden of leading the people (Num. 11:16–17). At first the elders had little or no governing power, but in time they were given authority as local magistrates.[164] The elders later also became

---

[157]In accordance with the matters referred to in the previous paragraph.

[158]Paul minces no words in this regard. Shortly after he said, "Do not neglect your gift," he added, "Watch your life and doctrine closely. Persevere in them, because if you do, you will save both yourself and your hearers" (1 Tim. 4:16 NIV). For any ordained minister of the gospel these are strong words indeed.

[159]Or "fan into flame" (NIV); KJV has "stir up."

[160]Note that Paul's words are in 2 Timothy, written several years after 1 Timothy.

[161]It is interesting that the first mention of elders in the Old Testament is in reference to Pharaoh and Egypt: "Joseph went up to bury his father; and with him went up all the servants of Pharaoh, the elders of his household, and all the elders of the land of Egypt" (Gen. 50:7). Note also "the elders of Moab and the elders of Midian" (Num. 22:7). However, the preponderance of references to elders relates to Israel.

[162]E.g., "Go and gather the elders of Israel" (Exod. 3:16); "Moses came and called the elders of the people" (19:7); "the elders of the city came to meet him" (1 Sam. 16:4).

[163]E.g., see Exodus 12:21–28.

[164]E.g., see Deuteronomy 19:11–13; 21:1–9.

involved in national affairs.[165] After the Exile the elders were active in rebuilding the temple and in local administration.[166] Throughout the Old Testament the elders played an important role in the life of Israel.

2. *Jewish elders*. In the New Testament Jewish elders are mentioned thirty-two times. The Gospels alone have twenty-four such references, and the Book of Acts has eight. The elders are frequently referred to as "the elders of the people"[167]—terminology similar to that of the Old Testament. Often the elders are spoken of in connection with the chief priests; for example, "the chief priests and the elders of the people came up to [Jesus]" (Matt. 21:23). The scribes are also often included; for example, "the chief priests and the scribes with the elders" (Luke 20:1), "the people and the elders and the scribes" (Acts 6:12). Together the chief priests, the scribes, and the elders composed the Sanhedrin, the high council of the Jewish nation.[168]

The Sanhedrin in some instances is referred to as "the assembly, or council, of the elders," with the chief priest and scribes as its two constituent parts: "the assembly of the elders[169] of the people gathered together, both chief priests and scribes; and they led him away to their council [*synedrion*]" (Luke 22:66). Paul speaks at one point of "the high priest and the whole council of elders"[170] (Acts 22:5).

In summary, on the national level Jewish elders are to be viewed from two perspectives. On the one hand, the entire high council, the Sanhedrin, is called the council of the elders. This probably had its origins in Moses' council of seventy elders, for the Sanhedrin was composed likewise of seventy members. On the other hand, the elders are depicted along with the chief priests and the scribes and are usually mentioned third. It was the priestly aristocracy first, the Pharisaic teachers of the law [the scribes] second, and the elders third. In all likelihood the elders represented influential lay families among the Jews.

Also the local synagogue had its own council of elders. It exercised general administrative oversight of the community. Such elders of the synagogue are mentioned in Luke 7:3–5. From this eldership the head of the synagogue was chosen. He was called "the ruler of the synagogue"[171] (Luke 13:14), not in the sense of having authoritative headship but of supervising the services, maintaining order, and so on.[172] Leadership often rotated among the elders without any one elder having superior authority. Moreover, the local council of elders was not hierarchically related to the high council of the Sanhedrin.

b. Biblical Data. There is no reference to church elders in the Gospels. For information on them we must turn to the Book of Acts and the Epistles.[173]

---

[165]E.g., see 1 Samuel 8:4–5; 1 Kings 20:7–8.

[166]See Ezra 6:7 and 10:8, 14. For the role of elders in this period see Y. Kaufmann, *History of the Religion of Israel*, 4:568.

[167]Matthew 21:23; 26:3, 47; 27:1; Luke 22:66. In one case they are called "the elders of the Jews" (Luke 7:3).

[168]E.g., see Mark 15:1: "The chief priests, with the elders, the teachers of the law [the scribes] and the whole Sanhedrin [*synedrion*], reached a decision" (NIV).

[169]The Greek word is *presbyterion*.

[170]The Greek word is *presbyteriou*.

[171]The Greek word is *archisynagōgos*.

[172]BAGD gives for *archisynagōgos* "leader or president of a synagogue."

[173]Twenty-four elders are depicted in the Book of Revelation twelve times. They appear to be a heavenly order of beings and in some sense representatives of the church on earth (see

1. *Acts*. There are ten references in Acts to church elders.[174] Eight of these relate to elders in the Jerusalem church. They are first mentioned in connection with a famine in Judea: "The disciples [in Antioch] determined . . . to send relief to the brethren who lived in Judea; and they did so, sending it to the elders by the hand of Barnabas and Saul" (11:29–30). Evidently the elders formed an official church group that was responsible for handling this financial relief throughout Judea. It is interesting that no reference is here made to the apostles, though they were still in Jerusalem.[175] The elders seemingly constituted a distinct body with authority to act.

The apostles and elders, however, are linked together later at the Jerusalem council to debate and decide the circumcision issue. "Paul and Barnabas and some of the others were appointed to go up to Jerusalem to the apostles and the elders about this question" (Acts 15:2). "The apostles and the elders," in that order, are mentioned together six times,[176] and seem to function in complete unity. For example, "the apostles and the elders were gathered together to consider this matter" (v. 6); "it seemed good to the apostles and the elders, with the whole church, to choose men from among them and send them to Antioch with Paul and Barnabas" (v. 22); "they[177] delivered to them [believers in various cities] for observance the decisions which had been reached by the apostles and elders who were at Jerusalem" (16:4). The apostles and elders not only worked in unity but also "the whole church" in Jerusalem participated in the choice of men to deliver the decision reached.

A further note of interest about the Jerusalem meeting: James, the brother of Jesus, presided. Peter, Barnabas, and Paul reported on their experiences among the Gentiles, after which James gave the deciding argument, beginning, "My judgment is. . ."[178] (Acts 15:19). A statement follows about "the apostles and the elders, with the whole church" (v. 22). James not only presided at the Jerusalem council but was already recognized as the leader in the Jerusalem church.[179]

The church elders are mentioned again later in Acts. Luke, discussing Paul's final trip to Jerusalem, states, "When we[180] had come to Jerusalem, the brethren received us gladly. On the following day Paul went in with us to James; and all the elders were present" (21:17–18). The apostles are not mentioned—only James and the elders. The apostles had by this time largely, if not altogether, departed from Jerusalem.[181]

---

p. 42, n.79). However, since our present concern is with church elders—elders on earth—we will not discuss the elders in Revelation.

[174]There are eight references in Acts to Jewish elders. This suggests that there are similarities between the two groups.

[175]See Acts 8:1, 14; 9:27; 11:1.

[176]Acts 15:2, 4, 6, 22, 23; 16:4.

[177]"They" now meant Paul, Silas, and Timothy (see context).

[178]Not "my decree" or "my decision." James did not dictate for the twelve apostles or the elders or the church what should be done; however, his judgment readily prevailed.

[179]Earlier in Acts after Peter had been set free from prison and had described his experience to a group of praying believers, he said to them, "Tell this to James and to the brethren" (12:17). (This James obviously was not John's brother, who had recently been killed by Herod [see 12:1–2].) James, the brother of the Lord, thus was early recognized as chief among the brethren in the Jerusalem church.

[180]This is one of the "we" passages in Acts implying that Luke was accompanying Paul.

[181]F. F. Bruce refers to "a tradition that the Lord commanded the apostles to stay twelve

Indeed, after Paul spoke to the elders about how God had blessed his ministry, "they glorified God" (v. 20) and then advised Paul on his next steps (vv. 20–25). It is clear from this passage that the elders, with James as their leader, were fully in charge of the Jerusalem church.

The data in Acts make it clear that the elders, with James, constituted the governing body of the church in Jerusalem. The apostles, though functioning closely with the elders at the Jerusalem conference, were not the continuing church authorities. James is elsewhere called an apostle,[182] but he was not one of the Twelve. James did *not* function as an authority over the elders but worked in close relationship with them. He could be called a "first among equals,"[183] perhaps even a "fellow elder."[184] As at the Jerusalem council he undoubtedly presided at the regular meetings of the elders and often made decisions when fully supported by them. The elders, however, were the official governing body.

We may ask, How did certain people in Jerusalem become elders? The Book of Acts gives no answer. They are first mentioned in Acts 11:30, but there is no word about their origin. Of course there was the Old Testament record of the elders of Israel who likewise appear in the accounts of Moses without any detail of their background or service: they simply represent the people. Even closer at hand, in New Testament times every local synagogue had its council of elders, or presbytery, from whom (as we have noted) the head of the synagogue was chosen. These elders of the synagogue, I might add, were elected by co-optation—i.e., by action of the synagogue members—and then ordained by prayer and the laying on of hands. Although nothing is directly said about the procedure in regard to church eldership, it is possible that the same thing occurred in the church at Jerusalem.

A parallel to this could be the way in which the "deacons"[185] in Acts 6:1–6 came into office. They were first of all selected by the Christian community, and then appointed, or ordained, by the apostles with prayer and laying on of hands. This quite possibly was the procedure followed in the selection of the Jerusalem elders.

Now we proceed beyond the Jerusalem elders to consider the two other places in Acts where elders are mentioned. The first is particularly relevant to the previous question regarding the origin of elders. Paul and Barnabas had returned to their recently established churches in Lystra, Iconium, and Antioch to strengthen them and to appoint elders. In regard to the latter, "when they had appointed ['ordained' KJV] elders for them in every church, having prayed with fasting, they commended them to the Lord in whom they had believed" (Acts 14:23 NASB). The churches already existed, but so that

years in Jerusalem and then go out into all the world" (*The Acts of the Apostles*, 391). Whatever the validity of such a tradition, the apostles are not mentioned again in Acts after the council in Jerusalem.

[182]Recall Paul's words in Galatians 1:19: "I saw none of the other apostles except James the Lord's brother."

[183]*Primus inter pares* is the Latin expression often used for this.

[184]Peter so describes himself in his first letter: "I exhort the elders among you, as a fellow elder" (5:1).

[185]They were men chosen to "serve [*diakonein*] tables" (Acts 6:2). There is some debate as to whether they should be called "deacons" in the sense of 1 Timothy 3:8–13. In any event those chosen in Acts 6 were, at the least, table "deacons." For fuller discussion of deacons see pages 207–10.

proper leadership might continue, elders were appointed. Probably, as in the case of the "deacons," there was congregational selection prior to the apostles' appointment.[186] In any event the elders became the acknowledged leaders of the local churches.

The other mention of elders in Acts outside the Jerusalem church is in regard to already-appointed elders in the church at Ephesus. Paul was on his final journey to Jerusalem and stopped at the port of Miletus, a short distance from Ephesus. "And from Miletus he [Paul] sent to Ephesus and called to him the elders of the church" (Acts 20:17). Upon their arrival Paul gave a farewell address, recommitting the elders to their guardianship of the church. Afterward he knelt and prayed with them. Then they wept and embraced him (vv. 18–38). These men had doubtless been elders for many years, but nothing is said in the text about the time and nature of their appointment. What stands out is Paul's faith in them and their deeply shared love.

2. *The Epistles*. Elders are mentioned ten times in the New Testament letters.[187] First to be noted are the Pastoral Epistles, Paul's letters to Timothy and Titus.

As we have earlier observed, Paul writes in 1 Timothy 4:14 about "the body of elders" or "the presbytery"[188] that laid their hands upon Timothy in his ordination.[189] Next Paul writes in 1 Timothy 5:17: "Let the elders who rule well[190] be considered worthy of double honor, especially those who labor in preaching and teaching." It is of particular interest that Paul depicts among the ruling elders a second group whose work is preaching and teaching. Hence there are elders who give general oversight[191] of the church as well as those who fulfill a preaching and teaching role. Next Paul writes, "Never admit any charge against an elder except on the evidence of two or three witnesses" (v. 19). However, Paul instructs Timothy, "As for those [elders] who persist in sin, rebuke them in the

[186]It is interesting that the word translated "appointed" above is a form of the verb *cheirotoneō*, which means literally to "elect by raising of hands" (BAGD). This suggests the same pattern as in Acts 6: congregational choice and apostolic appointment. The only other New Testament use of *cheirotoneō* is in 2 Corinthians 8:19, which speaks of a brother "appointed [*cheirotonētheis*] by the churches." This is clearly congregational choice. Perhaps, then, both the churches and the apostles were involved in the appointment of elders. S. J. Kistemaker, after a helpful discussion of the matter, says, "In the case of the elders in Lycaonia and Pisidia, the apostles approved the selections made by the churches, and, after prayer and fasting, appointed them" (*Acts*, NTC, 525). BAGD, however, in regard to Acts 14:23 states that "this does not involve a choice by the group." If it does not, I question why the word *cheirotoneō* is used, with its literal meaning of "elect by raising of hands." (See EGT also, which speaks of "a method [of appointment] in which the votes and voices of each congregation were considered" [2:313]; also cf. R. C. H. Lenski, *The Interpretation of the Acts of the Apostles*, 585–86.) A further word: Why would there be "prayer and fasting" (literally, "fasting*s*") before the appointments if the congregation were not involved in the process?

[187]After Acts there is no further mention of Jewish elders.

[188]*Presbyterion* is the same Greek word used for the Jewish high council of the elders, the Sanhedrin.

[189]See pages 205–7 for more on the presbytery and ordination.

[190]The NIV reads "direct the affairs of the church well." The relevant Greek word is *proestōtes*, likewise used in Romans 12:8 and 1 Thessalonians 5:12. Leadership is the basic theme. Recall the brief discussion of these verses on pages 131–32.

[191]Previously in 1 Timothy Paul spoke about oversight: "If anyone sets his heart on being an overseer, he desires a noble task" (3:1 NIV). For elders and overseers, see the next section.

presence of all, so that the rest may stand in fear" (v. 20). Thus elders are not to be lightly charged with wrongdoing; two or three witnesses are needed to verify the allegation. On the other hand, because of their leading position in the congregation, any elder proved continuing in sin must be severely rebuked.

Paul writes to Titus about the need to appoint elders: "I left you in Crete, that you might set in order what remains, and appoint ['ordain' KJV] elders in every city as I directed you" (Titus 1:5 NASB). Obviously churches already existed in these various cities, but there remained the need for elders. Appointing elders was necessary to set in order the church's life and activity. Thus the situation in regard to Titus was different from that of Timothy in Ephesus where elders were already appointed: The churches in Crete were still without elders, and Titus was charged with the task of moving ahead with their appointment. Incidentally, nothing is said here directly about the method of their appointment;[192] the stress is on getting the job done.

The letter of James[193] refers to elders in regard to one who is sick: "Is any among you sick? Let him call for the elders of the church, and let them pray over him, anointing him with oil in the name of the Lord; and the prayer of faith will save the sick man, and the Lord will raise him up" (5:14–15).[194] Reference here is clearly to elders of the local church and their pastoral responsibility to visit and pray for the sick.[195]

Next, we turn to Peter, who refers to elders in his first letter: "I exhort the elders among you, as a fellow elder" (5:1). Peter is writing to "the exiles of the Dispersion" (1:1) in a number of provinces of Asia Minor, and at this point addresses the elders in their churches.[196] Note that, as mentioned earlier, the elders are not addressed as "*over* them" but "*among* them." It is also important to bear in mind that Peter, although an apostle, calls himself "a fellow elder."[197] Thus Peter the apostle does not view himself as occupying a position of ecclesiastical authority above the local church eldership.

Finally, we move on to John's second letter, which begins, "The elder to the elect lady and her children," and the third, which begins, "The elder to the beloved Gaius." "The elder" is not identified, but probably refers to John

[192]The Greek word for "appoint" in Titus 1:5 is *katastēsēs*, a form of *kathistēmi*. The same word is used in Acts 6:3 for appointment, *after* the congregation had chosen, of the "deacons." Recall that in the appointment of elders by Paul and Barnabas another Greek word, a form of *cheirotoneō*, suggesting congregational involvement, was used. In regard to Titus, Lenski writes that "Paul speaks of placing them [elders] in office, having them elected by the congregations and then ordaining them" (*Interpretation of Colossians, Thessalonians, Timothy, Titus, Philemon*, 896). I believe this procedure is implied, though Paul does not directly so state it.

[193]Its author is generally regarded as the brother of Jesus, and the same James who presided at the Jerusalem council.

[194]It is interesting to recall how closely James worked with the elders at the Jerusalem meeting. In his letter, James speaks of the elders in regard to their pastoral role.

[195]Incidentally, there is no suggestion here that oil either has medicinal properties or is the spiritual channel for the healing to take place. It is *"the prayer of faith,"* not the oil, that will "save the sick man." (Also it is "the Lord," not faith, that will "raise him up"!)

[196]Peter does not use the word "church" or "churches" but implies it, especially in 1 Peter 2:9–10.

[197]The Greek word is *sympresbyteros*.

the apostle,[198] who may be calling himself "the elder" because of advanced years.[199] However, as earlier noted, Peter calls himself a "fellow elder" in relation to other elders. John may be doing the same in relation to his audience. Having said that, we are not able to gain any particular information from 2 and 3 John regarding the office of elder.

c. Nomenclature. Before proceeding further, let us summarize three basic names in the New Testament for the office of elder.

1. *Elders are presbyters.* Wherever "elders" are mentioned, the Greek word is *presbyteroi.* Moreover, the body of elders is the presbytery, the *presbyterion.*

2. *Elders are overseers.* The Greek word is *episkopoi.* When Paul charges Titus to "appoint elders" (Titus 1:5), he immediately adds the qualification that elders must be "above reproach" (v. 6 NASB). In the next verse Paul says, "The overseer[200] must be above reproach as God's steward" (v. 7 NASB). Paul is not here talking about another office; he is describing an elder from the perspective of his function as an overseer. The elder (or overseer) must be "above reproach."

That the elder and overseer are the same person is likewise apparent from these words of Paul to Timothy: "If anyone sets his heart on being an overseer, he desires a noble task" (1 Tim. 3:1 NIV). Then Paul immediately adds, "Now the overseer must be above reproach" (v. 2), the same language as used about the elder and overseer in Titus. The overseer is an elder.

This does not mean that elders function solely as overseers, for there is also the preaching/teaching function. We recall that in 1 Timothy Paul writes, "Let the elders who rule well be considered worthy of double honor, especially those who labor in preaching and teaching" (5:17). *All* elders "rule," that is, supervise and oversee, but some overseers have the additional responsibility of preaching and teaching.

This overseeing function of elders is pointed to in Acts 20:28 and 1 Peter 5:1–2. We have earlier observed that Paul called to himself the elders of the Ephesian church and spoke to them about "the flock, among which the Holy Spirit [had] made [them] overseers" (NASB). The Greek word here for "overseers" is *episkopous.* Similarly, as we have noted, Peter speaks of the elders' task as "exercising oversight" (1 Peter 5:2 NASB). The Greek word for "exercising oversight" is *episkopountes.* Elders, according to Paul and

---

[198]F. F. Bruce states that "the Epistles were written by . . . 'John the disciple of the Lord' " (*The Epistles of John*, 15). John Stott, after a lengthy discussion of authorship, concludes that "these epistles were . . . written by the apostle John" (*The Epistles of John*, TNTC, 41). There has been much debate about authorship, but I believe that the traditional view that John the apostle is the author is correct.

[199]Bruce writes, "A date [for the letters] toward the end of the first century is most probable" (*The Epistles of John*, 31). In that case John the apostle would be far advanced in years. The word "elder" does not necessarily point to an official office; it can mean simply an older person (see, e.g., Acts 2:17: "your old men [*presbyteroi*] will dream dreams"), or a man of great dignity.

[200]The Greek word is *episkopon.* The KJV, RSV, and NEB translate it "bishop." While this is possible etymologically ("bishop" derives from *episkopos*), "bishop" has now come to signify an official *above* the local congregation or the body of elders. J. N. D. Kelly in his commentary translates *episkopos* as "overseer" both here and in 1 Timothy 3:1, saying, "The traditional rendering 'bishop' for Gk. *episkopos* has been deliberately rejected as misleading" (*The Pastoral Epistles*, HNTC, 73). The NASB and NIV translation as "overseer" is much better.

Peter, clearly have an episcopal function: they are overseers of God's people.

3. *Elders are shepherds*. In the two passages just quoted from Acts 20 and 1 Peter 5, the shepherding function of elders is also stated. Following the words "has made you overseers," Paul adds, "to shepherd the church of God." The Greek word, as previously noted, for "to shepherd" is *poimainein*, from the noun *poimēn*. Peter, before mentioning "exercising oversight," exhorts the elders to "shepherd the flock of God among [them]." The Greek word is *poimanate*. Recall that Peter, who calls himself a "fellow elder," had been commanded by Christ, "Shepherd My sheep" (John 21:16 NASB). Elders unmistakably are shepherds of the flock.

This brings us back to the gifts of the exalted Christ, which include "some as pastors" (Eph. 4:11). Since "pastors," *poimenas*, is simply another form of *poimēn*, the words in Ephesians may equally well be read "some as shepherds." Thus elders are shepherds or pastors, and the words signify the same function.

Here we must guard against any idea that pastors are other than elders. *Elders are shepherds, and shepherds are pastors*. Hence what has been said earlier about pastors as exercising oversight and guarding refers to the role of elders. Pastors are elders in the New Testament: whatever their name, they are shepherds of God's people.

But now—lest there be confusion—we need again to make a *functional* distinction. Although all elders are overseers and shepherds, some among them also labor especially in preaching and teaching. Hence they may be designated as "preaching elders" or "teaching elders," or simply "ministers of the word." Moreover, because of this distinctive function within eldership, there may also be a particular ordination to the ministry of the word.[201] However, this does not place the minister of the word on a higher level than elders in general, because his very ordination is to eldership—a preaching/teaching eldership. Indeed, we may here recall that Timothy's ordination was by the body of elders, thus for specialized ministry within the office of eldership. All elders are ordained—not just teaching elders—but the latter ordination is for the more specific work of ministry of the word.

Thus we may speak of the eldership as serving on the one hand in an overseeing and shepherding, or pastoral, role, and on the other hand in a preaching and teaching, or ministry of the word, role. All are elders, whatever their function, and compose the one body of leaders that Christ has placed over and among His people.

d. Qualifications. In this section on qualifications of an elder we will focus primarily on those named by Paul in 1 Timothy 3:1–7 and Titus 1:5–9. It will be apparent that the emphasis lies on the elder's role as an *overseer*.[202] For 1 Timothy 3 begins, "If anyone sets his heart on being an overseer, he desires a noble task" (NIV); Titus 1:5 speaks first of appointing elders and then refers to one so appointed as "an overseer" in verse 7.

1. *Character*. In the two lists of qualifications one character trait heads both, namely, being *irreproachable*:

---

[201]Recall the discussion of such ordination on pages 191–96.

[202]Or overseer and shepherd. However, Paul uses the word "overseer" in these passages. We have already observed (on pp. 178–80) some of the things Peter said in 1 Peter 5:1–4 to elders about their responsibilities as shepherds and overseers. Our concern is now more with their qualifications as Paul sets them forth. There will inevitably be some overlap between responsibilities and qualifications.

"An overseer . . . must be above reproach"[203] (1 Tim. 3:2 NASB); "the overseer must be above reproach[204] as God's steward" (Titus 1:7 NASB).[205] This surely does not mean "sinless" (then who could qualify?), but it does mean solid in character so that reproach or censure cannot be brought against him. This is *the* basic character qualification of the overseeing elders.

2. *Domestic*. Next in importance is that the elder, or overseer, "must be . . . the husband of one wife" (1 Tim. 3:2, NASB; Titus 1:6). This statement by Paul may imply a number of things. First, the elder is to be *a married man*, so that with experience in family responsibilities he can better care for the church. Second, the elder should *not be a polygamist*, that is, having more than one wife. The NIV translation "the husband of but one wife" suggests this. Third, the elder must be *faithful to his wife* throughout marriage, never indulging in extramarital affairs or sexual promiscuity of any kind. He is to be a "one-woman man." Fourth, the elder should *not be a divorced person*, who has remarried and thus been the husband of more than one wife. Fifth, the elder must be a man who has *not married again* after his wife's death; hence he must have been married only once. He is the husband of one wife for life.[206] Whether all of these are implied by Paul's statement "the husband of one wife" may be debatable,[207] but the main thing Paul is stressing is the irreproachable ("above reproach") quality of the elder's married life. If the elder is off base here, whatever else may be said about his personal qualities (as described by Paul after that) has been undermined already. "The husband of one wife" is critical to all else.

Also, the elder's children must be

[203]The Greek word is *anepilēmpton*, "cannot be reprehended, not open to censure" (Thayer).

[204]The Greek word is *anegklēton*, "cannot be called to account, unreprovable" (Thayer).

[205]Also Titus 1:6 (NASB) reads, in regard to elders to be appointed, "if any man be above reproach."

[206]This point may be reinforced by Paul's later statement about "a widow . . . sixty years of age, having been the wife of one husband" (1 Tim. 5:9).

[207]The first statement above in regard to the necessity of an elder being a married man may be understood to mean "if he is married," in the same way as "if he has children" (see v. 4). The emphasis is not on being a *husband* but on being the husband of *one* wife. Still—to repeat what was said—there may be the thought that a married man, experienced in family responsibilities, would be better qualified to care for the daily life of the church. Incidentally, Paul never calls himself an elder, whereas Peter, a married man, does so speak of himself—recall the phrase "a fellow elder" (1 Peter 5:1). The fourth statement above, in regard to marriage after divorce, may be set in the light of Matthew 19:9: "Whoever divorces his wife, except for unchastity, and marries another, commits adultery"—thus teaching that divorce in this case and remarriage may take place. Accordingly, the argument follows, such a divorced person may legitimately be an elder. The fifth statement, regarding remarriage after the spouse's death, may be weighed in relation to Paul's words in Romans 7:1–3 about a woman being free to marry again: "If her husband dies . . . if she marries another man she is not an adulteress" (v. 3). This would apply to the husband in the event of his wife's death, namely, that he would be free to marry. The argument then follows that an elder may likewise be married again after his wife's death. Both of these arguments (in regard to the fourth and fifth statements) have some merit, and should not be readily dismissed. However, I believe that Paul's words in regard to an elder as being "the husband of one wife" refer ideally to a one-and-only marriage for those in church leadership. Such a single marriage makes for a total commitment that can be exemplary to the church. Indeed, has not our Lord Himself committed Himself totally and finally to one bride, one wife, namely the church?

"believers and not open to the charge of being profligate[208] or insubordinate"[209] (Titus 1:6). His children must have genuine faith, and there must be no charge of gross wildness and rebellion against them, for this would also bring reproach against the elder and his position in the church. Thus the elder "must manage[210] his own household well, keeping his children submissive and respectful in every way" (1 Tim. 3:4). The reason is that "if a man does not know how to manage[211] his own household, how can he care for God's church?" (v. 5).

In summary, the domestic side—the elder and his wife, the elder and his children—must be in order if the elder is properly to serve the household of God.

3. *Personal.* In regard to the elder, I will list a number of both *positive* and *negative* qualifications set forth in 1 Timothy and Titus.[212]

Positive—1 Timothy 3:2, 7: temperate, sensible (or prudent), dignified (or respectable), hospitable, an apt teacher,[213] well-regarded by outsiders; Titus 1:8–9—a lover of goodness, upright, holy (or devout), self-controlled, holding firm the sure word as taught.[214]

Negative—1 Timothy 3:3: not addicted to wine (or any intoxicant), not violent (or pugnacious) but gentle, not quarrelsome (or contentious), not a lover of money, not a recent convert; Titus 1:7: not arrogant (or self-willed, overbearing), not quick-tempered, not greedy for gain.

Paul thus mentions eleven[215] personal qualities to be present in, and eight to be absent from, an elder. Each quality should be carefully pondered by the person who, in Paul's language, "sets his heart" on being an elder. Also, these qualities need to be carefully considered by those who are responsible for elders' selection and subsequent ordination.

One further word: all that has been said about qualifications for the elder who is an overseer apply also to the elder whose primary responsibility is preaching and teaching. I have already discussed the quality of life that especially befits a person who is involved in the ministry of the word. Now I am emphasizing that all the qualifications for the overseeing elder must also be present in the teaching elder's life. For truly it is a high and noble calling to be a minister of the word of God.

e. Ordination. In regard to the ordination of overseeing elders, it is good to bear in mind a word of Paul to Timothy: "Do not be hasty in the laying on of hands" (1 Tim. 5:22). That Paul is here speaking of elders is apparent from the

[208]"Wild" (NIV). The reference is to "debauchery," "dissipation" (BAGD); cf. Ephesians 5:18.

[209]"Disobedient" (NIV) or "rebellious" (BAGD).

[210]Or "rule." The Greek word is *proistamenon*, a form of *proistēmi*. This is the same word that Paul used later (1 Tim. 5:17) in regard to "the elders who rule well"—*proestōtes*.

[211]Or "rule." The Greek word is *prostēmai*.

[212]I will omit qualifications that are repeated in Titus.

[213]Even though the qualities set forth are primarily those of an overseeing elder, he must also be "an apt teacher." Although his position is not that of a "minister of the word," he must still be able to teach.

[214]Paul adds, "so that he may be able to give instruction in sound doctrine and also to confute those who contradict it" (Titus 1:9). As an "apt teacher," he should be able to teach sound doctrine so as to refute any opponents. This again suggests that an overseeing elder, even though, strictly speaking, he is not a teaching elder (minister of the word), must be so sound in the faith that he can communicate it to others.

[215]Or twelve if "gentle" is included from the negative list.

context;[216] further, we have earlier observed Paul and Barnabas ordaining elders by the laying on of hands. Thus the warning is against moving too hastily to ordain elders. It is far better to delay ordination until there is assurance that the qualifications have been met.[217]

Who, then, does the ordaining, and what procedure is to be followed? We have earlier observed that Paul and Barnabas ordained the elders in various churches of Asia Minor and that Titus was instructed to ordain elders in Crete. Paul and Barnabas were apostles, and Titus was a kind of apostolic delegate carrying out Paul's charge. However, as we have previously observed, there was probably congregational participation in all these cases.[218] But now that Paul, Barnabas, and Titus have long departed the scene, do we need to look for apostles or some other outside authority to come into a local church today and, perhaps with congregational assent, ordain elders?

It is interesting that in turning from the New Testament to the document known as the *Didache* (or *The Teaching of the Twelve Apostles*) that one of its last injunctions reads, "Appoint for yourselves bishops [i.e., overseers] and deacons[219] worthy of the Lord, men who are humble and not avaricious and true and approved" (15:1).[220] Since this document may date around A.D. 70,[221] it was written shortly after Paul's letters to Timothy and Titus.[222] What the *Didache* implies is that it was the responsibility of the various congregations to appoint, or ordain, their own overseeing elders. Apostles are also mentioned in the *Didache*,[223] but there is no suggestion that they were to do the ordaining. If churches today follow the example of the *Didache*, then the congregation itself may ordain.[224]

But in the event that a church already has elders, would it not be in order for them to ordain other elders?[225] This is surely possible, because elders represent the people. If nothing else, since there should be the laying on of hands, a smaller group would need to be involved. Another early church document, *First Clement*, usually dated around A.D. 96, speaks about "the bishops and deacons" as appointed first by the apostles—the "bishops and deacons . . . were appointed by them" and later by others—"later on, by other reputable men with the consent of the whole church."[226] "Reputable men," however, does not necessarily mean elders—although they surely could have been such.

---

[216]See verses 17–20.

[217]Paul had expressed concern about an elder who so persisted in sin that a public rebuke was called for. Perhaps those who ordained him had not given sufficient consideration to his qualifications for the office.

[218]See notes 186 and 192.

[219]I will discuss deacons later.

[220]*The Apostolic Fathers*, 2nd ed., trans. by J. B Lightfoot and J. R. Harmer, ed. and rev. by M. W. Holmes, 157.

[221]There is wide difference of opinion about the dating of the *Didache*—anywhere from A.D. 50 to the third century or later! Holmes, in *The Apostolic Fathers*, writes that, whatever the date, materials from which the *Didache* was composed go back to approximately A.D. 70 (see p. 146).

[222]D. Guthrie gives A.D. 63–64 as "the most probable date" of these letters (ISBE, 3:685).

[223]See the *Didache* 11:3, which begins, "Now concerning the apostles and prophets. . . ."

[224]Recall that local synagogue elders were elected and ordained by the members at large (see pp. 198–200). It is quite possible that early churches, many of them growing out of synagogues, would follow the same procedure.

[225]As is the case in ordination of a minister of the word.

[226]*The Apostolic Fathers*, 52–53.

In summary, the ordination of overseeing elders is basically a local church function: "Appoint for yourselves." Elders already in office may surely participate in the ordination; however, other "reputable" persons may also be involved. Indeed, since the ordination of elders is done by the local church, the whole congregation (if not too large) could share in the laying on of hands. If this is done, there may be a heightened sense of the elders representing the whole community of God's people.

4. *Auxiliary*

In addition to those who serve as elders, we next consider the role of deacons and the ministry of women.

a. Deacons. 1. *Background.* The word "deacon" in Greek is *diakonos*. It basically means "servant." As such, Jesus Himself could be called *the* deacon. Jesus declared, "I am among you as one who serves"[227] (Luke 22:27); Paul writes, "Christ became a servant"[228] (Rom. 15:8). Paul describes himself and Apollos as "servants"[229] through whom the Corinthians came to believe (1 Cor. 3:5), and he speaks frequently of his fellow workmen as servants. For example, he refers to Timothy as "God's servant in the gospel of Christ" (1 Thess. 3:2), to Tychicus as "faithful servant[230] in the Lord" (Eph. 6:21 NIV), and to Epaphras as "a faithful servant[231] of Christ" (Col. 1:7 NASB). Indeed, in the broadest sense all Christians are servants. Jesus said about all who are His disciples: "If any one serves me, he must follow me; and where I am, there shall my servant[232] be also" (John 12:26). Further, the purpose of Christ's gifts of apostles, prophets, evangelists, pastors and teachers, is "for the equipping of the saints for the work of service"[233] (Eph. 4:12 NASB). It is apparent from all of these scriptures (and many more could be cited) that the theme of *diakonos* as servant pervades the Christian life.

2. *Scriptures relating to the office of deacon.* The two clearest references to the diaconate as a special office in the New Testament are Philippians 1:1 and 1 Timothy 3:8–10, 12–13.[234] In Philippians Paul writes, "To all the saints in Christ Jesus at Philippi, together with the overseers and deacons"[235] (NIV). Even though the same Greek word is used here that is usually translated "servants" elsewhere, it is apparent that the deacons are a different group from both "the saints" (the congregation at large) and "the overseers." In 1 Timothy Paul has just described the office of overseer, or elder, (3:1–7) and then continues, "Deacons[236] likewise. . ." (v. 8). Obviously deacons, again, are a separate category from overseers. The fact that deacons are addressed immediately after overseers in both passages suggests that they also have an important role to fulfill.

The commencement of the office of deacon is ordinarily viewed as occurring in Acts 6:1–6. Some of the church

[227]The Greek word is *diakonōn*, literally "serving."

[228]The Greek word is *diakonon*.

[229]The Greek word is *diakonoi*.

[230]The Greek word is *diakonos*; KJV, RSV, and NASB translate it "minister."

[231]The Greek word is *diakonos*; KJV, RSV, and NIV translate it "minister."

[232]The Greek word is *diakonos*.

[233]The Greek word is *diakonias*; KJV and RSV translate it "ministry."

[234]I should add here that the office of deacon seems to have no parallel in Judaism. As we have seen, the office of elder was represented in both the Sanhedrin—"the council of elders"—and the local synagogue. Also, Old Testament Israel did not have deacons.

[235]The Greek word is *diakonois*.

[236]The Greek word is *diakonous*.

widows were being neglected in the daily distribution of food; therefore, the twelve apostles called together the body of believers and said, "It is not right that we should give up preaching the word of God to serve tables" (v. 2). "To serve tables" is literally "to deacon[237] tables." The congregation, accordingly, was told to choose seven men whom the apostles would "appoint to this duty"[238] (v. 3). After the seven had been selected (Luke does not say how), they were set before the apostles who "prayed and laid their hands upon them" (v. 6). Although these men are not directly called deacons, their task was the serving, or "deaconing" of tables, thus the assistance of the apostles in a practical matter of the young church's life.

Two other texts in the New Testament may have a broader reference to deacons: Romans 12:7 and 1 Corinthians 12:28. In regard to Romans I have previously discussed the charismatic gifts of Romans 12, which include service—"if service, in his serving"[239] (v. 7 NASB)—and noted that such a gift is basically functional rather than official.[240] However, it is quite possible that the operation of this gift of grace might prepare someone for an appointment to the office of deacon. In 1 Corinthians 12:28 Paul lists various appointments including "helps": "God has appointed in the church, first apostles, second prophets, third teachers, then miracles, then gifts of healings, helps,[241] administrations, various kinds of tongues" (NASB). The word "helps" set in the context of appointments, while not ceasing to be a gift, may refer more largely to the office of a deacon,[242] or the diaconate.

3. *Responsibility*. Taking Acts 6:1–6 as our guide, we may say that the basic responsibility of deacons is practical affairs. The deacons were elected to the duty of providing assistance to neglected widows, thus to practical ministry. Such ministry doubtless included both wise handling of food distribution and the monetary matters involved. In the language of 1 Corinthians 12:28, we may call this the ministry of "helps"—helps that reach out in loving assistance to meet various kinds of practical needs.

It may be that Paul greets the deacons along with the overseers in his letter to the Philippians because of his later statement about the church's partnership in giving and receiving: "When I left Macedonia, no church entered into partnership with me in giving and receiving except you only; for even in Thessalonica you sent me help once and again" (4:15–16). This financial help was likely due to the work of the deacons.

The office of deacon, the diaconate, is closely associated with that of overseer, or elder. It is not an office of oversight or teaching but of practical service. Accordingly, it is an auxiliary office to that of elder, carrying forward the practical side of the overall responsibility of the eldership.

---

[237]The Greek word is *diakonein*.

[238]The Greek word is *chreias*; "business" (KJV); "task" (NASB); "office" is also possible (see BAGD).

[239]The Greek words are *diakonian* and *diakonia*.

[240]Recall my statement that in Romans 12 the reference to *diakonia* is more functional than official. See pages 128–29.

[241]The Greek word is *antilēmpseis* (or *antilēpseis*).

[242]Thayer, under ἀντιλήμψεις, refers to 1 Corinthians 12:28 as "the ministrations of the deacons, who have care of the poor and the sick." Dunn speaks of a probable "link between ἀντιλήμψεις and κυβερνήσεις [administrations] and the (later) more established positions of deacon and overseer respectively" (*Jesus and the Spirit*, 253).

4. *Qualifications*. We may first note that, according to Acts 6:3, deacons are to be "men of good repute, full of the Spirit and of wisdom." Their reputation should be good because they deal with practical matters, including monetary. Also, they should be Spirit-filled men who likewise are full of wisdom. The practical affairs of the church call for the Spirit's anointing so that the deacons' wisdom is more than worldly. What they do should be under the wise direction of the Holy Spirit.[243]

Next we turn to 1 Timothy 3:8–10 and 12–13. Here, as was done in the case of the overseers, we will list the given qualifications for deacons.

1 Timothy 3:8–10: serious (or worthy of respect), not double-tongued, not addicted to much wine, not greedy for gain, holding fast the mystery of the faith (the deep truths of faith) with a clear conscience, irreproachable (having so proved themselves).

1 Timothy 3:12–13: the husband of one wife, good managers of their children and household.

Observe that the same high character qualification required of elders—of being irreproachable—must likewise belong to deacons. However, as the Scripture reads, candidates for the office must "first be tested; then let them serve as deacons if they are beyond reproach" (1 Tim. 3:10 NASB). Such testing was not mentioned in regard to an overseer (elder) perhaps because he was not to be "a recent convert" (recall v. 6). Deacons, however, might be newer Christians and their character less well known, thus they need further testing or proving.[244]

In their domestic life there is the same requirement for deacons as for elders—that they be "the husband of one wife"[245] and their home life in good order.

The qualifications given for deacons are largely negative—in regard to the tongue, drinking, and money—and are particularly important for those whose responsibilities largely involve practical matters. Double-talk, addiction to wine, covetousness of money—all such will critically affect the outgoing service of deacons.

It is interesting that the qualification for the overseer of being an "apt teacher" is not required of deacons. However, deacons must be deeply committed to the Christian faith, holding it fast with a clear conscience.

A final word on the qualifications of deacons: They obviously must not be less spiritual or less moral than elders. To be sure, many more qualifications are listed for elders than for deacons, but none imply fewer spiritual and moral requirements. Both elders and deacons must be godly persons.

5. *Ordination*. As we have observed, the "table-deacons" of Acts 6, after their selection by the church, were ordained by prayer and the laying on of the twelve apostles' hands. It is important to bear in mind that the congregation, *not* the apostles, did the selecting. Here the same basic procedures for

[243]Incidentally, this same anointing of the Spirit resulted in at least two of the deacons going beyond practical ministry into witness and evangelism: Stephen (Acts 6:8–7:61) and Philip (Acts 8:4–40). This doubtless shows the freedom of the Spirit to move beyond any fixed office.

[244]This might call for a probationary period, or it may simply mean that the church, perhaps through the elders, needs first to examine carefully the candidate's personal life. Incidentally, this may correspond to the apostles' injunction to the church in Acts 6 about choosing seven men "of good repute" who would become deacons. The young church may have had to examine many persons carefully before they were ready to present candidates to the apostles.

[245]See the preceding discussion of this.

ordination of deacons as discussed in regard to the ordination of elders may be followed.[246] The prayer and laying on of hands remains a congregational responsibility, whether done through elders or other congregational representatives.

b. Ministry of Women. In the same passage where Paul discusses the office of deacon, he interjects this statement: "The women[247] likewise must be serious, no slanderers, but temperate, faithful in all things" (1 Tim. 3:11). This statement is both preceded by (vv. 8–10) and followed by (vv. 12–13) specific words about deacons. Thus it seems apparent that "the women" are also deacons, or deaconesses.[248] Paul could not have said "deaconesses" because there was no such separate word in Greek;[249] however, the word "women" in this context with deacons conveys the idea of deaconesses.

The diaconate therefore may include both men and women. The first qualification listed for deacons—that they "be serious" (1 Tim. 3:8)—is likewise stated for the women (v. 11). The other qualifications for the women deacons—"no slanderers [or 'scandal mongers'], but temperate, faithful in all things"—except for slander, parallel what is said of the deacons in verses 8 and 9—"not addicted to much wine" and holding "the mystery of the faith with a clear conscience." Thus there are essentially the same qualifications for deacons and deaconesses.

The work of women deacons, then, like that of the deacons, is basically practical ministry. In a third-century book of church order called the *Didaskalia Apostolorum*, the deaconesses are described as "assistants to the clergy with baptizing of women, ministers to the poor and sick among women, instruction of women catechumens, and in general intermediaries between the clergy and women of the congregation."[250] Surely there continues to be a need for similar ministry today.

Deaconesses, however, should not constitute a kind of third order or office in addition to elders and deacons.[251] For they are also deacons, women deacons, and therefore a part of the one church diaconate. This means also that they should be ordained just as the men are. Although their tasks may somewhat differ, they are fully deacons.

Following Paul's words about women deacons, we note that later in his letter Paul has much to say about widows (1 Tim. 5:3–16). At the outset, Paul

---

[246]See the previous section.

[247]The Greek word is *gynaikas*, a form of *gynē*. The KJV, NIV, and NEB read "their wives." However, "their" is not in the Greek text: it is only provided to support the translation of *gynaikas* as "wives." *Gynē* may be translated either "woman" or "wife" (see BAGD); however, the plural, "wives," seems unlikely in this passage. Why, for one thing, would Paul single out the wives of deacons rather than overseers (elders) for particular discussion?

[248]Walter Lock writes, "From the context and from the parallelism between the qualities required for them and for the deacons . . . these must be deaconesses (*not* wives of deacons), women who help" (*The Pastoral Epistles*, ICC, 40). Kelly describes them as "women deacons," and thereafter as "deaconesses" (*The Pastoral Epistles*, HNTC, 83–84).

[249]The word *diakonos* has no female equivalent. See BAGD under *diakonos*, where both "deacon" and "deaconess" are given.

[250]See the article "Deaconesses," *New International Dictionary of the Christian Church*, 285–86.

[251]A third order developed in the early church, with the deaconesses being viewed more as assistants to the clergy (see quotation above from the *Didaskalia*) than as women deacons. Incidentally, this order of deaconesses went into eclipse for many centuries, but has been revived in a number of Protestant churches.

writes, "Let a widow be enrolled if she is not less than sixty years of age" (v. 9). Paul seems to be referring to a special list of older widows in the church. To be on the list—besides the age requirement—a widow must have been "the wife of one husband; and she must be well attested for her good deeds . . . brought up children, shown hospitality, washed the feet of the saints, relieved the afflicted, and devoted herself to doing good in every way" (vv. 9–10). This graphically demonstrates Paul's teaching on the ministry of women in terms of practical content.[252] Also, although the earlier ministry of such widows may have been particularly related to other women, it includes a wide range of ministry to many kinds of needs.

Next we observe Paul's words to Titus about older women: "Bid the older women . . . to be reverent in behavior, not to be slanderers or slaves to drink; they are to teach what is good, and so train[253] the young women to love their husbands and children, to be sensible [or 'self-controlled'], chaste, domestic [or 'working at home'],[254] kind, and submissive to their husbands, that the word of God may not be discredited" (2:3–5). It is interesting that here Paul says similar things about the older women as he said in 1 Timothy 3:11 about the deaconesses not being "slanderers, but temperate"; only here the language is "not to be slanderers or slaves to drink."[255] But, and this is of particular relevance to the ministry of women, Paul here adds that they should "teach what is good." This is detailed through their training of younger women in a number of ways. Older women have a special ministry to young women that no one else—including ordained ministers of the word, overseeing elders, and male deacons—can fulfill. Because of their years of experience in marriage (marriage being presupposed), they can teach and train—counsel, advise, spur on—younger married women in all domestic matters, including proper submission to their husbands. When these older women teach the younger to so conduct themselves, the word of God will not be discredited but honored.

To sum up thus far: Paul depicts the ministry of women in the three passages noted to include "faithfulness in all things" (1 Tim. 3:11), "good deeds" in many practical ways (1 Tim. 5:10), and teaching "what is good" to younger women about their way of living (Titus 2:3–5).

Now for the sake of brevity I will delineate and summarize various ministries of women in the New Testament.

1. Financial support

Luke 8:3: that speaks of a number of women who traveled with Jesus and the apostles and "provided for them out of their means" (cf. Mark 15:40–42).

2. Witnessing to the gospel

John 4:39: the woman of Samaria—many "believed in him because of the woman's testimony" (cf., e.g., Acts 1:8, 14).

3. Homes open for prayer and worship

---

[252]What Paul said about deaconesses in 1 Timothy 3:11 is in terms of *qualifications* ("serious, no slanderers," etc.). Here in 1 Timothy 5:9–10 he is referring to the *actual ministry* of women (who may or may not have been deaconesses): hospitality, washing the feet of the saints, etc.

[253]The Greek word is *sophronizōsin*. According to BAGD, it means "to bring someone to his senses" (!); TDNT—"to spur on."

[254]The Greek word is *oikourgous*; KJV, "keepers at home"; NIV, "busy at home."

[255]W. H. Hendriksen comments that "wine drinking and malicious gossip often go together" (*I & II Timothy and Titus*, 364).

Acts 12:12: "the house of Mary . . . where many were gathered together and were praying." Also Colossians 4:15: "Nympha and the church in her house."

4. Good deeds and charity
Acts 9:36: "Tabitha [Dorcas] . . . was full of good works and acts of charity" (recall 1 Tim 5:10—a widow "must be well attested for her good deeds, as one who has . . . devoted herself to doing good in every way").

5. Hospitality
Acts 16:15: Lydia's hospitality to Paul and his companions—" 'Come to my house and stay.' And she prevailed upon us" (cf. 1 Tim. 5:10: "one who has shown hospitality").

6. Joint ministry with husband
Acts 18:26: "Priscilla and Aquila . . . took him [Apollos] aside and explained to him the way of God more accurately" (NASB) (cf. 1 Cor. 16:19: "Aquila and Prisca, together with the church in their house").

7. Deaconess (or servant) of the church
Romans 16:1–2: "Phoebe, a deaconess [or 'servant'—*diakonos*] of the church . . . helper of many" (recall 1 Tim. 3:11: "The women. . . ," probably deaconesses).

8. Female co-workers (possibly sisters)
Romans 16:12: "Greet those workers in the Lord, Tryphaena and Tryphosa."

9. Believing wives accompanying missionary husbands
1 Corinthians 9:5: "Do we not have a right to take along a believing wife, even as the rest of the apostles, and the brothers of the Lord, and Cephas?" (NASB).

10. Activity of praying and prophesying
1 Corinthians 11:5: a "woman who prays or prophesies" (cf. Acts 1:14: praying believers, including "the women and Mary the mother of Jesus"; 2:17: "your sons and your daughters shall prophesy"; also Acts 21:9: Philip's "four unmarried daughters, who prophesied").

11. Team ministry with men
Philippians 4:2–3: "Euodia and . . . Syntyche . . . women [who] . . . have labored side by side with me in the gospel together with Clement and the rest of my fellow workers" (cf. Rom. 16:3: Prisca and Aquila—"my fellow workers in Christ Jesus").

12. Teaching and training of younger women (discussed earlier).

It is apparent that a wide range of ministries was open to women in the New Testament and by projection should continue in the church. By a careful study of these twelve areas of ministry and reflection on their contemporary relevance, we can see the multiple ministry opportunities available for women. Unfortunately many of our churches have scarcely begun to recognize and activate the manifold ministries of women.

From the list of the twelve areas of ministry, we observe that women are largely depicted as functioning in supportive, cooperative, and auxiliary roles. Financial assistance, homes open for prayer and hospitality, joint and team ministries, etc., illustrate such roles. There is no suggestion of women being primary leaders, or in positions of authority: they are workers in the Lord, helpers of many, and may share a ministry without being in charge of it.

I must add a further word about the distinctive importance of women's ministries. Although there is much overlap with what men are called to do, the role of women by virtue of their own feminine nature cannot be identical with that of men. *What is needed in our churches is the further activation of women's ministries and not their involvement in male roles.* By God's determination, according to Paul, "the head of every man is Christ, and the head of the woman is man, and the head of Christ is God" (1 Cor. 11:3, NIV); and thus a woman must not in her ministry seek to take the leadership (= headship) or assume male authority, thereby violating her own nature. This applies not only to a married woman (whose head is her husband); it also relates to every woman because of her creation as "a helper"[256] (Gen. 2:18) for man. In Paul's words, "Neither was man created for woman, but woman for man" (1 Cor. 11:9). Hence, there is a natural limitation. Woman must not, especially in the church (with its knowledge of Scripture), presume in her ministry to assume man's God-given authority.[257]

Here we may return to Paul's letter in 1 Timothy. Paul writes, "I do not allow a woman to teach or exercise authority over a man" (2:12 NASB).[258] Obviously Paul is not excluding women from all teaching, because, as we have observed, he speaks of the older women teaching "what is good." However, their teaching is directed to women, not to men. Nor do Paul's words rule out the activity of a Priscilla and Aquila who, as we have noted, "took him [Apollos] aside and explained the way of God more accurately" to him; however, Priscilla did not presume to do this on her own.[259] In 1 Timothy 2:12, what Paul is prohibiting women from doing is teaching the Christian faith[260] in the setting of the church[261] and thus in a context where men are present. Such teaching is out of order: it is the exer-

---

[256]On woman as "helper," see *Renewal Theology*, 1:127–28; 130 n. 46 (especially); 203; 203 n. 17; 228; 237.

[257]Nor should men seek to minister in areas that more suitably belong to women, for example, the counseling of women. Women surely are better equipped to deal with problems relating to their own sex, also without the ever-dangerous possibility of sexual involvement. Incidentally, women will far more readily accept limitation if men will stay out of what properly belongs to them!

[258]Some people view Paul's words (including v. 11—which see) as culturally relative, and thus believe they should not be taken as a directive for the church today. Gordon Fee, for example, writes that "it is altogether likely that 1 Timothy 2:11–12 speaks to a local problem . . . [thus] the possibility that the prohibition in 1 Timothy 1:11–12 is culturally relative" (*How to Read the Bible for All Its Worth*, 69). Again, "It is hard to deny that *this* text prohibits women teaching men in the Ephesian church . . . a very ad hoc problem in Ephesus" (*Gospel and Spirit: Issues in New Testament Hermeneutics*). I find it difficult to pursue this line of thinking, for, whatever the cultural context, Paul seems clearly to be speaking to the church at large (note, e.g., v. 8: "in every place") and bases his statement in 1 Timothy 2:11–12 not on an ad hoc situation but on the biblical account of Adam and Eve (vv. 13–14). (I will say more on the latter point later.)

[259]Nor is the setting that of the church (see next sentence above). This was a private explanation.

[260]Paul, just a few words before, spoke of himself as "a teacher of the Gentiles in faith and truth" (v. 7). Clearly, this is not teaching in general but teaching the truth of the gospel. Hence, the teaching that women are forbidden to do refers to the same Christian truth. According to Douglas Moo, "In the pastoral epistles, teaching always has this restricted sense of authoritative doctrinal instruction" (*Recovering Biblical Manhood and Womanhood*, ed. by John Piper and Wayne Grudem, 185),

[261]Note that the background in verses 8–11 speaks about men "in every place . . . lifting up holy hands" in prayer (thus implying the church at worship) and follows by giving injunctions about women's adornment. Although Paul may be referring to the attire of women at any time, it seems more likely that he is focusing here on the church (see Kelly, *The Pastoral Epistles*, 66–67, for a good discussion of this).

cise of authority over men.[262] Rather, in church, as Paul says immediately prior to his words about not allowing a woman so to teach, "let a woman learn in silence with all submissiveness" (v. 11).[263] This means readiness to learn in silence rather than to teach, thereby to be in submissiveness to the proper place of male authority.[264]

To further emphasize this point Paul adds that "Adam was formed first, then Eve" (v. 13); hence the priority of authority, including teaching, belongs to men. Paul relates this to the church and thereby declares the impropriety of women occupying a superior teaching role.[265]

We may now refer again to the scriptural fact that church elders have the official responsibility of overseeing and instructing the congregation. To them and them alone belongs authoritative teaching in the church. Since an elder is male ("the husband of one wife"), for a woman to step into the role of an official teacher in church is to exceed her God-given authority. It is significant that just after the section in 1 Timothy 2 where Paul limits women's teaching he proceeds to speak about the qualifications of an overseer or elder (3:1–7) and these qualifications include being an "apt teacher" (v. 2). Thus Paul's basic reason for women not being permitted

---

[262]John Wesley translated 1 Timothy 2:12 in this way: "to usurp authority over the man—by public teaching" (*Explanatory Notes upon the New Testament*, 770).

[263]Parallel to this are Paul's words in 1 Corinthians 14: "As in all the churches of the saints, the women should keep silence in the churches" (vv. 33–34) Such silence obviously is not absolute, because Paul earlier speaks affirmatively of women prophesying—"any woman who prays or prophesies" (11:5). Paul is referring to silence as the proper attitude for receiving instruction. Accordingly, Paul adds in 1 Corinthians 14:34: "they [women] are not permitted to speak." Speaking here probably refers, as EGT 2:915 says, to "*Church-teaching and authoritative direction*" (italics EGT). This understanding is in basic accord with 1 Timothy 2:11.

[264]John Calvin writes about women that "to teach . . . is not permitted by their condition. They are subject, and to teach implies the rank of power or authority" (*Commentaries: Pastoral Epistles*, 68, Beveridge trans.). Calvin is not referring to teaching in general but to "the office of teaching" (p. 67).

[265]Following the words "Adam was formed first, then Eve," Paul adds, "And Adam was not deceived, but the woman was deceived and became a transgressor" (v. 14). Many biblical interpreters have viewed this statement as implying that, since Eve was deceived, women should not be trusted to teach. Donald Guthrie, for example, writes that Paul "may have in mind the greater aptitude of the weaker sex to be led astray" (*The Pastoral Epistles*, 77). J. N. D. Kelly writes that "his [Paul's] point is that since Eve was so gullible a victim of the serpent's wiles, she [woman] cannot be trusted to teach" (*The Pastoral Epistles*, 687). David Watson puts it more broadly: "By the very intuitiveness of their nature, women may see certain issues much more quickly and clearly than men—and by the same impulse be more strongly tempted to go off on a tangent and away from the biblical balance of the whole counsel of God" (*I Believe in the Church*, 285). Such interpretations, however, in applying Paul's words to female nature in general, may go beyond the apostle's intention. Susan Foh writes, "Paul is not speaking of women in general or the nature of woman but of Eve. . . . Paul contrasts the way in which Adam and Eve sinned: Adam was not deceived (he knew what he was doing), but the woman was completely deceived" (Bonnidell Clouse and Robert G. Clouse, eds., *Women in Ministry: Four Views*, 82). I agree that Paul does not actually state as a conclusion that Eve's deception points to a basic female tendency in the same direction. Rather, Paul declares that Eve's deception led to her becoming "a transgressor." Paul elsewhere writes about Eve's deception, "I am afraid that as the serpent deceived Eve by his cunning, your thoughts will be led astray from a sincere and pure devotion to Christ" (2 Cor. 11:3). It is obvious here that Eve's deception is by no means related to a general feminine tendency to deception but to the dangers of all believers being deceived and led astray from Christ.

to do authoritative teaching is their nonelder status. Such teaching—"apt teaching" as well as ruling—belongs to the office of elder.[266]

It should be added with emphasis that the negation of authoritative oversight and teaching by women in no way rules out women as teachers: it simply limits their sphere of operation. As I mentioned before, for them to teach other women is surely in order, and by implication that includes teaching young people and children. Teaching may be done by a woman nonofficially with her husband (recall Priscilla and Aquila),[267] for in so doing she is not in a position of superiority. Since Paul speaks of certain women (Euodia and Syntyche) as being among his "fellow workers," this suggests team ministries that include women whether or not they are in certain teaching roles. Indeed, there is no Pauline prohibition of women teaching outside the official church context of public worship (where elders carry oversight and teaching authority) even if that includes the teaching of men.[268]

What, then, about women proclaiming the gospel? We have already noted that the Samaritan woman so bore witness that many came to faith, and that, according to Acts 8:4, "those [believers in Jerusalem] who were scattered went about preaching ['evangelizing'] the word." All believers are called upon to bear witness, to proclaim the gospel to the lost, hence to evangelize. Such proclamation of the gospel is not the same as authoritative oversight and teaching[269] in a local congregation and is therefore the province of both men and women.

One further point: women may freely minister in charismatic gifts. I have already spoken of the activity of prophesying. Peter's message on the Day of Pentecost, announcing the fulfillment of Joel's words "Your sons and your daughters shall prophesy . . . my menservants and my maidservants . . . shall prophesy" (Acts 2:17–18), opens the door wide for ministry in this gift. Moreover, there is no biblical reason to exclude women from any of the other *charismata* mentioned in 1 Corinthians 12:8–10 or Romans 12:6–8 including, for example, word of knowledge and teaching. None of the *charismata* represent official church ministry,[270] and thus may operate through the total church, men and women alike. Women may be used in some gifts more than others, but the *charismata* are open to all.

Now a final word regarding women in ministry. The fact that some areas are closed to them by no means suggests that women are inferior to men. The issue is not equality of being but distinction of authority and practice. Even as Christ is equal to God the Father, but also is subordinate, not inferior, to Him; so is woman to man.[271] Paul also speaks of equality in terms of redemption: "There is neither Jew nor Greek, there is neither slave nor free, there is neither male nor female; for you are all one in Christ Jesus" (Gal. 3:28). However, equality in salvation and in the

[266]This means that not only women are excluded from authoritative oversight and teaching in the church but also men who are not elders. Paul can hardly be accused of gender bias!

[267]The instruction of Apollos by Priscilla and Aquila, as before noted, was done privately. Neither functioned as a church elder, though they were surely used by the Lord to impart to Apollos "the way of God more accurately."

[268]Hence today, for example, women teaching in church schools, Bible colleges, and seminaries, is in order.

[269]I have earlier spoken of this as "the ministry of the word."

[270]As do the *domata* gifts of Ephesians 4.

[271]Recall again 1 Corinthians 11:3: "the head of every man is Christ, and the head of the woman is man, and the head of Christ is God"(NIV).

unity that this brings about does not abolish creaturely distinctiveness.[272] Male is still male and female female. Christian man and woman, one in Christ, should all the more recognize and rejoice in the God-given positions of each and minister accordingly. Such ministry will indeed reflect the way of Christ Himself.

I close by emphasizing the manifold ministries of women. There is much need in our churches today for fresh reflection on the abundance of opportunities that should be available to women. As we have seen, the New Testament itself affords a wide range of examples that can give further impetus and guidance. Surely when women begin to fulfill their many roles, the church is all the more richly blessed.[273]

III. GOVERNMENT

In this concluding section we deal with the government of the church. What is the New Testament picture of how the church is to be governed? I have touched on this in earlier pages; here I will draw some of these refections together and add further details.

A. Autonomy of the Local Church

We begin with the glad affirmation of the one church of Jesus Christ throughout the world. The church includes people of all races, languages, and cultures. Although there are many denominations, there is and can be only one church. It is "the one, holy, catholic, and apostolic church" of all times and places.[274]

This universal church is invariably the gathering of believers in a particular place. It is the one church in individual expression. The local church is not simply a part of the whole church: it is the church of Jesus Christ.[275]

Christ made reference to the church twice in the Gospels: the first was to the universal church, "I will build my church" (Matt. 16:18); the second was to a local gathering of believers, "Tell it to the church" (Matt. 18:17). Christ's purpose is to build His church as bodies of believers throughout the world.

Thus in the New Testament we see individual churches coming into being. There is "the church in Jerusalem" (Acts 8:1), "the church at Antioch" (Acts 13:1), "the church of God which is at Corinth" (1 Cor. 1:2), and the church in many other locales. It may even be a house church, but such is still wholly a church—not just a part of some larger church body. The church is sometimes referred to in the plural: "churches"—for example, "the churches of Macedonia" (2 Cor. 8:1), "the churches of Galatia" (Gal. 1:2), and "the churches of Christ in Judea" (Gal. 1:22). These plural references make clear that the church consists of individual churches. This is shown also in the Book of Revelation, which is addressed "to the seven churches that are in Asia" (1:4). Note that it is not to the church of Asia but to the churches in Asia. Further, Christ speaks to each

[272]The distinction between slave and free may be abolished since slavery is not a given creaturely condition.

[273]There is much literature today on women in ministry. Two helpful books expressing different viewpoints are Alvera Mickelsen, ed., *Women, Authority, and the Bible*, and Bonnidell Clouse and Robert G. Clouse, eds., *Women in Ministry: Four Views*. In the latter book Susan Foh (earlier mentioned) has an interesting discussion entitled, "What May Women Do in the Church?" (94–102). Especially helpful is the book (earlier mentioned) *Recovering Biblical Manhood and Womanhood*, edited by John Piper and Wayne Grudem.

[274]Recall a discussion of this in chapter 2, pages 34–35.

[275]Recall a discussion of this in chapter 2, pages 38–41.

of the seven churches individually (chapters 2–3).

Accordingly, we refer to the autonomy of the local church. Each church, while under the lordship of Jesus Christ, operates in terms of its self-government and in distinction from all other churches. There cannot properly be the rule of one church over another. Of course, there may be a "mother church" such as the one in Jerusalem, but it does not exercise arbitrary authority over other churches. In the one recorded case in Acts where certain decisions were reached by the Jerusalem church council regarding the Gentile churches (Acts 15), both apostles and elders were present (hence a unique situation). But there is no record of further meetings or decisions; Jerusalem was not "headquarters" for all the other churches.

Further, there is no bishop or other church official over a number of churches. As we have seen, the word "bishop" in the New Testament is simply another translation for *episkopos*, and refers in every case to a local church official. Recall, for example, Paul's salutation in Philippians: "To all the saints in Christ Jesus who are at Philippi, with the bishops [or 'overseers'—*episkopois*] and deacons" (1:1). At the Jerusalem council James presided and delivered the judgment (Acts 15:19) that prevailed. But James did not presume to be an "overseer" for other churches; nor did he travel about to meet with local elders and churches to give advice and direction. Nor is there any reference to either Peter or Paul ordaining individual bishops to succeed them in office. The most that can be said is that Paul participated in the ordination of Timothy to serve as a teaching elder in Ephesus, and Titus was charged by Paul not to be a bishop but to appoint bishops (also called elders) in the churches of Crete. The word *episkopos* in the singular does appear in 1 Timothy 3:1: "If any one sets his heart on being an overseer. . ." (NIV); however, this is clearly a title for the office and does not imply that one person holds it. Bishops in the New Testament are invariably local church officials;[276] they are the overseeing elders.

We also note that there is no presbytery above the local church. The one New Testament reference to the presbytery relates to Timothy's ordination through "the laying on of hands by the presbytery" (1 Tim. 4:14 NASB). The presbytery (*presbyterion*) is "the body of elders" (NIV translation) in a local church. Indeed, there could not possibly have been an ordination through a higher presbytery or body of elders, for none existed. Hence not only could there not have been ordination by a presbytery above the local church (or even representing a number of churches), but also surely there could have been no supervision or control by such a body. The local presbyters, the elders, overseeing and teaching, made up the presbytery.

Thus, again, the local church is autonomous. There is no authority above it except the authority of Jesus Christ.

B. Plurality of Leadership

Leadership in the church is invariably plural. For example, in Hebrews

[276]I also call attention to I Clement, an early noncanonical letter that speaks of "bishops and deacons" as local appointees (see 42:4), and the *Didache*, which does the same: "Appoint for yourselves bishops and deacons" (15:1). In the letters of Ignatius, near the beginning of the second century, the office of bishop had come to be viewed as separate from those of elders and deacons—"the bishops and the presbyters and the deacons" (*Letter to the Philadelphians*, Intro.). This represents the beginning of the office of monarchical bishop, which increasingly became separated from the local churches and took on an authority above them.

13:17 is this injunction: "Obey your leaders and submit to them; for they are keeping watch over your souls, as men who will have to give account."[277] The leaders are unmistakably the elders or pastors who "keep watch."[278] To the leaders, *not* to a single leader, the church is enjoined to render obedience.

As we have earlier observed, in the Book of Acts there is invariably a plurality of elders. E.g., Paul and Barnabas "appointed elders . . . in every church" (14:23); "the apostles and the elders were gathered together" (15:6); Paul "called to him the elders of the church" (20:17). Elders—in the plural—are the leaders in the local church.[279] In the Epistles again there is plurality of leadership; e.g., "Let the elders who rule well" (1 Tim 5:17); "Appoint elders in every town" (Titus 1:5); "I exhort the elders among you" (1 Peter 5:1). There is *no* suggestion of one elder being over a church;[280] the leadership is always plural. There may be a duality in eldership—elders who, in addition to ruling, "labor in preaching and teaching" (1 Tim. 5:17).[281] However, again, no one elder, whether called pastor or teacher, overseer or minister of the word, is the leader of a given church. All the elders are ordained, set apart, to work as a unity under the one lordship of Jesus Christ.

Based on the New Testament pattern, a church is not fully in order until elders are in place. Paul charged Titus to "set in order" (Titus 1:5 NASB) the churches in Crete by appointing elders "in every town." Churches already existed there, but orderly church life calls for the rule of elders. Indeed, it may be better to delay for a while if qualified elders are not yet available; however, in time elders do need to be appointed. For a church to be without elders, or to allow one elder, the pastor, to assume the eldership to himself is out of order. This makes for one-man rule rather than a plurality of rule under Jesus Christ.

Deacons should not be in the position of leadership. Deacons in the New Testament are auxiliary persons who serve in various practical matters. They function in conjunction with the elders as church officers—"the bishops ['overseers'] and deacons" (Phil. 1:1). Deacons, however, are not essential to church order (Titus was charged only to appoint elders), but they do fulfill a valuable auxiliary role under the authority of the elders. This means, incidentally, that for a church to have deacons and not elders is also disorderly, because the true biblical office of rule is totally absent. The deacons then may assume too much authority or—the other extreme—may be allowed too little under the rule of a pastor who has assumed the eldership to himself. Further, a board of deacons can function properly only when it operates under the authority of a board of elders.

---

[277]Also, note 1 Thessalonians 5:12: "We request of you, brethren, that you appreciate those who diligently labor among you, and have charge over you in the Lord" (NASB).

[278]"They are pastors responsible to God" (TDNT 2:907, under ἡγέομαι, "to lead").

[279]The church in Jerusalem of course also had the apostles ("the apostles and elders"), with James as the leader among them. But even there they worked in conjunction with the elders; there is no suggestion that the apostles were over them.

[280]"Elder," in the singular, occurs in 1 Timothy 5:19 and 1 Peter 5:1, but in each case it occurs in the larger context of "elders" (see above quotations). "The elder to . . ." is the opening salutation of 2 and 3 John; however, it is questionable whether elder there refers to a church official.

[281]All elders in the New Testament are "ruling" elders, including those whose special work is preaching and teaching. Hence it is a mistake to refer to ruling elders and teaching elders; for all elders rule. Thus, for example, the teaching elder (or elders) should join with all the other elders in making decisions, voting, and the like.

Without eldership a diaconate ought not even to exist. It is urgent that many churches today reflect seriously upon this New Testament plan of church order.

Now, again, in regard to plurality of leadership, the question may be raised as to whether this can really work. Does not one person, after all, have to be in charge? Will there not be occasions when there is such division of opinion that without one person rendering a final decision no headway can be made? Recall again the Jerusalem council, where numerous apostles and elders met on the very divisive question of Gentile circumcision. What happened? One man, James, presided and even delivered a judgment: "My judgment is. . ." (Acts 15:19), but he did not make the final decision. For later in a letter prepared by the apostles and elders to be sent to the Gentiles, they said, "It has seemed good to the Holy Spirit and to us" (v. 28). Thus, one man (like James) may preside—and probably should for the sake of order—but progress and unity do not result from his rule but from *the uniting action of the Holy Spirit*. When Christ through His Spirit truly guides the meeting, a consensus will prevail. Indeed, it is the very plurality of leadership that, rather than being a cause of confusion and division, makes for the highest unity, because no one person has the answer. The Holy Spirit is the Spirit of unity and can bring out of the most difficult situation true harmony and peace.[282]

Plurality of leadership is the New Testament picture. With neither governing person nor governing body above another, it means that every body of elders is much like the original group of apostles, whose only authority beyond them was the Lord Himself. Serving Him unitedly is the high privilege of those He calls to leadership in His church.

C. The Lordship of Jesus Christ

This leads us to stress finally that Jesus Christ is the Lord of the church. All government therefore has its final authority in Him. He is the source of all rule in the local church. The church, while autonomous in relation to other churches, is theonomous[283] in relation to Christ; while under ordained leadership that leadership must be constantly led by His Spirit. Jesus Christ is the final and ultimate governor of the church.

Since Christ is also the head of the universal church—"He is the head of the body, the church" (Col. 1:18)—and thus is the Lord of each and every church, no local church ought to function in isolation from other churches. Rather, each should have a vital concern for the church worldwide. This means ongoing fellowship and cooperation with other churches, continuing effort to break down barriers that separate one church from another,[284] and, most of all, participating in every possible way in the fulfillment of Christ's prayer that "they may all be one" (John 17:21).

Hence, while no authority on earth is above the local church, this cannot mean dissociation from other churches.

---

[282]Incidentally, this means that all decisions by the elders should be *unanimous*. A divided decision is not the work of the Lord. It may take longer to arrive at unanimity than to proceed with a majority vote, but the extra time is well spent.

[283]Hence the autonomy is not that of self-rule but of rule under Christ. In its basic nature the church is theonomous (i.e., "governed by God [Christ]"), but in relation to other churches it is autonomous.

[284]Denominationalism is surely one of these barriers. Where particular churches assume that they uniquely contain the truth, thus becoming sectarian and exclusive, the cause of Christ suffers greatly.

Quite the contrary, since Christ is also present among all churches that call on His name,[285] there must be outgoing and loving concern for one another. For example, the church in Antioch blessed the church in Jerusalem by sending financial relief during a famine (Acts 11:27–30);[286] the church in Jerusalem in turn blessed the church in Antioch (and other Gentile churches) by giving relief on the matter of circumcision (Acts 15). Accordingly, without any sacrifice of local autonomy, churches should freely and gladly enter into fellowship with, and provide help for, one another.[287]

There is of course also the broader mission of every church to carry the gospel to all people. Christ, the Lord of the church, is concerned not only about unity among His people—that "they may all be one"—but also that they fulfill His commission—"Go therefore and make disciples of all nations" (Matt. 28:19). Thus among those who have been given equipping ministries (discussed earlier), there are some who function today in apostolic, prophetic, and evangelistic ministries that are largely translocal. Indeed, such ministries are necessary for the missionary outreach of the church. A local church that does not go and send is failing the Lord of the church and is sadly turned in upon itself. However, we must guard against the extreme of apostles (essentially missionaries), prophets, and evangelists functioning outside any local church connection, thus not being under its authority. Paul and Barnabas were commissioned by the church at Antioch (Acts 13:1–3) and reported back to the church there (Acts 14:26–27); Judas and Silas were sent out as prophets from the church in Jerusalem (Acts 15:22, 32). Thus the outreach of the church, which is essential to the Lord's command and its own true existence, needs to be connected with the local church.[288] This is the biblical and proven way.

Every true church throughout the world is under the lordship of Jesus Christ, and as He walks in their midst,[289] governing and guiding, the church will fulfill His mission to all mankind.

---

[285]Paul writes, "To the church of God which is at Corinth . . . together with all those who in every place call on the name of our Lord Jesus Christ, both their Lord and ours" (1 Cor. 1:2).

[286]See also Romans 15:25–28 for the contribution of the churches in Macedonia and Achaia to the saints in Jerusalem; similarly 2 Corinthians 8–9 in regard to the Corinthian church and Jerusalem; also 1 Corinthians 16:1 about the contribution from "the churches of Galatia."

[287]While avoiding the infringement of local autonomy, a number of churches may together appoint persons to represent them in a particular matter. In regard to the offering for the church in Jerusalem, Paul speaks of a brother who had been "appointed by the churches [possibly of Galatia] to travel with [Paul and his companions] in this gracious work" (2 Cor. 8:19). Thus churches in a local or larger area may—and often should—work together in various projects.

[288]Of course local churches may work together with other churches in a broader association of churches for cooperative endeavors, but this ought not to mean independence from local church connections.

[289]In the Book of Revelation Christ is seen "in the midst of the lampstands" (1:13)—the churches. He is still there.

6

Ordinances

Jesus Christ prescribed certain visible ordinances for His church to perform. Since an ordinance may be defined as a prescribed practice or ceremony, we may speak of two visible ordinances, namely, baptism in water and the Lord's Supper.[1]

The ordinance of baptism was declared by Jesus as a part of the Great Commission: "Go therefore and make disciples of all nations, baptizing them in the name of the Father and of the Son and of the Holy Spirit" (Matt. 28:19–20). In another account Jesus, after commanding, "Go into all the world and preach the gospel to the whole creation," stated, "He who believes and is baptized will be saved" (Mark 16:15–16). The prescription to baptize was clearly set forth by Jesus.

The ordinance of the Lord's Supper was likewise given by Jesus. He declared to His disciples in the Upper Room regarding the bread: "Take, eat; this is my body" (Matt. 26:26); and in regard to the cup, "Drink of it, all of you" (v. 27). Similar words are found in the other synoptic gospels (see Mark 14:22–24; Luke 22:17–19). Paul renders Jesus' words regarding the bread in this way: "Do this in remembrance of me" (1 Cor. 11:24); and the cup, "Do this, as often as you drink it, in remembrance of me" (v. 25). Thus the Lord's Supper is likewise an ordinance for the church to maintain.[2]

These two ordinances relate, on the one hand, to Christian beginnings—baptism—and, on the other, to Christian living—the Lord's Supper.[3]

---

[1]The word *sacraments* is the traditional term for these ordinances. Thus we could also speak of the sacraments of baptism and the Lord's Supper. However, since Christ specifically commanded the performance of baptism and the Lord's Supper, the word *ordinances* seems preferable.

[2]Many churches in the Anabaptist tradition (e.g., Brethren, Mennonites, and Amish, as well as some Baptists and Pentecostals) affirm footwashing as an additional ordinance. This is done in reference to Jesus' words "If I then, your Lord and Teacher, have washed your feet, you also ought to wash one another's feet" (John 13:14). However, since Jesus added, "For I have given you an example" (v. 15), it is questionable to view footwashing (whatever the value of the practice) as prescribed by Jesus in the same way as baptism and the Lord's Supper.

[3]The Roman Catholic Church, in addition to baptism and the Lord's Supper (or the

Let us now proceed to a consideration, in turn, of baptism[4] and the Lord's Supper.

I. BAPTISM

A. Definition

The word *baptism* is simply a transliteration of the Greek word *baptisma*, the verbal form being *baptizō*. The primary meaning of the word is immersion or submersion.[5] Hence, baptism is literally, in the case of baptism by water, a placing under the water.[6]

B. Formula

1. The Triune Name

The historic formula for Christian baptism is that found in Matthew 28:19: "in the name of the Father and of the Son and of the Holy Spirit." Since the New Testament period, the church has regularly practiced triune baptism.

2. The Name of Jesus Christ, or the Lord Jesus

In the Book of Acts baptism was performed in the name of Jesus Christ. Peter declared on the Day of Pentecost: "Repent, and be baptized every one of you in the name of Jesus Christ" (2:38). At a later date the Samaritans were "baptized in the name of the Lord Jesus" (8:16); then the Caesareans were "baptized in the name of Jesus Christ" (10:48); after that the Ephesians "were baptized in the name of the Lord Jesus" (19:5).[7] Other references to baptism in Acts do not specify the formula,[8] but presumably in those instances also it was likewise done in the name of Jesus Christ, or the Lord Jesus.

Both formulas, accordingly, are found in the New Testament and either of them may properly be used in a baptismal ceremony. The fact that the early church in Acts did not practice triune baptism is sufficient basis for the church today, despite centuries of baptismal practice, also to baptize in the name of Jesus only. Either practice is surely valid.[9]

In any event Christ is the vital center of all Christian baptism: whether in the triune or in the Jesus-only formula. Several references in Paul's letters also reinforce the centrality of Jesus Christ in baptism: Romans 6:3: "baptized into Christ Jesus"; Galatians 3:27: "baptized into Christ"; and Colossians 2:12:

Eucharist), includes confirmation, penance, marriage, holy orders, and extreme unction (the Council of Trent, "Decree concerning the Sacraments," Canon 1). These are all viewed as channels of grace, and actually go beyond Christ's ordinances, or commands, of baptism and the Lord's Supper.

[4]Baptism (in water) has been previously discussed in *Renewal Theology*, 2:38–39, 279–87, 291–93; also in this volume, pages 136–39. Hence the study of baptism in the present chapter will in some ways repeat past discussions (as will be noted); however, there will be additional material. It should prove helpful to view baptism in a total perspective.

[5]Thayer: "immersion, submersion." BAGD under *бαπτιζω* says, "dip, immerse, wash (in non-Christian lit. also plunge, sink, drench, overwhelm)." In the Old Testament LXX *baptizō* is found in 2 Kings 5:14, which states that Naaman "went down and dipped [*ebaptizato*] himself seven times in the Jordan."

[6]Later we will discuss the mode of baptism in more detail (see section E, pp. 225–28).

[7]The English preposition "in" is used above to translate *epi* (2:38), *eis* (8:16 and 19:5), and *en* (10:48). *Epi* often means "upon"; *eis*, "into"; *en*, "in." However, since there is little likelihood of a difference in meaning in the baptismal passages, "in" seems quite adequate. Moreover, there is clearly no difference between "the name of Jesus Christ" and "the name of the Lord Jesus."

[8]See Acts 9:18; 16:15, 33; 18:8; 22:16.

[9]See *Renewal Theology*, 2:286–87, for an earlier discussion of this matter (especially n. 48 in regard to extreme Trinitarian and "Jesus only" [Pentecostal] views). Also for more detail see the present volume, pages 138–39.

"buried with him [Christ] in baptism." It is clear that whatever the exact formula, Christ is the central reality.

C. Relationships

Baptism relates to a number of matters in Christian beginnings. Let us note several.

1. The Forgiveness of Sins

To Peter's words on the Day of Pentecost "Repent, and be baptized every one of you in the name of Jesus Christ" is added, "for the forgiveness of your sins" (Acts 2:38). The preposition "for"[10] suggests "with respect to," or "with a view to." Water often is used for cleansing, and so in relation to forgiveness of sins it is a vivid symbol.

2. Regeneration

Paul writes to Titus: "[God] saved us . . . by the washing of regeneration and renewing by the Holy Spirit" (Titus 3:5 NASB). "Washing" here refers to baptismal washing,[11] and thus is closely connected with regeneration, or the new birth. Recall also Jesus' words: "Unless one is born of water and the Spirit, he cannot enter the kingdom of God" (John 3:5).[12] There is undoubtedly a close connection between baptism and regeneration.

3. Buried With Christ and Raised With Him

Two passages in Paul's letters, earlier quoted in part, are relevant. First, Romans 6:3–4: "Do you not know that all of us who have been baptized into Christ Jesus were baptized into his death? We were buried therefore with him by baptism into death, so that as Christ was raised from the dead . . . we too might walk in newness of life." Second, Colossians 2:12: "You were buried with him in baptism, in which you were also raised with him through faith in the working of God, who raised him from the dead." Obviously baptism is closely related to burial with Christ into death and resurrection with Him to life.

4. Incorporation Into Christ and Unity With Other Believers

Another passage in Paul's letters quoted earlier in part—Galatians 3:27—reads, "As many of you as were baptized into Christ have put on Christ." Following that Paul adds, "You are all one in Christ Jesus" (v. 28). Baptism relates to both a union with Christ and in Him to all other Christians.

5. Engagement to Be the Lord's

The act of baptism expresses an irrevocable commitment to Jesus Christ. It is a public declaration that one henceforward belongs to Another; it is a visible demonstration "before men." Jesus declares, "Everyone who confesses Me before men, the Son of Man shall confess him also before the angels of God" (Luke 12:8 NASB). Baptism shows to the world one's confession of Christ and total dedication to Him.

D. Significance

Now that we have observed a number of relationships, let us next consider the question of significance. What is the significance of baptism in regard to the matters discussed? Baptism is a sign, a seal, and a means of grace.

---

[10]In the Greek, *eis*. See *Renewal Theology*, 2:284, for further details.

[11]The Greek word is *loutron*: "bath, washing of baptism" (BAGD).

[12]For an earlier discussion of this verse see *Renewal Theology*, 2:37–38. Not all agree that "born of water" refers to baptism, but see my comments in nn.15, 16.

1. A Sign

The ordinance of baptism may first be viewed as a visible *sign* of grace and salvation—that is, of God's forgiveness, of new birth, of burial and resurrection, of incorporation into Christ and unity with all believers, and of total dedication to Jesus Christ. A sign is a pointer. As we have observed, baptism is "for" the forgiveness of sins, hence it is a sign, a pointer, to that forgiveness. Baptism is a sign of the cleansing in forgiveness, of the washing in regeneration, of being buried with Christ, and so on. Augustine defined a sacrament as "a visible sign of a sacred thing."[13] Baptism verily is a visible sign of God's sacred and invisible grace in all these aspects of grace and salvation. Baptism does not bring about forgiveness of sins and the like, but it does point vividly in that direction.

2. A Seal

Baptism may be understood not only as a sign but also as a *seal*. It is noteworthy that Paul speaks about Abraham's circumcision[14] as both a sign and a seal of his faith. In regard to Abraham, Paul writes, "He received the sign of circumcision, a seal of the righteousness that he had by faith while he was still uncircumcised" (Rom. 4:11 NIV). Hence circumcision was not only a sign of God's grace already received; it was also a seal in the flesh of that same grace. Thus we may draw the parallel with baptism: not only does it signify a faith-righteousness already present, but it also seals that righteousness to the one being baptized. The seal is a visible ratification of God's grace in such a way that the spiritual reality of grace and salvation is confirmed bodily for the believer.[15] Thereafter the believer may continue to recall the occasion (even the day and hour of his confession) and the deeply confirming seal of baptism.[16]

3. A Means of Grace

Baptism may also function as a *means of grace*. Not only is God's grace of salvation signified and sealed in baptism, but also baptism is a channel of that grace. For example, Paul's words about "the washing of regeneration" imply that in the washing, which relates to water baptism, regeneration occurs. *Through* the act of baptism God's grace is given. It is not that the act of baptism regenerates but that baptism may be the channel, or means, by which the grace of regeneration is applied and received. Again, burial with Christ is not brought about by immersion in water, for such burial is a profoundly spiritual experience of dying to self. However, the very visible and tangible experience of going under the water (a kind of momentary death) can be a channel of God's grace in spiritual death and resurrection. Once again, to "put on Christ" is essentially an act of repentance and faith; however, the act of baptism may be a channel of grace in which the putting off of the old self and the putting on of the new occurs. Union with Christ, or for that matter with other believers, does not depend on baptism. But since baptism is a visible and tangible action, it can serve as a physical counterpart to the spiritual occurrence. Finally, in regard to one's

[13]*De catechizandis rudibus* xxvi.50 (tr. ACW II. 82).

[14]The relationship between circumcision and baptism will be discussed in more detail later.

[15]The Westminster Confession of Faith speaks in covenantal terms of baptism as one's personal sign and seal: "Baptism is . . . to be unto him a sign and seal of the covenant of grace, of his ingrafting into Christ, of regeneration, of remission of sins, and of his giving up unto God, through Jesus Christ, to walk in newness of life" (28.1).

[16]For more on baptism as sign and seal see *Renewal Theology*, 2:284–85.

engagement to be the Lord's—a profoundly spiritual commitment—baptism is an important component: it serves as the avenue for that engagement to be demonstrated.

In reflecting on baptism, two extremes must be avoided: on the one hand, viewing baptism only as a sign of salvation already received and, on the other hand, viewing it as the necessary means of grace. From the first of these perspectives baptism is understood only to be a pointer to the prior occurrence of salvation;[17] thus it is actually extraneous to that event. However, as we have noted, baptism is immediately related to salvation. It is not only a sign but also a seal and often a means or channel through which God's grace in salvation is received. From the second perspective, baptism is viewed as itself effectuating salvation, hence a necessary means of grace.[18] Baptism, when performed properly, confers grace and thus imparts salvation.[19] Thus there is baptismal regeneration. Such a view undoubtedly goes beyond Scripture, which, while emphasizing baptism even to the degree of its being a means of grace, does not affirm baptism as essential to salvation.[20]

E. Mode

Since the word *baptism* is simply a transliteration of *baptisma*, meaning "immersion," it follows that immersion is the normal mode of baptism. In addition to the etymology of the word, there are other reasons for considering immersion to be the proper mode. Three reasons may be mentioned.

1. Phraseology

In the Gospel of Mark, Jesus' baptism is described thus: "[He] was baptized by John in the Jordan. As Jesus was coming up out of the water. . ." (1:9–10 NIV). "In"[21] suggests the element (water) in which, or into which,

[17]For example, A. H. Strong (Baptist theologian) writes, "Baptism symbolizes the *previous entrance* of the believer into the communion of Christ's death and resurrection, or, in other words, regeneration through union with Christ" (italics added) (*Systematic Theology*, 940).

[18]The Roman Catholic Council of Trent declares, "If any one says that baptism is optional, that is, not necessary for salvation, let him be anathema" (*Canons on Baptism*, 5). In the earlier *Canons on the Sacraments in General*, grace is spoken of as "conferred *ex opere operato*" (Canon 8), meaning "by the work done" (i.e., the sacramental action). What this amounts to is baptismal regeneration.

[19]This may be described as *sacramentalism*, the view that grace is invariably conveyed through the religious rite.

[20]On this latter point—the necessity of baptism to salvation—several scriptures are frequently adduced. Among them are Acts 2:38; Romans 6:3–4; Galatians 3:27; Colossians 2:12; and Titus 3:5. However, these verses about baptism at most should be understood as means of grace (recall point 3 above: "A Means of Grace"). In addition there are other verses, particularly Mark 16:16; John 3:5 (earlier quoted); and 1 Peter 3:21, that are sometimes interpreted as likewise affirming the necessity of baptism. See *Renewal Theology*, 2:37–39, including nn.15–20, for relevant discussion of these verses. Incidentally, one of the most striking statements *dissociating* salvation and baptism is 1 Corinthians 1:17, where Paul says, "Christ did not send me to baptize but to preach the gospel." Paul surely baptized people (see the preceding three verses), but he does not stress baptism as integral to his preaching the gospel and by that means bringing people to salvation.

[21]The Greek preposition is *eis*. The ordinary meaning (as we have before noted) is "into"; however, "in" is sometimes the better translation. According to EGT, "the idea of descending into the river . . . [is] latent in *eis*" (1:342). Whether we translate the word "into" or "in," the idea of immersion is implied.

Jesus was placed; "coming up out of the water"[22] depicts an emergence from the water. The phraseology clearly implies that Jesus' baptism was by immersion.

Similar language is found in Acts regarding Philip's baptism of the Ethiopian eunuch: "Both Philip and the eunuch went down into[23] the water and Philip baptized him. When they came up out of[24] the water. . ." (8:38–39 NIV). Again, the phraseology points to immersion.[25]

Returning to the baptizing by John, we find another relevant statement: "John . . . was baptizing at Aenon near Salim, because there was plenty of water, and people were constantly coming to be baptized" (John 3:23 NIV). "Plenty of"[26] may imply the sufficiency of water for the practice of immersion.[27]

In regard to the three preceding scriptures, the phraseology of the first (Mark 1:9–10) presents the strongest case for baptism by immersion.

2. Symbolism

One of the most compelling reasons for viewing immersion as the normal mode of baptism is the symbolism involved.

For example, several of the Scriptures quoted earlier suggest immersion. Romans 6:4 and Colossians 2:12, which speak of being "buried" with Christ by baptism into death, point to a submersion of the whole body, even to symbolic drowning, and thereafter being raised with Christ from the dead. Even as a person in salvation undergoes a total spiritual renewal, so in immersion there is the total physical counterpart. It is total death and resurrection. Other scriptures quoted, such as "the washing of regeneration" and "born of water and the Spirit," likewise suggest immersion: a total washing, a total rebirth.

Two others verses, not quoted, may be mentioned. Paul writes to the Corinthians: "Our fathers were all under the cloud, and all passed through the sea, and all were baptized into Moses in the cloud and in the sea" (1 Cor. 10:1–2). This highly symbolic language regarding being "baptized into Moses" suggests a parallel with being "baptized into Christ," and "in the cloud and sea" points to Israel's being enveloped, even immersed, in God's surrounding glory in the cloud and in His total protection in the sea.[28] The other significant passage is found in Hebrews 10:22: "Let us draw near [in worship] . . . with our hearts sprinkled clean

[22]The Greek phrase is *anabainōn ek tou hydatos*. The parallel version in Matthew 3:16 has the preposition *apo*.

[23]*Eis*.

[24]The Greek phrase is *anebēsan ek*. EGT: "[This] indicates that the baptism was by immersion" (2:226).

[25]It could be argued, of course, that since both Philip and the eunuch went down into the water and both came up out of it, Philip was immersed also! However, this seems to push the language too far. I. H. Marshall also says that "there is not sufficient evidence to indicate whether the baptism took place by the immersion of the eunuch in water or by the pouring (affusion) of water over him as he stood in shallow water" (*The Acts of the Apostles*, TNTC, 165). My view, however, is that the evidence is stronger for immersion than for affusion, especially when compared with Mark 1:9–10.

[26]Literally, "many waters"—*hydata polla*; KJV, RSV, and NASB read "much water."

[27]EGT comments that "much water" suggests that "even in summer baptism by immersion could be continued" (1:719). Leon Morris holds that the "many waters" refers to "seven springs within a radius of a quarter of a mile" (*The Gospel According to John*, NICNT, 237). If so, the case for immersion in this passage may be not so strong (Morris, however, does not speak directly to that matter).

[28]As EGT says, "Paul sees a baptism in the waters of the Exodus" (2:857).

from an evil conscience and our bodies washed with pure water." Since the author of Hebrews seems to be referring to the original occurrence of salvation and accompanying baptism[29] when he uses the phrase "our bodies washed," the implication seems clearly to be a total immersion of the body.

Finally, in regard to symbolism even where baptism does not refer to water, immersion is often implied. I call attention to the baptism of suffering and the baptism in the Holy Spirit. Jesus declared, "I have a baptism to be baptized with; and how am I straitened till it be accomplished!" (Luke 12:50 KJV). This was to be a baptism of suffering even to death and an immersion in total grief and pain.[30] In regard to baptism in the Holy Spirit, John the Baptist spoke of Jesus as "the one who baptizes in[31] the Holy Spirit" (John 1:33 NASB). This suggests an immersion in the Spirit comparable to immersion in water.[32]

3. Church Practice

It is possible that the practice of immersion is related to the Jewish rite of proselyte baptism. Shortly before the appearance of John the Baptist, there emerged in Judaism the practice of not only requiring the circumcision of Gentile proselytes but also, because of their uncleanness in Jewish eyes, of their total immersion in water.[33] John the Baptist, of course, went farther than Gentile proselyte baptism because he also required baptism of fellow Jews. However, it seems quite likely that John would have followed the same practice of immersion, and that the disciples of Jesus would have done the same.[34] There is no biblical suggestion that the practice of immersion did not continue in Acts and the early church.

We may now turn briefly from the New Testament to an early teaching about baptism in the *Didache*.[35] It specifies immersion as the basic practice but also offers the option of pouring. "Now concerning baptism . . . baptize 'in the name of the Father and of the Son and of the Holy Spirit' in running water. But if you have no running water, then baptize in some other water; and if you are not able to baptize in cold, then do so in warm. But if you have neither, then pour water on the head three times 'in the name of the Father and Son and Holy Spirit.' "[36] Thus immersion is specified as the normal mode of baptism; only in excep-

---

[29]F. F. Bruce writes that the "reality which he [the author of Hebrews] has in mind is surely Christian baptism" (*Epistle to the Hebrews*, NICNT, 251).

[30]A. H. Strong writes, "Death presented itself to the Savior's mind as a baptism, because it was a sinking under the floods of suffering" (*Systematic Theology*, 932).

[31]The Greek preposition is *en*, which may also be translated "with" or "by." I believe, however, the NASB (likewise NEB) well catches the meaning. (See *Renewal Theology*, 1:169, nn.43–44; also 198–200, and nn.70–77.

[32]"Fire" is also connected with the baptism in the Holy Spirit in both Matthew 3:11 and Luke 3:16—"baptism in the Holy Spirit and fire." Since fire consumes totally, this figure also suggests total immersion.

[33]On the Jewish rite of proselyte baptism see R. E. O. White, *The Biblical Doctrine of Christian Initiation*, chapter 4, "Proselyte Baptism." Also note his quotation, "There is no adequate ground for doubting that Jewish baptism in the first century A.D. was by total immersion" (p. 63).

[34]Note the close connection between John's and Jesus' disciples baptizing in John 3:22–23 and 4:1–2.

[35]Probably a first-century document. See chap. 5, supra, n.221, on dating.

[36]*Didache*, 7:1–3 (*The Apostolic Fathers*, 2nd ed., trans. Lightfoot and Harmer, ed. and rev. M. W. Holmes, 153).

tional cases is another mode to be allowed.[37]

Immersion as the common church practice continued until the thirteenth century, and in the Eastern church immersion, even for infants, has continued to the present day.

EXCURSUS: POURING AND SPRINKLING

In addition to immersion, both pouring and sprinkling are widely practiced in Western Christendom. Pouring, as noted, was permitted in the *Didache*, but clearly this was a concession to situations where there was insufficient water for immersion. Sprinkling has also come to be practiced widely.[38] Indeed, pouring and particularly sprinkling have in some churches become the norm, with immersion much subordinated[39] or not practiced at all. This is a very unfortunate development. Immersion much needs to be reinstated as the normal mode of baptism, and therefore as the regular practice in all Christian churches.[40]

A final word: Let me emphasize that the matter of mode is not the critical issue. Baptisms are not invalid because some mode other than that of the New Testament is followed. Water, however applied and whatever the amount, is still a basic symbol for cleansing. Moreover, since baptism does not itself regenerate, even the omission of baptism does not basically affect a person's relationship with God. Still, although not a critical issue, there is much to be gained both for the church and its members if the original practice of total immersion is universally restored.

---

[37]The editors of *The Apostolic Fathers* add that "this appears to be the earliest reference to the Christian use of a mode of baptism other than immersion" (p. 153, n.26).

[38]Calvin justifies sprinkling thus: "Whether the person baptized is wholly immersed, and that whether once or thrice, or whether he is only to be sprinkled with water, is not of the least consequence: churches should be at liberty to adopt either, according to the diversity of climates, although it is evident that the term *baptize* means to immerse, and that this was the form used in the primitive church" (*Institutes*, 4.15.19, Beveridge trans.). It is significant that Calvin, while endorsing sprinkling and putting it on a parity with immersion, declares immersion to be the meaning of the word baptism *and* that the act of immersion was the early church practice. It seems to me a bit cavalier for Calvin to say that the matter is "not of the least consequence," that climatic consideration is what counts (were there no cold climates where the early church baptized by immersion?); so do what you like. We may be grateful, however, that Calvin goes beyond many Calvinists who are very loath to say, or admit, that immersion was the original church practice.

[39]The Westminster Confession states, "Dipping of the person into water is not necessary; but baptism is rightly administered by pouring or sprinkling water upon the person" (23.3). This is a very inadequate statement, elevating pouring and sprinkling above immersion. "Rightly," as used here, cannot help but suggest that there is really something wrong with the practice of immersion. If anything, the reverse should be the case! Incidentally, it is obvious that the Westminster Confession, a Calvinistic document, "out-Calvins" Calvin at this point!

[40]A further word about pouring and sprinkling. Pouring is a better symbol for the Holy Spirit who is "poured out" (Acts 2:17–18; 10:45) than it is for water baptism. Sprinkling may be connected with Ezekiel 36:25: "I will sprinkle clean water upon you, and you shall be clean from all your uncleannesses" and Hebrews 10:22: "our hearts sprinkled clean from an evil conscience." However, these verses seem to have little, if any, connection with the practice of baptism in the New Testament. Indeed, Hebrews 10:22 continues, as we have earlier noted, with the words "*and* our bodies washed with pure water." It is not the sprinkling but the washing that refers to baptism.

F. Subjects

The proper subjects of baptism are those who believe in Jesus Christ. This is apparent from all the relevant New Testament passages. Let us review a number of these in the Book of Acts.

Acts 2:41: "Those who received his [Peter's] word were baptized."

Acts 8:12: "When they [the Samaritans] believed Philip as he preached good news . . . they were baptized, both men and women."

Acts 8:35, 38: "Philip . . . told him [the Ethiopian eunuch] the good news of Jesus. And . . . he baptized him."

Acts 10:48: "He [Peter] commanded them [Gentile believers] to be baptized in the name of Jesus Christ."

Acts 16:14–15: "The Lord opened her [Lydia's] heart to respond to the things spoken by Paul. And when she and her household[41] had been baptized. . ." (NASB).

Acts 16:31–33: "And they [Paul and Silas] said, 'Believe in the Lord Jesus, and you [the Philippian jailer] shall be saved, you and your household.' And they spoke the word of the Lord to him together with all who were in his house. And . . . immediately he was baptized, he and all his household" (NASB).

Acts 18:8: "Crispus . . . believed in the Lord, together with all his household; and many of the Corinthians . . . believed and were baptized."

Acts 19:4–5: "Paul said [to the Ephesians], 'John baptized with the baptism of repentance, telling the people to believe in the one who was to come after him, that is, Jesus.' On hearing this, they were baptized in the name of the Lord Jesus."

Baptism in all these passages is clearly linked to faith: receiving the word, believing the good news, responding to the gospel message. The baptism was of believers. Their baptism was unmistakably connected with the preaching of the gospel and the response of faith.

In other New Testament references to Christian baptism it is apparent that believers are those who undergo baptism: Romans 6:4; Galatians 3:27; Colossians 2:12; and 1 Peter 3:21.[42] Although the word "believers" is not used in Matthew 28:19, the expression "make disciples . . . baptizing them" is the equivalent of baptizing those who have come to faith.

All of the passages noted underscore the personal and active faith of those who are baptized. Baptism belongs within the context of God's grace and human response. Believers' baptism is the New Testament way and should be the practice of the church at large.

EXCURSUS: INFANT BAPTISM

It is surely an important matter that across Christendom infant baptism (paedobaptism) is widely practiced. This is true for Eastern Orthodoxy, Roman Catholicism, and many Protestant denominations. Consideration of this, I believe, belongs to an excursus: a digression from the New Testament pattern of believers' baptism. Some of the arguments for infant baptism will be given with response following.

1. Household baptisms

The household baptisms in Acts in all likelihood included infants and children who were also baptized. Since Lydia "and her household" were baptized, this probably included children not yet of believing age. With the household as an organic unit, Lydia's faith would make valid the baptism of all members. The Philippian jailer was told by Paul,

---

[41]The Greek word here and in the following two references is *oikos*.

[42]Also kindred passages that do not directly mention baptism but probably imply it are John 3:5; Titus 3:5; and Hebrews 10:22.

"Believe in the Lord Jesus Christ, and you will be saved, you and your household," thus declaring that on the basis of the jailer's faith both he and his family would be saved. Hence, although household baptisms do not necessarily prove infant baptism, such baptism seems likely on the basis of family solidarity.[43]

We may first respond by observing that "household" in the New Testament does not necessarily include infants and small children. For example, in John 4, the servants of a Capernaum official brought word to him that his son was healed by Jesus; as a result "he himself believed, and all his household" (v. 53). "His household" probably included the servants and members of the official's family without reference to children. This is even clearer in the story of the Roman centurion Cornelius, who "feared God with all his household" (Acts 10:2). When Peter arrived to preach the gospel, Cornelius "had called together his kinsmen and close friends" (v. 24). It was they—household, kinsmen, friends—who later believed and were baptized (vv. 43–48). There is no suggestion that this faith and baptism encompassed children too young to believe.

Now looking particularly at the instance of the Philippian jailer, it is a serious misreading of the Scripture to say that his faith would suffice for his household. If we had only the words "Believe in the Lord Jesus, and you will be saved, you and your household," that might be claimed. However, immediately following this injunction is this statement: "And they [Paul and Silas] spoke the word of the Lord to him and to all that were in his house" (Acts 16:32). Clearly "all . . . in his house" were people of age capable of hearing and believing the word of God: thus likely his wife and older children. Shortly after that "he [the jailer] was baptized, he and all his household"[44] (v. 33 NASB). Finally, "he . . . rejoiced greatly, having believed in God with his whole household" (v. 34 NASB). In no sense whatever is this an account of one person's faith including others—a supposed solidarity. Rather, *all* in his household heard and believed and were baptized in connection with their own personal faith. Infants obviously were not included.

Lydia's household may or may not have included her own family. She was a business woman, a seller of purple goods, residing in Philippi; but she had come from the distant Asia Minor city of Thyatira. Her household (no mention is made of a husband) may then have included various business helpers, perhaps servants. Thus the baptism of Lydia and her household may not refer to family or children at all.[45] If it does, the same thing may apply as with the Philippian jailer: they would have been of age to hear and believe and thus be baptized along with Lydia.

Another significant household baptism (not previously mentioned) is that of Stephanas. Paul writes, "I did bap-

---

[43]Oscar Cullmann speaks of "solidarity in baptism" and refers to the incident of the Philippian jailer's conversion. Cullmann's argument is that if there were infants in the household (which he admits cannot be proved), they would also have been baptized. See his *Baptism in the New Testament*, 53.

[44]The RSV and NIV read "family." Literally, the Greek reads "he and all his" (so KJV). "Household" (as in NASB above), however, helps to maintain the connection with both verse 32 and verse 34.

[45]A distinction between household and children is to be noted in the early letter of Ignatius to Polycarp: "I greet everyone by name, including the widow of Epitropus with her whole household and children" (8:2). Similarly, reference to Lydia's household may point to individuals other than children.

tize also the household of Stephanas" (1 Cor. 1:16). It might be possible to visualize infant baptism in this statement *except* for the fact that Paul later says, "Now, brethren, you know that the household of Stephanas were the first converts in Achaia, and they have devoted themselves to the service of the saints" (1 Cor. 16:15). This household sounds rather adult!

All in all, the household evidence for infant baptism is very weak.[46] Its advocates usually admit that it is presumptive evidence (there is no direct statement anywhere that children were baptized); however, even to say that much is questionable. Incidentally, in one account that does not mention households, the wording, as we have noted, simply is this: "They were baptized, both men and women" (Acts 8:12). Are we to presume that children are included in "men and women"? The question hardly merits a serious answer. There is no adequate evidence—even presumptive—for infant baptism in any of the household narratives.[47]

2. Circumcision and baptism

Since infant boys received circumcision under the old covenant, so should infant children under the new covenant. For both circumcision and baptism are signs and seals of God's covenant of grace that includes not only adults but also their children. Baptism, which of course is still more inclusive—females as well as males—is nonetheless a parallel to Old Testament circumcision. Both practices demonstrate that a covenanting God includes the whole family.[48] Thus infant circumcision leads properly to infant baptism. The overarching concept is that of the one covenant of grace (Old Testament and New) to which children of Christian believers now belong; therefore, they should receive the sign and seal of baptism.[49]

By way of response it is important, first, to recognize that there is a connection between circumcision and baptism. Paul refers to both circumcision and baptism in Colossians 2:11–12: "In him you were also circumcised, in the putting off of the sinful nature, not with a circumcision done by the hands of men but with the circumcision done by Christ, having been buried with him in baptism and raised with him through your faith in the power of God" (NIV). Paul, however, is obviously not talking about physical circumcision "done by . . . men," which does include infants, but about spiritual circumcision "done by Christ," which includes only those who believe in Him—that is, those who are "buried with him in baptism." Thus the parallel is between spiritual circumcision and spiritual baptism,[50] both of which relate only to active believers in Jesus Christ. Accordingly, there is no way that this passage can be properly

[46]Karl Barth speaks of this evidence as "a thin thread to which one may perhaps hold," but adds, "then hardly!" (*The Teaching of the Church Regarding Baptism*, 44).

[47]Beasley-Murray states, "Luke, in writing these narratives, does not have in view infant members of the families. His language cannot be pressed to extend to them. He has in mind ordinary believers and uses language applicable only to them. Abuse of it leads to the degradation of Scripture" (*Baptism in the New Testament*, 315).

[48]Cullmann, for example, speaks of "a fundamental kinship between circumcision and Christian baptism" (*Baptism in the New Testament*, 56–57) and of "the analogy between infant circumcision and Christian infant baptism" (p. 65). Cullmann is a strong advocate of infant baptism.

[49]The Reformed theologian G. C. Berkouwer speaks of "the unity of the Old and New Covenants" as the "essential and profoundest basis for the defense of infant baptism" (*Studies in Dogmatics: The Sacraments*, 175).

[50]As we have observed, water baptism as immersion is a vivid symbol of this.

used to link infant circumcision and infant baptism.

Again, in reflecting on Old Testament circumcision of infants it is important to note that such was done purely on the basis of physical descent. Abraham, to be sure, received circumcision as a sign and seal of his own faith. Recall Paul's statement about this: "He [Abraham] received the sign of circumcision, a seal of the righteousness that he had by faith while he was still uncircumcised" (Rom. 4:11 NIV). However, not only Abraham was circumcised, for God had commanded, "Every male among you shall be circumcised . . . it shall be a sign of the covenant between me and you. He that is eight days old . . . every male throughout your generations" (Gen. 17:10–12). Thus regardless of the faith (or lack of it) among parents, the sign of the covenant must be made. Thus again there is a great difference between the sign and seal of circumcision based on physical birth and that of baptism, which relates to spiritual rebirth. Because circumcision was given to infant boys in the old dispensation is therefore utterly no reason for giving baptism to infant children in the new covenant.[51]

The basic error lies in the failure to recognize the *difference* between the old and new covenants. Doubtless there is a similarity, for it is the same covenanting God who graciously acts for His people. However, it is a great mistake to say, as many adherents of infant baptism do, that because God included the natural descendants of Abraham, adults and children alike, in the old covenant,[52] He includes the children of believers in the new covenant.[53] Rather, in the new covenant *in Christ* only those are included who come to personal faith in Him, and in that faith they are baptized.

3. Jesus' blessing of children

Jesus declared, "Let the children[54] come to me, do not hinder them; for to such belongs the kingdom of God. Truly, I say to you, whoever does not receive the kingdom of God like a child shall not enter it" (Mark 10:14–15). Then the text adds, "And he took them in his arms and blessed them, laying his hands upon them" (v. 16). The words of Jesus, plus His open reception of children, implies the validity of infant baptism.[55]

---

[51]Incidentally, when God told Abraham that this covenant included "every male throughout your generations," He added, "whether born in your house, or bought with your money from any foreigner who is not your offspring" (17:12). Paul Jewett makes this astute comment: "The insistence that every male attached to Abraham's house should be circumcised—even those who were slaves bought with money—is markedly different from anything in the New Testament regarding baptism" (*Infant Baptism and the Covenant of Grace*, 98).

[52]The Mosaic covenant, after Abraham, maintains the same necessity of circumcision (see Exod. 12:48; Lev. 12:3).

[53]See, for example, Pierre Ch. Marcel, *The Biblical Doctrine of Infant Baptism*: "Children are legitimately baptized, without faith or repentance, because they belong to the covenant" (209). This, I submit, is the Judaizing of Christian baptism.

[54]The Greek word is *paidia*. That these were infants is stated in Luke's parallel introductory statement, "They were bringing even infants [*brephē*] to him" (18:15).

[55]Calvin asks, "If it is right that children should be brought to Christ, why should they not be admitted to baptism, the symbol of our communion and fellowship with Christ?" (*Institutes*, 4.16.7, Beveridge trans.). Thus Calvin sees Christ's blessing of children as calling for their baptism. Even more vigorously in *The Biblical Doctrine of Baptism*, a study document issued by the Church of Scotland, this statement is made in italics: *"Our Lord, who stated so clearly that the Kingdom of God belongs to little children, could not have*

All of this, I submit, is special pleading. First, the main emphasis in the passage is not on Jesus' reception of children, but on the childlike attitude of trust and openness that one must have to receive the kingdom: "to such belongs the kingdom of God." Not to children but *"to such"* belongs the kingdom. Second, Jesus assuredly does bless the children, but blessing has no real connection with baptism. We may recall that Jesus' only recorded reference to water baptism was that it was to be given to "disciples"—"baptizing them" (Matt. 28:19). Thus those who come to Christ in active faith, not those who are brought to Him, as were the children, are to be baptized.[56] The attempt to relate Jesus' blessing of children to infant baptism is quite misguided.[57]

Actually the proper use of the texts regarding Jesus' blessing children and taking them in His arms is *not for infant baptism but for infant dedication.* It is altogether fitting that parents should bring forward their infants and small children for dedication to the Lord and that the pastor take the children up in his arms for a blessing. It is also altogether fitting that at some later time, when the child has arrived at a responsible decision of faith, he or she come forward and receive baptism.[58] As a matter of fact infant baptism as practiced in most churches is actually more of a dedication service than a baptism.[59] All that is needed is to omit the water, take the infant up in arms, and bless as Jesus did! Some years later, it will be the privilege and responsibility of one who was dedicated as an infant to come forward on his own and receive Christian baptism.

It is indeed important for infants and little children to be brought to Christ for

---

refused to allow them to share in the sacrament of initiation into that Kingdom, which is Baptism" (p. 49). Some New Testament scholars claim that this Scripture points to the validity of infant baptism. Jeremias, for example, writes, "We may state that the passage Mark 10. 13–16 and parallels in several places contains indirect references to baptism . . . the church took it as authority for the practice of infant baptism" (*Infant Baptism in the First Four Centuries*, 54–55). Cullmann similarly says about Jesus' blessing the children: "This story—without being related to baptism—was fixed [!] in such a way that a baptismal formula of the first century gleams through it" (*Baptism in the New Testament*, 78).

[56]As Karl Barth says, "In the sphere of the New Testament one is not brought to baptism; one comes to baptism" (*The Teaching of the Church Regarding Baptism*, 42). Barth also states, "It may be shown, by exegesis and from the nature of the case, that in this action the baptized is an active partner . . . plainly no *infans* [infant] can be such a person" (p. 41). Incidentally, Barth's exegesis of Mark 10:13–15 (with parallels), including brief critique of Cullmann, may be found in his *Church Dogmatics*, IV, 2, 181–82. See also Kurt Aland, *Did the Early Church Baptize Infants?* chapter 9, "The Blessing of Jesus," which includes a response to Jeremias.

[57]R. E. O. White, *The Biblical Doctrine of Initiation*, 331–38, contains a valuable study of Mark 10:13–15 (and parallels). His final statement: "The use of Mark 10:13f as support for paedobaptist practice . . . cannot be said to have lacked ingenious and scholarly defenders; but whichever way the argument is framed, the conclusion fails to stand. It is quite certain that infant baptism was not built, and cannot be supported on Mark 10:13f" (p. 338).

[58]Jesus Himself, although circumcised as a Jewish boy (Luke 2:21), was a few weeks later presented, or dedicated, to the Lord (v. 22), but not baptized until age 30 (Luke 3:21–23)! This of course does not mean that one dedicated to the Lord must wait thirty years for baptism, but it does plainly suggest that baptism belongs to an age of responsible decision.

[59]For example, in the Evangelical Presbyterian Church one of the questions that parents may be asked at the baptism of their infant begins, "Do you now unreservedly dedicate your child to God. . . ?" (*The Book of Order*, the Evangelical Presbyterian Church, III, The Book of Worship, 3, "The Sacraments"). A fine question indeed, but it belongs better to a service of infant dedication.

His blessing, but it is urgent that the church not confuse baptism with dedication.[60] Baptism belongs to the day—and only that day—when a person makes public confession of his faith in the Lord.

4. God's prevenient grace

The baptism of an infant magnifies God's prevenient grace in that the child is incapable of responding to God's action in this sacrament. The infant is unknowing and helpless, so in baptism he is totally the recipient of God's grace. Such baptism accordingly attests that long before a person is capable of decision God has already acted on his behalf.[61]

God's prevenient grace is a precious truth, namely, that God's grace is always primary (for example, in regeneration and sanctification), but grace calls for personal response. Infant baptism unfortunately denies this, because it affords no place for the response of repentance and faith.

5. The seed of faith and vicarious faith

In infant baptism, faith is operative either as a tiny seed planted in the child's heart or as a vicarious faith on the part of those who bring the child to baptism. From the former perspective it is affirmed that normally the seed will grow until the day when the child can make his own confession.[62] From the latter, it is held that the surrounding faith (of parents, godparents, and congregation) serves vicariously for the faith of the child so that he is truly renewed in baptism.[63]

Neither the seed of faith nor vicarious faith is adequate to the New Testament understanding of baptism. "He who believes and is baptized will be saved" (Mark 16:16). Only those who actively believe are to be baptized; thus saving faith is more than a seed and cannot be accomplished vicariously. Moreover, repentance is required at the time of baptism (recall Acts 2:38); this can hardly be done at the time of infant baptism or by proxy.[64] All in all, per-

[60]On this matter see *Infant Baptism and the Covenant of Grace* by Paul Jewett, "Jesus Blesses Little Children," 55–63. Jewett's whole book is an excellent refutation of the practice of infant baptism.

[61]Gustaf Aulèn, Swedish theologian and Lutheran bishop, refers to baptism as "the sacrament of prevenient grace," and says in regard to infant baptism: "If baptism is an act of God's prevenient grace, the validity of infant baptism is immediately established" (*The Faith of the Christian Church*, 335, 338). Aulèn adds, "The question whether infant baptism was practiced in the New Testament becomes, from this point of view, of secondary importance" (p. 338).

[62]So Calvin says, "Children are baptized for future repentance and faith. Though these are not yet formed in them, the seed of both lies hid in them by the secret operation of the Holy Spirit" (*Institutes*, 4.16.20, Beveridge trans.). Calvin, incidentally, seeks to guard against infant regeneration by speaking of *future* repentance and faith.

[63]Luther declares, "Infants are aided by the faith of others, namely, those who bring them to baptism. . . . The infant is changed, cleansed and renewed by inpoured faith, through the prayer of the church that presents it for baptism and believes" (*Works of Martin Luther*, II, "The Babylonian Captivity of the Church," 236). Luther's view, likewise, is not, strictly speaking, baptismal regeneration in the sense that *ex opere operato* the act of baptism regenerates: vicarious faith is required. However, Luther's position, like the Roman Catholic, does see regeneration—cleansing and renewing—taking place in baptism.

[64]One sometimes also hears the view (going beyond the seed-of-faith and vicarious-faith views) that an infant actually can believe. Even an unborn child is to some degree aware of outside impulses (e.g., John the Baptist in his mother's womb "leaped for joy"—Luke

sonal, conscious, even heartfelt faith is essential.[65]

6. Original sin

Since all persons born into this world come with the guilt of original sin, there is need for baptism as early as possible to remove this guilt and stain.[66] Otherwise infants who die prematurely will be forever cut off from the presence of God.[67] Infant baptism is essential to remove the inherited guilt of original sin so that babies if they die may go to heaven.

Even though it is true that infants are not born in innocence—the human race is sinful in nature[68]—baptism is surely not the way to remove the heritage of sin from infants. It is far better to say that even as Jesus blessed the infant children by taking them into His arms, if they die before an age of accountability, He will apply His saving work to them and receive them into heaven.[69]

Further, it is obvious that this view of the removal of the guilt of original sin in regard to infants again points to the error of baptismal regeneration.

7. Promise regarding children

The earliest proclamation of the gospel by Peter in Acts about repentance, baptism, and the gift of the Holy Spirit (2:38) continues with these words: "For the promise is to you and to your children and to all that are far off, every one whom the Lord our God calls to him" (v. 39). Since children, against a background that specifies baptism, are included in the promise, they rightly may be baptized.[70]

First, a careful reading of Acts 2:38–39 and the background of these verses will show that in the first place Peter is

1:44). All the more, an infant outside the womb, may sense God's grace at the moment of baptism and to some degree, even if unconsciously, believe. My response is simply that, without denying that infants may be more sensitive than we usually realize and that they may respond in some way at the time of baptism, this does not constitute a truly biblical understanding of the conscious repentance and faith required for Christian baptism.

[65]In the Acts narrative of the Ethiopian eunuch's baptism, the eunuch asked Philip, "What is to prevent my being baptized?" (8:36). According to some manuscripts, Philip replied, "If you believe with all your heart, you may" (v. 37 NASB). Such heartfelt faith cannot be held by infants.

[66]In Roman Catholic theology, original sin with which infants are born can be removed by baptism. The Council of Trent, in its *Decree concerning Original Sin*, declares, "From a tradition of the apostles, even infants, who could not yet commit any sin of themselves, are for this cause truly baptized for the remission of sins, that in them that may be cleansed away by regeneration, which they have contracted by generation."

[67]Infants dying without baptism, according to Roman Catholic theology, are consigned to limbo (*limbus infantium*), a place that is neither heaven nor hell but where infants are permanently excluded from eternal happiness.

[68]For a discussion of original sin see *Renewal Theology*, 1:267–73.

[69]Calvin states that when Jesus said, "For such is the kingdom of heaven," "he includes both little children and those who resemble them" (*Commentaries, Harmony of Matthew, Mark, and Luke*, 39, Pringle trans.). The Westminster Confession narrows this to "elect infants": "Elect infants, dying in infancy, are regenerated and saved by Christ through the Spirit, who worketh when, and where, and how he pleaseth" (10.3). This is a quite unfortunate statement, unavoidably implying that nonelect infants (who knows how many there are?) have no hope of salvation. Not even limbo is available for them!

[70]Jeremias writes, "The children are not the coming generations, but the sons and daughters of the hearers. Since the gift of the Spirit (2.38) is linked to baptism, 2.39 contains the challenge to have the children baptized also. Thus in Acts 2.38f we have before us a witness for the practice of infant baptism in apostolic times" (*Infant Baptism in the First Four Centuries*, 41). Jewett quotes Henry Alford as saying that Acts 2:39 contributes a

referring to the gift of the Holy Spirit, *not* salvation (contained in the words "repent," "be baptized," and "forgiveness of sins"), which is promised to all whom God "calls to him" (thus who have received salvation).[71] Hence it is misguided to view the baptism of anyone as included in the promise. Second, Peter's words about children cannot imply infant baptism, since the whole background of repentance and faith calls for conscious decision, and only in that context can baptism occur with the resulting promise of the gift of the Holy Spirit. Third, "your children" is properly understood as "your sons and your daughters" (v. 17)—not your infants—those of responsible age. In every way, to view Peter's words as undergirding the practice of infant baptism is without warrant.

8. Early church practice

Since there is sufficient evidence of early church practice of infant baptism,[72] we may safely assume the propriety of its continuation to the present day.

The problem with this statement is that the evidence for infant baptism in the first century is nonexistent[73] and meager, if at all, in the second century.[74] It is only at the beginning of the third century (ca. A.D. 200) that the first clearcut statement about infant baptism is found, namely, in the writing of Tertullian, in which he opposes what seemed to be a growing tendency toward infant baptism![75] After Tertullian—and despite his efforts—infant baptism became more and more the prevailing practice throughout Christendom. By the time of Augustine (fifth century), infant baptism was officially sanctioned by the whole church.

It is apparent that the propriety of infant baptism cannot be based on early-church evidence for its practice.

"providential recognition of infant baptism in the very founding of the Christian Church" (*Infant Baptism and the Covenant of Grace*, 119–20).

[71]Concerning this promise see *Renewal Theology*, 2:183–85, "The Promise of the Father."

[72]Calvin writes concerning infant baptism: "There is no writer, however ancient, who does not trace its origin to the days of the apostles" (*Institutes*, 4.16.8, Beveridge trans.) Jeremias, unlike Calvin, says, "For the first century we have no special evidence for the baptism of Christian children." However, Jeremias adds, "In the second century it was already taken for granted" (*Infant Baptism in the First Four Centuries*, 55). We may accordingly infer the practice of infant baptism from the earliest days.

[73]Contra Calvin, but affirming Jeremias. For example, the *Didache* has a section on baptism (as we have seen) that concludes with this statement: "And before the baptism, let the one baptizing and the one who is to be baptized fast. . . . Also, you must instruct the one who is to be baptized to fast for one or two days beforehand" (*The Apostolic Fathers* 7:4). Obviously none of this is applicable to infants.

[74]There is actually no concrete reference to infant baptism in the second century. The apostolic fathers (ca. A.D. 100–150) write nothing about infant baptism, and Justin in his *First Apology* (ca. A.D. 155) has a section (61) on baptism that clearly refers only to believers (see Aland, *Did the Early Church Baptize Infants?* 53–55, and Jewett, *Infant Baptism*, 39–41). Jeremias errs in saying that infant baptism was taken for granted in the second century. There may have been a growing practice of infant baptism toward the end of the second century, but there is no direct reference to it in any extant writings.

[75]Tertullian writes in his treatise *On Baptism*: "Our Lord says, indeed, 'Do not forbid them to come to me.' Therefore let them come when they are grown up; let them come when they understand, when they are instructed whither it is that they come; let them be made Christians when they can know Christ" (chap. 18).

Paedobaptists are often determined to find it there—even as they likewise search the New Testament for evidence—but it is all to no avail. Candidly, one suspects that the practice of infant baptism so dominates much biblical and historical research that it is a matter of seeking justification rather than truth.[76] Since the church at large (Roman Catholic, Eastern Orthodox, Protestant) practices infant baptism, this fact for some is basically all that is needed: surely the church could not be wrong in so important a matter.[77] Church tradition, no matter how widespread, *must* never become the norm of Christian truth and practice.

I have devoted a number of pages to this excursus on infant baptism, giving many of the arguments for its practice and some responses to them, because the matter is an important one. It is not my intention to exaggerate this matter, since baptism whenever it is done is not as fundamental as that to which it points, namely, salvation. However, infant baptism, if nothing else, does cloud the issue, and in many ways it affects both the church's witness and the practical experience of its members.[78] Hence, my concern is to call those churches that practice infant baptism to seriously reconsider what they are doing and make every effort to reinstate the baptism of believers.

G. Miscellaneous

1. Administrator

The New Testament designates no particular person to administer baptism. Jesus' command to baptize, included in the Great Commission, was given at least to His "eleven disciples" (Matt. 28:16). Perhaps others were included, as the words "some doubted" may suggest (v. 17). In any event, the important matter is that those designated as disciples received the commission to go and baptize.[79]

In the Book of Acts the first recorded baptisms were of some three thousand persons: "So those who received his [Peter's] word were baptized, and there were added that day about three thousand souls" (2:41). With such a large number being baptized, it seems likely that others besides the apostles may have shared in the baptizing.[80] If so, this further demonstrates that disciples in general were authorized to perform baptisms. Indeed, the next baptisms mentioned in Acts were performed not by an apostle but by Philip the evangelist; he baptized a number of Samaritans

---

[76]Jewett declares about paedobaptists that "their practice is a practice in search of a theology" (*Infant Baptism*, 209).

[77]N. P. Williams, who espouses infant baptism, candidly says, "That infants may and should be baptized is a proposition which rests solely upon the actual practice of the church; as in the fifth century, the sole argument for the fact is simply this: 'The Church does baptize infants, and we cannot suppose that the Church has acted wrongly or without good cause in so doing' " (*The Ideas of the Fall and of Original Sin*, 551). Williams says that in his view church practice is "a sufficient ground for affirming the legitimacy and laudability of Paedobaptism" (554). This, I submit, is a *wholly insufficient* ground!

[78]Barth speaks of infant baptism as "clouded baptism . . . a wound in the body of the church and a weakness for the baptized" (*The Teaching of the Church Regarding Baptism*, 40).

[79]D. A. Carson writes, "The injunction is given at least to the Eleven, but to the Eleven in their own role as disciples. . . . Therefore they are paradigms for all disciples" (*Matthew*, EBC, 596).

[80]I. H. Marshall conjectures, in light of the huge task of baptizing three thousand people, "that if the other disciples shared in the actual baptizing, there would have been plenty of time to accomplish the task" (*Acts of the Apostles*, TNTC, 82).

(8:12) and the Ethiopian eunuch (v. 38). Later it was a Christian brother Ananias who baptized Saul of Tarsus (9:18). In the next chapter is the account of the Caesareans' being baptized: Peter "commanded them to be baptized in the name of Jesus Christ" (10:48). Peter may have baptized these people; however, the language could imply that others in his company, "the believers . . . who came with Peter" (v. 45), did the actual baptizing.[81] Three further accounts describing Paul's ministry speak of the baptizing of certain people: Lydia and her household (16:15), the Philippian jailer and his household (16:33), and a number of Corinthians (18:8). But in none of these is Paul specified as the baptizer.[82] To be sure Paul did baptize,[83] but in his case—as that of Peter—it is very likely that other believers did most of the baptizing.

What all of this says to the church is that there should be no requirement beyond being a Christian in regard to who is authorized to baptize.[84] Even as every believer stands under the Great Commission to "go and make disciples," so likewise every believer is commanded to baptize: "baptizing them." To hold that every Christian is called to evangelize but only certain ones are allowed to baptize is wholly contrary to the command of the Lord.

However, it is important that "all things should be done decently and in order" (1 Cor. 14:40).[85] Such matters as inquiry into the faith of the one seeking baptism, the suitability of the water to be used, and the appropriate atmosphere of reverence and sincerity call for careful concern. It is no small thing to baptize someone in relation to his or her salvation.

2. *Validity*

The validity of baptism does not depend on the worth or dignity of the

---

[81]Marshall speaks of the likelihood that "the command was addressed to the other Christians present to perform the rite" (ibid., 195).

[82]In the case of Lydia, Paul was accompanied by Timothy, Silas, and Luke; the jailer was ministered to by Paul and Silas; and Silas and Timothy were with Paul in Corinth. In each of these incidents the statement is in the passive voice—"was baptized" and "were baptized"—without saying who did the baptizing. In regard to the Corinthians, Paul says in one of his letters to them: "I am thankful that I baptized none of you except Crispus and Gaius . . . also the household of Stephanas" (1 Cor. 1:14, 16). Thus all the rest were baptized by persons other than Paul.

[83]See preceding footnote.

[84]In the Roman Catholic Church the priestly office is viewed as ordinarily required for the performance of baptism: the priesthood is sacramentally endowed with the necessary power. According to the Decrees of the Council of Trent, "If anyone says that all Christians have the power to administer the word and all sacraments, let him be anathema" (*Canons on the Sacraments in General*, 10). Hence the power to baptize is not lodged in Christians at large. However, because baptism is viewed as essential to salvation, if no priest is available in an emergency situation, laymen are allowed to baptize. Many Protestant churches likewise limit officiating at the sacraments to certain ordained persons. The Presbyterian Church, U.S.A., for example, states that "for the sake of order the Sacraments are ordinarily to be administered only by those ordained to the ministry of Word and Sacrament" (*Book of Order*, Directory for the Service of God, 3.1). Thus it is not a matter of *power*, as in Roman Catholicism, but of *order* that invests the right to baptize in the ministerial office. However, in both Roman Catholicism and in much of Protestantism, believers in general are not authorized to perform baptism.

[85]Although Paul is talking about the exercise of spiritual gifts, his words, I believe, may be applied likewise to such a matter as the practice of baptism.

one who administers the rite.[86] If a person who has come to faith is baptized, the question of the character of the one officiating does not determine the validity of the act of baptism. If the baptism is done in the triune name or in the name of Jesus Christ,[87] and water is used,[88] and a person comes in faith, the baptism is proper. What makes a baptism ultimately valid is the Holy Spirit, not the human administrator, for it is the Spirit who performs His work through the faith of the one being baptized.

It is good to bear in mind the nondependence of baptism on the character of its administrant. People sometimes become concerned about their earlier baptism because of the one who administered it. Perhaps he was not a true believer or was actually living in immorality at the the time of the baptism. Now knowing what I do about his character, was my baptism genuine? Do I perhaps need to go through the baptismal rite again? Again, the answer, I submit, is that the validity of the sacrament does not rest on the worth or character of the administrant. One need not be anxious on that account.[89] To be sure, it is good to know that the officiant was a godly person; but even if he was not, the virtue and value of baptism is still not essentially affected.

In summary, the validity of baptism depends primarily on the work of the Holy Spirit, who signifies and seals the faith of the one who is baptized. On the human side, faith alone makes the sacrament valid.[90]

3. Once for All

The New Testament depicts baptism as occurring only once in the lives of those who received it. There is no evidence of additional Christian baptism.[91] Baptism was a once for all occurrence.

This corresponds to two things. First, Christ's work of redemption was once for all: "He has appeared once for all . . . to put away sin by the sacrifice of himself" (Heb. 9:26). Second, believers have been sanctified through that once for all offering: "We have been sanctified through the offering of the body of Jesus Christ once for all" (Heb. 10:10). Neither Christ's act of sacrifice nor our sanctification[92] is repeatable. Baptism,

[86]The fourth-century Donatists held that the validity of the sacraments depended on the personal character of the administrant. Augustine vigorously attacked them in his treatise *On Baptism, Against the Donatists*. It is interesting that the Westminster Confession of Faith contains the statement "Neither doth the efficacy of a sacrament depend upon the piety or intention of him that doth administer it" (10.7.3). This is well said.

[87]Recall our previous discussion of the different formulas in Matthew and Acts. The former highlights the formula in Matthew; the latter, the one in Acts.

[88]Although immersion is surely preferable (recall the earlier discussion), other modes are not illegitimate. Moreover, whether there is a threefold dipping, pouring, or sprinkling (recall the *Didache*'s reference to dipping three times), or a single act, is a secondary matter.

[89]Barth quotes Luther as saying, "If I should wait till I am certain that the one who baptizes is holy, then neither I nor anyone else would ever be baptized" (*The Teaching of the Church Regarding Baptism*, 57).

[90]Calvin declares about the sacraments (hence baptism): "They confer nothing, and avail nothing, if not received in faith" (*Institutes* 4.14.17, Beveridge trans.).

[91]According to Acts 19:1–6, the Ephesians were baptized twice; however, the first was "John's baptism" (v. 3), into which they had previously been baptized. Paul then baptized them "in the name of the Lord Jesus." There probably were many others who had earlier been baptized by John and later received Christian baptism.

[92]Sanctification, to be sure, is also a continuing process; however, it is a continuation of the initial sanctification that occurred at the moment of regeneration.

which corresponds to Christ's saving work and our entrance into salvation,[93] is on both counts a once for all event.

Moreover, since it is only through faith that salvation occurs, baptism is a demonstration of both the *objective* act of Christ's work in redemption and the *subjective* appropriation of it in faith. Hence, a person's baptism, on the one hand, is a testimony to Christ's redemptive action, and, on the other, it represents the response of saving faith. Both objective and subjective are once for all occurrences, and to these baptism corresponds.

Here we need to look once more at the practice of infant baptism. From what has been said, it is better not to perform such baptism at all. The proper rite for infants, as I have pointed out, is not baptism but dedication. Parents should be encouraged to bring forward their little ones for Christ's blessing and, along with the congregation assembled, to promise to bring them up in the spiritual nurture of the Lord. This will help to prepare children for the day when they can make a responsible decision for Christ and receive the ordinance of baptism. Moreover, the children, when baptism does occur, will themselves have the privilege and joy of active participation in the baptismal event, which marks their own entrance into the new life in Christ.[94]

What, however, should be done if a person has received the rite of infant baptism and now as an adult believer requests baptism? This doubtless is a complicated situation, especially in light of the once for all character of baptism. Let me mention three possible procedures. First, there is the radical possibility of *denying any validity* to infant baptism and thus baptizing any who later come to a responsible decision. Rather than viewing this as a second baptism—which is clearly unscriptural—it may be understood as the one and only baptism that corresponds to the decision of faith.[95] The former baptism is viewed as wholly an empty form; the reality occurs only when the person himself participates. Second, it is also possible, without denying the once for all character of baptism, to have an occasion of *baptismal renewal*.[96] In this case there is no question raised about the validity of infant baptism. However, since some persons desire to renew personally the vows taken for them as infants, they are now allowed to participate in the ritual, including water baptism, usually by immersion.[97] This renewal of baptism is often desired by those who have had a life-changing experience of conversion and/or spiritual renewal and now wish

[93]Whether this is called (initial) sanctification, regeneration (new birth), or justification, all are various ways of describing the beginning of salvation.

[94]I recall hearing someone say, "Infant baptism produces little conscripts for the Christian army when Christ really wants volunteers." To be a willing, knowing participant in baptism is a far greater incentive to go forth in Christ's army.

[95]At the time of the Reformation those who practiced such baptism were called Anabaptists, meaning those who baptize "again" (Greek, *ana*). However, this was a name their opponents gave them, thus implying a second baptism. The Anabaptists viewed infant baptism as a meaningless formality; thus the only valid baptism was that of believers.

[96]This is not unlike a service provided in some churches for the renewal of marriage vows.

[97]The Presbyterian Church of New Zealand has provided a "Service of Baptismal Renewal" for its members in which those who so desire may take their own vows and be baptized by immersion. The final question put to the member reads, "Do you submit to this act of immersion to show that you have put off the old man and been buried with Christ in His death; and to show that you are now alive with Christ in the power of the resurrection, as He clothes you with His life and His Spirit?"

personally to participate in the event of water baptism. Third—and somewhat intermediate between the two just described—there is the possibility of viewing the ceremony of infant baptism as objectively valid but calling for a *future subjective completion or fulfillment* in faith and repentance.[98] The rite of baptism will not be repeated, but it will be supplemented by personal confirmation. In many churches there is a recognized service of confirmation in which the person assumes the vows taken for him in baptism and makes his own public profession of faith.[99] Such confirmation may be viewed as the completion or fulfillment of his or her earlier baptism.[100]

In all three of the above possibilities, the once for all character of baptism is not denied.[101] The important thing, further, is that all such procedures are concerned to implement personal faith, which is critical to the validity of baptism.[102] If this is not recognized, the practice of baptism is injurious to the life of the church,[103] and misleading to all who receive the rite.

Let it be understood, however, that all of these approaches and possibilities would be *unnecessary if churches no longer practiced infant baptism*. The once for all character of believers' baptism would then be highlighted, the objective work of Christ in redemption and its subjective appropriation in faith would be unified, and personal participation in baptism would be a deeply renewing experience.

It is indeed important that the church at large make every effort to return to the biblical practice of baptism. This will not be easy because of centuries of tradition. However, the need is great, and with the blessed Lord's help such reformation can occur. Dare we wait any longer?[104]

II. THE LORD'S SUPPER

A. Terminology

There are a number of ways of designating this second ordinance of Christ,

[98]Calvin, as we have noted, speaks of infants as being "baptized for future faith and repentance." Although Calvin relates this to "the seed of faith" in infant baptism (which I have earlier questioned), it is significant that he suggests a future fulfillment. The Westminster Confession declares, "The efficacy of baptism is not tied to that moment of time wherein it is administered" (18.6); hence presumably there can be a future efficacious time.

[99]See, for example, the Episcopal Service of Confirmation in the Book of Common Prayer.

[100]There are three problems about confirmation as described: (1) to some degree it detracts from baptism, which should be the occasion of personal confession; (2) it separates the objective and subjective sides that baptism itself should represent; and (3) it detracts from what confirmation really should mean, not the assumption of baptismal vows or even for confessing personal faith, but rather the occasion for the reception of the Holy Spirit (see *Renewal Theology*, 2:289, and n.58).

[101]Even if strained a bit in the second and third!

[102]Along this line Barth writes, "The personal faith of the candidate is indispensable to baptism" (*Church Dogmatics*, IV, 4, 186).

[103]Calvin puts it bluntly: "What is a sacrament received without faith, but most certain destruction to the church?" (*Institutes*, 4.14.14, Beveridge trans.).

[104]I wrote this last paragraph on October 31, Reformation Day. What I am calling for is hardly of the magnitude of Luther's Ninety-five Theses posted on the door of the Wittenberg church on that October day in 1517. However, what the so-called Anabaptists of Luther's time stood for in regard to baptism (over against Luther, and later Calvin) needs to be brought to completion. We can be thankful for their witness and that of their Baptist successors to this day. It is now high time for all other churches to join with them in this reformation of baptismal practice.

the most common being the Lord's Supper. Interestingly, this language is found only in a negative statement by Paul: "When you meet together, it is not the Lord's supper[105] that you eat" (1 Cor. 11:20). Shortly thereafter Paul sets forth details regarding the institution and form of the Supper (vv. 23–26). Before saying more about the expression "the Lord's Supper," let us observe several other descriptions of it.

1. The Breaking of Bread

This expression goes back to an occasion in the Upper Room: "Now as they were eating, Jesus took bread, and blessed, and broke it, and gave it to the disciples and said, 'Take, eat; this is my body' " (Matt. 26:26).

A few weeks later, following Jesus' death, resurrection, and the coming of the Holy Spirit, some three thousand persons turned to the Lord and were baptized. From that time on, "they devoted themselves to the apostles' teaching and to the fellowship, to the breaking of bread and to prayer" (Acts 2:42 NIV). "The breaking of bread" in all likelihood signified the Lord's Supper.[106] The word "fellowship" (*koinōnia*) may refer in part to the fellowship meal that preceded the sacramental breaking of bread.[107] Hence "the breaking of bread" points in a special way to the Lord's Supper.[108] If this is the case, the Lord's Supper was celebrated by the early church at Pentecost.

It is interesting that the description of the church's activity continues shortly after in these words: "And day by day, attending the temple together and breaking bread in their homes [or 'from house to house'], they partook of food with glad and generous hearts" (Acts 2:46). Probably the breaking of bread again refers—in conjunction with their main meals—to the Lord's Supper.[109] If so, this demonstrates the importance of the Lord's Supper in the daily life of the early Christian community.

Let us note further references in Acts to the breaking of bread. Acts 20:7 reads, "On the first day of the week, when we were gathered together to break bread, Paul talked with them [believers in Troas]." This statement is doubly interesting: it shows that the believers gathered together on Sunday (the new Christian Sabbath) and that breaking bread was the purpose for which they assembled. This can hardly mean an ordinary meal—although it may have included such—but more

---

[105]The Greek phrase is *kyriakon deipnon*.

[106]I. H. Marshall writes, "The breaking of bread . . . is Luke's term for what Paul calls the Lord's Supper. . . . Luke is simply using an early Palestinian name for the Lord's Supper" (*Acts of the Apostles*, TNTC, 83). F. F. Bruce writes, "The 'breaking of bread' probably denotes more than the regular taking of food together: the regular observance of what came to be called the Lord's Supper seems to be in view" (*Book of the Acts*, rev. ed., NICNT, 73).

[107]In the words of J. Jeremias: "If the *κοινωνία* of Acts 2.42 refers to the Agape ['love feast'] then the breaking of bread must mean the subsequent Eucharist. . . . The designation of the Lord's Supper as 'the breaking of bread' arose as a consequence of the separation of the Eucharist from the meal proper" (*The Eucharistic Words of Jesus*, 120–21).

[108]Thus the words "Now as [or 'while'] they were eating, Jesus broke bread. . . ." Bread probably had already been used in the meal together; now Jesus broke it for another reason.

[109]Bruce declares in regard to verse 46: "They took the principal meal of the day in each other's houses, observing the Lord's Supper each time they did so" (*The Acts of the Apostles*, with Greek text, 100). For a similar understanding, see Jeremias, *Eucharistic Words*, 119; Marshall, *Acts of the Apostles*, 85; EGT 2:97. See also R. Otto, *The Kingdom of God and the Son of Man*, 312ff.; A. J. B. Higgins, *The Lord's Supper in the New Testament*, 57.

likely the Lord's Supper.[110] It is also possible that the further words in verse 11, "when Paul had gone up and had broken bread and eaten" (v. 11), refer to the Lord's Supper.[111] Breaking bread, it is noteworthy, is mentioned separately from eating.

Finally, in Acts there is the narration about Paul, his companions, and a number of sailors undergoing a fierce sea storm. Paul urged the hungry and battered men to eat something. Then the text reads, "He took bread, and giving thanks to God in the presence of all he broke it and began to eat. Then they all were encouraged and ate some food themselves" (27:35–36). There is a possible reference in these words to the Lord's Supper.[112]

The breaking of bread recalls Jesus' words and example and is thus an early way of characterizing the Lord's Supper. Although some of the uses of this expression in Acts are vague, the breaking of bread undoubtedly implies more than an ordinary meal. Since it can hardly be doubted that the church in Acts followed Christ's command to baptize, there is all the more assurance that the breaking of bread frequently refers to the Lord's Supper.

2. The Christian Passover

Paul writes to the Corinthians, "Christ, our Passover lamb,[113] has been sacrificed" (1 Cor. 5:7 NIV). This states, in vivid simplicity, that the Lord's Supper—with Christ as the Passover Lamb—is the Christian Passover.

Thus the Lord's Supper is the extension and fulfillment of the Jewish Passover. The Passover was the Jewish feast that recalled both the Lord's passing over the Israelites' houses the night He slew the Egyptians and the sacrificed lamb with its blood on the door that kept death from striking the homes of the Israelites.[114]

Jesus' close connection with the Passover is seen in that the Lord's Supper was basically a Passover meal. The Scripture reads, "Then came the day of Unleavened Bread, on which the passover lamb had to be sacrificed. So Jesus sent Peter and John, saying, 'Go and prepare the passover for us, that we may eat it' " (Luke 22:7–8). When preparations had been made and Jesus was at table with His apostles, He declared, "I have earnestly desired to eat this passover with you before I suffer" (v. 15). Thus it was a Passover

[110]Bruce: "The breaking of the bread was probably a fellowship meal in the course of which the Eucharist was celebrated" (*Acts of the Apostles*, NICNT, 384). Similarly Marshall, *Acts of the Apostles*, 325. See also Haenchen, *Acts of the Apostles*, 584.

[111]Jeremias holds that Acts 2:42, 46; 20:7, 11 concerning breaking bread are all Luke's way of referring "to the Lord's Supper exclusively" (*Eucharistic Words*, 133). Both Bruce (*Acts of the Apostles*, 385, n.30) and Marshall (*Acts of the Apostles*, 327) suggest the possibility that Acts 20:11 (above) refers to the Lord's Supper. Higgins sees both Acts 20:7 and 11 as "a eucharistic celebration" (*The Lord's Supper*, 57).

[112]Bruce speaks of this as probably "a eucharist meal in a limited sense: all shared the food, but to the majority it was an ordinary meal, while for those who ate with eucharistic intention (Paul and his fellow-Christians) it was a valid eucharist" (*Book of Acts*, NICNT, 492). Marshall, while admitting a eucharistic possibility, says that it "seems more probable that Luke is simply describing an ordinary meal" (*Acts of the Apostles*, 414–15). Jeremias' position is similar (*Eucharistic Words*, 133, n.6). Higgins states bluntly that there is no reference to the Eucharist here (*The Lord's Supper*, 46, n.1). I favor the view expressed in EGT that in regard to the Eucharist "St. Luke seems to intimate such a reference" (2:532).

[113]The Greek word is *pascha*. The word, strictly speaking, means simply "Passover" (so KJV and NASB read). However, it may also refer to the Passover (or Paschal) lamb or meal (see BAGD). Clearly in 1 Corinthians 5:7 the meaning is "Passover lamb."

[114]Recall Exodus 12:21–27.

meal, and the one to suffer and die was the Lamb of God.

The Lord's Supper is therefore the Christian Passover. Even as the Lord passed over the Israelites, saving them from physical death through the sacrificed lamb, so by Christ's infinitely greater sacrifice believers are saved from eternal destruction. As Christians we celebrate this on every occasion of the Lord's Supper.

3. Holy Communion

Paul also writes to the Corinthians in regard to the Lord's Supper: "The cup of blessing which we bless, is it not the communion of the blood of Christ? The bread which we break, is it not the communion of the body of Christ?" (1 Cor. 10:16 KJV). From these words derives the terminology of the Lord's Supper as Holy Communion.

The word translated "communion"[115] may also be rendered in this context as "participation" (RSV, NIV) or "sharing" (NASB), hence a participation in or sharing in the blood and body of Christ. Whatever the translation, the point is that in the Lord's Supper there is vital communication with Christ.

4. The Table of the Lord

A few verses later Paul refers to the Lord's Supper as "the table of the Lord" (1 Cor. 10:21): "You cannot partake of the table of the Lord and the table of demons." By the "table of demons" Paul refers particularly to sitting at table in a pagan temple where the food has been sacrificed to idols, hence demons, and then on another occasion to sit and partake at the Lord's table.

The Lord is host in His Supper and He invites His followers to participate at His table. The table of the Lord and the table of demons have utterly nothing in common.

5. The Eucharist

In all the biblical accounts of Jesus' words at the Last Supper, the note of thanksgiving is present. For example, "He took a cup, and when he had given thanks he said. . . . And he took bread, and when he had given thanks he broke it" (Luke 22:17, 19). The word for "given thanks" is a form of the verb *eucharisteō*, the noun form being *eucharistia*, or thanksgiving.

The name Eucharist for the Lord's Supper, while not used as such in the New Testament, is found in the *Didache*. Section 9:1 begins, "Now concerning the Eucharist, give thanks as follows." Then occur prayers of thanksgiving in regard to the cup and the bread, and it specifies that at the close of the service further thanksgiving is to be offered to the Lord.[116]

The word "Eucharist" for the Lord's Supper has come to be used in many of the churches of Christendom.[117]

B. Meaning

What is the meaning of the Lord's Supper? When Christians gather together in celebration of this ordinance, or sacrament, what is the significance of the event? Let us observe several things.

1. Remembrance

The Lord's Supper is, first of all, an occasion of *remembrance*. In the words of instruction, as given by Paul, Jesus

---

[115]The Greek word is *koinōnia*. Often the best translation is "fellowship" (as in Acts 2:42).

[116]*Didache*, 9:2–4 and 10:2–6. In regard to the Eucharist among the early church fathers see, for example, *Ignatius to the Smyrneans* 6:2 and Justin Martyr, 1 *Apology* 65–66.

[117]Two other nonbiblical terms for the Lord's Supper are "the Divine Liturgy" and "the Mass." The former is used in the Eastern Orthodox Church, and the latter largely in the Roman Catholic Church. The word *Mass* derives from the Latin word *missa*, meaning "dismissal," the closing blessing at the end of the Eucharist.

said, "This is my body which is for you. Do this in remembrance of me. . . .[118] This cup is the new covenant in my blood. Do this, as often as you drink it, in remembrance of me" (1 Cor. 11:24–25). The Lord's Supper is the recollection and showing forth of Christ's death. Paul adds, "For as often as you eat this bread and drink the cup, you proclaim the Lord's death until he comes" (v. 26). Hence the Lord's Supper is a representation, a re-presentation, of Christ's death, both vividly calling it to mind and showing it forth.[119]

The Lord's Supper is a perpetual memorial to the sacrificial death of Christ. Unlike most memorials that point to the outstanding lives of people, this is uniquely a memorial to a death. The bread broken represents the body of Christ, and the cup represents the blood: His total self-giving for mankind's redemption.

The Lord's Supper, accordingly, is an affirmation of a *historical* event. It points vividly to what happened on the earth almost two thousand years ago: Christ died on the cross for mankind's sin. The Supper, therefore, is not the dramatization of some mythological happening, as, for example, a god or goddess dying and later rising in an annual cycle of winter and spring. Rather, Christian faith is wedded to history, to what took place once for all in our world, in our flesh. The Lord's Supper is the earthly representation of a historical event: the death of Christ on a cross in ancient Judea.

Accordingly, the Lord's Supper is not an elaborate ritual. Rather, there is a kind of stark simplicity: the only action occurring through bread and a cup but dramatizing the most important event in history. Moreover, it is drama in an extraordinary way, for all who come to the Lord's Supper are "on the stage." Each participates by eating the bread and drinking the cup. All the human physical senses are involved: sight (beholding the elements), sound (hearing the words of institution), and touch, taste, even smell (the bread and the wine). Thus both spiritually and physically we experience Christ's death on the cross—the agony and the wonder. In the Lord's Supper it is as if we were present at the death of Christ.

The Lord's Supper is also the continuing reminder of *the new covenant* in Christ's death.

In a special way this is symbolized by the cup: "This cup is the new covenant in my blood." The old covenant with its sacrifices of animals was always insufficient for human salvation. Now in the death of Christ with the shedding of His blood, the new covenant of eternal life has been established. Thus the cup at the Lord's Supper is the vivid symbol and continuing reminder of that new covenant, which Christ's death made possible. Hence every celebration of the Lord's Supper is a reaffirmation of God's new covenant in Jesus Christ.

At the heart of the new covenant and its remembrance in the Lord's Supper stands *divine forgiveness*. According to Matthew's account, Jesus' words were: "Drink of it, all of you; for this is my

[118]The same words, "Do this in remembrance of me," are found in Luke 22:19 (NIV, NASB, cf. KJV).

[119]At the time of the Reformation Ulrich Zwingli particularly stressed the Lord's Supper as a representation. For example, "The Paschal Lamb represents the passing over of the angel of God; and 'This is my body,' that is, This represents my body, the eating of the bread being the sign and symbol that Christ, the soul's true consolation and nourishment, was crucified for us" ("On the Lord's Supper," *Zwingli and Bullinger*, LCC, 226). Since his day many followers of Zwingli have stressed almost totally the representational or commemorative aspect of the Lord's Supper (see, e.g., William Stevens, *Doctrines of the Christian Religion*, chap. 27, "The Lord's Supper," for a recent Zwinglian presentation).

blood of the covenant,[120] which is poured out for many for the forgiveness of sins" (26:27–28). Thus there is portrayed in every celebration of the Lord's Supper the immeasurable cost in the new covenant of divine forgiveness: the death of the Son of God. Christ's blood poured out in God's total forgiveness, hence complete salvation, is brought home through the ritual of the Lord's Supper.

Accordingly, there is a profound confirmation of God's gift of salvation in the Lord's Supper. For not only are the bread and cup a sign to us of this salvation but also through our eating the bread and drinking the cup, God's grace is *sealed* afresh in our hearts: truly we have been totally forgiven. Moreover, even as we receive the bread and cup we appropriate God's continuing grace in Christ. Thus the Lord's Supper is also a *means* of receiving and appropriating God's ever-present grace.[121]

Thus in the Lord's Supper we first of all remember Christ's death.[122] In that sense it is a very solemn occasion. For it points vividly to the most agonizing of all moments in history, to the One who in dying for our sins cried out, "My God, my God, why hast thou forsaken me?" (Matt. 27:46; Mark 15:34). Hence we initially come to the Lord's Supper with solemn, and indeed penitent, hearts. To be sure, there is the ensuing joy of fellowship with Christ and anticipation of His coming again,[123] but this joy can occur only against the solemn background of knowing that both the broken bread and the cup of wine represent the awesome and terrifying death of Jesus Christ our Savior.[124] We must first share with Christ in His death, partaking of the symbols of that death in order to rejoice in His life.

2. Communion

The Lord's Supper is also an occasion of *communion*.[125] Not only do we look to the past in remembrance of Christ's death; we also experience a present personal communion. We have earlier noted Paul's words "The cup of blessing which we bless, is it not the communion of the blood of Christ? The bread which we break, is it not the communion of the body of Christ?" (1 Cor. 10:16 KJV).

---

[120]Or "the new covenant." The textual evidence is about evenly divided between "the covenant" and "the new covenant." However, as we have seen, the word "new" is found in 1 Corinthians 11:25 (see also Luke 22:20) and thus is surely proper here.

[121]I previously discussed baptism as a sign and seal and means of grace (recall "Significance," pp. 224–25). As shown in this paragraph above, the Lord's Supper serves in a similar threefold manner.

[122]The Roman Catholic Church speaks not only of past remembrance but also of *present sacrifice*. The Council of Trent declares, "He [Christ] instituted a new Passover, namely, Himself, to be immolated [= 'offered in sacrifice'] under visible signs by the Church through the priests. . . . The victim is one and the same, the same now offering by the ministry of the priests who then offered Himself on the cross" ("Decree concerning the Sacrifice of the Mass," chaps. 1, 2). This view of the Sacrifice of the Mass, going far beyond remembering Christ's death, was earlier attacked by such Reformation leaders as Luther and Calvin (see, for example, Calvin's *Institutes*, 4. chap. 18, entitled "The Papal Mass, a Sacrilege by Which Christ's Supper was Not Only Profaned but Annihilated," Battles trans.). In the Vatican II Council, Rome continues to speak of sacrifice: "At the Last Supper . . . our Savior initiated the Eucharistic Sacrifice of His body and blood" ("Constitution on the Sacred Liturgy,"47).

[123]See the next two sections for further elaboration.

[124]In this connection an appropriate hymn for the observance of the Lord's Supper would be "O sacred Head, now wounded" (Bernard of Clairvaux, 12th century).

[125]Recall the brief earlier discussion of "Holy Communion" as one of several terms for the Lord's Supper.

The words of Paul betoken a very close relationship with Christ in the Lord's Supper. It is a sharing in His body and blood, and this points not only to the death of Christ but also to His living presence. We remember Christ's death through the bread and cup; we also experience Him as active and present in our midst. We receive the elements of bread and wine to reappropriate His saving forgiveness; we also partake of them to be nourished by His life. Moreover, since we have not only been crucified with Christ but also raised with Him, every Lord's Supper is also an occasion of fellowship and communion with the living Lord.

a. Communion between Christ and His church. In terms of communion the Lord's Supper is first an occasion of *Christ's communing with His people*. We may begin by recalling His words in the Upper Room: "I have earnestly desired to eat this passover with you before I suffer" (Luke 22:15). In the words "with you" Jesus spoke of desiring close fellowship with His disciples, and through the personal symbols of the cup and bread, He shared Himself with them. Jesus was the host at the table, not as a distant person but as One who communicated intimately with His disciples. Thus the atmosphere created was that of close communion with those who belonged to Him.

We may also recall two other occasions after the gathering in the Upper Room when the risen Jesus shared bread with His disciples. One occasion was at the home of two disciples in Emmaus. "When he was at table with them, he took the bread and blessed, and broke it, and gave it to them.[126] And their eyes were opened and they recognized him" (Luke 24:30–31). Thus "He was known to them in the breaking of the bread" (v. 35). A second occasion took place by the Sea of Tiberias (Galilee). Jesus gave an invitation to several of his disciples, who at first had not recognized Him: "Come and have breakfast. . . . Jesus came and took the bread and gave it to them" (John 21:12–13). Although neither of these events was, strictly speaking, the Lord's Supper, they were occasions of meal fellowship in which the risen Christ was present and made Himself known to His disciples. It surely seems possible that on the later occasions in Acts when the early church "broke bread"[127] there was a vital sense of the resurrected, living Lord in their midst. Thus, we may conclude that in many ways the Lord's Supper was also a celebration of the Resurrection.[128]

Since Christ is now the risen and exalted Lord, we may view every occasion of the Lord's Supper as an opportunity for the living Christ to communicate closely with His people. The bread and wine, while they remain symbols of His death, also represent the Christ who in glory has not given up His bodily reality. He still has flesh and bones,[129] hence a real human body. Thus under the visible symbols of bread and wine on the table, His glorious presence is all the more manifest among

---

[126]Note the similarity of the words to Jesus' earlier action in the Upper Room (Luke 22:19).

[127]Recall Acts 2:42, 46; 20:7, 11.

[128]Cullmann writes, "The Lord's Supper in the early Church was a feast of the Resurrection" (O. Cullmann and F. J. Leenhardt, *Essays on the Lord's Supper*, 23). This may be an overstatement, for the Lord's Supper basically relates to Christ's death; however, Cullmann is surely stressing a matter that is often overlooked.

[129]The risen Christ is not a disembodied spirit. Recall Jesus' words to His disciples on Resurrection evening: "A spirit has not flesh and bones as you see that I have" (Luke 24:39).

His people. He is concretely and tangibly present in fellowship and communion with those who belong to Him.

Hence we move from the death of Christ to His living reality. Indeed, there always is the need to sense again and again the somber reality of Christ's death and likewise reappropriate divine forgiveness. But there is also the joyous reality of Christ's risen and continuing presence that ministers new life. The Christ who was both crucified and raised from death is host at the Holy Communion!

b. Communion between the Church and Christ. I have been speaking of communion in terms of Christ's presence with His people; now we turn to the consideration of *our communion with Christ*. The Lord's Supper is an opportunity for close and vital communion of His people with Him.

Here we may reflect on these striking words of Jesus in the Gospel of John: "Truly, truly, I say to you, unless you eat the flesh of the Son of man and drink his blood, you have no life in you; he who eats my flesh and drinks my blood has eternal life" (6:53–54). Although these words were not spoken at the Last Supper, they seem much related to the inner content of Jesus' words in the Upper Room.[130] In a larger sense Jesus in John 6 was talking about the meaning of faith. Earlier He had said, "I am the bread of life; he who comes to me shall not hunger, and he who believes in me shall never thirst" (v. 35). These words are similar to others in the Fourth Gospel where Christ is depicted, for example, as living water (4:10), as the light of the world (8:1), and as the door (10:9). Faith means drinking the water, coming to the light, and entering the door. Thus the words about Jesus as "the bread of life" are essentially the same: believing means coming to Jesus in faith and never hungering or thirsting again. So when Jesus proceeds with the words about eating His flesh and drinking His blood, He does not leave the realm of faith behind but is stressing even more intensely that to believe is to partake of Him inwardly. Believing is not only a satisfying of spiritual hunger by coming to Christ; it is also a coming in which one receives Christ into his or her inmost being.

Thus the words of Jesus about eating "the flesh of the Son of man" and drinking "His blood" must be understood not literally but *spiritually*. Shortly after Jesus had spoken these words, many of His own disciples, taking them literally, began to murmur and take offense (6:61). Then Jesus replied, "The words that I have spoken to you are spirit and life" (v. 63). He did not mean for them to partake literally of His body and blood but to partake spiritually of Him through faith.

This brings us, then, to the deep meaning of the Lord's Supper. When Jesus says about the bread, "Take, eat; this is my body," and about the cup, "Drink of it, all of you" (Matt. 26:26–

[130]The Gospel of John contains no direct depiction of the Lord's Supper. Later, in John 13, the setting is clearly the Upper Room with the Passover at hand and Jesus at supper with His disciples (vv. 1–2). However, instead of making any reference to Jesus taking bread, John writes that Jesus took a towel and a basin of water, then washed and wiped His disciples' feet (vv. 3–20). John's Gospel thereby focuses on the need of the disciples to learn humility. This parallels the account in Luke where Jesus stresses the importance of humble service (22:24–27); but in Luke this *follows* the account of the Lord's Supper (vv. 14–23). Thus we must look elsewhere in John for a reference to the Lord's Supper, and this we find in John 6. The setting is different: it is not the Upper Room but Capernaum, the background is Jesus' feeding of the five thousand, and the discourse is with both unbelieving Jews and Jesus' own disciples. Nonetheless, the inner significance of what Jesus said then is closely related to the Lord's Supper.

27), the language is almost identical with Jesus' words in the Gospel of John: "Unless you eat the flesh of the Son of man and drink his blood. . . ." Since these words in John cannot be understood as a literal eating of Christ's flesh and drinking His blood, no more can Jesus' words at the Supper be understood as a call for a literal partaking of Christ's body and blood.[131] Only *a spiritual understanding will again suffice*. In line with Jesus' statement "The words that I have spoken to you are spirit and life," the same is true of the words at the Table. It is a matter of our spiritual communion with Jesus Christ.

Accordingly, this means that at the Lord's Supper as we partake of the elements of bread and wine, we partake spiritually of Christ. The bread and wine are important because they symbolize Christ. In that sense Jesus called them His body and blood. Indeed, when Jesus said, "This is my body . . . my blood," He was obviously speaking symbolically because He was not the bread and wine He spoke about: He sat at the table with them. Further, not only are the bread and wine symbols of Christ but also by partaking of them physically the believer has an opportunity to gain a deeper spiritual experience: the appropriation of physical bread and wine leading to a deeper spiritual appropriation of Christ. There is indeed a correspondence between the physical and the spiritual. At the same time that we physically partake of the bread and wine and receive them into our bodies, we likewise partake of Christ spiritually so that He has fuller entrance into our souls and spirits.

Thus the Lord's Supper is an *enhancement* of spiritual communion. There can be spiritual communion without the Lord's Supper, as in times of prayer and worship. Some would even urge that true spiritual communion calls

[131]Accordingly, any view of a literal partaking of Christ's body and blood at the Lord's Supper is erroneous. Such a view, for example, follows from the Roman Catholic doctrine of *transubstantiation*. The Council of Trent declares, "By the consecration of the bread and wine a change is brought about of the whole substance of the bread into the substance of the body of Christ our Lord, and of the whole substance of the wine into the substance of His blood. This change the holy Catholic Church properly and appropriately calls transubstantiation" ("Decree concerning the Most Holy Sacrament of the Eucharist," chap. 4). By virtue of this presumed total change, recipients of the Eucharist are said to partake literally of the substance of the body and blood of Christ. Luther held a view that likewise affirmed a literal and physical partaking of Christ: "In the Supper we eat and take to ourselves Christ's body truly and physically" (*Works*, 37.53). This occurs, however, Luther claimed, not as a result of the miracle of transubstantiation, but because of Christ's glorified body and blood being "in, with, and under" the bread and wine: "It is the true body and blood of our Lord Jesus Christ, under the bread and wine, given to us Christians to eat and drink" (*Luther's Smaller Catechism*, VI, "The Sacrament of the Altar"). This view, often called *consubstantiation*, though more adequate than transubstantiation, nonetheless also fails to recognize that the basic partaking at the Lord's Table is not physical but spiritual. Christ is bodily in heaven, but through the Holy Spirit (spiritually) His *real* presence is communicated at the Eucharist. Calvin, while disavowing both transubstantiation and consubstantiation, also held to a substantive partaking—we are "partakers of his substance" (*Institutes*, 4.17.11, Beveridge trans.) and of "the wondrous communion of his body and blood," but then adds these important words: "provided we understand that it is effected by the power of the Holy Spirit" (4.17.26). This is a strong affirmation of the real presence of Christ in the Supper by the Holy Spirit. I submit, however, in reflecting on the views of both the Council of Trent and the Reformers, that it is better not to speak of partaking of Christ's substance but of communing with Christ spiritually through partaking of the elements of bread and wine.

for no physical elements.[132] However, since we are not in this life disembodied creatures, it is good to have corporeal realities through which we reach out into the realm of the spiritual. Holy communion is not ill-served by physical aids: it is all the more enhanced.

This communion with Christ at His Supper is so meaningful that we should exercise due care not to allow anything to block it. Shortly after Paul's words about our participation in the body and blood of Christ, he declares, "You cannot drink the cup of the Lord and the cup of demons. You cannot partake of the table of the Lord and the table of demons" (1 Cor. 10:21). As we have noted, Paul was urging the believers in Corinth not to eat in pagan temples where the food and drink presumably were offered to idols (v. 19), hence to demons (v. 20), and after that to sit down at the Lord's Table to eat and drink. This means, by implication, that any participation in the realm of the demonic makes impossible the partaking of Holy Communion with Christ. Paul's words are quite relevant in a world today where demonic forces and influences in many forms—such as witchcraft, the occult, and "new age" phenomena—abound. Christians cannot share in any of these things—"tables of demons"—and sit also at the Lord's holy Table.

By extension, if anything else is dominating one's life rather than devotion to Christ, it is not possible to have true communion with Him. While most Christians are repelled by overt idolatry and demonism (as just described), they are often prey to more subtle forms of idolatry—for example, allowing money or power or pleasure to dominate their lives. However, in Jesus' words, "You cannot serve both God and Money" (Matt. 6:24 NIV)—or power, or pleasure, or any other idol. If we attempt to do so, we cannot truly recognize God, and the lordship of Christ is usurped by idols that actually are tools of Satan. To serve any such forces is to partake of "the table of demons" and prevent true communion with the Lord.

Now turning to the more positive side: it is also critically important to come *in faith* to the Lord's Table. Although the Lord's Supper is "the communion of the body and blood of Christ," and therefore Christ is truly present as Host, we can receive Him only as we come in true faith.[133] There is no automatic guarantee that because we say certain words or offer certain prayers we will receive Christ. Earlier I spoke of spiritual partaking and I emphasize it as *partaking through the Holy Spirit in faith*. Through the Holy Spirit Christ is present, but only to the faith of those open to receive Him. Indeed, since the very elements depict Christ's body and blood, there can be a heightened experience of His spiritual and real presence—but again only to and through faith.[134]

In regard to faith and the Lord's Supper, the invitation of Christ in the Book of Revelation is appropriate: "Be-

[132]The Quakers, for example, reject the use of outward elements (in both baptism and the Lord's Supper), viewing them as "survivals" of the Old Testament and hence contrary to the true inward spiritual worship instituted by Christ (John 4:24).

[133]Calvin says it well: "Men bear away from the Sacrament no more than they gather with the vessel of faith" (*Institutes*, 4.17.33, Battles trans.). The Westminster Confession speaks of the body and blood of Christ being "not corporally or carnally in, with, or under the bread and wine, but spiritually present to the faith of believers . . . as the elements are, to their outward senses" (29.7).

[134]As the Evangelical Presbyterian Church puts it, "Christ is spiritually present in the elements and is discerned by the faith of the believer" (*The Book of Worship*, 3–3, B).

hold, I stand at the door, and knock: if any man hear my voice, and *open* the door, I will come in to him, and will sup[135] with him, and he with me" (3:20 KJV). Although this is not directly a statement about the Lord's Supper, the Lord does invite us to "open the door"—an invitation to open up the heart in faith—and thereby to "sup with Him." It follows that if the door is not opened in faith, then regardless of how truly Christ is present, there can be no Holy Communion with Him. Let us then come in true faith to the Table of the Lord.

c. Communion and union with one another. The Lord's Supper is also an occasion of communion and union with one another. Immediately after his words about the communion of Christ's blood and body, Paul continues, "Because there is one loaf, we, who are many, are one body, for we all partake of the one loaf" (1 Cor. 10:17 NIV). Since the loaf, before it is broken into pieces to be eaten, is one, the Lord's Supper, regardless of the plurality of participants, is a meal affirming the unity of all. United in Christ at the Lord's Table, all are united with one another.

This means that the Lord's Supper has not only a vertical dimension, uniting believers and Christ mutually, but also a horizontal dimension, namely, communion and union with one another. In a human family, whatever the usual differences, the table meal, sometimes likewise called "breaking bread," is the expression of an underlying family relationship. This is much more the case when the spiritual family, the church, comes together to break bread at the Table of the Lord, for in so gathering God's people have a deeper sense of community and union. For the Lord, not some family member, is the One who through human hands dispenses the bread and cup to the church family and thus binds them together in fellowship and unity.

This communion and union presupposes that those who share in the Lord's Supper are truly believers. No one should participate, or be allowed to participate, if he or she does not belong to Christ. From the beginning, Christ ordained the sacrament for His own disciples, not for the world; thus believers are the proper persons to sit at His Table. Only those who confess faith in Christ should be invited to receive the elements. There can be no unity at the Table where belief and unbelief are mixed together. Paul, in a later letter to the Corinthians, asks rhetorically, "What fellowship [*koinōnia*] has light with darkness? . . . Or what has a believer in common with an unbeliever?" (2 Cor. 6:14–15). Accordingly, the Lord's Supper cannot include fellowship between light and darkness, or communion between believers and unbelievers. Thus, while all people—believers and unbelievers alike—are welcome to be in church together, only believers belong at the Lord's Table.

Some further words in this regard should be added. If believers themselves become involved in certain evil practices, there is no place for them at Holy Communion. Paul had earlier written, "You must not associate with anyone who calls himself a brother but is sexually immoral or greedy, an idolater or a slanderer, a drunkard or a swindler. With such a man do not even eat" (1 Cor. 5:11 NIV). If we are not even to eat with such a person, it is all the more urgent that he be restrained from partaking at the Lord's Table. There may be cases in which even

[135]The Greek word is *deipnesō*, a cognate of *deipnon*, the word used in regard to the Lord's Supper.

excommunication[136] should take place. In the same chapter Paul writes the Corinthians concerning a man involved in incest: "Let him who has done this be removed from among you" (vv. 1–2). Paul was also concerned that the church had become too tolerant of evil and needed to take strong action in regard to this perverse situation. There is no place in the church for such gross evil, and all the more so in regard to the Lord's Table.

Another concern of Paul that relates to fellowship at the Lord's Table is divisiveness. Paul writes to Titus, "As for a man who is factious [or 'divisive' NIV],[137] after admonishing him once or twice, have nothing more to do with him . . . he is self-condemned" (Titus 3:10–11). Such a person who is dividing the church in any way should not be allowed to come to the Lord's Table, the focal point of Christian unity. This divisiveness may also be doctrinal in nature. Paul writes to the Romans, "I urge you, brethren, keep your eye on those who cause dissensions and hindrances contrary to the teaching [or 'doctrine'] which you learned, and turn away from them" (16:17 NASB). To "turn away from" means to withdraw fellowship; this surely applies to the Lord's Table. False doctrine, which serves only to divide the body and to produce schism, is a critical barrier to communion and unity. Such persons do not belong at the Table of the Lord.

There is one other negative factor so significant that if it exists, there really can be no Lord's Supper at all. I am not now speaking of unbelief, immorality, or divisiveness (which I have discussed in turn), but lack of love. After Paul speaks of divisiveness in relation to the church at Corinth (see 1 Cor. 11:18–19), he then adds, "When you meet together, it is not the Lord's supper that you eat. For in eating, each one goes ahead with his own meal, and one is hungry and another is drunk. . . . Do you despise the church of God and humiliate those who have nothing?" (vv. 20–22). It is apparent that the meal held in connection with the Lord's Supper was anything but an *Agapē*, or "love feast."[138] It was such a travesty of love that no matter what was said or done in a presumed Lord's Supper, the Supper simply did not exist. Lack of love—selfishness, greed, and thoughtlessness—had emptied it of all validity and significance. It was in no sense whatever a Communion service.

Paul's negative words about the Corinthians' "Lord's Supper" should be a continuing warning to the church. Far too often it is assumed that if a properly ordained minister is officiating and the right words and actions transpire, the Lord's Supper is thereby celebrated. This is far from the truth. It is Paul who gives us the Communion ritual usually followed in 1 Corinthians 11:23–26 (often read apart from the context); however, this is preceded by his words about the Corinthian "Lord's Supper,"

---

[136]Excommunication refers to exclusion from the fellowship of the church and particularly from the Lord's Supper. See Calvin's *Institutes*, 4.12, "The Discipline of the Church: Its Chief Use in Censures and Excommunication" for a helpful presentation. While excommunication is severe punishment, the ultimate purpose is "reconciliation and restoration" (sec. 10).

[137]"A heretic" (KJV, NEB). The Greek word is *hairetikon*, literally "heretical." However, the Greek word in Paul's day more likely meant "factious" or "divisive" (see BAGD, Thayer).

[138]The language of "love feast," or *Agapē*, is specifically used in Jude in reference to certain "godless men" (v. 4 NIV), of whom Jude said, "[They] are blemishes at your love feasts [*agapais*], eating with you without the slightest qualm" (v. 12 NIV). The *Agapē* was a common meal in conjunction with, or ending with, the Lord's Supper.

which was no Lord's Supper at all! Does this not strongly suggest that our major concern in coming to the Lord's Table should be the proper attitude of all the participants? The Lord's Supper is the vivid portrayal of Christ's love for us—His body and blood sacrificially given. How can we come to His Table except in responsible love to Him and in love for one another?

Finally, I want to reaffirm the value and importance of the Lord's Supper. It is the paramount occasion in the church of our communion and union with other believers. There is church fellowship in many ways, but none can approximate Holy Communion. Augustine called the Lord's Supper "the bond of love."[139] Surely it is that, for it binds believers all the more closely to one another in what love requires.[140] By partaking of the communion of the body and blood of Christ, whose love we share, we are constrained to a fuller and deeper love for one another.

3. *Expectation*

The Lord's Supper is, finally, an occasion of *expectation*. It is a looking forward to the messianic Supper in the future kingdom. The Lord's Supper is not only a meal of remembering the Lord's death and of present communion; it is also an anticipation of a glorious fulfillment when Christ returns. Every celebration of the Lord's Supper is a foretaste and expectation of what will happen in the age to come.

Jesus Himself spoke of a future fulfillment. Immediately following His words in the Upper Room about earnestly desiring to eat the Passover with His apostles, He declared, "I tell you, I will not eat it again until it finds fulfillment in the kingdom of God" (Luke 22:16 NIV). Then, after taking the cup and giving it to the disciples, He said, "I tell you I will not drink again of the fruit of the vine until the kingdom of God comes" (v. 18 NIV). In another account the latter words are more personal—"until that day when I drink it anew with you in my Father's kingdom" (Matt. 26:29 NIV). Thus the Passover that Christ celebrated—and is now our Christian Passover—will find its fulfillment in the coming kingdom. Only then will Christ again eat and drink with those who belong to Him.[141]

In Paul's delineation of the institution of the Lord's Supper, he also refers to a future event. After quoting Jesus about remembrance—"in remembrance of me"—Paul adds, "For as often as you eat this bread and drink the cup, you proclaim the Lord's death until he comes" (1 Cor. 11:26). The emphasis is on the continuing observance of the Supper until Christ returns. Paul says nothing about what will happen when the Lord comes back; however, there is clearly a forward look—"until he comes." Hence, the Lord's Supper in every observance contains a note of expectation. This is shown again near the close of his letter when Paul cries out, "Our Lord, come!"[142] (16:22). Al-

[139]*John's Gospel*, 26.13 (NPNF 7.172).

[140]Calvin writes, "As often as we partake of the symbol of the Lord's body . . . we reciprocally bind ourselves to all the duties of love in order that none of us may permit anything that can harm our brother, or overlook anything that can help him" (*Institutes*, 4.17.44, Battles trans.).

[141]I have earlier commented on Jesus' breaking bread for the two disciples in Emmaus and for several of His disciples by the Sea of Tiberias; however, Jesus Himself did not partake. Moreover, neither account mentions that Jesus drank with them. *Both* remain unfulfilled until the consummated kingdom of God.

[142]Or "Maranatha" (KJV, NASB), an Aramaic expression (*Marana*, "our Lord"; *tha*,

though it is possible that Paul's words have no direct eucharistic reference, the language seems to catch up his earlier words in connection with the Lord's Supper, "until he comes," by a fervent "Our Lord, come!"[143] For, somehow (Paul does not say how), with the return of Christ the earthly Supper will find its ultimate fulfillment.

We move, then, to this fulfillment. In terms of a climactic Supper, the Book of Revelation depicts it vividly as a marriage supper. The Scripture reads, "Let us rejoice and exult and give him [God] the glory, for the marriage of the Lamb has come, and his Bride has made herself ready. . . . Blessed are those who are invited to the marriage supper of the Lamb" (19:7, 9). The Lamb of course is Christ and the Bride is His church; together they will partake of the Supper that is the climax and fulfillment of every earthly Supper. This is the Supper of the kingdom to which Jesus pointed at the Last Supper: the heavenly banquet to which every earthly celebration points and the glorious fulfillment of the cry of faith and hope, "Our Lord, come!"

Because of the prospect of this final Supper, every occasion of the Lord's Supper should be marked by joy. I have spoken of the Lord's Supper as a solemn time, since it calls to mind the Lord's death. It surely is that, but we have observed further that the Supper is also a witness to the resurrected Lord's presence in our midst. Thus already His presence is a matter of joy and thanksgiving (hence a "Eucharist"). The early church experienced this, as Luke points out: "Attending the temple together and breaking bread in their homes, they partook of food with glad and generous hearts" (Acts 2:46). Now as the church, the people of God, continue to experience the risen Lord's presence in their midst, they can further realize that this is but a small token of what is yet to come!

The Lord's Supper has been called "a mystic banquet" in which by feasting at the Lord's Table we even now ascend to the joy and glory of heaven.[144] However, all the joy and glory we may now know in Christ's spiritual presence at the Table serve only to intensify our yearning for the day when we will see Him face to face and sit with believers of all ages and places at the eternal Supper of our Lord.

Thus at every celebration of the Lord's Supper our hearts cry out, "Our Lord, come," for we long to share with Him in the glorious marriage Supper of His kingdom that has no end.

C. Observance

We come to the actual observance of the Lord's Supper. Now that we have discussed both terminology and meaning, let us consider a number of matters related to its proper observance.

1. Administrator

First, there is the question of who is to administer the Lord's Supper. Imme-

"come"). Paul's use of Aramaic rather than Greek suggests the early use of this phrase at the Lord's Supper in Aramaic-speaking churches in Palestine.

[143]It is interesting to note that the *Didache* (9 and 10), after relating various prayers to be used at the Eucharist, climaxes them with "Maranatha! Amen" (*The Apostolic Fathers*, 155). Thus there is all the more likelihood that Paul's words belong to a eucharistic setting.

[144]In words from one of the Wesleys' eucharistic hymns:

To heaven the mystic banquet leads:
Let us to heaven ascend,
And bear this joy upon our heads
Till it in glory end.

(J. Ernest Rattenbury, *The Eucharistic Hymns of John and Charles Wesley*, p. 226, hymn 99).

diately we can say two things from the New Testament perspective: Christ Himself is *the* chief administrator and by implication any who truly believe in Him may administer the Supper in His name.

We have only the synoptic gospels and Paul's account in 1 Corinthians to go by. In the former, Christ is the Host and administers the bread and cup to His apostles; in the latter, Paul rehearses the words and event of the Upper Room without saying anything about who may validly administer the elements.[145] This suggests that any true believer in Christ may do so.[146]

It is important, of course, as with baptism, that any administration of the Lord's Supper be done in a proper and fitting manner.[147] For surely, since every occasion of its celebration is a high and holy time, those who lead should be especially prepared in heart and mind to minister in Christ's name.

2. Time and Place

It is apparent from the Book of Acts that in the early days of the church there was frequent "breaking of bread,"[148] and this occurred in many places. This could have been daily—"day by day . . . breaking bread"—and in various homes—"in their homes," or "from house to house"[149] (2:46). Another reference suggests a Sunday observance in a house: "On the first day of the week . . . we were gathered together to break bread" (20:7). This took place in an upstairs room—"the upper chamber where we were gathered" (v. 8). Thus there was frequent occurrence of the Lord's Supper, with specific mention of a Sunday gathering, in various house locations.

The Corinthian believers were meeting—the day of the week not mentioned—in some place separate from their various houses. Paul clearly refers to their gathering as a church, for shortly before declaring, "It is not the Lord's Supper that you eat" (1 Cor. 11:20), he said, "When you assemble as a church. . ."[150] (v. 18). Then after Paul's negative statement about the Lord's Supper, he vigorously speaks out: "What! Do you not have houses to

---

[145]We may recall that Paul's concern with validity had nothing to do with administration but everything to do with the situation of a presumed Supper that, because of lovelessness, was no real Lord's Supper at all! *It was invalid not because of improper administration but because of a totally wrong attitude.*

[146]The Roman Catholic Church limits the administration of the Eucharist to those who have received the sacrament of orders. By virtue of this sacrament only priests of the church are said to be qualified to celebrate the Mass and thereby enable people to receive the substantive body and blood of Christ. This means, incidentally, that Protestant churches without the sacrament of orders (as Rome defines such) cannot fully celebrate the Eucharist. Vatican II declares that "ecclesial communities [i.e., non–Roman Catholic churches] . . . because of the lack of the sacrament of orders they have not preserved the genuine and total reality of the Eucharistic mystery" (*Documents of Vatican II*, "Decree on Ecumenism," 22).

[147]Many Protestant churches assign the administration of the Lord's Supper to ordained ministers, not because of any particular power inherent in their ordination, but for the sake of order (recall n.84). Exceptions may usually be made if no ordained minister is available.

[148]Recall the earlier discussion of "breaking bread" in Acts as likely referring to the Lord's Supper.

[149]Both are possible translations of Acts 2:46.

[150]The Greek phrase is *en ekklēsia*, literally "in church"; however, this can be a misleading translation suggesting a church building. Fee indicates that the meaning of this Greek phrase is "in assembly" (*First Epistle to the Corinthians*, NICNT, 537, n.29). "As a church" (RSV, NIV, NASB) catches up the note of the church as not being a building but an assemblage of believers.

eat and drink in?" (v. 22). We are not told that the Corinthians assembled in a church building (there were none in the early church) but "as a church."[151] It could have been an assemblage in any place that was large enough to accommodate them all.

This early church record in Acts and 1 Corinthians suggests that in view of the frequency of meetings in which the Lord's Supper was observed, we may do well likewise to meet often for a similar purpose. A weekly—"on the first day of the week"—observance would surely be in order.[152] However, this can be more, or less, frequently done, depending in part on the nature of church gatherings. For example, the Supper can be celebrated in house gatherings during the week or in visits to shut-ins and sick at any time. Once a week may be too often for a Sunday gathering, especially if the congregation is large; perhaps once a month will suffice. Another important matter is that the Lord's Supper not become a formality, which can happen through frequent repetition. However, if there is proper preparation[153] and care given, frequent observance can be a rich blessing to any body of believers.

The place of the Lord's Supper is the Christian community. It cannot be a solitary matter: private communion is self-contradictory. The Lord's Supper, to be sure, is first with the Lord; but it is also communion with one another, or it is not communion at all.[154] Moreover, since originally the Lord's Supper occurred in the context of a fellowship meal, churches today may occasionally use ordinary church suppers as an opportunity to climax with the sharing of the Lord's Supper. Indeed, to make use of the common bread on the table later for the Eucharist can be a rich experience in the fuller meaning of Holy Communion.

Finally, in regard to place, since the Lord's Supper is a high occasion of the community's worship of God, it is fitting that it most often be held in connection with that worship. It should not be an unrelated addendum to public worship but its climax. The Lord's Supper is the culmination of the church's worship of God.

3. *Participants*

All who participate in the Lord's Supper should be believers in Jesus Christ. He is the Host who from the beginning in the Upper Room ordained this service for His own disciples. It is an occasion for those who trust in Christ to sit at His holy Table.

All believers who are present, whether or not they are a part of the local body, should be invited to participate. Since every local body is an expression of the universal church of Jesus Christ, all believers, regardless of denomination or distance from their home church, should be included.

---

[151]The church in the New Testament is the meeting, not the meeting place, of believers.

[152]Calvin writes, "The sacrament might be celebrated in the most becoming manner, if it were dispensed to the church very frequently, at least once a week" (*Institutes*, 4.17.43, Beveridge trans.). Indeed, Calvin adds, "We ought always to provide that no meeting of the Church is held without the word, prayer, the dispensation of the supper, and alms" (4.17.44). Later Calvin moderates this by saying that "each week, at least" (4.17.46) the Supper should be held.

[153]Especially in terms of opportunity for self-examination (see 4, below).

[154]Even where the Lord's Supper is administered to an individual (shut-in, sick, etc.), it is important to maintain the community aspect by having at least two other persons participate. In the Presbyterian Church, it is usually the ordained minister with another elder, who serves the elements. Thus community is represented: it is not a private affair but a shared fellowship.

Christ is the Head of the whole church and so invites all His people to participate. Thus there should be no "fencing of the Table" in an unreadiness to share at Table with other Christian brothers and sisters.[155] All who confess faith in Christ and come in true repentance should be included at His Table.[156]

There are, however, certain exclusions. First, unbelievers obviously should not be invited to participate.[157] They are surely welcome to attend the occasion of worship, but until they have made a public profession of faith, they do not belong at the Table of the Lord. Thus it is a mistake to invite all people to partake of Holy Communion. Christ continually invites sinners to come to Him—and so should the church—but an invitation to the Lord's Supper is different. It is only for those who truly belong to Him and thus are able to remember His death, commune with His life, and await His future return.

Second, children who have not yet made a profession of faith should not participate. Even though children are in a different category from that of unbelievers, especially if they are children of believers, they should wait until the day when they make a public confession. It is a mistake to assume that because of family ties a child should be allowed to receive Communion along with his parents. For the Lord's Supper is not in essence the gathering of a natural family but a gathering of the spiritual church family. Moreover, a child cannot possibly follow the injunction of Paul "But let a man[158] examine himself, and so let him eat of the bread and drink of the cup" (1 Cor. 11:28 NASB). Actually, by withholding Holy Communion from a child, he can be better taught the higher significance of the spiritual family. Instead of feeling left out, the child may look forward to the day when he can make his own confession of faith and likewise become a communing member of the body of Christ.

Third, unrepentant believers should not be invited to the Lord's Table. We have earlier talked about Paul's warning not to eat with a brother who is "sexually immoral or greedy, an idolater or a slanderer, a drunkard or a swindler" (1 Cor. 5:11 NIV). Thus all who are continuing in such evils should be warned *not* to come to Holy Communion. We may also recall Paul's admonition about avoiding persons who are factious in manner or doctrine and excluding them from a table expressing communion and unity. If, on the other hand, such persons come after repenting of their sins, they should surely be allowed—indeed, encouraged—to participate.

In connection with this last point, let me emphasize that all believers who come in a spirit of repentance are

[155]The Baptist theologian A. H. Strong, however, speaks affirmatively of "fencing the tables" (*Systematic Theology*, 970) and raises a number of objections to "open communion" with those who are paedobaptists (pp. 977–980). This makes the Table an exclusively Baptist Table.

[156]Alan Schreck, a Roman Catholic theologian, on the contrary, writes, "For us, it would be a scandal for Christians to gather together in this 'sacrament of unity' while we remain in basic disagreement over important points of Christian faith, especially as regards the Eucharist itself" (*New Covenant* magazine, Sept. 1988, 31). If the Lord is the Host, I would reply, what "scandal" is there—regardless of many differences—in gathering together as Christians at His Table? Is it not a far greater scandal to insist on staying apart when *He* invites?

[157]Recall some earlier discussion of this on pages 251–53.

[158]Even though "man" should be understood broadly (NRSV reads, "Examine yourselves"), the idea of self-examination excludes children who have not yet reached the age of accountability.

welcome at the Lord's Table. One does not have to be immoral, greedy, a slanderer, or a factious person to need repentance: all Christians, because of continuing sin in their lives, need to come in genuine repentance. If we come, recognizing and confessing our sins, the Lord truly and gladly receives us at His holy Table.

4. Self-Examination

What was just said leads to the importance of self-examination on the part of believers. I have previously quoted these words of Paul: "But let a man examine himself, and so let him eat of the bread and drink of the cup" (1 Cor. 11:28 NASB). Now let us note in more detail what Paul is saying. Immediately it is obvious that Paul is calling for self-examination to precede the partaking of Holy Communion.

Furthermore, the fact that self-examination is critical is shown by Paul's preface to his call: "Whoever, therefore, eats the bread or drinks the cup of the Lord in an unworthy manner will be guilty of profaning[159] the body and blood of the Lord" (v. 27). The word "therefore" points back to the Corinthians' profanation of the Supper by their greed and selfishness. Even though they were believers in Christ, they had reduced the whole occasion of Holy Communion to a farce. But even worse, as Paul now declares, they—and any other believers ("whoever") who act similarly in partaking of the elements—are guilty of profaning Christ's body and blood. This is unmistakably a very serious charge.

That is the background of Paul's call to personal self-examination before receiving the elements: "But let a man [a person] examine *himself*." The word "but" is critical because it provides the alternative to profaning Christ's body and blood—the way of self-examination. One's sins may not be the same—or as serious—as those of the Corinthians, but they must be recognized and confessed.

Self-examination is also the way of coming to Holy Communion in a *worthy* manner. Sincere believers have sometimes been disturbed—even anguished—by Paul's prior statement about eating and drinking "in an unworthy manner."[160] Who is really worthy to come to the Table? Who, if he comes, will not profane the body and blood of Christ? Would it not therefore be better to stay away from the Lord's Table altogether than to risk such a terrible occurrence? The answer, according to Paul, lies in self-examination. To be sure, none of us is worthy to come: we are all sinners saved by grace. But the relevant matter is *not our worthiness but our coming in a worthy manner,* namely, by examining ourselves. If we do this, we will then partake worthily of the Lord's Supper.

Such self-examination may occur shortly before the Supper—either immediately prior to receiving the elements or, if the Supper takes place at the climax of a worship service, at an earlier time given to self-examination and confession. Or, again, it may occur on some occasion prior to the Supper in a period of private prayer or in a special church service of penitence and preparation.[161] Whenever and however self-

---

[159]The Greek text does not actually contain the word "profaning": it reads simply "guilty of the body and blood of the Lord" (as in KJV, NASB). However, such a word as "profaning" (or "desecrating" NEB) is implied.

[160]Or "unworthily" (KJV, NEB). The Greek word is *anaxiōs*.

[161]Some churches provide a separate service of self-examination. For example, the Episcopal Church in its Book of Common Prayer has "A Penitential Order"—two of them—preceding two rites for "the Holy Eucharist." Each is "for use at the beginning of

examination is done, it prepares the way for receiving Holy Communion worthily.

Such examination also leads to a better discernment. Paul next says, "For any one who eats and drinks without discerning the body[162] eats and drinks judgment[163] upon himself" (1 Cor. 11:29). If there is no spiritual self-examination, a person is actually blind to the spiritual reality of the body of Christ. He may eat and drink, but the food and drink are not the conveyers of blessing but of judgment. One cannot partake of the holy in an unholy manner without negative results.

Let us consider two final statements by Paul: "But if we examine[164] ourselves, we should not thus fall under the judgment," and "When, however, we do fall under the Lord's judgment, he is disciplining us, to save us from being condemned with the rest of the world" (1 Cor. 11:31–32 NEB). Thus Paul repeats the need for self-examination and adds further that if we do experience "the Lord's judgment" through weakness, sickness, or even death, it is for positive ends: our discipline and ultimately *our noncondemnation*.

This last statement by Paul should remove any fear or trepidation about partaking at the Lord's Table. Surely we should previously examine ourselves—this is very important. But even if we fail, or do it poorly, God does not condemn us. Whatever negative consequences may occur are ultimately for our good, our salvation, and never for our condemnation. We may praise the Lord for this!

Still—back to where we began: "Let a man examine himself." This truly is important as anyone makes ready to partake of Holy Communion.

5. Words of Preparation

Now we look more specifically at the administration of the Lord's Supper. We are here concerned with the procedure. Our first consideration involves the words of preparation.

It is important that such words precede the administration of the sacrament. Since the Lord's Supper is a *visible* showing forth of God's grace in Jesus Christ, it needs *audible* preparation. If the Lord's Supper is celebrated in a regular worship service, whatever is said in the preceding sermon should provide background. When the word of God goes forth and His truth in Christ is audibly proclaimed and heard, such proclamation better prepares the congregation for visible demonstration and personal reception in the Eucharist.

However, whether or not there has been a previous proclamation of the word, there is need for reading, and perhaps commentary on, the words of institution of the Supper. When this is done, the Lord's Supper becomes

---

the Liturgy, or a separate service." The Presbyterian Church (U.S.A.) in its Book of Common Worship contains two orders of "Preparation for Holy Communion." As a former pastor, I have found much advantage in having a Saturday night "Pre-Communion Service" in which self-examination was usually based on reading the Ten Commandments or the Sermon on the Mount with a pause at various moments for reflection and confession.

[162]The Greek phrase is *diakrinōn to sōma*. *Sōma*, I believe, refers to the body of the Lord (as in v. 27). Some people understand Paul to be speaking of the church (as in 1 Cor. 10:17, and later in 12:12ff.); however, because of the immediate background, the body of Christ (a metonymy for body and blood) seems more likely. For this interpretation especially see I. H. Marshall, *Last Supper and Lord's Supper*, 114–15 (similarly, C. K. Barrett, *The First Epistle to the Corinthians*, 275; Leon Morris, *1 Corinthians*, rev. ed., TNTC, 161). Contrariwise, Fee views the body as the church (*First Epistle to the Corinthians*, 562–64).

[163]Rather than "damnation" (KJV). The Greek word is *krima*.

[164]Better than "judged" (in most translations). The Greek word is *diekrinomen*, from the same root as *diakrinōn* in verse 29.

meaningful. Augustine well said, "Let the word be added to the element and it will become a sacrament."[165] It is by reading and hearing the words about the bread and the cup that God's people are better prepared to receive them.

Incidentally, this means that the words should be clearly understood. If the words of institution are read hurriedly or in a strange language,[166] they do not adequately prepare the way for participation in the Lord's Supper.

6. Prayers of Blessing and Thanksgiving

After the words of preparation, prayers of blessing and thanksgiving should be offered. According to the Gospel of Mark, "while they were eating, He took some bread, and after a *blessing*[167] He broke it, and gave it to them. . . . And when He had taken a cup, and *given thanks*, He gave it to them" (14:22–23 NASB). Jesus' blessing and thanksgiving preceded the apostles' reception of the bread and cup.

We may focus particularly on the note of thanksgiving.[168] In the *Didache*, which contains the earliest use of the word *Eucharist*, the text reads, "Now concerning the Eucharist, give thanks as follows: First, concerning the cup:

> 'We give you thanks, our Father,
> for the holy vine of David your
> servant,
> which you have made known to us
> through Jesus, your servant,
> to you be glory forever.'[169]

Similar words follow about the bread,[170] with an additional prayer for the unity of the church.

Hence prayers of blessing God and giving Him thanks, prayers that focus particularly on Jesus, "the holy vine of David," are appropriate before the serving of the elements.

The prayers here offered may also include supplication for God to bless with His Word and Spirit[171] the bread and wine soon to be distributed and received. It is appropriate especially to pray that the elements will be set apart from a common to a sacred use, so that both bread and wine will be channels for Christ to come to His people.

7. The Bread and the Cup

Now that prayers of blessing and thanksgiving have been offered, the assembly may proceed with the minis-

---

[165]*John's Gospel*, 53.3 (tr. NPNF VII. 344).

[166]One of the concerns of the Reformation was that of celebrating the Lord's Supper in the common language. It is significant to observe that the Roman Catholic Church, while still preserving the Latin rite in the Mass, since Vatican II has opened the door for use of "the mother tongue" (see *Documents of Vatican II*, "Constitution on the Sacred Liturgy," 36).

[167]A. J. B. Higgins points out that in the Jewish Passover ritual the leader "takes unleavened bread, blesses God in the words, 'Blessed art thou who bringest forth bread from the earth,' and breaks it in pieces which he hands to the guests" (*The Lord's Supper in the New Testament*, 46).

[168]The words for blessing, *eulogeō*, and for giving thanks, *eucharisteō*, are used interchangeably. In his account of the institution of the Supper Paul uses *eucharisteō* instead of *eulogeō* in regard to the bread.

[169]*The Apostolic Fathers*, 153–54.

[170]This order of the cup first and then the bread follows the pattern in Luke 22:17–19.

[171]In many of the early church liturgies there was a special invocation of the Holy Spirit called the *epiclesis* (from *epikaleō*, "to call upon"), which was to consecrate the eucharistic elements. For example, in Hippolytus's *Apostolic Tradition* (c. A.D. 215), this prayer is offered: "We ask you to send your Holy Spirit into the offering of Holy Church; grant, as you gather them together, to all the saints receiving, to be filled with the Holy Spirit so as to affirm their faith in truth, that we may praise and glorify you through your child Jesus Christ. . . . Amen."

try and reception of the bread and the cup.

First, in regard to the bread, it is appropriate to use a single loaf to represent Christ Himself and our unity with one another. This accords with Paul's words: "Because there is one loaf, we, who are many, are one body, for we all partake of the one loaf" (1 Cor. 10:17 NIV). The table minister may hold up the loaf in the sight of all who will participate, and then break it. This accords with Jesus' action: He "took bread,[172] and blessed, and broke it" (Matt. 26:26). Then the minister may give it to all, saying, "Take, eat; this is my body" (v. 26) or "This is my body which is [broken][173] for you. Do this in remembrance of me"[174] (1 Cor. 11:24). If the number of participants is too many for one loaf, other loaves may be broken and shared.[175] Each communicant may then break off a piece,[176] and hold it in hand until all have been served. This gives further time for reflection and self-examination. Then at the leader's word all may partake together.[177]

Second, regarding the cup, it is appropriate to have a single large cup, or chalice, containing the "fruit of the vine."[178] The one ministering may hold up the cup and then quote the words of Jesus: "Drink of it, all of you; for this is my blood of the covenant, which is poured out for many for the forgiveness of sins" (Matt. 26:27–28), or "This cup is the new covenant in my blood. Do this, as often as you drink it, in remembrance of me" (1 Cor. 11:25). The contents of the cup may then symbolically be poured into another cup (or cups); this act represents Jesus' blood being poured out in His work of redemption. Distribution of the sacrament then follows. If the number of participants is relatively small, one cup may appropriately be used, with each person in turn drinking from it. This best symbolizes the action of Jesus and His apostles in the Upper Room, and also, even as with the one loaf, the union and communion of all gathered together. However, for practical reasons, individual cups taken from the same table may be distributed. Again, as with the bread, this can afford time for further con-

---

[172]This bread was doubtless unleavened because at the Passover (which Jesus was celebrating—and transforming!) only unleavened bread was used. However, since Christ is our Passover now, it hardly seems necessary to insist on having unleavened bread: it may or may not be used.

[173]KJV includes the word "broken." However, "broken" (*klōmenon*) is "an early gloss" (EGT), hence not in the original text.

[174]The equivalent of these words may also be spoken, since, as quoted, the New Testament has no set pattern (note also the variation in Luke 22:19–20).

[175]Practically, in many church settings this will call for persons to distribute the bread.

[176]This is more meaningful than having each person receive pieces already broken or individually baked, such as small cubes or round wafers. The actual breaking of bread better represents the death of Christ.

[177]In some churches people partake individually, either after being served or by going forward one by one to receive the bread. Although such individual practice is surely valid, the emphasis tends to be more on personal communion than on united participation.

[178]In the three synoptic accounts of the Lord's Supper the content of the cup is called the "fruit of the vine" (Matt. 26:29; Mark 14:25; Luke 22:18). This doubtless was wine; however, since wine is not directly mentioned in any of these accounts, it is irrelevant to insist (as some do) that wine must be used. Grape juice equally comes from "fruit of the vine." Incidentally, to use some other liquid (milk, tea, etc.) may be necessary in places where there is no viticulture. However, if possible, "fruit of the vine," resembling blood, should be used.

templation and self-examination.[179] Following the distribution of the cup, all may drink together.

Additional comments:

1. It is appropriate that the celebration of the Lord's Supper be around a table or tables. If the number of participants is large and there is only one table, communicants may come forward at various times to sit at the table and pass the elements to one another.[180] If the use of tables is impractical, communicants may remain seated and pass the elements.[181]

2. It is important that both the bread and the cup be received by all participants. There is no suggestion in the Gospels that Jesus withheld one element or the other from His apostles or in the Corinthian account that only the bread was to be eaten by believers. Thus both bread and cup are essential to attest fully the body and blood of Jesus in His death and to receive spiritually the whole Christ in His living reality.[182]

3. At the close of the service there should be a disposition of the remaining elements. Since the bread and the wine do not actually constitute the body and blood of Christ but were only set apart (not consecrated) for the occasion of Communion, they contain no continuing sacramental significance. If, on occasion, the bread and cup are taken to persons unable to attend the Communion service, it is not as if they receive already consecrated elements. Each serving of Communion is a new occasion, calling for words of institution, prayers of blessing, and the like. Whatever remains after any celebration of the Lord's Supper is ordinary bread and "fruit of the vine."[183] They may be

---

[179]According to the *Book of Order* of the Presbyterian Church (U.S.A.), "it is proper that a part of the time occupied in the distribution of the elements should be spent by all in communion with God, confession, thanksgiving, intercession, and in renewing the believer's personal covenant with the Lord" (5–3.0500).

[180]This also eliminates any idea that the table is an altar. The Lord's Supper is not "the sacrament of the Altar" (an expression often used) but "the sacrament of the Table." When an altar is emphasized, the appropriate action is to come forward, not to sit but to kneel. The apostles sat, not knelt, around a table, not an altar.

[181]Much valuable symbolism is lost if communicants receive singly from the one, or ones, leading in the administration of the elements. This, incidentally, further underscores the value of sitting rather than kneeling.

[182]The Roman Catholic Council of Trent, however, affirms a doctrine of "Concomitance," namely, "that Christ is whole and entire under the form of bread and under any part of that form; likewise the whole Christ is present under the form of wine and under all its parts" ("Decree concerning the Most Holy Sacrament of the Eucharist," chap. 3). Thus a person may communicate "under one species" (bread or wine) and receive the total Christ. An additional statement, entitled "Doctrine concerning the Communion under Both Species," reads in part: "Mother Church . . . induced by weighty and just reasons, has approved . . . communicating under one species and decreed that it was to be Law" (chap. 3). Practically speaking, this means that the laity receives only the bread, but are told that they have received, by concomitance, the whole Christ. It is interesting that Vatican II adds, "The dogmatic principles which were laid down by the Council of Trent remaining intact, communion under both kinds may be granted when the bishops see fit. . ." ("Constitution on the Sacred Liturgy," 55). Regardless of this slight moderation in doctrine, the Roman Catholic Church still remains basically committed to an unbiblical and deleterious viewpoint. For Calvin's critique of "Concomitance" see *Institutes*, 4.17.18; also the Lutheran Augsburg Confession, 22, which specifies "Both kinds in the Sacrament."

[183]Thus any idea that the contents of the cup must be totally consumed (usually by "priests") or that the sacrament, being viewed as actually the body and blood of Christ, is to

eaten and drunk, or otherwise disposed of.

8. Offering of Praise

The Lord's Supper may appropriately close with the offering of praise to God. Immediately following the Supper in the Upper Room, Jesus and His disciples began to sing: "And when they had sung a hymn, they went out to the Mount of Olives" (Matt. 26:30; Mark 14:26). We are not told directly what they sang; however, in all likelihood it was the singing of various praise, or "hallelujah," psalms of the Old Testament.[184] Hence it was more than "*a* hymn" that they sang; there was singing and praising God for some time. Only after this offering of praise did Jesus and His apostles go out.

This indeed speaks a relevant word to us. When we likewise have partaken of the bread and cup, our praises should also break forth. We may sing Old Testament psalms, but surely we may also sing other hymns and choruses of praise to God.[185] Since we live beyond the occasion of the Upper Room and in addition have experienced the resurrected and exalted Lord in Holy Communion, we have all the more for which to offer praise. Thus there could be song after song, praise upon praise, to express our joy in the Lord.

This is further appropriate because, following the celebration of the Lord's Supper, we look forward to the coming *great Supper* in the kingdom. It is noteworthy that just after Jesus spoke about not drinking again "of this fruit of the vine until that day when I drink it new with you in my Father's kingdom" (Matt. 26:29; cf. Mark 14:25), they sang together. Hence this forward look to the coming Marriage Supper of the kingdom can make the singing of praise all the more meaningful and joyful. Since we may be living very near to the return of the Lord[186] and His glorious Supper, which will include believers of all ages and places, our praise should mightily sound forth.

The Book of Hebrews encourages us to "continually offer up a sacrifice of praise to God" (13:15). The offering of praise at the conclusion of the Lord's Supper can highlight the rich and abounding praise that should constantly be manifest in all God's people.

---

be reserved, and even worshiped, is quite wrong. On the latter point, the Council of Trent, in a chapter entitled, "The Worship and Veneration to be Shown to This Most Holy Sacrament," declares, "There is no room for doubt that all the faithful of Christ may . . . give to this most holy sacrament in veneration the worship of *latria*, which is due to the true God" ("Decree concerning the Most Holy Sacrament of the Eucharist," chap. 5). This view is not only wrong; it is also sacrilegious.

[184]The Greek word for "sung a hymn" is *hymnēsantes*, literally "singing a hymn." This word, according to BAGD, refers to "the second part of the Hallel [Ps. 113–18 Heb.], sung at the close of the Passover meal." These Hallel (or, Hallelujah) psalms include, for example, Psalm 117, which begins, "Praise the LORD, all nations! Extol him, all peoples!" and has many other expressions of praise to God.

[185]In many churches, there is little more than a brief hymn before dismissal.

[186]See the discussion of the return of Christ in part 2.

7

The Church and Civil Government

One final concern about the church calls for consideration—namely, its relationship to civil government. This is an arena of frequent misunderstanding and conflict. Church and state: how are they properly related?

I. THE TWO SPHERES

Old Testament Israel was a theocracy. There was no separation between Israel as a religious entity and the state as a civil government. From the beginning of their existence as God's special people, Israel stood under His total rule. Through Moses God established not only all the religious rituals but also all judicial functions. Later when kings ruled over the nation of Israel, they did so as God's vice-regents to enforce His will for every aspect of national and personal life. Israel as a people were called by God to reflect His rule and purpose in all areas of their social, political, and religious existence. The ongoing responsibility of government was to see that the whole of life moved under the rule of God.

However, although Israel was a theocracy, there was nonetheless the recognition at the time of Moses of division of authority. Aaron and his sons were priests, and Moses was not authorized by God to perform their priestly role. After Saul became king there was a clear division between the authority of the king and that of judge/priests. So even in the Old Testament theocracy there were seeds of two spheres.

With the establishment of the church, there came into being two distinct spheres: the church and the civil government. The church, composed of Jews and Gentiles alike, was no longer identical with any political configuration but was a new people of God drawn from all races and tongues. Hence wherever Christians were gathered, in whatever land or nations, they were a separate entity from the civil government under which they existed.

In a sense two spheres existed in Israel at the time the church appeared. The people of Israel lived as a part of the Roman Empire under its overarching authority. The Jews had their own secondary authority centered in the Sanhedrin, which, under Rome, acted in both civil and religious matters. Hence there were two spheres of government—the Roman Empire and the Jewish nation, with the latter subordinate to the former.

The church, however, represented a further separation of the two spheres.

For although the church had, and has, its form of government, it operates in a separate arena from that of the state. Political and social affairs of state are no longer its realm of operation. The church, composed of people from many states and nations, is in no sense a subset of any civil government but, drawn out of the whole earthly sphere, exists for an entirely different purpose.[1] Thus in a profound sense the church is a heavenly colony: in Paul's language "our citizenship is in heaven" (Phil. 3:20 NIV, NASB). This does not, however, deny earthly citizenship as well. Paul himself also declared his Roman citizenship. For example, "Is it lawful for you [a Roman centurion] to scourge a man [Paul himself] who is a Roman citizen?" (Acts 22:25).[2] Thus for the Christian there is dual citizenship—in heaven and on earth.

Next it is important to observe that both spheres are under the rule of God. He is Lord of heaven and earth, hence over both church and state. Church and civil authority have both been established by God. The church is "the church of God";[3] it has been brought into being as a part of His eternal plan and is under His rule and direction. But likewise civil authority is under the rule of God. Let us observe this latter point in more detail.

In the Book of Daniel are these words: "Blessed be the name of God for ever and ever, to whom belong wisdom and might. . . . He removes kings and sets up kings" (2:20–21). Again, note the words addressed to Nebuchadnezzar, king of Babylon: "The Most High rules the kingdom of men, and gives it to whom he will, and sets over it the lowliest of men" (4:17). The "kingdom of men," Babylon and all others, are under God's rule, and, accordingly, those who rule do so by His ordination. Indeed, Nebuchadnezzar elsewhere is even called God's servant: "I have given all these lands into the hand of Nebuchadnezzar, the king of Babylon, my servant" (Jer. 27:6; cf. 25:9; 43:10). Cyrus, king of Persia, moreover, is called God's "anointed": "Thus says the LORD to his anointed, to Cyrus, whose right hand I have grasped, to subdue nations before him" (Isa. 45:1). All such statements emphasize that God establishes and rules over the kingdoms of men and nations.

In the New Testament Paul's words to the church in Rome follow a similar pattern. He writes about "the governing authorities" that "there is no authority except from God, and those that exist have been instituted by God" (Rom. 13:1). Jesus Himself had earlier declared to Pilate: "You would have no authority over Me, unless it had been given you from above" (John 19:11 NASB). Hence all governing authority, surely including that of Rome, is under God and answerable to Him.

Next we observe that there is a separation in the New Testament between the church and the civil government but not necessarily an opposition between the two. If both the church and "the governing authorities" exist by the will of God, each has its proper function to fulfill. God is at work in and through both to carry out His purpose. Accordingly, it is a mistake to view civil government simply as the realm of Satan. Satan may indeed seek to influence and take control, and civil authorities may serve him, but ultimately God is sovereign over all. There is now a "kingdom of the world," which

[1]See Marcellus Kik, *Church and State in the New Testament*, chapter 2, "Two Distinct Jurisdictions."

[2]See also Acts 16:37–39; 23:27.

[3]1 Corinthians 1:2; Galatians 1:13, and elsewhere.

indeed is Satan's realm that will some day become "the kingdom of our Lord and of his Christ" (Rev. 11:15). However, Satan's kingdom is the domain of darkness that, despite its penetration of all earthly kingdoms, is not to be identified with them. Hence, civil government—whatever may be its capitulation to Satan—is not the same as Satan's kingdom, the domain of darkness.

So then, there are two spheres: civil government and the church, each set in place by God. The former deals with mankind's political, economic, and social existence, the latter basically with man's spiritual existence.[4] In the Old Testament theocracy the two spheres ideally were held together; however, Israel's rebelliousness against God increasingly brought a recognition of the necessity of inward spiritual redemption. Thus without denying the fact that mankind's existence must have a political and social dimension, there came to be the reality of the church in which the spirit of man is set right with God. Therefore, rather than a theocratic unity, which, because of human sin, is unworkable in the present order, separation had to occur so that God's purposes could be fulfilled.

One further word: civil government is a part of God's providential order for human life. This is not unlike the human family, which, regardless of all the problems and rifts that may occur, is still God's basic providential arrangement for human welfare. Similarly, the church, which may be called mankind's spiritual family, can never replace the physical family. A far deeper spiritual relationship between members in the church may exist than between family members in the home, but this does not eliminate the continuing need for the human family. So God providentially has set in place human governments, and nothing that the church represents can obviate their continuing importance in the sustaining and ordering of human life.[5]

II. THE FUNCTION OF CIVIL GOVERNMENT

We turn now to a consideration of the function of civil government. Let us observe a number of matters.

A. The Establishment of Justice in Society

In the Book of Proverbs "wisdom"[6] declares, "By me kings reign, and rulers decree what is just; by me princes rule, and nobles govern the earth" (8:15–16). This statement stresses the point that justice—"rulers decree what is just"—is fundamental to the purpose of civil government. This concern for justice is frequently found in the Old Testament. For example, Moses declared to Israel, "You shall appoint judges and officers in all your towns . . . and they shall judge the people with righteous judgment. You shall not pervert justice; you shall not show partiality. . . . Justice, and only justice, you shall follow" (Deut. 16:18–

[4]By "spiritual existence" I do not mean an existence unrelated to the political, moral, and economic sphere, for the spiritual surely has significant effects on the public arena. However, the spiritual signifies such a profound reorientation of life as to represent a separate sphere.

[5]John Calvin speaks highly of civil governments with these words: "Civil authority is, in the sight of God, not only sacred and lawful, but the most sacred, and by far the most honorable, of all stations in mortal life" (*Institutes of the Christian Religion*, 4.20.4, Beveridge trans.).

[6]"Wisdom" is personified throughout Proverbs 8. This is obviously God's wisdom, even a second person alongside Him (note especially vv. 22–31), and probably a foregleam of Christ the Incarnate Wisdom of God (cf. 1 Cor. 1:24–30).

20). King Jehoshaphat later "appointed judges in the land . . . and said to the judges, 'Consider what you do, for you judge not for man but for the LORD; he is with you in giving judgment . . . take heed what you do, for there is no perversion of justice with the LORD our God, or partiality, or taking bribes' " (2 Chron. 19:5–7). Impartial and even-handed justice must be the primary obligation of leaders and judges. "Justice, and only justice" is to be the guideline for all. In addition to the multiple references to justice in the Old Testament,[7] there is also a foretelling of the Messiah to come: "Of the increase of his government and of peace there will be no end, upon the throne of David, and over his kingdom, to establish it, and to uphold it with justice and with righteousness from this time forth and for evermore" (Isa. 9:7).

All the above passages depict a theocracy in which there is no separation between the secular and religious spheres. However, as we have noted, with the New Testament emergence of the church as a separate entity, the two spheres have become distinct.[8] The church represents a redeemed community of grace within the overall secular order. Its concern is to proclaim the gospel of salvation, to live as a holy people, and to fulfill Christ's commands. Moreover, justice, while surely recognized as needed,[9] is transcended by the operation of love and mercy.[10] Yet—and this is quite important to add—the concern of the church by no means eliminates God's requirement of justice among people. This requirement is also emphasized by the church; however, it is the primary concern of the state, or civil government.

B. The Punishment of Wrongdoers

Let us observe this concern for justice in terms of the punishment of wrongdoers. Here we turn again to Romans 13 and note Paul's further words about a governing authority: "If you do wrong, be afraid, for he does not bear the sword in vain; he is the servant of God to execute his wrath on the wrongdoer" (v. 4). Several things are said here. First, there is a proper fear of the governing authority, for he has power to execute divine justice; second, such an authority is God's servant or minister[11] (even though this is not an ecclesiastical office); and, third, he executes God's wrath upon the evildoer. The state, by virtue of its governing authority, is God's servant of wrath against wrongdoing. What Paul is saying applies to all people, unbelievers and believers, pagans and Christians alike. Thus the state performs a necessary, God-given function, not only beyond the sphere of the church but also one that uniquely expresses the wrath of God against wrongdoing.

On this matter of punishment of wrongdoers, Peter writes similarly of the role of civil government. He speaks of "governors as sent by him [the

---

[7]There are hundreds of these.

[8]Oscar Cullmann writes that "the Jewish theocratic ideal is expressly rejected by Christianity" (*The State in the New Testament*, 9).

[9]I refer here to justice for people. E.g., there is Jesus' question, "Will not God bring about justice for his chosen ones, who cry out to him day and night?" Jesus continues, "I tell you, he will see that they get justice, and quickly" (Luke 18:7–8 NIV). The church likewise is concerned with justice (see e.g., 1 Cor. 5 and 6).

[10]In the parable of the Prodigal Son (Luke 15:11–32), for example, the wayward son justly deserves nothing, but through his penitence he receives the loving embrace of his father. Justice is transcended by love.

[11]The Greek word is *diakonos*. This means that the service of God *includes* political service!

emperor] to punish those who do wrong" (1 Peter 2:14). This, we need to emphasize, is *not* the basic purpose of the church. Leaders in the church are not "sent by" God to punish wrongdoers but to seek to bring them to repentance, forgiveness, and new life.[12] Of course, punishment by the church may be involved (even to excommunication for persistent sinners), but it is neither as primary nor final (e.g., capital punishment) as that of the civil government. Punishment of wrongdoers is, on the other hand, a basic function of the state.

The presence of evil in the world requires that there be a forceful governing power. Civil government, accordingly, at best represents God's providential order to restrain and punish evil. Thus while its punitive function is an aspect of God's judgment, it also indirectly shows God's mercy. For without such restraint and punishment no civilized life is possible: society would degenerate into barbarism and chaos.[13]

C. The Public Good

Civil government, however, is instituted by God not only for punishment of wrongdoers but also for the public good. Paul speaks in Romans 13 of the civil authority as "God's servant for [our] good" (v. 4). So it is that the public good has often been recognized by the church as the legitimate and proper concern of the state. For example, the Westminster Confession of Faith (Presbyterian) declares, "God, the supreme Lord and King of all the world, hath ordained civil magistrates to be under him, over the people, for his own glory and the public good."[14] The Augsburg Confession (Lutheran) similarly states, "It is taught among us that all government in the world and all established rules and laws were instituted by God for the sake of good order."[15] The public good, good order, is the concern of the state.

In a broader sense we may say that the civil government exists to protect whatever good God has given man in creating him. For example, God gave mankind first and foremost life itself; He offered human beings freedom and choice; He desired happiness and joy for them. These God-given endowments are called "rights" by the American Declaration of Independence. "All men . . . are endowed by their Creator with certain unalienable rights . . . among these are Life, Liberty, and the pursuit of Happiness." Further, "to secure these rights, Governments are instituted among men. . . ." Of course, not all governments have been faithful in protecting such rights, but the Declaration stakes out the important fact that government is related to God as Creator and thus to His concern for the genuine good of mankind.[16]

But now we must recognize a further point. Civil government, while a part of God's divine order, also exists in a fallen world: it operates therefore as a fallen entity in a world of fallen humans. Thus the public good can be secured only, first, by checks and balances on the power of civil government itself—else tyranny can result—and second, by such action of civil govern-

[12]The words of Jesus in John 8 to the adulterous woman are to the point: "Neither do I condemn you; go, and do not sin again" (v. 11).

[13]F. F. Bruce speaks about the difference between "the preservation of the world" and "the salvation of the world" (*Romans*, TNTC, 238). It is with the former that God's order in civil government is concerned.

[14]Chapter 23, "Of the Civil Magistrate."

[15]Chapter 16, "Civil Government."

[16]See Gary T. Amos, *Defending the Declaration*, chapter 4, " 'Unalienable Rights' Endowed by the Creator," for a helpful study.

ment regarding human affairs as to adjudicate between manifold and competing self-interests. In the latter case, the restraining power of civil government on human society is essential to prevent anarchy. The public good in an unfallen world would be the direct and voluntary concern of civil government; however, in our present fallen existence the public good can occur only through the proper, often involuntary, application of checks and restraints on both civil government and society at large.

Society at large also includes the church. The church is composed of God's redeemed people, essentially delivered from a fallen condition; however, sin—self-seeking and self-interest—remains. Wrongdoing still occurs, indeed is sometimes of such a kind that it may call for more than repentance and forgiveness or even temporary exclusion from the church. The public good may be so affected that the civil government needs to step in to render proper judgment and mandate punishment. Even a civil government that has little or no recognition of God, and thus operates out of its own self-interest, may be required for its own and the public order to express God's wrath and judgment on Christian offenders.

D. Provision for Exercise of Religious Faith

The public good, just described, also ideally includes provision for the exercise of religious faith. Paul's words are relevant: "I urge that entreaties and prayers, petitions and thanksgivings, be made on behalf of all men, for kings and all who are in authority, in order that we may lead a tranquil and quiet life in all godliness and dignity" (1 Tim. 2:1–2 NASB). Thus the purpose of these manifold prayers for those in authority is that people of faith may live in godliness and dignity. The civil government, without endorsing the Christian faith or any other particular religious expression,[17] should make room for its religious exercise.

It is interesting that this resembles the First Amendment clause of the United States Constitution that reads, "Congress shall make no law respecting an establishment of religion, or prohibiting the free exercise thereof." The prayers urged by Paul in regard to Christian faith were not that civil authorities would establish or even endorse that faith, but that they would simply allow its "free exercise." In later church history there would be, first, the attempt to prohibit Christian expression through bitter Roman persecution of the church (by Nero and others); second, still later would come the establishment of the church as the state religion (by Emperor Constantine). *Neither* of these is what Paul held in prospect, for the church functions best when it is neither prohibited nor established by governing authorities. Moreover, the state should not be in the role of enforcing religious exercise, suppressing heresy, and the like.[18] Such activity by civil government—in regard

[17]In 1 Timothy 2:1–2 Paul is of course speaking specifically of Christian faith. However Paul's concern surely may be applied to all other religions that likewise desire free expression.

[18]Such a role for the state was set forth in the original 1647 edition of the Westminster Confession of Faith in the chapter entitled "Of the Civil Magistrate." It declared that "he hath authority, and it is his duty to take order, that unity and peace be preserved in the

to any religious group—unquestionably contravenes the First Amendment clause and is inimical to the best interests of both church and state.

Since all civil government derives its true authority from God, it should be only natural for the state to support religious practice. Unfortunately, civil governments have often gone either to the extreme of self-deification (the state *is* God) or total secularization (the state *rejects* God). A government that falls into either extreme has denied its own authority under God and its duty to permit free religious expression.

This leads to the critical point that when civil government recognizes its existence under God, it will both publicly recognize God and ensure the people's right to full religious practice. There is indeed a separation of church and state (the two spheres), but the separation is not from religion but from any particular expression of it. The American Declaration of Independence, as earlier noted, affirms God as Creator—"all men are . . . endowed by their Creator with certain unalienable rights"—and speaks of divine providence—"a firm reliance on the Protection of Divine Providence."[19] Accordingly, there is a proper, indeed continuing, need in the public arena for the recognition of God as Creator and Provider; for example, through national days of prayer, in opening sessions of Congress, and in public school classrooms. Such evidences of recognition of God *must* not be obliterated by a destructive secularism that seeks to separate the nation from God.[20] This recognition does not mean the establishment of any particular religion (including the Christian), but it does demonstrate a nation's basic religious orientation and its essential congeniality to the various religious expressions that it guarantees. Indeed, a nation that publicly recognizes God, for its own good purpose, will foster religion,[21] while at the same time seeking to secure for its people freedom in their varied practice of it.

E. Promotion of Moral Standards

I have earlier quoted the words of Peter about "governors, who are as sent . . . to punish those who do wrong"; now I add Peter's further words: "and to commend those who do right" (1 Peter 2:14 NIV). In the same vein Paul writes, "Do what is right and he [the one in authority] will commend you" (Rom. 13:3 NIV). Thus it is an

Church, that the truth of God be kept pure and entire, that all blasphemies and heresies be suppressed . . . he hath power to call synods, to be present at them, and to provide that whatever is transmitted in them be according to the mind of God." Let me add that I am thankful that this has been changed in the United States version of the Confession to read, in part: "It is the duty of civil magistrates to protect the church of our common Lord, without giving the preference to any denomination of Christians." Nothing is said later in the Confession about the civil magistrate suppressing blasphemies, heresies, etc. The word "protect" far better expresses the properly functioning relationship between civil government and the church.

[19]Words referring to those who signed the Declaration.

[20]As Bob G. Slosser writes emphatically, *"Separation of church and state is not separation of God and state"* (*Changing the Way America Thinks*, 193).

[21]Calvin declared, "No polity [i.e., political order] can be successfully established unless piety be its first love" (*Institutes*, 4.20.9, Beveridge trans.). This may be extreme—"its first love"—but it contains a valuable nugget of truth.

additional function of civil government to commend its citizens for doing the good and the right.

This means that civil government is not only in the business of establishing justice, punishing wrongdoers, promoting the public good, and providing for the exercise of religious faith;[22] it also should act as a moral stimulus to its citizenry by commending right and good actions. Public commendation for faithful citizenship, for valorous and rightful deeds in war and peace, for standing heroically against crime and vice—and other such actions—helps to promote a higher level of citizenship.

All of this implies that civil government is in some sense a moral entity. This is true because civil government has been "instituted by God" and thus has a given moral character.[23] Hence, civil government inherently knows what is right. Although it has no way of changing human nature (only the gospel can do this), it can encourage and stimulate its citizens to moral activity.

Moral values *are* a responsibility of the state. Merely to govern by finding a way through competing self-interests is actually self-defeating. Civil government, as an entity ordained by God, must always have as its larger interest the right of all its citizens. When government does the right and commends the right, it governs well.

III. DUTIES TOWARD CIVIL GOVERNMENT

What, next, are the duties that the church owes to the civil government? We have observed a number of functions of the civil government, the state, and how these functions relate to the church. Our concern now is in regard to the church's obligation to the state.

A. Subjection to Authority of the Civil Government

All citizens, including those in the church, owe subjection, honor, and respect to the ruling authorities in the state. Let us recall several Scriptures.

Paul's words in Romans 13 stand out: "Let every person be in subjection to the governing authorities . . . he who resists authority has opposed the ordinance of God; and they who have opposed will receive condemnation upon themselves" (vv. 1–2 NASB). Later Paul adds, "Wherefore it is necessary to be in subjection, not only because of [God's] wrath, but also for conscience' sake" (v. 5 NASB). Both of these passages strongly call for obedience to civil authority and warn against God's judgment upon those who resist. Likewise the consciences of the disobedient will reflect guilt.[24] Further on Paul speaks of "respect to whom respect is due, honor to whom honor is due" (v. 7). Hence, subjection, respect, honor—all are due the governing authorities.

Another related admonition of Paul was given to Titus: "Remind them to be subject to rulers, to authorities, to be obedient" (Titus 3:1 NASB). Titus had been left by Paul on the island of Crete with responsibility for the churches there. Most of Paul's letter to Titus

[22]As discussed in the preceding paragraphs.

[23]To this may be added the fact that the moral law is basically known by all people. Paul in Romans 2:15 writes about the Gentile nations that "what the law requires is written on their hearts." This means that the ethical demands of the Law (i.e., the Ten Commandments) are written deep in human nature (the heart), so that all people, and therefore governments, have some knowledge of what is just and right.

[24]The conscience is an inward moral monitor. Just after his words about "the law . . . written on their hearts," Paul adds, "their conscience also bears witness" (Rom. 2:15). Since the state in some sense represents God's moral order, and the conscience bears witness to this fact, an unwillingness to be subject to the state will have repercussions on the conscience.

deals with matters of the church and Christian living; however, he throws in this important reminder about the state: "be subject . . . be obedient." Paul obviously sees no conflict between this action and the people's devotion to Christ.

Next we turn to Peter. He writes, "Submit yourselves for the Lord's sake to every authority instituted among men: whether to the king, as the supreme authority, or to governors, who are sent by him to punish those who do wrong and to commend those who do right. . . . Show proper respect to everyone: Love the brotherhood of believers, fear God, honor the king" (1 Peter 2:13–14, 17 NIV). Here he exhorts the same submission and subjection to governing authorities as does Paul. Likewise the stress is on such authorities as "instituted" by God; however, Peter emphasizes this subjection not because of God's wrath or for conscience's sake but "for the Lord's sake." The Lord has ordained these authorities, and so it is for His sake that Christians, the church, should willingly[25] submit to them.

Based on the above passages, let me make a few observations:

1. The kind of government in power has no bearing on the required subjection. Reference is basically to governing authorities, whoever or whatever they may be. Peter mentions "the king" (doubtless the Roman emperor at that time) but also other "governors." Whether the government be a monarchy, oligarchy, or even a democracy is essentially irrelevant. Christians are to be in subjection to whatever governing authority is in place.

2. There is no suggestion that the character of the ruling authority has any bearing on submission. The king, governor, ruler—indeed the whole government—may be overbearing, even pagan, but obedience and respect are still due. Peter's words are followed by two other passages regarding submission, beginning, "Servants, be submissive to your masters" (1 Peter 2:18) and "Wives, be submissive to your husbands" (3:1). Servants owe submission "not only to the kind and gentle but also to the overbearing"[26] (2:18); wives owe submission to husbands even "though they do not obey the word" (3:1), hence are unbelievers. Thus, in the same manner Christians are to submit even to governing authorities that are harsh, unjust, possibly pagan.[27] The point is that civil government is similar to other societal arrangements that likewise call for submission regardless of the character of those in authority.

3. Finally, as was previously mentioned, the basic reason for subjection is neither the kind of governing authority nor its character, but "for the Lord's sake." The fact that governing authority is an ordinance of God—an aspect of His providential arrangement for mankind—means that Christians should willingly submit to its authority. The church, knowing the special providence of God by which it exists under

[25]Just prior to Peter's statement that culminates in "honor the king," he writes, "Live as free men" (v. 16). These words apply, in part at least, to the church's willing submission to governing authorities.

[26]Or "unjust." The Greek word is *skoliois*—"harsh, unjust" (BAGD).

[27]Calvin writes, "Even an individual of the worst character, one most unworthy of all honour, if invested with public authority, receives that illustrious divine power which the Lord has by his word devolved on the ministers of his justice and judgment, and that, accordingly, in so far as public obedience is concerned, he is to be held in the same honour and reverence as the best of kings" (*Institutes* 4.20.25, Beveridge trans.). The Westminster Confession declares, "Infidelity or difference in religion doth not make void the magistrate's just and legal authority, nor free the people from their due obedience to him" (chap. 23.4).

its own authorities, should gladly be submissive to God's general providence in undergirding the authorities of state. Indeed, far more than the citizenry at large, the church should freely submit itself to civil government.[28]

B. Intercession for Those in Authority

Here we return to Paul's words in 1 Timothy 2:1–2: "I urge that entreaties and prayers, petitions and thanksgivings, be made on behalf of all men, for kings and all who are in authority"[29] (NASB). Paul's concern is that believers should intercede, first, for all people—interceding along with giving thanks—and, second, for kings and all others in high places.

Thus the church is obligated to intercede for civil government. That Christians are subject to the state does not mean that their prayers should be directed elsewhere. Quite the opposite: since civil government is ordained by God to fulfill certain of His purposes, the church must not shirk its obligation of intercession for the state.[30] Three reasons may be given.

First, since civil government, although ordained by God, is basically involved in temporal and secular matters, it needs the prayers of the church. The responsibilities of executing justice, punishing wrongdoers, providing for the public good, and so on, are weighty indeed. Those in authority may have little or no sense that they are servants of God and may seldom, if at all, turn to prayer. The church therefore must in a sense "stand in the gap" (Ezek. 22:30 KJV) for the civil government and intercede earnestly on its behalf.

Second, civil government, operating necessarily in a fallen world, is itself prone to evil action. Whereas civil authority is "instituted by God" and is "God's servant for [our] good," that authority by no means always fulfills God's purpose for it. Paul's words to the Romans just quoted, as well as those about "kings and all who are in authority" in 1 Timothy, related at that time to the Roman Empire, its emperor (or king), lesser kings (such as Herod), provincial governors, and the like. Basically such authorities are of God, for without them anarchy would follow; however, their actions are often pervaded by evil so that tyranny results. Thus the church needs to intercede for civil government that it may properly be God's servant for good. What can the church do when governments go wrong? The answer is surely neither self-isolation nor interference in government affairs, but continually, and profoundly, to intercede on behalf of kings, presidents, prime ministers, and all lesser officials, that they may turn to the good and right. An interceding church can powerfully affect the ways of civil government.

Third, civil government can stand in the way of Christian living and the spread of the gospel, and this needs the

---

[28]That the authority of civil government is not absolute will be discussed in the next section, "A Higher Loyalty."

[29]Or "high positions" (RSV). The Greek word is *hyperochē*, "a place of prominence or authority" (BAGD).

[30]I quote here a beautiful prayer for "rulers and governors" in I Clement: "You, Master, have given them the power of sovereignty through your majestic and inexpressible might, so that we, acknowledging the glory and honor which you have given them, may be subject to them, resisting your will in nothing. Grant to them, Lord, health, peace, harmony, and stability, that they may blamelessly administer the government which you have given them. . . . Lord, direct their plans according to what is good and pleasing in your sight, so that by devoutly administering in peace and gentleness the authority which you have given them they may experience your mercy" (*The Apostolic Fathers*, 2nd. ed., 61:1–2).

church's intercession. Following Paul's words about interceding for those in authority so that Christians may live a peaceful life, he adds, "This is good and acceptable in the sight of God our Savior, who desires all men to be saved and to come to the knowledge of the truth" (1 Tim. 2:3–4 NASB). For the civil government to allow the church to practice its faith without government interference, hence to "lead a tranquil life" (v. 2), should be continually a matter of intercession. Since the church is the instrument of One who "desires all men to be saved," prayers should also be regularly offered for civil government to clear the way for the proclamation and extension of the gospel everywhere. On this latter point, there have been, and often are, civil governments that either through their antipathy to religious faith (e.g., in Marxist countries) or capitulation to a particular religious formulation (e.g., in Moslem states) seek to prevent the propagation of the Christian gospel. Indeed, the church must continually intercede for doors to open. Since God Himself desires salvation for "all men," He will surely hear and bless the prayers of His people in that regard.

May the prayers of the church on behalf of civil government rise constantly to the Lord, especially in these critical days. No other intercessions by the people of God are more important.

C. Payment of Taxes

Another responsibility to the civil government is the payment of taxes. Shortly after Paul spoke about subjection—"one must be subject" (Rom 13:5)—he added, "For the same reason you also pay taxes, for the authorities are ministers[31] of God. . . . Pay all of them their dues, taxes[32] to whom taxes are due, revenue[33] to whom revenue is due, respect to whom respect is due, honor to whom honor is due." (vv. 6–7). Civil government, ordained by God, cannot exist without the financial support of its citizens. Regardless of the merits of individual rulers[34] or governments, taxes and revenues are to be paid by all.

Jesus Himself paid taxes. We read in Matthew 17: "When they [Jesus and His disciples] came to Capernaum, the collectors of the half-shekel tax[35] went to Peter and said, 'Does not your teacher pay the tax?' He said, 'Yes' "[36] (vv. 24–25). Later, the Pharisees, through some of their own disciples, tried to tempt Jesus by asking, "Is it lawful [or 'right'] to pay taxes to Caesar, or not?" Whereupon Jesus had them bring him a coin stamped with Caesar's portrait and inscription; then

[31]The Greek word here is *leitourgoi*. According to BAGD, "in our literature always [used] with sacral connotations." Dunn writes that "taxes could be regarded as the secular equivalent of the offerings and sacrifices brought to the altar; within the state as ordered by God, tax officials are the equivalent of priests within the cult!" (*Romans 9–16*, WBC, 772).

[32]Or "tribute" (KJV). The Greek word is *phoron*. According to Thayer, *phoros* refers especially to "the annual tax levied upon houses, lands, and persons." C. K. Barrett speaks of it as "direct taxation" (*The Epistle to the Romans*, HNTC, 242).

[33]Or "custom" (KJV). The Greek word is *telos*. According to Barrett, "indirect taxation, such as customs dues" (*Epistles to the Romans*, 248).

[34]E. F. Harrison states, "The man in authority may be unworthy, but the institution is not, since God ordained it" (*Romans*, EBC, 139).

[35]The Greek word is *didrachma*, "the sum required of each person annually as the temple tax" (BAGD).

[36]In the verses that follow, Jesus—after speaking of freedom *not* to pay—tells Peter, so as not to give offense, to cast a hook into the sea "and take the first fish that comes up, and when you open its mouth you will find a shekel; take that and give it to them for me and yourself" (v. 27). So Peter paid the tax both for himself and Jesus.

He said to them, "Render therefore to Caesar the things that are Caesar's, and to God the things that are God's" (Matt. 22:17–21). Thus Jesus, even if indirectly, affirmed the propriety of paying taxes to Caesar, the Roman emperor, as well as the importance of rendering to God what belongs to Him. This of course does not mean that Caesar and God are in comparable spheres, for Caesar would have no power at all if God did not give it.[37] But it does signify that there is a temporal realm, which Caesar represents and to whom taxes are due, as well as the spiritual realm for which God's children also have responsibility.

It surely was not always easy to pay taxes to a government that glorified Caesar more than God and whose tax collectors often defrauded the people. It is interesting that John the Baptist had early told tax collectors who came to be baptized, "Collect no more than is appointed you" (Luke 3:13). Thus John did *not* deny the validity of collecting taxes but only the abuse that had set in. In Jesus' ministry many tax collectors (including Matthew) were numbered among His disciples. Not once did Jesus suggest that their office was wrong,[38] only the misuse of it.[39]

Hence, today Christians may declaim about taxes being too much or not always used for proper ends, but the obligation remains. Taxes, unlike contributions to the church, are not voluntary: they are exactions. However, when there is the fresh realization that civil government is instituted by God and that, whatever its faults, it exercises an irreplaceable role in human affairs, taxes should be much less painful. It may be too much to suggest that one exult over the obligation, but at least there should be a readiness and willingness to pay!

D. Participation in Public and Civic Affairs

We have earlier noted these words of Paul to Titus: "Remind them to be subject to rulers, to authorities, to be obedient." To this statement Paul adds, "to be ready for every good deed" (3:1 NASB). This suggests that beyond the call for willing subjection to civil authorities, there is also the call to civic responsibility. Subjection could of course be viewed as a kind of negative acquiescence; however, the positive side is that of readiness for "every good deed." Christians should be active citizens.[40]

Peter writes similarly: After speaking about governors "who are sent by him [the king] to punish those who do wrong and to commend those who do right," he continues, "For it is God's will that by doing good you should silence the ignorant talk of foolish men" (1 Peter 2:15 NIV).[41] This suggests again the

---

[37]Recall Jesus' words to the Roman governor Pilate: "You would have no power over me unless it had been given you from above" (John 19:11).

[38]Matthew, of course, did give up his tax office to follow Jesus (see Matt. 9:9). However, because of Matthew's call to be an apostle, this was an exception.

[39]This comes out indirectly in the case of the rich tax collector Zacchaeus who, upon turning to Jesus, said, "If I have defrauded any one of anything, I restore it fourfold" (Luke 19:8).

[40]E. F. Scott writes in this connection: "Christians should be among the foremost in showing public spirit" (*The Pastoral Epistles*, MNTC, 172). D. E. Hiebert puts it well: "As good citizens, believers must . . . 'be ready to do whatever is good'—prepared and willing to participate in activities that promote the welfare of the community. They must not stand coldly aloof from praiseworthy enterprises of government but show good public spirit, thus proving that Christianity is a constructive force in society" (*Titus*, EBC, 11:443).

[41]I. H. Marshall writes that "what starts off, then, as apparently a lesson in political

importance of good deeds in the civic arena, especially because such deeds will help to silence those who may accuse Christians of being uninvolved in public and community life.

Here we must differentiate between the activity of Christians in the church and their activity in the state. The church's function is essentially nonpolitical; it represents the spiritual realm: people born of the Spirit who worship together, build up one another in the Lord, and seek to extend the gospel of salvation to all mankind. Accordingly, the sphere of the church does not encompass the political and civic arena; thus the church itself ought not to become involved in affairs of the state.[42] However, individual Christians are not only citizens of heaven, the spiritual commonwealth; they are also citizens of earth and of the God-ordained realm of the state. Therefore, Christians need to do more than submit, pray, and pay taxes: they should also assume their rightful role of "readiness for every good [civic] deed" and "doing good [in society]," wherever they can make an impact.

This surely includes the possibility of political office. Since civil government is also instituted by God, for a Christian to serve in such government is indeed appropriate.[43] The Christian knows God (many civil authorities do not) and thus should be all the more concerned to fulfill the cause of justice and to work for the public good. The Christian, however, must not seek any preferential role for his own church and faith; nor, for example, should a Christian magistrate seek to apply specific biblical laws in the civil arena.[44] However,

---

passivity [in Peter's preceding words] culminates in an injunction to take an active role in society" (*1 Peter*, 84).

[42]The Westminster Confession of Faith, in regard to church synods and councils, calls this "intermeddling"! "Synods and councils are to handle or conclude nothing but that which is ecclesiastical; and are not to intermeddle with civil affairs that concern the commonwealth" (chap. 31.5).

[43]Herbert W. Titus, dean of the Law School at Regent University, writes, "There is a ministry in politics, just as sure as there is a ministry in evangelism. If a nation's legal and political structure does not reflect the law of God, it is bound to fail. It is because of God's grace that we have the opportunity to participate in the public affairs of nations, and we ought to do so in accordance with the plan God has for America and nations all over the world" (*The Biblical Basis of Public Policy*, National Perspectives Institute, 10).

[44]Contemporary Reconstructionism, however, affirms that this is what any civil magistrate should do. For example, Greg L. Bahnsen writes, "The magistrate today *ought* to obey and enforce God's Law" (italics his) (*Theonomy in Christian Ethics*, expanded ed., 433). By "God's Law" is meant the Old Testament laws—all the civil statutes revealed to Moses. In regard to capital punishment, for example, "civil magistrates are under obligation to execute all those who commit capital crimes as defined by God's authoritative law" (442). Bahnsen later lists as "capital offenses" (I will omit the Scriptures he gives): "adultery and unchastity . . . sodomy and bestiality . . . homosexuality . . . rape . . . incest . . . incorrigibility in children . . . sabbath breaking . . . kidnapping . . . apostasy . . . witchcraft, sorcery, and false pretension to prophecy . . . and blasphemy" (445). This is indeed a rather shocking portrayal of a civil magistrate's penal obligations in a society reconstructed along Old Testament lines. Obviously, from this viewpoint, Christian civil magistrates should be even more concerned that persons who commit such capital offenses be executed. (This is a kind of Christian parallel to Islamic fundamentalism that upholds the right and duty of the Moslem magistrates to "obey and enforce God's [Allah's] Law" in detail as set forth in the Koran.) Reconstructionism, by definition, calls for reconstruction, i.e., of the state, to move from whatever its present form (pluralistic democracy in the United States) to a biblical theocracy in which Old Testament laws are the law of the land and civil magistrates "obey

the Christian in political office[45] should rightly strive to strengthen the nation's historical commitment to God (e.g., represented by God as "Creator" in the Declaration of Independence, "in God we trust" on our coins and currency, "one nation under God" in the Pledge of Allegiance) and stand firm on the recognition of God in every sphere of public and civil life. Today, I hardly need add, this is of urgent importance because of the increasing efforts by many to exclude from civil life all reference to God.

IV. THE CHURCH BEYOND CIVIL GOVERNMENT

A. A Higher Ethic

The civil government, as we have observed, is concerned primarily with *justice*. Every human society has friction and tension that are brought about by self-interest and result in abuse of the rights of others. Civil government must exist to restrain expressions of violence, to adjudicate between competing claims, to punish lawbreakers, to protect life and property, to maintain peace and order. In all of this, justice is the supreme goal. It is the heart of the concern of civil government.

The church, while affirming justice, goes beyond justice to *love*. One of the best examples of this is the teaching of Jesus in the Sermon on the Mount where He first quotes the Old Testament commandment "You have heard that it was said, 'An eye for an eye and a tooth for a tooth.'" Then Jesus adds, "But I say to you, Do not resist one who is evil. But if any one strikes you on the right cheek, turn to him the other also; and if anyone would sue you and take your coat, let him have your cloak as well" (Matt. 5:38-40). "An eye for an eye and a tooth for a tooth"[46] was an Old Testament prescription for justice. This was not vengeance but retribution—the *lex talionis*, law of retaliation—and met the demand for equivalence: the punishment to fit the crime. By such punishment justice was served in giving the offender what he deserved and protecting society against acts of lawlessness. The Old Testament law of retaliation with various modifications, of course, continues to be a rule of justice in contemporary life.

Jesus' words "But I say to you" do not contradict the Old Testament law but fulfill it. Indeed, He had earlier said, "Do not think that I have come to abolish the Law or the Prophets; I have not come to abolish them but to fulfill them" (Matt. 5:17 NIV). However, Jesus' words belong to the *new* ethic of the kingdom of heaven (or of God)[47] and can be fulfilled only by those who belong to it. Thus this is not an ethic for the state but for the church that embodies God's kingdom. It does not contradict law but goes *beyond* it and in so doing fulfills it. Retributive justice is entirely proper for the state. But for the church, the born-again people of the spiritual kingdom, there is a higher way—the way of love. Thus a blow to the cheek, while rightly calling for a response in kind, is transcended by the Christian's turning the other cheek; and if sued for something he owns, rather than going to court, he will give the

---

and enforce" them. Such a goal, I must add, has no New Testament support, and is an infringement in regard to separation of church and state.

[45]Here I refer particularly to the American scene.

[46]See Exodus 21:24; Leviticus 24:19–20; Deuteronomy 19:21.

[47]Jesus' opening words in the Sermon on the Mount are "Blessed are the poor in spirit, for theirs is the kingdom of heaven [or "God"–see next chapter in *Renewal Theology*]." "Poor in spirit" refers to those who "acknowledge spiritual bankruptcy" (D. A. Carson, *Matthew*, EBC, 8:132) and thus are recipients of the kingdom.

plaintiff what he demands and more.[48] The Christian does not stand for his rights but views whatever happens to himself at the hands of another as an opportunity to show love and compassion.

Jesus makes this even stronger a few words later in saying, "You have heard that it was said, 'You shall love your neighbor and hate your enemy.' But I say to you, Love your enemies and pray for those who persecute you, so that you may be sons of your Father who is in heaven" (Matt. 5:43–45). Persecution by an enemy rightly calls for retribution, but for the Christian, love is the higher way. Why? Because by love the believer demonstrates his sonship to God the Father who, as Jesus adds, "makes his sun rise on the evil and on the good, and sends rain on the just and on the unjust" (v. 45). Thus Jesus goes even beyond nonretaliation (as expressed in the preceding verses in Matt. 5:38–42) to positive love (vv. 43–45).

This higher ethic of love may seem like a denial of justice by capitulation to evil. However, it is actually the way to right human relations by changing the enemy! Here we move to Paul's words in Romans 12:20–21: " 'If your enemy is hungry, feed him; if he is thirsty, give him drink; for by so doing you will heap burning coals upon his head.'[49] Do not be overcome by evil, but overcome evil with good." While justice may be served through retaliation, the enemy remains the enemy. Far better is the exercise of outgoing love that may so overwhelm him that he will no longer be an adversary!

We are moving deeply into the arena of interpersonal relationships and to a quality of life infinitely far removed from legalistic achievement. It is not a matter of securing one's rights by bringing an offender to justice but of allowing the offense to be an opportunity of expressing God's love to the offender and thereby possibly bringing about his restoration. Does this mean dealing lightly with an offense? Not at all. For the way of love does *not* overlook the offense or the just deserts of the offender, but, in spite of the hurt, reaches out to him in forgiveness and love. This totally undeserved act of love and forgiveness has the power to do far more than the law can achieve—such as justice, redress, perhaps rehabilitation—because it can restore a relationship, even change the offender, and bring to him new life.

Ultimately we are talking about the way of the cross. Jesus had every right to retaliate against his vicious offenders. Moreover, He could have done so when one of His disciples, to protect Him, began slashing with a sword; but Jesus quickly intervened, saying, "Put your sword back in its place . . . for all

---

[48]R. T. France speaks of this as Jesus' calling for "a radically unselfish attitude to one's own rights and property" (*Matthew*, TNTC, 127). This cannot, of course, be the attitude of the state, which exists in part to protect people's rights and property. Lawsuits, for example, are appropriate to the state as a way of abetting justice. The Christian, as a citizen of the state, accordingly, may participate in the legal defense of others' rights—including other believers—while personally refraining from defending his own. However, Jesus' words about the willing defenselessness of His disciples should not be applied to the state or Christian activities within the state at large. Now one further word: If there is some ambiguity here in regard to Christians and lawsuits in general, there should be none in relation to inter-Christian and interchurch affairs: *lawsuits are wrong*. Paul makes this clear in writing, "To have lawsuits *at all* with one another is defeat for you. Why not rather suffer wrong? Why not rather be defrauded?" (1 Cor. 6:7). Perhaps as we put Paul's words into practice, we may also better learn how to deal with the more complex matter of church and state.

[49]Quotation from Proverbs 25:21 (LXX).

who draw the sword will die by the sword. Do you think I cannot call on the Father, and he will at once put at my disposal more than twelve legions of angels?" (Matt. 26:52–53 NIV). In the cause of justice God could properly have sent angels to punish, even destroy, the enemies of Jesus. But Jesus did not ask; *for there was something much higher at stake than justice*. On the cross He demonstrated it for the whole world to see, crying out to God, "Father, forgive them; for they know not what they do" (Luke 23:34). Whereas this could have been the day of God's righteous and total judgment upon an evil and offending world, it was the day of mankind's forgiveness and ensuing salvation. It was the higher and redeeming way of love.

Some day in the future God's righteous anger and vengeance will be totally unleashed[50] against all who have spurned the forgiveness offered at the Cross,[51] and there are numerous evidences of people receiving just retribution even now.[52] But the way of the Cross, the way of forgiving love, is the way of the present kingdom. Justice is not denied, because Christ Himself at the Cross received God's righteous judgment and punishment for all people, thus unleashing the awesome power of love and forgiveness. Hence for the church, those who themselves have been forgiven, the high way is the way of love to all who may cause offense.

It is important to add that this higher ethic of love in no way invalidates the responsibility of the state to operate on the level of justice. Since the civil government—even if there are many Christians serving in it, or if it is entirely pagan as was the Roman Empire for centuries—is not the kingdom of God, it cannot operate on the basis of forgiving love. In an unredeemed society ridden with evil and injustice, it is important that civil government seek to restrain evil and punish injustice, and thus work for the public good. Civil government is not in a position to follow such words of Jesus as "Do not resist one who is evil," but it must resist evildoers in every possible just way. The *lex talionis* also includes "life for life,"[53] thus at times there must be the imposition of capital punishment. Such punishment cannot be ruled out in a still sinful world. Further, this resistance by the civil government may on occasion not be simply against individuals but against groups within[54] or nations without[55] when the cause of justice is at stake. "Do not resist," while applying to the way of the kingdom and referring to interpersonal relationships, cannot be the way of the state. The civil authority does execute God's vengeance. Indeed, according to Paul, "he does not bear the sword in vain; he is the servant of God to execute his wrath on the wrongdoer" (Rom. 13:4). Such is the God-given role of the state.

Now obviously there will be some

[50]The words of Paul earlier quoted, beginning, "If your enemy is hungry, feed him," are prefaced by Paul's statement, "Vengeance is mine, I will repay, says the Lord" (Rom. 12:19).

[51]See discussion of "the Day of the Lord" in part 2, pages 305–7.

[52]Paul mentions some examples in Romans 1:18–32.

[53]See Exodus 21:24 and Deuteronomy 19:21. Also, even prior to the Mosaic law of "life for life" in these two passages, there was God's word to Noah, and through him to all mankind: "Whoever sheds the blood of man, by man shall his blood be shed; for God made man in his own image" (Gen. 9:6).

[54]For example, the United States against the South with its institutionalized slavery in the nineteenth century.

[55]For example, the United States and its allies against Germany in World Wars I and II.

tension for the Christian, who is necessarily a citizen both of the state and of the kingdom of God. For the state the "sword" of authority is proper and necessary—it "does not bear the sword in vain"; for the kingdom it is improper and self-defeating—"put your sword back in its place." The only sword the church has is the Word of God: "the sword of the Spirit, which is the word of God" (Eph. 6:17). This means that the Christian must operate on *both* levels: one level calls for justice to be done, and the other calls for love to be exercised. The Christian, for example, cannot therefore properly forego military duty because of the kingdom command of nonresistance and love for enemies. Although this is a higher ethic, it does not invalidate the call to service of the state in a just war.[56] If a Christian, however, is involved in military duty, it is important for him in every way possible to embody love for the very enemy he is fighting against. This is not easy, but it is surely the Christian way.

In conclusion, the higher ethic of love in this present sinful world must operate alongside the ethic of justice. The state is God's servant; so is the church. Where the two function harmoniously together, the purposes of God are being justly and lovingly fulfilled.

B. A Higher Loyalty

One of the most memorable scenes in the Old Testament is that of the three Hebrew young men—Shadrach, Meshach, and Abednego—who defied King Nebuchadnezzar of Babylon by disobeying his royal decree to bow down and worship his golden image. After being threatened by death in a fiery furnace, they replied, "If it be so, our God whom we serve is able to deliver us from the burning fiery furnace; and he will deliver us out of your hand, O king. But if not, be it known to you, O king, that we will not serve your gods or worship the golden image which you have set up" (Dan. 3:17–18). Thus, even though Nebuchadnezzar is called God's servant[57] and was placed in power by God,[58] the three Hebrews defied his order. "We will not," they told him, and—as the narrative continues—they were delivered by God from the fiery furnace.

This story brings together seemingly disparate elements: a reign by God's appointment, an imperial or state decree, and defiance of that decree—a defiance that God Himself sustained! How can this be? Despite a ruler's holding office by God's ordination and thus properly calling for submission to his rule and authority, if an ordinance (or ordinances) is contrary to God's will, those under that rule may properly disobey. Such disobedience is not disloyalty to civil authority but, with due respect to it, gives a higher loyalty to God. Earlier in Daniel is the statement that God "removes kings" (2:21), hence no civil authority, despite its God-given position, is as permanent as God's continuing will and command. In time God may remove the unjust governing power.

The classic New Testament example of this is the statement of Peter and the

---

[56]Some would argue that there is no such thing as a just war, especially in light of all the bloodshed in modern warfare. However, in the larger picture of the securing of justice and the protection of liberty, most churches today recognize the principle of the just war. In this matter, however, a pacifist stance is taken by such denominations as the Church of the Brethren, Quakers, and Mennonites, whereas most other Protestant churches, as well as the Roman Catholic Church, adhere to a just war viewpoint.

[57]Recall the earlier quotation from Jeremiah 27:6: "Nebuchadnezzar, the king of Babylon, my servant."

[58]God "sets up kings" (Dan. 2:21).

apostles to the high priest and the members of the Sanhedrin,[59] who had commanded them not to teach further about Jesus: "We must obey God rather than men" (Acts 5:29). This does not mean that the high priest and council were viewed only as "men,"[60] hence with no authority from God, but that God and the gospel had a higher claim on the apostles' lives and actions. Even though threatened with death, the apostles and the young church could not submit to an authority that forbade expression of their ultimate commitment to God.

Jesus, as we recall, had said, "Render . . . to Caesar the things that are Caesar's, and to God the things that are God's."[61] This does not mean giving unqualified obedience to Caesar—it is impossible to give such to both Caesar and God. Rather, it means giving to Caesar all that is his due—"the things that are Caesar's"—but no more. The paying of taxes to Caesar (Rome) was proper, even if Caesar was ruthless and despotic; but if he should begin to demand worship of himself, the church could only disobey. This of course is exactly what was later to happen: the deification of the Roman emperor, the demand for Christians to worship him, and countless numbers of believers being put to death.

Thus Paul in all that he says about the governing authorities as being "instituted by God," and in his statement that "he who resists the authorities resists what God has appointed, and those who resist will incur judgment" (Rom. 13:1–2), does not speak of unqualified submission. Even though Paul calls them "ministers [or servants] of God," he does not accord them more than honor, adding, after speaking about taxes, that the Christian believers should give "respect to whom respect is due, honor to whom honor is due" (vv. 6–7). Respect and honor are entirely appropriate; not adulation and worship. Likewise, Peter, after speaking of submitting—i.e., "submit yourselves"—to king and governors, climaxes with these words: "Fear [or 'reverence'] God, honor the king." To go beyond submission and honor is unwarranted. Thus if kings, governors, and rulers of any kind exceed their God-given limits, their subjects may, even ought to, disobey.

To review thus far: no unqualified obedience to the civil government is called for. Authorities that either demand worship or seek to prevent the proclamation of the the gospel have gone far beyond their God-given limits.

There is also the matter of conscience. We have noted Paul's words about being subject to civil authority "for the sake of conscience" (Rom. 13:5), namely, because rulers as appointed by God represent His external moral order, even as the conscience is a moral judge within. Hence the two mesh. However, if civil authority acts immorally—for example, by engaging in vicious, self-serving warfare and therein drafting citizens for military service—it is right and proper to object "for the sake of conscience" and even to disobey if need be, regardless of the personal consequences. Submitting to government ends at the point where it sanctions or demands activity that is contrary to conscience.[62] "God alone is

[59]The Sanhedrin, though a religious council, operated also as a functionary of the Roman civil government.

[60]Later in Acts Paul shows deference to the high priest in saying, " 'You shall not speak evil of a ruler of your people' " (23:5; quoting Exod. 22:28 LXX).

[61]Recall the earlier discussion of this in regard to taxes.

[62]Conscience is not to be thought of as an invariably sure guide. It needs purification

Lord of the conscience"[63]—never the state.

Beyond "for the sake of conscience," as we have noted, there is also submission to civil authority "for the Lord's sake" (1 Peter 2:13). The Lord enjoins such submission. But also, even as conscience may inwardly protest against unwarranted intrusions, the Lord as head of the church may call for civil disobedience. Surely this was the case when Peter and the Eleven declared, "We must obey God rather than men." The church is also guided by the written Word of God, so that if government authority requires activity contrary to what the Scriptures prescribe, the church may protest and disobey. Martin Luther's famous words of defiance—"Here I stand, I can do no other, God help me"—spoken before Roman Catholic Church officials and the Roman emperor, were based on his statement "My conscience is bound by the Word of God." This was a case of both conscience and Scripture calling for a higher loyalty than to any earthly powers. Ultimately, it is a matter of loyalty to the Lord Himself.

A cautionary word: Christians ought not to expect a perfect civil government on this earth. They must always recognize that the state, however constituted, basically represents order (against anarchy and chaos), and that as citizens of that state their first duty is submission, payment of taxes, and the like. Civil disobedience, accordingly, should occur only in situations where there is a clear conflict between the state's demands or laws and the church's higher loyalty to God. Even if conflict ensues, the first response should be to intercede for those in authority rather than to disobey them, and then to work for changes in the law rather than flagrantly to break it. Only at the extreme point where the state is clearly disregarding God's law ought there to be rebellious action. But, to repeat, since there is no perfect civil government, Christians should exercise patience before defying their government's laws and ordinances.

Still there remains a higher loyalty. This is particularly the case if the civil government increasingly degenerates from its true function as a servant of God. The same Roman government that Paul speaks of as "God's servant to do . . . good" may even become so dominated by evil forces that it becomes the tool of Satan. The "beast" in Revelation 13 represents political power that blasphemes God and wars against Christians (see vv. 6–7). The same Roman government instituted "to do good" now is totally determined to do evil. Romans 13 and Revelation 13 are not too far apart! If and when the state takes on Revelation 13 proportions, there can be no doubt that Christians owe a higher loyalty to God.

V. CHRIST OVER ALL

Finally, it is important to recognize that Christ is over both the church and the civil government. I have already spoken of how both church and state are under the rule of God.[64] Now let us observe this from the aspect of Christ's lordship over all.[65]

This means, first, that Christ is Lord *over all earthly kingdoms and powers.* According to Paul, Christ is "the head

---

through "the blood of Christ" (see Heb. 9:14). However, conscience exists in all people (recall Rom. 2:15); but in the Christian, whose conscience has been purified, it is much more trustworthy.

[63]The opening words in the Westminster Confession of Faith, chapter 20.2.

[64]Recall section I, "The Two Spheres," pages 265–67.

[65]In chapter 5, regarding the government of the church, I dealt with Christ's lordship over the church, pages 219–20.

of all rule and authority" (Col. 2:10).[66] In the Book of Revelation are the striking words that Christ is "the ruler of the kings of the earth" (1:5 NIV). Hence all earthly governing authorities are under the lordship of Christ.

This does not mean, of course, that earthly authorities recognize Christ's lordship; they usually do not. We could say, therefore, that the state generally is the realm of Christ's *unacknowledged* lordship, even as the church is the realm of His *acknowledged* lordship. The church is privy to the secret of a lordship that is much larger than over itself, namely, a lordship that is over all the nations. This means, for example, that when the church proclaims the gospel to the nations, it is not as if the church is, so to speak, taking Christ to them. *He is already there!* The message is simply: Acknowledge Him, accept Him, receive Him, as your own true Lord. Let go of your idols, open your eyes, "do homage to the Son"[67]—for He is Lord even now.

Second, the lordship of Christ over kings and nations is *the result of His death and resurrection.*[68] In Ephesians Paul declares that God "raised him [Christ] from the dead . . . far above all rule and authority and power and dominion . . . and he has put all things under his feet and has made him head over all things" (1:20–22). All the kingdoms of earth had been under the control of Satan,[69] but now Christ by His death, resurrection, and exaltation has won a victory over Satan, so that the control is now ultimately in Christ's hands. This means that, despite the continuance, even increase, of evil[70] in the nations, Christ overrules whatever Satan may try to accomplish.

Here we may recall the words of the resurrected Lord: "All authority in heaven and on earth has been given to me" (Matt. 28:18). The authority "on earth" surely includes all the nations and governments of mankind. In the Book of Revelation, Christ the Lamb is depicted as having "the scroll" (5:8) of history in His hand. He is the One whose "blood . . . purchased men for God from every tribe and language and people and nation" (v. 9 NIV). Later, as the Lamb opens the seals of the scroll (6:1), the future unfolds to the final day of wrath and destruction (vv. 2–17). Thus the crucified, risen, and exalted Lord, "the ruler of the kings of the earth" (1:5)—hence over all governing authorities—is the Lord of history! He is the Lord over all that happens, even to the end.

Third, the lordship of Christ over all earthly authorities is *for the church.* Paul's words in Ephesians 1 continue: "He [God] has made him the head over all things for the church, which is his body, the fulness of him who fills all in all" (vv. 22–23). Christ's headship over

[66]"All rule and authority" may also refer to angelic authorities. Colossians 2:15 declares that Christ "disarmed the principalities and the powers" at the Cross. Nonetheless, "all" suggests authorities not only in heaven but also on earth.

[67]The messianic Psalm 2 declares, "Now therefore, O kings, show discernment, Take warning, O judges [or 'rulers'] of the earth. Worship the Lord with reverence, And rejoice with trembling, Do homage to [or 'kiss'] the Son" (vv. 10–12 NASB). (The RSV reads "kiss his feet," a less likely translation.)

[68]Of course, the preincarnate Christ, as second person of the Trinity and fully God, essentially rules over all.

[69]Recall in the temptation of Jesus that Satan "showed him all the kingdoms of the world and the glory of them; and he said to him, 'All these I will give you, if you will fall down and worship me' " (Matt. 4:8–9). Jesus did not dispute Satan's claim; rather, He proceeded step by step to overthrow his power and authority.

[70]See "The Increase of Evil," pages 326–27.

all powers, established through His victory on the cross, is directed to the church. Christ has the authorities in heaven and on earth in His control so that no matter what they do, the church will prevail. The state may even seek to destroy the church, but it cannot possibly succeed. Moreover, since Christ "fills all in all," and the church is His "fulness," His *plērōma*,[71] then all earthly authorities will one day affirm the triumph of Christ's church and kingdom.

We should not, however, expect a final merger of the nations with the church into some kind of theocracy. Earthly rulers and authorities, while under Christ, have their God-given role of restraining wrongdoers and establishing justice in a sinful world. Since there will be continuing evil to the very end of this age, the task of civil government remains. While the state should support the church, indeed all religious expressions, its business is different from that of worshiping God, upbuilding believers in faith and love, and carrying the gospel to all people. The urgent matter for civil government is to do its own job faithfully and well.

[71]The Greek word for "fulness" is *plērōma*; "sum total, fulness, even (super) abundance" (BAGD).

Part Two

LAST THINGS

8

The Kingdom of God

BACKGROUND: THE PATTERN OF HISTORY

Christian faith affirms that all of history moves to a definite end or goal. History is by no mean a series of endless cycles but moves ever to a definite climax. Christian faith is time-conscious and end-conscious. While it looks backward to many decisive events, there is also the forward look to "how it will all come out." Thus a pattern in history is in the process of being fulfilled.

This movement in history may be noted first in relation to creation and consummation. The whole of history moves forward between these two poles.

In the language of Scripture the movement is from the creation of "the heavens and the earth" "in the beginning" (Gen. 1:1) to "a new heaven and a new earth" (Rev. 21:1). Even as the first two chapters in the Bible (Gen. 1 and 2) depict the original creation, so the last two chapters (Rev. 21 and 22) portray the future consummation. Everything else occurs in between—the fall of man, salvation through Jesus Christ, the destruction of evil, and the triumph of righteousness. But the movement forward is unmistakable.

A transition has taken place in that Christians are no longer living B.C.—"before Christ"— spiritually but are now living A.D.—"in the year of our Lord." There will not be another radical shift into some kind of post-A.D. era. What believers look forward to is the consummation of Christ's lordship.[1]

History's movement may be represented under the caption of "The Kingdom of God." This term refers to God's rule or reign—His kingship, His sovereignty. On the one hand, it is *the great present fact of history*: "Say among the

---

[1]We may diagram the pattern of history in this way:

The Kingdom of God

Creation ______________ Christ ______________ Consummation

B.C. A.D.

nations, 'The LORD reigns!'" (Ps. 96:10). It is *everlasting*: "Thy kingdom is an everlasting kingdom, and thy dominion endures throughout all generations" (Ps. 145:13). It is *universal*: "The LORD has established his throne in the heavens, and his kingdom rules over all" (Ps. 103:19). Although human history might seem to evidence otherwise, the kingdom of God is supreme. On the other hand, the kingdom of God is *to be established*. It is God's intention that His rule become effective among people and nations. Thus Jesus taught His disciples to pray, "Our Father who art in heaven. . . . Thy kingdom come, Thy will be done. . ." (Matt. 6:9–10).

We may now view the kingdom of God in terms of preparation, establishment, and completion.[2]

I. PREPARATION

Although the expression "the kingdom of God" is not directly used in the Old Testament, Israel was clearly a people called in a special way to live under the rule of God: to acknowledge His kingship, His reign, His commandments. E.g., "The LORD became king in Jeshurun, when the heads of the people were gathered, all the tribes of Israel together" (Deut. 33:5). Again, "I am the LORD, your Holy One, the Creator of Israel, your King" (Isa. 43:15). Israel, accordingly, was a theocratic nation, first without human kings, then with kings, but in every situation expected to acknowledge God's ultimate kingship and reign.

Indeed Israel was called by God to be a "kingdom of priests and a holy nation"—in that sense to be the kingdom of God—if the people would truly serve Him. "If you will obey my voice and keep my covenant, you shall be my own possession among all peoples; for all the earth is mine, and you shall be to me a kingdom of priests and a holy nation" (Exod. 19:5–6). Israel, though under God's sovereignty, was not as such His kingdom but would become so if the people obeyed His voice and kept His commandments. Over and over again in the Old Testament God's call to obedience rang out through prophets, priests, and kings. Truly, the general establishment of God's rule, His kingship, was *the* great concern. But it was to no avail. Israel's heart was not right; their will was stubborn. Israel only rebelled all the more. The one hope was an inward renewal: God's law written on mind and heart with a corresponding new orientation of the will.

The Old Testament began to point forward to the coming of a king, a Messiah, who would enable God's rule to be established. So did Isaiah declare prophetically: "For to us a child is born, to us a son is given; and the government will be upon his shoulder. . . . Of the increase of his government and of peace there will be no end, upon the throne of David, and over his kingdom, to establish it, and to uphold it with justice and with righteousness from this time forth and for evermore" (Isa. 9:6–7). By the end of the Old Testament era, such a One had not yet been born—a Messiah to establish God's kingdom so that true justice and righteousness will evermore abound.

[2]The previous diagram may now be filled out:

The Kingdom of God

	Preparation		*Establishment*		*Completion*	
Creation	______		Christ	______		Consummation
	B.C.				A.D.	

Thus the Old Testament was a time of preparation and hope.[3] The kingdom had not yet come, nor could it come until a radical change occurred in human nature. This change must be connected with the coming of the promised Messiah who would reign over a kingdom of people of transformed lives.

II. ESTABLISHMENT

One of the first declarations in the New Testament was the angel's to Mary that THE child was at last to be born: "You shall call his name Jesus . . . the Son of the Most High; and the Lord God will give to him the throne of his father David, and he will reign over the house of Jacob forever; and of his kingdom there will be no end" (Luke 1:31–33). The messianic king was to be named Jesus—He would also be the Son of God! At last the kingdom was to be established—and forever! But—and this is important to emphasize—the King would also be Savior! For when the child was born, he was given the name Jesus—"Jehovah saves." Moreover, an angel of the Lord announced to some shepherds: "Behold, I bring you good news of a great joy which will be for[4] all the people; for to you is born this day in the city of David a Savior, who is Christ the Lord" (Luke 2:10–11).

The record of that fulfillment begins with the opening declaration of Jesus: "The time is fulfilled, and the kingdom of God is at hand; repent, and believe in the gospel" (Mark 1:15). The promise of long ago was now on the threshold of taking place, and it would come about for those who "repent, and believe in the gospel." (The gospel, of course, is the good news of salvation, even as Jesus Himself is the Savior.) Hence, for those who put their trust in Him and receive His salvation, the kingdom of God will become a reality.[5]

In multiple ways throughout His ensuing ministry, Jesus described the kingdom of God for his hearers. This called for a great shift in their thinking, because, unfortunately, the Jews had come to believe that the kingdom belonged to them as a nation, and that the Messiah—when he came—would overthrow foreign rule and establish Israel's dominion both universally and perpetually. Consequently, Jesus again and again depicted the kingdom in a radically different fashion.

In the first words of the Sermon on the Mount Jesus declared that the kingdom[6] belongs to the "poor [or humble]

---

[3]John Bright writes in his book *The Kingdom of God* that "the hope of Israel was the hope of the coming kingdom of God" (p. 181). See chapters 1 through 4 for a helpful presentation of the Old Testament understanding of the kingdom of God.

[4]Rather than "come to" (in RSV). Note also that the "to you" in the second clause corresponds with the "to us" of Isaiah 9:6.

[5]John Calvin writes concerning Jesus that "by the kingdom of God which he declared to be at hand, he meant forgiveness of sins, salvation, life, and every other blessing which we obtain in Christ" (*Institutes of the Christian Religion*, III.3.19, Beveridge trans.).

[6]Matthew reads "the kingdom of heaven." The parallel in Luke is "the kingdom of God" (6:20). In the Gospel of Matthew "kingdom of heaven" is frequently used as a synonym for "kingdom of God." The expression "the kingdom of heaven" is never found in Mark, Luke, and John whereas it occurs thirty-two times in Matthew. Obviously no distinction should be made—for the Gospels make none—between the two expressions for the kingdom. Incidentally, the Scofield Reference Bible's declaration that the "the kingdom of God is to be distinguished from the kingdom of heaven" (note 1 to Matt. 6:33) is an invalid scriptural distinction. The New Scofield Reference Edition (the same footnote), while now recognizing that "the kingdom of God" is "used in many cases" synonymously with "the kingdom of

in spirit" (Matt. 5:3). No doubt to the shock of all His disciples, He said a little later: "I tell you, unless your righteousness exceeds that of the scribes and Pharisees, you will never enter the kingdom of heaven" (Matt. 5:20). Thereupon Jesus described this higher righteousness in one piercing statement after another—no anger with a brother, no lust, no swearing, and no resistance of evil; also love your enemies, pray in secret, forgive others their trespasses, and on and on. It is clearly a righteousness of the heart, truly an impossible righteousness for sinful human beings. But without it there is no entrance ("you will never enter") into the kingdom of God!

If anyone is going to enter *this* kingdom, something radical must happen within. Indeed, there can be nothing less than a new birth, as impossible as that sounds. On another occasion Jesus said to Nicodemus, a ruler of the Jews: "Truly, truly, I say to you, unless a man is born anew, he cannot see the kingdom of God . . . he cannot enter the kingdom of God" (John 3:3, 5). Then even more bluntly: "You must be born anew" (v. 7). Jew and Gentile alike are placed on the same plane regarding the kingdom; no one has a monopoly. Entrance into and membership in the kingdom are only by a radical new birth: a re-generation.[7]

Sadly, the Jews as a nation rejected Jesus' message—though they had been the very people called to be God's kingdom, and although it was primarily to them that Jesus was now speaking. They viewed His message as a threat to their status and would not repent and believe. Thus Jesus finally could only say, "I tell you that the kingdom of God will be taken away from you and given to a people[8] who will produce its fruit" (Matt. 21:43 NIV). Rejecting His message, the Jewish nation finally crucified Him. Thus any claim to the kingdom was completely relinquished through their perverse action.[9] Yet at the same time, Jesus' very death on the cross opened a way into the kingdom for all people who would believe.

Further, Jesus' death and resurrection overcame the kingdom of Satan, in which all men—Jew and Gentile alike—had been bound. Over against this, the kingdom of Christ was established. Already Jesus had declared that the inbreaking of this kingdom was the breaking of Satan's power: "If it is by the Spirit of God that I cast out demons, then the kingdom of God has come upon you" (Matt. 12:28). As a result of the establishment of the kingdom, believers may now rejoice with the apostle Paul: "He has delivered us from the dominion of darkness and transferred us to the kingdom of his beloved Son, in whom we have redemption, the forgiveness of sins" (Col. 1:13–14).

The kingdom of God, in summary, can no longer be identified with a partic-

heaven," adds that "it is to be distinguished from it in many instances." No instances are given, for the simple reason that there are none.

[7]Geerhardus Vos writes that "the kingdom . . . is constituted by the regenerate; the regenerate alone experience in themselves its power, cultivate its righteousness, enjoy its blessings" (*The Teaching of Jesus Concerning the Kingdom of God and the Church*, 86).

[8]Many other translations read "nation" (so KJV, RSV, NASB, and NEB). The Greek word is from *ethnos*, which may be translated either "nation" or "people" (see BAGD). "People" is preferable in this context because it refers to a people drawn from all nations.

[9]Thus the idea of a postponement of the kingdom for Israel (as in "dispensational" teaching) is totally unwarranted. For dispensational teaching on postponement see, for example, L. S. Chafer, *Systematic Theology*, 4:266–67; C. C. Ryrie, *Dispensationalism Today*, 162–65; and J. F. Walvoord, *The Millennial Kingdom*, 227–30. (Walvoord holds the dispensational view that the church age is a parenthesis between the Old Testament promise of the kingdom to Israel and its fulfillment in a millennium to come.)

ular race or nation. Such an identification belonged to a time of preparation for Old Testament Israel, but Israel as a people never truly measured up. The kingdom of God now belongs to the "poor in spirit," to persons whose righteousness is of the heart—hence to those who have been miraculously "born anew." The kingdom that Jesus established is not a kingdom that derives from, or is a part of, the order of this world. Jesus clearly stated this before Pontius Pilate: "My kingdom is not of this world. . . . My kingdom is not from here"[10] (John 18:36 NASB mg.). In that sense, it comes from above[11] and is a totally new order within human existence.

We need to add quickly that the reality of God's kingdom as being "not of this world" does not mean that it is "other-worldly," that is, having nothing to do with ordinary human affairs. Quite the contrary, it affects *every* relationship both with God and with man. Recall, for example, the words of Jesus in the Sermon on the Mount. Truly God rules over a transformed people who essentially are eager to do His will, a people who are now able to love both Him and their neighbor, a people who yearn to see the whole world living in His kingdom.[12]

This kingdom Jesus established, and all who belong to him are "sons of the kingdom" (Matt. 13:38). We have "received" a kingdom—"let us be grateful for receiving a kingdom that cannot be shaken" (Heb. 12:28).[13] Indeed, through Jesus Christ we have been *"made"* a kingdom, as John writes in the Book of Revelation: He "made us a kingdom, priests to his God and Father." So we may declare with John, "To him be glory and dominion for ever and ever. Amen" (1:6)!

This means that Christ is presently reigning over His people. He *is* Lord! And in a real sense, we reign with Him! Paul speaks of how those who "receive the abundance of grace and the free gift of righteousness reign in life through the one man Jesus Christ" (Rom. 5:17). Satan no longer reigns—he has been cast down—and we have the victory in Christ! This is what it means to be in the kingdom of God.

III. COMPLETION

We now move to the climax, for the day is yet to come when God's kingdom will be consummated.[14] Although the

---

[10]Rather than "from the world." The Greek word is *enteuthen*, literally "from here" or "hence."

[11]Reference was earlier made to the necessity of being "born anew" if one is to enter the kingdom of God. "Born anew" may also—perhaps even preferably—be translated "born from above" (the Greek word is *anōthen*). Thus, correspondingly, both the new birth and the kingdom of God originate from a higher realm.

[12]Pat Robertson writes in his book *The Secret Kingdom* that this kingdom "is the rule of God in the hearts, minds, and wills of people—the state in which the unlimited power and blessing of the unlimited Lord are forthcoming" (p. 48).

[13]C. H. Dodd writes that "to 'receive His kingdom' is to 'enter into life' " (*The Parables of the Kingdom*, 76). Dodd speaks of this as "realized eschatology" (p. 51), or as he says elsewhere, "the age to come has come" (*The Apostolic Preaching and Its Development*, 85). The kingdom is, therefore, a present reality.

[14]George Eldon Ladd in his book *The Presence of the Future* speaks of "the consummation of the kingdom" (the title of chap. 13). In an earlier chapter he writes of "fulfillment without consummation" (the title of chap. 4). These topics closely correspond to the headings of sections II and III in this chapter: "Establishment" and "Completion." The important matter to recognize (as Ladd well does) is that the kingdom is both present and future. (Incidentally, Ladd takes Dodd to task for his view of "realized eschatology" which makes little room for a kingdom also yet to come [see pp. 17–19].) See also Vos, *The*

kingdom has been established among those who have been born "from above," there are many who do not belong. They are still dominated by evil, by worldly passions, by Satan—who for them is still "the god of this world" (2 Cor. 4:4). Hence there remains a kingdom of the world, which has not yet become the kingdom of God.

It is important to note that the kingdom of God continues to grow from its original establishment. Jesus compared it to "a grain of mustard seed . . . the smallest of all seeds, but when it has grown it is the greatest of shrubs" (Matt. 13:31–32), and to "leaven which a woman took and hid in three measures of meal, till it was all leavened" (Matt. 13:33). Here is depicted both the inward and the outward growth of the kingdom. It can refer, on the one hand, to what happens in the life of a person who has entered the kingdom and continues to grow spiritually and, on the other, to the overall growth of the kingdom within the world. The truth of these parables is demonstrated by countless people who have matured in Christian faith and whose lives display the leavening influence of the grace of Jesus Christ. This may also be seen in the present worldwide scope of the kingdom of God, with the number of professing Christians today being the largest in all of history.

Two further matters need to be noted in this progress of the kingdom of God. First, what is genuinely present is largely hidden (as in the three measures of meal); it does not reveal itself to the outward eye. Accordingly, on one occasion when Jesus was asked by certain Pharisees when the kingdom would come, He replied, "The kingdom of God does not come visibly,[15] nor will people say, 'Here it is,' or 'There it is,' because the kingdom of God is within[16] you" (Luke 17:20–21 NIV). Here we find a parallel to the invisible spiritual

Teaching of Jesus Concerning the Kingdom of God and the Church, chapter 4, entitled "The Present and the Future Kingdom." For more on Vos's "realized eschatology," see infra, chap. 9, n. 57.

[15]The Greek phrase is *meta paratērēseōs*, "with observation."

[16]The Greek word is *entos*. The KJV also translates it "within." The RSV has "in the midst of"; NASB, "in your midst"; NEB, "among." *Entos*, however, is usually "inside" or "within" (see Matt. 23:26—"inside [*entos*] of the cup" [the only other NT occurrence of *entos*]; *entos* is also used in the LXX where the only possible English translation is "within" or "in" [see, e.g., Pss. 38 (39):3; 102 (103):1; 108 (109):22]). The other translations suggest that the kingdom of God was in their midst because of Jesus' presence and activity. This is also a possibility (recall Matt. 12:28 supra); however, the context of an invisible coming of the kingdom points more evidently to its spiritual and internal reality. R. C. H. Lenski writes, "It is wholly and altogether a spiritual kingdom. . . . The phrase [*entos hymōn*] does not locate the kingdom but states its character as being something internal and not, like earthly kingdoms, external" (*Interpretation of St. Luke's Gospel*, 882). Incidentally, the idea of "among" or "in the midst of" would be better expressed by the Greek word *mesos* (e.g., John 1:26—"among you [*mesos hymōn*] stands one whom you do not know"). G. R. Beasley-Murray writes that "while it is possible to understand *entos* as 'among,' it must be considered a doubtful interpretation" (*Jesus and the Kingdom of God*, 102). In regard to the translation "within you," it is sometimes argued that since Jesus is speaking to the Pharisees, "in the midst of" or "among" you is much more fitting; however, the "you" may be understood in an indefinite or general sense (so, e.g., I. Howard Marshall who, although he translates the word as "among," views "you" as "quite indefinite" [*The Gospel of Luke*, 655]).

essence of the church.[17] The true kingdom of God cannot be specifically pointed to with a "Here it is" or "There it is," because it is a hidden, profoundly internal reality.[18] And the number of its members submits to no human calculation: this is known by God alone.

Second, and this follows, as the kingdom grows through the ages it is admixed with many persons who are not truly of the kingdom; and there is no possible way of uprooting them or sorting them out until the end. In this connection Jesus gave two parables of the kingdom: the parable of the wheat and the tares (or weeds) (Matt. 13:24–30, 36–43) and that of the fishnet drawing in both good and bad fish (Matt. 13:47–50). In the former, "the Son of man" sowed good seed or wheat (the "sons of the kingdom"); then in the same field the enemy, the Devil, sowed tares. But the wheat and the tares become so intermingled that only at "the close[19] of the age" (v. 39) can they be disentangled: "The Son of man will send his angels, and they will gather out of his kingdom all causes of sin and all evildoers. . . . Then the righteous will shine like the sun in the kingdom of their Father" (vv. 41, 43). In the latter parable, the fishnet gathered in every kind of fish; so when it was full, "men drew it ashore and . . . sorted the good into vessels but threw away the bad. So it will be at the close of the age" (vv. 48–49). To summarize, the intermixture of good and evil in this age can be overcome only at the end time when the kingdom stands forth in all its beauty and perfection.

This brings us to the future consummation of the kingdom. At the end of history a voice will cry, "The kingdom of the world has become the kingdom of our Lord and of his Christ, and he shall reign for ever and ever" (Rev. 11:15). At that time Jesus will say to His own, "Come, O blessed of my Father, inherit the kingdom prepared for you from the foundation of the world" (Matt. 25:34). We will eat and drink with our Lord Jesus in the consummated kingdom, for He said at the Last Supper, "I shall not drink again of this fruit of the vine until that day when I drink it new with you in my Father's kingdom" (Matt. 26:29).

This event will happen only when at the end the "kingdom of the world," namely, Satan's kingdom, is utterly destroyed. For the apostle Paul says, "Then comes the end, when he delivers the kingdom to God the Father after destroying every rule and every authority and power. For he must reign until he has put all enemies under his feet. The last enemy to be destroyed is death" (1 Cor. 15:24–26).

Then comes the glorious climax: "When all things are subjected to him, then the Son himself will also be subjected to him who put all things under him, that God may be everything to every one" (v. 28)![20] Such a consummation transcends our most vivid and joyous imagination. But truly it awaits all those who belong to His eternal kingdom.

[17]See the prior discussion of this on page 21. Vos writes that "Jesus plainly leads us to identify the invisible church and the kingdom. It is impossible to be in the one without being in the other" (*The Teaching of Jesus Concerning the Kingdom of God and the Church*, 86). A. H. Strong writes similarly that "the church is identical with the spiritual kingdom of God" (*Systematic Theology*, 887).

[18]Paul writes that "the kingdom of God does not mean food and drink but righteousness and peace and joy in the Holy Spirit" (Rom. 14:17). This description fits the picture of the kingdom as an internal, spiritual reality.

[19]The Greek word is *synteleia*. It may also be translated "completion," "end," or "consummation" (BAGD).

[20]Or "all in all," the Greek phrase is *panta en pasin*.

9

The Return of Jesus Christ

The great event at the close of the age is the return of Jesus Christ. This is the crown of history. All things move to the coming day of Jesus Christ the Lord. It has been computed that 318 verses[1] in the New Testament refer to His return,[2] and many of the great creeds and confessions of Christendom include this event. For example, the Apostles' Creed at a point of climax declares, "From thence [heaven] he shall come to judge the quick and the dead." Without the return of Christ, history would be incomplete. With His return all things reach their final destination.

I. THE CHRISTIAN ATTITUDE

The Christian attitude is essentially that of hope: the hope of Christ's return. Paul speaks of "awaiting our blessed hope, the appearing of the glory of our great God and Savior Jesus Christ" (Titus 2:13). Peter writes about this hope: "Set your hope fully upon the grace that is coming to you at the revelation of Jesus Christ" (1 Peter 1:13). Hoping is the Christian's forward look; it is not a mere wishful or uncertain thinking[3] but focuses on the sure return of Christ.

A. Eager Waiting

The note of eager waiting belongs to the Christian hope. To be sure, there is waiting,[4] but, according to the New Testament, this waiting is not passive. Rather, it is an eager and active waiting for the return of the Lord.

---

[1]"All but four of the New Testament books refer to it, with a total of 318 verses in which it is set forth within the 216 chapters of the New Testament . . . one-fifth of the Bible is prophecy . . . one-third of the prophecy relates to Christ's return . . . one-twentieth of the New Testament deals with the subject." So writes William M. Arnett in *Basic Christian Doctrines*, 277–78.

[2]The word "return" is not itself actually used (except indirectly in the parable of the pounds [Luke 19:11–27] where the Scripture speaks of a "nobleman" who went "into a far country to receive kingly power [or 'a kingdom'] and then return" [12]\this of course refers to Jesus); however, I believe it is a good word to express Jesus' final coming again. He who was once manifested in the Incarnation *will* return.

[3]In ordinary speech, hope is a *desire* for the future, or something future; for example, "I hope it will come about." Thus it may or may not happen. However, hope in regard to Christ's return is the forward look to an assured occurrence.

[4]Recall Titus 2:13 above.

Paul writes, "Our citizenship is in heaven, from which also we eagerly wait for a Savior, the Lord Jesus Christ" (Phil. 3:20 NASB). We as believers are already spiritually citizens of heaven, where Christ is now, but we yearn to see Him face to face. Accordingly, we eagerly await the return of our Lord.

In one of his letters to the Corinthians, Paul speaks of the church there as "not lacking in any [spiritual] gift." Then he adds immediately, "awaiting eagerly the revelation ['coming' KJV] of our Lord Jesus Christ" (1 Cor. 1:7 NASB). This suggests that the more the spiritual gifts are present and operating in a community of believers, the more there is expectation of the Lord's return. Christ was so present in the spiritual gifts—for example, in word of wisdom and word of knowledge, in gifts of healing and working of miracles, in prophecy and speaking in tongues[5]—that the Corinthians could hardly wait until His full personal revelation occurred. So it continues to be: the spiritual presence of Christ through the gifts (and of course in many other ways), despite all its wonder, is but a foretaste of His return. "Our Lord, come!" (1 Cor. 16:22).[6]

One more Scripture passage on eager waiting is Hebrews 9:28: "Christ, having been offered once to bear the sins of many, will appear a second time, not to deal with sin but to save those who are eagerly waiting for him." The salvation to come will no longer relate to sin but to the fullness of blessing in Christ. The blessings now experienced will be completed when Christ returns. These will surely include salvation from the wrath of God (Paul speaks in 1 Thessalonians 1:10 of Jesus as the One "who delivers us from the wrath to come," a wrath to be poured out on a sinful and disobedient human race), but even more a salvation from all that remains in our lives of sin and death into a perfect fulfillment when Christ returns. Surely our waiting now must be one of eager expectancy!

B. Loving Christ's Appearing

Here is another beautiful New Testament touch: not only eager waiting but loving His appearing. Paul, toward the end of his life and ministry, wrote to Timothy about "the crown of righteousness" to be awarded not only to himself "but also to all who have loved his [Christ's] appearing" (2 Tim. 4:8). To love Christ's appearing is the deep note of eager waiting. This may be illustrated from human relationships. We may have beloved family members away in a far country. Not only do we eagerly await their return, but also upon their arrival we will greet them with a deep embrace of joy and happiness. We love their appearing—how much more the appearing of Christ our Lord and Savior!

C. Exercising Patience

The Christian attitude of eager waiting, loving His appearing, includes the exercise of patience. James, the brother of Jesus, writes, "Be patient . . . brethren, until the coming of the Lord" (James 5:7). It is not always easy to await the return of the Lord; it may seem like an endless delay. Indeed, from where we stand today it has been nearly two thousand years! However, Peter reminds us, "Do not ignore this one fact, beloved, that with the Lord one day is as a thousand years, and a thousand years as one day" (2 Peter 3:8). Moreover, the Lord's seeming delay is not a failure in His promise to

[5]See 1 Corinthians 12:8–10 for a listing of these and other spiritual gifts.

[6]Paul closes this letter to the Corinthians with the Aramaic words, *"Marana tha!"* meaning "Our Lord, come!"

return, but it is His giving time that "all should reach repentance" (v. 9). Our eager desire and love for the Lord's appearing should be tempered by the realization that His timetable is much different from ours and that the Lord Himself is giving more time for people to repent. When He returns, the day of salvation will forever be past; so let our yearning for His return be mixed with compassion now for the lost. "Be patient. . . !"

D. Purifying Ourselves

There is much stress in the New Testament on the importance of self-purification and holiness in awaiting Christ's return.[7] Let us hear a word from John: "Abide in him [Christ], so that when he appears we may have confidence and not shrink from him ['away from Him,' NASB] in shame at his coming. . . . Every one who thus hopes in him purifies himself as he is pure" (1 John 2:28; 3:3). Will we be ready when the Lord returns? Will we be living in such sin that although His arrival is "our blessed hope" (which indeed it is), we will shrink in shame at His presence? The Lord who comes is holy and pure; shall we meet Him in unholiness and impurity of life? To be sure, none of us will be perfect when the Lord returns, but we can make better preparation, as John says, by seeking in every way possible to "purify ourselves as he is pure." Hebrews puts it quite strongly: "Strive for peace with all men, and for the holiness without which no one will see the Lord" (12:14). If we are striving and seeking for holiness and purity of life, we need not shrink in shame at the Lord's appearing. Are you—am I—making ready?

E. Being Watchful

One of the strongest New Testament emphases in regard to the return of Christ is the importance of being watchful. Jesus Himself lays heavy stress on the necessity of watching, being on the alert for His return. In the Gospel of Mark, after Jesus said, "But of that day and hour no one knows,[8] not even the angels in heaven, nor the Son, but only the Father," He adds, "Take heed, watch, for you do not know when the time will come"[9] (13:32–33). Then a few words later Jesus again speaks strongly: "Watch therefore—for you do not know when the master of the house will come, in the evening, or at midnight, or at cockcrow, or in the morning—lest he come suddenly and find you asleep. And what I say to you I say to all: Watch" (vv. 35–37). In the Gospel of Matthew, after making a similar statement (in chap. 24), Jesus reinforces the importance of watchfulness in His parable of the ten virgins. Only five of them had oil for their lamps when the bridegroom suddenly arrived at midnight, and so they were able to go into the marriage feast. At the close of the parable Jesus said, "Watch therefore, for you know neither the day nor the hour" (25:13). In all of these statements watchfulness—alertness, readiness, preparedness—is the truly critical matter.[10]

A further word of Jesus about watchfulness is found in the Book of Revelation. The kings of the earth are being gathered for the Battle of Armageddon when suddenly the scene is interrupted

[7]In addition to the Scriptures in 1 John and Hebrews quoted in this paragraph, see also Philippians 1:10–11; 1 Thessalonians 3:13; 5:23; 1 Timothy 6:14.

[8]This refers to Jesus' earlier words about seeing "the Son of man coming" (Mark 13:26).

[9]In Matthew the parallel to Mark 13:33 is "Watch . . . for you do not know on what day your Lord is coming" (Matt. 24:42).

[10]See also Jesus' words in Luke 12:35–40, which climax with this statement: "You also must be ready; for the Son of man is coming at an hour you do not expect."

by Jesus' declaring, "Behold, I come as a thief. Blessed is he that watcheth, and keepeth his garments, lest he walk naked, and they see his shame" (16:15 KJV).[11] As the time draws very near for the Lord's return, it is all the more important to be on the alert, with "garments"[12] ready at hand. A person who is so waiting is truly blessed by the Lord.

Paul himself echoes many of Jesus' words in writing to the Thessalonians: "You . . . yourselves know perfectly that the day of the Lord so cometh as a thief in the night" (1 Thess. 5:1–2 KJV). Then after describing how that day will catch unbelievers by surprise, with its "sudden destruction," Paul adds, "But ye, brethren, are not in darkness, that that day should overtake you as a thief. Ye are all the children of light, and the children of the day. . . . Therefore let us not sleep, as do others; but let us watch and be sober" (vv. 4–6 KJV). Thereby Paul compares the situation of a world in perilous darkness not expecting the return of the Lord with believers who as "children of light" will not be surprised by that day. Thus, similar to Jesus' frequent injunctions, Paul urges his readers to be always on the watch.

Being watchful suggests alertness at all times. A watchman is one who is alert to his surroundings. It may be that certain signs not recognized by others afford the watchman suggestions or signs of an event to come. So it is with believers; we are to be watchful and alert, seeking to discern the signs of the Lord's coming and being ready whenever He will appear.

F. Exercising Faithfulness

Another important New Testament emphasis is exercising faithfulness. This refers to the importance of being good stewards of what the Master has given us to do, so that whenever He comes He will find us faithfully doing our tasks. In this regard we may call to mind Jesus' parable of the talents. Immediately following His parable of the ten virgins and His warning to all: "Watch therefore, for you know neither the day nor the hour" (Matt. 25:13), Jesus tells about a master who entrusted various talents of money to three servants. After a long time the master returned, and to each of the two who have multiplied their talents he says, "Well done, good and faithful servant; you have been faithful over a little, I will set you over much; enter into the joy of your master" (Matt. 25:21, 23). Accordingly, the ones rewarded at Christ's return will be those who have been faithful stewards of what has been committed to them.

In the similar parable of the pounds Jesus again stresses the importance of faithfulness. A certain nobleman, before going away into a distant country, calls his servants together and entrusts to them ten pounds saying, "Occupy till I come" (Luke 19:13 KJV).[13] When the master returns, he calls the servants to accountability, and to one of them who has multiplied his pound tenfold, the master says, "Well done, good servant! Because you have been faithful in a very little, you shall have authority over ten cities" (v. 17).[14] Faithful stewardship is again the critical matter before the Lord's return.

---

[11]I quote the King James Version because of the word "watcheth" (RSV reads "is aware"; NIV and NASB, "stays awake"). This is a form of the same Greek word *gregoreō* used in the previous quotations from the Gospels.

[12]This is similar to the picture of the virgins having oil ready for trimming their lamps.

[13]The RSV reads "trade with these till I come." The basic idea is to "do business" (so NASB) with the pounds.

[14]Similar words are spoken to another servant who has multiplied his pound fivefold.

This matter of faithfulness must not be neglected. The Lord has given all of us tasks to perform and responsibilities to be fulfilled, and He expects us to faithfully "occupy" until that day when He returns. Indeed, we should be all the more faithful because the Master of our house in His coming will call us to give an account of what we have done. Although He is the loving Savior whom we earnestly desire to see, He is also a stern Lord who will have little toleration for slothfulness. In the parable of the talents one servant who had buried his talent in the ground is addressed by the returned master as a "wicked and slothful servant"[15] (Matt. 25:26) and is then cast into "outer darkness" (v. 30). This is a severe picture, but in light of the coming of the Lord it underscores the urgency of our being active and faithful in what He has given us to do.[16]

It does not matter how seemingly small or great our God-given task is; the returning Lord will require of us faithfulness. Knowing that He will surely return, we should be all the more diligent to be found faithful at His coming.[17] "Occupy till I come" is the Lord's word to all believers.

G. Proclaiming the Gospel

Paul writes to Timothy, "In view of his [Christ's] appearing and his kingdom, I give you this charge: Preach the Word" (2 Tim. 4:1–2 NIV). This injunction to Timothy surely applies to all Christians. We are not only to eagerly await and purify ourselves and, in addition, to be expectant and faithful in our God-given tasks, we are also called upon to proclaim the gospel. In view of Christ's appearing, and while there is yet time and opportunity, we are to bear witness. Paul adds, "Be ready in season and out of season" (v. 2 NASB). Whether or not the situation seems opportune—hence on any and every occasion—we are to be ready to proclaim the word about Jesus.

Here we may recall Acts 1:6–11. The disciples first asked Jesus about a restoration of the kingdom to Israel (v. 6). Jesus replied, "It is not for you to know times or seasons which the Father has fixed by his own authority" (v. 7). He then added, "But you shall receive power when the Holy Spirit has come upon you; and you shall be my witnesses in Jerusalem and in all Judea and Samaria and to the end of the earth" (v. 8). Then, while the disciples were observing, Jesus was taken up into heaven. Afterward two angels spoke: "Men of Galilee, why do you stand looking into heaven? This Jesus, who was taken up from you into heaven, will come in the same way as you saw him go into heaven" (v. 11). This Scripture passage sets such matters as the timing of the coming kingdom and the nature of the Lord's return within the context of the prior urgency of bearing witness to the gospel. We are not to remain gazing into heaven—however eager we may be—but to move forward under the injunction to be a witness to Jesus Christ even to the farthest reaches of the earth.

Now I add a word about the relation of this witness, this proclaiming the gospel, to being faithful in our daily tasks. *Both* are important. As we have observed, Christ calls us to faithful stewardship in our ongoing tasks and responsibilities, but He also calls us to

[15]Similarly, in the parable of the pounds one servant who laid away his pound in a napkin is addressed by the Lord as a "wicked servant" (Luke 19:22).

[16]Earlier I spoke of the need of purifying ourselves in making ready for the return of Christ. This remains necessary even as we now emphasize faithfulness. Actually, it is holiness allied with faithfulness that marks the proper Christian preparation.

[17]This should be our stance whether or not Christ returns in our lifetime. It is the same Lord who will some day call us to render account.

be His witnesses "to the end of the earth." It is as we both discharge our stewardship responsibilities *and* proclaim the Word that we truly fulfill the Lord's intention and make ready for His return.

But surely the climactic activity in prospect of the Lord's return is that of bearing witness to Him. For through our witness, Christ adds people to His kingdom, and as the coming Lord and King He will return to receive all His people to Himself. Surely there can be no greater challenge, no more compelling urgency than that of being the Lord's witnesses until He comes.

II. LANGUAGE OF THE RETURN

A number of terms in the New Testament relate to the return of Christ. It should prove helpful to note the variety of expressions. Both the meaning and use of these terms, as well as their context, can provide insight into this climactic event.

A. *Parousia*—"Arrival," "Presence"

The word *parousia* is most often used today as the technical term for the return of Christ. It is advantageous in some ways to speak simply of "the parousia of Christ," because translation from the Greek is not easy. Usually the English word "coming" is used (as we will note below); however, the Greek word contains the aspects of both arrival and presence. It is a coming that is both a "becoming present" and a "being present" for a shorter or longer period. It is also a coming that is a personal arrival and presence. The word *parousia*, incidentally, is used in the New Testament not only in relation to Christ but also in reference to others: e.g., "the coming of Titus" (2 Cor. 7:6), "my [Paul's] coming to you again" (Phil. 1:26), "my [Paul's] presence" (Phil. 2:12), also "the coming of the lawless one by the activity of Satan" (2 Thess. 2:9). Despite the wide range of uses and persons mentioned, the word *parousia* in relation to Christ always refers to His *future* coming and presence. Let us now observe some of the relevant Scripture passages.

In the four Gospels the only place where the word *parousia* occurs is in Matthew 24. Here it is used four times in connection with the return of Christ. The first is found in the question of the disciples to Jesus: "Tell us, when will this[18] be, and what will be the sign of your coming [*parousia*] and of the close of the age?" (v. 3). The first part of the question, "when will this be," refers to the future destruction of the temple, which Jesus had just declared (vv. 1–2). The second part relates to the coming of Christ, the *parousia*, and the close, or end, of the age.[19] In the discourse that follows, Jesus says concerning His *parousia*: "As the lightning comes from the east and shines as far as the west, so will be the coming [*parousia*] of the Son of man" (v. 27); "as were the days of Noah, so will be the coming [*parousia*] of the Son of man" (v. 37); and "they did not know until the flood came and swept them all away, so will be the coming [*parousia*] of the Son of man" (v. 39).

In the accounts of Mark 13 and Luke 21, which also begin with the question about the destruction of the temple and cover many of the same sayings as Matthew 24, there is no use of the term

---

[18]Or "these things" as in NASB. The Greek word is *tauta*, a plural. Since the antecedent of the pronoun is a singular subject, namely, the fact that "there will not be left here one stone upon another, that will not be thrown down" (v. 2), the RSV (also NIV, NEB) translation above seems grammatically proper in English.

[19]The Greek word is *aiōnos*. "Age" is preferable to "world" (the latter being the KJV translation).

parousia. The question in Mark and Luke begins as in Matthew: "When will this be. . ." (Mark 13:4; Luke 21:7), but does not mention the *parousia* of Christ. Rather, Mark continues, "And what will be the sign when these things are all to be accomplished?" Luke continues, "And what will be the sign when this is about to take place?" "These things" (Mark) and "this" (Luke) specifically refer to the destruction of the temple. We may infer, however, that the matter of the *parousia* is implied, since it is included in the question in Matthew's Gospel. Nonetheless, the term *parousia* is used only in Matthew.

Turning to the Epistles, we discover that the word *parousia* is used twelve times in relation to Christ.[20] It is not to be found in the Book of Revelation. A careful reading of the verses in the Epistles shows that all references, except one (2 Thess. 2:8), relate in some way to the situation of believers. For example, "Christ the first fruits [of all who are to be 'made alive'], then at his coming those who belong to Christ" (1 Cor. 15:23); "that he may establish your hearts unblamable in holiness . . . at the coming of our Lord Jesus" (1 Thess. 3:13); "concerning the coming of our Lord Jesus Christ and our assembling to meet him" (2 Thess. 2:1); "establish your hearts, for the coming of the Lord is at hand" (James 5:8); "abide in him, so that . . . we may have confidence and not shrink from him in shame at his coming" (1 John 2:28). The reference mentioned as an exception (2 Thess. 2:8) concerns the situation of "the lawless one" whom "the Lord Jesus will overthrow with the breath of his mouth and destroy by the splendor of his coming" (NIV). In conclusion, the coming (*parousia*), which relates primarily and centrally to the expectation and future of believers, will *also* be the destruction of the man of lawlessness. The focus of *parousia* remains, however, on believers—as the multiplicity of passages above clearly testify.

B. *Phanerōsis*—"Manifestation"

Another term used for the return of Jesus Christ is *phanerōsis*, which is best translated "manifestation." Actually only the verbal form, *phaneroō*, is used in relation to the return of Christ, and the verb in each of its occurrences is in the passive voice.[21]

Paul writes that "when Christ, who is our life, is manifested, then you too will be manifested with him in glory" (Col. 3:4 NEB). It is significant that believers will be manifested with Christ at the same time.[22] Peter writes, "When the chief Shepherd is manifested you will obtain the unfading crown of glory" (1 Peter 5:4). Finally, John writes, "Abide in him, so that when he is manifested[23] we may have confidence and not shrink in shame at his coming. . . . We know that when he is manifested we shall be like him" (1 John 2:28; 3:2).

In all of these cases the manifestation is in relation to the future of believers.

---

[20]1 Corinthians 15:23; 1 Thessalonians 2:19, 3:13, 4:15, 5:23; 2 Thessalonians 2:1, 8; James 5:7, 8; 2 Peter 1:16, 3:4; 1 John 2:28.

[21]Colossians 3:4; 1 Peter 5:4; 1 John 2:28; 3:2. The translation frequently is "appears." However, that translation fails to convey the passive voice; moreover, the basic meaning of *phaneroō* is "to make manifest" (Thayer), or "to make known" (BAGD).

[22]This will be discussed later.

[23]In these two verses I substitute "manifested" for "appears" (as in the RSV and most other modern translations). The Greek word is *phanerōthē*, a passive voice (as in the previously quoted words of Paul and Peter), so that "is manifested" again seems to be the preferable translation. The American Standard Version (ASV) of 1901 reads "manifested."

C. *Epiphaneia*—"Appearance"

In the Pastoral Epistles a term used by Paul for Christ's return is *epiphaneia*. The usual translation is "appearance"; however, the Greek word also contains the idea of brightness, radiance, even splendor. Literally, *epiphaneia* means "shining upon." From *epiphaneia* the English word "epiphany" is derived.

We have earlier noted that at the return of Jesus the "lawless one" will be destroyed by "the splendor[24] of his [Christ's] coming" (2 Thess. 2:8 NIV). So overwhelmingly bright and radiant will be the appearance of Christ that, like fire, it will consume and even annihilate this final concentration of evil.[25] Such will be the *epiphaneia* of Christ's presence. As far as believers are concerned, the same *epiphaneia* will be an appearance of glory—"the glorious appearing[26] of our great God and Savior, Jesus Christ" (Titus 2:13 NIV). In preparation for this we are "to say 'No' to ungodliness and worldly passions, and to live self-controlled, upright and godly lives in this present age, while we wait for the blessed hope—the glorious appearing. . . " (Titus 2:12–13 NIV). In other words, although the Christian should have no fear of harm at this glorious epiphany, there is need for spiritual preparation. In this same connection are these words of Paul to Timothy: "I charge you to keep the commandment unstained and free from reproach until the appearing of our Lord Jesus Christ" (1 Tim. 6:14). This again is a call to personal godliness in light of Christ's coming *epiphaneia*. Further, Paul exhorts Timothy that a sense of this coming should also affect his whole ministry: "I charge you in the presence of God and of Christ Jesus who is to judge the living and the dead, and by his appearing and his kingdom: preach the word, be urgent in season and out of season . . . be unfailing in patience and in teaching" (2 Tim. 4:1–2). The urgency of proclaiming the truth in Christ is all the more heightened by the sense of His coming epiphany.

A further note, added by Paul to Timothy, tenderly refers to loving Christ's appearing: "Henceforth there is laid up for me the crown of righteousness, which the Lord, the righteous judge, will award to me on that Day, and not only to me but also to all who have loved his appearing" (2 Tim. 4:8). To love Christ's *epiphaneia* greatly deepens the expectancy of the coming event.

Truly the glorious appearance of Christ at His return is our "blessed hope." For His coming will mark the ultimate destruction of all evil and the fulfillment of the long awaited coming of Christ in His kingdom.

D. *Apokalypsis*—"Revelation"

The Greek word *apokalypsis* is also frequently used in relation to the return of Christ. The word is usually translated "revelation." It means literally "an uncovering,"[27] thus a bringing to light what has not before been known or perceived. Hence, for example, the Book of Revelation, or the Apocalypse, is a book containing many things long hidden but now being disclosed. Apoca-

[24]The RSV reads "his appearing"; NASB, "the appearance"; NEB, "radiance"; KJV, "brightness." The latter two, as well as NIV "splendor" above, much better capture the meaning of *epiphaneia*.

[25]The NEB vividly translates this as "that wicked man whom the Lord Jesus will destroy with the breath of his mouth, and annihilate by the radiance of his coming."

[26]NEB translates the word as "splendour."

[27]From the Greek preposition *apo*, signifying "away from," "off," and the verb *kalyptein*, "to cover."

lyptic literature is a type of religious writing that purports to reveal secret information about God and His kingdom.[28] Specifically, in the New Testament, *apokalypsis* refers to the revelation centering in Christ.

In relation to Christ's return we may note several passages that contain this term. The first is found in the words of Jesus Himself. He speaks of the time of Noah when the flood destroyed an unsuspecting, unprepared people and of the time of Lot when fire and brimstone did the same. Then He adds, "So will it be on the day when the Son of man is revealed" (Luke 17:30). Paul uses the word *apokalypsis* twice in his letters. First, in writing to the Corinthians he says to them, "You are not lacking in any gift, awaiting eagerly the revelation of our Lord Jesus Christ, who shall also confirm you to the end, blameless in the day of our Lord Jesus Christ" (1 Cor. 1:7–8 NASB). Second, in writing to the Thessalonians Paul says, "It is only just for God to repay with affliction those who afflict you, and to give relief to you who are afflicted and to us as well when the Lord Jesus shall be revealed[29] from heaven with His mighty angels in flaming fire, dealing out retribution . . . the penalty of eternal destruction . . . [and] to be glorified in His saints on that day, and to be marveled at among all who have believed" (2 Thess. 1:6–10 NASB). Peter refers three times to this coming *apokalypsis*: first, he speaks of various sufferings so that the believers' "faith, more precious than gold . . . may redound to praise and glory and honor at the revelation of Jesus Christ" (1 Peter 1:7); again, "Gird up your minds, be sober, set your hope fully upon the grace that is coming to you at the revelation of Jesus Christ" (1 Peter 1:13); and finally, "To the degree that you share the sufferings of Christ, keep on rejoicing; so that also at the revelation of His glory, you may rejoice with exultation" (1 Peter 4:13 NASB).

Based on the Scripture passages quoted and the use of the word *apokalypsis*, several observations may be made. First, the very word itself conveys a note of suddenness and unexpectedness; second, it is a disclosure of a terrifying kind of retribution on the wicked; and third, it is the occasion when the saints richly glorify Christ, receive abounding grace, and rejoice with great joy.

The *apokalypsis*, therefore, is the day when all things will at last be fully revealed.[30]

E. *Hēmera*—"Day"

The term that is used quite often in relation to the return of Christ is *hēmera*, always translated "day." The word "day" in this connection does not so much refer to the natural day (of twelve or twenty-four hours) but to the period of Christ's return. In one sense it is "the last day" of the present age, but since it represents the inauguration of the age to come, the word "day" transcends ordinary terminology.

The use of "day" in relation to the return of Christ varies considerably. Scriptures that specifically connect Christ with "day" are found in Paul's letters to the Corinthians and Philip-

[28] *The Apocalypse of Baruch*, for example, was written after the fall of Jerusalem in A.D. 70 to explain why tragedy had befallen God's people.

[29] Literally, "at the revelation [*apokalypsis*] of the Lord Jesus."

[30] Thus the final book of the Bible is well named as the Revelation, or the Apocalypse. Significantly the book begins with the words *Apokalypsis Iēsou Christou*: "[the] Revelation of Jesus Christ." The word *apokalypsis* never appears again in the book, because the whole essentially is a book of revelation. The opening of the seals (chap. 6 and following) signifies an "unsealing," an "uncovering," of what is hidden and thus one continuing revelation after another.

pians: "the day of our Lord Jesus Christ" (1 Cor. 1:8); "the day of the Lord Jesus" (1 Cor. 5:5; 2 Cor. 1:14); "the day of Jesus Christ" (Phil. 1:6); and "the day of Christ" (Phil. 1:10; 2:16). In these verses, Paul is referring particularly to the believers' future blessedness. For example, "[God] . . . will sustain you to the end, guiltless in the day of our Lord Jesus Christ" (1 Cor. 1:8) and "He who began a good work in you will bring it to completion at the day of Jesus Christ" (Phil. 1:6).

Often in the New Testament the expression omits any direct reference to Christ and is simply "that day" (Matt. 24:36; Mark 13:32; 1 Thess. 5:4; 2 Thess. 1:10, 2:3; 2 Tim. 1:12, 18; 4:8); "what day" (Matt. 24:42); "a day" (Matt. 24:50); "the day" (Matt. 25:13); "his day" (Luke 17:24). Finally, there are references to "the day of the Lord" (1 Thess. 5:2; 2 Thess. 2:2; 2 Peter 3:10); "the day of God" (2 Peter 3:12); and "the great day of God the Almighty" (Rev. 16:14).

The indirect references—"that day," "a day," etc.—in the Gospels are invariably Jesus' own words about His future return. For example, "But of that day and hour no one knows. . ." (Matt. 24:36; Mark 13:32), and "Watch . . . for you do not know on what day your Lord is coming" (Matt. 24:42). It is a day that will be unknown ahead of time to anyone. Although it will catch an unwatchful world by complete surprise (see the continuation of Matt. 24:36), believers are told to be constantly on the alert for it. In Paul's letters where "that day" is used, similar motifs are found. He writes to believers, "You are not in darkness . . . for that day to surprise you like a thief" (1 Thess. 5:4). Also, Christ will come "on that day to be glorified in his saints" (2 Thess. 1:10), and "May the Lord grant him to find mercy from the Lord on that day" (2 Tim. 1:18).

Similar are the "day of the Lord" expressions. For an unsuspecting world "the day of the Lord will come like a thief in the night. . . . Sudden destruction will come." However (as we have previously noted), Paul says, "You are not in darkness . . . for that day to surprise you like a thief" (1 Thess. 5:2–4). Again, "[Do not] be quickly shaken . . . to the effect that the day of the Lord has come" (2 Thess. 2:2). Paul writes these words in relation to "the coming [*parousia*] of our Lord Jesus Christ and our assembling to meet him" (v. 1) and then describes a coming apostasy, in which "the man of lawlessness" will appear before that day will come (vv. 3–8). The day of the Lord is both the day of our "assembling to meet him" and the day when the lawless one will be destroyed by the "splendor" (*epiphaneia*) of His coming (*parousia*).

It is apparent from the above quotations (and others could be added) that "the day"—whatever the terminology used—has a double aspect. It is both the day of believers' future blessedness and a fearful day for all the wicked; it is the day that will take the world by surprise, but believers are to be on the alert, ever watching; it is the longed-for day of our being gathered to meet Him even as it is the day of destruction upon the incarnation of evil.[31]

---

[31]Clearly these are not two separate days. According to the *Scofield Study Bible*, there is first "the day of Christ" which "in the N.T. is described as relating to the reward and blessing of the Church at the rapture in contrast with the expression 'the day of the Lord' . . . which is related to judgment upon unbelieving Jews and Gentiles, and blessing on millennial saints" (note 1 to 1 Cor. 1:8). According to this reckoning, since "the rapture" of the church is viewed as occurring prior to the period of "the great tribulation" (see pages 360–70 for a discussion of "pretribulationism") and the return of Christ in judgment as occurring after the Tribulation, the two "days" are distinct and separated by a number of

Climactically, it is "the great day of God the Almighty" (Rev. 16:14). It will be a day of fearsome destruction upon the world—even "Armageddon" (v. 16). But on the other hand the message to believers is "Lo, I am coming like a thief! Blessed is he who is awake . . . " (v. 15). It is even "the day of God" (2 Peter 3:12) in which "the heavens will be kindled and dissolved." But believers should be prepared with "lives of holiness and godliness, waiting for and hastening the coming of the day," because the glorious result is a "new heavens and a new earth in which righteousness dwells" (vv. 11–13). The day of God, the day of the Lord—whatever the name—will be that great day when the old will completely pass away and the new will gloriously come.

F. *Erchomai*—"Coming"

Finally we turn to the verb *erchomai*, which is often used to refer to the return of Christ. For example, the Book of Revelation, in the next to the last verse, records the Lord Jesus saying: "Surely, I am coming [*erchomai*] soon," and the ringing response of the faithful: "Amen. Come [*erchou*], Lord Jesus!" (22:20).

In the Gospel of Matthew we find these words of Jesus: "For the Son of man is to come with his angels in the glory of his Father, and then he will repay every man for what he has done" (16:27). Later Jesus says, "All the tribes of the earth will mourn, and they will see the Son of man coming on the clouds of heaven with power and great glory" (Matt. 24:30). In the next chapter various pictures of His coming are given—the bridegroom arriving at midnight, a man coming back after a long journey to settle accounts with his servants, and the Son of man coming to judge all nations ("When the Son of man comes in his glory" [25:31]). In the Gospel of Luke Jesus states, "Blessed are those servants whom the master finds awake when he comes. . . . He will come and serve them. If he comes in the second watch, or in the third, and finds them so, blessed are those servants. . . . The Son of man is coming at an hour you do not expect" (12:37–38, 40). In a later passage Jesus asks rhetorically, "When the Son of man comes, will he find faith on earth?" (18:8). According to the Gospel of Mark, Jesus declares, "Whoever is ashamed of me and of my words in this adulterous and sinful generation, of him will the Son of man also be ashamed, when he comes in the glory of his Father with the holy angels" (8:38). In the Gospel of John Jesus speaks to Peter concerning John's future: "If it is my will that he remain until I come, what is that to you?" (21:22). In his first letter to the Corinthians Paul declares concerning the Lord's Supper: "You proclaim the Lord's death until he comes" (11:26).

All of the above quotations are examples of the use of some form of *erchomai* in relation to the Lord's return. Many additional passages could be quoted. One other verse in the Book of Revelation may be cited: "Look, he is coming with the clouds, and every eye will see him, even those who pierced him; and all the peoples[32] of the earth will mourn because of him" (1:7 NIV).

---

years. However, in response to such a view, it is apparent, from the Scriptures I have cited, that there is no legitimate way of distinguishing temporally between "the day of Christ" and "the day of the Lord." It is the same "day" containing both blessing and judgment, and not two different "days." (For a helpful discussion of this matter see George Eldon Ladd, *The Blessed Hope*, 92–94, in which he speaks of "the identity of the day of the Lord and of the day of Christ.")

[32]Instead of "tribes" (as in RSV and NEB). The Greek word is *phylai* and can mean either

It is apparent from these quotations that the return of Jesus is the climactic event in the New Testament: "Come, Lord Jesus!"[33] His coming will be the occasion for judging the nations, for recompense and reward to all people. The "peoples of the earth" will mourn because the day of penitence will be past. Those who have been ashamed of Christ will find Christ ashamed of them. Now those who belong to Christ are called to render faithful stewardship and always be on the alert, for no one knows the hour of His return. His coming for those who are wakeful will be a special blessing: "He will come and serve them" (Luke 12:37). There is also the warning against apostasy, a lack of faith on the earth at His return. The future coming of the Lord has many aspects.

Those who sincerely belong to Christ continue to look for His coming. Indeed, each celebration of the Lord's Supper is not only a commemoration of Christ's death, but also a looking forward "until he comes" (1 Cor. 11:26).[34] There is the yearning to behold Him face to face and to know His glorious presence. This is the primary thing. But also it is the deep desire to see evil at last totally removed and righteousness forever prevail.

In summary, from this study of the various words used for the return of Christ, certain conclusions may be drawn.

1. The variety of terms—*parousia, phanerōsis, epiphaneia, apokalypsis, hēmera*, and *erchomai*—exhibits the richness and fullness of Christ's return. These many terms, signifying "arrival," "manifestation," "appearance," "revelation," "day," and "coming," convey something of the wealth of meaning involved in the event. By looking at these terms one at a time, we behold increasingly the glory of this climactic event in history.

2. The focus of the first two terms, *parousia* and *phanerōsis*, is on Christian believers. *Parousia*—the technical term most often used now—refers in most cases to Christ's return in relation to believers. *Phanerōsis*, or "manifestation," is invariably used of Christ's return in relation to Christians. *Epiphaneia* and *apokalypsis* are used in relation to both believers and nonbelievers. Christ's "epiphany" and "apocalypse" is the believer's blessed hope and is eagerly to be awaited. But for unbelievers these terms signify the "brightness" of destroying fire and the revelation of retribution upon all evil. *Erchomai* is likewise used in reference both to blessing and to judgment.

3. *Hēmera*, or "day," is the scriptural term for the event of Christ's return. It will be the occasion of both blessing for Christian believers and judgment upon unbelievers. It is both the "last day" of this age and the breaking in of the new age. On that "day"—"the day of Christ," "the day of the Lord," "the day of God"—whatever the terminology—there will be the final consummation of all things.

4. Christ's future coming will therefore be a single event. Each term used—*parousia, phanerōsis, epiphan-*

"tribes" or "peoples" (see BAGD). "Peoples" seems more appropriate to this worldwide context.

[33]In 1 Corinthians 16:22 are similar words: "Our Lord, come!" These words are a translation of the Aramaic *"Marana tha"* that Paul uses here. The fact that Paul uses Aramaic words in a Greek setting doubtless shows how deep and fervent was the early church's cry for the return of the Lord.

[34]"Christ's death is not itself the End, but the beginning of the End. . . . By these final words Paul is reminding the Corinthians of their essentially eschatological existence" (Gordon Fee, *The First Epistle to the Corinthians*, NICNT, 557).

eia, apokalypsis, hēmera, or *erchomai*—points to the unique and final returning of Jesus Christ. These are different aspects[35] of Christ's return, for there is only one final day of Christ's return at the end of history.

EXCURSUS: THE COMINGS OF CHRIST

A striking fact of the New Testament witness is not only that Christ's coming is the climactic event at the consummation of history, but also that there have been previous comings.[36] There are some references to a coming that is an event at that time, some that seem to point to events in the near future, and still others (as we have observed) that clearly refer to Christ's final coming.[37] These comings can be called *erchomai* events, for some form of this verb is often used in these accounts.[38]

A number of comings relate clearly to the period of Christ's life and death, His resurrection, and possibly Pentecost. For example, His incarnation: "He came to his own home, and his own people received him not" (John 1:11); His triumphal entry: "Behold, your king is coming to you" (Matt. 21:5); and His resurrection: "Jesus came and stood among them" (John 20:19). Jesus possibly made a reference to Pentecost when He said, "There are some standing here who will not taste death before they see the Son of man coming in his kingdom" (Matt. 16:28).[39] All of these are past, "*erchomai*," comings.

But there are also comings of Jesus that seem to relate to early events subsequent to His life, death, resurrec-

[35]Some biblical interpreters believe that there will be a future coming of Christ in relation to believers and at a later day a coming in judgment on the world. (Recall the earlier footnote regarding a similar distinction between "the day of Christ" and "the day of the Lord.") For example, this has been popularized in books by Hal Lindsey. In his *There's a New World Coming*, Lindsey speaks of "two stages in Jesus' second coming." The first is "Christ's coming *in the air* and *in secret*"; the second is "Christ's coming in power and majesty *to the earth*, with every eye seeing Him" (italics his). Lindsey then adds, "Both of these can be true only if there are separate appearances of Christ in the future" (pp. 77–78). Two future stages, or appearances, however, is biblically incorrect. There are indeed *two aspects but not two stages* (I will later comment on the presumed earlier "secret" coming). Lindsey's view actually makes for two final comings of Christ.

[36]See G. B. Caird, *The Revelation of St. John the Divine* (HNTC), pages 32, 49, 58 in regard to some previous localized comings.

[37]The "Second Coming," an expression popularly used for the return of Jesus, is therefore not altogether appropriate. Incidentally, the Book of Hebrews does say that Christ "will appear a second time, not to deal with sin but to save those who are eagerly waiting for him" (9:28). This is the closest approximation in the New Testament to "second coming" language; however, "appear" (*ophthēsetai*) is more related to other "return" terminology and thus is distinctive of Christ's final advent.

[38]Thus the word *erchomai*, unlike the other terms (*parousia, phanerōsis*, etc.) that refer only to the return of Christ, has a much broader range of reference.

[39]There are two other possible interpretations of this verse: first, that it was fulfilled in the transfiguration of Jesus six days later (Matt. 17:1–8); second, that it occurred in the destruction of Jerusalem in A.D. 70. The first interpretation places the coming within a week, which seems difficult in the context. The second gives a range of time more fitting for the clause "*some* standing here who will not taste death," in that the destruction of Jerusalem occurred about forty years later. R. H. Lenski writes that "in the judgment on the Jews the royal rule of Jesus would become visible. In this calamity some of the hearers were actually to 'see' the Son of man coming in his kingdom, i.e., clothed with the royal majesty as the King that he is" (*The Interpretation of St. Matthew's Gospel*, 649). W. E. Biederwolf in his *Second Coming Bible Commentary*, 322, agrees with this interpretation.

tion, and Pentecost. In Matthew 10:23 Jesus charges the twelve disciples: "When they persecute you in one town, flee to the next; for truly, I say to you, you will not have gone through all the towns of Israel, before the Son of man comes." The charge, which begins in 10:1, is related to much more than a brief journey. No doubt a fairly long period is envisaged in such words as "you will be dragged before governors and kings for my sake, to bear testimony before them and the Gentiles" (v. 18). This coming seems to represent God's visitation upon the Jews by the Romans in A.D. 70.[40] Indeed, the language of being "dragged before governors and kings for my sake" is almost identical with that of Luke 21:12: "You will be brought before kings and governors for [His] name's sake." This is followed by a prediction of the destruction of Jerusalem—"when you see Jerusalem surrounded by armies, then know that its desolation has come near" (Luke 21:20). Thus the coming referred to in Matthew 10:23 was likely fulfilled in the desolation and destruction of Jerusalem.

Another significant reference to a future coming, perhaps identical with that of Matthew 10:23, is the statement of Jesus before the Sanhedrin. The high priest declared, "I adjure you by the living God, tell us if you are the Christ, the Son of God" (Matt. 26:63). Jesus replied, "You [singular] have said so. But I tell you, hereafter[41] you [plural] will see the Son of man seated at the right hand of Power, and coming on the clouds of heaven" (v. 64). Jesus' words apparently refer to an occurrence within the lifetime of the members of the Jewish high council. The fulfillment—at least in the primary instance[42]—would again occur in the coming judgment upon and destruction of Jerusalem in A.D. 70.[43] For this happened within forty

[40]Biederwolf writes concerning this coming that the "expression here is most certainly a direct reference to the destruction of Jerusalem which historically put an end to the old dispensation and which is of course a type of the final coming of the Lord" (*The Second Coming Bible Commentary*, 314). Similarly, J. Barton Payne says, "In Matthew 10:23 . . . the concept which is forecast by 'the coming of the Son of man' seems to be that of God's visitation upon the Jews through the Romans in 70 AD" (*Encyclopedia of Biblical Prophecy*, 127). Likewise, D. A. Carson writes about Matthew 10:23: "They [the disciples] will have not finished evangelizing the cities of Israel before the Son of man comes in judgment on Israel" (*Matthew*, EBC 8:253).

[41]The Greek *ap' arti* means literally "from now." Weymouth's New Testament in Modern Speech translates this as "later on." In a footnote Weymouth remarks, "Or before long, in the near future." The NIV translation, "in the future," does not convey the sense of nearness. The parallel text in Mark 14:62 has no *ap' arti*, but simply reads, "Jesus said, 'I am; and you will see the Son of man sitting at the right hand of Power, and coming with the clouds of heaven.'" All in all, "hereafter" (RSV, KJV, and NASB) seems to be the best translation.

[42]This does not deny the final coming of Jesus in even more fearful judgment at the end of the age. Indeed, the coming in A.D. 70 is a preliminary fulfillment of the final fulfillment yet to occur. The divine visitation upon an unbelieving Jewish nation represents the final visitation yet to come upon an unbelieving world. Biederwolf entitles his discussion of Matthew 26:64 "The Second Coming of Jesus in a Figurative and Ever Present Sense" (*The Second Coming Bible Commentary*, 360). Hence, while Jesus' words point ultimately to "the awful time of the end when every eye shall see him . . . the reference is not specifically to this . . . but rather . . . to the whole judicial administration of Christ, which commences immediately after His resurrection, but more especially at the destruction of Jerusalem, and shall be completed in the end of the world" (p. 361).

[43]The language of "coming on the clouds" might seem to rule out any idea of Matthew 26:64 as referring to A.D. 70. I will say more about this language later.

years of the time Jesus spoke the words.

Let us now reconsider Jesus' words in Matthew 24:30 about His coming. Jesus, speaking to the disciples, says, "They will see the Son of man coming on the clouds of heaven with power and great glory" (cf. Mark 13:26; Luke 21:27). It is noteworthy that the language is almost identical with that of Matthew 26:64: "They [instead of 'you'] will see the Son of man . . . coming on the clouds of heaven." This suggests that Jesus is referring basically to the same event. If Matthew 26:64 refers primarily to an event within the lifetime of the Sanhedrin members (as seems likely), then Matthew 24:30 could do so as well. This seems to be confirmed by the later words of Jesus in Matthew 24:34 (cf. Mark 13:30; Luke 21:32): "Truly, I say to you, this generation[44] will not pass away till all these things take place."

A review of Jesus' earlier words in Matthew 24 reveals that "all these things" finds its primary focus in the destruction of the temple. There Jesus declares, "Truly, I say to you, there will not be left here one stone upon another, that will not be thrown down" (v. 2). The first question the disciples asked Jesus concerned the temple: "When will this be?" Hence, "all these things" would unmistakably include the temple destruction and thus occur within the first generation. The destruction of the temple is, by no means, God's final judgment, for that will occur at "the close of the age" (a part of the disciples' second question). However, the destruction of the temple (and of Jerusalem) is signified as the primary coming of the Son of man in judgment.[45]

This fact is important to keep in mind in light of two additional matters. First, the coming of the Son of man in Matthew 24 (and in the Mark 13 and Luke 21 parallels) is unquestionably depicted on a larger scale than the Jewish nation, Jerusalem, and the temple. I have commented on the near identity between the "*you* will see the Son of man . . . " (Matt. 26:64) and "*they* will see" (Matt. 24:30). That reference thereby basically alludes to the same event—namely the visitation of judgment upon and destruction of Jerusalem. However, "they"—as the context shows—includes far more than the Jewish nation. Although the reference to "all the tribes[46] of the earth" (Matt. 24:30) essentially refers to the tribes of Israel, it refers ultimately to all the peoples[47] of the earth. Thus the focus on Jerusalem broadens to a worldwide perspective,

[44]The Greek word here translated "generation" is *genea*. "This generation," accordingly, signifies the approximate lifetime of people then living. Earlier in Matthew 23, Jesus had repeatedly denounced the Jewish leaders, the scribes and Pharisees, climaxing His denunciation by saying, "Upon you [will] come all the righteous blood shed on earth, from the blood of innocent Abel to the blood of Zechariah the son of Barachiah, whom you murdered between the sanctuary and the altar. Truly, I say to you, all this will come upon this generation" (vv. 35–36). Then Jesus adds concerning Jerusalem, "Behold, your house is forsaken and desolate" (v. 38). Hence, the focus of the judgments in Matthew 24 (Mark 13, Luke 21) indisputably centers on the Jewish nation and Jerusalem its center. Thus before "this generation" was to "pass away," "all these things" would happen.

[45]In Mark 13 and Luke 21 the only *explicit* question concerns the destruction of the temple. Hence, Jesus' words about "all these things" must even more be recognized as fulfilled in the first generation at A.D. 70. This does not mean that the account in Mark and Luke relate to nothing beyond this destruction, for *implicitly* they do relate to something more, as will be observed shortly. Nonetheless, it would be a serious error to ignore the fact that the primary focus is Jerusalem at the time of Christ.

[46]The Greek word is *phyla*—its primary meaning "the twelve tribes of Israel" (BAGD).

[47]The secondary meaning of *phylai* is "nations, peoples" (BAGD).

and the prophecy, accordingly, relates also to the final judgment at the close of the age. Since "this generation" (Matt. 24:34) can also mean, expansively, "this race,"[48] then the "coming of the Son of man" refers ultimately to His coming at the end of history.

The second matter concerns the language that describes the coming of the Son of man. Would not such terminology point exclusively to Christ's final advent? Did He—we may ask—actually come "on the clouds of heaven" in A.D. 70? The answer seems to be yes—in a real, though figurative, sense. The Old Testament frequently uses similar language. Isaiah 19:1 reads, "An oracle concerning Egypt. Behold, the LORD is riding on a swift cloud and comes to Egypt; and the idols of Egypt will tremble at his presence." "Riding on a swift cloud" is obviously figurative, not unlike Psalm 104:3, where God is addressed: "[Thou] who makest the clouds thy chariot, who ridest on the wings of the wind." Another psalm, traditionally attributed to David as a "song to the LORD on the day when the LORD delivered him from the hand of all his enemies, and from the hand of Saul,"[49] reads, "He bowed the heavens, and came down. . . . He rode on a cherub, and flew; he came swiftly upon the wings of the wind" (18:9–10). The "clouds" with their parallelism "wings of wind" represent God coming majestically to the earth,[50] especially for the destruction of evil and the establishment of righteousness. Because of such Old Testament imagery, it is possible to say that Christ came "on the clouds of heaven" in the devastation of Jerusalem and the further victory of his kingdom.

In addition to the language of "the clouds" Matthew 24:29 (parallels in Mark 13:24–25; Luke 21:25–26) has other apocalyptic language such as the sun being darkened, the moon not giving light, the stars falling, the powers of the heavens being shaken—all prior to the coming on the clouds. In the Old Testament, as we have similarly noted, this is frequently the language of God's judgment upon a nation. One of the most vivid examples is the judgment on the pharaoh of Egypt: "Son of man, raise a lamentation over Pharaoh king of Egypt, and say to him. . . . When I blot you out, I will cover the heavens, and make their stars dark. I will cover the sun with a cloud, and the moon shall not give its light. All the bright lights of heaven will I make dark over you. . ." (Ezek. 32:2, 7–8). This will happen by "the sword of the king of Babylon" (v. 11). What is vividly pictured here in unforgettable language is the utter destruction to occur in Pharaoh's own time. Many other Old Testament pas-

[48]A second possible translation of *genea* is "race" (as in NASB and NIV margins on Matt. 24:34; Mark 13:30; Luke 21:32) or "family." (For *genea* Thayer suggests also "men of the same stock, a family" and "in a bad sense a perverse race"—e.g., Matt. 17:17.) Hence "this *genea*" could also refer to the Jewish race, which did not pass away before all the things Jesus spoke were fulfilled. This other translation expands the picture far beyond the destruction of the temple in A.D. 70 down through history, even to the present day. This secondary meaning of *genea*, I believe, is likewise included in Jesus' prophecy.

[49]The caption of Psalm 18 in the RSV (similarly NIV, NASB).

[50]"The clouds are an emblem of God's sovereign power and majestic glory moving to the earth." So writes Paul Minear in his *Christian Hope and the Second Coming*, 124. Minear also states, "Wherever the cloud appeared, there the invisible transfigured the visible surface of man's existence, giving to it the depth dimension of eternity" (p. 127). Minear further comments that a person must avoid either a literal or a purely metaphorical understanding of Scripture's use of "clouds": "By insisting on either a literal or a purely metaphorical meaning he may be depriving the Word of its power to convey living truth concerning the depths of reality" (p. 127).

sages similarly portray such a day of judgment upon a particular nation or upon the whole earth.[51]

With even greater intensity than against the pharaoh of Egypt, the king of Babylon, or any other, is the judgment of God—and all heavenly forces—upon the nation of Israel. God had spoken through the prophet Amos to Israel: "You only have I known of all the families of the earth; therefore I will punish you for all your iniquities" (Amos 3:2).[52] In other words, because Israel was "known" by God, blessed specially by Him, His "chosen" one, her sin and rebellion were all the more heinous in God's sight, and so her punishment would be all the greater. And now that she had spurned God's own Messiah, His very Son, the judgment upon her would be far more severe than upon any other nation. Indeed, immediately before He depicted the devastation in Matthew 24, Jesus proclaimed, "Behold, your house is forsaken and desolate" (Matt. 23:38). Thus the destruction dealt out upon Israel would be far vaster than anything the world had ever before known.[53] Celestial phenomena will be evidenced far beyond those of the Old Testament—and this, of course, is exactly what is depicted in Matthew 24 (and parallels).[54] For then, almost forty years later, Israel's desolation would be complete; the kingdom taken from her spiritually would be destroyed politically. Thus it would be the dawning of a new

[51]E.g., Jeremiah 4:23–24: "I looked on the earth, and lo, it was waste and void; and to the heavens, and they had no light . . . all the hills moved to and fro" (judgment on Jerusalem). Note also Isaiah 34:2–5 (all the nations/Edom) and Joel 2:28–31, both a picture of the universal outpouring of God's Spirit as well as "portents in the heavens and on the earth. . . . The sun shall be turned to darkness, and the moon to blood, before the great and terrible day of the LORD comes" (cf. Acts 2:16–21). The use of such imagery is at least as old as the judges of Israel, e.g., the song of Deborah and Barak: "From heaven fought the stars, from their courses they fought against Sisera" (Judges 5:20; note also the earth trembling and the mountains quaking: 5:4–5). J. Adams, commenting on Christ's words in Matthew 24 and Peter's in Acts 2, speaks of this as language "used to describe the fall of the old order and the entrance of a new one" (*The Time Is at Hand*, 63, n.). This would apply also to the many passages already cited.

[52]Note also the apocalyptic imagery in Amos 8. God declares, "The end has come upon my people Israel" (v. 2), and "on that day I will make the sun go down at noon, and darken the earth in broad daylight" (v. 9).

[53]Josephus, Jewish historian and eyewitness of the destruction, estimated that 1.1 million Jews were slain in the siege and destruction of Jerusalem. "Accordingly," wrote Josephus, "the multitude of those that therein perished exceeded all the destructions that either men or God ever brought upon the world." Those not killed in Jerusalem were sent into the provinces "as a present to them, that they might be destroyed upon the theatres by the sword, and by the wild beasts. . . . Those under seventeen years of age were sold for slaves . . . [some] 97,000" (*Wars of the Jews*, 6.9.3–4). (It is also estimated that more than 1.3 million Jews in Judea and bordering countries were slain in the seven years preceding the destruction of Jerusalem.) The result was that not a single Jew was left alive in Jerusalem, and that all buildings, including the temple, were totally demolished.

[54]It is interesting that Josephus speaks of such phenomena as "a star resembling a sword, which stood over the whole city, and a comet that continued a whole year"; on another occasion "before sunsetting, chariots and troops of soldiers in their armor were seen running about among the clouds, and surrounding cities"; again "at that feast which we call Pentecost, as the priests were going by night into the inner [court of] the temple . . . to perform their sacred ministrations, they said, that . . . they felt a quaking, and heard a great noise, and after that they heard the sound of a multitude, saying, 'Let us remove hence.' " Josephus expressed his vast sorrow that the Jews "did not attend nor give credit to the signs that were so evident, and did so plainly foretell their future desolation" (6.9.3).

age in which the kingdom of God, broken free of all identification with one nation, would be released into the whole world.

Let me make two summary remarks about the "coming" of Jesus in Matthew (with parallels in Mark and Luke) which climaxes with the language, "this generation will not pass away until all these things take place." First, this is a coming that refers primarily to the visitation in judgment upon Jerusalem in A.D. 70. Hence, the generation that was alive when Jesus spoke would not have passed away by the time of fulfillment. Some would live through all the things described in Matthew 24:4–34, and thus experience "the coming of the Son of man." Second, although the desolation of Jerusalem in A.D. 70 is the primary focus, the words of Jesus extend far beyond the first generation, indeed to the very end of history. This "generation"—now to be understood as "race"—will not pass away before all things are accomplished. Hence, the events leading up to the destruction of Jerusalem in A.D. 70 are the paradigm on a smaller scale (as vast as those events were!) of that which is yet to come.

Finally, one verse in the Book of Revelation may be cited. Although it seems to focus primarily on the end, it may also refer to events of an earlier generation. The passage reads, "Behold, he is coming with the clouds! Every eye shall see him, and among them those who pierced him; and all the peoples of the world shall lament in remorse" (1:7 NEB). Insofar as this prophecy also relates to events that refer to a coming judgment upon Rome,[55] it is possible that these words have a tentative fulfillment in the early centuries of the church. "Every one who pierced him" could, in addition to the Jews, also include the Romans who shared in Christ's crucifixion.[56] But beyond that, mankind at large is involved. For all the "peoples" of the earth—not just Jews and Romans—are guilty through their sin and evil of putting to death the Son of God. Thus, "every eye will see him" and all unbelievers will lament in anguish upon His return. Hence, the ultimate reference of these words about the coming of Christ points to the final generation.

III. A REAL EVENT

The return of Christ is the event that ushers in the climax of history. The last words of Jesus in the Book of Revelation are unmistakable: "Surely I am coming soon" (22:20). These words, yet to be fulfilled, are the assurance of a real future event.

This needs to be emphasized over against any view that Christ has already finally come. To remove all futurist elements in favor of a "realized eschatology"[57] is to do radical disservice to

---

[55]The latter chapters of Revelation speak of a judgment upon "Babylon the great" (17:5), which undoubtedly includes judgment upon Rome, the city of "seven hills" (17:9).

[56]Zechariah 12:10 depicts a future day when "the house of David and the inhabitants of Jerusalem . . . look on him whom they have pierced [and] they shall mourn . . . ." In his Gospel, following the description of a Roman soldier at the cross piercing Jesus' side with a spear, John quoted the words from Zechariah thus: "They shall look on him whom they have pierced" (19:37).

[57]As, e.g., held by C. H. Dodd. In his book *The Apostolic Preaching and Its Developments*, Dodd writes, "The Age to Come has come. The Gospel of primitive Christianity is a Gospel of realized eschatology" (p. 85). Later in his writing Dodd made more room for a real future (see his *Gospel and Law: The Relation of Faith and Ethics in*

the overall biblical witness. Christ surely has come—and this is the central fact of history—but He is also to come. Without the reality of the latter, history has no conclusion. This also needs to be said over against the "demythologizing"[58] view, which regards all language of a return of Christ as being mythical. This view calls for reinterpretation in terms of the believer's own future possibilities. Even more radical than either of these views is that of "consistent eschatology,"[59] which very bluntly says that the New Testament (including Christ Himself) was simply wrong about a future real event. The consummation was expected to take place upon Jesus' death, but it did not, so there is nothing yet to happen.

Milder, perhaps, than the preceding views are those that do not deny a future event, but look upon it as the general fulfillment of God's purpose. For example, history will end with a vindication of Christ's life and teachings: this is His "return." The message of Christ, while only now partially realized, will at some future time be fully recognized and put into practice.[60] That will be the day of the Lord: His truth acknowledged by all mankind.

Over against all the previously mentioned views—whether moderate or more radical—we do, and must, affirm that there is to be a *real* return of Jesus

Early Christianity). However, Dodd will likely remain best known for his stress on "realized eschatology."

[58]This is Rudolf Bultmann's well known term. For example, in his essay "New Testament and Mythology," Bultmann speaks at the outset of "the mythical view of the world and the mythical event of redemption." He includes in such "mythology" the belief that Christ "will come again on the clouds of heaven to complete the work of redemption, and [that] the resurrection and judgment of men will follow" (*Kerygma and Myth*), 2). Because, says Bultmann, such is mythology, and yet contains a kernel of truth, "theology must undertake the task of stripping the Kerygma [the gospel message] from its mythical framework, of 'demythologizing' it" (p. 3). For "the real purpose of myth is not to present an objective picture of the world, but to express man's understanding of himself in the world in which he lives" (p. 10). This is a radical reduction of the supernatural to the natural, and a reinterpretation in terms of human life and possibilities. Eschatology, accordingly, has nothing to do with objective events such as a real return of Christ. This is pure mythology, and needs to be radically "demythologized" in terms of human existence. To be blunt: Bultmann totally subjectivizes and thereby destroys the factuality of an eschatological event.

[59]Albert Schweitzer held that Jesus' message was eschatological throughout and that only by a "consistent" application of the eschatological category are we able to understand Jesus at all. Jesus' only concern was the preaching of the coming kingdom. So He sent out His disciples in the belief that they would cause the kingdom to come. When this failed, Jesus offered Himself on the cross in the mistaken conviction that God would thereby bring all history to its consummation and his parousia forcibly be brought to pass. Here are some of Schweitzer's best-known words: "In the knowledge that He is the coming Son of Man, [Jesus] lays hold of the wheel of the world to set it moving on that last revolution which is to bring all ordinary history to a close. It refuses to turn, and he throws Himself upon it. Then it does turn; and crushes Him. Instead of bringing in the eschatological conditions, He has destroyed them" (*The Quest for the Historical Jesus*, 368). Obviously, there is no future coming of Jesus Christ.

[60]For example, William Adams Brown writes, "Not through an abrupt catastrophe, it may be, as in the early Christian hope, but by the slower and surer method of spiritual conquest, the ideal of Jesus shall yet win universal assent . . . and his spirit dominate the world. This is the truth for which the doctrine of the second advent stands" (*Christian Theology in Outline*, 372). In this view we do not look forward to an "abrupt catastrophe" (i.e., the events associated with an actual return of Jesus), but toward the day when His ideal has "universal assent."

Christ. Any view that detracts from His actual coming again in glory is less than the true witness of Christian faith. Indeed, He *Himself* is our hope of the future—nothing else; He is the "blessed hope." Without Him and His final advent, there can be no assurance of God's ultimate triumph.

10

Signs

Prior to the return of Christ, a number of things will take place. The Scriptures make clear that certain events will happen that point to the final coming of Christ and the consummation of history. Recall that the disciples asked Jesus, in addition to the question about the destruction of the temple, "What will be the sign of your coming [*parousia*] and of the close of the age?" (Matt. 24:3). Christ's future coming and the completion of the age are so closely connected that the question is really a single one. Hence, we may speak of "the sign," or "signs,"[1] that will particularly point to this final consummation.

Another way of putting the question is this: Are there evidences that the climactic event that centers in Christ's return is near? Do the signs point in that direction? We need to examine carefully the witness of Scripture concerning the events in the end times and to view all such testimony in the light of world affairs.

I. THE OUTPOURING OF THE HOLY SPIRIT

The outpouring of the Holy Spirit is a basic sign of the "last days." On the day of Pentecost Peter quoted the prophet Joel to this effect: "And in the last days it shall be, God declares, that I will pour out my Spirit upon all flesh, and your sons and your daughters shall prophesy. . ." (Acts 2:17). Peter clearly was referring, first of all, to what had just taken place in the effusion of the Spirit upon the believers in Jerusalem. In that sense the "last days"—signified by the coming of the Spirit—had now begun. After speaking these and other words about the outpouring of the Holy Spirit (vv. 17–18), Peter proceeded to state what God had prophesied through Joel: "And I will show wonders in the heaven above and signs on the earth beneath, blood and fire, and vapor of smoke; the sun shall be turned into darkness and the moon into blood, before the day of the Lord comes, the great and manifest day" (vv. 19–20). Hence, there is a close and vital connection between the outpouring of the Spirit and "the day of the Lord." Both belong to the "last days," with the effusion of the Spirit preceding the coming day.

While signaling the "last days" and

[1]It is relevant to note that Jesus in His reply spoke of a number of signs and also focused on particular ones (Matt. 24:4–30).

the approach of "the day of the Lord," the events of Pentecost were only the presaging of things yet to come. In a real sense, the outpouring of the Spirit at Pentecost was but the beginning of fulfillment, for it is apparent that the effusion was limited to Jerusalem and some Jews dwelling there. Later there would be an outpouring of the Holy Spirit on some half-Jews in Samaria (Acts 8:14–17), some Romans in Caesarea (Acts 10:44–47), some disciples in Ephesus (Acts 19:1–7),[2] and doubtless on others far beyond. Accompanying the gospel there would be "signs and wonders and various miracles and . . . gifts of the Holy Spirit" (Heb. 2:4). But as surely as the prophecy of Joel is universal—relating to "all flesh"[3]—its comprehensive fulfillment would occur at a later time in history prior to the day of the Lord.[4] When such a universal outpouring occurs, it will be an unmistakable sign of the near advent of Jesus Christ.

This brings me, then, to comment on the contemporary Pentecostal effusion of the Holy Spirit. In a manner unprecedented since New Testament times there is an outpouring of the Holy Spirit across the body of Christ and around the world. With the dawn of the twentieth century the "Pentecostal Reality"[5] has increasingly been breaking in upon the churches. People in many places are experiencing a fresh outpouring of the Holy Spirit, prophecy (as at Pentecost) is recurring, extraordinary manifestations of the Spirit are happening. Although we cannot be certain, this present-day outpouring of the Holy Spirit—unparalleled in past history—could be a profound sign of the near return of the Lord and the consummation of history.[6]

It is undoubtedly a fact that the more fully the Holy Spirit is known and experienced among believers, the greater is the sense of the Lord's being at hand. For the Holy Spirit is also the Spirit of Christ. To the degree that the Spirit is dynamically present, Christ is spiritually present, and there is an increased expectation of His corporeal

[2]The word "outpouring" occurs only in Acts 10:45: "The Holy Spirit had been poured out upon the Gentiles also" (NASB). However, the same basic action is conveyed in the use of the word "fallen" in Acts 8:16 and the statement "The Holy Spirit came on them" in Acts 19:6. For a study of these and other terms that parallel "outpouring," see *Renewal Theology*, 2:181–207.

[3]" 'All flesh' signifies all men. . . . We must not restrict the expression 'all flesh' to the members of the covenant nation" (C. F. Keil and F. Delitzch, *Commentary on the Old Testament*, 10:210).

[4]"Peter was right in taking Pentecost with its accompanying miracles as the fulfillment of Joel's prophecy. It was the beginning of its fulfillment, the beginning of the signs of the end, and then, as Alford says, 'follows the period, known only to the Father, the period of waiting—the Church for her Lord's return—and then the signs shall be renewed and the day of the Lord shall come' " (Biederwolf, *The Second Coming Bible Commentary*, 405).

[5]See my book *The Pentecostal Reality*. E.g., "Truly an extraordinary spiritual renewal is beginning to occur across Christendom. We are seeing the release of the primitive dynamism in our century. . . . At the first Pentecost, people were gathered together 'from every nation under heaven' in *one place*, Jerusalem; but now Jerusalem is the world, with Christians in almost *every place*. As the Holy Spirit moves in mighty power over the earth, baptizing people from on high, we can but rejoice exceedingly!" (pp. 53–54). For further specific information on the Pentecostal outpouring, see Vinson Synan, *In the Latter Days: The Outpouring of the Holy Spirit in the Twentieth Century*, and idem, *The Twentieth-Century Pentecostal Explosion*.

[6]"In prophetic eschatology the consummation of the Kingdom of God is to be marked by a great revival of charismatic happenings. Both leaders and people will be Spirit-filled and Spirit-empowered on a scale hitherto unknown" (G. E. Wright, *The Rule of God*, 104).

return.[7] Since the manifestation of the Holy Spirit may be described as "powers of the age to come" (Heb. 6:5) breaking in upon the present age, the very experience of these powers can but create a lively sense of the near approach of that age.[8] All in all, the building up of spiritual intensity could move to such a peak that like a lightning flash between heaven and earth would be the Parousia of the Lord.

It is not the absence of the Lord but His presence—intensified—that is preparation for His return. Through the activity of the Holy Spirit, Christ becomes so manifest that a thin line separates this from His final manifestation (*phanerōsis*). For He will not come as a distant stranger, but as One who is our very life. Hence Paul can say, "When Christ who is our life appears. . ." (Col. 3:4): not "when *Christ* appears," but "when *Christ who is our life* appears." Thus—to repeat—it is not Christ's absence that is the deep note calling out for His return but His presence in the Spirit: He is so real now we can hardly wait for His full appearance![9]

There are several reasons that the outpouring of the Spirit is a sign of the "last days" and the Lord's return. For one thing, the power (and powers) of the Holy Spirit is much needed by believers to stand against the heightened activity of Satan and evil forces in the end times. Paul speaks of "deceitful spirits" and "doctrines of demons" because of which "in later times some will depart from the faith" (1 Tim. 4:1). Hence, one highly important reason for the outpouring of the Holy Spirit and the multiplication of genuine spiritual manifestations is to provide the divine power and strategy necessary to cope with the increasing tide of evil. If today, amid the flood of occult practices, cult proliferation, even Satanism and witchcraft, the church seems almost helpless, it will remain that way unless there is a fresh endowment of spiritual resources. Only this latter-day outpouring of the Holy Spirit and the church's participation in it will provide adequate fortification against the assaults of evil. Satan is having his own "counterfeit Pentecost" by increasingly pouring out his evil spirits. Thus nothing can suffice except a true Pentecost to turn back the crescendo of evil in these difficult hours. The fact that God is providing an outpouring of fresh spiritual resources in our time is undoubtedly an "end-time" sign.

Another, yet related, reason for the outpouring of the Spirit is to provide courage and wisdom for Christian believers to endure whatever trials may come. Jesus emphasized that all who follow Him will endure persecution, but

---

[7]"The more powerfully life in the Spirit of God is present in it [the church], the more urgent is its expectation of the coming of Christ; so that the fullness of the possession by the Spirit and the urgency of expectation are always found together" (Emil Brunner, *Dogmatics III*, 400).

[8]"The 'Pneuma' was in the mind of the Apostle [Paul] before all else the element of the eschatological or the celestial sphere, that which characterizes the mode of existence and life in the world to come and of that anticipated form in which the world to come is even now realized in heaven" (Geerhardus Vos, *The Pauline Eschatology*, 59). Hence when the Spirit becomes active in the present—in the sphere of the church, the believing community—this is the breaking in of the "world to come."

[9]How sad, then, is the view of some today who emphasize His absence, or—what amounts to much the same thing—His powerlessness. In this view Satan is the dominant figure through his presence, power, and rule—not Christ. Thus the coming of Christ will be that of a veritable stranger to earth. To be sure, Satan's activity will be increasingly felt as the end draws near (as will be discussed later), but it will remain subordinate to the lordship of Christ.

the Holy Spirit will be their help: "And when they bring you to trial and deliver you up, do not be anxious beforehand what you are to say; but say whatever is given you in that hour, for it is not you who speak but the Holy Spirit" (Mark 13:11). Persecution will intensify as the end draws near;[10] hence a full investment of the Holy Spirit is all the more needed. Those who rely on the Holy Spirit—regardless of what may come at the end—will find wisdom and courage that none can stand against.

The final reason for the outpouring of the Holy Spirit is for the empowerment of the gospel proclamation. Jesus tells us, "This gospel of the kingdom will be preached throughout the whole world, as a testimony to all nations; and then the end will come" (Matt. 24:14).[11] In order for this end-time proclamation to be effective, the plenitude of the Spirit's endowment is called for. If the first disciples had to receive power to witness—"You shall receive power when the Holy Spirit has come upon you; and you shall be my witnesses in Jerusalem and in all Judea and Samaria and to the end of the earth" (Acts 1:8)—then all the more so do we as the final testimony goes forth. Human strategies and efforts (though necessary) are insufficient in a time of increasing secularism, materialism, and pseudo-religions of many kinds. Only the endowment of "power from on high" (Luke 24:49) can provide the resources for completing the final task.

To conclude: the outpouring of the Holy Spirit is undoubtedly a sign—perhaps the primary sign—of the return of Jesus Christ. For as surely as the Holy Spirit is "the Spirit of glory" (1 Peter 4:14 NIV) who comes from the Lord in heaven, there is but a short step from this coming to the final coming in glory of Christ Himself.

II. THE GOSPEL TO ALL THE WORLD

The time between the Ascension and the Parousia is peculiarly the time for the spread of the gospel. The Great Commission of Matthew 28 is unmistakable: "Go therefore and make disciples of all nations, baptizing them in the name of the Father and of the Son and of the Holy Spirit, teaching them to observe all that I have commanded you; and lo, I am with you always, to the close of the age" (vv. 19–20). Hence, the church has one basic mission: to bring the nations to Christ through discipling, baptizing, and teaching, with the assurance of Christ's continuing presence in this mission even to "the close [or 'end'] of the age."

A. Universal Proclamation

In connection with this mission to reach all nations, the "sign of the end" will be the universal proclamation of the gospel. As Jesus earlier declared, "This gospel of the kingdom will be preached throughout the whole world, as a testimony to all nations; and then the end will come" (Matt. 24:14). What is said is *not* that all nations will turn to Christ—though this is the goal (as Matt. 28 states)—but that all will hear and have opportunity to turn. When this occurs, the end will come.

Let us look more closely. The Great Commission is not only to proclaim but also to reach—and this refers to "all nations" (in both Matt. 24 and 28)—so that people are discipled, baptized, and taught. The goal is testimony plus con-

[10]As the context of Mark 13:11 demonstrates. Jesus had just declared, "The gospel must first be preached to all the nations" (v. 10), and later adds, "But he who endures to the end will be saved" (v. 13).

[11]See the next section for a discussion of this proclamation of the gospel as a sign of the end, or the return of the Lord.

version: it can never be anything less than that. And as surely as Christ is with His church throughout the ages, there will be—and unquestionably has been—the turning of many "nations" to Him. However, Christ does *not* say in the Great Commision that this goal will be fully reached. Nor—and here we return to the matter of "sign"—did He earlier say that all nations must be converted before the end of the age and His return. *But,* when the church universally proclaims the gospel as a testimony (or witness) so that all may hear and believe, then the end will come. The "sign," therefore, is not universal salvation but universal witness with opportunity for decision.

Now let us examine more closely Jesus' words "the whole world" and "all nations." The word translated "world" is *oikoumenē*, meaning literally "the inhabited earth."[12] Hence the gospel of the kingdom is to be proclaimed wherever there are people. The word translated "nations" is from *ethnos*, meaning not necessarily a political entity but a large number of people who make up a cohesive group socially, culturally, and racially.[13] To all such *ethnē*[14]—wherever they are across the face of the earth—the gospel must be proclaimed as a testimony. Then the end will come.

A question that naturally follows is this: Has this proclamation been accomplished, or are we perhaps very close to fulfilling the task? One obvious problem is that no one is sure how many *ethnē* there are. If this refers only to "nations" in a larger sense, it is probably correct to say that all nations have now had some gospel testimony. But if it refers to cohesive groups of people within or without nations, there may be large numbers who have not yet heard. Indeed, there are many "unreached peoples"[15] in the world who might be called *ethnē* and to whom the gospel has not yet been proclaimed. Whether or not they are *ethnē* and therefore must hear the gospel before the end can come, it is still the mission of the church to keep on preaching and witnessing to everyone everywhere. For as surely as God "desires all men to be saved and to come to the knowledge of the truth" (1 Tim. 2:4) and as truly as "the love of Christ compels us" (2 Cor. 5:14 NIV) to seek every lost soul, the church must continue—sign or no sign—to witness to the good news as long as time remains. But, returning to the point of inquiry, the only proper answer must be that we simply do not know for certain. From God's perspective it is quite possible that the witness to the *ethnē* has been accomplished, or is now being accomplished, so that the end could quickly come. It may be, on the other hand, that we have a long way yet to go before all *ethnē* have had a chance to hear and respond.

---

[12]So NASB margin. *Oikoumenē* is "the *world* in the sense of its inhabitants, *humankind*" (BAGD).

[13]*Ethnos* signifies "a multitude of people of the same nature or genus" (Thayer); it means "the natural cohesion of a people in general" (TDNT). From *ethnos*, of course, is derived the English word "ethnic," which may be defined as "relating to races and large groups of people classed according to common traits and customs" (*Webster's Ninth New Collegiate Dictionary*). I should add that in other contexts the *ethnē* are "the Gentiles." For example, see the discussion below regarding Israel (or Jews) and Gentiles.

[14]Since the word *ethnos* is difficult to translate adequately ("nations," as noted, conveys too much the image of a political configuration), I am here using the plural of *ethnos* instead of attempting further translation.

[15]"Unreached peoples" is a term sometimes used by missiologists to refer to peoples who have no indigenous church. According to some estimates, at the beginning of the last decade of the twentieth century, there were some twelve thousand such groups.

B. Growth of the Kingdom

The Scriptures emphasize the growth of the kingdom all the way to the end. Here we turn back to Jesus' earlier parables of the kingdom—as recorded in Matthew 13—particularly those concerning the mustard seed (vv. 31–32) and the leaven (v. 33). In the former parable, Jesus likens the kingdom of heaven to the small grain of mustard seed, which "when it has grown it is the greatest of shrubs and becomes a tree, so that the birds of the air come and make nests in its branches"; in the latter parable, He likens it to "leaven which a woman took and hid in three measures of meal, till it was all leavened." Both parables unmistakably teach the growth of the kingdom from very small and hidden beginnings to a large and significant place. The kingdom externally will be great and expansive in size; internally it will be a force that permeates and pervades all.

Such parables might seem to suggest that the kingdom will be all-inclusive and gradually overcome every alien force; thus all the world will finally hear "the gospel of the kingdom" and believe. But such is not Jesus' teaching. There will be—and, of course, there has been over the past two thousand years—much growth and much leavening influence. From its minute beginnings in a small nation, the gospel has gone forth—as Jesus commanded—"from Jerusalem" to "all Judea and Samaria and to the end of the earth."[16] The kingdom of heaven, in the sense of the Christian church, now embraces approximately one-third of the world's population.[17] Its influence extends far beyond its own boundaries with striking growth in recent years. It is possible that we are now on the verge of even greater increase and development.[18] Therefore in accordance with Jesus' parables, the kingdom of heaven will be unmistakably "the greatest of shrubs" and the "meal" will be yet further "leavened." For this we may hope and pray—and believe. However, to repeat what was said shortly before, Jesus does not teach that before "the end" the kingdom of God will be all in all. "The greatest of shrubs" is not the only shrub, nor is "leaven" the meal it leavens. Indeed, to the very end there will be those who do not respond. Also, another parable in Matthew 13 declares that there will be both wheat and tares (vv. 24–30, 36–43) to the very end.

Hence, the kingdom of God filling the earth is *not* the sign of the end. This is no more the case than is the turning of all nations to Christ. There is the Great Commission to minister the gospel to all nations, and there is also the assurance that the kingdom will grow mightily. But the sign is not total conversion or total expansion. The sign is total witness—the proclamation of the gospel "throughout the whole world" (recall-

---

[16]These words of Jesus in Acts 1:8 define the Great Commission in terms of the movement of the gospel from its beginnings in Jerusalem through an ever widening circle to "the end [KJV—'uttermost part'] of the earth."

[17]According to David Barrett, editor of the *World Christian Encyclopedia*, "the total of all Roman Catholic, Orthodox, and Protestant believers is now an estimated 1,758,777,900 or about 33 percent of the world's 5.3 billion people" (as quoted in *Christianity Today* [May 14, 1990], 51). That a large number of these "believers" may be only nominally so (as will be discussed later) does not detract from the fact that the kingdom of God is truly worldwide.

[18]According to Peter Wagner, professor of church growth at Fuller Theological Seminary, "Every day sees 78,000 new converts. Each week 1600 new churches start." In regard to third-world nations, Wagner adds, "In 1900 there were 50,000 evangelical Christians in Latin America; by 2000 that figure will be 137 million. In 1900 there were 10 million Christians in Africa; by 2000 that figure will reach 324 million" (as reported in *Ministries Today* [May-June 1990], 45).

ing Matt. 24) "as a testimony to all *ethnē*." When the witness has been accomplished the end will come.

C. The Fullness of the Gentiles and of Israel

Climactically, the fullness (or full number) of both the Gentiles and Israel is to come to salvation. For the first time, we specifically note the two groups. I have referred before to the proclamation of the gospel to the "nations"—the "nations" being understood essentially as the "Gentiles"[19]—and to the growth of the kingdom. The latter include all who have entered the kingdom through faith in Christ, Jews and Gentiles alike. Now consider the important fact that along with the fullness of Gentiles coming to faith, there will also be a full-scale turning of Israel to Christ and finding salvation through Him.

Here, with Paul as our guide, we recognize an extraordinary sequence of events regarding Israel and the Gentile world. Paul speaks of the gospel as "the power of God for salvation to every one who has faith, to the Jew first and also to the Greek" (Rom. 1:16). Israel had a definite priority—"to the Jew first"—and this, of course, is a historical fact. The first proclamation in Jerusalem was to Jews only on the Day of Pentecost, and Paul himself first preached to the Jews (Acts 9:20–22 and elsewhere) before turning to the Gentile world (whether Greek or Roman). Although many Jews responded, there was from the beginning bitter and ever growing opposition. Gentiles, on the other hand, soon began to come in increasing numbers into the kingdom. Jesus Himself had said to Israel, "The kingdom of God will be taken away from you and given to a people who will produce its fruit" (Matt. 21:43 NIV). Paul finally said to Jews who continued to oppose him, "From now on I will go to the Gentiles" (Acts 18:6). Although the Jews were first to hear the message, a hardness rapidly set in, so much so that the Gentiles largely became the recipients of the kingdom. Thus Paul later declared, "Through their [Israel's] trespass [or 'transgression'][20] salvation has come to the Gentiles" (Rom. 11:11).

Hence the focus of gospel proclamation throughout the centuries has been to the "nations" or "Gentiles" primarily. When they have all had an opportunity to hear and respond, the end will come. But—and this is an additional highly significant fact—the end will not occur without Israel's coming to salvation. Paul continues, "Lest you [Gentiles] be wise in your own conceits, I want you to understand this mystery, brethren: a hardening has come upon part of Israel,[21] until the full number [or 'fullness'][22] of the Gentiles come in, and so all Israel will be saved" (Rom. 11:25–26). Paul had pointed in this direction earlier: "Now if their [Israel's] trespass means riches for the world, and if their failure means riches for the Gentiles, how much more will their full inclusion [or 'fullness'][23] mean!" (Rom 11:12). Thus the fullness of the Gentiles—through proclamation of the gospel to the *ethnē*, and the growth of the kingdom (largely Gentile growth)—is not the last word! Indeed, there will finally be such a fullness of

---

[19]*Ethnē*, as we have observed, means both "nations" and "Gentiles."

[20]The Greek word is *paraptōmati*—"false step, transgression" (BAGD).

[21]Instead of "upon part of Israel." The Greek reads *apo merous tō Israēl*—literally, "in part to Israel" (so KJV).

[22]The Greek word is *plērōma*; KJV and NASB read "fulness."

[23]Again *plērōma*.

Israel when their hardness and blindness[24] is overcome as to vastly enrich the whole world. For the almost unbelievable truth is that *all Israel will be saved*. The first shall be last! The fullness of Gentiles will climax with the fullness of Israel.

All of this belongs to the realm of "mystery."[25] Moreover, it shows that God is not done with Israel. Paul had earlier said, "God has not rejected his people whom he foreknew" (Rom. 11:2). Although for a time Israel has been cut off, like branches, through unbelief, and the Gentiles grafted in, God will "graft them in again" (11:23). When this happens, truly the end is at hand!

The "fullness" of Israel—"all Israel"—will come in exactly as does the fullness of the Gentiles: through faith in Jesus Christ.[26] For, says Paul, "if they do not persist in their unbelief, [they] will be grafted in" (Rom. 11:23); and later he speaks of all Israel being saved. Likewise, just after the statement about Israel's salvation, Paul quotes freely from the Old Testament: "The Deliverer will come from Zion, he will banish [or 'remove'][27] ungodliness from Jacob; and this will be my covenant with them when I take away their sins" (Rom. 11:26–27). The Deliverer is undoubtedly Christ,[28] and "ungodliness" will be removed with the taking away of sin.

Does the saving of "all Israel" mean every individual Jew? Paul does not say. It would seem likely, however, that he is referring to a wide-ranging cross-section of Israel, including the leadership, that would represent the whole people.[29] "All Israel" in the Old Testament could mean representatives of the people, for example, "all Israel had come to Shechem to make him [Rehoboam] king" (1 Kings 12:1). In any

---

[24]Paul speaks elsewhere of a "veil" being over Israel's face: "For to this day, when they read the old covenant, that same veil remains unlifted" (2 Cor. 3:14).

[25]Paul writes to the Ephesians concerning another "mystery," namely, that "Gentiles are fellow heirs, members of the same body, and partakers of the promise in Christ Jesus through the gospel" (3:4–6). I suggest that the "mystery" he describes in Romans is a complementary one, and a humbling one, lest the Gentiles become too proud—"wise" in their "own conceits"! That the Gentiles are partakers of the promise—a matter not made known, says Paul, "to the sons of men in other generations" (Eph. 3:5)—is a glorious truth. But the mystery beyond this is that Israel will likewise some day come in.

[26]"The salvation of all Israel is distinguished from that of the Gentiles, but the manner of salvation will nevertheless be the same, namely, it will be the victory of the free grace of God that will save Israel" (Günter Wagner, "The Future of Israel: Reflections on Romans 9–11" in W. Hulitt Gloer, ed., *Eschatology and the New Testament*, 105).

[27]As in NASB and NEB. The Greek word is *apostrepsi*.

[28]Some interpreters speak of the conversion of Israel as occurring *at* the return of Christ and thus identify this return with the "Deliverer" coming "from Zion." For example, E. F. Harrison states that "the conversion of Israel will occur at Messiah's return" (EBC, 10, 124). But "from Zion" is hardly the origin of Christ's return. (It is interesting that Isaiah 59:20, which Paul quotes, does have "to Zion." He would surely have quoted the phrase if he were thinking of Christ's final return). Moreover, such a view contradicts one of the basic motifs in Christ's return, namely, that He comes in final salvation and judgment (see later discussion). There is no more "banishing" of "ungodliness." Also, if the conversion of Israel were delayed until Christ's return, salvation would come to the Jews in a way different from all others—not through the proclamation of the gospel in the power of the Holy Spirit but by the supernatural intervention of Jesus Christ.

[29]F. F. Bruce writes, " 'All Israel,' is a recurring expression in Jewish literature, where it need not mean 'every Jew without a single exception' but 'Israel as a whole' " (*Romans*, TNTC, 222). C. E. B. Cranfield similarly states, "The most likely explanation of 'all Israel' is that it means the nation Israel as a whole, though not necessarily including every individual member" (*Romans: A Shorter Commentary*, 282).

event, this future conversion of Israel will be the reversal of that terrible day when, at Jesus' trial, the people cried, "His blood be on us and on our children" (Matt. 27:25), and the chief priests, scribes, and elders "mocked him" (Matt. 27:41) as He hung dying on the cross. Against such a background the prospect is glorious indeed: all Israel will be saved!

That this will happen before Christ returns is also suggested in the words of Jesus Himself. Just after pronouncing the forsakenness of Jerusalem ("Behold, your house is forsaken and desolate") He said, "For I tell you, you will not see me again,[30] until you say, 'Blessed is he who comes in the name of the Lord' " (Matt. 23:39). When the Lord returns, it will be to an Israel who is blessing His name—indeed, along with Gentiles from all over the world.

Since we are considering "signs" of Christ's return—and surely the turning of Israel to the Lord is an end-time event—it is noteworthy that presently there are increasing evidences of Jews turning to Christ. The "Jews for Jesus" movement in the United States,[31] the growth of "Messianic Judaism"[32] throughout the world, the enlarging number of "completed Jews"[33] serving as missionaries of the gospel—while none of this is yet a groundswell, all could be the initial evidences of a truly significant breakthrough. It is also quite possible that the establishment of the nation of Israel is a prelude to a wide-scale national conversion that could include the leadership of the people. If (when?) it happens there in the ancient homeland, the effects will be felt around the world—among both Jews and Gentiles alike. There are, to be sure, far more Jews outside than inside Israel; however, if the *nation* should turn to Christ (through its prime minister, rabbis, and various other ruling authorities), it would be the reversal of the *nation's* turning *from* Christ almost two thousand years ago. Truly all Jewry around the world would be mightily affected. Paul goes so far as to say, "If their [Israel's] rejection means the reconciliation of the world, what will their acceptance mean but life from the dead?" (Rom. 11:15). When Israel is "grafted" back in as "natural branches" (unlike Gentiles who are "cut from what is by nature a wild olive tree and grafted, contrary to nature, into a cultivated olive tree"—Rom. 11:24), it will have such a vitality ("life from the dead") as is hard to imagine. The Jewish people will at long last turn to their own natural brother Jesus—accepting Him, believing in Him, obeying Him. Truly it will be riches to all the world—and what more fitting final preparation could there be for the return of the Lord in glory!

If this en masse turning of the Jews to Christ seems almost unbelievable against the background of their centu-

[30]The Greek is *ap' arti*, literally "from now," thus "henceforth" (KJV). This expression is found also in Jesus' words to the high priest in Matthew 26:64 (see prior discussion in chap. 9).

[31]Founded in 1973 by converted Jew Moishe Rosen in San Francisco as an outgrowth of the "Jesus Movement." There is now a staff of over one hundred, offices in fourteen cities in six countries, and some fifty volunteer chapters. As Jewish Christians, they are concerned about evangelizing Jews. Other organizations reaching out to Jews include the American Board of Missions to the Jews, the Messianic Jewish Alliance of America, and the International Alliance of Messianic Congregations and Synagogues.

[32]This includes many Messianic congregations that seek to retain their Jewish heritage while at the same time accepting Jesus—"Yeshua"—as the Messiah.

[33]Many Jewish believers in Christ prefer to call themselves "completed [or 'fulfilled'] Jews" rather than Christians. Others, less desirous of retaining cultural Jewish ties, simply call themselves "Hebrew Christians."

ries-long opposition to Him—not to mention, on the Gentile side, the long history of bitter anti-Semitism—then we need today to count all the more on the power of the Holy Spirit to bring about a total change. This, I believe, is where the first sign, the outpouring of the Holy Spirit, stands as background for the second, the preaching of the gospel to all the world—and especially to the Jews. It will take a powerful anointing of the Holy Spirit, in terms of courage, wisdom, boldness, patience, and much else, upon those who witness if the gospel is to be heard and received by Israel. But it *did* happen at the beginning: the Spirit was poured out, and three thousand Jews came to salvation! It *can* happen—and by God's word it *will* happen again!

III. THE INCREASE OF EVIL

The return of Christ will also be preceded by an increase of evil throughout the world. Along with the wide extension of the gospel there will be a corresponding growth of evil and evil forces. So Jesus spoke regarding the wheat and the tares: "Let both grow together until the harvest" (Matt. 13:30). Both good and evil will increase to the very end.[34] We will now consider the nature of this evil and to what degree it approximates the evil to be expected at the close of the age.

We begin with Paul's graphic statement "There will be terrible[35] times in the last days" (2 Tim. 3:1 NIV). Then he proceeds to portray something of what it will be like: "People will be lovers of themselves, lovers of money, boastful, proud, abusive, disobedient to their parents, ungrateful, unholy, without love, unforgiving, slanderous, without self-control, brutal, not lovers of the good, treacherous, rash, conceited, lovers of pleasure rather than lovers of God—having a form of godliness [or 'religion' RSV] but denying its power" (vv. 2–5 NIV). This picture of "the last days" could, in some sense, apply to any period in Christian history—the Christian dispensation itself being "the last days."[36] For there has never been a time since Christ came that the world has not included many people who could be characterized by Paul's words. Although many are nominally religious ("holding the form of religion"), it is only a cover-up for what they really are. But, as Paul says later, the situation will get no better: "Evil men and impostors will go from bad to worse" (v. 13). Hence, as we draw still closer to the end, there will be no improvement. The times will become even more "terrible."[37]

---

[34]This is not just a numerical fact due to increase of population, so that the measure of good and evil will proportionately increase. It is also due to the fact that the growth of good brings forth the counterattack and growth of evil. (In the above parable the devil comes along and sows tares among the good seed.) If there is a "Pentecost" today (as was discussed earlier) with the Holy Spirit and His gifts being poured out, Satan will—and does surely—have his counterfeit Pentecost with his evil spirits let loose. A. H. Strong observes, " 'Wherever God erects a house of prayer, the devil always builds a chapel there.' Every revival of religion stirs up the forces of wickedness to bring opposition. As Christ's first advent occasioned an unusual outburst of demoniac malignity, so Christ's second advent will be resisted by a final desperate effort to overcome the forces of good" (*Systematic Theology*, 1009).

[35]The Greek word is *chalepoi*—"perilous" (KJV), "difficult" (NASB), "(times of) stress" (RSV). *Chalepoi* conveys the note of "hard to bear," even "dangerous" or "fierce" (Thayer). *Chalepoi* so describes the two demoniacs in Matt. 8:28.

[36]Recall Acts 2:17 (also cf. Heb. 1:2).

[37]We might also note the words in Jude 17–19. Jude first quotes "predictions of the

Paul's catalog of evil surely seems to correspond to our present days. Only a brief reflection on the intensive commitment of society at large to self-love and self-gratification, the passion for money and pleasure, the surrender of self-control to instant satisfaction, widespread brutality marked by lessening concern for human life—and on and on—makes one realize how close we are to collapse. The breakdown of morals, through increasing and open adultery, divorce, homicide, homosexuality, abortion, and the like, seems imminent. The "form of religion," without genuine substance, is not only the situation in society around us, but also—far worse—is increasingly prevalent in the Christian church. A growing number today are tacitly denying the power of faith by spurning the dynamism of the Spirit while going through the motions of religiosity. Thus along with gross immorality there is an ever more pervasive spiritual vacuum. Chaos seems near at hand.

That these are "terrible times" does not mean that everything is bleak and evil. Forces of righteousness and goodness are standing over against the violence and immorality of our day. Many people deplore the ubiquitous evil in society and seek both to rectify it wherever possible and personally to live godly lives. Also, as we have noted, the kingdom of God is continuing to grow in the world, and opportunities for witness abound. Nonetheless, evil is resurging and becoming increasingly virulent in the world at large. In that sense Paul's words about "terrible times" seem vividly to denote our present situation.

IV. RELIGIOUS APOSTASY

We focus next on the matter of religious apostasy. In Jesus' answer to the disciples' question about "the close of the age," He says at one point, "Because wickedness is multiplied, most men's love will grow cold" (Matt. 24:12). Then Jesus adds, "But he who endures to the end will be saved" (v. 13). This suggests that the decline of Christian love—the love toward God and all people that Christ makes possible[38]—will be prevalent toward "the end." This points to a falling away, or apostasy. Jesus' concern about this matter is also shown in His words in the Book of Revelation to the church at Ephesus: "I know you are enduring patiently and bearing up for my name's sake, and you have not grown weary. But I have this against you, that you have abandoned the love you had at first. Remember then from what you have fallen, repent and do the works you did at first" (2:3–5). Of course, these words are addressed to one church,[39] but they also underscore Jesus' concern about a departure from love. We see from Matthew 24 that it is the multiplication of wickedness that stands behind the growing dearth of love. As wickedness abounds—a wickedness[40] that cares for neither God nor man—love diminishes. This departure from love is the core of apostasy, for when love is gone, there is little left. Toward the end of the age such tragic lovelessness will be true of "most men."

---

apostles": "In the last time there will be scoffers, following their own ungodly passions." Then he adds, "It is these who set up divisions, worldly people, devoid of the Spirit."

[38]R. T. France writes that the words "most men's love will grow cold" mean "that the majority . . . will cool off in their love, whether for God or for their fellow-men. It is a somber picture of a church in decline" (*Matthew*, TNTC, 338–39).

[39]Nonetheless they are applicable to the church at large, as are all seven letters in the Book of Revelation though they are addressed to particular churches.

[40]Some of this we noted in preceding paragraphs.

What shall we say about today? On the one hand, the love of many Christians has actually intensified. Struggling against the wickedness of the world around, and seeking to be open constantly to the love of God in Christ, they have an ever-deepening love and compassion. They have come to experience profoundly the content of Paul's words in Romans 5:5: "God has poured out his love into our hearts by the Holy Spirit, whom he has given us" (NIV). Through the gift of the Holy Spirit they know the abundant love of God and grow daily in a personal relation to Him, to brothers and sisters in Christ, and to all people. But this is *far* from the total picture. The balance has tipped quite the other way: for many there was a love at first (at the time of their affirming commitment to Christ), but that love has decreased over the years. Love of the world, love of money, love of pleasure, love of self—all of which is the seedbed of wickedness—has driven out that first affection. This is the *primal* apostasy—departure from love. It far too often marks the church in our time.[41]

Apostasy can also include a departure from the truths of Christian faith. Paul writes Timothy: "The Spirit clearly says that in later [or 'the latter' KJV][42] times some will abandon[43] the faith and follow deceiving spirits and things taught by demons. Such teachings come through hypocritical liars, whose consciences have been seared as with a hot iron" (1 Tim. 4:1–2 NIV). This abandonment of "the faith," this apostasy, which is demonically inspired, comes through persons of calloused consciences who do not hesitate to substitute a lie for the truth. Paul accordingly is speaking against false teachers who subtly lead people farther and farther from the truth until at last they have totally departed from it. "The faith" is the body, or corpus, of Christian truth[44]—indeed, its essence. This "faith" is at last laid aside.[45]

Because such apostasy is caused by demonically inspired teachers, people who desert the faith scarcely realize what they are doing. It is delusion and deception that leads them to commit apostasy. Paul speaks of this apostasy as happening "in later times." Such times were obviously, in some sense, already present, because a little later the apostle tells Timothy to "fight the good fight of the faith" (1 Tim. 6:12). Throughout this letter Paul has much to say about the importance of "the words of the faith . . . the good doctrine" (4:6), about Timothy's taking heed to himself and to his teaching (4:16), and about the need for carefully proclaiming

---

[41]We earlier observed that some one-third of the world's population can be designated as Christian. However, it is also undoubtedly true that a large number of these are not only nominal Christians but that many who were once truly believers and knew the love of Christ have lost their earlier devotion.

[42]The Greek word is *hysterois*. BAGD renders *hysterois* here as "last," "in the last times."

[43]The Greek word is *apostēsontai*; literally, "apostatize," "depart from" (also KJV), "fall away from" (NASB), "desert from" (NEB).

[44]Jude speaks of "the faith which was once for all delivered to the saints" (v. 3). There *is* a body of truth that does not vary through the ages. Jude, by the way, urges his Christian readers in the same verse to "contend for" this faith.

[45]It is true that after this Paul speaks only of teachings that forbid marriage and enjoin abstinence from certain foods—matters that may seem less than central to the faith. However, such teachings (due to certain Gnostic influences that viewed the body itself and its natural appetites as evil) falsified God's good creation and had to be dealt with. Before long other subtle attacks on such matters as the Incarnation (see later discussion on the Antichrist, pages 330–34) and salvation would no doubt work their way in.

"the sound words of our Lord Jesus Christ and the teaching which accords with godliness" (6:3). Times of apostasy have frequently appeared in church history since Paul's day. This is the reason that early church councils declared "the faith" over against heretical teachings, that the Reformation occurred so as to steer the church back into many vital truths, and that even today numerous churches struggle to reaffirm the faith despite increasing secularism and liberalism.

What about the late twentieth century? Paul said that "in later times some will abandon the faith"; and if ever this statement was true, it seems to be vividly so today. Many of the major denominations have become less and less concerned about doctrinal integrity, so much so that we may legitimately question whether some have not become largely apostate.[46] An evangelical upsurge occurring both outside[47] and, to some degree, inside[48] the mainline denominations has come into being largely as an attempt to counter these deviating forces. Still the departure from biblical faith continues, and the end scarcely seems to be in sight.[49]

There is also New Testament reference to apostasy that is graphically called "*the* apostasy" and that is definitely related to the Parousia of Christ. Paul writes to the Thessalonians "with regard to the coming [*parousia*] of our Lord Jesus Christ . . . the day of the Lord" thus: "Let no one in any way deceive you, for it will not come unless the apostasy[50] comes first" (2 Thess. 2:1–3 NASB). This Scripture speaks of an apostasy so specific in nature as to be

---

[46]For example, the former United Presbyterian Church (at that time the largest Presbyterian denomination in America) in one situation was charged with apostasy by one of its seminary professors. When certain conservative actions were taken at its General Assembly in 1981, this charge was withdrawn. However, these actions (partly at least to fend off further local church defections) seem to have been only a momentary pause before further drifting away. (For further comment on the case see note 70 below.)

[47]Outside the mainline denominations in recent years there has been a large increase in the number of evangelical churches (e.g., those taking a strong stand on such matters as the authority of Scripture, the necessity of regeneration, and biblical morality). Such churches are generally growing in size and influence, whereas the traditional denominations are gradually decreasing.

[48]To illustrate: Inside the United Presbyterian Church a group called "Presbyterians United for Biblical Concerns" long strove for more biblical and theological integrity. A number of churches in 1981 broke away from both the United Presbyterian Church (UPUSA) and the Southern Presbyterian Church (PCUS) to form the Evangelical Presbyterian Church (EPC). Since the merging of the United Presbyterian and Southern Presbyterian Churches in 1983 to form the Presbyterian Church (U.S.A.), the liberal drift has continued, with the result that an increasing number of churches within the merged body have felt conscience-bound to withdraw.

[49]What has been described about the Presbyterian situation is to be found similarly in most other Protestant denominations. For example, the Southern Baptist Church, the largest denomination in the United States, at this writing has managed to stem the liberal tide. But the pressures to move away from a solid evangelical stance are intense.

[50]The Greek is *hē apostasia*. This is translated as "the rebellion" in RSV and NIV, "a falling away" in KJV, and paraphrased as "the final rebellion" in NEB. "The apostasy" is a more literal and a more accurate translation. "Rebellion" is a possible rendering of the term in a political context, but misses the religious meaning here (cf. Acts 19:19, the other N.T. use of *apostasia*, which has a definitely religious connotation). "*A* falling away" fails to show that Paul is talking not about *an* act but *the* act of falling away, that is total apostasy. Schlier writes that *hē apostasia* is not the state but "the act" of turning away, and signifies "complete apostasy" (TDNT, 1:513). In the Greek Old Testament (LXX) *apostasia* is particularly used in a religious sense (e.g., Josh. 2:22; 2 Chron. 29:19; 33:19; Jer. 2:19).

the apostasy. Further, it is more than an apostasy of "later times," or even "the last times"; it is "the apostasy" that is closely connected with the return of the Lord.[51] Indeed, the second advent will not happen without the apostasy preceding it: "Let no one . . . deceive you. . . ."[52]

Unmistakably we are here dealing with a sign of the return of Jesus Christ—or, it might be said, a definite precursor. Unless "the apostasy" has occurred, it is a deception to claim that the Parousia of the Lord is imminent.[53]

What, then, is "the apostasy"? Paul does not specifically answer. However, it seems to follow that whatever is most central to Christian faith, if that is abandoned, this would be *the* apostasy. The center undoubtedly is the Lord Jesus Christ, who came in the flesh and wrought mankind's salvation; hence the denial of Christ as God incarnate would be the very essence of apostasy. This brings us in a roundabout way from Paul to John and to John's language about "the antichrist." Let us now turn briefly to John's letters.

V. THE ANTICHRIST

The antichrist is one who deceives others by denying that Christ is God come in the flesh. "For many deceivers have gone out into the world, those who do not acknowledge Jesus Christ as coming in the flesh. This is the deceiver and the antichrist"[54] (2 John 7 NASB). This is the ultimate deception, namely, that the Incarnation did not occur; anyone who denies this is "the deceiver," "the antichrist." By such deception the ultimate in apostasy occurs: Jesus Christ, the Word become flesh, is spurned.

I have quoted from John's second letter. In his first letter, John emphasizes that it is "the last hour" because of the many antichrists that have appeared: "As you have heard that antichrist is coming, so now many antichrists have come; therefore we know that it is the last hour" (2:18). Later he adds, "Who is the liar but he who denies that Jesus is the Christ? This is the antichrist, he who denies the Father and the Son" (v. 22). Still later in this letter John speaks about "the spirit of antichrist" (4:3) being now present in the world.[55]

From these statements there is no suggestion that "antichrist" or "the antichrist" is a particular person. *Anyone* who denies the coming of Christ from the Father, that "the Word became flesh" (John 1:14)—the central truth of Christian faith—is "the antichrist." Thus, many antichrists have come, and many more will come. For "the spirit of antichrist" is in the world—all the way to the end. What, then, about "the last hour"? It is "the

---

[51]This does not mean that this apostasy is different from the one mentioned earlier (e.g., in 1 Tim. 4:1–2 and 2 Tim. 3:1); however, Paul is here focusing on its final manifestation.

[52]One further word might be said about *apostasia*. The claim of some that *apostasia* means "departure" (see e.g., E. Schuyler English, *Re-Thinking the Rapture*, 67–71; Kenneth S. West, *Bibliotheca Sacra*, 114:63–67), and therefore is to be understood as "rapture" (i.e., the "catching up" of believers) has utterly no biblical basis. See R. H. Gundry, *The Church and the Tribulation*, 114–18, for a clear refutation.

[53]Along with this deception is the appearance of "the man of sin." This will be discussed later.

[54]The Greek phrase is *ho antichristos*, literally "the antichrist" rather than "an antichrist" (KJV).

[55]There are no other occurrences of the word *antichrist* in the New Testament. I have mentioned all of them: 1 John 2:18, 22; 4:3; 2 John 7.

hour" of the multiplication of antichrists (again see 1 John 2:18).[56]

The antichrist, then, is not one who commits such sins as murder, adultery, and theft to the maximal degree, nor is he one who tortures and kills Christians in some gruesome, physical manner. He is actually far worse than any of this, for he deceives people about Jesus Christ. In this wicked deception (which ultimately goes back to *the* Deceiver—Satan),[57] he shuts the door to eternal life. He is "*anti*"—opposed to—"*Christ.*" This is the ultimate evil, and his activity is the ultimate deception.[58] For there is no greater tragedy in the world than that of turning people aside from Christ, the Son of God, who has wrought mankind's salvation.

Now let us seek to bring the language of Paul and John together about "the apostasy" and "the antichrist." It seems apparent that they are two sides of the same dark situation. "The antichrist" is the deceiver, and "the apostasy" is the falling away through deception. And at the heart of it all lies the denial of the inmost essence of faith: the eternal Word, the Son of God, became flesh for the redemption of mankind.

Here we need to mention also those who are called by Jesus "false Christs." Jesus declares in a passage that culminates with His Parousia (Matt. 24:23–27): "False Christs [pseudo-Christs][59] and false prophets will arise and show great signs and wonders, so as to lead astray, if possible, even the elect" (v. 24; cf. Mark 13:22). These "pseudochrists" are actually "antichrists" because they presume to be Christ,[60] and will be increasingly evident as the end draws near.[61] Jesus adds, "So, if they say to you, 'Lo, he [Christ] is in the wilderness,' do not go out; if they say, 'Lo, he is in the inner rooms,' do not believe it. For as the lightning comes from the east and shines as far as the west, so will be the *parousia* of the Son of man" (vv. 26–27).

It is a fact of history that many times over the centuries claimants to be Christ have arisen and have drawn large numbers of people away to follow them, even to wait for their manifestation. In the late twentieth century such claims

---

[56]Hence the word "hour" should not be understood literally. John Stott puts it well in saying that John "was expressing a theological truth rather than making a chronological reference. . . . It is still 'the last hour,' the hour of final opposition to Christ" (*The Epistles of John*, TNTC, 108–9). F. F. Bruce, in regard to this text, writes, "In the Christian era it is always five minutes to midnight" (*The Epistles of John*, 65).

[57]"Satan, the deceiver of the whole world" (Rev. 12:9).

[58]In the history of the world after the time of the New Testament there has been no more vivid demonstration of this deception than in the seventh-century rise of the religion of Muhammad, namely Islam. According to the Koran (presumably dictated to Muhammad), all are infidels who claim that Jesus Christ was the Son of God (e.g., "Surely now they are infidels who say, 'God is Christ the son of Mary. . . . Christ, the son of Mary, is no more than an apostle"). Muhammad, by denying that Jesus Christ was the Son of God, was wholly antichrist, and by this teaching has deceived untold millions of people down through the centuries.

[59]The Greek word is *pseudochristoi*.

[60]*Anti* can mean not only "against," or "opposed to" Christ (as in the previous passages quoted from John's letters), but also "in the place of" (BAGD: "for, instead of, in place of").

[61]F. F. Bruce writes, "Like the Antichrist of 1 John 4:3, the false Christs here are linked with false prophets; like the Antichrist of 2 John 7, the false Christs here are deceivers" ("Antichrist in the Early Church," *A Mind for What Matters*, 182).

have multiplied,[62] all of which could signal that the Parousia of the *real* Christ is near at hand.

It is important to recognize that the false Christs actually are also opposed to the Incarnation. The true Christ, who came in the flesh to effect mankind's salvation, is replaced by a pseudochrist who claims to bring final truth. Thus there is no need to look back to Jesus Christ as Savior when *the* Christ is at hand. The pseudochrist therefore by actually denying the decisive significance of the Incarnation is also an antichrist:[63] he has taken the place of the true Christ.

What has been said above about "false Christs" is one of the aspects of the so-called New Age Movement.[64] Jesus is viewed by many New Age devotees as only one of many manifestations or appearances of the Christ. There have been innumerable incarnations through the ages and there will be many more. This thinking is rooted in the Hindu idea of the avatars who again and again embody themselves in human form. Jesus accordingly is not "*the Word*" that "became flesh" (as in John 1:14) but one among many. Such "New Age" teaching is likewise antichrist in its opposition to the once-for-allness of the Incarnation and its essentiality for mankind's salvation.[65]

---

[62]On this latter point, a frequently recurring claim of New Age devotees is that Christ now secretly waits somewhere but will soon manifest Himself. For example, in the major newspapers of the world on April 25, 1982, a full page advertisement declared in large letters, "THE CHRIST IS NOW HERE," adding that his name is "Lord Maitreya" ("the World Teacher"), whose "location is known to only a very few disciples" (recall Jesus' words about "the inner rooms"!) but who "*within the next two months* will speak to humanity through a worldwide television and radio broadcast" (italics theirs). Despite the obvious fact that this pseudochrist never so spoke or appeared does not prevent such a claim from continually recurring. Incidentally, I have recently heard it announced that "Maitreya" is secretly in London but will soon declare himself to the world! So it goes . . . from deception to deception.

[63]Another full page ad of response appeared a week later (May 2, 1982) in the *Los Angeles Times* declaring "ANTICHRIST IS NOW HERE." This ad, produced by a number of Christians in southern California, was an important, and true, perception of the "Lord Maitreya" as not the Christ but representing the antichrist. The ad continued in bold letters, "THE TRUE CHRIST HAS ALWAYS BEEN HERE," and pointed out that He will not come back in hiding but as suddenly as a flash of lightning.

[64]"The New Age Movement" is an umbrella term for a variety of persons, organizations, and practices that proclaim the alteration of human consciousness so as to recognize humanity's oneness with God and affirm the emerging unity of all religion and government in a new "Aquarian" age of peace and love. This movement draws heavily on various Eastern religions (especially Hinduism), the occult (e.g., channeling/mediumship), and humanistic psychology. The book that particularly heralded the "new age" was Marilyn Ferguson's *Aquarian Conspiracy: Personal and Social Transformation in the 1980's*. See also David Spangler, *Revelation: the Birth of a New Age*; Mark Satin, *New Age Politics*; Jessica Lipnack and Jeffrey Stamps, *Networking* (cataloging some 1,500 diverse New Age networks); George Trevelyan, *A Vision of the Aquarian Age*. Shirley MacLaine, a Hollywood celebrity, through her autobiography, *Out on a Limb*, and subsequent television miniseries, is one of the best-known New Age exponents. For critiques of New Age thinking, see, e.g., Walter Martin, *The New Age Cult*; Karen Hoyt, ed., *New Age Rage*; Douglas R. Groothuis, *Unmasking the New Age*; Ruth Tucker, *Another Gospel: Alternative Religions and the New Age Movement*; and Tal Brooke, *When the World Will Be as One: The Coming New World Order in the New Age*.

[65]Instead of emphasizing that Jesus was one of the embodiments of the divine, New Age thinking often stresses that He was simply an embodiment of the universal and impersonal

Now let us more specifically address the church. For within it recently leaders and teachers have arisen who radically question the Incarnation, often labeling it mythology[66] or denying its uniqueness.[67] This is far more serious than when an outsider—for example, an avowed atheist or secular humanist—makes a similar statement, for that is to be expected and there is no pretense of its being somehow a Christian statement. But when this kind of questioning comes from theological and ecclesiastical leaders who still claim to represent the Christian faith, it is much harder to cope with. For deception is now occurring with the result that many of the faithful are led into departure from truth. Thus do "the spirit of antichrist" and "apostasy" tragically go hand in hand.

Perhaps we have not arrived at "the apostasy"—but who really knows? We have earlier noted with gratitude the outpouring of the Holy Spirit and the growth of the kingdom in our present day—and this includes a rising tide of affirmation of the central truths of Christian faith.[68] The percentage of church members who affirm the deity of Christ, the Incarnation, and the Resurrection has seemingly reached an all-time high.[69] But—and this is the dark side—many of our denominations, theological schools, church colleges, and ecclesiastical boards have moved far to the left, and, if at all, hold only loosely to the historic Christian faith.[70] What people, both outside and inside the church, do not fully realize, however, is how far this defection has really

"Christ consciousness." This exists in all people and needs only to be recognized. Benjamin Creme in his book *The Reappearance of Christ and the Masters of Wisdom* writes, "The christ is not God, he is not coming as God. . . . He is the embodied soul of all creation. . . . He would rather that you didn't pray to him, but to God within you, which is also within him" (p. 135).

[66]Rudolf Bultmann, German Lutheran New Testament scholar, has stood out prominently in our time. See his essay, "New Testament and Mythology" in *Kerygma and Myth*, where he makes this statement: "What a primitive mythology it is, that a divine being should become incarnate, and atone for the sins of men through his own blood!" (p. 7). Also within recent years a number of British churchmen and theologians (all Anglicans) have come forth with a collection of essays entitled *The Myth of God Incarnate*. These question the basic, ontological reality of the Incarnation. For example, in the preface, the editor calls for "a recognition that Jesus was . . . 'a man approved by God' for a special role within the divine purpose, and that the later conception of him as God incarnate, the Second Person of the Holy Trinity living a human life, is a mythological or poetic way of expressing his significance for us" (p. ix). These are but a few evidences (illustrations could be multiplied) of an ever-growing "spirit of antichrist" within the church in our time.

[67]For example, Matthew Fox, a Roman Catholic theologian, claims that the "cosmic Christ" has become incarnate in all of us. Fox asks, "Does the fact that the Christ became incarnate in Jesus exclude the Christ's becoming incarnate in others—Lao-tzu or Buddha or Moses or Sarah . . . or Gandhi or me or you?" (*The Coming of the Cosmic Christ*, 235). This is a violent antichrist statement, for it denies Jesus as *the* Christ and views all people as incarnate "cosmic" Christs.

[68]On the matter of *The Myth of God Incarnate*, it should be added that in the same year as this work by Anglican theologians was published, a number of evangelical church leaders and scholars responded with a series of essays entitled *The Truth of God Incarnate*, edited by Michael Green. These essays strongly affirm the historic faith, and for this we may be profoundly grateful. In regard to Matthew Fox's book *The Coming of the Cosmic Christ*, it is encouraging to note that Fox in 1988 was ordered silenced by the Vatican's Congregation for the Doctrine of the Faith.

[69]As recent polls have shown.

[70]The focal point of the United Presbyterian Church controversy, mentioned earlier, was the deity of Christ. The problem centered in a pastor who was unwilling to affirm that Jesus

gone. Seminaries particularly are often at fault, for despite occasional public statements to pretend orthodoxy, the situation in many places is really an ominous one.[71] For it is in the seminaries that the pastors and leaders of the church most often receive their basic training and orientation. Truly "a spirit of antichrist" is abroad in many of the churches.

Once again: Is *the* apostasy here? Let me try to give no further answer. Perhaps enough has been said to suggest that, however this question may be answered, it is a perilous moment in the life of faith. We *could* be in the last days before the return of the Lord.

VI. THE MAN OF SIN

We have been considering the increase of evil as one of the signs of the Parousia of Christ and have noted both the general picture of the last days—"terrible times"—and the growth of apostasy. It is now in order to reflect on the disclosure of "the man of sin"—or "man of lawlessness." According to Paul, not only will there be "the apostasy," but also the revelation of this man before the Lord returns. Referring to the day of the Lord, he writes, "It will not come unless the apostasy comes first, and the man of lawlessness[72] is revealed. . ." (2 Thess. 2:3 NASB).

It is particularly relevant that the appearance of this man of sin closely relates to the return of Christ. For a few verses later Paul says, "Then the lawless one will be revealed whom the Lord will slay with the breath of His mouth and bring to an end by the appearance of His coming [*parousia*]" (v. 8 NASB). Hence, we may add, when this man of wickedness is revealed, the final advent of Christ is at hand.

Let us examine more closely the identity of this man. In the first place it is possible that he emerges from apostasy, since Paul speaks of his appearance immediately after mentioning "the apostasy." He could represent some-

is God. To the ordination question, "Is Jesus God?" he replied, "No, God is God." His case went through six church tribunals with the result that his status as a minister was left intact. The General Assembly declined to take action, but did draw up a statement on the deity of Christ. The pastor still rejects, he says, the "notion of Jesus being God"; rather, He is "one with God." Such a statement, I would urge, remains a departure from, and a dilution of, historic Christian faith.

[71]For example, a survey in 1977 of the theological viewpoint within a number of seminaries on the deity and resurrection of Christ revealed that many faculty members deny both. In an article in the *Los Angeles Times*, John Dart cited one example among many: "For instance, at the nine-school Catholic and Protestant Graduate Theological Union in Berkeley, which has the largest theological faculty in the world, New Testament professor Edward Hobbs said he didn't know of one school there in which a significant part of the faculty would accept statements that Jesus rose physically from the dead or that Jesus was a divine being" ("Did Jesus Rise Bodily? Most Scholars Say No," Sept. 5, 1977). The situation has hardly improved within recent years.

[72]The Greek phrase is *ho anthrōpos tēs anomias*. The KJV reads "the man of sin"; RSV, NIV, and NASB read "the man of lawlessness." Although *anomia* is literally "lawlessness," it frequently is best translated "sin," "wickedness," or "iniquity" (see, e.g., Matt. 23:28; 24:12; Rom. 4:7; 6:19; 2 Cor. 6:14; and Heb. 10:17 in various translations). According to TDNT, in 2 Thessalonians 2:3 "ἀνομία has in fact no meaning other than that of ἁμαρτία [sin]" (4:1086). It is interesting that some ancient Greek manuscripts have *hamartia* rather than *anomia*. This evidence all the more reinforces the view that "the man of sin" is preferable to "lawlessness," because it better signifies the concentration of evil he represents. So while retaining "lawlessness" as a possible translation, I will also render *anomia* as "sin," "wickedness," or "iniquity."

one who has become so utterly apostate that he is now the very embodiment of sin and wickedness.[73] He may be the climactic stage where "the antichrist" and "the apostasy" are combined.[74] Thus, from such a dark situation in which "the spirit of antichrist" is regnant and apostasy abounds, the man of sin who is the very incarnation of evil could readily emerge. In Christian tradition he has frequently been called "the Antichrist";[75] however, more accurately, he is the man of sin, the man of lawlessness, the man of total wickedness.[76]

It is also possible that rather than being directly related to apostasy, the appearance of "the man of sin" is a parallel phenomenon. Paul speaks of both happening[77] before the Parousia of Christ. What he does specify, as we have observed, is that the appearance of this man occurs in very close connection with the return of Christ. So let us look more carefully at Paul's description of this man and the nature of his appearance.

Immediately he is spoken of as "the son of perdition": ". . . and the man of lawlessness is revealed, the son of perdition" (continuation of 2 Thess. 2:3).[78] This title suggests both his origin, the offspring of all that is evil,[79] and his destination, eternal damnation. He is not the devil but his instrument, for what he does is totally activated and empowered by Satan. Thus Paul later speaks of "the coming of the lawless one by[80] the activity of Satan . . . with all power" (2 Thess. 2:9).

Now let us return to the statement about "the son of perdition." This man—"that Wicked"[81]—shows his devilish character at once. For, Paul continues, he "opposes and exalts himself against every so-called [or 'everything that is called'] god or object of worship, so that he takes his seat in the temple of God, proclaiming [or 'showing' KJV] himself to be God" (2 Thess. 2:4). Here truly is the devil's own way: the way of standing against God, seek-

---

[73]The NEB translation suggests this: "That day cannot come before the final rebellion against God, when wickedness will be revealed in human form."

[74]Or, as TDNT has it: "The apostasy makes possible the power of the man of sin, and this in turn increases the apostasy" (1:514).

[75]It is important to bear in mind that, strictly speaking, "the antichrist" (as we have noted) is one who denies the Incarnation. There is nothing said in John's letters about the antichrist being "the son of perdition" or proclaiming himself "to be God" (as Paul proceeds to describe "the man of sin"). Hence—whatever the long tradition to the contrary—I will not make a simple identification between the two.

[76]The NEB later calls him "that wicked man" (2 Thess. 2:8).

[77]Note the conjunction "and" in 2 Thessalonians 2:3.

[78]The Greek word is *apōleias*. The NASB reads "destruction"; NIV, "the man doomed to destruction." The Greek word usually means "destruction," and frequently (as here) "eternal destruction." For example, 2 Peter 3:7 speaks of "the day of judgment and destruction [*apōleias*] of ungodly men." The traditional translation "perdition" (KJV as well as RSV), meaning "eternal damnation," vividly sets forth the picture. (Judas Iscariot is called "the son of *apōleias*" in John 17:12.)

[79]Cf. Isaiah 57:4: "Are you not children of transgression, offspring of deceit?" Jesus addresses the Jews who oppose Him: "You are of your father the devil, and your will is to do your father's desires" (John 8:44). He also condemns the scribes and Pharisees for proselytizing a person and making him "twice as much a child of hell as [them]selves" (Matt. 23:15).

[80]The Greek word is *kata*—"in accord with" (NASB).

[81]The KJV uses this title for the man in translating 2 Thessalonians 2:8.

ing to exalt himself above God.[82] Wherever God, or anything called God, is worshiped, "that Wicked" enters "the temple,"[83] "takes his seat," and calls for worship of himself. This has been Satan's one vast ambition and compulsion from the beginning—and he will seek to have it fulfilled on earth through his vicar, the man of total iniquity.

Although this man of wickedness will emerge just prior to the Parousia of Christ, "the mystery of wickedness" is now present: "Already the secret power[84] of wickedness is at work. . ." (2 Thess. 2:7 NEB). It is not as if the man of wickedness will bring wickedness on to the scene, for it is "already" operating. This sounds much like "the spirit of antichrist," which is "in the world already";[85] then comes its full manifestation. In the present situation, Paul suggests, there is a restraint upon the working of this "secret power"; otherwise he would be fully revealed. Paul says to the Thessalonians, "You know what is restraining him[86] now so that he may be revealed in his time" (v. 6). After speaking of the secret power of wickedness already operating, Paul adds, "Only he who now restrains it will do so until he is out of the way [literally, 'comes out of the midst']"[87] (v. 7). Who the restrainer is, Paul does not directly state, nor is it clear how the restrainer is out, or comes out, of the way. It has been suggested that Paul is referring to the order and fabric of society that restrains evil, so that when it breaks down, evil will have full sway.[88] Insofar as the Holy Spirit in the world provides the "cement" of society and the restraint

[82]Recall the words of "Lucifer" in Isaiah 14: "I will ascend into heaven. I will exalt my throne above the stars of God. . . . I will be like the most High" (vv. 12–14 KJV). Cf. also "the little [horn]" in Daniel 7:8 with "a mouth speaking great things," and the willful king in Daniel 11:36–37 who "shall exalt . . . and magnify himself above every god, and shall speak astonishing things against the God of gods." (Also cf. Ezek. 28:2ff.)

[83]"The temple" may be viewed as a literal temple, perhaps Jerusalem, but more likely this is a metaphor for the usurpation of God's authority. F. F. Bruce writes, "The Jerusalem sanctuary is meant here . . . but meant in a metaphorical sense . . . he ['the son of perdition'] demands not only the obedience but also the worship due to God alone" (*1 & 2 Thessalonians*, 169). Leon Morris, contrariwise, affirms a more literal understanding of the temple (see *The First and Second Epistles to the Thessalonians*, NICNT, 4). I believe Bruce's view better represents the text. Another view is that "the temple" represents the church. Paul refers to the church likewise as "the temple of God" in 2 Corinthians 6:16 (cf. Eph. 2:21–22). It is possible that the usurpation of God's authority includes both world and church (see below concerning the two beasts). Incidentally, about a decade before Paul wrote the Thessalonians, the Roman emperor Caligula in A.D. 40 had attempted to place his statue in the temple at Jerusalem to assert his claim to divinity. Although this attempt failed, it may have provided Paul background for his teaching about the eschatological temple and the man of sin.

[84]The Greek word is *mystērion*—"mystery" as in KJV, RSV, NASB. The NIV, like NEB, translating the word as "secret power" seems proper in this context.

[85]As John says in 1 John 4:3. See the earlier discussion.

[86]The Greek word is simply *katechon*—"restraining," "holding back." There is no "him" in the Greek. So the KJV has "what withholdeth" without an object.

[87]The Greek phrase is *ek mesou genētai*. There is no word "taken" ("taken out of the way") as in KJV, NIV, NASB. The NEB puts it well: "until the Restrainer disappears from the scene."

[88]In regard to "the restrainer," Dietrich Bonhoeffer writes, "The 'restrainer' is the force which takes effect within history through God's governance of the world, and which sets due limits to evil. The 'restrainer' is not God; it is not without guilt; but God makes use of it in order to preserve the world from destruction. . . . The 'restrainer' is the power of the state to establish and maintain order" (*Ethics*, 44).

upon evil and disruptive forces, this is also possibly Paul's meaning.[89] To come "out of the midst" would signify that near the Parousia the restraining influence of the Spirit of God will be so removed from the midst of human society that the man of sin is free to express himself fully and at the same time be revealed in his totally evil reality.[90]

We read next that this release of restraint upon the man of sin will initiate his revelation, even his *parousia*. Words that usually apply to Christ in His final advent now are applied to him: "And then the lawless one will be revealed . . . the *parousia* of the lawless one by the activity of Satan"[91] (vv. 8–9). Suddenly he will be out in the open for all to see. "That Wicked"—the man of sin, of lawlessness, of total iniquity—will have come on the scene!

We further read that the coming of this man of wickedness by Satan's activity will have two aspects: (1) it will be "with all power and signs and false wonders"; and (2) it will be "with all the deception of wickedness for those who perish" (vv. 9–10 NASB). The Wicked One will have power over all those who do not belong to Christ ("those who perish"); they will be dazzled by his counterfeit miracles; they will be utterly deceived by his wicked deeds. Indeed, as Paul proceeds to say, because they have "refused to love the truth and so be saved . . . God sends upon them a strong delusion to make them believe what is false. . ." (vv. 10–11). Those who know salvation in Christ, however, will not be thus deluded.

Finally the revealing of the man of sin will be brief, for immediately following the words "the lawless one will be revealed," Paul adds, "whom the Lord will slay with the breath of His mouth and bring to an end by the appearance of His coming" (2 Thess. 2:8 NASB). This is the total and final end of the Wicked One.

Now let us summarize this teaching about the man of sin in relation to the return of Christ:

1. The man of sin must appear before the return of Christ. His appearance immediately precedes "that day." Recall the words "The lawless one will be revealed whom the Lord Jesus will slay." The appearance of the man of wickedness belongs to the final moments in history.

2. His appearance is in close conjunction with *the* apostasy. The man of sin may emerge from that apostasy or be a parallel phenomenon. Indeed, he may make use of the apostasy to achieve his own ends.

3. The man of sin is "the son of perdition." He is the offspring of evil, wholly activated by Satan, and is on his way to destruction.

4. He totally opposes every object of worship, takes his seat "in the temple," and declares himself to be God. In his self-deification there is no room for the true God.

5. At the present time this secret power of wickedness is already at work. This suggests that the God-defying, God-identifying attitude operates throughout history. It is possible that just before the appearance of the man of

[89]L. Berkhof writes, "He [the Holy Spirit] restrains for the present the deteriorating and devastating influence of sin in the lives of men and society" (*Systematic Theology*, 426). It is possible that Paul is referring both to the state (as exemplified by Rome in his day) as an order given by God and the Holy Spirit's restraint through the state (cf. Rom 13:1).

[90]This could correspond to the "loosing" of Satan (Rev. 20:7). See later discussion.

[91]Paul's use of the word *parousia* for the coming of the man of sin suggests that he is Satan's false christ. "He is Satan's messiah, an infernal caricature of the true messiah" (EGT, 4:49).

sin this attitude will be reaching a climax.

6. He will emerge on the scene when the present restraint upon this secret power is removed. This may mean the collapse of the social/moral order as held together by the Holy Spirit.

7. The appearance of the man of sin will also be that of a *parousia*. While he previously has been restrained and not known, he will now be revealed and present for all to see. (An additional note: Since the word *parousia* in relation to Christ always refers to His future coming, the Scripture suggests that the man of sin is the final counterfeit appearance of Christ.)

8. The man of sin will dazzle the world with his powerful deeds, including miracles, and various deceptions. These will lead those who do not truly believe in Christ to be so deluded as to follow him to destruction.

9. The *parousia* of the man of sin will be brief, for closely connected to his appearance will be the return of Jesus Christ.

Next we must ask, Is the scenario previously described relevant for our time? Does any, or all, of it suggest we may be near the time of the Lord's return? Again, as with apostasy, we cannot be sure. However, there is at least one line of increasing evidence that the appearance of the man of sin and therefore the return of Christ could be near at hand.

Let us focus on one particular point. It is apparent from what has been said that the man of sin is one who elevates himself to deity. He is not described (any more than "the antichrist") as a thief, a murderer, an immoral person, but as one who puts himself in the place of God. God is simply shunted aside in human pride, and man declares himself to be God. Since "the secret power" of this deep sinfulness is "already" at work—and has been over the centuries—are there evidences of its presence and perhaps increase in our time?

We could pursue many lines and seek to check out much historical data, but rather than doing so (an impossibly complex task in our limited space), I will focus on the recent growth of secular humanism and the so-called New Age movement.[92]

By secular humanism I refer to various views of human existence that have no place for God. For example, the thought of such men as Karl Marx, Charles Darwin, and Sigmund Freud has made a strong impact on the twentieth century. Materialistic communism, an evolutionary interpretation of the world and human life, and Freudian psychological analysis have all served to view God at best as expendable, but most often as a liability. Secular humanism, as, for example, set forth in *Humanist Manifesto I* and *Humanist Manifesto II*, has no place for God, faith, or moral law.[93] As we have noted, Paul speaks of the man of sin as one "who opposes and exalts himself against every so-called God or object of worship." This sounds similar to secular humanism, which opposes every trace of religion and puts man and his self-fulfillment as the only legitimate concern. Thus, without saying so, secular humanism deifies man. Humanist man, accordingly, to use Paul's further words, is one "proclaiming himself to be God."

On the American scene, despite the high percentage of people who claim to believe in God, there is an ever-growing secularity. The constitutional freedom

[92]Recall the brief discussion of the latter in Section V.

[93]See *Humanist Manifesto I* (1933) and *Humanist Manifesto II* (1973). Also note *A Secular Humanist Declaration* (1980). For a fuller discussion of the two manifestos, see *Renewal Theology*, 1:247–49.

for religion has become increasingly a freedom *from* religion. For example, the use of the name of God in the public arena is increasingly forbidden. Moral values in the public schools are now frequently made subject to "values clarification," by which the student is called upon to make his or her own moral choice. Abortion presumes the right to kill the unborn and is protected by law. Homosexuality, a profound human perversion, has come more and more to be viewed as a viable lifestyle. The critical orientation in all such aberrations as these is not God and objective moral principles but man's own selfish preferences. Many of our churches have likewise become so secularized that, despite the verbal avowal of God, they simply go along with, indeed often even encourage, the secular tide. In a strange way, the secular man therefore "takes his seat in the temple of God."

The New Age movement goes the further step of specifically identifying man with God. Whereas secular humanism declares there is no God and then proceeds to make man into God, New Age thinking quite bluntly speaks of man as one with God and urges all people to realize their true identity. To be more precise, the New Age movement views all things as one—man, the world, God—so that we need look nowhere else than our inner selves to discover God. As one contemporary New Ager puts it: "The myth of the savior 'out there' is being replaced by the myth of the hero 'in here.' Its ultimate expression is the discovery of *the divinity within us*."[94] Another declares, *"Know thyself and that will set you free; to thine own self be true; to know self is to know all; know that you are God; know that you are the universe.;"*[95] If we know that we are God, then we may even apply such biblical words about God as "I AM" to ourselves.[96] When this happens—and it is occurring in various shapes and forms throughout the New Age movement—surely we are not far removed from the man of sin who proclaims himself to be God.

VII. THE TWO BEASTS

We turn now to a consideration of the two beasts in Revelation 13: the beast out of the sea and the beast out of the earth. As will be apparent, they represent in a quite dramatic manner much of the same reality as "the man of sin."

Let us first note the background. The dragon (Satan) has been making war on believers, "those who keep the commandments of God and bear testimony to Jesus," and now he stands "on the sand of the sea [i.e., 'on the seashore']" (Rev. 12:17). As he stands there, one beast begins to emerge "out of the sea" (13:1) and later another "out of the earth" (13:11). Thus from the outset a

---

[94]Words of Marilyn Ferguson, author of *The Aquarian Conspiracy*, in the *Yoga Journal* (July/August 1981), 10. (For this quotation I am indebted to Tal Brooke, *When the World Will Be One*, 206.)

[95]Shirley MacLaine, *Dancing in the Light*, 350 (emphasis hers).

[96]David Spangler, spiritual leader of the Findhorn New Age community, writes about himself: "I AM now the life of a new heaven and a new earth. Others must draw upon Me and unite with Me to build its forms" (*Revelation: The Birth of a New Age*, 110). Shirley MacLaine at one point speculates whether the statement "I AM THAT I AM" (Exod. 3:14) could well mean that she was her own creator, even that she had created God (see her book *It's All in the Playing*, 192). In the television production of *Out on a Limb*, Shirley is shown on the beach at Malibu with her occultist spiritual adviser, their arms flung open to the universe, shouting out, "I am God! I am God! I am God!" Here is the absolute zenith of human pride and self-deception.

connection is suggested between the dragon and the two beasts.

A. The Beast out of the Sea

This beast "out of the sea"[97] is obviously a full representative of the dragon, for it has "ten horns and seven heads" (Rev. 13:1), identical with the "great red dragon" with his "seven heads and ten horns" (Rev. 12:3).[98] Since the dragon is the depiction of Satan,[99] the beast out of the sea is Satan's identical representative. Indeed, "to it the dragon gave his power and his throne and his great authority" (13:2). This hideous looking beast is Satan's surrogate and plenipotentiary.

Next we observe that the beast had received a mortal wound in the past, but now it was healed. "And I saw one of his heads as if it had been slain,[100] and his fatal wound was healed" (v. 3 NASB). This suggests the continuing vitality of the beast, for even with a mortal wound it had now been healed.[101] This calls to mind the fact that Satan himself had received a mortal blow at Calvary—indeed in fulfillment of the ancient promise that "the seed of woman" would crush the serpent's

---

[97]"Out of the sea" probably signifies out of the peoples and nations of the world. Cf. Isaiah 17:12: "Ah, the thunder of many peoples, they thunder like the thunder of the sea! Ah, the roar of nations, they roar like the roaring of many waters!" Also note Revelation 17:15 where the "waters" (i.e., the sea) are described as "peoples and multitudes and nations and tongues." Biederwolf writes, "By the vast majority of commentators the sea is taken, and rightly, as symbolic of the disordered and confused life of the Gentile nations of the world" (*The Second Coming Bible Commentary*, 630).

[98]The ten horns find their background in Daniel 7. There four great beasts come up "out of the sea" (v. 3), in turn like a winged lion, a bear, a leopard, and the last unnamed but described as "terrible and dreadful and exceedingly strong" and having "ten horns" (v. 7). Horns represent power, and ten horns in apocalyptic language the completeness of power. Because Revelation 13:2 describes the beast as looking like a leopard, bear and lion ("the beast . . . was like a leopard, its feet were like a bear's, and its mouth was like a lion's mouth"), thus a combination of the three fierce animals in Daniel 7, it portrays all the more the intensity of terrifying power in the ten horned beast of Revelation 13. "Seven heads" suggest the tremendous vitality of the beast—as we will observe. (Later we will note how the references to seven heads and ten horns are specifically applied to earthly kings, according to Rev. 17.)

[99]In Revelation 12 the dragon is specifically called Satan "the great dragon . . . who is called the Devil and Satan, the deceiver of the whole world" (v. 9).

[100]The Greek word is *esphagmenēn*. This is the same word used in Revelation earlier for the Lamb (Christ): "I saw a Lamb standing, as though it had been slain [*esphagmenon*]" (5:6; see also v. 12), and again in chapter 13 again about "the Lamb that was slain" (v. 8). The above text does not mean that the head of the beast was only apparently slain (any more than that the Lamb was only apparently killed). No, the head was mortally wounded, but the death wound had been healed.

[101]Although only one of the seven heads is said to have been slain, it was a mortal blow to the whole beast. Later in the chapter, reference is made to "the beast [not just one of its heads] which was wounded by the sword and yet lived" (v. 14). Incidentally, some commentators have seen in the slaying of one of the heads and its healing a reference to the Roman emperor Nero, who, after a career of violently persecuting Christians, committed suicide. The legend later developed that Nero still lived and returned again and again in succeeding brutal emperors, climaxing with Emperor Diocletian. Although this interpretation is possible, it is noteworthy that the text in verse 14 (as just quoted) does not say that the beast died and lived on but that the whole mortally wounded (v. 3) beast "yet lived." As Robert H. Mounce puts it, "It was the *beast* who recovered from the death-stroke upon one of its heads" (*The Book of Revelation*, NICNT, 253). (For further references to Nero, see infra.)

head (Gen. 3:15 NIV).[102] Satan is therefore a mortally wounded force, even though he is alive in the world today. Likewise, the beast as his identical representative has a crushed head, but is very much alive and active in the world.[103]

One might think that this hideous beast would be anything but attractive to people. However, Revelation adds that "the whole world went after the beast in wondering admiration" (v. 3 NEB), and they "worshipped the dragon because he had conferred his authority upon the beast; they worshipped the beast also, and chanted, 'Who is like the Beast? Who can fight against it?' " (v. 4 NEB). There is both great adulation of the beast and the conviction that none can withstand its power.

The beast next is shown as having been "given a mouth uttering haughty and blasphemous words . . . against God, blaspheming his name and his dwelling" (vv. 5–6). Since it was earlier said that "each head had a blasphemous name" (v. 1 NIV), this means that all seven heads were united in blaspheming God. The beast, by blaspheming, speaks contempt against God, arrogates to itself divine attributes; by blaspheming against His name,[104] it speaks evil against everything God represents, including His laws; by blaspheming His dwelling, it even denounces those who dwell in heaven, both angels and human beings. This last-mentioned blasphemy may also be against believers whose true home is in heaven, even while they still dwell upon the earth.[105]

Moreover, the beast has authority over all who dwell on earth *except* the true believers: "Authority was given it over every tribe and people and tongue and nation, and all who dwell on earth[106] will worship it, every one whose name has not been written before the foundation of the world in the Book of life of the Lamb that was slain" (vv. 7–8). The authority, however, is for a limited period of time: "It was allowed[107] to exercise authority for forty-two months"[108] (v. 5). For this relatively

---

[102]The words in Genesis apply to the serpent who, in Revelation, is also the dragon. The "great dragon" is likewise called "the ancient serpent" and both are identified as "the Devil and Satan" in Revelation 12:9.

[103]The mortal wounding of the beast, accordingly, must be traced back, prior to any Roman emperor, to the mortal wounding of Satan himself. (On this, see especially Paul S. Minear, "The Wounded Beast," in *The Journal of Biblical Literature* 72, (1953), 93–101.) Although wounded fatally, Satan continues his diabolical activity.

[104]According to George E. Ladd, "to blaspheme . . . in connection with God [is] to do or say anything that desecrates his divine name or violates his glory and deity" (*The Revelation of John*, 180).

[105]This whole picture of the beast uttering haughty words calls to mind Daniel 7. From the last beast—"terrible and dreadful and exceedingly strong" with its ten horns—there emerged a little horn that "pulled out by the roots" three of the horns and "possessed eyes like the eyes of a man, and a mouth uttering great boasts" (vv. 7–8 NASB). The "great boasts" are not specified as blasphemies in Daniel, but this seems to be implied.

[106]"All who dwell on earth," from what follows, obviously does not include believers. In Revelation, wherever "earth-dwellers" are mentioned, the reference is to unbelievers. See also Revelation 6:10; 8:13; 11:10; 13:12, 14; 14:6; 17:2, 8.

[107]The word "allowed" (or "given" as in KJV, NIV, NASB; the Greek word is *edothe*) refers not to Satan but to God. Although Satan had "great authority" (v. 2), it was by God's permissive will that the beast was allowed to exercise that authority. God remains sovereign!

[108]Mounce speaks of forty-two months as "a conventional symbol for a limited period of time during which evil would be allowed free reign" (*The Book of Revelation*, NICNT, 221). It is the same period as 1,260 days (see Rev. 11:2–3; 12:6), or "a time, and times, and half a

short time the beast is in complete control over all persons except those whose names are in "the Book of life," namely those who belong to Jesus Christ.

However, during this same period the beast is also "allowed[109] to make war on the saints [believers in general] and to conquer them" (v. 7). The saints, not bending to the beast's authority over the world with its adulation and worship, not willing to accept the beast's dominion, are overcome. Thus the beast, unable to claim believers for itself, turns to their persecution and destruction, and for a time (forty-two months), it is successful. The saints are conquered by it.[110]

How should believers react during this time of the beast's persecution? Are they to fight against it? The next verses emphatically answer: "If any one has an ear, let him hear:[111] If any one is to be taken captive, to captivity he goes; if any one slays with the sword, with the sword must he be slain" (vv. 9–10). If captivity is the result of the beast's persecution, believers should not seek to avoid it; moreover, if they seek to slay with the sword through self-defense, it will only result in their being slain.[112] The important thing for believers is to stand firm and endure whatever comes. So the exhortation concludes: "Here is a call for the endurance and faith of the saints" (v. 10).

Next we need to reflect further on the identity of the beast out of the sea. Later in Revelation 17, a woman[113] is depicted sitting on the beast described as "a scarlet[114] beast . . . full of blasphemous names, and it had seven heads and ten horns" (v. 3). Afterward John is told, "The beast that you saw was, and is not, and is to ascend [or 'is about to come up' NASB] from the bottomless pit [or 'the abyss' NASB] and go to

time" (cf. 12:6 and 14), or 3 + 2/2 years (a time = one year, times = two years, half a time = six months). Also again see Daniel 7 where it is said that "a little horn" comes up among the ten horns with "eyes like the eyes of a man, and a mouth speaking great things" (v. 8); further, "he shall speak words against the Most High, and shall wear out the saints of the Most High . . . and they shall be given into his hand for a time, two times, and half a time" (v. 25; cf. Dan. 12:7).

[109]Note the word "allowed" again. What happens to the saints is by God's sovereign permission.

[110]Again returning to Daniel 7, we read later in the chapter about the little horn: "As I looked, this horn made war with the saints, and prevailed over them" (v. 21). Daniel's fourth beast with its little horn obviously in some sense prefigures the beast out of the sea in the Book of Revelation, for this beast likewise conquered (= "prevailed over") the saints.

[111]Earlier in Revelation, John declares, "Blessed are those who hear" (1:3), and each of the letters to the seven churches (chaps. 2–3) contains the words "He who has an ear, let him hear what the Spirit says to the churches."

[112]The words about the sword are sometimes interpreted as referring to the beast or its followers who slay with the sword and who, in turn, will be slain. However, I believe that the words refer to believers. Recall Jesus' injunction to Peter: "Put your sword back into its place; for all who take the sword will perish by the sword" (Matt. 26:52). Note also John 18:11: "Put your sword into its sheath; shall I not drink the cup which the Father has given me?" Even as Jesus would not take the sword, but rather submitted to captivity and death, so should His disciples at all times and particularly in the end time of evil's (seeming) victory.

[113]The woman is described as "Babylon the great, mother of harlots and of earth's abominations" and "drunk with the blood of the saints and the blood of the martyrs of Jesus" (Rev. 17:5–6) and also as "the great city which has dominion over the kings of the earth" (v. 18).

[114]"Scarlet" suggests its master, "the great *red* dragon" of Revelation 12:3.

perdition" (v. 8). This cryptic statement refers to the fact that the beast, like Satan, did exist ("was"), received a mortal blow[115] ("is not"), is going to break forth in totally evil fury ("is to ascend from the bottomless pit"),[116] and is now on his way to final perdition.[117] The verse ends by saying, "It [the beast] was and is not and is to come" (v. 8). Thus the coming of the beast is in some sense a future event.

Let us examine this more closely, for it is apparent from what follows that the beast is both present and future. The Book of Revelation now identifies the seven heads: "The seven heads are seven hills on which the woman is seated; they are also seven kings, five of whom have fallen, one is, the other has not yet come, and when he comes he must remain only a little while. As for the beast that was and is not, it is an eighth but it is of[118] the seven, and it goes to perdition" (vv. 9–11). The "seven hills" doubtless refer primarily to Rome,[119] the famed city of seven hills, thus the beast with its seven heads, in part, refers to the imperial city. But then the seven heads also refer to "seven kings," or emperors, that have reigned, one who is now reigning, and another yet to come who will have a short reign.[120] Still this is by no means

[115]Recall Revelation 13:3, 14.

[116]Ladd writes about the beast: "He once existed in one or more of his heads; he ceased to exist when one of the heads received a mortal wound; but he will have a future existence when the wound is healed. The healing . . . will involve a satanic embodiment that will exceed anything that has yet occurred" (*A Commentary on the Revelation*, 226). According to Mounce, "In the broadest sense the beast is that satanically inspired power that, although having received the stroke of death, returns to hurl himself with renewed fury against the forces of God" (*The Book of Revelation*, NICNT, 312).

[117]Regarding this "perdition" see Revelation 19:20.

[118]I have substituted "of" (as in KJV) for "belongs to." The Greek word is *ek*. "Of" better expresses the idea of being of the same spirit and attitude as the preceding seven without being a part of them.

[119]As Leon Morris puts it, "This does not mean that Rome exhausts the meaning of the symbol . . . the great city is every city and no city. It is civilized man apart from God" (*The Revelation of St. John*, 209). "Babylon" and "Rome" are essentially the same.

[120]Much effort has been expended to identify these seven emperors. At the time John received the Revelation, as noted, five had preceded, the sixth was presently reigning, and the seventh was still to come. The sixth is sometimes identified as Nero. Preceding him were Julius Caesar, Augustus, Tiberius, Caligula, and Claudius. Nero reigned subsequently, from A.D. 54–68, and brought to a peak the bitter persecution of Christians that was later to become the official policy of the Roman Empire. (For more on Nero see the next section, "The Second Beast.") Galba succeeded Nero and reigned less than a year (A.D. 68–69), hence "only a little while." However, most New Testament scholars date the writing of the Book of Revelation much later toward the end of the reign of Domitian, who was emperor from A.D. 81 to 96. According to G. R. Beasley-Murray, "from Irenaeus on, the tradition of the church has maintained that John 'saw the Revelation . . . at the close of Domitian's reign' " (*Revelation*, NCBC, 37; the inner quotation is from Irenaeus, *Against Heresies*, v.30.3). To get to Domitian in John's reckoning of the emperors it has been suggested that only the five emperors deified by an act of the Roman Senate be included (Julius Caesar, Augustus, Claudius, Vespasian, and Titus) and, as the sixth, Domitian, who demanded the worship of himself as *Dominus et Deus noster* ("our Lord and God") and actively persecuted the church. Domitian was succeeded by Nerva, who reigned for less than two years (hence another possibility for the other king "who has not yet come"). Whatever the reckoning—whether Nero or Domitian, or some other emperor at the time of the Revelation, with short-lived emperors immediately following them—the important matter is the eighth (as I will discuss in the next paragraph). A further note: It is important to

the entire picture, because the beast that was and is not will finally be an eighth: he will be of the seven in the sense that he will share their kind of rule, but he will be separate from and beyond them. This clearly is the final, eschatological beast for whom the Roman emperors (as beastly figures!) are the prototypes. This beast will epitomize all the evil of the deified and deifying[121] emperors and especially of those who did everything possible to ravage the Christian church. The beast out of the sea is therefore *the final concentration of evil in worldly form*,[122] for after that "it goes to perdition." This is its divinely destined end.

It is important to note that with the eighth beast we have finally gone beyond the Roman Empire into the final days of history. The seven heads of the beast representing seven emperors of ancient Rome have been left behind: an eighth has come to take their place and go far beyond them in its evil power. Moreover—and now we move on—the ten horns previously mentioned also become future! John is told, "And the ten horns that you saw are ten kings who have *not yet* received royal power [literally, 'a kingdom'], but they are to receive authority as kings for one hour, together with the beast. These are of one mind and give over their power and authority to the beast; they will make war on the Lamb" (17:12–14). The ten kings represent the totality of earthly powers[123] that in the time of the end will be wholly subservient to the beast and make final warfare against Christ. The authority of these "ten kings" and the beast is short-lived. In "one hour"[124] it is all over, and the victory is the Lamb's—"the Lamb will conquer them, for he is Lord of lords and King of kings!" (v. 14).

Thus we have come full circle. The beast out of the sea in Revelation 13 is ultimately this eschatological beast at the consummation of history. In one

---

recognize that seven is more a number of totality all through the Book of Revelation than necessarily an exact figure (e.g., "the seven spirits" [1:4], the seven churches, the seven seals, the seven trumpets, etc.), so that the seven kings may not call for particular identification as much as recognition that they signify the totality of God-defying authority *represented* by the Roman emperors.

[121]See note 120.

[122]Mounce writes, "He is Antichrist, not simply another Roman emperor. . . . He belongs to the cosmic struggle between God and Satan which lies behind the scenes of human history. Yet he will appear on the stage of history as a man. He is of the seven—not *one* of the seven—in that he plays the same sort of role as his earthly predecessors. He, himself, however belongs to another sphere of reality" (*The Book of Revelation*, NICNT, 316). The fact that the eighth beast is *not* another head is important to bear in mind. Thus, according to I. T. Beckwith, this describes "Antichrist not as an eighth head but as the eighth world ruler coming up after the 7 world rulers impersonated in the Roman emperors have fulfilled their course" (*The Apocalypse of John*, 708). Thus the eighth beast will appear at the climax of history.

[123]Some interpreters view these earthly powers as ten political entities in a revived Roman Empire. In our time much attention has been given in some circles to the formation of the European Economic Community, which until 1981 consisted of ten nations. However, in 1986 Spain and Portugal joined the E.E.C., thus bringing the number to twelve. Thus the interest in this possibility has somewhat waned. I agree with Beckwith's statement: *"The ten kings are purely eschatological figures representing the totality of the powers of all nations on earth which are to be made subservient to Antichrist"* (italics his) (*The Apocalypse of John*, 700). Recall that the dragon himself (Satan) is depicted as having ten horns. To repeat, ten is a symbolic number in Revelation for completeness or fullness.

[124]"One hour" signifies a short period. See also Revelation 18:10, 17, 19 for a similar use of this expression.

sense the beast represents the Roman emperors who increasingly took on evil proportions, through both prideful deification of themselves and vicious persecution of the church. Thus what John saw rising out of the sea was a terrifying reality already experienced in his day.[125] Rome was the beast: its seven heads and ten horns depicting the Roman emperors in their successive power. But the beast was more than a Roman symbol;[126] it surely further represents all earthly powers that have risen up and, seeking to assume divine proportions, have found Christians and Christian faith intolerable. Still, beyond that, there is also the beast to come (the "eighth") who will be the final manifestation of evil on earth in its God-defying and Christian-persecuting reality.

Now a critical question. Does this necessarily mean a totalitarian state (such as, for example, Stalinist Russia or Nazi Germany)? Such a state seems to closely approximate Roman self-glorification and ruthless domination. There can be little question of this. However, the Book of Revelation focuses more on "the kingdom (singular) of the world" than on "the kingdoms (plural) of the world." I call attention to the triumphant climactic words in Revelation 11:15: "The kingdom of the world has become the kingdom of our Lord and of his Christ, and he shall reign for ever and ever." The kingdom of the world signifies more than, and perhaps other than, any earthly kingdom, however violent or debased it may be. It is the whole world as dominated by the power of Satan, the power of evil, arrayed against the kingdom of "our Lord and of his Christ."[127]

Now let us observe a number of similarities between the man of sin and the beast out of the sea.

1. Both the man and the beast operate under the total power of Satan. The coming of the former is "by the activity of Satan . . . with all power" (2 Thess. 2:9); to the latter "the dragon gave his power and his throne and great authority" (Rev. 13:2). They both are earthly embodiments of Satan.

2. Both the man and the beast are totally anti-God. The former "exalts himself against every so-called god or object of worship" (2 Thess. 2:4); the latter "opened its mouth to utter blasphemies against God" (Rev. 13:6) and everything connected with God.

3. Both the man and the beast make themselves into God. The former "takes his seat in the temple of God, proclaiming himself to be God" (2 Thess. 2:4); in the latter case people worshiped the beast, saying, "Who is like the beast?" (Rev. 13:4).

4. Both the man and the beast have only a short time to function. In the same statement about the man being revealed, the text reads that "the Lord Jesus will slay him" (2 Thess. 2:8); the beast is given authority "for forty-two months" (Rev. 13:5).

5. Both the man and the beast are on the way to "perdition." The man is called "the son of perdition" (2 Thess. 2:3); and the beast "goes to perdition" (Rev. 17:11). The end of both is eternal destruction.

---

[125]John received the Revelation while exiled on the Isle of Patmos, as part of a churchwide experience of "tribulation": "I John, your brother, who share with you in Jesus the tribulation and the kingdom and the patient endurance, was on the island called Patmos on account of the word of God and the testimony of Jesus" (Rev. 1:9).

[126]Earlier I mentioned the four beasts of Daniel 7. It is generally recognized that the four represent different earthly empires (usually Babylonia, Medo-Persia, Greece, and Rome). Since the beast in Revelation 13 is a composite of the four Danielic beasts (see earlier), it may well represent more than the Roman Empire.

[127]I will say more about this later.

Unmistakably, the man of sin and the beast out of the sea represent the same malign reality.

B. The Beast out of the Earth

The beast out of the earth,[128] which John next beholds emerging, has none of the terrifying appearance of the beast out of the sea: "It had two horns like a lamb" (Rev. 13:11). When compared with the first beast's ten horns and seven heads, body like a leopard, feet like a bear, and mouth like a lion,[129] this beast seems positively innocuous. Surely it can do no one any harm. But then it speaks. Rather than a little lamblike "baa," its voice was that of a dragon: "It spoke like a dragon" (v. 11). Hence this second beast is another embodiment of Satan. Likewise it "exercises all the authority of the first beast" (v. 12). Thus the evil triumvirate is now fully on the scene: the dragon on the seashore, the beast out of the sea, and the beast out of the earth.[130]

The important matter to underscore here is the deceptive character of the beast out of the earth. It looks anything but threatening, and its appearance as a lamb suggests a Christlike figure. Christ is called the Lamb (or a lamb) many times in the Book of Revelation.[131] Hence there is the suggestion of a representation of Christ in the figure of the two-horned lamb.[132] Deception is undoubtedly involved, for although the lamb's speech is like that of the dragon (hence, satanic), the lamb appears to all as a guileless and trustworthy figure.

Next we observe that this second beast is wholly a henchman of the first beast. It indeed has all the authority of the first beast (as noted before), but this authority is "in its presence" (Rev. 13:12). Therefore, even as the first beast was worshiped by "the whole earth" (vv. 3–4), the second beast in the presence of the first is constantly engaged in making that worship happen. It "makes the earth and those who dwell in it[133] to worship the first beast, whose fatal wound was healed" (v. 12 NASB). Thus the sole purpose of the second beast is to direct the worship and glorification of the first.[134]

In order to further this adulation of the first beast,[135] the lamblike beast engages in deceptive practices. First, in the presence of the other beast, "he performs great signs [or 'miracles']," so

---

[128]The "earth" may represent that which is sensual and deceptive. James speaks of a "wisdom" that "does not come down from heaven but is earthly, unspiritual, of the devil" (3:15 NIV). This beast out of the earth, as we will note, is the epitome of falsehood. In no sense does his "wisdom" "come down from heaven."

[129]Recall note 98 for this description and reference to Daniel 7.

[130]This evil triumvirate, or evil trinity, is the exact opposite of the Holy Trinity. Even as each member of the Holy Trinity has equal authority so does each member of the unholy trio.

[131]Twenty-seven times, against the background of Revelation 5:6: "I saw a lamb standing, as though it had been slain." Thereafter, in Revelation, "a lamb standing" is invariably called "the Lamb."

[132]Significantly, however, Revelation 5:6 specifies that the "lamb standing" had "seven horns and . . . seven eyes" so that ultimately the two-horned lamblike beast out of the earth will be no competitor for the Lamb of God.

[133]Recall that "earth-dwellers" are those whose names are *not* written in "the Book of life of the Lamb that was slain" (v. 8).

[134]This is evidence of another diabolical parallel to the Holy Trinity. Even as the Holy Spirit constantly focuses on Christ ("He will glorify me"—words of Jesus about the Holy Spirit and Himself in John 16:14), so the second beast's total concern is the glorification of the first beast.

[135]I say "further" because, as we noted, the first beast is already an object of adulation—"the whole world went after the [first] beast in wondering admiration" (v. 3, NEB).

that he "even makes fire come down out of heaven to the earth in the presence of men"[136] (Rev. 13:13 NASB). Second, because of these signs that deceive the "earth dwellers," the second beast tells those "who dwell on the earth[137] to make an image" (v. 14 NASB) to the first beast. Third, the second beast gives breath to the image so that "it might even speak" and "cause as many as do not worship the image of the beast to be killed"[138] (v. 15 NASB). Believers—those neither deceived by the great signs nor involved with the image made by "earth-dwellers"—are subject to death.

What do we make of all this? First, in line with the interpretation that the first beast initially signifies first-century Roman emperors, the second beast seems primarily to represent the religious cult around the emperors, whose basic purpose was to further the worship and even the deification of the emperor.[139] Not having the vast (ten-horned) power of the emperor, the pagan priests of Rome (with only two horns) seemed to be almost harmless (lamblike). But by their magical practices and sorceries they further duped the pagan world—the "earth-dwellers"—into making an image of the emperor in various places that could even speak.[140] Christians, who, unlike the rest of the world, were not deceived by the godlike imperial image, were nonetheless required to pay homage or be subject to persecution and death. Genuine believers could not salute the emperor as *"Dominus et Deus noster"* ("our Lord and God"),[141] for Christ was the only Lord and God. As a result, untold numbers of Christians were put to death.

Let us reflect briefly on the image of the beast. It is significant that it is not the second beast but the "earth-dwellers" themselves who make the image. To be sure, this is at the instigation of the second beast, but they all do it: they voluntarily capitulate. Since reference here is to all "earth-dwellers," hence even beyond the reach of the Roman Empire of John's day, there must be some further meaning than literally constructing images of the Roman emperors. Since, as we have observed, the first beast is ultimately the "eighth king" who represents a final power and is the focal point of admiration ("the whole earth followed the beast in won-

---

[136]Thus the beast seemingly operates like the prophet Elijah in whose presence the fire from heaven fell (1 Kings 18:20–39). However, Elijah's miracle was for the glorification of God, the beast's for the glorification of Satan. The second beast is therefore also "the false prophet," the designation given later in Revelation 16:13; 19:20; 20:10.

[137]Once again, the earth-dwellers are the unbelieving world.

[138]Note the similarity here to Daniel 3, which records the Babylonian King Nebuchadnezzar's demand that everyone worship his "golden image," with death the certain penalty for refusing to do so.

[139]Henry B. Swete writes, "The Caesar [i.e., emperor]-worship was a State function at which the Proconsul and the other magistrates assisted, and the pagan priesthood wrought their *σημεῖα* ['signs'] before these representatives of the Empire" (*Commentary on Revelation*, 170). Since John is addressing seven churches in Asia Minor (chaps. 2–3), it is also noteworthy that the imperial cult was strong there and many temples had the ruling emperor's statue in place for the people to come and worship. Pergamum was the center of the imperial cult. As Hemer notes, "The provincial temple at Pergamum is portrayed on many coins of the city and of the Commune. It served as a precedent for the cult in other provinces" (*The Letters to the Seven Churches of Asia in Their Local Setting*, 84).

[140]Beasley-Murray writes that "sorcery and trickery were part of the stock-in-trade of pagan priesthoods" (*Revelation*, NCB, 217). Ventriloquism was a common practice in the various temples.

[141]Recall note 120. This was the title by which Domitian later demanded he be saluted.

der") and worship ("they worshiped the beast and chanted, 'Who is like the beast? Who can fight against it?' "), the second beast is his continuing religious support. In every way possible the lamblike beast intensifies the adulation of the first beast by performing great signs. Thus the "earth-dwellers" make or, to put it a bit differently, conjure up an image of the beast that is almost overwhelming and takes on life in itself (the religious beast giving breath and speech to the image). They worship not only the beast but also the very image of it.[142] The image "speaks" in such fashion as to demand total obedience.

We have seen this phenomenon in the twentieth century to a limited degree in such countries as Germany and Russia. In regard to Nazi Germany, there was an approximation to the worship of Adolf Hitler and the images (pictures, paintings, etc.) made of him. This near worship was accentuated both by those who made a pagan religion of German blood and destiny and by the so-called German Christian Church that expressed devotion to Hitler and the Nazi state. Russia has had a long history in which the Russian Orthodox Church, the state church, has given support to both czarist and communist leaders. Indeed, in almost every established church there is the strong tendency to give religious support to the governmental authorities. Of course, this may not be worship of the state (as represented by kings, queens, and the like), but inflated images of leadership (with all its pomp and ceremony) often intensify devotion to the political powers.

Thus it is possible that this political and religious coalition will reach its zenith at the close of the age. In any event, the Roman emperors whose deification was supported by the religious cultus is the paradigm in the Book of Revelation of what will yet fully occur.

But there is more to this "beastly" situation than is found in the political/religious arena alone. For, as earlier noted, the first beast is more than a political entity. It signifies also the whole world—"the kingdom of the world"—as dominated by the power of evil. It is this world that is deeply anti-God and anti-Christian and denies divine truth as a basis for law and morality. A profoundly sinful perversity is at work not only in the political arena but also in all human society, making an "image" out of evil and following it "religiously." This applies to every area of life in which mankind substitutes idols for God, an image for reality. People may not directly worship Satan (though many do), but before the images of him they readily bow: self-glorification (even to self-deification),[143] self-gratification (through money, sexual license, pleasure hunting, power seeking), and self-fulfillment (seeking one's own fulfillment as the goal of life). Much more could be added to describe this "beastliness" that grips all "earth-dwellers." But now the truly grotesque feature is that the harmless-appearing lamb, the religious beast, wholly approves of this demonic self-orientation, indeed blesses these images, and fully undergirds the worldly enterprise.

The second beast may be called an "ecclesiastical beast." For here we behold representatives of the worldly church, whatever their outward differ-

---

[142]R. C. Lenski writes, "By bowing down before the antichristian world power all the dwellers on the earth make an idol of it and worship that idol" (*Interpretation of St. John's Revelation*, 414).

[143]The apex of this, as earlier mentioned, is to be found in New Age thinking (cosmic humanism) in which man is acclaimed as God: "I am God." However, such self-deification practically exists in the world at large.

ences, endorsing and demonstrating many things secular. Leaders vie with one another for position and acclaim, many church denominations sprinkle "holy water" on such immoral practices as homosexuality and abortion, and people are taught that success and prosperity are the right of every believer. When this occurs, the world is all the more secure in its sinfulness, for the church is doing the same thing and granting total encouragement to others. The worldly beast is in all its glory as the ecclesiastical beast vents its approval!

Let me add a further word about the second "ecclesiastical beast." It has actually no interest in true faith. With sanctimonious (lamblike) and stentorian (dragonlike) utterances it points away from good and gives justification to evil. This is done very subtly, because it uses God-language in such a way as to deceive people into thinking that it speaks truly. Later in Revelation the second beast is described as "the false prophet";[144] for indeed he pretends to speak for God while leading people astray.

In many ways this is "the apostasy" come to full flower. Rather than standing for God, biblical truth, and moral values, the church is more and more deceived into walking the way of the world and, in turn, endorsing that way. It is a tragic situation that can only end in chaos and destruction.

Returning to the Scripture about the second beast, let us observe further that "it causes all, both small and great, both rich and poor, both free and slave,[145] to be marked on the right hand or the forehead" with "the name of the beast or the number of its name" (Rev. 13:16–17). The worship of the beast and its image results inevitably ("it causes all") in economic activity being wholly marked by the beast: "No one can buy or sell unless he has the mark" on his right hand or forehead (vv. 16–17). The mark of the beast on the right hand or forehead denotes the capitulation of self to be Satan's instrument—the right hand signifying activity, the forehead implying mental power.[146] The result is that only those who have so capitulated—hence have been so marked—can buy or sell in the marketplace of the world.[147] It is the way of selfish con-

---

[144]Revelation 16:13; 19:20; 20:10.

[145]This is a more expansive way of describing the "earth-dwellers": the classes mentioned represent all people who are not believers.

[146]"A prostration of bodily and mental powers to the beast's domination is implied" (*The Second Coming Bible Commentary*, 241, quoting A. R. Fausset). Hence this does not mean that one has to have a physical mark—name or number—of the beast on the hand or forehead (as some biblical commentators say). Such is too external and superficial. What is intended here is not a physical but a spiritual imprint. The same thing is true of those in the next scene who have the name of the Lamb and the Father on their foreheads—"a hundred and forty-four thousand who had his name [the Lamb's] and his Father's name written on their foreheads" (Rev. 14:1). Incidentally this imprintation by God is likewise God's "seal." Earlier 144,000 were "sealed" for protection (7:3–4) and the seal is "upon their foreheads" (9:4). The devil "marks," but God "seals"! Both are profoundly spiritual. The question comes to this: *Which way will it be—the devil's "marking" or God's "sealing"?* The outcome is of ultimate significance, with eternity finally at stake.

[147]It would be an error to infer from this that buying and selling are bad in themselves (they are not), or that believers (those without the mark of the beast) are excluded from the marketplace. Rather, it is that all who have received the mark (that is, who are committed to the way of Satan)—and this signifies all "earth-dwellers"—cannot buy or sell without the

cern, exploitation, and self-aggrandizement: there is no other way to go for those who bear the mark of the beast.

Yet both are the way of ultimate destruction. An angel later cries out a terrible warning: "If anyone worships the beast or its image, and receives a mark on his forehead or on his hand, he also shall drink the wine of God's wrath, poured unmixed into the cup of his anger, and he shall be tormented with fire and brimstone . . . for ever and ever" (Rev. 14:9–11). Such a person has sold out to the devil: the devotion of his heart (worship), mind (forehead), strength (hand) to Satan. This is just the opposite of true devotion to the Lord: "Love the Lord your God with all your heart, and with all your soul (or mind), and with all your strength" (Deut. 6:5 NIV).[148] Such a one will live forever in the presence of the Lord, enjoying His love and blessing. If the Lord is not the center of devotion, another—Satan, the beast, the "man of wickedness"—will be. The terrible result is eternal destruction.

A final word regarding the mark of the beast. The mark is said to be "the name of the beast or the number of its name" (Rev. 13:17).[149] Then this cryptic comment is added: "This calls for wisdom: let him who has understanding reckon the number of the beast, for it is a human number,[150] its number is six hundred and sixty-six" (v. 18). Many attempts have been made to identify this number with a particular known emperor[151] or some other person in later history;[152] however, this procedure is probably ill-advised. Six hundred and sixty-six (like many other numbers in Revelation) is a symbolic figure, and most likely signifies the beast in its most evil human manifestation[153]—the eschatological beast at the consummation of

---

mark upon them. They operate in the world of buying and selling *as those already committed* to the way of Satan: the way of exploitation, self-interest, etc.

[148]Recall also that in the Old Testament the Israelites were told to bind these words on their "hands" and "foreheads" (Deut. 6:8). This is the outward sign of total devotion to God, even as the mark of the beast likewise on the hands and foreheads means total commitment to Satan.

[149]In Greek (also in Hebrew and in Latin) every letter was also viewed as a number (as though a = 1, b = 2, c = 3, etc.). Thus any word could be computed as a numerical sum by adding up all the letters.

[150]Or "the number of (a) man." The Greek phrase is *arithmos anthrōpou*.

[151]The most common suggestion is Nero. The name "Nero Caesar" when transposed into Hebrew comes out to 666 (although an extra *n* must be added to "Nero"—"Nero*n*"). Because of the ruthlessness of Nero's persecutions of Christians, it is possible that 666 represents him or any later "Neronic" oppression—a kind of "return of Nero." However, Domitian's full Latin title in an abbreviated Greek form also equals 666. By another computation the initials of the Roman emperors from Julius Caesar to Vespasian add up to 666. It is also interesting that Irenaeus, writing in the second century, shows along with other suggestions that the word *Lateinus* (the Roman Empire) translates into 666 (incidentally Irenaeus makes no reference to Nero). In regard to Nero, it is questionable whether John would have expected his Greek readers to know Hebrew also, and further, even if they did know, to make a transposition from the Greek text of Revelation into Hebrew.

[152]Including such disparate figures as the Pope, Martin Luther, Napoleon, and Hitler—to mention only a few.

[153]In biblical numerology the number seven symbolizes completeness and perfection (e.g., see Rev. 1:4 where "the seven spirits" doubtless signify the completeness and perfection of the Holy Spirit). Six in sequence is before seven but never reaches or equals it. Three sixes, 666, may then signify the final, but abortive effort of the beast in human form to attain divine status.

history. Roman emperors in John's time doubtless represented this evil,[154] but John foresaw another yet to come[155] so totally evil that even as it is being described, John says, "It goes to perdition." This is the final God-boasting, world-acclaiming, Christian-persecuting beast that, supported by the devil, is in human form.

Now in retrospect concerning what has been said about "the man of sin," "that Wicked" (KJV), it is apparent that the second beast is quite similar to him in various aspects. One aspect in particular stands out: both the man of sin and the second beast are masters of deception. Recall the statement that the *parousia* of the man of sin would be "by the activity of Satan . . . with all power and with pretended signs and wonders, and with all wicked deception for those who are to perish" (2 Thess. 2:9–10). Compare similar words about the second beast: "It works great signs, even making fire come down from heaven . . . [thus] it deceives those who dwell on earth [i.e., 'those who are to perish']" (Rev. 13:13–14). False signs and vicious deception are hallmarks of both the man of wickedness and the second beast.

This brings up an interesting question: Is the second beast only similar to the man of sin, or is it somehow identical with at least one aspect of him? I have earlier commented on many similarities between the man of sin and the first beast and concluded that the two figures represent the same evil reality. It is interesting, we may now observe, that there is one striking feature about the man of sin that is not depicted in the first beast, namely the performing of counterfeit miracles and wicked deception. With the second beast, such activity is elaborated in vivid detail.

The man of sin, the Wicked One, I submit, is therefore actually a kind of composite beast. In himself he represents both the secular and the religious components: the man of sin is at one and the same time the ten-horned and seven-headed beast out of the sea *and* the two-horned, one-headed lamb out of the earth. Each is the counterpart of the other. He is both terrifying and seemingly harmless; he both blasphemes God Almighty and demonstrates miraculous powers. He is the awesome combination of worldly power and idolatrous veneration; he is a kind of wholly secular entity supported by the religious (non-Christian) forces of the earth.

Finally, it should be clear that what is being represented by these eschatological figures is man. Neither the Wicked One nor the beast(s) is Satan, however much each is his instrument. Nor is any of them a demon under Satan's direction, however demonically activated they may be. They are both man: the Wicked One is "the man of sin"; the beast has "the number of a man." Here is man inspired by Satan—*man in open and final revolt against Almighty God.*

EXCURSUS: THE BEAST IN REVELATION 11 AND THE TWO WITNESSES

In the discussion about the two beasts I have not commented on an earlier account in the Book of Revelation that likewise speaks of "the beast." We have observed the emergence of the beast "out of the sea" and the beast "out of the earth" in Revelation 13 and also the "eighth" beast in

[154]Recall the seven heads of the beast being identified as seven Roman kings (emperors); thus 666 in a sense applies to all of them.

[155]The eighth beast of Revelation 17:11.

Revelation 17 who ascends "from the bottomless pit."[156] This last depiction of the beast, as observed, is manifestly the climactic appearance of demonic evil in its effort to destroy all Christian witness from the earth. For along with "the ten kings" it "will make war on the Lamb"; but "in one hour" it is all over, and the victory is the Lamb's. Now we note, for the first time, that this beast "from the bottomless pit" was earlier shown in Revelation 11 as emerging on the scene: "the beast that ascends from the bottomless pit" (v. 7). It is obvious that this is the same eschatological beast—up from the pit—and that it is doing essentially the same thing: it "will make war" (v. 7). And, as in Revelation 17, the war is against Christianity (against "the Lamb," v. 14); in Revelation 11 it is against Christ's "two witnesses" (vv. 3, 7): the war will be "upon them" (v. 7).

Revelation 11 earlier depicts a trampling of "the holy city" by "the nations" and two witnesses prophesying during that same period: "The nations . . . will trample over the holy city[157] for forty-two months. And I will grant my two witnesses power to prophesy for one thousand two hundred and sixty days, clothed in sackcloth" (vv. 2–3). The witnessing covers the same period as the trampling,[158] and belongs to the end of history immediately preceding the beast's making war upon them. It is the period of the persecuted (trampled) church's final witness.

The two witnesses who prophesy during this period are described as "the two olive trees and the two lampstands which stand before the Lord of the earth" (v. 4). The "two olive trees" relate to Zechariah 4, where they precede these words spoken to Zerubbabel: "Not by might, nor by power, but by my Spirit, says the Lord of hosts" (v. 6). The olive trees are later declared to be "the two anointed who stand by the Lord of the whole earth" (v. 14). These words refer to the task of rebuilding the temple amid many difficulties, not by human strength but by the power of the Holy Spirit. The "two anointed"[159] become in Revelation the two Spirit-anointed witnesses who, as the church,[160] bear witness at the end of

[156]Or "the abyss" (as in NIV, NASB, NEB). The Greek word is *abyssos*.

[157]"The holy city" in Revelation is best understood as "the church" (see also Rev. 21:10, 11, 19, where the glorified church, the "new Jerusalem," is called "the holy city"; likewise see "the beloved city" in Rev. 20:9). So Mounce writes, "In John's imagery the holy city is yet another designation for the church" (*The Book of Revelation*, 221). The background of the "trampling" may be seen in Daniel 8:9–14, which contains the earliest reference to "the transgression that makes desolate" (i.e., "the abomination of desolation") and "the giving over of the sanctuary and host to be trampled under foot" (v. 13). Also recall Daniel's reference to "the holy people" in 12:7 as background for "the holy city."

[158]The 42 months = 1260 days (computing the year, or 12 months, as 360 days). This is, of course, likewise 3½ years. The period of 1,260 days also corresponds with the 1,290 days of Daniel 12:11. (In regard to the latter, the 30 days of difference may reflect the difference between lunar and solar calendar reckoning [see John Goldingay, *Daniel*, WBC, 310].)

[159]The "two anointed" in Zechariah in the first instance probably refer to both Zerubbabel the governor and Joshua the high priest (on Joshua see Zechariah 3).

[160]The two lampstands represent the church. The churches are depicted in Revelation as lampstands: "The seven lampstands are the churches" (1:20). The number two does not mean that only two churches bear witness. Rather "two" probably is used because two witnesses signify a valid and complete testimony (e.g., see Deut. 19:15: "Only on the evidence of two witnesses, or of three witnesses, shall a charge be sustained"; cf. also Jesus' words in Matt. 18:16 and Paul's in 2 Cor. 13:1). Some biblical interpreters, however, view the two as that portion (two out of seven) of the church that will suffer martyrdom in the end

history. As noted, they appear in sackcloth, symbolizing a call to repentance and the approaching judgment. But also, as the text continues to show, during the days of their witnessing they have great miracle-working power.[161] No foe can stand against them.

What this suggests is that the church in the time of the end will be Spirit-anointed to a high degree. It will witness with great authority and effectiveness. Its message of repentance and coming judgment, its proclamation of the gospel,[162] its miraculous deeds all will point to the church successfully carrying forward the gospel commission to its final climax. This is indeed a challenging and wonderful prospect!

When—and only when—the witness is complete, does the beast ascend from the bottomless pit: "And when they have finished their testimony, the beast that ascends from the bottomless pit will make war upon them[163] and conquer them and kill them" (Rev. 11:7). The gospel has been testified to all the world; the task assigned by Jesus to His witnesses (also recall Matt. 24:14) has been done. The beast is too late on the scene! He conquers and kills utterly to no avail![164]

The beast in Revelation 11 accordingly is the same as the beast(s) in Revelation 13. The first beast conquers (v. 7) and the second beast kills (v. 15). What is not said in Revelation 13 is that the saints have already won the victory through their witness. So whatever calamities may happen to the church when the beast breaks onto the scene, the Great Commission will already have been gloriously fulfilled.

VIII. THE ABOMINATION OF DESOLATION

Our concern continues to be the increase of evil as a sign and precursor of the return of Christ. We have earlier noted the words of Jesus about apostasy: "Most men's love will grow cold" (Matt. 24:12).[165] This is followed by His statement about "the gospel of the

---

(see, e.g., Morris, *The Revelation of St. John*, TNTC, 148; G. B. Caird, *The Revelation of St. John the Divine*, 134). Others view the two as literal individuals who in the last days will bear powerful witness (see J. M. Ford, *Revelation*, AB, 177–78 for various possibilities that have been suggested).

[161]Their miracles described in verses 5–6—"fire from their mouth" to protect their witness, "power to shut the sky" from rain falling that would dampen their witness, "power over the waters to turn them into blood, and to smite the earth with every plague"—are reminiscent of Elijah (see 2 Kings 1:10–12; 1 Kings 17:1) and Moses (Exod. 7–12). But see also Jeremiah 5:14: "Behold, I am making my words in your mouth a fire . . . and the fire shall devour them."

[162]This is suggested by the two witnesses having "power to prophesy" (v. 3). Prophesying in Revelation refers particularly to testifying to Jesus: "The testimony of Jesus is the spirit of prophecy" (19:10; cf. John 1:7).

[163]The language of making "war upon them" is further evidence that the two witnesses are *not* individuals. One would hardly make war against two people!

[164]This is all the more apparent in the verses that follow, for after a short time ("3½ days," v. 11) the witnesses stood on their feet and "in the sight of their foes went up to heaven in a cloud" (v. 12). This may be a parallel to "the rapture" of the church. See later discussion.

[165]Incidentally, before moving on, we should observe that Jesus prefaces this statement thus: "And because wickedness is multiplied. . . ." The word translated "wickedness" is *anomia*, the same as in 2 Thessalonians 2 ("the man of wickedness," "the mystery of wickedness"). We have noted the close connection between *anomia* and *apostasia* in Paul's letter, although apostasy was there mentioned first; in Jesus' words *anomia* is first mentioned and given as the reason that most people's love will grow cold.

kingdom" and "the end"[166] (Matt. 24:14). Next we come to the words of Jesus about "the abomination of desolation" (Matt. 24:15 NASB)—and to this we now give our attention.

The text reads, "So when you see the ABOMINATION OF DESOLATION[167] which was spoken through Daniel the prophet, standing in the holy place[168] (let the reader understand). . ." (NASB).[169] Then will follow a period of "great tribulation"[170] (Matt. 24:21), which Jesus describes, and then declares that "immediately after the tribulation of those days" (v. 29) He will come "on the clouds." Hence, the event of the "abomination of desolation" will be a sign ("when you see") of the coming of the Lord.

We have previously observed how this coming (*erchomai*) of Jesus was fulfilled initially in the destruction of Jerusalem in A.D. 70.[171] Now we note that the words of Jesus concerning "the abomination of desolation" also had their near fulfillment in that same event. By observing what occurred then we should be better able to understand the meaning of such an "abomination" before His final coming.

However, in looking at the significance of "the abomination of desolation," we need to turn even farther back, to the Book of Daniel. The words of Lord Jesus are quite specific on this: ". . . spoken through Daniel the prophet . . . (let the reader understand)." So first we will observe what Daniel himself had to say about this expression.

There are three references in Daniel to "the abomination of desolation," though the language in the first account is slightly different. First, Daniel 9:27: "And he will make a firm covenant with the many for one week, but in the middle of the week[172] he will put a stop to sacrifice and grain offering; and on the wing of abominations will come one who makes desolate, even until a complete destruction, one that is decreed, is poured out on the one who makes desolate" (NASB). Next, Daniel 11:31: "And forces from him will arise, desecrate the sanctuary fortress, and do away with the regular sacrifice. And they will set up the abomination of desolation ['the abominable thing that causes desolation' NEB]" (NASB). Finally, Daniel 12:11—"And from the time that the regular sacrifice is abolished, and the abomination of desolation is set up, there will be 1,290 days"[173] (NASB).

It is generally recognized that references to "the abomination of desolation" have an initial fulfillment in the desecration of the Jewish temple by the

---

[166]See the prior discussion on this.

[167]The Greek phrase is *bdelugma tēs erēmōseōs* = "the detestable thing causing the desolation" (BAGD). The NIV translates this as "the abomination that causes desolation"; RSV, "the desolating sacrilege."

[168]Thus the abomination, the detestable thing, brings about the desecration of the holy place by standing in it. Instead of "in the holy place," Mark 13:14 reads "where it should not be."

[169]The NASB capitalizes ABOMINATION OF DESOLATION, not for emphasis, but because it is an Old Testament expression.

[170]See the discussion in the next section.

[171]See the preceding chapter.

[172]"Week" here is translated "seven" in NIV. Actually this is a week of years, "seven of years," sometimes called a hebdomad. Hence the covenant is for seven years, and "the middle of the week" (next mentioned) refers to the midpoint of three and a half years.

[173]1,290 days = approximately 3½ years (see n.158).

Syrian king Antiochus Epiphanes.[174] Antiochus, after making a covenant with many apostate Jews, captured the city in 170 B.C. He plundered it, set it ablaze, stripped the temple of its precious vessels, and in 167 B.C. caused all sacrifices to cease. A few months later Antiochus placed a pagan altar in the temple, offering swine and other unclean beasts. To climax it all, he set up in the temple an image to the pagan deity, Zeus Olympius. This was "the abomination of desolation."[175] The next three and a half years after the sacrifice stopped were years of severe oppression and continuing sacrilege against the temple until Judas Maccabeus restored the worship of God and rededicated the temple[176] in 164 B.C.[177]

Now the words of Jesus that relate to the desecration of the temple in A.D. 70 can take on more concrete significance: "When you see the abomination of desolation . . . spoken through Daniel the prophet . . . then let those who are in Judea flee to the mountains. . ." (Matt. 24:15–16 NASB). For that will be the time of Jerusalem's total destruction, and of great tribulation to follow. What then was this "abomination of desolation"? Actually, it was not unlike what happened under Antiochus Epiphanes, except that in this case the desolator was Titus, the Roman emperor. As the temple was being destroyed, the Roman legions under Titus brought their military standards of eagles to the holy precincts, offered up sacrifices to them, and saluted Titus as imperator.[178] Thus Roman eagle ensigns rising over the Jewish temple, the offering of sacrifice to them, and the adulation of Titus—all represented "the abomination of desolation." Later, as further desecration, the statue of Titus was erected on the site of the destroyed and desolated temple. Thus did the Roman emperor assume the place of God.

This brings us again to the close of the age. For as we have previously observed, all that is said about Jerusalem—its destruction and desolation—refers ultimately to events prior to the return of Christ. Antiochus Epiphanes and Titus with their sacrilegious practices and blasphemy against the holy temple and the living God are types and precursors of the final abomination.[179]

---

[174]Also called Antiochus IV.

[175]See The Apocrypha, 1 Maccabees 1, which describes this tragic situation for Jerusalem. Verse 54 specifically mentions "the abomination of desolation": "On the fifteenth day of the month Kislev. . . . 'the abomination of desolation' was set up on the altar" (NEB). See also Josephus, *The Antiquities of the Jews*, 12.5.4., for another vivid account.

[176]Jews to this day celebrate the victory over Antiochus and the rededication of the defiled temple in the Feast of Hanukkah (also called the Feast of Lights).

[177]See 1 Maccabees 4:52–59.

[178]"And now the Romans . . . brought their ensigns to the temple; and set them over against the eastern gate; and there did they offer sacrifices to them, and there did they make Titus imperator, with the greatest acclamations of joy" (Josephus, *The Wars of the Jews*, 6.6.1.) It is also interesting that Josephus viewed the words of Daniel as applying to the desolations wrought both by Antiochus and the Romans: "Our nation suffered these things under Antiochus Epiphanes, according to Daniel's vision. . . . In the very same manner Daniel also wrote concerning the Roman government, and that our country should be made desolate by them" (*The Antiquities of the Jews*, 10.11.7.). F. F. Bruce also notes, "In Josephus' eyes the abomination of desolation—the profanation of the sanctuary and of the priestly office [by the insurgent zealots]—was manifested increasingly as the war went on; he records, in fact, a succession of 'abominations' " ("Josephus and Daniel," *A Mind for What Matters*, 24).

[179]C. F. Keil, focusing on Antiochus Epiphanes and the final assault of the Antichrist,

Thus we come once more to "the Wicked" who will carry the abomination of desolation to its ultimate height. Exalting himself over all gods and objects of worship, and taking his seat in "the temple of God," he will proclaim to all the world his deity. This Wicked, this composite beast, this mouthpiece of Satan, is man in his final, and promethean, exaltation of himself as God.

Now we raise the question, For how long a period will this "abomination" be manifest? We have previously observed, first, that "forty-two months" are mentioned for the time of the beast. This, of course, is the equivalent of 3½ years, or "half a week"[180] (in Daniel's terminology). Since the desolator in Daniel's prophecy causes sacrifice to stop "in the middle of the week"[181] and his abominations continue thereafter, this is a period of 3½ years, or 42 months.[182] Later, as we observed in Daniel, the statement is made that there will be 1,290 days from the time the abomination of desolation is set up until the end: this again is approximately 3½ years, or 42 months. Hence, the time the beast exercises authority and the extended period from the appearance of the desolation of abomination is the same.

Thus the various figures given in days, months, or years signify the same period of time. There is, I might add, yet another designation for the same period, namely, "a time, and times, and half a time," (a "time" = one year, "times" = two years, and "half a time" = six months) in Revelation 12:14[183] and similarly "a time, two

writes, "The rage of Antiochus Epiphanes against the Jewish temple and the worship of God can be a type of the assault of the Antichrist against the sanctuary and the church of God in the time of the end" (*Commentary on the Old Testament*, 8:370). I would only change "can be" to "is"!

[180]Half a hebdomad. See note 172.

[181]I should mention here that some biblical interpreters view the stopping of sacrifices "in the middle of the week" as the work of Christ, who by His death brought to an end the necessity of other sacrifices. (See e.g., E. J. Young, *The Prophecy of Daniel*, 208.) However, the immediate background points not to Christ but to an adversary: "The people of the prince to come will destroy the city and the sanctuary. And its end will come with a flood; even to the end there will be war; desolations are determined" (9:26 NASB). Then these words follow: "And he will make a firm covenant with many for one week, but in the middle of the week he will put a stop to sacrifice. . . ." It is true that "the Messiah" (or "an anointed one" [RSV]) is referred to—"the Messiah will be cut off and have nothing" (v. 26a NASB)—just prior to the statement about "the people of the prince to come." However, it is more natural to connect "he will make a firm covenant" with the immediate antecedent, "the prince." Moreover, this understanding better accords with Daniel 11:31 and 12:11.

[182]I have not sought to deal with the complex issue of Daniel's "seventy weeks," beginning with 9:24 (which see). For our purpose the important matter is that the seventieth, or last, week refers to the activity of the Desolator. Some interpreters have held that the seventieth week is totally fulfilled in the activity of Antiochus Epiphanes, *or* Titus, *or* the final Antichrist. In the last case, dispensationalists claim that there is a large gap (a parenthesis) between the sixty-ninth week, understood as the Incarnation, and the seventieth week viewed as the future coming of the Antichrist. I submit, however, that there is nothing in the text to suggest such a gap. It is far better to view both Antiochus and Titus as *types* of the Antichrist. According to some computations, the seventy weeks wholly end with Antiochus; others view these weeks in closer connection with Christ's coming and being completed with Titus. However, if these two events are typological (which seems apparent), there is no need to posit a gap between the sixty-ninth and a long-delayed seventieth week.

[183]This is the period given for the nourishment of "the woman" away from "the dragon." See later discussion.

times, and half a time" in Daniel 7:25 and 12:7. Daniel 7 contains a vivid portrayal of the anti-God person: a "little one" who comes up among ten horns with "eyes like the eyes of a man, and a mouth speaking great things" (v. 8); further, "he shall speak words against the Most High, and shall wear out the saints of the Most High . . . and they shall be given into his hand for a time, two times, and half a time" (v. 25). Daniel asks, "How long shall it be to the end of these wonders?" (12:6).[184] The reply is that "it would be for a time, two times, and half a time; and that when the shattering of the power of the holy people comes to an end all these things would be accomplished" (v. 7). Again, it is evident that the same time period is being spoken of—the time of the anti-God's total sway and the desolation of God's people.

It is important to recognize that the time—whether measured in days, months, years, or "times"—is a relatively short period totaling three and a half years. This may be a literal calendar designation, or it may symbolically refer to a limited time of Satan's final power.[185] Since three and a half is one-half of seven—the symbolic number of wholeness—reference may be to an abbreviated, even broken period. Satan (through the man of sin, beast, desolator, "little horn"), though seemingly great, cannot completely destroy. His power is always broken and incomplete. However, during this brief time there will be great devastation.

Finally, in regard to "the abomination of desolation," there will be this culminating manifestation. Rather than putting an end to Jewish sacrifice and offering or desecrating the temple sanctuary, the desolator will seek to end Christian worship and abolish all testimony to Jesus Christ. The attack will no longer be on the physical city of Jerusalem but on the city of God, the church of the living God. The armies and weapons and strategies will not be directed against earthly strongholds but against God's holy people. It will be Satan's final effort to erase every trace of Christian witness from the earth.

It is apparent that as this age draws to an end, there will be an intensification of the attack of evil upon Christian faith. We have earlier discussed the matter of the growth of the gospel and its successful proclamation to all the nations (the *ethnē*) before the end comes. But along with this ongoing fulfillment of the Great Commission, evil becomes, and will become, all the more vicious. This we have observed in terms of increasing violence and immorality, of religious apostasy, in the emerging spirit of antichrist, and in the man of sin with whom all this culminates. At present the full release of this evil is restrained. Thus society is checked from its total expression, and Christian faith is not wholly opposed by the surrounding secular culture. Nonetheless, there are ominous signs both of near total moral collapse and of an increasing virulence against all things Christian.

In America this virulence is expressed in a growing undercurrent of opposition to Christian faith and morals as *the* truth of God. This stems not only from secular humanism and New Age thinking—however bitter their opposition—but also from a spirit of religious pluralism that steadily dilutes Christian

[184]This question refers to a time of great trouble for God's people followed by the wonders of their deliverance, resurrection from the dead, and eternal life.

[185]According to Beckwith the reference is to "the indefinite but short period . . . preceding the end . . . *the period of the last terrible sway of Satan and his agents in the world before the second coming of the Lord*" (italics his) (*The Apocalypse of John*, 252).

uniqueness. Further, Christ is often defamed on the screen and in art,[186] ministers and priests are frequently depicted as corrupt and immoral,[187] biblical morality is replaced by situational ethics, sexual promiscuity is now being redefined as "safe sex" (no moral questions asked), and on and on. Although millions of Americans still stand firm in faith and morality (and that number is growing), there is an ever-deepening hostility by millions of others against all things essentially Christian. The church is becoming a beleaguered garrison in a hostile land.

This of course does not mean that Christian faith cannot influence the secular world. It is important to recall some words of Jesus to His disciples: "You are the salt of the earth" and "You are the light of the world" (Matt. 5:13–14). As salt, Christians must continue to press for high standards in political life, economic affairs, education, the arts, and in society at large, and in this way seek to preserve society from destroying itself. As light, Christians must seek to shine brightly in the midst of a world of corrupt practices and not hesitate to turn the light on all that is shady and dark. *Christians must not withdraw from the world*, for none of us knows what changes can occur by energetic participation. Doubtless, the most significant changes in the secular realm will be personal. Through the faithfulness of Christians who overcome frequent ridicule and persecution, many people will turn to Christ and experience salvation. Changed people can cause changes in society by their faithfulness.

A further positive word needs to be spoken. The basic order of society, particularly the political, is God-given. The first beast in Revelation 13 was not Rome itself with its imperial rule, but *the perversion of that rule* by lust for power, ruthlessness, and deification. We must also bear in mind that "governing authorities" are "instituted by God" (Rom. 13:1). Hence public office ought to be viewed as a trust from God. Therefore godly people should seek to participate in it, and all Christians should be concerned about government's proper and good functioning. Despite the "beastly" tendencies of the state, Christians are not simply to forswear involvement in the political arena. The state first of all belongs to God, not Satan!

But having said these things, we must face the biblical truth that, whatever the impact the church can make on the world, things in society will become progressively worse as the end draws near. Christians, despite their growing numbers, will more and more be vilified and persecuted. This is the result of a number of factors. For example, the secular world, through its acts of violence and perversion, is increasingly in radical opposition to everything Christian. There is the growing antagonism of anti-Christian religions (including resurgent Islam, the New Age movement, and a multiplicity of cults).[188] Growing secularism gladly expunges all references to God and the Bible from every-

[186]Recent examples include the film *The Last Temptation of Christ,* videos by the rock star Madonna, and an art work that features a crucifix submerged in a jar of urine.

[187]Unfortunately there has been some recent justification for this, but Hollywood has taken this as opportunity for the further vilification of things religious. In an article entitled "Does Hollywood Hate Religion?" film writer Michael Medved describes what he calls "the pervasive hostility to religion and religious values in Hollywood. . . . If someone turns up in a film today wearing a Roman collar or bearing the title Reverend, you can be fairly sure that he will be crazy or corrupt—or both" (*Reader's Digest*, July 1990, 100–101).

[188]See, for example, Walter Martin, *The Kingdom of the Cults*, and Ruth A. Tucker, *Another Gospel*.

day life. Subtle attacks have arisen within the nominal church, which espouses worldly values and is bitter against the true church of Word and Spirit. None of this will decrease in the time of the end; rather, the opposition and attacks will grow more and more pronounced.

Indeed, before the end comes, a vastly heightened demonic attack will be unleashed against the church of Jesus Christ. The restraint on "the man of sin," of total lawlessness and iniquity, will be removed. The two "beasts" who combine political and religious power will temporarily be victorious over the people of God. The "desolator" will forbid Christian worship, education, and missionary outreach from occurring. The saints—the believing church—will be ruthlessly fought against, and for a time vanquished.

Martyrdom, like that experienced by the early church under the Roman emperors, will again be common. Already in the twentieth century more believers have paid the ultimate price than in any previous period in history. Today, as I write, there has been a reprieve in such countries as Russia and China. For this we may be extremely grateful, not only for the lessening of persecution but also for fresh opportunities to proclaim the gospel. But the doors could close again in those countries and elsewhere, with increased persecution even to death.[189] Of course, we do not know whether such persecution is imminent or not, but the "changing of the guard" in totalitarian countries is no assurance of continued freedom.

Whether or not there is increased physical persecution and martyrdom, the deeper issue, doubtless, is spiritual. What the secular world desires is not so much the physical death of Christians as their being stripped of all voice and influence. They want no Christian faith on the earth[190] to bar their way to total self-expression. The world desires the neutralization, the isolation, the enervation—in very fact, the death of Christian witness. This by no means excludes physical martyrdom, but spiritual isolation can be even more severe. In any event, evil will for a time prove victorious.

Ultimately the important thing for Christians to realize is that God is in it all! It is not that the gospel has failed, or will fail, when evil breaks forth in full power. God *allows* the evil beast to emerge, exercise authority, and conquer the faithful.[191] This is not always easy for believers to understand. Most of us would probably prefer that the beast be smashed before it can raise its ugly head. But this is not God's way. It was smashed once at Calvary *only after* the beast had done its worst in the crucifixion of the Son of God. The beast received a mortal wound then, but God in His omniscience has allowed it to live

[189]Earlier in the Book of Revelation seven seals were opened. With the opening of the fifth, John beholds "the souls of those who had been slain for the word of God and for the witness they had borne" (6:9). These souls cry out for God to execute justice and vengeance, and they are "each given a white robe and told to rest a little longer, until the number of their fellow servants and their brethren should be complete, who were to be killed as they themselves had been" (v. 11). Death and martyrdom are continuing facts of Christian history.

[190]Jesus Himself raises the rhetorical question, "When the Son of man comes, will he find faith on the earth?" (Luke 18:8 NIV). His question does not intend to suggest that when He returns there will be no believers but that faith may have no place on earth—in the language of Revelation, among the "earth-dwellers."

[191]Recall the words of Revelation 13:5, 7: "It was allowed to exercise authority. . . . It was allowed to make war on the saints and conquer them."

on until the time of the end. The passion of Christ ending in seeming defeat and death by the beast will likewise be the passion of the church. Satan will make his last deadly attack and will again seemingly succeed. We cannot really expect it to be otherwise.

But, finally, as with the Resurrection, there will be victory. The Christ who rose from the grave triumphant over death and hell will return this time not only as victor but also as the One who will utterly destroy all evil. The man of sin, the deadly beast(s), the Antichrist, the desolator of God's people—however named—will be out in the open. *Totally exposed*, it will receive God's own total deathblow. The victory will be not ours, but the Lord's!

Meanwhile, knowing the final outcome, we must be patient, keep on with the proclamation of the gospel to the ends of the earth, seek to be salt and light in an evil world, and be prepared to endure evil's expanding power and influence. The last will not be easy, for it will mean much faith and endurance.[192] But by God's grace *His* triumph is sure.

IX. GREAT TRIBULATION

Another sign of the end, the near advent of the Lord, is that of great tribulation. This is to be understood primarily from Jesus' words: "Immediately after the tribulation of those days the sun will be darkened, and the moon will not give its light, and the stars will fall from heaven . . . then will appear the sign of the Son of man in heaven . . . and they will see the Son of man coming on the clouds of heaven. . ." (Matt. 24:29–30).[193] The word "immediately" places the tribulation referred to—described as "great tribulation" in verse 21—in close proximity to the final advent of Christ.

Before looking specifically into "great tribulation" mentioned above, which is unmistakably a sign of the end, we will first examine the broader picture of tribulation. Tribulation is frequently declared in the New Testament to be a fact of Christian existence. Jesus speaks to His disciples elsewhere: "In the world you have tribulation. . ." (John 16:33)—not *will have*, but *have*. In this sense tribulation is a continuing reality of Christian life and witness, because the "world" is basically in opposition to what Christianity represents. Hence persecution is to be expected: "If they persecuted me, they will persecute you" (John 15:20). Paul says much the same thing later: "All who desire to live a godly life in Christ Jesus will be persecuted" (2 Tim. 3:12). Thus tribulation—in the sense of persecution, affliction, oppression[194]—is invariably the lot of the believer who truly follows his Lord.

Let us look a bit further. Paul and Barnabas visited various churches in Asia Minor "strengthening the souls of the disciples, exhorting them to continue in the faith, and saying that through many tribulations we must enter the kingdom of God" (Acts 14:22). Tribulation thus is not only a fact of Christian life in this world; it is also a *necessary* one. Similarly Paul later urges the Thessalonians that "no one be moved [or 'unsettled' NIV] by these afflictions [or 'tribulations' KJV].[195] You yourselves know that this is to be our lot" (1 Thess. 3:3). Paul also speaks to

---

[192]Bear in mind what John said after depicting the victory of the first beast over the saints: "Here is a call for the endurance and faith of the saints."

[193]Mark 13:24 reads, "But in those days, after that tribulation. . . ."

[194]The Greek word usually translated "tribulation" is *thlipsis*. "Affliction" is also a frequent translation.

[195]Again, the Greek word here and in verse 4 below is from *thlipsis*.

the Thessalonians of their "persecutions" and "afflictions [or 'tribulations' KJV]" as avenues by which they are "made worthy of the kingdom of God" (2 Thess. 1:4–5). In such language the emphasis is unmistakable: tribulation is not only an inevitable fact of Christian life—the believers' lot—but it is also the proving ground for genuine existence in the kingdom of God. Does one truly belong to Christ and willingly suffer with Him,[196] risk life, even lay it down if need be?

In his letter to the Romans Paul affirms the significance of tribulation for Christian hope. Against the background of being "justified by faith" and having "peace with God," Paul states that "we exult in hope of the glory of God" (5:1–2 NASB). Then he adds, "We also exult[197] in our tribulations, knowing that tribulation brings about perseverance [or 'endurance'];[198] and perseverance, proven character;[199] and proven character, hope. . ." (vv. 3–4 NASB). The progression is noteworthy: Beginning with hope, Paul moves through tribulation to the endurance that follows and the proven character that develops, and on to hope again. However, this hope is obviously far richer and deeper because it is the fruit of tribulation, endurance, and developed character. Hence tribulation, far from dimming hope of the glory ahead, is the primary stage in leading to an even greater hope. Instead of feeling disturbed by tribulation—affliction, persecution—"*we exult*" in it! Paul, it may be supposed, could add that "the worse it gets, the more radiant that hope of glory becomes"!

Later in Romans Paul has an extraordinary statement about the love of Christ. Already he had said (and this I did not mention above) that "hope does not disappoint, because the love of God has been poured out within our hearts through the Holy Spirit who was given to us"[200] (Rom. 5:5 NASB). Now referring later in his letter to the love of God, or Christ, Paul asks, "Who shall separate us from the love of Christ? Shall tribulation, or distress, or persecution, or famine, or nakedness, or peril, or sword?" (8:35). Then Paul adds, freely quoting Psalm 44:22: "For thy sake we are being killed all the day long; we are regarded as sheep to be slaughtered" (v. 36). Then—against what seems like an impossibly dreary picture of tribulation, even death—Paul triumphantly affirms: "No, in all these things we are more than conquerors[201] through him who loved us!" (v. 37). Therefore, whatever may seem to conquer the Christian believer—tribulation, persecution, famine, sword, even death itself—is actually "overconquered"!

---

[196]Paul speaks about his earnest desire: ". . . that I may know Him . . . and the fellowship of his sufferings, being conformed to his death; in order that I may attain to the resurrection from the dead" (Phil. 3:10–11 NASB). Thus suffering, i.e., tribulation, and conformity to Christ's death, is even said to be necessary to attain the resurrection. This resembles Paul's statement, previously quoted, about being "made worthy" through "persecutions and afflictions . . . of the kingdom of God."

[197]The Greek word is *kauchōmetha*—"glory" (KJV), "rejoice" (RSV, NIV), "exult" (NASB, NEB).

[198]The Greek word is *hypomonēn*, frequently translated "endurance."

[199]The Greek word is *dokimēn*, literally, "the quality of being approved" (BAGD), or tested—hence "character." The NEB translation—"proof that we have stood the test"—is excellent. (The KJV's "experience" is an unsatisfactory translation.)

[200]This is actually the climax of Paul's statement relating to the hope that stems from tribulation, endurance, and proven character.

[201]The Greek word *hypernikōmen* is literally "we overconquer." The NASB excellently translates this as "we overwhelmingly conquer"; the NEB paraphrase is "overwhelming victory is ours."

Here, then, is a new motif: not only do all these things, if patiently endured, make for a deeper and richer hope of the coming glory, but we are also, both now and in the life to come, "more than conquerors"! The climax is beautiful: "For I am sure that neither death, nor life, nor angels, nor principalities ['demons' NIV],[202] nor things present, nor things to come, nor powers, nor height, nor depth, nor anything else in all creation, will be able to separate us from the love of God in Christ Jesus our Lord" (vv. 38–39). In that vast love—"poured out within our hearts through the Holy Spirit"—nothing can separate us: we overwhelmingly conquer all.

Here we return briefly to Matthew 24 and observe an earlier reference to tribulation.[203] Jesus says to His disciples, "They will deliver you up to tribulation, and put you to death; and you will be hated by all nations for my name's sake. . . . But he who endures to the end will be saved" (vv. 9, 13).[204] Thus the primary mention of tribulation and endurance, also of death and salvation, is to be found in the words of Jesus. This is quite similar to Paul's later emphasis (in Acts 14:22) that "through many tribulations we must enter the kingdom of God." By holding firm through all tribulation—including death itself—the followers of Jesus have the victory: "He who endures to the end will be saved." In Paul's words again: We are "more than conquerors."

Some of the emphases on tribulation thus far noted are to be found also in the Book of Revelation. John, to whom the revelation was given, says, "I John, your brother, who share with you in Jesus the tribulation, and the kingdom and the patient endurance, was on the island called Patmos on account of the word of God and the testimony of Jesus" (1:9). Note that "tribulation" is immediately followed by "endurance"[205] as in Romans 5:3. John says that he is sharing both (also "the kingdom")[206] with his readers, who are "the seven churches that are in Asia" (1:4). John has obviously been exiled to the island of Patmos—just off the coast of Asia Minor—since he speaks of being there as a result of his testimony. Thus John shares the tribulation with the seven churches.

Now we come to the words of Jesus who Himself speaks directly to the church in Smyrna: "I know your tribulation. . . . Do not fear what you are about to suffer. Behold, the devil is about to throw some of you into prison, that you may be tested, and for ten days you will have tribulation. Be faithful unto death, and I will give you the crown of life" (2:9–10). Tribulation—fairly short ("ten days") but unmistakably intense, even "unto death"—was to be the lot of some of the Smyrneans. Again, similar to Paul's teaching in Romans 8, there is tribulation, suffering, and death; but even more patently

[202]The Greek word is *archai*—earthly rulers and authorities; but it is also used in reference to "angelic and demonic powers" (BAGD). Since "angels" have just been mentioned, "demons" is the likely meaning, as translated in NIV.

[203]Earlier, that is, than the reference to "great tribulation" previously noted (to which we will later return).

[204]The parallel Markan passage gives other details, e.g., "They will deliver you up to councils; and you will be beaten in synagogues . . . brother will deliver up brother to death, and the father his child, and children will rise against parents and have them put to death" (13:9–12; cf. Luke 21:12–19).

[205]The Greek word again is *hypomonē*, whether translated "patient endurance" (RSV above and NIV), "perseverance" (NASB), or simply "endurance" (NEB). ("Patience," the KJV translation, is misleading.)

[206]See the earlier discussion of "the kingdom of God." We will return to this later.

here the devil is declared to be the source. (Recall the "principalities," or "demons," in Romans 8.) Nonetheless, the devil cannot win, because finally they will receive "the crown of life." Thus, one might add, the Smyrneans, like the Romans, will be "more than conquerors."

Now we move to another expression of tribulation, sometimes designated "great tribulation," which is sent upon the forces of evil. This is not the tribulation visited upon God's people (which I have been describing) that makes for persecution, suffering, and death and whose roots are in the opposition of the world to Christian faith.[207] Rather, this is tribulation from God Himself sent upon those who do the works of evil. Here we may refer back for a moment to 2 Thessalonians where Paul, in speaking of persecutions and afflictions (or tribulations) by which we are made worthy for the kingdom of God,[208] also speaks of "the righteous judgment of God . . . since indeed God deems it just to repay with affliction [or 'tribulation'] those who afflict [us]" (1:5–6). Hence, so to speak, there will be tribulation upon the "tribulators"—and this will be greater and more intense.

In this connection we again take up the Book of Revelation and continue with further words of Jesus. In this case He addresses the church at Thyatira, which, despite its "patient endurance" (Rev. 2:19), is putting up with the false prophetess Jezebel, who, by Satan's devices, is leading some of the believers into immorality. Jesus warns, "Behold, I will throw her on a sickbed, and those who commit adultery with her I will throw into great tribulation, unless they repent of her doings; and I will strike her children dead" (vv. 22–23). This tribulation is quite unlike the tribulation that is the lot of every true believer. It is rather "great tribulation" that God sends as punishment upon evil—those who are involved in "the deep things of Satan" (2:24), who seek to prevent and destroy the good, and who are distorting the true Christian witness. The church at Thyatira has endured and suffered much (as have all the churches of Asia Minor), hence has experienced much tribulation, but upon those who follow Satan's devices, there will come "great tribulation."

Now we again return to Matthew 24, this time to the place where Jesus also speaks of "great tribulation." This may be referred to as the Great Tribulation.[209] Jesus had earlier spoken of tribulation that would occur to His followers ("they will deliver you up to tribulation," v. 9) and the need for endurance to the end. After this He speaks of a time when the "desolating sacrilege" (or "the abomination of desolation") will stand "in the holy place" (v. 15) and a little later He adds, "Then there will be great tribulation" (v. 21). It is clear that this great tribulation is due to divine vengeance—"these are days of vengeance, to fulfil all that is written" (Luke 21:22).[210] It is God's judgment primarily upon unbelieving Jerusalem,[211] *but also* ultimately upon an unbelieving world. Thus there will be "great distress[212] . . . upon the earth

---

[207]This opposition we have further observed in the guise of "the man of sin" and the two "beasts" in preceding sections.

[208]See supra.

[209]For specific language of "the great tribulation" see Revelation 7:14 (discussed infra).

[210]These words in the parallel passage in Luke 21, not found in Matthew and Mark, make it clear that the Great Tribulation is vengeance upon the enemies of God.

[211]Recall the earlier discussion of this matter.

[212]"Great distress" (*anankē megalē*) is the parallel expression in Luke to "great tribulation" (*thlipsis megalē*) in Matthew.

and wrath upon this people" (Luke 21:23). Hence all will know severe distress, or tribulation, even as divine judgment is poured out upon "this people" who are to receive God's vengeance. This great tribulation or distress is not described, but that it will be *intense* is unmistakable; for it will be "such as has not been from the beginning of the world until now, no, and never will be"[213] (Matt. 24:21). That it will be universal is clear from Jesus' next words: "And if those days had not been shortened, no human being would be saved; but for the sake of the elect those days will be shortened" (v. 22). There is no suggestion that "the elect"—God's people—will be removed from the Great Tribulation; rather they will live through it. But God in His mercy will shorten the days for their sake.[214] It is important to recognize that "the days of vengeance" in this Great Tribulation refer to days of judgment. They are consequently days of the wrath of God upon all who work iniquity, who have spurned His ways. What happened to an unbelieving Jerusalem in the first generation will happen manifoldly to an unbelieving world in the last generation. Those who have spurned God's offer of grace, persecuted God's servants, and gloried in themselves will receive the full measure of divine judgment.[215] Such will be something of the "great tribulation" they will endure.

What of God's servants during this time? By no means is this Great Tribulation a time of judgment upon them, nor is the operation of God's wrath directed against those who believe. How then can God's "elect" endure a devastation and judgment so vast as to engulf an unrighteous world? The answer may be seen first in the instructions Jesus gave in relation to the destruction of Jerusalem. The key word is *flight*: "Let those who are in Judea flee to the mountains, and let those who are inside the city depart, and let not those who are out in the country enter it" (Luke 21:21).[216] Since the visitation of divine judgment was in that case local (upon Jerusalem and the immediate environs of Judea), the word then was: Flee quickly, get out, do not enter the area of devastation. Believers alive at the time of that tribulation, while in a sense living through it, did have a way of escape.[217]

But now what about the vastly larger situation in which, instead of an unbelieving city and nation, the judgment will be on an unbelieving and hostile world? What will be the case when it is

---

[213]I have earlier commented on the destruction of Jerusalem in A.D. 70 and the anguish, suffering, and tribulation involved. Truly it was "great," and in magnitude nothing like it had been experienced before. Still, for all its devastation, there will be a tribulation near the end that will be far more intense. Thus the desolation of Jerusalem is the precursor of the final and ultimate devastation.

[214]The parallel in Mark 13:20 concludes, "He shortened the days."

[215]Thus all the forces leading up to the appearance of "the man of sin" (the composite beast, the desolator—whatever the name) will undergo divine judgment. The climax, at the conclusion of Christian witness, will be total destruction (see chap. 12).

[216]The immediate background is: "When you see Jerusalem surrounded by armies. . ."; in Matthew and Mark: "When you see the desolating sacrilege . . . standing in the holy place [Mark—'set up where it ought not to be']. . . ." We will return to this later.

[217]Christians living in Jerusalem and environs did escape. Norval Geldenhuys writes, "When the first signs appeared that Jerusalem was going to be surrounded by the Roman forces practically all the Christians fled from the city and its environs across the Jordan to . . . Pella . . . where they remained until after the destruction of Jerusalem" (*The Gospel of Luke*, NICNT, 528). It is interesting that Eusebius, an early church historian, says that they went out in response to "an oracle given by revelation" (*Ecclesiastical History* 3.5.3).

no longer divine vengeance on Jerusalem and Judea or on the Roman Empire in its idolatry and immoralities and its intense persecution of Christians—but when it is matter of the whole world? In such a time of far greater and broader tribulation, how can believers possibly be spared the judgments of God? Yet somehow this must happen, since the wrath of God is not on them but on the world.

We turn again to the Book of Revelation where the answer becomes clearer. I have already called attention to the "great tribulation" that God was to send upon the evil forces perverting many in the church of Thyatira. Of course, that was local,[218] but it does demonstrate that God will not allow evil to go unavenged. We next observe that in the message to His church in Philadelphia, Jesus says, "Because you have kept my word of patient endurance, I will keep you from the hour of trial which is coming on the whole world, to try those who dwell upon the earth" (Rev. 3:10). These words of Jesus, although including the local scene, also extend far beyond it to "the whole world." Whether this is viewed as the Roman Empire (which, in a sense, was the whole world[219] at the time the messages in Revelation were spoken) or the entire earth, (wherever people are) does not matter. In any event the trial will come upon "those who dwell on the earth" (the "earth-dwellers"), an expression that, as we have earlier noted, refers particularly to the earth in its godlessness. The "hour of trial" thus refers not to a time of testing of God's people but to "*the* hour of trial," thus to *the* Great Tribulation that will come upon the world in its opposition to God.[220] It points to that awful time at the end when God's final judgments will be poured out.[221] After speaking of this "hour of trial," Jesus proceeds to say, "I am coming quickly"[222] (Rev. 3:11 NASB). "Quickly," it might be added, accords with the "immediately" of His statement in Matthew 24:29: "Immediately after the tribulation of those days. . . ."

But now we must return to the question, How will God keep His people from this "hour of trial"? If it points to the time of God's judgments coming upon an unbelieving world, and such judgments are universal, how can believers avoid them? The answer is "God will keep them from. . . ," meaning that whatever may happen to the "earth-dwellers," Christian believers

---

[218]While this tribulation is local in a sense, a proper understanding, I believe, of the Book of Revelation sees in the message to Thyatira (as well as to all the seven churches) a message to the church and world at every stage in history, including the final time.

[219]The "whole world" (*oikoumenē*), for example, is clearly the Roman Empire in Luke 2:1: "In those days a decree went out from Caesar Augustus that all the world [*pasan tēn oikoumenēn*] should be enrolled."

[220]Accordingly, Ladd writes, "This prophecy [Rev. 3:10] refers to the Great Tribulation, and it is directed not against God's people but against 'earth-dwellers.' This phrase is a recurring one in Revelation by which the author designates the people of a godless society . . . and who are to suffer the wrath of God (cf. 6:10; 8:13; 11:10; 13:8, 12, 14; 14:6; 17:2, 8)" (*The Blessed Hope*, 85).

[221]Thus the word translated "trial" (*peirasmos*) cannot here refer to God's people. Hence the translation "temptation" (KJV) or "testing" (NASB), while appropriate for *peirasmos* in other contexts, is unsatisfactory here. Seeseman says in his article on *peira* and its cognates that the *peirasmos* in Revelation 3:10 refers to "the total eschatological terror and tribulation of the last time" (TDNT, 6:30).

[222]Rather than "soon" (as in KJV, RSV, NIV, and NEB). The Greek word is *tachu*. Thayer renders *tachu* as "quickly, speedily"; BAGD suggests "quickly" as preferable to "soon" in this context.

will somehow be protected. "Because you have kept my word of patient endurance, I will keep you. . . ." Thus believers are called not to be catapulted out of the world but to endurance within it.[223] As they patiently endure the persecution and affliction that the world brings against them, believers will be kept by God from the judgments He will release upon His foes and those who oppose His people.

To be kept "from," it bears repeating, is not to be removed from.[224] It is, of course, true (as we have noted) that the Christians who were in Jerusalem at the time of its destruction were told to flee from the devastation (in that sense to "remove" themselves). However, there can be no flight when it is a matter of the whole world, for there is no place to go. The answer again is God's keeping from, or safekeeping. If we patiently endure, He will keep us safe. If we hold fast, regardless of the attacks of the world—persecution, affliction, suffering, even death—all of which will multiply as the end draws near,[225] God will shield His own from the judgments that are to be poured out upon the oppressors. There is no need for removal—a kind of escape hatch into the beyond—for God promises to protect those who belong to Him.

Let us look further in the Book of Revelation. For as important as the passage in Revelation 3 is, the most vivid picture is that of "the great tribulation" multitude in Revelation 7. John has now been transported in the Spirit to heaven, a voice having said, " 'Come up hither, and I will show you what must take place after this.' At once I was in the Spirit. . ." (4:1–2). After a number of visions, John beholds "a great multitude which no man could number . . . clothed in white robes . . . crying out with a loud voice, 'Salvation belongs to our God who sits upon the throne, and to the Lamb' " (7:9–10). Then one of the "elders" in heaven identifies this multitude clothed in white: "These are they who have come out of the great tribulation;[226] they have washed their robes and made them white in the blood of the Lamb" (vv. 13–14). Then follows a beautiful picture of these Great Tribulation saints before the throne of God, serving Him day and night and knowing the blessings of the Lamb with tribulation forever over: "God will wipe every tear from their eyes!" (vv. 15–17). This is a preview of the climactic pictures of eternal bliss as shown in Revelation 21 and 22.[227]

Regarding a point of prior concern, it is obvious that those so richly blessed in heaven—the "great multitude which no man could number"—are those who

---

[223]Recall the word spoken to believers attacked by "the beast" in Revelation 13:10: "Here is a call for the endurance and faith of the saints."

[224]As held by those who view this verse as affirming a rapture of the church whereby the hour of trial is avoided. (See, e.g., René Pache, *The Return of Jesus Christ*, "The Removal of the Church," 118–19.) But keeping from is not removal; it rather means protection. A good illustration of this may be found in Jesus' prayer to the Father for His disciples: "I do not pray that thou shouldst take them out of the world [hence 'remove them'], but that thou shouldst keep them from the evil one" (John 17:15). See, e.g., Eldon Ladd, *The Blessed Hope*, 85–86, and especially Robert Gundry, *The Church and the Tribulation*, 54–61. See also my Excursus on pretribulationism, pages 370–82.

[225]Recall previous sections.

[226]The Greek phrase is *erchomenoi ek tēs thlipseōs tēs megalēs*, literally, "coming out of the great tribulation."

[227]This is obvious from the many similar details; e.g., cf. Revelation 7:15 and 22:3, both referring to "the throne of God" and those who "serve [or 'worship'] him"; 7:17 and 21:6, speaking similarly of the "spring(s) of the water of life" (NASB); and 7:17 and 21:4, both saying that God "will wipe away every tear from their eyes."

have *come out of* the Great Tribulation. They did not avoid it, nor were they snatched from it, but they went through it, emerging victorious on the other side. Since these Great Tribulation saints doubtlessly represent the believers of the end times[228] (any local designation such as believers dwelling in Jerusalem and Judea, or the church in Philadelphia—both already noted—having dropped away), we are all the more ready to ask what happened to them during this climactic tribulation.

For an answer we need to look back in the chapter to the *sealing* of the servants of God. The scene is vivid: four angels are about to release the four winds that will devastate the world when another angel, who has "the seal of the living God," cries out, "Do not harm the earth or the sea or the trees, till we have sealed the servants of our God upon their foreheads" (Rev. 7:3). The sealing is unmistakably for protection—to prevent them from being harmed when the judgments of God are released upon the world. This is doubly confirmed later when, after the judgments have begun, locusts with fearsome power to torture people are told "not to harm the grass or earth or any green growth or any tree, but only those of mankind who have not the seal of God upon their foreheads" (9:3–4). The seal, therefore, marks out those who are "the servants of our God" so that no harm will come to them, regardless of the injury to nature or man.[229] Those sealed, according to Revelation 7:4, are said to be "a hundred and forty-four thousand . . . out of every tribe of the sons of Israel," with twelve thousand sealed out of each tribe. It seems apparent that this is a composite figure and that "Israel" here represents Christian[230] believers sealed from the final judgments of God.

---

[228]It is important to recognize that these tribulation believers are *not* martyrs. To be sure, as we have earlier observed, persecution and death may indeed be the lot of believers especially in the end time; however, the focus of Revelation here is that of believers sealed and therefore emerging unscathed from the judgments of God. Beasley-Murray writes, "It is a puzzling feature to the present writer that the majority of commentators on the Revelation in this century identify the *great multitude* with the martyrs. Of this there is not a hint in the text" (*Revelation*, NCBC, 145). Similarly I. T. Beckwith says, "The redeemed here are . . . in no way distinguished as martyrs. These latter are described as 'those who have been slain for the word of God' (6[9]), and 'those who have been beheaded for the testimony of Jesus' (20[4]); but the multitude in this vision are those who 'have washed their robes in the blood of the Lamb' (v. 14), a characterization of all saints alike, cf. 1[5], 5[9]. The vision then is a revelation of the whole Church brought in safety through the great tribulation into the blessedness of its finished salvation" (*The Apocalypse of John*, 539). I agree wholeheartedly with these statements.

[229]The parallel with God's judgments upon Pharaoh in Exodus 7–11 is apparent. Whatever God sends upon Pharaoh and Egypt—blood, flies, boils, hail, locusts, etc.—Israel is each time spared. Recall also the account in Ezekiel 9 where a mark is placed on the foreheads of those who "sigh and groan over all the abominations that are committed" (v. 4) in Jerusalem; all others are to be slain. The command to the executioners: "Pass through the city . . . and smite; your eye shall not spare, and you shall show no pity . . . but touch no one upon whom is the mark" (vv. 5–6).

[230]The fact that the next mention of those sealed in Revelation 9 makes no reference to "Israel" but simply to "those who have not the seal of God upon their foreheads"; also the fact that the next reference to 144,000 in Revelation 14:1–5 again makes no reference to "Israel" but speaks of them as "redeemed from mankind as first fruits for God and the Lamb" (v. 5) suggests that these are Christians, whether Jewish or Gentile. (Believers are called "first fruits" in James 1:18; also cf. Rom. 8:23.) Furthermore, that Revelation 7 does not literally deal with the twelve tribes of Israel is apparent for a number of reasons: (1) not

The picture, then, is one of divine protection. No matter how great the tribulation upon the world, the servants of God are sealed from the divine judgments. This does not in any way mean that they are exempt from the persecution of the world. Such tribulation including suffering and death is their lot. In fact, in another scene, in Revelation 6, we see "under the altar the souls" of those "who had been slain for the word of God and for the witness they had borne" (v. 9). Many more, they are told, will likewise be killed for the sake of the gospel—and as the Book of Revelation shows, this martyrdom continues to the very end.[231] However, whatever their lot of persecution, suffering, or even death, the saints of God are *totally* shielded from the judgments of God. Indeed, these very judgments are God's vindication of His "elect"—those "under the altar" who cry out, "O Sovereign Lord, holy and true, how long before thou wilt judge and avenge our blood on those who dwell upon the earth?" (v. 10). He does hear their cry; He releases His judgments and preserves His own in the midst of His outpoured wrath.

As the judgments of God are released upon the world and with far greater intensity toward the end, those who are truly His servants will be untouched. The Book of Revelation depicts ever-increasing calamities: with the opening of the seals and the horsemen riding forth, death and Hades are given power over *one-fourth* of the earth, and so kill with sword, famine, and pestilence (6:8); with the blast of the trumpets *one-third* of the earth, sea, rivers, heavenly bodies, and mankind are smitten (8:7–9:19); with the outpouring of the bowls of wrath *all* the earth, sea, rivers, sun, and mankind at large receive the divine judgment (16:1–10).[232] These are patently not just natural disasters;[233] else

all the tribes are included (there is no mention of Dan or Ephraim; in their place are Levi and Joseph); (2) that exactly 12,000 from each tribe are numbered—the same from tribes large and small—seems improbable; (3) the tribes as such do not exist today; and (4) if Gentile Christians are not included in the 144,000 of Israel, they are nowhere spoken of as sealed at all. If 144,000 on the other hand is a symbolic number of completion—possibly 12 x 12 x 1000—then this would signify *all* Christians, Jews and Gentiles alike. Incidentally, if Paul's expression in Galatians 6:16, "the Israel of God," refers to Christians in general (which seems likely), then there is a significant parallel with Revelation 7. On Revelation 7:4ff., see Mounce, *The Book of Revelation*, NICNT, 168–70; Ladd, *Commentary on Revelation*, 111–17.

[231]For example, Revelation 11:7; 12:11; 13:7; 14:13; 18:24.

[232]A basic theme in the Book of Revelation is the judgments of God as the expression of His wrath. The "seven bowls of the wrath of God" (16:1) are the climactic expression of this (they are "bowls full of the wrath of God"—15:7). Prior to this, however, with the opening of the sixth seal, people cry out to the mountains and rocks, "Fall on us and hide us from the face of him who is seated on the throne, and from the wrath of the Lamb; for the great day of their wrath has come" (6:16–17). Similarly, when the seventh trumpet has sounded forth, there is the statement that "the nations raged, but thy wrath came" (11:18). Likewise, there is the picture of the angel who "gathered the vintage of the earth and threw it into the great wine press of the wrath of God" (14:19). Following the pouring out of the seven bowls "full of the wrath of God," there is the awesome scene of One whose name is "the Word of God," who "will tread the wine press of the fury of the wrath of God the Almighty" (19:13, 15). The wrath of God is depicted throughout Revelation as the motivating reality behind the climactic judgments of God upon the evil world.

[233]The very fact that the imagery above moves from one-fourth to one-third to totality is evidence enough that these are not merely increasing natural incidents. Moreover, a literal understanding is impossible; for example, "a third of the sun was struck, and a third of the moon, and a third of the stars . . . a third of the day was kept from shining, and likewise a

the servants of God would be as afflicted as anyone else. Rather, they are divine visitations in which the godless increasingly feel the severity of divine judgment upon their sin and evil. They are also a call to repentance, but to no avail. Even when one-third of mankind is slain, "the rest . . . did not repent" (9:20–21); even when the total sun scorches people with fierce heat, they curse God—"they did not repent and give him glory" (Rev. 16:8–9).[234]

Hence at the time of the end there will be increasing tribulation across the face of the earth. It will be upon all the "earth-dwellers," even to a point of such intensity as to be designated as the Great Tribulation.[235] The saints will not be affected by it, for they will "come out of" it, having "washed their robes and made them white in the blood of the Lamb" (Rev. 7:14). Moreover, they have been willing to endure, even unto death, whatever travail and persecution has been their lot. Hence the judgments of God do not fall upon them. But upon all who are not "sealed" by God, the judgments will be increasingly fearsome.

What, finally, are we to say about the Great Tribulation, which will immediately precede the return of the Lord? Are there signs that it is at hand? Although it is difficult to answer definitely, there can be little question but that God's judgments are upon the earth, whether or not they are fully recognized as such. We live in an age of increasing rebellion against the rule of God, the gospel of Jesus Christ, and principles of law and morality. Turning instead to a totally self-serving view of life, spurning the life-giving gospel, many are walking in the way of the world—the way of death. Although there may be outward success and achievement, there is much inward disturbance. There is a gnawing inward sense that somehow things are not right, as well as widespread deep anxiety and foreboding. These result from the judgments of God—whether yet partial (only "one-fourth" or "one-third") or nearing totality.[236] The call to repentance goes unheeded—as people move on in increasing opposition to the things of God while ever intensifying judgment comes upon them from heaven.

Doubtless we can expect this situation to intensify in these latter days as the gospel goes forth in final testimony to all the nations. Either people will be drawn by the proclamation of salvation to Christ or they will be repelled and hardened by it. The message will be "a fragrance from life to life" for many, but for others it will be "a fragrance from death to death" (2 Cor. 2:16). This means, in the latter case, condem-

---

third of the night" (8:12). Besides the obvious fact that none of this makes literal sense, the sun later, with a bowl of wrath poured on it in totality, scorches men with fire (16:8). Many other examples could be cited. Regarding 8:12 Beasley-Murray writes, "The astronomy is less important than the thing signified. John wishes to affirm that people will experience darkness in the day and intensified darkness in the night because of their sins. But the Lord is merciful in sparing them light both by day and by night—that they may forsake their moral darkness in the unending light of his presence" (*Revelation*, NCBC, 158).

[234]"When the conscience of man has been seared and deadened by deliberate and persistent sin, there is nothing softening or converting in the judgments of God. . . . The heart may become so hardened that even the torture of the burning sun of divine wrath cannot burn into it the saving fear of God which leads to repentance and confession of guilt" (D. W. Richardson, *The Revelation of Jesus Christ*, 97).

[235]Or "the hour of trial." See earlier comments.

[236]Recall Revelation 6 (one-fourth), Revelation 8 (one-third), and Revelation 16 (totality).

nation and judgment,[237] for "he who does not obey the Son . . . the wrath of God rests upon him" (John 3:36). Opposition will grow toward the gospel and hatred against those who represent it. And God's judgments consequently will be increasingly severe. The divine judgments still call to repentance (they are not merely punitive) and sternly warn concerning the ultimate end of all who oppose God's way and truth. But the "earth-dwellers" will not hear; they continue to bow to the beast and bear his number in the marketplace of the world. So they move, step by step, into ever accelerating judgment and ultimate destruction.

EXCURSUS: PRETRIBULATIONISM[238]

Since the mid-nineteenth century a number of evangelical biblical interpreters have espoused the view that the church of true believers will not have to endure the Great Tribulation.[239] The church throughout history does experience general tribulation, but when the time of the Great Tribulation arrives, the church will be removed[240] from earth to heaven. Unbelievers, however, will remain on earth during this time of unprecedented trouble.

Pretribulationists generally affirm that Revelation 4–19 describes the period of the Great Tribulation. John F. Walvoord writes, "The major Scripture portion in the New Testament on the [great] tribulation is the Book of Revelation, chapters 4–19."[241] The claim is that since the church is not mentioned by name in these chapters (whereas it is mentioned seven times in chapters 2 and 3), and since the various scenes in chapters 6–19 are filled with pictures of unparalleled devastation and destruction that God in His wrath pours out on the earth, the church must have been earlier removed from the scene. Wal-

[237]The gospel condemns no one: "God sent the Son into the world, not to condemn the world." However, "he who does not believe is condemned already. . ." (John 3:17–18).

[238]This excursus will also briefly touch on midtribulationism. I will not by name deal with the other main tribulational view— posttribulationism—since what has been written in the previous section is from that perspective, namely that Christ will return *after* the Great Tribulation. However, in the critique that follows, the reasons for the posttribulational perspective should become still clearer. (A helpful study of all three tribulational positions may be found in Richard R. Reiter, ed., *The Rapture: Pre-, Mid-, or Post-Tribulational?* Proponents of each perspective describe their positions and then respond to one another. See also Millard J. Erickson, *Contemporary Options in Eschatology,* part 3, "Tribulational Views," for a thoughtful presentation.)

[239]J. N. Darby (1800–1882), leader of the Plymouth Brethren movement, was largely responsible for promulgating the pretribulational viewpoint. Darby taught that Christ's second coming would occur in two stages: first, before the Great Tribulation and, second, at its close. This was part and parcel of his "dispensational" teaching that divided history into several distinct eras or dispensations. The next to the last dispensation, according to Darby, is the present church age, which will climax with the return of Christ to rapture the church prior to the Great Tribulation. The second coming will occur seven years later and usher in the Millennium and kingdom age. Dispensationalism as a scheme of biblical interpretation is best known today through the *Scofield Reference Bible* (seven dispensations are outlined in the footnote to the heading of Genesis 1:28). Dallas Theological Seminary is the chief center of dispensational teaching.

[240]Recall my earlier reference to the chapter title, "The Removal of the Church," in Pache's book, *The Return of Jesus Christ*.

[241]*The Rapture Question*, 48. Walvoord, former president of Dallas Theological Seminary, is a leading spokesman for pretribulationism. He, like all others to be quoted in this excursus (except Blackstone), is also a graduate of Dallas Seminary.

voord quotes Revelation 6:17, "For the great day of their [God and Christ's] wrath is come and who is able to stand?" and later adds, "The only way one could be kept from that wrath would be to be delivered beforehand."[242] Against those who might argue for God's preservation in this time of wrath, Paul Feinberg writes that "if the wrath is falling *everywhere*, it is difficult to see how preservation could be by any other means than the Rapture, or removal."[243] Both Walvoord and Feinberg claim that the words in Revelation 3:10 to the church at Philadelphia, "I will keep you from the hour of trial which is coming on the whole world, to try those who dwell upon the earth," promise the removal of the church before the Great Tribulation begins.[244] This verse, it is claimed, points to a pretribulation removal of the church. Some pretribulationists cite Revelation 4:1, just following John's letters to the seven churches (chaps. 2–3), where John is told to "come up hither," as referring to the church's being taken up to heaven.[245] Hal Lindsey, popular pretribulation writer, says, "I believe, along with many scholars, that the apostle John's experience here is meant to be a prophetic preview of what the living church will experience in the Rapture."[246] This prepares the way for the church's not being mentioned in Revelation 4–19.

Other passages often claimed by pretribulationists to affirm that the church will not go through the Great Tribulation are Luke 21:36: "Be always on the watch, and pray that you may be able to escape all that is about to happen" (NIV); Romans 5:9: "We are now justified by his blood, much more shall we be saved by him from the wrath of God"; 1 Thessalonians 1:10, which speaks of waiting "for his Son from heaven . . . who delivers us from the wrath to come"; and 1 Thessalonians 5:9: "God has not destined us for wrath, but to obtain salvation through our Lord Jesus Christ."[247] The last

---

[242]Ibid., 69. Gerald B. Stanton writes similarly: "The Church is expressly promised deliverance from the wrath of God" (*Kept from the Hour: A Systematic Study of the Rapture in Biblical Prophecy* [see 4, 30–32, 43 quoted]).

[243]*The Rapture: Pre-, Mid-, or Post-Tribulational?* 70. In this volume Paul Feinberg writes chapter 2, entitled "The Case for the Pretribulation Rapture Position."

[244]See Walvoord, *The Rapture Question*, 70, 142, 194. Feinberg has a more lengthy discussion of Revelation 3:10 in *The Rapture: Pre-, Mid-, or Post-Tribulational?* 63–72.

[245]In the earlier *Scofield Reference Bible* (1909), the footnote to this verse says, "This call [to John] seems clearly to indicate the fulfillment of 1 Thes. 4:14–17 [the rapture]." This statement in the present Scofield Bible has been modified to read, "the catching up of John from earth to heaven *has been taken* to be a symbolic representation of the translation of the church" (italics mine).

[246]*The Rapture: Truth or Consequences*, 90. Walvoord is more guarded, saying, "Though many pretribulationists find in the catching up of John a symbolic presentation of the rapture of the church, the passage obviously falls short of an actual statement of the rapture" (*The Blessed Hope and the Tribulation*, 136). Charles L. Ryrie more bluntly says that the words "come up hither" "do not teach the rapture of the church; however . . . the rapture of the church would occur at this point in the book" (*Revelation*, 33–34). It seems that pretribulationists would like to claim Revelation 4:1 as a prooftext for a pretribulation rapture of the church but are now hesitant to take this as a valid exegetical interpretation.

[247]On all these passages, see Walvoord, *The Rapture Question*, 194 (also note index references to his previous fuller discussion of these passages). Paul Feinberg says, "The texts that express this promise [of deliverance for the church from wrath] are: 1 Thessalonians 1:10; 5:9; Revelation 3:10; and possibly Romans 5:9; Ephesians 5:6; Colossians 3:6" (*The Rapture, Pre-, Mid-, or Post-Tribulational?* 52). Walvoord in *The Rapture Question* gives as a possibility 2 Thessalonians 2:3 with the suggested translation of *apostasia* as

passage is especially emphasized against the background of 1 Thessalonians 5:3, which speaks of "sudden destruction" coming upon the world. Walvoord, in viewing the overall biblical picture, does not hesitate to say, "The Scriptures reveal no evidence that the church of the present age will go through the tribulation."[248]

But what then, we may ask—returning briefly to the Book of Revelation—are we to make of the many references in chapters 4–19 to "saints" being present on the earth?[249] For example, Revelation 13:10 reads, "Here is a call for the endurance and faith of the saints." Walvoord claims that these saints are *not* the church or any part of it. He writes, "The omission of the phrase 'unto the churches' in 13:9 is most significant and tends to support the teaching that the church, the body of Christ, has previously been raptured and is not in this period . . . the message is not addressed to the church as such but to the entire world."[250] References, therefore, to "the saints" in Revelation never refer to the church but to believers in the time of the Great Tribulation. Walvoord declares, "The church has a distinct place in God's plan and program and as such is contrasted to saints who will come to know Christ in the tribulation period or in the future millennium[251] . . . [the church] must not be confused with those described as saints or with Israel or with the elect in the tribulation period . . . never are tribulation saints referred to as a church."[252]

This brings us to a consideration of Matthew 24 where "the elect" are definitely said to be present in the Great Tribulation. The Scripture reads, "Then there will be great tribulation . . . for the sake of the elect those days will be shortened" (vv. 21–22). However, according to pretribulationists, "the elect" here are *not* the church. Walvoord again: "While the term 'elect' is found in Matthew 24:22, 31, no mention is made of the church or of any other term which would identify the believers of that period as belonging to the present dispensation."[253] Hence "the elect" are not the church, but future believers living during the time of the Great Tribulation.[254] Thus when in Matthew 24 Jesus adds that "immediately after the tribulation of those days" (v. 29), He will return (vv. 29–31), the church will not have been involved in the prior tribulation. It will have been removed from the earth.

Now this does not mean that the professing, or apostate, church will not be in the Great Tribulation. Indeed, the professing church during that time will "form the nucleus of the ungodly, apostate church of the tribulation which becomes the state religion of that

"departure" (instead of the usual "apostasy" or "rebellion")—thus a departure from earth of the church before "the man of sin" is revealed. (See my earlier note 50 for a discussion of the translation of *apostasia*.) Later Walvoord came to recognize the error in such a translation and interpretation (see *The Blessed Hope*, 125).

[248]*The Rapture Question*, 61.

[249]See Revelation 5:8; 8:3, 4; 11:18; 13:7, 10; 14:12; 16:6; 17:6; 18:20, 24.

[250]*The Revelation of Jesus Christ* (a commentary on the Book of Revelation), 203–4.

[251]On "the future millennium," see chapter 13, "The Millennium."

[252]*The Rapture Question*, 38–39.

[253]Ibid., 47.

[254]The elect may be thought of primarily as Jews who will come to salvation during the tribulation. Charles Feinberg, referring to the days being "shortened," says that this will be "for Israel's sake" (*Millennialism: The Two Major Views*, chap. 10, "The Tribulation Period," 164). Matthew 24 is "Israel's age [not the church's] depicted in its last stages" (pp. 288–89).

time."[255] The true church, the church of the regenerate, will be in heaven throughout the entire period.

Next, it is apparent that the pretribulational viewpoint presupposes the coming of Christ prior to the Great Tribulation to remove, or rapture,[256] the church from the scene. Walvoord's opening chapter in *The Rapture Question*, entitled "The Promise of His Coming," emphasizes that this coming of Christ is prior to the Great Tribulation. Indeed, this is "the blessed hope": "The blessed hope is the rapture of the church before the great tribulation."[257] Again: "The hope offered . . . in the New Testament is the hope of rapture before the tribulation, not the hope of survival through the tribulation."[258] But, we may ask, if Christ returns *before* the Great Tribulation to rescue the church, what about Scriptures that seem to point to the coming of Christ *after* the Great Tribulation? For example, in Matthew 24 Jesus declares that "immediately after the tribulation of those days" (i.e., the "great tribulation" referred to in verse 21) "they will see the Son of man coming on the clouds of heaven" (vv. 29–30). Thus there would seem to be *two* returns: one for the church, the other in relation to the world ("*they* will see"). Pretribulationists do not hesitate to affirm *both* as returns of Christ, though they usually refer to the first as "the rapture" and the second as "the second coming."[259] Thus there is a posttribulational return of Christ, but, since the Great Tribulation has intervened, it has nothing to do with the church. The hope of the church is deliverance from this tribulation by the first return of Christ.

One of the chief arguments of pretribulationism relates to the imminency of Christ's return. If there is to be a period of great tribulation before Christ comes back, how can we truly speak of Christ's any-moment return? So Walvoord writes, "If the church is destined to endure the persecutions of the tribulation, it is futile to proclaim the coming of the Lord as our imminent hope."[260] Indeed, says Paul Feinberg, "There is no mention of any signs or events [including the Great Tribulation] that precede the Rapture of the church in *any* of the Rapture passages" (italics

[255]Walvoord, *The Rapture Question*, 66.

[256]On "rapture," see my chapter 12, "The Purpose of Christ's Return," page 407, notes 38, 39.

[257]*The Blessed Hope*, 163. The importance of this point for Walvoord is evidenced in the very title of his book.

[258]Ibid., 72.

[259]Or "the revelation." See the early pretribulational book by W. E. Blackstone, *Jesus Is Coming*, chapter 9, "Rapture and Revelation." Also see Charles Feinberg, *Millennialism: The Two Major Views*, chapter 17, entitled "The Rapture and the Revelation." It is interesting that Feinberg admits that on the basis of the Greek words this distinction cannot be demonstrated; but he then adds, "The differentiation between the rapture and the revelation is made clear by a comparative study of the Scriptures on the coming of the Lord Jesus Christ" (p. 287). It seems that pretribulationists would like to avoid the idea of a double Second Coming and thus prefer "rapture" for the church and "revelation" for the world. Accordingly, Charles Feinberg still uses the terminology despite its exegetical inadequacy. Paul Feinberg (his son) seems to have dropped the terminology of "rapture" and "revelation" and speaks instead of "rapture" and "second coming" (see his lengthy discussion entitled "The Differences between Rapture Passages and Second Coming Passages," in *The Rapture Pre-, Mid-, or Post-Tribulational?* 80–86).

[260]*The Rapture Question*, 11. Also Walvoord later says, "The doctrine of imminency . . . is the heart of pretribulationism" (55).

his).[261] Pretribulationists thus claim that theirs is the only position that adequately affirms an any-moment return of Christ.

Furthermore, pretribulationists seek to assure the church, that is, the church of true believers, that it has nothing to fear about all the terrors of the Great Tribulation to come. Terrors, indeed, there will be. Charles Feinberg declares, "The plagues of Egypt will be insignificant in comparison with it, and the Reign of Terror in France during the French Revolution or the unspeakable atrocities of the Spanish Inquisition will not even remotely approximate it. Even the diabolical Nazi holocaust will not equal it."[262] It is little wonder that the return of Christ to rescue His church from such horror is the believer's "blessed hope." In regard to the tribulation saints (those who turn to Christ during the Great Tribulation), "only a small portion of them will survive."[263] Obviously believers today are far more fortunate, for *all* of them will be raptured when Christ returns.

For pretribulationists this is far more than a minor theological point. The pretribulational rapture is an antidote to personal despair. Lindsey writes, "The hope of the rapture keeps me from despair in the midst of ever-worsening world conditions."[264] In fact, there is the excitement or hope that at any time Christ will return and take believers far beyond all that will happen on earth below.

A further point in pretribulationism is that the church will be removed from the scene not only to avoid the terrors of the Great Tribulation but also to make room for a transitional period between God's dealing with the church and His dealing with Israel. Charles Ryrie writes, "The distinction between Israel and the Church leads to the belief that the Church will be taken from the earth before the beginning of the tribulation (which in one major sense concerns Israel)."[265] The church age, our present age, has nothing to do with the fulfillment of Old Testament prophecies about Israel's glorious future, but, in Walvoord's words, it is a "parenthesis in the divine program."[266] The church age is both "an *unexpected* and *unpredicted* parenthesis as far as Old Testament prophecy is concerned"[267] (emphasis mine). God's basic (unparenthetical?) program for the future is the establishment of the earthly kingdom of Israel.[268] This will be initiated in the period of the Great Tribulation with the church first raptured out. God will renew His dealings primarily with Isra-

---

[261]*The Rapture, Pre-, Mid-, or Post-Tribulational?* 80.

[262]*Millennialism: The Two Major Views*, 163. In this connection, Lindsey states that "those who say that the believers in the Church are going to go through all these horrors never really bring out what that means" (*The Rapture*, 24). Pretribulationalists ask, How can one really get excited about the return of Christ if all these terrors must first be faced? In Charles Feinberg's words, "How can the church be looking for the blessed hope when she is looking for the Tribulation period?" (*Millennialism: The Two Major Views*, 161).

[263]Walvoord, *The Blessed Hope*, 55.

[264]*The Rapture*, 210.

[265]*Dispensationalism Today*, 159.

[266]*The Rapture Question*, 23.

[267]Ibid., 23–24.

[268]This program includes the rebuilding of the temple, the reinstitution of Old Testament sacrifices, etc. In Charles Feinberg's words, "The land will be redistributed among the twelve tribes, and the Temple will be rebuilt with the sacrifices, as memorials, reinstituted. . . . Israel will also rule over the nations" (*Millennialism: The Two Major Views*, 186).

el. The tribulation accordingly is "a prelude to Israel's restoration and exaltation in the millennial kingdom."[269]

Also during the Great Tribulation a remnant of Israel, who have come to salvation when their spiritual blindness is removed at the rapture of the church, will proclaim the gospel to the nations.[270] According to J. Dwight Pentecost, "the result of their [Israel's] testimony is seen in the great multitude of Gentiles saved"[271] (Rev. 7:9–17). In summary, with the church removed from the scene, not only will Israel be readied for her exaltation in the Millennium, but also she will be used by God to bring multitudes of peoples to salvation.

During the Great Tribulation there will also be terrible persecution by the Antichrist so that vast numbers of believers will be put to death. During the same period God will pour out His wrath upon all the forces of evil. According to Charles Feinberg, "It will be the period of the most intense judgments and the greatest activity of the beast, the false prophet, or the Antichrist, and Satan himself. So horrendous will they be that unless they were shortened, no one would be saved."[272] The church, however, is safely in heaven while "tribulation saints" on earth are going through indescribably horrible times.

Such in general is the picture of events as portrayed by pretribulationism. It is interesting that there is also today a suggested modification of this system often known as *midtribulationism*.[273] According to this view, the church will go through a part of the future tribulation but will be removed before the worst occurs. Rather than viewing the rapture of the church as occurring prior to Revelation 6–19, the midtribulationist holds that it occurs prior to the outpouring of the "bowls of wrath" in Revelation 16. Midtribulationism, like pretribulationism, envisions two future comings of Christ, though for midtribulationism the time period separating the two is briefer.

I will mention three representatives: Norman B. Harrison, J. Oliver Buswell, and Gleason L. Archer, Jr. Harrison holds that the Great Tribulation, properly speaking, refers only to the latter portion of Revelation, where the words "wrath" and "judgment" are frequently repeated. Harrison writes, "Let us get clearly in mind the *nature of the Tribulation*, that it is divine 'wrath' (11:18; 14:8, 10, 19; 15:1, 7; 16:1, 19) and divine 'judgment' (14:7; 15:4; 16:7; 17:1; 18:10; 19:2)."[274] Since Harrison identifies this later period with the Great Tribulation and says that Christ will return for His church just prior to that tribulation, he views himself as a pretribulationist.[275]

Buswell, on the other hand, identifies the Great Tribulation as the period preceding the outpouring of wrath. This climaxes in Revelation 11 with the destruction of God's two witnesses (representing the true church) and their ascension to heaven: "The ascension of the two witnesses in the cloud (Rev.

[269]Walvoord, *The Rapture Question*, 65.

[270]See, e.g., J. Dwight Pentecost, *Things to Come*, chapter 18, "Israel in the Tribulation." Pentecost speaks of "the setting aside of the 144,000, the calling out of the believing remnant, and Israel's ministry to the nations during the tribulation period" (p. 304).

[271]Ibid., 162.

[272]*Millennialism: The Two Major Views*, 164.

[273]The term is not exact, as will be seen in what follows. Moreover, persons who espouse a midtribulational viewpoint do not usually designate it as such.

[274]*The End: Re-Thinking the Revelation*, 111.

[275]Harrison speaks of "His [Christ's] pre-Tribulation coming" (ibid., 118).

11:12) synchronizes precisely with the rapture of the church."[276] Thus Buswell could be called posttribulational in that Christ will return after the Great Tribulation. However, since the period of God's wrath follows, after which Christ will return, Buswell retains (as does Harrison) the basic pretribulational view that there will be two stages in Christ's return separated by a number of years.

Archer prefers to speak of "the mid-seventieth-week" rapture of the church.[277] He refers to Daniel 9:27, which reads, "And he will make a firm covenant with the many for one week [i.e., a heptad of years], but in the middle of the week he will put a stop to sacrifice and grain offering; and on the wing of abominations will come one who makes desolate" (NASB). "In the middle of the week," i.e., a week of seven years, the Antichrist will appear, and God's terrifying judgments will follow. Thus "the raptured church will not be present on earth to experience the unparalleled disasters and afflictions of the last three and a half years while the wrath of God is poured out in successive judgments upon the guilty earth."[278]

Midtribulationism, it is apparent, seeks to give more space to the church's enduring tribulation. However, in the larger sense, it remains pretribulational throughout.[279]

Critique of Pretribulationism

Much of what I have written preceding this Excursus contains, at least indirectly, a critique of pretribulationism. But now I will focus on some of the specific points raised in the Excursus.

1. *The scriptural basis for a pretribulational removal of the church.* The claim that the Book of Revelation evidences such a pretribulation removal cannot be substantiated. For example, to claim that the many references to "the saints" in Revelation do not refer to the church is a serious error. "Saints" throughout the New Testament are believers in Christ: they are the church. Moreover, throughout all of history since the time of Christ the saints have had to face persecution. When, for example, the "beast" in Revelation 13 is "allowed to make war on the saints" (v. 7), this refers to a climactic persecution of the church at the end of history. Even to suggest that they are some other breed of saints ("tribulation saints") and that the church has already been removed from the scene borders on the incredible. To be sure, the word "church" is not used in Revelation 4–19, but, incidentally, the term is not used either for those in heaven who are depicted a number of times in these chapters.[280] Why, then, are the (presumably) raptured ones not called "the church"?

That Revelation 3:10—"I will keep you from the hour of trial which is

[276]*A Systematic Theology of the Christian Religion*, 2:391.

[277]See his article, "The Case for the Mid-Seventieth-Week Rapture Position" in *The Rapture: Pre-, Mid-, or Post-Tribulational?*

[278]Ibid., 134.

[279]Another pretribulational view is known as "partial rapture." This minority view holds that only faithful and watchful believers will be raptured prior to the Great Tribulation. The rest will be raptured during or at the end of the Tribulation. See Erickson's *Contemporary Options in Eschatology*, 169–73, on this viewpoint. An additional view has recently emerged called the "pre-wrath rapture." This view is propounded by Marvin Rosenthal in his book *The Pre-Wrath Rapture of the Church*. Both pre-wrath rapturism and partial rapturism are summarized in Robert P. Lightner, *The Last Days Handbook*.

[280]Also in the critical rapture passage in 1 Thessalonians 4:13–18 the word "church" is not used. But surely this is the rapture of the church.

coming on the whole world"—refers to the removal, or rapture, of the church prior to the Great Tribulation is a misreading of the text. To "keep from" is *not* to be "removed from," but to be "kept through," or "protected from."[281] Moreover, the suggestion of some pretribulationists that the words in Revelation 4:1—"Come up hither"—refer (symbolically or otherwise) to a pretribulational rapture of the church is utterly without exegetical validity. A final remark on the pretribulational view that Revelation 4–19 refers to the period following the removal of the church: Since this removal obviously has not happened yet, those chapters would have relevance *only for a future time*. It is hard to see what value these chapters would have been to the seven churches addressed in Revelation 2 and 3 almost two thousand years ago![282]

Similarly the claim by pretribulationists that "the elect" in Matthew 24—"for the sake of the elect those days will be shortened" (v. 22)—are not the church is as indefensible as the view about "the saints" in the Book of Revelation. "The elect" in the New Testament are often identified with the church;[283] moreover, in Matthew 24 Jesus is clearly talking about the future of His own disciples who will constitute the church. Already, according to Matthew 21, Jesus had said to the Jerusalem leaders, "I tell you that the kingdom of God will be taken away from you and given to a people who will produce its fruit" (v. 43 NIV). Why then would Jesus not be dealing with the church, a new "people," in Matthew 24?[284] The obvious reason that the pretribulationist cannot say this is that these "elect" are suffering "great tribulation" (v. 21); thus the church must already have been removed from the earth! Matthew 24, however, in no way suggests such a prior removal of the church any more than does Revelation 6–19.

2. *The matter of the wrath of God*. Pretribulationists, as we have noted, emphasize that the church must be removed before the Great Tribulation begins because the church is not to be subjected to God's wrath. In a section entitled "The Church Promised Deliverance from the Tribulation,"[285] Walvoord initially quotes 1 Thessalonians 5:9: "For God appointed us not unto wrath, but unto the obtaining of salvation through our Lord Jesus Christ" (ASV). Since the wrath of God is depicted as being poured out during the Great Tribulation, it follows that since the church is not "appointed . . . unto wrath," it must have already been removed to heaven. Indeed, since God's wrath is poured out many times in the Book of Revelation, beginning with 6:17—"the great day of their wrath has come"—the church cannot be on the scene. But such is faulty

---

[281]See the previous discussion of this, pages 365–69, and note 224 (especially referring to John 17:15).

[282]By this I do not mean that these chapters make no reference to future events, for they surely do. However, these chapters were *also* a summons to the first-century church in Asia Minor to bear up under tribulation and persecution. It is these churches who were promised a blessing for reading and keeping the *entire* prophecy (1:3), not just chapters 1–3.

[283]See, e.g., Romans 8:33, 2 Timothy 2:10; Titus 1:1. Also note Jesus' words in Matthew 22:14: "Many are called, but few are chosen [or "elect"—*eklektoi*]." Why would "the elect" in Matthew 24 not also refer to God's "elect" in the present age?

[284]For a helpful discussion of Matthew 24 see Douglas J. Moo, "The Olivet Discourse" in *The Rapture: Pre-, Mid-, or Post-Tribulational?* 190–95. Indeed, there is much of value in all of Moo's chapter, entitled "The Case for the Posttribulation Rapture Position."

[285]*The Rapture Question*, 69.

reasoning. To be sure, the church will *never* be subjected to the wrath of God that always falls upon God's adversaries, but it will be sustained in the midst of it all. The sealing of the 144,000 in Revelation 7:1–8, who unquestionably are saints in the time of the Great Tribulation,[286] is testimony to this fact. The saints are protected from, I repeat, not removed from, the wrath of God.[287]

It follows, therefore, that the church, believing Christians, need fear nothing in the time of God's outpoured wrath. Pretribulationists, however, in reading about all the expressions of God's wrath in the Book of Revelation, question whether anyone could avoid it. Recall Paul Feinberg's words that "if the wrath is falling *everywhere*, it is difficult to see how preservation could be by any other means than the Rapture, or removal." But that *entirely* misses the point: the "other means" is not Rapture but sealing. Nowhere in the Book of Revelation are saints pictured as being even touched by God's judgments; only the "earth-dwellers" are affected.[288] The parallel to all of this is the Book of Exodus where again and again the Israelites are protected from God's wrath upon Pharaoh. *Never once* does a plague fall on them. How God preserved then, and how He will do it in the coming Great Tribulation, we cannot tell. This does not mean there will be no persecution ahead for believers. Quite the contrary, as we have noted, it will be worldwide and devastating. But in the matter of the Great Tribulation, which is *not* persecution suffered by believers but God's wrath on the world, there will be total protection. Hence, rather than shuddering or even despairing[289] at the possibility of such fearsome expressions of God's wrath, we should rejoice in God's assured protection.[290]

Now a further word: for a pretribulationist to say that "the blessed hope is the rapture of the church before the great tribulation" (Walvoord) is grossly to misstate what the "blessed hope" really is. Paul speaks of "awaiting our blessed hope, the appearing of the glory of our great God and Savior Jesus Christ" (Titus 2:13). *The "blessed hope" is Christ's glorious appearing:* it is *that* that we await—not His presumed rapture of us from tribulation. Indeed there is something quite self-centered about desiring Christ to come to rescue us from danger, rather than to behold Him in all His glory and grace.

3. *Christ's return in two stages.* Let us move on to an even more serious matter: the dividing of Christ's return into two stages. As we have noted, according to pretribulationists, Christ will come *before* the Great Tribulation to remove, or rapture, the church; He will also come again *after* that tribula-

---

[286]As Revelation 7:14 shows, they "have come out of the great tribulation." This is true whether they are viewed as the church or as "tribulation saints" after the supposed removal of the church.

[287]Paul Feinberg erroneously states that "the means of protection is *removal* from this period by the Rapture" (italics his) (*The Rapture: Pre-, Mid-, or Post-Tribulational?* 59). Removal is not protection; sealing is.

[288]Recall that in the picture of the invasion of mankind by fiendish locusts who torture people so much that "they will long to die, and death will fly from them" (Rev. 9:6), not a single "sealed" person is affected. The locusts are "told not to harm the grass or the earth or any growth or any tree, but only those of mankind who have not the seal of God upon their foreheads" (v. 4). This sealing doubtless applies to all other woes that follow.

[289]Recall Hal Lindsey's words, "The hope of the rapture keeps me from despair."

[290]Some words in Isaiah may speak to this: "Come, my people, enter your chambers, and shut your doors behind you; hide yourselves for a little while until the wrath is past. For behold, the LORD is coming forth out of his place to punish the inhabitants of the earth for their iniquity" (26:20–21).

tion to establish His kingdom. But, I submit, there is utterly no biblical justification for a twofold future coming. We have observed that some early pretribulationists tried to distinguish between "the Rapture" and "the Revelation" (this is now seldom attempted), thereby to avoid two future comings. Now the attempt is to differentiate between "the Rapture" and "the Second Coming."[291] However, in reply, let me say that the Rapture as described in 1 Thessalonians 4:15-17 is *also* the Second Coming. Paul speaks in this passage of "the coming of the Lord" (v. 15). In 2 Thessalonians 2:8, a recognized Second Coming passage relating to the destruction of "the man of sin," Paul says that "the Lord Jesus will slay him with the breath of his mouth and destroy him by his appearing and his coming." In both passages the word "coming" is *parousia*. Thus there are two aspects of the one and same event of the Second Coming, but not a distinction or separation between a "Rapture Coming" and a Second Coming.[292] Such a division is biblically and theologically out of the question.[293]

4. *The view of imminence*. One of the arguments used to support a pretribulational coming of Christ, as we have noted, is that such a coming, and rapture, can occur at any time. If, for example, the Great Tribulation is future, we cannot expect an imminent coming. Recall Walvoord's words: "If the church is destined to endure the persecutions of the tribulation, it is futile to proclaim the coming of the Lord as an imminent hope." Thus there must be a pretribulation return if there is to be an imminent hope. But such an argument fails to recognize that the New Testament does not actually teach a return at any moment. Jesus does declare, "Watch . . . for you do not know on what day your Lord is coming" (Matt. 24:42). However, shortly after that Jesus tells the parable about the master who entrusted his property to three servants and then "after a long time" (Matt. 25:19) returns to settle accounts with them. Since this parable is one of several in connection with the injunction to "watch," the point is not a return at any moment but that all must be prepared for the future coming of the Lord.[294] The same thing can be said about the Great Tribulation: it must happen first. However, its duration may be rather brief (more intensive than

[291]E.g., Paul Feinberg has a section entitled "The Differences Between Rapture Passages and Second Coming Passages" (*The Rapture: Pre-, Mid-, or Post-Tribulational?* 80–86).

[292]Pretribulationists also seek to distinguish between "the Rapture" as a secret coming and "the Second Coming" as public. It is hard to imagine anything more public than the scenario in 1 Thessalonians 4:16–17—"a cry of command," an "archangel's call," and "the sound of the trumpet of God"!

[293]I might add that it is out of the question historically too, for until the nineteenth century there is no recorded reference to a pretribulational coming of Christ. George Ladd writes, "The hope of the church throughout the early centuries was the second coming of Christ, not a pretribulation rapture" (*The Blessed Hope*, 19). This is a quotation from Ladd's chapter entitled "The Historic Hope of the Church." This chapter and the next, entitled "The Rise and Spread of Pretribulationism," are well worth reading.

[294]Much else could be added on this point. For example, the parables of the kingdom in Matthew 13 about the mustard seed growing to become "the greatest of shrubs" (vv. 31–32) and the leaven in meal increasing "till it was all leavened" (v. 33) imply a lengthy period of time before Christ will return. Also the command of Jesus "You shall be my witnesses . . . to the end of the earth" (Acts 1:8) requires many years, even centuries, to be fulfilled. Obviously Christ will not return until this task has been completed. Thus His return was not imminent in the first generation or in many thereafter. We are surely much closer to its occurrence now.

extensive) and its profile so indeterminate that we could be in the first stages of the Great Tribulation even now.[295] Surely we could easily see the Lord's return in the very near future.

5. *Israel and the church.* Nothing is more disturbing about pretribulationism than its view that the church is a parenthesis in God's plan to bless and glorify Israel. The church presumably is nowhere predicted or foreseen in the Old Testament; hence after the present parenthetical church dispensation, God will move ahead to fulfill various Old Testament prophecies. Thus—and this is critical—the church *must* be removed from the scene in order for the divine program to get underway again and be consummated. Recall Ryrie's words: "The distinction between Israel and the church leads to the belief that the church will be taken from the earth before the beginning of the tribulation." The controlling motif for pretribulationism, accordingly, is not what Scripture teaches about the "horrors" of the Great Tribulation or even the return of Christ, but the distinction between Israel and the church. To put it more bluntly, it elevates Israel and minimizes the church. Dispensationalists might deny this relegation of the church to second-class status, since they recognize it to be truly God's vehicle of heavenly salvation. However, in their view the Old Testament is concerned with another program entirely. Thus there is the parenthetical church age and the necessary removal of the church before God's program for Israel can be carried through. It is sad indeed that this is essentially what pretribulationism is all about.

Now a word about midtribulationism. As we have observed, whatever terminology is used, this position seeks to give more space for the church's being present during a part of the tribulation period. Thus Revelation 6–19 is not viewed wholly as the future time of the Great Tribulation. In some ways, midtribulationism is an improvement over pretribulationism in that it sees the church as still on earth throughout a large portion of the book, and thus during at least some of the coming tribulation. However, midtribulationism makes a serious double mistake in holding that the church will not be on earth when the wrath of God is poured out and that this outpouring of wrath is limited to the later chapters in Revelation. The first part of this mistake midtribulationists share with pretribulationists; on the second they stand alone. Regarding this second part, pretribulationists do have the better position since the expression of God's wrath is vividly portrayed in Revelation 6:17—"the great day of their [God and the Lamb's] wrath has come"—and thus relates to the unfolding of events before "the bowls of wrath" are depicted in Revelation 16. However, the critical matter is that midtribulationism, just like its pretribulational counterpart, errs in its view that the church will be removed prior to the time when God's wrath is progressively poured out. Thus, again, in contradiction to the Scriptures, there must be both an earlier coming of Christ to remove the church and a later one to culminate His wrath. The only difference is that midtribulationism views the time between the two events as being shorter. However, pretribulationism and midtribulationism are essentially the same in their misapprehension of the church's situation regarding the wrath of God and in their misunderstanding of the *one* coming of Jesus Christ.

---

[295]Recall some of the things said in the preceding section on the Great Tribulation in answer to the question, "Are there signs that it is at hand?" (pp. 369ff.).

Finally, in regard to pretribulationism I must express a definite alarm. I wonder if pretribulationists are aware of the danger of misleading believers into thinking that when things get *really bad*, they will not be here to have to face them. If the persecutions of "saints" described in Revelation refer only to saints after the Rapture—as pretribulationists claim—then what will happen to the faith of present believers who have embraced the pretribulation rapture teaching if increased persecution and the Great Tribulation lie ahead?[296] Rather than being prepared to meet whatever may come, such believers run the risk of profound disillusionment and despair. Also, as I suggested earlier, there is a touch of self-centeredness in wanting to "go up" when, as pretribulationists say, there will be "tribulation saints" on earth that must endure everything that the raptured believers have avoided. One pretribulationist actually writes about having "a balcony seat in heaven"[297] to view the terrible events below. Surely there is something terribly misplaced, almost a smug self-satisfaction, in this kind of pretribulational thinking.

A further word must be said in regard to the Great Tribulation. Since this is not (as I have earlier discussed) the church undergoing persecution but God's judgment upon the "earth-dwellers," we really have nothing to fear. God will preserve His own from whatever spiritual and natural disasters may occur. God's wrath is a terrifying thing, but we are not "appointed unto" it. We will in no way be subjected to God's wrath, not because we have been raptured to heaven but because He keeps us safe on earth.

I close with the words of the psalmist: "God is our refuge and strength, an ever-present help in trouble. Therefore we will not fear, though the earth give way and the mountains fall into the heart of the sea[298]. . . . Come and see the works of the LORD, the desolations he has brought on the earth.[299]. . . . The LORD Almighty is with us; the God of Jacob is our fortress" (46:1–2, 8, 11, NIV). Verily *we will not fear* in the midst of all this, for God is, and will be, our refuge and fortress.

X. EXTRAORDINARY PHENOMENA

The last of the signs before the return of Jesus Christ is that of extraordinary phenomena in the heavens and on the earth. Jesus Himself describes how

[296]Corrie ten Boom, who endured prison and persecution under the Nazis, has said, "I have been in countries where the saints are already suffering terrible persecution. In China the Christians were told, 'Don't worry, before the tribulation comes, you will be translated—raptured.' Then came a terrible persecution. Millions of Christians were tortured to death. Later I heard a bishop from China say, sadly, 'We have failed. We should have made the people strong for persecution rather than telling them Jesus would come first.' " Corrie ten Boom added, "I feel I have a divine mandate to go and tell the people of this world that it is possible to be strong in the Lord Jesus Christ. We are in training for the tribulation. . . . " This, I submit, is the voice of tried and true wisdom.

[297]Thomas S. McCall writes, "My hope is that you are rejoicing that, as a believer, you will not have to go through the awesome tribulation, and that you will be able to observe those events from a balcony seat in heaven. See you at the rapture!" (Hal Lindsey et al., *When Is Jesus Coming Again?* 41–42).

[298]Recall many scenes in the Book of Revelation of earth and mountains giving way and collapsing under the impact of God's judgments and wrath.

[299]The "desolations" could signify the sum total of the results of God's wrath and devastation in Revelation 6–19. God's people, totally protected, are invited to "come and see" them.

after "great tribulation" and just prior to His return, certain signs will appear. The fullest account is in Matthew: "Immediately after the tribulation of those days the sun will be darkened, and the moon will not give its light, and the stars will fall from heaven, and the powers of the heavens will be shaken; then will appear the sign of the Son of man in heaven. . ." (24:29–30). In the Lukan account, just after the statement that "there will be signs in sun and moon and stars and upon the earth distress of nations in perplexity at the roaring of the sea and the waves, men fainting with fear and with foreboding of what is coming on the world; for the powers of the heavens will be shaken" (21:25–26), certain earthly aspects are added, namely 'the roaring of the sea and the waves." These apparently follow the heavenly occurrences in the sun, moon, and stars, which have their counterpart in the waters below (tidal waves, tempestuous sea winds, and the like). The result of the shaking of the "powers of the heavens" is a disturbance on earth that increases fear and foreboding among people in general.

At this juncture we may turn to the Book of Revelation and observe a still more vivid picture. With the opening of the sixth seal John writes, "I looked, and behold, there was a great earthquake; and the sun became black as sackcloth, the full moon became like blood,[300] and the stars of the sky fell to earth . . . the sky vanished like a scroll that is rolled up, and every mountain and island was removed from its place" (6:12–14). As a result, the people of earth cry out to the mountains and rocks, "Fall on us and hide us from the face of him who is seated on the throne, and from the wrath of the Lamb" (Rev. 6:16). Here, even more vividly, cosmic and earthly convulsions are depicted immediately preceding the return of Christ.

As I mentioned in the section on the Great Tribulation, when we reflect on many of the phenomenal descriptions in the Book of Revelation, it is apparent that not everything can be understood with a strict literalism.[301] Moreover, as we have also earlier observed, the passages quoted in Matthew and Luke also apply, in a preliminary way, to what

---

[300]A parallel to this may be observed in Peter's words, quoting the prophet Joel, on the Day of Pentecost: "I will show wonders in the heaven above and signs on the earth beneath, blood, and fire, and vapor of smoke [perhaps from an earthquake]; the sun shall be turned into darkness and the moon into blood, before the day of the Lord comes. . ." (Acts 2:19–20).

[301]"In connection with this apocalyptic picture strict literalness must be avoided." So writes William Hendriksen regarding the language in Matthew (*The Gospel of Matthew*, NTC, 863). He then adds, "Until this prophetic panorama becomes history we shall probably not know how much of the description [in Matt., Mark, and Luke] must be taken literally and how much figuratively." Ladd writes in relation to the above passage in Revelation: "The language of cosmic catastrophe . . . is the Bible's picturesque way of describing the divine judgment falling on the world. The language is 'semi-poetic': i.e. it is symbolic language which can hardly be taken with strict literalness. . . . However, the language is not merely poetic or symbolic of spiritual realities but describes a real cosmic catastrophe whose actual character we cannot conceive. Out of the ruins of judgment will emerge a new redeemed order. . ." (*The Revelation of John*, 108). In sum, neither the word "literal" nor the word "symbolic" is adequate to describe the phenomena depicted as preceding the coming of Christ, for they are the immediate backdrop of the unimaginable day of the Lord, of the final irruption of God into history through Jesus Christ, and hence portray the dissolution of the old world in preparation for the coming of the new heavens and new earth.

happened in Jerusalem in A.D. 70.[302] Also, as we have noted, some of the language in the Old Testament about occurrences in the sun, moon, and stars has to be understood in a figurative sense, since it applied to a local situation of that time.[303] However, even with all this recognized, such language concerning the end cannot be understood in a purely figurative or symbolic way: it has a profound spiritual and cosmic base.

In this connection observe that the extraordinary phenomena in all these instances relate particularly to the coming of Christ in judgment. For example, just after Jesus said, "Then will appear the sign of the Son of man in heaven," He added, "[and then] all the nations of earth will mourn" (Matt. 24:30 NIV). This mourning is not one of sorrow or penitence but of remorse and fear at the impending judgment.[304] The "fainting with fear" (in Luke) and the "fall on us and hide us" (in Revelation) also bespeak attitudes, not of believers, but (to use the expression from Revelation) of "earth-dwellers" who are about to experience the wrath of the Lord's appearing.

Indeed, the Old Testament writers attribute the cosmic phenomena of darkened sun, moon, and the like to the coming day of the Lord as the day of God's wrath. For example, the prophet Zephaniah cries, "A day of wrath is that day, a day of distress and anguish, a day of ruin and devastation, a day of darkness and gloom, a day of clouds and thick darkness, a day of trumpet blast and battle cry. . ." (Zeph. 1:15–16).[305] Isaiah speaks for the Lord, saying, "Behold, the day of the LORD comes, cruel, with wrath and fierce anger, to make the earth a desolation and to destroy its sinners from it. For the stars of the heavens and their constellations will not give their light; the sun will be dark at its rising and the moon will not shed its light. I will punish the world for its evil. . ." (Isa. 13:9–11). The prophet Joel cries out, "Multitudes, multitudes, in the valley of decision![306] For the day of the LORD is near in the valley of decision. The sun and the moon are darkened, and the stars withdraw their shining" (Joel 3:14–15). In these (and many other) accounts the apocalyptic language of extraordinary cosmic phenomena is part and parcel of the visitation of God's wrath on "the day of the LORD."

The consummation of all this is, of course, found in the New Testament depictions of that day. What is described in the Old Testament is carried forward with increasing intensity in the apocalyptic language of the New, climaxing in the Book of Revelation. The description in the sixth seal (Rev. 6) of total disturbance in the heavens and vast cataclysms on earth—although portrayed relatively early in the Apocalypse—actually brings to a climax not

---

[302]See the discussion on pages 354–56 particularly the quotations from Josephus.

[303]See earlier quotations, e.g., from Jeremiah 4:23–24 and Ezekiel 32:7–8.

[304]Cf. Revelation 1:7 (NIV): "All the peoples of the earth will mourn because of him" (Christ "coming with the clouds"). Mounce writes, "The mourning of Revelation is the remorse accompanying the disclosure of divine judgment at the coming of Christ" (*The Book of Revelation*, NICNT, 72). This is also the case in Matthew.

[305]That this prophecy relates to all the earth is apparent from these later words: "In the fire of his [the LORD's] jealous wrath, all the earth shall be consumed; for a full, yea, sudden end he will make of all the inhabitants of earth" (1:18). In some Old Testament instances "the day of the LORD" may refer to a more local action of God's judgment upon a people or nation; however, there is usually the implication of an ultimate day to which this action points. See, e.g., Isaiah 13 for a picture of both the final "day of the LORD" (vv. 1–16) and a local event (vv. 17–22) in regard to Babylon.

[306]Meaning *God's* decision (see NASB margin: "i.e. God's verdict").

only the words of Jesus in the Synoptics but also the sequence of ever-increasing cosmic and earthly catastrophe related to the approaching day of wrath.[307]

Finally, we should note again the last word of Jesus *after* speaking of the phenomena in sun, moon, stars, and powers of heaven, and immediately *prior to* the statement about His coming "on the clouds," namely, "Then will appear the sign of the Son of man in heaven"[308] (Matt. 24:30). We have observed that this precipitates mourning: "and all the nations of earth will mourn"—the mourning of remorse and misery. But just what, we may ask, is this very last sign before His final coming? Jesus does not say; hence, we cannot really know until it happens. One suggestion I like is that it is "the dawning of the Messianic glory, growing brighter and brighter until Christ appears in the midst of it."[309] It will surely be a sign of glory!

If such a final sign brings remorse to the world—as surely it will—it will also bring great rejoicing to all believers who yearn for the Lord's return. For truly, as the apostle has said, "we wait for the blessed hope—the glorious appearing of our great God and Savior Jesus Christ." We await the final sign, but even more His "glorious appearing"!

---

[307]Recall, e.g., the discussion supra, pages 360–65.

[308]Or "in the sky" (NASB, NIV). The Greek word *ouranos* may be translated either "sky" or "heaven." However, "heaven" (also in KJV and NEB) seems more appropriate in conveying the supernatural character of this great event.

[309]As stated in *The Second Coming Bible Commentary*, 344. Since Jesus says earlier in Matthew that His coming will be like a flash of lightning—"for as the lightning comes from the east and shines as far as the west, so will be the coming [*parousia*] of the Son of man" (24:27)—it is also possible that something like a flash of lightning is the sign. If this is the case, the glory (mentioned above) would not be a gradual "growing brighter and brighter" but a sudden, electrifying flash across heaven and earth!

11

The Manner of Christ's Return

We will now consider the manner of Christ's return. Our concern thus far has been with various names or terms used in the New Testament to express His return and with a number of signs that point to this great event. Thus we are ready to look at the actual event itself: What will the return of Christ be like?

I. THE CLOUDS OF HEAVEN

Christ will return on the clouds of heaven. Following the words about "the sign of the Son of man in heaven" and the resultant mourning of "the tribes of the earth," the text in Matthew adds, "And they will see the Son of man coming on the clouds of heaven" (24:30). The exact wording varies within the Synoptic Gospels: "in clouds," Mark 13:26; "in a cloud," Luke 21:27; and, according to Revelation 1:7, "he is coming with the clouds."[1] Whether "on,"[2] "in," or "with" "clouds" or simply "a cloud," all these are obviously variable expressions to declare the wonder and mystery of an event that transcends exact description.

Let us reflect for a moment on this latter point. The return of Christ will have no counterpart in anything in ordinary experience; hence no precise conceptualization is possible. It will not be a movement from cosmic space to earthly space (like the return of an astronaut) but *from heaven to earth*; thus whether on, in, or with one cloud or many clouds makes no difference, since this is a movement between heaven and earth of Him who is both God and man. It cannot be contained by the language of ordinary space or de-

[1]The Book of Daniel uses similar language: "Behold, with the clouds of heaven there came one like a son of man" (7:13). However, rather than moving toward earth, he "came to the Ancient of Days and was presented before him." Nevertheless, the background (v. 11) is similar to that of the New Testament in that there is the slaying of the beast—"the beast was slain" (a prototype of the beast[s] of Revelation and the "man of sin" of 1 Thessalonians, et al.) prior to the reign of the "son of man."

[2]Revelation 14:14, similar to Daniel (see note 1) in its use of the "son of man" terminology, has the preposition "on": "Lo, a white cloud, and seated on the cloud one like a son of man." This passage does not specify His coming on the cloud, although it is unmistakably a depiction of Christ's final action, for afterward He is described with a sickle in hand to reap the earth (vv. 14–16).

picted on even a three-dimensional canvas: it is the incomprehensible transection of the mundane by the supramundane, the earthly sphere by the heavenly sphere.

This return of Christ from heaven to earth will end the long period between His ascension almost two thousand years ago and His Parousia. When Jesus departed from His disciples, the situation was the same except that the movement was in the opposite direction: *from earth to heaven.* "As they were looking on, he was lifted up, and a cloud took him out of their sight"[3] (Acts 1:9). Hence, it was not a trip from earthly to cosmic space, or even beyond, but from visibility to invisibility, from earth to heaven. Likewise it will be, in reverse, upon His return. Thus two angels said to the watching disciples, "This Jesus, who was taken up from you into heaven, will come in the same way as you saw him go into heaven" (Acts 1:11). As a cloud "took him" before, "in the same way" He will come back.

It is apparent that the clouds (whether one or many) in all these accounts are clouds of heaven. They are from heaven, and while they are beheld by human eyes, their origin is from beyond. Indeed the clouds are of the same order as the clouds that are frequently depicted in the Bible as accompanying a divine visitation or action. For example, at Mount Sinai there is the memorable scene of the Lord coming to the mountain "in a thick cloud" (also with thunder and lightning) in the sight of all Israel and communicating His commandments (Exod. 19:9–19; 20). On another occasion the cloud covered the mountain, and God spoke with Moses "out of the midst of the cloud" (Exod. 24:15–18). Yet again, Moses went up Mount Sinai and "the LORD descended in the cloud and stood with him there" (Exod. 34:5). At the conclusion of Moses' building the tabernacle an extraordinary event occurred: "Then the cloud covered the tent of meeting, and the glory of the LORD filled the tabernacle" (Exod. 40:34). Thus God came in "the cloud." Similarly many years later when Solomon had finished the temple, "a cloud filled the house of the LORD" (1 Kings 8:10). Another vivid instance is that of the prophet Ezekiel; he beheld "a great cloud, with brightness round about it, and fire flashing forth continually, and in the midst of the fire, as it were gleaming bronze" (Ezek. 1:4)—the awesome divine presence. In a memorable New Testament scene, while the close disciples of Jesus were on the top of a mountain, suddenly "a bright cloud overshadowed them, and a voice from the cloud said, 'This is my beloved Son, with whom I am well pleased; listen to him' " (Matt. 17:5). And so, in multiple ways, throughout both Old and New Testaments, clouds are frequently shown as vehicles[4] of the divine presence and activity.[5]

Thus Christ's return on the clouds of heaven will be in continuity with the past, but also it will be at the climax of history. The cloud will be like one never seen before. But more important than the cloud will be He who comes to bring history to its consummation. Even so, come Lord Jesus!

[3]See the discussion of this in *Renewal Theology*, 1:390–95.

[4]The psalmist puts it in beautiful poetry: "O LORD my God, thou art very great! Thou art clothed with honor and majesty, who coverest thyself with light as with a garment . . . who makest the clouds thy chariot, who ridest on the wings of the wind" (104:1–3).

[5]Paul Minear says it well: "The cloud on which the Son of man returns is continuous with the cloud that hovered over men in the Deluge, the Exodus, the wilderness, the Temple, the prophet's [i.e., Ezekiel's] ecstasy, and the Messiah's ministry" (*Christian Hope and the Second Coming*, 129).

Finally, to come on (or with, or in) the cloud(s) means to *return in glory*. We have noted that in the Old Testament "the cloud covered the tent of meeting, and the glory of the LORD filled the tabernacle." Thus closely connected are the cloud and the glory. And that glory was so awesome that "Moses was not able to enter the tent of meeting, because the cloud abode upon it, and the glory of the LORD filled the tabernacle" (Exod. 40:35). In a similar manner, just after the cloud filled the temple built by Solomon, "the priests could not stand to minister because of the cloud; for the glory of the LORD filled the house of the LORD" (1 Kings 8:11). In the New Testament, Peter, looking back to that awesome day on the mount when God spoke out of the overshadowing cloud, declares that "the voice was borne to him [Christ] by the Majestic Glory" (2 Peter 1:17). The cloud is the emblem of the glory of God—a glory awesome and majestic.

So it is that when Christ returns "on the clouds," He will return in glory. According to the apocalyptic narrative of Matthew 24, Jesus speaks of "the Son of man coming on the clouds of heaven with power and great glory" (v. 30). At an earlier date in His ministry Jesus refers, according to the Lukan account, to His future coming "in his glory and the glory of the Father and of the holy angels" (9:26). Hence He will come both with "great glory" (Matthew) and in multiplied glory (Luke): His own, that of the Father, and also that of the holy angels!

What a source of blessedness and rejoicing is this return in glory for those who belong to Christ! Truly our blessed hope "is the appearing of the glory of our great God and Savior Jesus Christ" (Titus 2:13). Indeed, with this hope ever before us, we may gladly endure all present travail and pain. So Paul declares, "I consider that the sufferings of this present time are not worth comparing with the glory that is to be revealed to us" (Rom. 8:18). And Peter writes, "Rejoice in so far as you share Christ's sufferings, that you may also rejoice and be glad when his glory is revealed [literally, 'at the revelation of his glory']" (1 Peter 4:13). The revelation of that future glory is so full of blessedness and joy that in comparison any present trial or suffering pales into insignificance.

Such is the glory of Christ's presence as He comes "in clouds." But it is also *the glory of His power*. He will return "with great power and glory" (Mark 13:26);[6] thus the two are closely conjoined. It will take His mighty power to gather the elect by awakening the dead and translating the living, to destroy evil totally, and to bring all things to their consummation.

According to Paul, "the Lord himself will descend from heaven with a cry of command"[7] (1 Thess. 4:16), and it is that mighty "cry of command" that will set in operation all forces leading to the consummation. In the Book of Revelation, in the climactic scene of Christ's return, John says, "I saw heaven opened, and behold, a white horse!"[8] (19:11)—the horse representing power and might. Christ is followed by "the

---

[6]In Mark the word "great" relates to "power"; in Matthew, to "glory" (supra).

[7]The KJV and NASB have "shout." If "shout" is used, it means a "shout of command" (see TDNT, 3:657). The "cry" or "shout" in 1 Thessalonians 4:16 is particularly related to the resurrection and translation of believers. However, in a broader sense it refers to *all* the dead, for, according to the words of Jesus in John 5:28, "the hour is coming when all who are in the tombs will hear his voice. . . ." (Some of these points will be discussed later in this chapter.)

[8]No mention here is made of the "white cloud" (as in Rev. 14:14), for the emphasis in this passage is wholly on Christ's coming in power.

armies of heaven" (v. 14). Here the focus is on the fact that all power is at His disposal for the final destruction of everything evil.

Finally, Christ's coming in glory on the clouds has the dual effect of being so brilliant and bright as to destroy evil[9] by its very presence and power and to produce great marveling and glorification among believers. Regarding the latter, Paul speaks of the day "when he [Christ] comes . . . to be glorified in his saints, and to be marveled at in all who have believed" (2 Thess. 1:10).

Surely we cannot even begin to imagine the magnitude, the marvel, and the wonder of Christ's return in glory.

II. ACCOMPANIMENTS

It is apparent, first, that the return of Christ will be with *angels*. According to Mark 8:38, Jesus will come "in the glory of the Father with the holy angels."[10] Paul speaks of the Lord Jesus as "revealed from heaven with his mighty angels" (2 Thess. 1:7). The angels, accordingly, are "the angels of his power."[11] They come with Him to effectuate His purposes.

Paul also makes reference, in the context of Christ's return, to "the voice of the archangel." After saying that the Lord "will descend from heaven" with "a cry of command," Paul adds, "with the voice of the archangel" (1 Thess. 4:16 KJV).[12] Nothing is further stated regarding either the identification of the archangel or what he says.[13] The relevant point is that, in addition to mentioning the angels who accompany Jesus, Scripture also refers to the presence and activity of an archangel.

The return of Christ is also described as occurring in the company of the *saints*: "the coming [*parousia*] of the Lord Jesus with all his saints"[14] (1 Thess 3:13). In the same connection Paul says that "through Jesus, God will bring with him those who have fallen asleep" (1 Thess. 4:14). Hence, the return of Christ will be in company with not only the holy angels but also those believers who have died.

There is one other passage of particular relevance here—Colossians 3:4: "When Christ who is our life appears, then you also will appear with him in glory." The background for this appear-

[9]Recall the words of Paul that "the man of sin" will be destroyed by the *epiphaneia*, the outshining, of Christ's *parousia* (2 Thess. 2:8).

[10]The parallel account in Matthew 16:27 speaks of the Son of man coming "with his angels in the glory of his Father." The angels are *His* angels: they represent and serve Him.

[11]This is the literal reading of 2 Thessalonians 1:7.

[12]Also NASB, NIV; RSV has "with the archangel's call." The archangel possibly is Michael. The only other references in the New Testament to an archangel by name are in Jude 9 ("the archangel Michael") and Revelation 12:7 ("Michael and his angels"). According to EGT in loco, "Michael . . . in Jewish tradition not only summoned the angels but sounded a trumpet to herald God's approach for judgment (e.g., in *Apoc. Mosis*, xxii)." It is also noteworthy that Daniel's prophecy of the tribulation and resurrection in chapter 12 begins: "At that time shall arise Michael, the great prince who has charge of your people" (v. 1).

[13]It is possible that the "voice of the archangel" is a summons to all the other angels.

[14]The Greek word is *hagion*. The NIV translates it "holy ones"; the KJV and NASB (like RSV) read "saints." "Saints" here, as elsewhere in the New Testament, ordinarily refers to believers in general. Robert L. Thomas writes that "universally in Paul and perhaps the entire NT (Jude 14 is debatable) it is a term for redeemed humanity" (EBC, 11:268). Leon Morris, while affirming that *hagioi* "seems always elsewhere to refer to men," adds that "it is best to understand the 'holy ones' as all those bright beings who will make up His train, be they angels or the saints who have gone before" (*First and Second Epistles to the Thessalonians*, NICNT, 115). I submit that, whereas it is true that angels will accompany Christ in His return, the *hagioi* are distinctively believers (see especially 2 Thess. 1:10, a somewhat parallel passage, where "his saints" are unmistakably people).

ance with Christ "in glory" is the fact that, says Paul, "your life is hid with Christ in God" (v. 3). Hence when He appears, we will appear with Him because we are already with Him. The coming of the saints with Christ, accordingly, is the manifestation to the world that our lives are hid with Christ in God. He comes with His saints because they belong to Him; they are a part of Him, and hence will appear with Him in glory.[15]

It is also possible that the "armies of heaven" (mentioned earlier) signify the saints. We have observed that He who comes on "a white horse" is followed by "the armies of heaven." The armies are further described as "arrayed in fine linen" (Rev. 19:14). Nothing is said here specifically as to whether the armies are angels or people, but several verses earlier it was declared of the bride of Christ that "it was granted her to be clothed with fine linen" (19:8). It would seem to follow that the "armies of heaven" are saints in glory who will be with Christ in the final victory over evil.[16]

Finally, the return of Christ will be accompanied by a great *trumpet call.* Following the statement in Matthew about the Son of man "coming on the clouds of heaven with power and great glory," the text reads, "and he will send out his angels with a loud trumpet call [literally, 'with a great trumpet']" (24:31). Paul's words about the Lord descending "with a cry of command, with the voice of the archangel" continue: "and with the sound of the trumpet of God" (1 Thess. 4:16). It will be a great trumpet call—indeed, the very trumpet of God.

Without referring directly to the return of Christ,[17] Paul speaks elsewhere of "the last trumpet" and adds, "for the trumpet will sound. . ." (1 Cor. 15:52). This "last trumpet" seems identical with the seventh trumpet in the Book of Revelation. After six trumpet calls have gone forth, the announcement is made "that there should be no more delay, but that in the days of the trumpet call to be sounded by the seventh angel, the mystery of God . . . should be fulfilled" (10:6–7). The climax comes when "the seventh angel blew his trumpet, and there were loud voices in heaven, saying, 'The kingdom of the world has become the kingdom of our Lord and of his Christ, and he shall reign for ever and ever' " (11:15). Truly the last trumpet will have sounded, for the mystery of God will be complete and His kingdom come in power and glory.

This sounding of the trumpet at the return of Christ calls to mind the sounding of a trumpet at the awesome descent of God to Mount Sinai just before the giving of the Ten Commandments. In addition to thunder, lightning, and the

[15]See also Paul's words in 1 Thessalonians 4:14: "For since we believe that Jesus died and rose again, even so, through Jesus, God will bring with him those who have fallen asleep."

[16]The admitted difficulty of this interpretation is that if "the armies of heaven" are the saints, there seems to be no reference in this passage to the angels who (as we have earlier observed) are clearly said to accompany Christ. Moreover, since the angels are elsewhere described as "mighty" (as in 2 Thess. 1), they could well be spoken of as "armies." (Indeed, there are many references in the Scriptures to angels as warriors, fighters, etc.) However, on the other side, an earlier scene in Revelation shows Christ along with saints in the final victory over the forces of evil: "The Lamb will conquer them, for he is Lord of lords and King of kings, and those with him are called and chosen and faithful" (17:14). A possible resolution of the difficulty is that both angels and saints are included in the "armies of heaven" that accompany Christ in His return.

[17]That the return of Christ is the context, however, is apparent, for Paul is writing about the resurrection to come and the changes that will occur at that time (see later discussion).

"thick cloud," there was "a very loud trumpet blast," with the result that "all the people who were in the camp trembled" (Exod. 19:16). A short time later, "as the sound of the trumpet grew louder and louder, Moses spoke, and God answered him in thunder" (v. 19).

The sounding of the trumpet, accordingly, is an announcement or declaration that God is at hand: He has drawn near.[18] In relation to Christ and His return, it is a proclamation to all the world that God's final action in Jesus Christ is about to occur. The trumpet sound heard at Mount Sinai, growing ever louder and louder, is but a dim prefiguring of that final trumpet blast,[19] which will declare the consummation of all things.

III. TOTAL VISIBILITY

The return of Christ will be in total visibility. The Book of Revelation declares, "Behold, he is coming with the clouds! Every eye shall see him, and among them those who pierced him; and all the peoples of the world shall lament in remorse" (Rev. 1:7 NEB).[20] Since "every eye shall see him," the return of Christ will be visible to the whole world.

Hence, the return of Christ is public; it is no hidden or secret coming. Indeed, there is a twofold purpose in His return: the redemption of His own and the destruction of His enemies. Thus there are two attitudes: one of lamentation (mourning, wailing) among "the peoples of the earth" (= the "earth-dwellers")[21] and one of rejoicing among believers. In the Gospel of Matthew we read, "Then all the tribes ['peoples'] of the earth will mourn, and they will see the Son of man coming on the clouds of heaven" (24:30). This text declares the lamentation of nonbelievers—"*they* will see. . . ." But following similar words in the Gospel of Luke is this affirmative message to Jesus' disciples: "Now when these things begin to take place, look up and raise your heads, because *your* redemption is drawing near" (21:28). In the coming of Jesus there is both redemption and destruction, rejoicing and wailing: such is the day of the Lord's visitation. But that the return is public, therefore visible to all, is unmistakable.

A further word of clarification: some New Testament passages so focus on one aspect of Christ's return that they have led some biblical interpreters to

---

[18]In the Old Testament the coming day of the Lord is also depicted as a day of trumpet sounding: "The great day of the LORD is near. . . . A day of wrath is that day . . . a day of clouds and thick darkness, a day of trumpet blast and battle cry. . ." (Zeph. 1:14–16).

[19]Since this is, ultimately, "the trumpet of God" (as in 1 Thess. 4:16), the sounding forth will go far beyond that of any earthly trumpet. Much like "the clouds of heaven," "the trumpet of God" belongs to the realm of the presently unimaginable. But when it sounds, *all will know it!*

[20]The RSV translation, I believe, is misleading at a critical point in this verse above. It reads, "Every eye will see him, every one who pierced him." This suggests that the visibility will be limited to those who "pierced him." The NIV and NASB make the limitation more pronounced: "Every eye will see him, even those who pierced him." Granted, "even those" is a possible translation of the *kai hoitines* of the Greek text. However, the primary meaning of *kai* is "and," and *hoitines*—"such as," "among them those who" (as above)—suggests in addition a second, more limited group. Exegesis is an important matter here, for if RSV, NIV, and NASB are correct, there will not be total visibility (unless "those who pierced him" is given universal application—which seems to strain the text). The KJV puts it well: "Every eye shall see him, and they also which pierced him."

[21]Recall that in Revelation the "earth-dwellers" are those who are *not* believers.

claim a double return.[22] The first coming is usually said to be private, for believers only. A key scripture in this connection is 1 Thessalonians 4—the "rapture" passage—in which Christ's Parousia is said (by these interpreters) to be unobserved by the world (although the effects, they say, will be experienced, e.g., the absence of many persons). However, although it is true that such a passage relates only to the resurrection and rapture of believers, it is hard to visualize the event as private. The "cry of command," the "voice of the archangel," the "sound of the trumpet of God"—can these events happen without the whole world being aware? A private, invisible rapture and a public, visible coming are clearly not two events, but two aspects of the *one* return that "every eye shall see."

On the matter of the public visibility of Christ's return, Jesus also speaks of it in connection with those who will claim that He has already come but His presence is invisible to most of the world,[23] or, having come, He is in hiding and will soon reveal Himself.[24] All such thinking is totally erroneous even as Jesus Himself declared in a strong warning: "If any one says to you, 'Lo, here is the Christ!' or 'There he is!' do not believe it. . . . Lo, I have told you beforehand. So, if they say to you, 'Lo, he is in the wilderness,' do not go out; if they say 'Lo, he is in the inner rooms,' do not believe it" (Matt. 24:23, 25–26). Then Jesus adds, "For as the lightning comes from the east and shines as far as the west, so will be the coming [*parousia*] of the Son of man" (v. 27). In other words, even as lightning flashes across the whole sky from east to west so that no one can fail to see it, so will the coming of Christ be. It will be wholly visible, a public coming: all will behold it as it happens.

Finally, the question is sometimes asked, How will it be possible for everyone to see the return of Christ? We today, many centuries after the New Testament was written, are far more aware of the wide expanse of the earth than early Christians were and, accordingly, may wonder how all people can possibly behold such an event. Moreover, we also know that the earth's curvature would seemingly rule out a visibility from all parts of the globe at the same time. A relatively small and flat earth—which we do not have—would seem to be a more probable arena for the viewing of this climactic event in history.[25]

---

[22]Recall my reference to this in note 35, page 309, in terms of "two stages in Jesus' second coming" (Lindsey), hence the view of a double return. See also my critique of the pretribulationist view that Christ's return will be in two stages (p. 379).

[23]Jehovah's Witnesses claim that Christ came in A.D. 1914 invisibly and is directing His organization from theocratical headquarters in Brooklyn, New York. E.g., see *Let God Be True* (publication of the Watch Tower Bible and Tract Society, 1952), "Christ Jesus came to the Kingdom in A.D. 1914, but unseen to men" (p. 300).

[24]See the discussion (p. 332, n.62) of the declaration by some in the New Age movement that Christ (or "Lord Maitreya") has now come but in secret (with location known to only a few of His disciples) before His imminent manifestation and declaration to the world.

[25]In our modern age of television, it is, of course, now possible for people any place on earth to view live by satellite what is happening anywhere else. Hence—it is sometimes suggested—the return of Christ could be seen through television by "every eye." This suggestion has many obvious problems (TV sets are hardly available to everyone, such viewing would not have the directness of "every eye will see him," etc.). I might add that modern television, which has actually made possible the viewing of any event on our globe as it happens, could well be an earthly sign of the far greater, television-transcending, event

The answer to this carries us back to some things said earlier about Christ's coming on the clouds. The clouds are "clouds of heaven," and therefore the return of Christ is not from cosmic space to earthly space, but from a supramundane dimension (heaven), invisible and inaccessible, that breaks into our earthly sphere. Moreover, since the clouds are not clouds of earth but of heaven, and heaven is *not* a place above the earth nor does it have any spatial relation to it, when Christ appears "on the clouds of heaven," He will truly be visible to all. This, to be sure, is presently unimaginable because of our three- (or possibly four-) dimensional consciousness. We are simply not accustomed to traffic between heaven and earth and the trans-spatial aspect of its occurrence.

One additional reflection: Since Christ will return in His glorified body (in which He now reigns "at the right hand" of the Father), a body no longer subject to the usual limitations of space,[26] it is quite possible that all could see Him at the same moment. In a way presently unimaginable to us—because we have no experience of a glorified or spiritual body—He will make Himself visible to every person on earth.

But however we seek to understand the total visibility of Christ at His return, we are inevitably stopped short by the realization that here, if anywhere, we see "through a glass darkly." There is simply no way prior to His appearing that we can adequately conceive of the nature of an event that represents the unique and ultimate incursion of heaven into earth and the transition from the present age into the age to come. The return of Christ stands on the boundary line between the known and the unknown, hence it is now beyond our comprehension. "Every eye shall see him"—that we *know*. But to *understand* it remains for the day of His revelation.

IV. PERSONAL AND CORPOREAL

The return of Christ will be personal and corporeal. Let us note each of these aspects in turn.

A. Personal

It is important to emphasize that the future coming of Christ will be personal: He will return as the same Jesus who lived on earth many years ago. For example, to the disciples who had just observed the Lord's ascension into heaven the angels said, "*This same Jesus*, who has been taken from you into heaven, will come back" (Acts 1:11 NIV). It will be the same person they had known.

Thus there is no Christ to come who is other than the Jesus who has come. To a Jewish audience that was still expecting a future Messiah, Peter declared, "Repent therefore, and turn again, that your sins may be blotted out, that times of refreshing may come from the presence of the Lord, and that he may send the Christ [= Messiah] appointed for you, Jesus, whom heaven must receive until the time for establishing all that God spoke by the mouth of his holy prophets. . ." (Acts 3:19–21). The coming Messiah is the one who has come, even Jesus Himself.[27]

Hence it will be the return of One whom we have already known as our Lord and Savior. In the words of Paul:

---

of the return of Christ. Total disclosure and instant communication, which are aspects of this late twentieth-century video era, may well be preparation for the Parousia.

[26]See the discussion of this in *Renewal Theology*, 1:381–413.

[27]This, of course, distinguishes the Christian faith from Judaism. Both Christians and Jews look forward to the coming of Christ (or the Messiah)—indeed, among many on both sides there is a growing conviction of its imminent occurrence—but for Jews it is surely not Jesus. For Christians it is the Jesus who came before who will come again.

"Our commonwealth is in heaven, and from it we await[28] a Savior, the Lord Jesus Christ" (Phil. 3:20). For the believer who is already joined to Christ by faith, it will be a deeply personal occasion. Let us also recall the words of Jesus to His disciples: "Let not your heart be troubled. . . . I go to prepare a place for you. And if I go and prepare a place for you, I will come again and receive you to Myself; that where I am, there you may be also" (John 14:1–3 NASB). The first-person pronouns, the sense of closeness, the warm promise of the future—all point to the day of Christ's return as the day of personal reunion to be with Him forever.

Thus the Christ who returns on the clouds of heaven will be the same person who formerly walked on the earth. He will seem distant, even forbidding, to the unbeliever, but for those who belong to Him it will be a joyous occasion. In both cases, however, He will return in person: the Jesus of Nazareth being verily the Christ of glory.

B. Corporeal

We need also to stress that the return of Christ will be corporeal: He will come in the body. On the day of His ascension the disciples saw Him leave in the body, and so He will return. It will be in "the body of His glory" (Phil. 3:21 NASB)[29]—hence beyond usual earthly limitations.[30] Nonetheless, He will return in the body.

The return of Christ, therefore, will not be a spiritual coming. Truly He came in the Holy Spirit at Pentecost, and so comes again and again. But coming in the Paraclete is quite different from His coming in the Parousia.[31] Through the Holy Spirit Christ is with His people in presence and power, but this is a spiritual presence.[32] The coming at the end of history is of a different order; it will be the coming of Christ Himself in His glorious body.

It has been popular in some circles to interpret the Parousia as wholly spiritual. What we therefore look forward to at the consummation of history, according to this view, is a greatly increased sense of the spiritual presence of Christ. At long last there will be the spiritual triumph of the gospel of Christ over the world—and this will be the Parousia. Indeed—as it is also sometimes urged—since *parousia* basically means "presence," we should not look for a bodily return but an intensified spiritual presence.

To respond to the latter point first: *parousia*, to be sure, does mean "presence." But it also carries the note of "arrival,"[33] hence an arriving presence. It refers to someone who comes, hence it is much more concrete than a purely spiritual presence. On the other point, it is simply incorrect to speak of a spiritual triumph of the gospel as the return of Christ. For one thing, the Scriptures depict no such triumphant climax of the gospel (although there will be a witness to all the nations). For another, the return of Christ is of a Person (as we have noted) in His corporeality, and not of a spiritual occurrence that has reached its consummation.

In conclusion, I would add that from

---

[28]Or "eagerly await" (as in NIV, cf. NASB). The Greek word is *apekdechometha*.

[29]Or "his glorious body" (KJV, RSV, NIV).

[30]As we noted above.

[31]I like the words of A. J. Gordon: "Observe this difference: In the Paraclete, Christ comes spiritually and invisibly; in the *Parousia*, he comes bodily and gloriously" (*The Ministry of the Spirit*, 49).

[32]This is true also of the "real presence" of Christ in the Eucharist. He is truly present not corporeally but spiritually.

[33]See the earlier discussion of this.

the perspective of the believer, what is earnestly desired is the coming of the *whole* Christ—and this includes the body. "Without having seen him you love him," Peter writes (1 Peter 1:8). Indeed, we do. But the very fact that we love Him and believe in Him now without seeing Him only intensifies our desire to see Him in person. Hence, our earnest expectation—as well as the biblical assurance—is that at His return we will behold Him in the body of His glory. For *that* we yearn—and pray, "Our Lord, come!"[34]

V. SUDDEN AND UNEXPECTED

Finally, Christ will return suddenly and unexpectedly. Jesus Himself makes it unmistakably clear that no one knows the exact time of His coming. In his Olivet address He declares, "Of that day and hour no one knows, not even the angels of heaven, nor the Son, but the Father only" (Matt. 24:36). In this extraordinary statement Jesus Himself claimed ignorance of the precise day and hour of His coming[35] and He included in this ignorance the angels in heaven as well as all mankind! Regarding mankind at large, Jesus compares the suddenness of His future coming with the suddenness of events in the time of Noah. Even as people then "did not know until the flood came and swept them all away, so will be the coming [*parousia*] of the Son of man" (v. 39). In like manner, Jesus adds, "two men will be in the field; one is taken and one is left"; likewise "two women will be grinding at the mill; one is taken and one is left" (vv. 40–41). To his own disciples Jesus then adds, "Watch therefore, for you do not know on what day your Lord is coming" (v. 42). Similar are Jesus' words in Mark: "Take heed, watch; for you do not know when the time will be" (13:33). Then, using the figure of a "thief" (Matt. 24:43) who unexpectedly breaks into one's house, Jesus adds, "Therefore you must also be ready; for the Son of man is coming at an hour you do not expect" (v. 44). The Parousia will be a sudden and unexpected event.

Paul carries forward this imagery of a thief, saying to the Thessalonians, "You yourselves know well that the day of the Lord will come like a thief in the night" (1 Thess. 5:2). Peter echoes the same note: "The day of the Lord will come like a thief" (2 Peter 3:10). Finally, in the Book of Revelation, as the battle of Armageddon is about to occur, a voice speaks from heaven: "Lo, I am coming like a thief" (16:15). Just as a thief comes suddenly and unexpectedly, so the Lord Himself will return.

Nonetheless, there is a striking difference in this connection between believers and unbelievers. The same element of suddenness and unexpectedness exists for both; however, the difference lies in the element of surprise. Believers look forward to the day of the Lord's coming and so will not be surprised when it happens; unbelievers will be caught completely off guard. So Paul writes to the Thessalonians, "You are not in darkness, brethren, for that day to surprise you like a thief. For you are all sons of light and sons of the day; we are not of the night or of darkness" (1 Thess. 5:4–5). Although a thief comes unexpectedly, believers will not be surprised when this occurs. In summary, the difference lies in being asleep (the world) and awake (believers). Paul adds, "So then let us not sleep as others do, but let us keep awake and be sober" (v. 6). If we are awake and alert, there

[34]First Corinthians 16:22—the expression is in Aramaic: *Marana tha.*

[35]Jesus, of course, said this in the days of His *kenosis* (self-emptying) on earth. Now in His glorification He surely shares this knowledge with God the Father.

will be no surprise in the returning of the Lord.

I have earlier discussed the Christian attitude toward Christ's return and noted such things as earnestly desiring that it happen, loving Christ's appearing, and patiently waiting.[36] Indeed, all of this belongs to the Christian hope, a hope that is solid and sure. So there will be no surprise—even if it happens suddenly and unexpectedly—when the hoped-for Lord returns. Moreover, believers are (or should be) aware of the various signs of the Lord's coming,[37] hence, although not knowing the exact time of the Parousia, they can be aware of the proximity of His return.

A further word: the sudden and unexpected return of the Lord does not necessarily mean a return at any moment.[38] Certain things must happen first (as we have seen); then the Lord will return. In our present day much is occurring that may point to a near coming, so that we may properly say that the Lord's return is impending.[39] Moreover, even if the event is yet future or indeed even if all signs seem totally fulfilled, the return of Christ will still be sudden and unexpected.

It is interesting to reflect on the fact that the Lord's first coming in the Incarnation was likewise sudden and unexpected. Although there were abundant Old Testament prophecies and signs, Christ came at a moment no one expected. This is a good warning to believers today not to be overconfident about the signs, and certainly not to seek to pinpoint the exact time or season.[40] Christ will return suddenly and unexpectedly.

A further illustration of this is the Day of Pentecost. As the disciples were gathered in one place, "suddenly a sound came from heaven like the rush of a mighty wind" (Acts 2:2). This refers to the Holy Spirit who came suddenly and unexpectedly. The disciples surely were not surprised, for they were faithfully awaiting His coming; but they had not been told the exact time. That was in the hands of the Lord, who sovereignly came in the Spirit when He willed. The disciples sought to calculate nothing;[41] but they were ready when the memorable day arrived.

Indeed, the very fact that Christ will return suddenly and unexpectedly adds to the majesty and wonder of the event. This will be *God's* sovereign action even as in the Incarnation and at Pentecost. Christ's coming on the clouds, accompanied by angels and saints, in total visibility, personally and corporeally, is such an incomprehensible incursion of heaven into earth that there is no way, prior to the event, that we can

---

[36]Recall pages 297–302, concerning the Christian attitude to the return of Christ.

[37]Chapter 10 deals with these.

[38]See pages 379–80 regarding the pretribulational view of imminence.

[39]"Impending" is a better term than "imminent." "Imminent" implies the idea of an any-moment return; "impending" implies the idea of approaching, or being near at hand.

[40]History is laden with the miscalculations of those who have sought in vain to calculate and name the time. One attempt, among many, in the recent past was that of the man who claimed he had irrefutable proof that Christ would return in the fall of 1988. When this did not happen, he changed the date to September, 1989, all of course to no avail. Frequently, those who make such predictions seek to avoid Jesus' words about not knowing the "day and hour" by claiming "only" to know the season and the year. However, Jesus' words include *all* predictions of time (recall also His words: "You do not know when the *time* will be"). We may by virtue of the signs believe the time is near, but we will not seek to be too specific about what ultimately belongs to God's hidden counsel. Beware, then, of anyone who claims to know more than the Lord intends for us to know!

[41]The disciples did not even calculate when the Day of Pentecost it was likely to happen! How different were they from some of our modern day calculators about the Parousia.

fully comprehend what it will be like or know its exact moment of occurrence. When eternity invades time, all human calculations come to nought. Nor, I submit, should we want it otherwise, for it will be the Day of the Lord, His day not ours, that will suddenly break forth across the earth.

Suddenly, unexpectedly—therefore we can only give God all the glory.

12

The Purpose of Christ's Return

The return of Christ will be for the purpose of bringing all things to their consummation. In order to accomplish this end there will be the final redemption of believers, the total destruction of all that is evil, and the last judgment of the living and the dead. Whatever happens will be an aspect of God's climactic purpose in the consummation of His kingdom.

I. FINAL REDEMPTION

In relation to believers the purpose of Christ in His return is to bring about their *final redemption*. Christians, to be sure, have received redemption through Jesus Christ, as Paul says, for example, in Ephesians 1:7: "We have redemption through his blood, the forgiveness of our trespasses." But there is also the final redemption yet to come. Here we may recall the words of Jesus in Luke 21:28 that follow a depiction of various eschatological events that climax in the coming of Christ from heaven: "Now when these things begin to take place, look up and raise your heads, because your redemption is drawing near."

The return of Christ means the "drawing near" of our redemption. Let us examine in some detail what this signifies and how it is accomplished.

A. Gathering

We may observe, at the outset, that Christ returns for the gathering of His own. This is declared particularly in these words: "He will send out his angels with a loud trumpet call, and they will gather his elect from the four winds,[1] from one end of heaven to the other" (Matt. 24:31).[2] These words immediately follow the statement that "they will see the Son of man coming on the clouds of heaven with power and great glory" (v. 30).[3] This gathering of

[1]"The four winds" signifies all points of the compass (on "the four winds," cf. Jer. 49:36; Ezek. 37:9; Dan. 7:2; 8:8; 11:4; Zech. 2:6; 6:5).

[2]Mark 13:27 reads, ". . .from the ends of the earth to the ends of heaven." Thus the "gathering" will be from all over heaven and earth.

[3]I earlier commented on the primary applicability of these words to the judicial visitation upon Jerusalem in A.D. 70: "they will see" referring to the Jewish nation. However, it is clear now that the words of Jesus that refer to the gathering of "the elect" "from the four

God's "elect" will be the climactic gathering at the final advent of Jesus Christ.

In the Old Testament God had promised Israel, "If your outcasts are in the uttermost parts of heaven, from there the LORD your God will gather you" (Deut. 30:4). Also the psalmist prayed, "Save us, O LORD our God, and gather us from among the nations" (106:47); and again: "The LORD builds up Jerusalem; he gathers the outcasts of Israel" (147:2). Isaiah also wrote, "Thus says the Lord GOD, who gathers the outcasts of Israel, I will gather yet others to him besides those already gathered" (56:8). Such passages as these, which point to the gathering of Israel, could surely have been fulfilled during Jesus' ministry on earth. But the nation of Israel would not allow it to happen. So Jesus cried, "O Jerusalem, Jerusalem, killing the prophets and stoning those who are sent to you! How often would I have gathered your children together as a hen gathers her brood under her wings, and you would not! Behold, your house is forsaken and desolate" (Matt. 23:37–38). Hence, Israel as a nation is no longer truly God's people; others will be gathered to Christ who receive Him in faith.

One of the most extraordinary scriptures concerning Christ's role in gathering is a New Testament prophecy by Caiaphas, the high priest, followed by John's comment. Caiaphas spoke to the Jewish council: "'It is expedient for you that one man should die for the people, and that the whole nation should not perish.'" Then follows John's comment: "He did not say this of his own accord, but being high priest that year he prophesied that Jesus should die for the nation, and not for the nation only, but to gather into one the children of God who are scattered abroad" (John 11:50–52). Thus the gathering of God's people will move far beyond what Caiaphas and his fellow Jews understood.

With the destruction of Jerusalem in A.D. 70, Israel's "house"—as Jesus Himself prophesied—was made "forsaken and desolate." This was shown publicly not only in Christ's coming in power to devastate the unbelieving Jewish nation, but also in His launching a new era of gathering "the children of God . . . scattered abroad." Thus, in part, the prophecy that "they will gather his elect from the four winds" was fulfilled in the aftermath of the desolation of Jerusalem and has continued to be fulfilled down through the ages.

The climax of this gathering will be at the return of Jesus Christ. This is the gathering of "the wheat" into "the barn." John the Baptist early declared about Jesus: "He will gather His wheat into the barn" (Matt. 3:12 NASB). And Jesus Himself in a parable says, "At harvest time[4] I will tell the reapers . . . Gather the wheat into my barn" (Matt. 13:30). In John's language it will be a separation of wheat from chaff; in Jesus' words it will be a separation of wheat from tares (or weeds). For John adds, "but the chaff he will burn with unquenchable fire" (Matt. 3:12), and Jesus says, "Gather the weeds first and bind them in bundles to be burned" (Matt. 13:30). Whoever they are, and wherever they are, they will be gathered into the presence of the returning Lord. "Then," as Jesus so beautifully puts it, "the righteous will shine like the sun in the kingdom of their Father" (Matt. 13:43).

It is this gathering that Paul speaks of in a statement beginning, "Concerning

winds" move beyond the first century and a Jerusalem locus to the final advent and a worldwide scene.

[4]"Harvest time" is "the close of the age" (Matt. 13:39).

the coming [*parousia*] of our Lord Jesus Christ and our being gathered to him. . ." (2 Thess. 2:1 NIV). This is the great gathering at the end of the age when the Christ of glory will send forth His angelic messengers to "gather his elect from the four winds, from the ends of the earth to the ends of heaven" (Mark 13:27). This, indeed, will be the climactic and glorious gathering of all believers at the Parousia of the Lord.

Finally, this gathering is possibly referred to in the Book of Revelation where John beholds "a white cloud, and seated on the cloud one like a son of man, with a golden crown on his head, and a sharp sickle in his hand" (14:14). With "the harvest of the earth . . . fully ripe," Jesus swings His sickle "on the earth, and the earth was reaped" (vv. 15–16). That this occurs through Him "on the cloud" and at harvest time clearly relates it to the return of Christ.[5] If this refers—as I believe it does—to the "reaping" of Christians at the end, then this final book in the Bible points to the gathering of the true people of God.

B. Resurrection

At the return of Christ there will be the resurrection of those in Christ who have died.[6] For, says Paul, "the Lord himself will descend from heaven with a cry of command, with the archangel's call, and with the sound of the trumpet of God. And the dead in Christ will rise" (1 Thess. 4:16). Similarly Paul writes elsewhere, "The trumpet will sound, and the dead will be raised imperishable" (1 Cor. 15:52).

The resurrection of believers is affirmed by Jesus particularly in the Gospel of John. On one occasion—after the feeding of the five thousand—Jesus repeats three times that He Himself will perform this resurrection: "I will raise him up at the last day" (6:40, 44, 54). The context in each instance makes clear that this concerns the believer, for example, "This is the will of the Father, that everyone who sees the Son and believes in him should have eternal life; and I will raise him up at the last day."[7] This resurrection will take place "at the last day"—the day of Christ's return.

The Gospel of John makes a further statement about resurrection. Lazarus had died, and Jesus said to Martha, "Your brother will rise again." After Martha's reply, "I know that he will rise again in the resurrection at the last day," Jesus responded, "I am the resurrection and the life; he who believes in me, though he die, yet shall he live, and whoever lives and believes in me shall never die" (11:23–26). There is a significant difference here, however: resurrection does not refer to the "last day" (as in the prior verses quoted and in Martha's words) but to the fact that through belief in Christ there is resurrection life even now—hence "though he die, yet shall he live." "Resurrection" in this case does not refer to "the last day," but to a living in the present. Since this is true, death, although still a

---

[5]There is a second reaping in this picture in Revelation (vv. 17–20), which unmistakably refers to the reaping of evil ("the vintage of the earth," which is afterward thrown into "the great wine press of the wrath of God"). Some commentators hold that the first reaping (mentioned above) refers to the same category of people as the second, since the Book of Revelation focuses largely on the Day of the Lord as a day of wrath and judgment. Also, in this passage Christ does not send forth angels to do the reaping, but does it Himself. This seems to me of little consequence, especially since Christ is the ultimate Reaper either way. I am strongly inclined to the interpretation that the first reaping is of the good.

[6]I will discuss the resurrection of unbelievers later.

[7]John 6:40. The other verses, 44 and 54, vary somewhat in background statements, but the reference is unmistakably to believers.

fact, is of no consequence—for "whoever lives and believes in me shall never die." To sum this up: in addition to—actually prior to—the resurrection of the last day, there is a spiritual resurrection for the one who believes, because death is no longer a barrier. For Christ Himself is "*the* resurrection and the life."

Before returning to "the last day," I must emphasize the important New Testament teaching that a believer also is alive in the period between his own physical death and "the last day"; for the resurrection life of Christ continues to animate him. Thus Paul could write, "For to me to live is Christ, and to die is gain," because death is "to depart and be with Christ" (Phil. 1:21, 23). It is not merely a living on after death, but living *with* Christ; it is, as Paul puts it elsewhere, to be "at home with the Lord" (2 Cor. 5:8). This calls to mind the promise of Christ to the repentant thief on the cross: "Truly, I say to you, today you will be with me in Paradise"[8] (Luke 23:43). Those who believe in Christ, who belong to Him, are "with" Him immediately upon death.

We must further recognize that the resurrection life after death is *not* that of the body. Bodily resurrection (as I will discuss more fully later) belongs to the day of Christ's return—"the last day." To be with Christ after death is to be "away from the body," but says Paul, "we would rather be away from the body and at home with the Lord" (2 Cor. 5:8).

Thus at death the believer is in heaven without his body; he is there in his spirit or soul.[9] According to Hebrews, heaven—"the heavenly Jerusalem"—is the abode of "the spirits of righteous men made perfect" (12:22–23 NASB). Hence, believers ("righteous men" through what Christ has done for them) at death are made perfect in their spirits.[10] As spirits, they are present with the Lord.[11] In Revelation 6:9–11 the souls of those who have been slain for their witness are depicted as being "under the altar,"[12] thus living on and crying out for God's judgment upon the earth. They are given "a white robe," possibly denoting blessedness, and told to "rest a little longer," thereby suggesting that rest is an important aspect of the believer's life after death. To sum up, the spirit or soul of the believer at death is in heaven.

Accordingly, there is no thought of "soul sleep" in the biblical record. After death, the believer is fully conscious and knows the presence of the Lord in heaven.[13] The Bible speaks of death as "falling asleep,"[14] and this

---

[8]For other references to "Paradise," see also 2 Corinthians 12:3 and Revelation 2:7.

[9]"Spirit" and "soul" in many cases are interchangeable terms. See the discussion of this in *Renewal Theology*, 1:197–219.

[10]This, incidentally, contravenes any idea of a "purgatory" (as in Roman Catholic teaching) after death before the believer can enter heaven. There is no need for an extended period of purgation of sin, since at death the believer's spirit is "made perfect."

[11]Recall also the similar words of Jesus and Stephen at their deaths: "Father, into thy hands I commit my spirit!" (Luke 23:46); "Lord Jesus, receive my spirit" (Acts 7:59). The spirit unmistakably continues after death.

[12]"Under the altar" signifies both that they have given their lives as a sacrifice and that they are in the heavenly realm. The altar in Revelation stands before the throne of God (cf. 8:3; 9:13; 14:18; 16:7).

[13]Seventh-day Adventists thus err in their teaching that death is "a state of temporary unconsciousness while the person awaits the resurrection" (*Seventh-day Adventists Believe. . .*, 352). They interpret "sleep" literally rather than figuratively, as the biblical writers use it in speaking of death.

[14]See e.g., Psalm 90:5 (NIV); Daniel 12:2; Matthew 27:52; John 11:11; Acts 7:60; 13:36; 1 Corinthians 15:6; 1 Thessalonians 4:13.

implies that death, like sleep, is not a permanent matter. From sleep one awakens—and so it will be for those who know the sleep of death.[15]

Hence, there is an interim period between death and the final resurrection. Those who have died in Christ are present with Him in their spirits[16] (or souls), but they have not experienced the final resurrection, which, accordingly, must be of the body. In this sense, for all the joy and rest in heaven that believers know after death, they yet look forward to "the last day" when their bodies will likewise be raised.[17]

Although countless numbers of believers are already "with Christ" (in Paradise, in heaven), having preceded those alive today, all, both living and dead, may look forward to the same great day when together they will experience the resurrection or transformation[18] of the body. For all the joy to be known after death—fellowship with Christ, rejoicing, and rest—that climactic moment when all things are complete and every "elect" person comes to faith and salvation cannot occur until spirit and body are rejoined in preparation for entrance into His glorious and eternal kingdom.

As we next consider the last day and the resurrection of the body, it is apparent that when Paul says that "the dead in Christ will rise," he is referring to their bodies. For already their spirits are with Christ in heaven. What will happen on that glorious day is a dual operation: believers will both come with him from heaven in their spirits and be raised from the dead in their bodies! Earlier we observed that Christ will return "with all his saints" (1 Thess. 3:13), and that "through Jesus, God will bring with him those who have fallen asleep" (1 Thess. 4:14). The "saints" are those who "have fallen asleep," who as spirits are in heaven with Christ, and as such they will return with Him. Shortly after that and immediately following other words that describe the return of Christ, Paul says, "And the dead in Christ will rise. . ." (v. 16). Accordingly, the last day is portrayed as the time when the spirits of the returning saints are reunited with their resurrected bodies.

Thus as rich as the time in heaven with Christ is now, there will finally be the completion, the fullness. No longer will the martyrs cry "How long?"; no longer will there be the wait for the full number of the faithful to come in; no longer will saints be separated from the bodily aspect of their nature.[19] At last

[15]This applies to both believer and nonbeliever. I will later discuss the situation of the unbeliever at death.

[16]The spirit is not simply a part of man, so that at death the believer is only partly present with God. No, the spirit is the whole person in his inwardness (the "inner man" of 2 Cor 4:16 [NASB]), hence his essential reality. So it was with Jesus, who was "put to death in the flesh but made alive in the spirit; in which [spirit] he went and preached to the spirits in prison" (1 Peter 3:18–19). Jesus—not just a part of him—preached to the spirits; but He did it as spirit.

[17]On the interim period see particularly Oscar Cullmann, *Immortality of the Soul or Resurrection of the Dead?* chapter 4: "Those Who Sleep."

[18]This will be discussed in the next section.

[19]Paul speaks in 2 Corinthians 5:4 of his desire not to be "unclothed" in the life beyond but to be "further clothed, so that what is mortal may be swallowed up by life." Hence, despite all the joy of going to be "with Christ" (as Paul expresses elsewhere), there is a yearning—which, by implication, will continue to be felt after death—for being "further clothed." Paul speaks of this as being "clothed with our dwelling from heaven" (v. 2 NASB).

the glorious realm of the new heaven and the new earth can be entered. For it is in this eternal realm of the spiritual and the corporeal that spiritual bodies will live forever!

Let me now make several summary statements about the resurrection of the body:

1. Christian faith holds vigorously to the resurrection of the body and not simply to spiritual immortality. In the beginning God made man soul and body (or spirit-soul and body); accordingly God's purpose includes both soul and body in the consummation. The body is neither "the prison-house of the soul," nor is it simply a shell containing "the real thing" (i.e., the spirit), nor is it somehow—being matter—less pure than the soul.[20] God made the body, He also took on the human body in Jesus Christ, and it is in the body that the Holy Spirit tabernacles in believers—the body therefore has a highly significant place in God's future for His creation.

The body is not just a part of man, but it is his totality under the aspect of his relationship to the given order of creation. Man is not man in the earthly sphere without a body that relates him to it: he is an earthling. The heavenly sphere has no place or need for a body (hence the believer's existence as spirit there). But on this earth there is, *and* on the new earth there will be, a proper and essential place for the body. Thus do we look forward to the resurrection of the body for the life of the world to come.

2. Christian faith affirms that the body of the resurrection to come is not a natural body but a spiritual one. In the language of Paul, "it [the body] is sown [in death] a natural[21] body; it is raised a spiritual body" (1 Cor. 15:44 NASB). It will be a body adapted to the new order of things that lies beyond.

We note next that there is both continuity and discontinuity between the natural body and the spiritual body. On the one hand, it is still the same body: the person raised from the dead is not a different person; he is the same individual as before.[22] He will not assume another body.[23] On the other hand, the resurrection body will be different, for it will be spiritual, not natural (or physical). There will be qualities of the body appropriate to the new order: not those of the present earth and earthly relationships but of the world to come.

Jesus made precisely this point with the Sadducees who, not believing in a resurrection, tried to trap Him with a question concerning a complex marriage situation in which one woman was married, in sequence, to seven brothers (each in turn having died). "In the resurrection, therefore, to which of the seven will she be wife?" (Matt. 22:28). By this question the Sadducees craftily attempted to demonstrate the absurdity

That this "dwelling" (*oikētērion*) is a body is clear from the overall context. According to BAGD, *oikētērion* refers here to "the glorified body of the transfigured Christian."

[20]All of these are basically non-Christian (particularly Greek) views of the nature of the body.

[21]The Greek word is *psychikon*, also translated in KJV and NIV as "natural." The RSV has "physical"; NEB, "animal." Whatever the translation, *psychikon* refers to man's earthly existence. "Man . . . is essentially ψυχή under the present order, and his body throughout is essentially ψυχικόν as determined by that order" (EGT, 2:937).

[22]"Every man will rise again in his own likeness, his own unchangeable individuality" (E. Brunner, *Eternal Hope*, 149).

[23]As is held by those religions and philosophies that teach reincarnation (rebirth in a new body or other form of life). This false teaching abounds in the New Age movement of our time.

of a resurrection. Jesus' reply—doubtless to their complete surprise and discomfiture—was, in part: "In the resurrection they neither marry nor are given in marriage, but are like angels in heaven" (v. 30). The error of the Sadducees was to view life in the (supposed) resurrection as being under the same conditions of corporeality as it is on earth. However, while marriage is a constituent of earthly relationships and serves as the God-given vehicle for procreation, it is transcended in heaven by the new order of things.

Now returning to the matter of identity and difference in the resurrection, we observe both in Jesus' own resurrection appearances.[24] He was the same Jesus the disciples had known; indeed, He strongly emphasized that by appearing to them and saying, "See my hands and my feet, that it is I myself; handle me, and see; for a spirit has not flesh and bones as you see that I have" (Luke 24:39). Hence there was identity and continuity with the past—underscored further when Jesus took a piece of broiled fish and ate it "before them" (v. 43). He had not become a spirit (e.g., an angel); He was the same Jesus with a human body. However, there was also a great difference. Although He unmistakably was still corporeal, it was a strange, unexperienced form of corporeality. Indeed, two of the disciples walking earlier on the road to Emmaus had been accompanied by the risen Jesus for some time. But they did not recognize Him until He broke bread with them. Then He suddenly "vanished out of their sight" (Luke 24:31). Later they began to share this strange and obviously mysterious experience back in Jerusalem with the other disciples. But "as they were saying this, Jesus himself stood among them" (v. 36), appearing suddenly through closed doors. As John's Gospel puts it, "The doors being shut . . . for fear of the Jews, Jesus came and stood among them" (20:19). Although Jesus' body in the resurrection was the same as before—He had not become a spirit—He was operating in a new dimension that transcended the previous mode of earthly limitations. Thus His body had become, in the language of Paul, "a spiritual body."

From this background of Jesus' own resurrection body, we can better perceive the meaning of a "spiritual body."[25] Believers will be the same persons with the same bodies in the age to come. But these bodies will have qualities representing a different, even higher, mode of existence. Believers will not become angels. While finite like human beings, angels have no bodies at all because they are incorporeal, purely spiritual beings. Yet believers will be akin to angels in that their bodies will be spiritual, or pneumatic. Believers in their spiritual bodies will be inhabitants of a sphere *never* before existing—not simply heaven (the sphere of God and the angels), but "a new heaven and a new earth" (Rev. 21:1)! Thus being both spiritual (heavenly) and corporeal (earthly) in their nature, they will be adapted to live forever in this wondrous new creation.

This leads to a final point: although the present, natural body passes away, the future body of the resurrection remains forever. For, says Paul, "the dead will be raised imperishable. . . . For this perishable nature must put on the imperishable, and this mortal nature

---

[24]See also *Renewal Theology*, 1:382–90.

[25]That it is proper to move from Christ's resurrection to the believer's is due to the fact that Christ is "the first fruits": "Christ has been raised from the dead, the first fruits of those who have fallen asleep" (1 Cor. 15:20). Again, Christ is "the first-born from the dead" (Col. 1:18; cf. Rev. 1:5).

must put on immortality" (1 Cor. 15:52–53). Since the body will not perish, all sickness, all debilitation, all decay will be no more. Moreover, since mortality will be a thing of the past, all that surrounds the misery of death will be gone. By God's grace we shall thus live forever!

3. Christian faith also attests to the fact that the resurrection of the body occurs wholly by the action of the Triune God. It will not take place by virtue of some resident vitality or force in the human person, nor is it the result even of the new life in Christ. Regarding the latter, surely the redemption of the soul (or spirit) has occurred—we are freed thereby from spiritual death—but the body has not yet been changed. Paul says that we "groan inwardly as we wait for adoption as sons, the redemption of our bodies"[26] (Rom. 8:23). Redemption is an act of God, whether of the soul now or the body on the day of Christ's return.

First, the resurrection of the body will be brought about by God the Father. In the words of Jesus, "the Father raises the dead" (John 5:21). He does this by His power, and because He is the living God. Jesus, in His response to the Sadducees (discussed previously), not only demonstrated the total inadequacy of their understanding of the resurrection, but he also spoke to their condition of disbelief: "You know neither the scriptures nor the power of God. . . . He is not God of the dead, but of the living" (Matt. 22:29, 32). The power of God, almighty and unlimited, will raise the dead: He alone can do it. Since by His very nature He is the living God,[27] He is God of the living. To know these things about God is to know that there will be a resurrection from the dead. Truly God is behind it all: "the Father raises the dead."

Second, Jesus Himself is the means or instrument of this resurrection. As we have earlier observed, Jesus three times says, "I will raise him [the believer in Christ] up at the last day." Then, also as noted, Paul speaks of the Lord (Jesus) descending from heaven with a "cry of command" that—along with the archangel's call and the trumpet sounding forth—immediately precedes the resurrection of "the dead in Christ" (1 Thess. 4:16). Jesus is unmistakably the "command-er"—as His cry of command rings forth.

Jesus displayed this commanding voice at the grave of Lazarus. Once the gravestone had been removed, Jesus "cried out with a loud voice, 'Lazarus, come forth'" (John 11:43 NASB). The next line reads, "He who had died came forth." Doubtless this is, in part, a preview[28] of what will happen at the last day. Indeed, we may recall an earlier statement of Jesus: "The hour is coming when all who are in the tombs will hear his voice and come forth, those who have done good, to the resurrection of life, and those who have done evil, to the resurrection of judg-

---

[26]"Bodies" is simply "body" in the Greek text (so the KJV, NASB, and NEB translate).

[27]The "I am." Jesus prefaces His statement that God is the God of the living by the words of Scripture, "I am the God of Abraham, and the God of Isaac, and the God of Jacob" (Matt. 22:32)—hence the God of the living.

[28]I say "in part, a preview" because Lazarus's being raised from the dead was actually more of a resuscitation than a resurrection. Lazarus's body was revived from death; he did not receive a spiritual body; and he died again. Nonetheless, the authority of Jesus over death and the grave that was demonstrated in the raising of Lazarus is a presage of the resurrection yet to occur.

ment'' (John 5:28–29).[29] It is the commanding voice of Jesus that will be instrumental in bringing about the resurrection.

We can sense in all of this the authority of Jesus as the Word of God. Even as in the beginning God created all things through the Word (John 1; cf. Gen. 1), and through the word of Christ new resurrection life occurs now—''Truly, truly, I say to you, the hour is coming, and now is, when the dead will hear the voice of the Son of God, and those who hear will live''[30] (John 5:25)—so at the end it is that same Word (word) that will bring about the resurrection of the dead. For Christ truly is ''the Alpha and the Omega, the first and the last, the beginning and the end'' (Rev. 22:13).

Third, the resurrection will occur through the enlivening power of the Holy Spirit. One of the great empirical facts of the Christian life is that believers are indwelt by the Spirit of God. When we become children of God by faith, the Holy Spirit becomes the inner reality of our being—''Because you are sons, God has sent the Spirit of his Son into our hearts, crying 'Abba! Father!' '' (Gal. 4:6). According to Paul, it is this same indwelling Spirit who will some day move upon our mortal remains and bring immortality to them: ''If the Spirit of him who raised Jesus from the dead dwells in you, he who raised Christ Jesus from the dead will give life to your mortal bodies also through his Spirit which dwells in you'' (Rom. 8:11).

When the Lord comes back and the summons goes forth for the dead in Christ to be raised, the great event will occur by the inward efficacy of the Holy Spirit. Thus—it is important to add—the natural body will become a spiritual body, which signifies in a profound sense a body totally enlivened[31] by the Holy Spirit. On the last day when the voice of the Lord goes forth calling people from the grave, the Holy Spirit will simultaneously move upon our mortal remains,[32] invigorating and empowering them to rise to meet the Lord as He comes. Such is the marvel and wonder of the resurrection.

C. Translation

When Christ returns, believers who are living will be translated, that is,

[29]Although I have been discussing the resurrection of believers in this section, it is apparent from this text that there will also be a resurrection of unbelievers (or ''those who have done evil''). This other resurrection will be discussed later.

[30]These words affirming a present spiritual resurrection—''now''—were spoken just before Jesus' words about the resurrection to come: ''All who are in the tombs . . . will come forth.''

[31]Hence, the spiritual body of the resurrection not only operates in a new dimension (beyond our spiritual world)—which I have discussed—but it is also a body that has been quickened by the Holy Spirit. The same Holy Spirit who gave life to dead spirits in regeneration will some day give life to dead bodies in the resurrection!

[32]We may add, wherever these remains are and whatever they have become. It is, of course, a fact that the mortal remains of countless believers have been scattered far and wide. But surely the Holy Spirit is not dependent on enlivening intact bodies (every part in place, as in a grave), or even putting scattered parts together. For the resurrection body will *not* be a rejuvenated material body (hence dependent on intact remains—as in the resuscitation of Lazarus) but a spiritual body in continuity with the past (the same essential self, i.e., spirit or soul). Yet there will be a radical difference: the body will be ''pneumatic''—not constituted by past material. So Paul can say, ''What you sow [in death] is not the body which is to be, but a bare kernel. . . . God gives it a body as he has chosen'' (1 Cor. 15:37–38).

conveyed into the life of the age to come, without ever dying physically.[33] In the words of Paul: "We who are alive, who are left, shall be caught up together with them [the dead in Christ] in the clouds to meet the Lord in the air; and so we shall always be with the Lord" (1 Thess. 4:17). "We shall not all sleep," says Paul elsewhere (1 Cor. 15:51). Thus believers living when Christ returns will never experience death: they will be translated.

This translation involves, first, a basic change. After Paul said, "We shall not all sleep," he writes, "but we shall all be changed, in a moment, in the twinkling of an eye, at the last trumpet. For the trumpet will sound, and the dead will be raised imperishable, and we shall be changed" (15:51–52). The change for the living will be the same as for the dead: as earlier noted, "this perishable nature must put on the imperishable, and this mortal nature must put on immortality" (v. 53). In another place Paul writes, "We await a Savior, the Lord Jesus Christ, who will change our lowly body to be like his glorious body, by the power which enables him even to subject all things to himself" (Phil. 3:20–21). The change thus beautifully depicted is the transformation of our bodies into the likeness of "his glorious body."

Hence, living believers at their translation will go through a transformation[34] from their natural bodies to spiritual bodies. When Christ returns, even as the dead in Christ will rise in their spiritual bodies, so living believers will be translated in their spiritual bodies. This latter point needs special emphasis, namely, that living believers will not simply be translated in their natural bodies. They will be translated in transformed bodies.[35]

Second, this transformation will occur instantaneously. The transformation that, for example, takes place in sanctification covers a believer's lifetime and is not complete until glory. But the transformation into the new spiritual body will take place "in a moment." The word for "moment" in the Greek points to a time so brief as to be indivisible into a shorter period![36] It will occur "in the twinkling of an eye"—another way of stating an extremely brief moment. Hence, there will be utterly no time of transition from the natural body of the living believer to the spiritual body: it will happen suddenly and instantaneously.

Third, it is important to add that in the relation between resurrection and translation, the former has priority. Before the words "we who are alive," Paul says, "The dead in Christ will rise

[33]The Old Testament depicts two persons, Enoch and Elijah, as likewise not passing through death; both were translated. "Enoch walked with God; and he was not, for God took him" (Gen. 5:24; cf. Heb. 11:5), and "Elijah went up by a whirlwind into heaven" (2 Kings 2:11). Enoch's translation is not described; it is said simply (and movingly) that "God took him." Elijah's going "into heaven" is vividly described in 2 Kings 2:12, though only Elisha saw it happen.

[34]In the quotations above from 1 Corinthians 15 and Philippians 3 containing the word "change," the former is from *allassō*, meaning to "change" or "alter," and is used in the New Testament also in relation to the heavens: "as a garment they will also be changed" (Heb. 1:12 NASB); the latter is from *metaschēmatizō*, meaning literally to "change the form of" (*schēma* = "form"). Hence, "trans-formation" of a radical, though external, kind is the meaning (on *schēma* cf. 1 Cor. 7:31—"the form of this world [*to schēma tou kosmou toutou*] is passing away").

[35]In contrast to some popular pictures of believers being translated in natural bodies.

[36]"In a moment" is *en atomō*. This means "indivisible because of smallness" (BAGD). Compare our English word *atom* (from the Greek word). No separation, or cutting apart (*atomos* = *a* [not] + *temnein* [to cut]) is possible.

first'' (1 Thess. 4:16). A little earlier, Paul had stated, ''We declare to you by the word of the Lord, that we who are alive, who are left until the coming of the Lord, shall not[37] precede those who have fallen asleep'' (v. 15). Indeed, Paul is here primarily referring to those who, ''through Jesus, God will bring with him'' (v. 14), that is, the spirits of believers who at last are to have their bodies raised from the dead.[38] His point is that the translation of living believers will not precede this resurrection.

There is undoubtedly a sense of divine proportion in this arrangement. Those who have long looked forward to the day of resurrection will be afforded priority over those who are living at that time. This is also a salutary arrangement because it is far too easy to assume that being alive when Christ returns is a preferential position.[39] But this is not at all the case: those who are living will not precede believers of the past.

This matter of priority, however, seems to be more of a logical than a chronological matter. For we are next told by Paul that the translation of living believers will occur in connection with the resurrection of dead believers. After saying that ''the dead in Christ will rise first'' he declares, ''Then we who are alive, who are left, shall be caught up together with them in the clouds to meet the Lord in the air'' (1 Thess. 4:17). The word *''then''* implies sequence no doubt, but *''together with them''* denotes simultaneity. Since all this happens at the sudden Parousia of the Lord, and since both the resurrected dead in Christ and transformed living believers go to meet Him, it seems apparent that it is essentially one great event with various aspects.

Fourth, the translation of living believers will be that of a ''catching up'': ''We . . . shall be caught up.''[40] This is often referred to as ''the rapture.''[41] This ''catching up'' points to the sovereign action of God and the passivity of the believer. It is totally of God in Christ—His doing, His timing, and we contribute absolutely nothing. The pic-

[37]Or ''by no means'' (*ou mē*); ''certainly not'' (NIV).

[38]This means that those ''fallen asleep'' (who live on as spirits in heaven) are the same as the ''dead in Christ'' (whose bodies have died).

[39]It is clear that the Thessalonians actually grieved over the situation of fellow believers who had passed on, so much so as to question whether they would share in the event of Christ's return. Paul responded, ''We would not have you ignorant, brethren, concerning those who are asleep, that you may not grieve as others do who have no hope'' (1 Thess. 4:13). This is the background statement for Paul's succeeding words about Christ's resurrection and how God would bring through Jesus those who have ''fallen asleep.'' Not only was that true, but also those alive would ''by no means'' precede those who had passed on.

[40]The Greek word is *harpagēsometha*. The verb *harpazō* can signify violent seizure—a stealing, carrying off, a snatching. However, here and in a number of other places the word conveys the note of simply being ''caught up'' nonviolently. Cf. Acts 8:39: ''The Spirit of the Lord caught up [*hērpasen*] Philip''; 2 Cor. 12:2: ''a man . . . caught up [*harpagenta*] to the third heaven''; Rev. 12:5: ''her child [Jesus] was caught up [*hērpasthē*] to God and to his throne.'' Hence, one should avoid the language, sometimes heard, of this being a ''great snatch'' or ''seizure'' (often thought of in the sense of snatching one out of some threat or danger). Since this ''catching up'' accompanies the resurrection of the dead in Christ, which surely has no relation to a violent seizure (or a desperate situation), all the more reason exists to avoid such misleading language.

[41]In the Latin text ''we shall be caught up'' is *rapiēmur*, hence ''rapture.'' Although ''rapture'' is the usual designation for this extraordinary event, two possible misimpressions should be guarded against: (1) forcible seizure (akin to the root idea of ''rape'') or (2) mystical or ecstatic delight. It is neither of these.

ture, then, is of living believers at the time of Christ's return. They will have been immediately changed—transformed—and in their changed bodies will be "caught up" at the Parousia of the Lord.

This "catching up" is possibly referred to by Jesus in His words to the disciples in the Upper Room: "In my Father's house are many rooms. . . . I go to prepare a place for you. And when I go and prepare a place for you, I will come again and will take you to myself, that where I am you may be also" (John 14:2–3). The "taking to"[42] is an idea similar to "catching up." Since it is Jesus who is described as the agent in both passages, the reference could also be to what occurs at His return.[43]

We also should note the use of the same word "take" in Jesus' discourse concerning His Parousia. The background relates to the time of Noah—"As were the days of Noah so will be the coming of the Son of man"; also as "Noah entered the ark" but people in general "did not know until the flood came and swept them all away, so will be the coming of the Son of man" (Matt. 24:37–39). These relevant words follow: "Then two men will be in the field; one is taken[44] and one is left. Two women will be grinding at the mill; one is taken and one is left" (vv. 40–41). The "taking" can scarcely mean to "sweep away" or "take away" in the sense of destruction,[45] but a "taking to" someone. That someone is the Lord Himself, especially in light of the warning that follows: "Watch therefore, for you do not know on what day your Lord is coming" (v. 42). The overall picture is that of Noah entering the ark—hence in a sense "taken to" the Lord—as the prototype of believers who are "taken" at the Parousia. The "all" who are "swept away" in the Flood represent those who are "left" for the judgment at the end.[46]

Fifth, returning to the passage in 1 Thessalonians, we observe that the "catching up" will be "together with them." Living believers, while second in order to the resurrected dead, will not be a later group to go to the Lord. Rather, they will be fully a part of the one great company of the dead and living who are gathered[47] to meet the coming Christ. Such a picture is truly a marvelous one: all the saints of all times, past and present, as one vast multitude totally united at the glorious Parousia!

I must emphasize again that all of this

[42]The Greek word is *paralēmpsomai*, a form of *paralambanō*.

[43]Also, the statement in 1 Thessalonians 4 concludes with the words "and so we shall always be with the Lord" (v. 17). This is not unlike the picture conveyed in the wording "that where I am you may be also."

[44]The Greek word is *paralambanetai* (like *paralēmpsomai*, a form of *paralambanō*).

[45]Some interpreters view the "swept away," or "took away" (KJV, NASB, NIV) of verse 39 as being the same as the "taken" of verses 40–41. However, the Greek words are quite different, the former being *ēren* (from *airō*) pointing to forcible removal, hence "swept away" (or "took away"), the latter, *paralambanetai*, signifying "taken" for the purpose of blessing (cf. Matt. 1:20; 17:1; 20:17). According to R. H. Gundry, " 'One will be taken' in rapture and 'one will be left' for judgment" (*The Church and the Tribulation*, 138).

[46]In the parallel passage in Luke 17:26–37, in addition to Noah and the Flood, Lot and Sodom are also mentioned, with Lot (like Noah) being saved and the Sodomites destroyed. There is one addition regarding the taking—the Lukan text also gives another example: "There will be two men in one bed; one will be taken and the other left." Again the word for "taken" is a form of *paralambanō*: *paralēmphthēsetai*.

[47]Paul writes in 2 Thessalonians about "the *parousia* of our Lord Jesus Christ, and our gathering together to Him" (2:1 NASB). (See the earlier discussion of "gathering," pp. 397–99.)

will take place in resurrected and transformed bodies. This means spiritual bodies that are no longer subject to past earthly restriction (recall Christ in His resurrection body), hence now moving together in a supramundane dimension of existence. Thus the "togetherness" will be of a kind that utterly transcends our present imagination.

Sixth, we observe that this "catching up" will be "in the clouds." This is another beautiful touch; for even as Christ comes "on the clouds," or "in clouds,"[48] believers will also be taken up "in the clouds." The clouds undoubtedly are clouds of glory,[49] and are depicted here as vehicles[50] carrying believers to their meeting with the Lord. Again, we are dealing with the realm of the presently inconceivable, for these are heavenly clouds that alone can convey these glorified saints.[51]

There is a possible allusion to the "catching up" of the saints in the clouds in Revelation 11:11–12. In this passage the "two witnesses" who prophesied on earth have been slain.[52] But after a brief period they come to life and hear a heavenly voice saying, "Come up here." Then the text continues, "And they went up into heaven in the cloud, and their enemies beheld them" (NASB). Since the two witnesses likely represent the witnessing church that is outwardly overcome by evil[53] but is victoriously taken up by the Lord, this may be a symbolic reference to the "rapture." However, in this case (not so specified in 1 Thessalonians), the going up "in the cloud" is beheld by the believers' foes.[54] Still this could be a part of the total picture; for even as "every eye" will behold Christ in His return, it is quite possible that the going to meet Him will be visible to all.[55]

Seventh and finally, the catching up will be to "meet the Lord in the air." Here truly is the high and glorious point in the resurrection of the dead and the translation of the living: as one vast multitude they go to meet the Lord! Not having seen Him, they nevertheless have believed in Him and have yearned to behold Him. Now at last in the company of all God's saints of all ages they see Him face to face. Never again will there be a separation; for the climax is—"so we shall always be with the Lord."

But now a critical question relates to

---

[48]Recall that the New Testament has various ways of depicting Christ's relationship to the cloud(s).

[49]See the earlier discussion of Christ's return in the clouds.

[50]The psalmist speaks of the clouds as the "chariot" of the Lord (104:3).

[51]For their "lowly" bodies have now been made "like his glorious body" (see Phil. 3:20–21).

[52]See the Excursus, "The Beast in Revelation 11 and the Two Witnesses," pages 351–53, especially note 160.

[53]As depicted by "the beast from the bottomless pit."

[54]Hendriksen in his book *More Than Conquerors* views this passage in Revelation as referring to the church at the return of Christ: "The church—still under the symbolism of the two witnesses–now hears a voice: 'Come up hither.' Thereupon the church ascends to heaven upon a cloud of glory. 'And their enemies *beheld* them.' No *secret* rapture!" (p. 158).

[55]Incidentally, viewing Revelation 11:11–12 as referring to the rapture of believers (or in connection with it) is often done by those who affirm a mid-tribulation rapture and thus do not see the church as being on earth during the visitations of wrath and judgment in the latter portion of the book (recall the earlier discussion). Although I myself do not hold a mid-tribulation viewpoint (rather, I believe that Christians will be on earth during the full period of tribulation), I believe there is a strong possibility that Revelation 11:11–12 does symbolically refer to the "catching up."

this meeting. It is said to be "in the air," which refers, it would seem, to the space immediately surrounding the earth.[56] Does the Scripture mean that the Lord takes us from there into heaven, so that we will "always" be with Him? But this hardly seems right because the Lord is depicted as descending "from heaven," bringing those "fallen asleep" with Him. It thus points to a continuing movement of descent.

Here it is relevant to turn back for a moment to what may be further implied in meeting the Lord. "To meet the Lord" is literally "to a meeting of the Lord."[57] The word "meet" is used elsewhere in the New Testament in only two places—Matthew 25:6 and Acts 28:15. In Matthew 25 it occurs in the parable of the bridegroom who comes at midnight when the ten virgins are asleep. A cry rings out, "Behold, the bridegroom! Come out to meet ['to a meeting'][58] him" (v. 6). Then the virgins who have oil for their lamps are prepared and go "in with him to the marriage feast" (v. 10). In Acts 28, some Christian brethren who have invited Paul's company to stay with them in Rome "came as far as the Forum of Appius and Three Taverns to meet ['to a meeting'][59] us" (v. 15). Then they accompanied Paul into the city. In both Matthew and Acts the implication of the word "meeting" is that of joining the person (the bridegroom or Paul) on his continuing journey (to a marriage feast, to Rome).[60] From this brief word study alone, it seems clear that the meeting with the Lord in the air is to join Him in His continuing descent.[61] Further, the fact that Paul had earlier said, "The Lord himself will descend from heaven," hardly suggests that the descent will be only to "the air" (where the saints meet Him). Rather, they will accompany Him in the final stage of His journey to the earth itself.

Thus, from this perspective, to "always be with the Lord" after meeting Him does not mean an immediate return to heaven, certainly not a long continuance in the air, but includes being with Him in His mission to earth and forever thereafter.

Now all that has been said in the preceding pages about *translation* and *resurrection* relates to the matter of *gathering*. I began with "gathering" as

---

[56]"Air," however, may signify more than the surrounding atmosphere. Satan is spoken of by Paul elsewhere as "the ruler of the kingdom of the air" (Eph. 2:2 NIV), hence air is not merely a physical but also a spiritual realm. Morris makes this interesting comment: "The fact that the Lord chooses to meet His saints there, on the demons' home ground so to speak, shows something of His complete mastery over them" (*The First and Second Epistles to the Thessalonians*, NICNT, 146). "Air," like "clouds," may refer to more than a natural sphere. BAGD, under *aēr*, speaks of "the kingdom of the air."

[57]The Greek word for "meeting" is *apantēsin*.

[58]Again, *apantēsin*.

[59]Again, *apantēsin*.

[60]Concerning the word *apantēsis*, Bruce says, "When a dignitary paid an official visit (*parousia*) to a city in Hellenistic times, the action of the leading citizens in going out to meet him and escort him back on the final stage of his journey was called the *apantēsis*" (*1 & 2 Thessalonians*, WBC, 102). According to the *Interpreter's Bible*, "the word *meet* is found in the papyri in the sense of an official welcome" (11:307).

[61]Bruce, despite his statement (in the preceding note) adds that "there is nothing in the word *apantēsis* which demands this interpretation . . . whether the Lord (with his people) continues his journey to earth or returns to heaven" (*1 & 2 Thessalonians*, 103). However, because of both the Hellenistic background and the Scriptures (Matt. 25:6 and Acts 28:15), I believe that *apantēsis* strongly suggests meeting Christ in His continuing descent. (See also Ladd, *The Blessed Hope*, 91–92, and Gundry, *The Church and the Tribulation*, 103–5).

the basic term because in many ways it is the most inclusive, for it signifies the bringing together of believers from every place in heaven and on earth. According to Mark 13:27 (as we observed earlier), Christ "will send out the angels, and gather his elect from the four winds, from the ends of the earth to the ends of heaven." This is all-inclusive—saints in heaven and saints on earth—all will be gathered to Him. It includes the dual aspects of resurrection and translation, but the important thing is that the saints are gathered to Him.

One further word: in reviewing the discussion about resurrection and translation, I am aware that little was said about the role of angels. Yet at the Parousia it is the angels, according to Christ, who will gather the elect, whether in heaven or on earth, whether "dead in Christ" or alive. Why are they not mentioned in such key Scripture teachings on resurrection and translation as 1 Corinthians 15 and 1 Thessalonians 4? The answer, I believe, is that indirectly they are mentioned by the references to the sounding of the trumpet (1 Cor. 15:52: "for the trumpet will sound"; 1 Thess. 4:16: "with the sound of the trumpet of God"). For according to Matthew 24:31 (the parallel to Mark 13:27), Christ "will send out his angels with a loud trumpet call, and they will gather his elect." Thus by implication, the angels are involved in both resurrection and translation (without the manner being described) in gathering the saints to the returning Christ.

Further, as I have suggested, all these terms—*gathering, resurrection, translation*—may appropriately be subsumed under the heading of *redemption*. For in the same context, according to Luke 21:28, "when these things [things leading to and climaxing in the return of Christ] begin to take place, look up and raise your heads, because your redemption is drawing near." Now we need to stress, in a larger sense, that this redemption has to do with deliverance from the world before its final destruction.[62]

Accordingly, the word *salvation* is also appropriate here. Salvation has already been accomplished in the life of the believer, but there is also a salvation yet to come.

Let us call to mind a few relevant Scripture passages. According to Hebrews 9:28, "Christ, having been offered once to bear the sins of many, will appear a second time, not to deal with sin but to save [literally, 'unto salvation'][63] those who are eagerly waiting for him." Patently salvation here has nothing to do with Christ's first coming, but His second (or final), and therefore must signify a salvation in relation to what happens at His appearing. Peter declares concerning those "born anew" that by God's power they are "guarded through faith for a salvation ready to be revealed in the last time" (1 Peter 1:3, 5). What that salvation is Peter does not say, but it unmistakably belongs to the "last time" of final revelation—i.e., the revelation (*apokalypsis*) of Christ. Paul is the most specific, for he writes to the Thessalonians, shortly after his words about the resurrection and translation of believers: "God has not destined [or 'appointed'][64] us for wrath, but to obtain salvation through our Lord Jesus Christ" (1 Thess. 5:9). The salvation to which we are destined, or appointed, is

[62]Redemption of the soul and body applies to most of what has been written in the previous pages. Redemption may also take on a broader meaning in relation to the situation of the world at the return of Christ.

[63]The Greek phrase is *eis sōtērian*.

[64]The Greek word is *etheto*, translated "appointed" in KJV and NASB.

deliverance from the coming wrath of God.[65] The implication is that even as we have been saved eternally from God's wrath, we will also be saved from its final expression at the end of the age.

D. Glorification

The climax of what happens to believers at Christ's return is their *glorification*. For in going to meet the Lord they will be glorified in His presence.

Paul speaks of our being "glorified[66] with him" (Rom. 8:17). Christ has already been glorified in His resurrection, ascension, and exaltation at the right hand of the Father and will manifest that glory at His Parousia. But when He returns, we will participate in that glory. Indeed, says Paul elsewhere, one aspect of Christ's return is that He "comes on that day to be glorified[67] in his saints, and to be marveled at in all who have believed" (2 Thess. 1:10). Thus the saints at His return in glory will share and reflect that glory. Here we may recall Paul's beautiful words in Colossians 3:4: "When Christ, who is our life, is manifested, then you too will be manifested with him in glory" (NEB). Therefore when Christ—in whom our lives are hid—appears, His glory will be manifested through us. Christ will glorify[68] His own at His coming.

Hence all our previous discussion about resurrection and translation may be summed up as glorification. In regard to resurrection, this is the glorification of the body that has died. Paul, comparing death of the body to the sowing of a seed in the ground, writes, "It is sown in dishonor, it is raised in glory" (1 Cor. 15:43). Thus the bodies of dead believers will be raised to glorification. In regard to translation, this is the glorification of the living body. Let us recall again the striking statement "Our commonwealth is in heaven, and from it we await a Savior, the Lord Jesus Christ, who will change our lowly body to be like his glorious body" (Phil. 3:20–21). Thus the bodies of living believers will be transformed into the likeness of Christ's glorious body.

The total picture, however, goes far beyond the body, because glorification is of the total person—body, soul, and spirit. This means another thing of signal importance, namely, that glorification will include the final *sanctification* of believers living at the return of Christ. I have spoken at some length about the transformation of the body from a natural to a spiritual one at the Parousia. Now I must add that this also includes the perfecting of holiness. The saints in heaven have already been perfected (recall that presently in heaven there are "the spirits of righteous men made perfect" [Heb. 12:23 NIV]). But living saints on earth, whatever their state of sanctification, are not completely free of sin[69] at death. This obviously is a critical impediment, since the believer with sin remaining in him will not be able to face the coming holy Lord. Thus Paul, shortly after his teaching on the rapture in 1 Thessalonians 4, writes, "May God himself, the God of

[65]See also 1 Thessalonians 1:9–10, where Paul speaks of turning away from idolatry "to serve a living and true God, and to wait for his Son from heaven . . . Jesus who delivers us from the wrath to come."

[66]The Greek word is *syndoxasthōmen*—to be "glorified together . . . to be exalted to the same glory to which Christ has been raised" (Thayer).

[67]The Greek word is *endoxasthēnai*—"to be adorned with glory." Christ will come "that this glory may be seen in the saints, i.e. in the glory, blessedness, conferred on them" (Thayer).

[68]The word "glorify," *doxazō*, may be defined as "to clothe in splendor" (BAGD). Such a definition vividly expresses the marvel of what is to occur.

[69]See the discussion of sanctification in *Renewal Theology*, 2:83–117.

peace, sanctify you through and through. May your whole spirit, soul and body be kept blameless at the coming of our Lord Jesus Christ'' (5:23 NIV). There Paul adds—and this is our assurance—"The one who calls you is faithful and he will do it'' (v. 24 NIV).[70] Even as "the spirits of righteous men'' now in heaven have been made perfect by God's action and not by their own doing, so it will be at the Parousia of Christ: God will do it again! On this point I conclude with the praise benediction of Jude 24: "Now to him who is able to keep you from falling and to present you without blemish before the presence of his glory with rejoicing [literally, 'exultation'],[71] to the only God, our Savior through Jesus Christ our Lord, be glory, majesty, dominion, and authority, before all time and now and for ever. Amen.'' He is able not only to keep us, but also to present us blameless—and it will be with great rejoicing, even exultation. What a glorious God!

Such is something of the picture of the glorification of believers that will occur at the return of Jesus Christ: the resurrection of bodies, the translation of those bodies into the likeness of Christ's glorious body, and the sanctification of spirit for those who go to meet Him. But, most of all, our glorification will be the reflection of His glory. Even as in this life—in Paul's words—"we all . . . beholding the glory of the Lord, are being changed into his likeness from one degree of glory to another'' (2 Cor. 3:18), so when we behold Him face to face at His coming, our glory will be complete: we will reflect Him totally.

I close with the words of Peter who speaks of being "a partaker in the glory that is to be revealed'' (1 Peter 5:1). This is God's gracious intention for all who belong to His Son Jesus Christ.

II. TOTAL DESTRUCTION

A second aspect of Christ's return is His coming for *total destruction*. Christ comes to destroy all that is evil and to usher in the kingdom of righteousness.

In the Scriptures, "the day of the Lord'' is frequently depicted as a day of destruction. The prophet Joel laments, "Alas for the day! For the day of the LORD is near, and as destruction from the Almighty it comes'' (Joel 1:15). Similarly Isaiah cries, "Wail, for the day of the LORD is near; as destruction from the Almighty it will come!" (Isa. 13:6). Jesus speaks of "that day'' as one similar to the time of Noah when "the flood came and swept them all away'' (Matt. 24:36, 39). Paul calls "the day of the Lord'' a day of "sudden destruction'' (1 Thess. 5:2–3). According to Peter, it will be "the day of judgment and destruction of ungodly men'' (2 Peter 3:7).

In the Book of Revelation when the seventh angel blows his trumpet and voices in heaven proclaim the victory of Christ's kingdom, then others cry forth, "The nations raged, but thy wrath

[70]Shortly before the rapture passage, Paul writes, "May the Lord make you increase and abound in love to one another and to all men . . . so that he may establish your hearts unblamable in holiness before our God and Father, at the coming of our Lord Jesus with all his saints'' (1 Thess. 3:12–13). Without the further reading of 1 Thessalonians 5:24 (above), the matter of complete (unblamable) holiness might seem dependent on the measure of our love ("to one another and to all men"); however, the climax in chapter 5 vigorously affirms that God Himself "will do it.'' How eternally grateful we may be, for whatever depends on us will surely prove inadequate.

[71]The Greek word is *agalliasei*, "exultation'' (BAGD). The KJV translates it as "exceeding joy''; NIV and NASB, "great joy''; NEB, "jubilation.''

came, and the time for . . .[72] destroying the destroyers of earth" (11:18). We have previously observed that the blowing of the (last) trumpet is directly associated with Christ's return—the gathering, resurrection, and translation of believers. In Revelation it is also unmistakably related to destruction: "destroying the destroyers of earth." Christ will return to bring about total and final destruction.

The most frequent biblical depiction of this destruction is its occurring by *fire*. Isaiah prophesies, "For behold, the LORD will come in fire . . . to render his anger in fury, and his rebuke with flames of fire. For by fire will the LORD execute judgment. . ." (Isa. 66:15–16). In the words of Zephaniah, "the great day of the LORD" is "a day of wrath . . . a day of ruin and devastation . . . a day of trumpet blast," and, the prophet adds, "In the fire of his jealous wrath, all the earth shall be consumed; for a full, yea, sudden end he will make of all the inhabitants of the earth" (1:14–18). Malachi, in the closing chapter of the Old Testament, declares, "For behold, the day comes, burning like an oven, when all the arrogant and all evildoers will be stubble; the day that comes shall burn them up . . . it will leave them neither root nor branch" (Mal. 4:1).[73] It is apparent that the fire of God's wrath, while executed upon all the earth, will actually be upon "the arrogant" and "evildoers," and of them nothing will be left ("neither root nor branch").[74]

As the New Testament opens, John the Baptist proclaims about Jesus that He will "thoroughly clear His threshing floor; and He will gather His wheat into the barn, but He will burn up the chaff with unquenchable fire" (Matt. 3:12 NASB). Hence whatever is not gathered[75] will be burned up, consumed by an unquenchable fire—thus utterly destroyed. John the Baptist does not say when this conflagration will occur; but Jesus does. In His parable about the good seed (or wheat) and the tares (or weeds), Jesus concludes, "Let both grow together until the harvest; and at harvest time I will tell the reapers, 'Gather the weeds first and bind them in bundles to be burned. . .' " (Matt. 13:30). "Harvest time" (as earlier discussed) will occur at the return of Christ, for Jesus later adds, "Just as the weeds are gathered and burned with fire, so it will be at the close of the age. The Son of man will send his angels, and they will gather out of his kingdom all causes of sin[76] and all evildoers, and throw them into the furnace of fire; there men will weep and gnash their teeth" (Matt. 13:40–42). Similarly Jesus, using the imagery of sorting good and bad fish from a full net, declares, "So it will be at the close of the age. The angels will come out and separate the evil [men] from the righteous, and throw them into the furnace of fire;

---

[72]I have omitted a portion that reads, "[The time came] for the dead to be judged, for rewarding thy servants, the prophets and saints. . . ." I will deal with these matters later.

[73]The Old Testament closes with these words: "Behold, I will send you Elijah the prophet before the great and terrible day of the LORD comes. And he will turn the hearts of fathers to their children and the hearts of children to their fathers, lest I come and smite the land with a curse [or 'ban of utter destruction' RSV mg.]" (Mal. 4:5–6). Elijah did come, in the figure of John the Baptist, and through his message that prepared the way for Christ's gracious first advent, "utter destruction" was restrained until the final "great and terrible day."

[74]For other Old Testament Scriptures that depict the fire of God's judgment, see, e.g., Psalms 50:3; 97:3; Isaiah 24:6; Jeremiah 5:14; Nahum 1:6.

[75]Recall the earlier discussion of the "gathering" of believers (pp. 397–99).

[76]The Greek word is *skandala*—"stumbling blocks" (NASB), "everything that causes sin" (NIV), "whatever makes men stumble" (NEB), "all things that offend" (KJV).

there men will weep and gnash their teeth'' (Matt. 13:49–50). In these various instances, whether the figure is chaff, tares, or bad fish, evildoers will be consumed by fire.

Turning to the Epistles, we find that when Paul speaks of ''eternal destruction'' in 2 Thessalonians, he also describes Christ as coming in ''flaming fire.'' ''Affliction''[77] will come upon ''those who afflict'' believers ''when the Lord Jesus is revealed from heaven with his mighty angels in flaming fire, inflicting vengeance upon those who do not know God and upon those who do not obey the gospel of our Lord Jesus. They shall suffer the punishment[78] of eternal destruction and exclusion from[79] the presence of the Lord and from the glory of his might'' (1:6–9).

Regarding Paul's account, several comments may be made. First, fire is related directly to Christ Himself: He will be revealed from heaven with His angels in ''flaming fire'' bringing vengeance. The ''flaming fire'' will come ''from heaven'' upon the evil world. In the Gospel accounts of the chaff, tares, and bad fish, the fire relates more to the result of Christ's action—a gathering out and then burning. However, there is basically no difference: fire and destruction are elements in both the Gospel and Epistle narratives. Fire—burning—is the result (Gospel), but it is also present in the very action of Christ Himself who comes in flaming fire (Epistle). This, then, is similar to the Old Testament accounts, which frequently show the Lord as coming in fire and thereby bringing destruction.

Second, vengeance is inflicted on those who bring ''affliction'' to believers: God will repay them with ''affliction'' at the end. Then Paul adds the broader categories of ''those who do not know God'' and ''those who do not obey the gospel.'' At first thought, such persons might seem less reprehensible than the ''afflicters,'' and those who—in the language of Matthew—are ''causes of sin'' and ''evildoers'' (supra). Yet, in speaking of these broad categories, Paul includes all sinful humanity. For, as he says elsewhere, the root problem of the human race is its turning from the knowledge of God, indeed suppressing that knowledge, with the result that all manner of evil follows.[80] Hence, Paul pinpoints the origin of sin and evildoing as mankind's lack of knowledge of God, which lack is the given situation of all people. Thus blatant ''afflicters'' and ''evildoers'' are not by any means the only practitioners of evil. Rather *all persons* are guilty, for all humanity has turned aside from the true knowledge of God. ''Those who do not obey the gospel'' doubtless are those who spurn the gospel, even when it is offered to them:[81] they will suffer vengeance. Thus, afflicters of Christians, despisers of the gospel, and those who do not know God—all will be subjected to the vengeance of God in Jesus Christ.

Third, it is apparent, in Paul's account, that the ''flaming fire'' is the

[77]Or ''tribulation'' (KJV; see the prior discussion of the Great Tribulation, pp. 360–70).

[78]Or ''penalty'' (NASB). The Greek word is *dikēn*.

[79]The Greek reads simply *apo*—''from.'' The word ''exclusion'' may, however, be implied.

[80]Recall the picture that Paul sets forth in Romans 1:18–32, beginning, ''for the wrath of God is revealed from heaven against all ungodliness and wickedness of men who by their wickedness suppress the truth'' (v. 18). Thus, not honoring God, their thinking becomes vain, their hearts darkened, their desires and actions immoral; they become ''filled with all manner of wickedness'' (v. 29) and cause others to sin.

[81]Paul may have had primarily the Jews in mind; however, his language could surely include Gentiles as well.

very presence of Christ Himself that inflicts vengeance. Thus vengeance is not only His action—which to be sure it is—but also an outflow from the fire of His presence. It is the awesomeness and brilliance of His sudden coming upon people that in itself strikes terror. Here we may again call to mind the cries of the "earth-dwellers" in Revelation to the mountains and rocks: "Fall on us and hide us from the face of him who is seated on the throne and from the wrath of the Lamb" (6:16). The "face" of God in the coming of Christ, far more terrifying than falling mountains and rocks, brings vengeance and retribution. Also recall this statement in Hebrews: "Our God is a consuming fire" (12:29). Hence the very revelation of Christ from heaven in "flaming fire" consumes all things evil.

This becomes even more apparent in Paul's vivid depiction in 2 Thessalonians of the visitation of Christ upon "the man of sin"[82] (lawlessness, wickedness, iniquity, evil) who is the very incarnation of evil.[83] The text reads, "The Lord Jesus will slay him with the breath of his mouth and destroy him by his appearing and his *parousia*" (2:8)—or "by the brightness[84] of his *parousia*" (KJV). The climactic fact, set forth in the latter part of the statement, is that Christ's very presence (his Parousia—"arriving presence") is of such overwhelming brightness that "the man of sin" is totally destroyed by it.[85]

This, then, is the analogue to Paul's earlier picture of Christ's being revealed "in flaming fire." The "flaming fire" and the "brightness" (splendor, brilliance) of His person are one and the same. For both humanity at large and "the man of sin," it is destruction by fire: the fire of God's arriving presence. In the intensity of that fire nothing, absolutely nothing impure, evil, or unholy can remain. Our God is, and will be, a consuming fire.

All this destruction is powerfully captured in the final scene of the Book of Revelation. Satan has worked his deception upon the nations, gathered them in number "like the sand of the sea" for battle. But when they surrounded "the beloved city," suddenly "fire came down from heaven[86] and consumed[87] them" (20:7–9). There is utterly nothing left of them.[88]

The "flaming fire" of "the Lord Jesus from heaven" upon sinful mankind at large (2 Thess. 1), "inflicting vengeance" and causing "eternal destruction"; the fiery "brightness" of the Parousia bringing to total destruction "the man of sin" (2 Thess. 2); and now, climactically, "fire from heaven" (Rev. 20) upon the nations: it is all of a piece—a terrifying one. It is the fire of God's total destruction.

Now I must add a sobering word. For, according to the New Testament, the fire will also come upon those who affirm the gospel, but thereafter sin

[82]Chapter 2, verse 3. See the earlier discussion of this "man" on pages 334–39.

[83]The same word, *anomia*, is used in the Greek for this man—*ho anomos*, "the evil one" (2 Thess. 2:8) as for "evildoers" (see e.g., Matt. 13:41)—*tous poiountas tēn anomian* ("the ones doing evil").

[84]The Greek word is *epiphaneia*—"splendor" (NIV), "radiance" (NEB). See the earlier discussion.

[85]The word translated "destroy" above is *katargēsei*, which means also "bring to an end" (NASB).

[86]According to the RSV margin, "other ancient authorities read *from God, out of heaven*, or *out of heaven from God*." The KJV has "from God out of heaven."

[87]The Greek word is *katephagen*. "Devoured" (KJV, NASB, NIV) means totally consumed.

[88]The "destroyers of earth" (Rev. 11:18) have been destroyed. Also, this fulfills the words of the prophet Zephaniah: "In the fire of his jealous wrath . . . a full, yea, sudden end he will make of all the inhabitants of the earth" (1:18).

willfully and deliberately. The same Book of Hebrews that speaks of "our God" as a "consuming fire" also has strong words to believers to "encourage one another . . . all the more as you see the Day approaching"; and then the following: "If we deliberately keep on sinning after we have received the knowledge of the truth, no sacrifice for sins is left, but only a fearful expectation of judgment and of raging fire[89] that will consume the enemies of God" (10:25–27 NIV). If we who have received knowledge of the truth—through the blessing of the gospel—deliberately and willfully continue to sin, the prospect is fearful indeed. The raging fire of God's fury that will consume His enemies will likewise fall upon us.[90]

This leads us to a further—and truly more joyful—reflection. When Christ returns, there will indeed be consuming fire upon mankind at large, the "man of sin," the nations of the earth, and upon deliberate sinners. None of these will escape the fearful brightness of His Parousia: all will be destroyed. But—and here we return to things said earlier—the fury of fire will not be upon those who are found in Him. For as He comes, faithful believers will go to meet Him, to be transformed bodily and spiritually into His likeness, then to glorify Him and He in turn to be glorified in them. The antithesis is total: the same day when Christ is "revealed from heaven . . . in flaming fire, inflicting vengeance," He also "comes on that day to be glorified in his saints and to be marveled at in all who have believed" (2 Thess. 1:7–8, 10). His awesome presence, which is a consuming fire against every force and trace of evil, will be for the saints of God a reality of inexpressible glory and marvel.

Let us proceed to note two terms in the Scripture often associated with the fiery destruction that Christ will perform: *word* and *breath*. A background text for both of these may be found in the messianic prophecy of Isaiah 11:4: "He shall smite the earth with the rod of his mouth, and with the breath of his lips he shall slay the wicked." We will consider these in order.

First, the reference to "the rod of his mouth": this rod is unmistakably His tongue or, more specifically, the word proceeding from it. By such a "rod" the Messiah will "smite the earth." Another comparable, and quite graphic, picture is later given by Isaiah: "See, the Name of the LORD comes from afar, with burning anger and dense clouds of smoke; his lips are full of wrath, and his tongue is a consuming fire. . . . He shakes the nations in the sieve of destruction" (Isa. 30:27–28 NIV). His lips, His tongue, hence His word, goes forth in destructive power against the nations. Thus it is a rod to smite the earth. Psalm 2, in which the Lord speaks to His "anointed," similarly declares, "Ask of me, and I will make the nations your heritage, and the ends of the earth your possession. You shall break them with a rod of iron, and dash them in pieces like a potter's vessel" (vv. 8–9). Thus in a composite picture "the rod of iron" becomes "the rod of his mouth"—His mighty word.

Now all of this comes to a focus in the Book of Revelation where Christ is shown returning from heaven with His armies to make war against the kings of earth and their armies (19:11–21). His name is "the Word of God" (v. 13), and "from his mouth issues a sharp

[89]Or "a fury of fire" (RSV). *Puros zēlos* is the Greek phrase.

[90]One thinks also of these very sobering words of Jesus: "If a man does not abide in me, he is cast forth as a branch and withers; and the branches are gathered, thrown into the fire and burned" (John 15:6).

sword with which to smite the nations, and he will rule[91] them with a rod of iron" (v. 15). The kings of earth and their armies—indeed "all men, both free and slave" (v. 18)—are gathered for battle against Christ and His heavenly armies, but utterly to no avail. For the beast and the false prophet, who had assembled the enemy host, are "thrown alive into the lake of fire" (v. 20). Then comes the conclusion: "And the rest [i.e., 'all men'] were slain by the sword of him who sits upon the horse, the sword that issues from his mouth" (v. 21). The destruction is total: no one is left alive, except Christ and those with Him.

It is clear from this picture that not only are Christ and the Word of God one, but also that the sword of victory is none other than the word. The sword is not swung by the hand, as in an earthly battle, but issues from the mouth.[92] Again, although "the armies of heaven" come with Christ, there is no mention of their participating in the battle: the total victory belongs to the Word. Further, there really is no battle or struggle; all, however, are immediately slain. Christ does not move around the vast multitudes of the nations gathered against Him, slaying one and then another. The destruction is a single, undivided, instantaneous event.

Actually, therefore, it is the very presence of Christ, the Word of God, that destroys everything contrary to truth. His word, proceeding from His mouth, is Christ Himself in His movement against evil. Even as all good things were created through the Word (Genesis 1 and John 1), so all evil things will be destroyed by the same Word. Even as the "Word became flesh" for mankind's salvation from sin, so the Word will finally return for the obliteration of all that is sinful and evil.

Second, we may now reflect on the other image—"the breath of his lips." And here also is an approximation to the word. For, "with the breath of his lips he shall slay the wicked." Two other passages may be mentioned: Job 4:9, referring to those who "plow iniquity and sow trouble" (v. 8), reads, "By the breath of God they perish, and by the blast of his anger they are consumed"; and Isaiah 30:33, where "the breath of the Lord" is described as being "like a stream of brimstone." Thus the breath of God the Lord can cause all to perish:[93] it is itself a consuming fire.

---

[91]"Rule"—from the Greek word *poimainō*—here does not mean to govern but to break or destroy. "To rule with a rod of iron means to destroy rather than to govern in a stern fashion. The shepherd not only leads his flock to pasture but defends the sheep from marauding beasts. His rod is a weapon of retaliation. The Messiah's rod is a rod of iron; that is, it is strong and unyielding in its mission of judgment" (Mounce, *The Book of Revelation*, 347). The truth of this is further confirmed by the words in Psalm 2 (as quoted): "You shall break them with a rod of iron," and by the words in Isaiah 11 (as quoted): "He shall smite the earth with the rod of his mouth." Accordingly, the statement in Revelation about the "sharp sword" and "rod of iron" do not refer (as many have interpreted) to separate events—i.e., a smiting of the nations with the sword and an iron rule after that, but to the one event of their being smitten and broken (or destroyed). Incidentally, this is clarified in the next statement: "He will tread the wine press of the fury of the wrath of God the Almighty" (19:15). This is surely not a description of a later event (after a supposed iron rule, or even during it), but one further portrayal of what will happen when Christ returns. He will *smite* the nations, *break* (destroy) them, and *tread* upon them in His fury.

[92]This picture calls to mind this messianic statement in Isaiah: "He made my mouth like a sharp sword" (49:2).

[93]Another verse from Isaiah: "The grass withers, the flower fades, when the breath of the LORD blows upon it; surely the people is grass" (40:7).

This brings us again to the description of the destruction of "the man of sin." For, according to Paul, when Christ returns, He will "slay him with the breath of his mouth." I have already commented on the words that follow: "and destroy with the brightness of his coming" (2 Thess. 2:8 KJV). Actually, from this description we can see that there is no real difference between the two statements: "slaying" and "destroying"[94] can hardly be distinguished. Thus, "the man of sin" is destroyed *both* by "the breath" of Christ's mouth *and* by "the brightness" of His coming. The former—which we are now discussing—does, however, reiterate the fact that no battle or concerted effort is involved: simply the breath of the returning Lord upon him. Yet that very breath, like "a stream of brimstone" (to use the language of Isaiah), brings about the total destruction of the wicked.

In the beginning of creation it was the breath of God that brought man to life—He "breathed into his nostrils the breath of life; and man became a living being" (Gen. 2:7). It was the breath of God upon dry bones that made them live—"breath came into them, and they lived" (Ezek. 37:10). It was the breath of Christ that brought new life in the Spirit—"he breathed on them, and said . . . 'Receive the Holy Spirit' " (John 20:22). It will be that same divine breath in the end that—so powerful, so near, so holy—will consume the very incarnation of evil: "the man" of utter wickedness.

In reflecting on the *word* by which all evil persons—"all men, slave and free"—are to be slain (Rev. 19), and the breath by which the evil man—"the man of sin" is to be destroyed (2 Thess. 2), it is evident that both word and breath are inseparable from the Parousia: the awesome "arriving presence" of the Lord Jesus Christ. Whether it is the *totality* of evil (Revelation) or the *concentration* of evil (Thessalonians), nothing evil can stand before the Lord on the day of His return in glory.

Let us look again at the imagery of fire. For whether we speak of Christ Himself, His word, or His breath in relation to the coming destruction, it is all a fearsome and fiery consuming of evil. This recalls the words of the psalmist: "Our God comes . . . before him is a devouring fire" (50:3). Again, "Fire goes before him, and burns up his adversaries round about" (97:3). So Christ Himself will return "in flaming fire"; it goes "before him" and "burns up" His enemies. Also, His word and breath are a flame of fire. "The voice of the LORD flashes forth flames of fire" (Ps. 29:7), and "the breath of the LORD" is "like a stream of brimstone" (Isa. 30:33). So Christ in His return, through a voice that flashes forth flames of fire and a breath that streams forth brimstone, will utterly destroy every trace of evil on the earth.

Although this coming event transcends our capacity to understand how it will occur, there could be some parallel to it in the approach of a celestial body—a star, the sun itself, a huge flaming meteorite—that would burn away everything living on the earth. Or in this age of a potential nuclear holocaust, it might not be unlike the explosion of nuclear warheads with such vast force as to obliterate the human race and all other life.[95] Yet neither of these—the approach of a celestial body nor the explosion of

---

[94]"Slay" is from the Greek word *anaireō*, which can also be translated "destroy" (as in NEB). Like the word above translated "destroy" (*katargeō*), *anaireō* can also mean to "do away with" (BAGD). So there is no basic difference.

[95]In an article, "Living with Mega-Death," *Time* magazine predicted that if most of the

nuclear warheads—for all their vast force and resulting devastation, would approximate the return of God in Christ. For this is the Almighty Himself, not some cosmic body that He has made or some forces resident in the nucleus of the atom, who will be coming in judgment and destruction.[96]

Now a final note is in order concerning the situation of those who belong to Christ—"the saints," believers—at His coming in destruction. As earlier discussed, there will be the resurrection of "the dead in Christ" and the translation of living believers. Both groups will be "caught up together in the clouds to meet the Lord in the air" to be forever with Him.[97] Since, however, this glorious occasion is at the outset a meeting with continuing descent to the earth, the saints will accompany Him in His coming. Thus they—all the saints of all ages—will be in His company as Christ comes to earth to bring about the final and total destruction of all evil.[98]

The saints, of course, will not be consumed by the fire of His presence, for there will be no evil in them. They will come with Him as the "spirits of righteous men made perfect" and in bodies now "like his glorious body." They will be wholly like Him.

Further, since Christ returns to make war against all evil powers, the saints who will attend Him are doubtless included in "the armies of heaven."[99] Hence they will be present at the final conflict, even as the "kings of earth" seek to do battle against them and their Lord.[100] However, the saints are merely there; they are not touched by the forces of darkness any more than Christ is. And He alone wins the victory.

No scripture perhaps puts it more vividly than that concerning the "ten kings": "They will make war on the Lamb, and the Lamb will conquer them, for he is Lord of lords and King of kings, and those with him are called and chosen and faithful" (Rev. 17:14). "With him" in the last battle—but the victory is the Lord's!

---

strategic warheads that are at the disposal of Russia and the United States were discharged in a nuclear war exchange, "the earth would momentarily flicker back at the distant stars—and then perhaps go out, the very life of the planet extinguished" (March 29, 1982, p. 19).

[96]This by no means rules out the possibility that God could make use of a celestial body or a nuclear explosion as a cosmic or earthly counterpart to His own activity. In the instance of "mega-death," the human race through the accumulated result of its own evil would self-destruct. The "fiery flame" of Christ's appearing would be at one with the "fiery holocaust" of man's own devising.

[97]I will not here repeat matters discussed in some detail earlier, such as the transformation of the natural body to a spiritual body, the spirits of believers in heaven being reunited with new bodies, and the perfecting of holiness in raptured believers.

[98]In Jude we find this prophecy of the ancient Enoch: "Behold, the Lord cometh with ten thousands [or 'myriads'—an 'innumerable multitude'] of his saints, to execute judgment upon all" (vv. 14–15 KJV). This is similar to Paul's statement in 1 Thessalonians 3:13 concerning "the coming of our Lord Jesus with all his saints." Some commentators, however, hold that the reference in Jude is to angels (e.g., Michael Green, *The Second Epistle of Peter and the Epistle of Jude*, TNTC, 177) or to angels and men (e.g., John Calvin: "By saints he means the faithful as well as angels; for both will adorn the tribunal of Christ, when he shall descend to judge the world" [*Commentaries on the Catholic Epistles*, 443]). The text is debatable; however, since the critical word *hagioi* is used regularly in the NT to refer to believers, I am inclined to affirm the same for Jude 14. (See p. 388, n.14, on *hagion*.) This, of course, does not mean that only believers will accompany Christ, for, as we have earlier noted, the holy angels will also be in the company.

[99]Revelation 19:14 (see the earlier discussion of Revelation 19:11–21 on p. 389).

[100]"And I saw the beast and the kings of earth with their armies gathered to make war against him who sits upon the horse and against his army" (Rev. 19:19).

13

The Millennium

Before considering the third purpose of Christ's return, namely, to execute the Last Judgment,[1] we may here address the question of the Millennium. I do this because interposed between Christ's return in reference to destruction in Revelation 19:11–21 and the Last Judgment in Revelation 20:11–15 is the depiction of a thousand years, or millennium, in Revelation 20:1–6, with subsequent related events in verses 7–10. Satan is bound for a thousand years (vv. 1–3); there is a reign with Christ for a thousand years (vv. 4–6); and after a thousand years the final battle is fought (vv. 7–10). The question is: How are we to understand all this?

It hardly needs saying that the question of the Millennium has been one of the most perplexing biblical and theological issues in the history of Christendom. So it is in all humility that I will set out a pattern of interpretation that I hope will be of value. I will be straightforward while at the same time mentioning some of my differences with other interpretations. At the end of this chapter, an Excursus will focus more directly on alternative interpretations. I urge the reader—especially if another pattern is more familiar—to follow my words closely in the attempt to understand God's truth in this important matter.

At the outset I suggest that Revelation 20:1–10 is to be viewed as relating to the entire Christian era, namely, from the initial coming of Christ to His return. Accordingly, from this perspective these events do not chronologically follow Revelation 19:11–21,[2] which depicts the final destruction wrought by Christ. Revelation 20:1–10, I submit, concludes with this destruction, but goes back to prior events.[3]

[1]The first two purposes, as already discussed, are for final redemption and total destruction.

[2]If my thesis is correct, a chapter on the Millennium should not necessarily appear at this point in *Renewal Theology*. However, because of the locus in the Book of Revelation, I will now turn to the "thousand years."

[3]For a similar viewpoint to that expressed in the paragraph above see, e.g., R. H. Lenski: "[The] 1000 years extend from the incarnation and the enthronement of the Son (12:5) to Satan's final plunge into hell (20:10), which is the entire New Testament period" (*The*

Before detailing these events, it is important to note that Revelation 20:1–10 opens with the words "And I saw."[4] This suggests a succeeding vision, not necessarily a succeeding event or series of events.[5] Indeed, even as Revelation 12 is a vision[6] that goes back to the birth of Christ and then forward to the last days[7] and is immediately preceded by 11:18–19, which declares total destruction ("destroying the destroyers of earth"); so Revelation 20 and 19 are related. Chapter 19 likewise depicts total destruction, and chapter 20 goes back to the beginning of the Christian era and forward to the end times. This may be seen by a careful study of Revelation 20:1–10.

I. THE BINDING OF SATAN

According to Revelation 20:1–3 Satan is bound for a thousand years. The key words are "And he [an angel] seized the dragon . . . who is the Devil and Satan, and bound him for a thousand years and threw [or 'cast' KJV] him into the pit, and shut and sealed it over him, that he should deceive the nations no more, till the thousand years were ended. After that he must be loosed for a little while" (vv. 2-3).

First, we are to understand the binding of Satan as having occurred during the ministry of Jesus Christ. On one occasion when Jesus was casting out demons, He said, "How can anyone enter the strong man's house and carry off his property, unless he first binds[8] the strong man? And then he will plunder his house" (Matt. 12:29 NASB). The "strong man"[9] undoubtedly represents Satan,[10] for it is only by first binding him that his "house" may be plundered, that is, his demons cast out. The work of binding Satan actually began in the wilderness of temptation when at the beginning of Jesus' ministry He rebuffed Satan at every point; it continued through His ministry as demons were again and again cast out and Satan spurned; it climaxed in Jesus' death when He rendered Satan powerless. On the latter, we may recall the words in Hebrews how Christ partook of our

---

Interpretation of St. John's Revelation, 564–65). Philip E. Hughes similarly states that "the thousand years may be defined as the period between the two comings of Christ, or, more strictly, between the return of the ascended Son to glory, his mission to earth completed, and the loosing of Satan for a little while" (*The Book of Revelation*, 212).

[4]As in KJV, NIV, and NASB. The Greek phrase is *kai eidon*.

[5]Henry B. Swete writes: "The formula *καὶ εἶδον* ['and I saw'] does not, like *μετὰ ταῦτα εἶδον* ['after these things I saw'], determine the order of time in which the vision was seen relative to the visions which precede it. . . . It must not, therefore, be assumed that the events now to be described chronologically follow the destruction of the Beast and the False Prophet and their army" (*Commentary on Revelation*, 259). Incidentally, *μετὰ ταῦτα εἶδον* occurs in Revelation 4:1; 15:5; 18:1. In regard to order of time Leon Morris writes that "John says nothing to place this chapter in the time sequence" (*Revelation*, TNC, rev. ed., 228).

[6]Revelation 12 begins, "And a great sign was seen [*ōphthē*] in heaven" (ASV). This language is quite similar to Revelation 20:1, "And I saw." Both accounts are visions.

[7]Revelation 12 depicts the birth of "a male child, one who is to rule all the nations" (v. 5) and then the attempt by the dragon (Satan) first to devour the child and afterward to destroy "those who keep the commandments of God and bear testimony to Jesus" (v. 17). This carries us to the end times when, in Revelation 13, the two beasts appear on the scene.

[8]The Greek word is *dēsē*, from the verb *deō*. In Revelation 20 where Satan is said to be bound, the Greek word is *edēsen*, likewise from *deō*.

[9]Actually there is no "man" in the Greek, only "strong" (*ischyron*). Thus it would be better to translate the word as "the strong one" (so ASV).

[10]See also Mark 3:26–27, where Satan is specifically mentioned by Jesus. In Luke 11:21–22 Jesus declares himself "stronger" than "the strong man."

flesh so that "through death He might render powerless him who had the power of death, that is, the devil" (2:14 NASB). To "render powerless" is to "bind": it is to relativize Satan's power, indeed essentially to nullify it. According to Revelation 20, this was done for a thousand years—"bound him for a thousand years," which means that throughout the whole Christian era Satan remains bound[11] and rendered essentially powerless by Jesus Christ.[12] This, of course, does not mean that Satan has become inactive—far from it. But a critical limitation has been placed on his power.

Second, the statement that Satan was "cast" into the pit (or "abyss") likewise is to be understood as happening through the work of Christ in His first coming. Speaking of His own imminent death, Jesus declares, "Now is the judgment of this world, now shall the ruler of this world be cast out;[13] and I, when I am lifted up from the earth, will draw all men to myself" (John 12:31–32). This signifies that by Christ's death on the cross Satan will be deposed from his high position and cast out of his place as world ruler. As a result, from that same cross Christ will be able to draw "all men" to Himself. Satan will be "cast out" with utterly no power to stop the successful proclamation of the gospel. It will reach out to all people, Jew and Gentile alike.[14] In that sense Satan has been cast into the pit,[15] and totally confined in it, for, as Revelation 20 puts it, the pit has been "shut . . . and sealed . . . over him." Whatever else Satan may do, he cannot prevent Christ's drawing people to Himself: he cannot destroy the gospel witness. The restraint—the "shutting" and "sealing"—of him in this regard is total.

---

[11]In regard to the figure 1000, see note 44 below.

[12]In Revelation it is said that "an angel" (20:1) did the binding. An angel as representing Christ is also found in Revelation 14:19: "So the angel swung his sickle on the earth and gathered the vintage of the earth, and threw it into the great wine press of the wrath of God." Ladd comments, "In apocalyptic thought angels often play a role which we might attribute to the Messiah" (*A Commentary on the Revelation of John*, 199). Ladd also refers to Revelation 12:7ff., commenting, "It is Michael and his angels who win the victory over the Dragon . . . , although in the rest of the New Testament, the victory is won by Christ."

[13]The Greek word for "cast out" is *ekblēthēsetai*, from the verb *ekballō*. In Revelation 20 where Satan is said to be "cast," the word is *ebalen*, from *ballō*. It is the same root except for the *ek*—"out."

[14]Quite significantly, Jesus speaks the words about casting out Satan and drawing all men to Himself (John 12:31–32) *after* some Greeks had come to one of Jesus' disciples saying, "Sir, we wish to see Jesus" (John 12:21). Thus will all people—Gentiles included—be able to come to Christ.

[15]According to Revelation 12:9, there is another casting of Satan not to the "pit" but to the "earth": "And the great dragon was thrown [or 'cast'—*eblēthē*—from *ballō*] down, that ancient serpent, who is called the Devil and Satan, the deceiver of the whole world—he was thrown down to the earth, and his angels were thrown down with him." It is significant here again that Satan as "deceiver" is "cast," and this action is described as occurring by angelic force ("Michael and his angels" [v. 7]), similar to Revelation 20 ("an angel" [v. 1]), hence ultimately occurring by Christ's power and victory. But in Revelation 12 the picture is of "earth" and primarily relates to Satan's ongoing attack against the church. However, Satan is *totally incapable* of a victory. On the one hand, we read that believers, even should they die as martyrs, are really the victors: "They have conquered him by the blood of the Lamb and by the word of their testimony, for they loved not their lives even unto death" (v. 11). Again, Satan (the dragon) is portrayed as continuously pursuing and fighting the church but not able truly to conquer (vv. 13–17). Thus whether Satan is depicted as on earth or in the pit, he is equally unsuccessful in overcoming God's people and God's message. One may recall also the relevant and powerful words of Christ in Matthew 16:18: "I will build my church; and the gates of hell shall not prevail against it" (KJV).

Third, because of Christ's victory over Satan and His present rule, the nations will all hear the gospel! In the Great Commission, Jesus had declared, "All authority in heaven and on earth has been given to me. Go . . . and make disciples of all nations" (Matt. 28:18–19). This command can be fulfilled because of the powerlessness of Satan. Surely Satan would like to maintain his former deception over the nations—that he, not Christ, is the ultimate ruler—but he is utterly incapable. For Satan has been confined by Christ (as Revelation 20 continues) so "that he should deceive the nations no more." The nations, whatever Satan may attempt, will hear the gospel. As Jesus again said, "This gospel of the kingdom *will be preached* throughout the whole world, as a testimony to *all nations*" (Matt. 24:14). Since Christ has been given all authority in heaven and *on earth*—and Satan has been cast out—the gospel will be proclaimed, whatever Satan's attempted deceptions, to all mankind!

It is important to recognize that this casting out of Satan, his being shut and sealed in the pit, and his inability to deceive the nations relates essentially to only one thing: the proclamation of the gospel. Satan may, and does, continue to pervert mankind, and many a nation has granted him a false[16] dominance, but none of this can really hold out against the powerful gospel witness. In that all-important matter Satan is totally impotent: he is in the "pit," wholly "shut" and "sealed" away. For since Christ deposed Satan, and was Himself "lifted up" on the cross, the former deception of the nations[17] has been done away during all the time of the final sending forth of the gospel proclamation.[18]

Finally, according to Revelation 20:1–3, Satan will be released for a short time. As we have noted, his inability to deceive the nations extends "till the thousand years were ended. After that he must be loosed for a little while."[19] As the Scriptures declare in countless and various ways, our present age is to witness an unparalleled breaking forth of evil at the conclusion of the proclamation of the gospel. Revelation itself depicts this (as we have earlier observed) in the emergence of "the beast" from the "bottomless pit" after the "two witnesses"[20] have ended their testimony: "And when they have finished their testimony, the beast that ascends from the bottomless pit will make war upon them and conquer them and kill them" (11:7). This ascent from the "pit" correlates with Satan's "loosing"; moreover, it is only for a brief

[16]"False" because Christ is now over all the nations; hence nations or people that surrender to Satan do so to a defeated foe who no longer has any real dominance.

[17]From the fall of man until the coming of Christ the truth of God had got through to *no* nations (including Israel who never really could cope with it). They lived under Satan's grip and deception. With Christ's victory everything is essentially changed.

[18]For further helpful reading on the binding and casting of Satan, as depicted in Revelation 20:1–3, see W. Hendriksen, *More Than Conquerors*, 222–29; D. W. Richardson, *The Revelation of Jesus Christ*, 166–70; W. E. Cox, *Biblical Studies in Final Things*, 160–64; R. C. H. Lenski, *The Interpretation of St. John's Revelation*, 574–77; Floyd E. Hamilton, *The Basis of Millennial Faith*, 129–31; Anthony A. Hoekema, *The Bible and the Future*, 228–29. St. Augustine's *City of God*, 20. 7–9, is a valuable early presentation.

[19]The Greek phrase is *mikron chronon*; KJV, "little season"; NASB, NIV, "short time"; NEB, "short while."

[20]Mounce speaks of the two witnesses as "a symbol of the witnessing church in the last tumultuous days before the end of the age" (*The Book of Revelation*, NICNT, 223). Morris writes that "the words have relevance to every persecution the church has suffered, though especially that in the last days" (*Revelation*, TNTC, 145).

period. According to Revelation 13, where the two beasts emerge from sea and land, their destructive power is limited to a short time: forty-two months[21]—hence a "little while." Thus there is an unmistakable parallel between the loosing of Satan at the end of a thousand years and his breaking forth at the climax of our present age.

In Matthew 24 it is significant to observe that just *after* the statement that the "gospel of the kingdom will be preached throughout the whole world, as a testimony to the nations; and then the end will come," "the desolating sacrilege" (or "the abomination of desolation") stands "in the holy place" (vv. 14–15). This parallels the loosing of Satan at the end of the age of gospel proclamation to the nations during which time Satan is powerless to "deceive" the nations and thereby prevent its happening. With restraints removed, he enters upon his final time of deception. Similarly, Paul writes in 2 Thessalonians 2:3–10 that the "man of sin" is under restraint now (paralleling Satan's present "binding"). But when the restraint is removed (paralleling Satan's "loosing"), "the lawless one will be revealed," and it will be with "all wicked deception." The deceiver, no longer under restraint, will then be fully upon the scene. But this loosing and deception will occur only a little while before final destruction: "the lawless one" slain by the Lord—by "the breath of his mouth . . . his appearing and his coming."

In our discussion of Revelation 20:1–3, it is apparent that this Scripture does not refer to a future thousand years. Rather, the text covers the era of gospel proclamation extending from Christ's binding of Satan to the conclusion of the gospel witness. During this time Satan—whatever else his diabolical machinations—is incapable of preventing the gospel message from getting through to the nations. Hence, his loosing at the end of the gospel era has no reference to a period after a future reign of Christ on earth,[22] but to the climax of the present age when, restraints removed, he will be set free for a short season. Indeed, that time could be near at hand.[23]

II. REIGNING WITH CHRIST

The next verses, Revelation 20:4–6, depict a reigning with Christ for a thousand years. The last words climax the passage: "They shall be priests of God and of Christ, and they shall reign with him a thousand years" (v. 6). The passage begins, "And I saw thrones, and they sat upon them, and judgment was given to them" (v. 4 NASB). This opening statement also depicts reigning: sitting upon "thrones";[24] and the fact that "judgment was given to them" indicates that rule[25] belongs to them. Thus the passage both opens and closes with the picture of people reigning.

Let us continue with verse 4: "And I saw the souls [or 'lives'][26] of them that

---

[21]Recall the earlier discussion regarding the significance of "forty-two months."

[22]As is the case in much millennial thinking. We will return to this later.

[23]Recall the previous discussion in chapter 10 of the many signs.

[24]"Thrones" is a figure of speech signifying reigning.

[25]The Greek word *krinō*, usually translated "judge," can also have the meaning of "rule." See TDNT, 3:923, especially note 4: "In Rev. 20:4 the activity of those who sit on thrones and hold *κρίμα* is *βασιλεύειν*, 'reigning.' "

[26]The Greek word is *psychas*. "Lives" may be preferable here. Cf., e.g., Revelation 12:11: "they loved not their lives [lit. 'the life of them'—*tēn psychēn auton*] even unto death." See also Revelation 8:9 and 16:3. In the Gospel of John *psychē* is most often used for life: see John 10:11, 15, 17; 12:25; 13:37, 38; 15:13. Also see 1 John 3:16; cf. 1 Peter 3:20.

had been beheaded for the testimony of Jesus, and for the word of God, and such as worshiped not the beast, neither his image, and received not the mark upon their forehead and upon their hand; and they lived,[27] and reigned with Christ a thousand years'' (v. 4 ASV).[28] Here we are told that those who lived and reigned with Christ for the thousand years were martyrs for the sake of Christ and ''such as'' did not worship the beast nor receive his mark.[29] Neither the most brutal martyrdom (by beheading) nor the most vicious temptations and attacks from ''the beast'' cause them to waver. To use the words of Paul, they ''reign in life'' (Rom. 5:17), whatever the suffering and death they have to endure—or, to use John's words in Revelation, they ''sat'' upon ''thrones.'' Hence, ''they'' who reigned seem to include all believers of all ages who remained faithful to Christ to the very end.[30]

For further specification of those who lived and reigned with Christ, we may next observe that they are participants in ''the first resurrection.'' Looking ahead to verse 6 we read, ''Blessed and holy is he who shares in the first resurrection! Over such the second death has no power, but they shall be priests of God and of Christ, and they shall reign with him a thousand years.'' What, then, is ''the first resurrection''? Because ''the second death has no power'' over such persons, the most obvious answer is that it refers to those who no longer have to face eternal death[31] but who have come into eternal life—indeed have been ''resurrected'' from death to life. Here we may refer to the Gospel of John where Jesus says, ''For as the Father raises the dead and gives them life, so also the Son gives life to whom he will . . . he does not come into judgment, but has passed

Psychē in none of these instances refers to ''soul'' as distinct from the body—hence disembodied—but to the person, or creature, as a living being.

[27]The Greek verb is *ezēsan*. The RSV, NASB, and NIV read ''came to life''; however, *ezēsan*, from *zaō*, basically means ''lived'' (as in ASV above; also in KJV). Cf. Revelation 13:14—''the beast which was wounded by the sword and yet lived [*ezēsan*].''

[28]I use the ASV here because it not only (as also KJV) translates *ezēsan* as ''lived'' (rather than ''came to life'') but also because it properly translates *prosekynēsan* as ''worshiped not'' and *elabon* as ''received not'' (both are in the aorist tense) and accordingly places them in the same time reference as the ''lived'' and ''reigned'' (also both aorist). Thus as Marcellus Kik writes, ''The time of sitting on the thrones and reigning with Christ is the same as that of not worshiping the beast'' (*An Eschatology of Victory*, 45).

[29]While worshiping the beast and bearing its mark will culminate in the period immediately before the end (as we have seen), they are prefigured throughout Christian history. Hence, the saints who do not capitulate to the ''beast'' are saints throughout the centuries—even as martyrs belong to every period of time since Christ first came. Also the expression ''such as'' (*hoitines*), if nothing else, broadens the statement to include all true believers.

[30]I realize that some interpreters view Revelation 20:4 as referring to disembodied ''souls'' of believers—martyrs especially—and view this as their reigning in heaven. William Hendriksen, e.g., says that John in Revelation ''describes these souls [i.e., martyrs]—together with those of all departed Christians who had confessed their Lord upon earth—as reigning with Jesus in heaven'' (*More Than Conquerors*, 230). The difficulty with this interpretation is that there is no other biblical warrant for a present heavenly reign of disembodied souls or spirits. Indeed, according to Revelation 6:9–11, souls of martyrs are depicted as ''under the altar'' and, crying out for vengeance; they are told to ''rest a little longer.'' This is hardly a portrayal of reigning. Also, in Revelation 14:13 the picture is likewise of ''rest'' for the ''blessed'' dead. Incidentally, this interpretation—namely, of souls as presently reigning in heaven—obviously does not visualize a future thousand-year period of reigning on earth.

[31]''This is the second death, the lake of fire; and if any one's name was not found written in the book of life, he was thrown into the lake of fire'' (Rev. 20:14–15).

from death to life.[32] Truly, truly, I say to you, the hour is coming, and now is, when the dead will hear the voice of the Son of God, and those who hear will live" (5:21, 24–25). This is clearly a resurrection, the same that Jesus refers to later in saying, "I am the resurrection and the life . . . whoever lives and believes in me shall never die"[33] (John 11:25–26). Such words refer to a "first resurrection"—a spiritual one, from spiritual death—over which "the second death" will *never* have any power. There will also be a second resurrection, a bodily one. To this Jesus refers in saying, "Do not marvel at this; for the hour is coming when all who are in the tombs will hear his voice . . . those who have done good, to the resurrection of life, and those who have done evil, to the resurrection of judgment" (John 5:28–29).[34] Concerning the spiritual (first) resurrection Jesus declares (as noted), "The hour is coming, and now is . . ."; concerning the bodily resurrection, he does not add, "and now is," because it belongs to the future when all the dead shall be bodily raised.[35]

Let me add a further word about "the first resurrection." Since it is a spiritual resurrection, those who are not so raised remain spiritually dead. Thus the next verse reads, "The rest of the dead lived not[36] (ASV) until the thousand years were ended" (Rev. 20:5). They did not live spiritually:[37] they remained dead, as do all persons whom Christ has not yet made alive. Throughout the thousand years such persons never saw life—and this was true all the way to

[32]The Greek word is *zōēn*. This is a cognate of *zaō* and *ezēsan*. Hence, we may say that the ones who "lived" (*ezēsan*, Rev. 20:4) are those who had "passed from death to life" (*zōēn*, John 5:24).

[33]"Die" here refers to "the second death."

[34]Augustine in *The City of God* puts it vividly: "Oh, rise then in the first resurrection all you who will not perish in the second!" (20.9). Chapter 9, from which this quote is taken is entitled "What the first resurrection is, and what the second"; it is invaluable reading.

[35]There are many students of the Scriptures who view "the first resurrection" as a bodily resurrection; however, this seems unlikely in light of the overall context. Such a view usually designates "the first resurrection" as of believers who are to be raised bodily to reign with Christ in a future millennium. The Greek word *ezēsan* is understood to mean "came to life" (so RSV, NASB, NIV translate, as noted before) in a bodily sense, hence *after* physical death at a future time. The immediate difficulty of viewing this as a bodily resurrection is that "souls" are thereby perceived as "coming to life." This, of course, is impossible, since "souls" continue to live on in spite of death.

Many other students of Scripture view the "first resurrection" as the immediate translation of the believer at death to heaven, there to reign with Christ in his soul (spirit) even now (see previous note 31). A. A. Hoekema, for example, says in regard to "the first resurrection" that "we must understand these words as describing not a bodily resurrection but rather the transition from physical death to life in heaven with Christ" (*The Bible and the Future*, 236–37). The critical difficulty with this view is that it depicts the believer's presence with Christ in heaven as a resurrection. There is, to be sure, a spiritual resurrection of believers now, and a future bodily resurrection of both believers and unbelievers. But there is no Scriptural basis for viewing the believer's presence after death with the Lord as a resurrection.

[36]The RSV, NAB, NIV, and NEB read, "The rest of the dead did not come to life." However, the critical Greek word again is *ezēsan*, meaning basically "lived" (KJV reads, "lived not again"; however the "again" is superfluous and misleading). Hence, the better translation is that of ASV, "lived not," or "did not live."

[37]They are the "dead," according to John 5:21, 24–25; they have not "passed from death to life."

the end: "until the thousand years were ended."[38]

To return to the matter of reigning, it follows that the reign of the saints in Revelation 20 is another way of describing the present victorious living of Christian believers. *Made alive by Christ* and *reigning in life* are specified in the statement "They lived, and reigned with Christ a thousand years." This is hardly a future event, even though the subsequent words affirm, "They shall reign with him a thousand years." This latter statement is similar to the words in John 5:25: "The hour is coming, and now is, when the dead will hear the voice of the Son of God, and those who hear will live." The "will live" by no means refers to a future period, but to the present ("now is")—so likewise the "shall reign."

That this reigning refers to the present is further attested by earlier statements in Revelation. In the opening chapter John joyously speaks about Jesus: "To him who loves us and has freed us from our sins by his blood and made us a kingdom, priests to his God and Father, to him be glory and dominion for ever and ever. Amen" (vv. 5–6). He "*made us* a kingdom," which means that all who have been freed from sins *are* also a kingdom, hence they reign as kings[39] even now. John is not so much saying that we are *in* His kingdom (however true that is) but that we *are* a kingdom.[40] Thus, we reign in life—*now*. Later in this chapter John declares, "I, John, your brother . . . share with you in Jesus the tribulation and the kingdom and the patient endurance" (v. 9). This is not the kingdom to come, but the present situation of his—and of all saints—victoriously reigning over every earthly trial and tribulation with "patient endurance."

Note also the imagery of "priests." We have not only been "made . . . a kingdom" but we have also been made "priests" to His God and Father. Hence, as believers we are presently both a kingdom (or kings, reigning) and priests to God. Now we turn again to Revelation 20 and observe that "they" are also called priests: "They shall be priests of God and of Christ, and they shall reign with him a thousand years" (v. 6). It seems unmistakable, therefore, that both kingdom—reigning—and priesthood refer in both Revelation 1 and 20 to the present victorious lives of all who have been freed by Christ from their sins. It is not a fact of the future, but a present joyous reality.

One further scripture relating to kingdom and priests and their victorious reigning is found in Revelation 5. In heaven a "new song" is sung to "the Lamb": "Worthy art thou to take the book, and to open the seals thereof: for thou wast slain, and didst purchase unto God with thy blood men of every tribe, and tongue, and people, and nation, and madest them to be unto our God a

[38]Hence the text should not be read as meaning that they "lived"—or "came to life"—*after* the thousand years. "Until" does not here refer to a time *beyond* but to a time *within*. Hoekema puts it well: "The Greek word here translated 'until,' *achri*, means that what is said here holds true during the entire length of the thousand-year period" (*The Bible and the Future*, 236). A further illustration of this may be observed in Romans 11:25: "A hardening has come upon part of Israel, until [*achri*] the full number of the Gentiles come in." The *achri* does not point to a hardening *after* the Gentiles come in, but throughout and *up to* the time when the full number of Gentiles have come to Christ. In like manner the (spiritually) dead remain so even to the end of the thousand years. So did Augustine write, " 'Until the thousand years be finished' implies that they were without life all the time that they should have had it, attaining it by passing through faith from death to life" (*The City of God*, 20.9).

[39]The KJV reads, "made us kings." Although "kingdom" (*basileian*) is a more literal rendering of the text, the KJV well conveys the idea of reigning as "kings."

[40]The kingdom, in this context, is not so much *realm* as it is *reign*.

kingdom and priests; and they reign upon [or 'over'][41] the earth" (vv. 9–10 ASV).[42] In accordance with Revelation 1:5–6 (which, as noted, likewise speaks of salvation by the blood of Christ and being "made a kingdom, priests . . .") this reigning refers to the present. Reigning over the earth therefore signifies the victorious reign of believers "in life" over everything that formerly held them captive. It is—in the language of Paul—to be "in all these things . . . more than conquerors" (Rom. 8:37).

One further matter: The reign of the saints with Christ is said to be for a thousand years. How are we to understand the figure of a thousand? Does this refer to a literal calendar period? In light of the symbolic use of figures in the Book of Revelation,[43] it is more likely to express a complete but indeterminate period of time.[44] Indeed, the reference to a thousand years in regard to the reign of the saints sets it apart from the age to come when "they shall reign for ever and ever" (Rev. 22:5), and places it within the limits of the present age. Hence, the thousand years specifies the period of reigning with Christ between His first coming and His final advent—that is, the gospel age. Upon Christ's return the thousand years will be complete, and the eternal reign begun.

The thousand-year period—or "the Millennium"—is therefore a *present* reality. It cannot be placed in a future time prior to the eternal kingdom. The Bible is silent regarding an interim age; it speaks only of the present age and the age to come. The teaching of Jesus is unmistakable in this matter;[45] likewise Paul[46] and other New Testament writers

---

[41]The more likely translation (as in Weymouth). The Greek preposition *epi* can mean "upon" or "over"; however, in a similar later passage that also relates to reigning—"And the woman whom thou sawest is the great city, which reigneth over [*epi*] the kings of earth" (Rev. 17:18 ASV)—the only possible translation is "over" (all translations). Also cf. Luke 1:33: "He will reign over [*epi*] the house of Jacob for ever," and Luke 19:14: "We do not want this man to reign over [*epi*] us." "Upon" would make no sense. BAGD translates *epi* as "over" in Revelation 5:10.

[42]In regard to the ASV translation "they reign," we must recognize, as Mounce says, that "textual evidence is rather equally divided between 'they reign' (ASV) and 'they shall reign' (RSV)" (*The Book of Revelation*, NICNT, 149). My preference is the ASV rendering because it points more clearly to the reign as being in the present. However, the translation "shall reign" (most commentaries) does not necessarily call for a future reign any more than the "will live" of John 5 (as discussed earlier) points to a future situation.

[43]See, e.g., the previous discussion of 3½ years (also 42 months or 1,260 days). Recall also the 144,000 "sealed" in the time of "the great tribulation."

[44]Ladd speaks of "the symbolic use of numbers in the Revelation." Then he adds, "A thousand equals the third power of ten—an ideal time. While we need not take it literally, the 'thousand years' does appear to represent a real period of time, however long or short it may be" (*A Commentary on the Revelation of John*, 262). This is what Hoekema speaks of as "indeterminate length." In a statement similar to Ladd's, he writes, "Since the number ten signifies completeness, and since a thousand is ten to the third power, we may think of the expression 'a thousand years' as standing for a complete period, a very long period of indeterminate length" (*The Bible and the Future*, 227).

[45]It is interesting that Ladd, who himself affirms a future millennium, writes, "I can find no trace of the idea of either an interim earthly kingdom or of a millennium in the Gospels" (Robert G. Clouse, ed., *The Meaning of the Millennium: Four Views*, 38).

[46]In regard to Paul, Ladd states, "There is, however, one passage in Paul which may refer to an interim kingdom if not a millennium. In 1 Corinthians 15:23–26 Paul pictures the triumph of Christ's kingdom as being accomplished in several stages" (ibid.). The stages are Christ's resurrection, the resurrection of believers, and after that the end. In addition, says

give scant reason[47] for any other view. The Old Testament has many beautiful pictures of a coming messianic age, but it is very difficult—if not impossible—to discover a future earthly millennial period.[48] Indeed, the whole idea of such a future earthly reign seems out of harmony with the rest of Scripture. But when the thousand years is viewed as a present reality, all Scripture fits together in its basic portrayal of two ages (*not* three): the present age and the age yet to come.

When it is also realized that Revelation 20:4–6 does not call for a future millennium, but emphasizes, along with Revelation 1 and 5, the present reign of the saints with Christ, then everything falls in place. Moreover, such an understanding highlights the victory that saints down through the years, even to the present day, have in Christ. They have sat on thrones—hence reigned—and by their lives the world has been judged. Many have been martyred, but this has not prevented them from living and reigning with Christ. Indeed, whatever the persecution, the saints have not bowed before the beast or received its mark on forehead or hand. They have reigned victoriously. Death has meant nothing, for they have already known the "first resurrection" from spiritual death; hence over them the "second death"—eternal death—has utterly no power. What a blessing to share in the resurrection to life, and thereby to become "priests" of God and of Christ and to reign with Him throughout the thousand years!

III. FINAL DESTRUCTION

Finally, we come to Revelation 20:7–10, which climaxes with the destruction

Ladd, there is "an unidentified interval . . . between Christ's resurrection and his parousia; and a second undefined interval . . . between the parousia and the *telos*, when Christ completes the subjugation of his enemies" (p. 39). Ladd's delineation of an interval between the Parousia and the *telos* (end), however, is hardly Paul's teaching. The subjugation of Christ's enemies climaxes at the Parousia, not afterward. When Paul says, "For he must reign until he has put all enemies under his feet," this is better understood not as referring to a future reign but to a present reign that will end *at* His Parousia with the final subjection. (On this see particularly G. Vos, *The Pauline Eschatology*, 244–46.) It is significant that Mounce, also a premillennialist, writes that "the attempt to attribute to Paul a belief in the millennium on the basis of 1 Cor. 15:20–28 is unconvincing" (*The Book of Revelation*, NICNT, 357, n.15).

[47]Revelation 20 is the only conceivable possibility! However, as Richardson says, "If verses four, five, and six had been omitted from this chapter no one would ever have dreamed of a literal thousand years of Christ's reign on earth; of his setting up a temporal kingdom and inaugurating a millennial reign as an earthly monarch" (*The Revelation of Jesus Christ*, 157). Both the very limited evidence and the even more serious disharmony with other Scriptures makes highly questionable a future millennium.

[48]According to the Old Testament, there is surely an age to come, but it is essentially undifferentiated. Indeed, there is depicted only *one* coming of the Messiah, and His reign will by no means be for a thousand years but forever. Some of the earthly images of the coming messianic reign are frequently viewed as referring to a limited reign, but this is quite unwarranted. The reason for such a view, incidentally, is not hard to find. Since the Messiah did not literally reign on earth in His first coming, nor will this happen in the eternal kingdom, there must be then a limited period in between when Old Testament pictures and promises will be fulfilled. Thus the Millennium as such a period seems to be the solution. However, the Old Testament in no instance has such a limited prospect in view. It is far better to understand the Old Testament messianic blessings as fulfilled both in the church age and in the age to come. This includes both spiritual and material blessings. In regard to the latter (which the Old Testament often mentions), it is better to view many of them as fulfilled eternally in "the new heaven" and "the new earth" of Revelation 21–22 rather than in a limited thousand-year period.

of the nations and Satan himself. The passage begins, "And when the thousand years are ended, Satan will be loosed from his prison and will come out to deceive the nations . . . ." Revelation 20:1–3 ended with the preview that after the thousand years Satan "must be loosed for a little while." This loosing—to review for a moment—will bring about the final flood time of evil in the world, vast and widespread persecution of the saints, and the seeming destruction of the gospel witness. Further, the nations formerly open to the proclamation of the gospel (recall verse 3) will be totally closed, and Satan will have them wholly at his disposal. The Deceiver, frustrated during the thousand years by the reign of Christ and the saints, will at last be freed for a short time to work his deception among the nations.

And what is that deception? The answer is unmistakable: "The nations" will attempt to make a final assault upon Christ and His saints that will bring about their seeming overthrow and destruction. We have already seen depicted Satan's ascending from the pit and the resultant killing of the "two witnesses"; we have also seen the emergence of the first and second "beasts" with their conquering and slaying of the saints. All of this is part and parcel of the final picture of the nations—the peoples of earth (the "earth dwellers") who are captivated by the delusions of Satan[49] and are now seeking total obliteration of Christ and those who belong to Him. The tragic thing is that Satan will be able to deceive them into thinking it can be done.

Let us now read Revelation 20:7–9: "And when the thousand years are ended, Satan will be loosed from his prison and will come out to deceive the nations which are at the four corners of the earth, that is, Gog and Magog, to gather them for battle [literally, 'the battle'];[50] their number is like the sand of the sea. And they marched up over the broad earth and surrounded the camp of the saints and the beloved city; but fire came down from heaven and consumed them." The nations across the earth will be totally deceived into thinking they can destroy the "camp of the saints and the beloved city," that is, the community of true believers.[51] However, when they gather for the battle and success seems all but assured, suddenly fire from heaven will come down and totally consume them. Actually there is no final attack, no assault upon "the beloved city": the invading forces of the nations will simply be wiped out.

This immediately calls to mind two earlier pictures in Revelation of "the battle." In Revelation 16 Satan ("the dragon") and his henchmen, the first and second beasts, through demonic and deceptive spirits, "go abroad to the

[49]"The man of sin" being the epitome of Satan's final deluding power.

[50]The Greek phrase is *ton polemon*.

[51]"The camp of the saints" and "the beloved city" are the same. Together the terms signify the totality of those who belong to Christ: His people, His true church. "Camp of the saints" calls to mind a pilgrim people, for this is always what the saints of God are in this world; "the beloved city" signifies the community of God's people on earth. In the Book of Revelation there is also "the great city which has dominion over the kingdoms of the earth" (17:18). This is "Babylon the great" (17:5)—the concentration of all evil. In total contrast is "the beloved city," which has God for its Maker (recall Heb. 11:10: "the city which has foundations, whose builder and maker is God"); it is the beloved church of Christ (recall Eph. 5:25: "Christ loved the church and gave himself up for her"). Incidentally, to view either of these cities—"the great city" or "the beloved city"—as particular geographical localities, such as Babylon and Jerusalem, would be an egregious mistake.

kings of the whole world, to assemble them for battle [literally 'the battle'][52] on the great day of God the Almighty" (vv. 13–14). In Revelation 19 "the beast and the kings of the earth with their armies gathered to make war [literally, 'the battle'][53] against him who sits upon the horse [Christ] and against his army" (v. 19). But there is actually no battle; all "were slain by the sword of him who sits upon the horse, the sword that issues from his mouth" (v. 21). These statements—along with Revelation 20—are all unmistakably pictures of the same final assault—"the battle," indeed the one climactic battle on "the great day of God the Almighty." The final destruction is portrayed in Revelation 19 through the sword issuing from Christ's mouth, that is, the word of God, and in Revelation 20 through fire coming down from heaven.[54] The result is complete: all men and nations will be totally destroyed.[55]

A review of Revelation 20:7–10 indicates that this passage again represents the final activity of Satan at the end of the present age. This clearly is not an occurrence after a future thousand-year rule of Christ and the saints on earth. It is *the* battle—not a second battle—but the same battle as in Revelation 16 and 19.[56] According to the Book of Revelation (as everywhere else in the New Testament), Christ will not return to establish a "rod of iron" rule[57] for a thousand years at the close of which there will be a worldwide assault of the enemy. Rather, He will come back to redeem His own, destroy all forces of evil, sit upon His throne of judgment, and usher in the eternal kingdom in a new heaven and a new earth.

Incidentally, the whole concept of a future reign of Christ on earth with His saints for a thousand years and Satan's leading a multitude of nations finally in attack is laden with difficulties. First, it depicts Christ as an earthly, even political ruler—the role Christ never claimed for Himself while on earth two thousand years ago. It is hard to imagine that what He turned down, namely earthly kingship[58] and worldly dominion, He would some day exercise for a thousand years. Second, it is difficult to conceive how, after a thousand years of Christ's rule on earth, there would be multitudes of nations and people—"their number . . . like the sand of the sea"—who would make an assault on "the beloved city." This scarcely seems like a glorious reign when rebellious people, presumably long held in

[52]As in Revelation 20:8, *ton polemon*.

[53]As in Revelation 20:8 and 16:14, *ton polemon*.

[54]Recall the earlier discussion of the final destruction under the imagery of "word" and "fire." It might further be suggested that both "word" and "fire" are caught up in the figure of "the breath of his [Christ's] mouth" (2 Thess. 2:8), by which "the man of sin" will be destroyed.

[55]The two beasts and the dragon (Satan) are not slain (such is impossible because they are evil forces, not human beings), but are "thrown" into "the lake of fire" (Rev. 19:20; 20:10). This occurs in separate scenes of destruction by the sword and fire. Incidentally, this does not point to separate occasions (as some millennialists urge) but to different aspects of God's final riddance of all evil forces that have long wrought havoc with mankind. The forces under Satan's command (Satan's henchmen) go first to their eternal destruction, followed by Satan himself.

[56]Indeed, the same as also in Revelation 17 (not discussed above) where it is said that the beast along with ten kings "will make war [or 'do battle'—Gr. *polemēsousin*] on the Lamb, and the Lamb will conquer them, for he is Lord of lords and King of kings, and those with him are called and chosen and faithful" (vv. 12–14).

[57]Recall the previous discussion of the "rod of iron."

[58]Recall that of Jesus said, "My kingship is not of this world" (John 18:36).

check, become vast in number and powerful enough to make a worldwide attack. Third, and even more problematic, where do all these nations come from? According to Revelation 19, when Christ returns with the armies of heaven, everyone is killed.[59] It will not do to say that some escaped, perhaps distant nations, whom Satan at the end of a thousand years will assemble from the "four corners of the earth." *None* escaped—and the "four corners" does not mean far distant people, but the *totality* of people.[60] Fourth, assuming that somehow there are nations on the earth that Satan will assemble at the end of a future millennium, how could there possibly be a battle? Christ and His returned saints would be in their glorious bodies—all existing in a spiritual/corporeal dimension. How could they be attacked by earthly weapons or foes? Indeed, the whole picture of a future millennium in which glorified and sanctified saints in resurrected and spiritual bodies, fitted for a new order of existence, share the same earth with unholy sinners in natural bodies is so bizarre as to strain credibility to the limit. Fifth, and finally, it seems increasingly apparent that this idea of a Satanic attack at the end of the Millennium (viewed as earthly and future)—with all its attending difficulties (a few just mentioned)—is a case of what may be called double vision. It makes a double image of the Satanic period of evil that precedes the return of Christ and recurs after Christ has returned: thus the picture is out of focus.[61] The New Testament, contrariwise, throughout depicts only *one* climactic period of evil and that *before* Christ returns. There can be no other such period; for in His return Christ destroys all evil upon the earth.

Let me add a brief further word about the Old Testament and millennialism.[62] One of the reasons often cited for a future earthly reign of Christ and the saints is that many Old Testament prophecies speak of an earthly fulfillment. Hence, whatever may be the difficulties in finding other New Testament teaching of an earthly millennium, Revelation 20 would seem to provide an opportune context. Several objections, however, may be raised.

First, Old Testament passages concerning a future messianic reign nowhere depict this as a limited period of time. The kingdom to come, the reign of God, His blessing on the world will be without end. Second, these same Old

[59]"The rest were slain" (Rev. 19:21). "The rest" does not mean that some remained alive. The background is that after the two beasts (or beast and false prophet) were thrown into the lake of fire, "the rest" were killed. "The rest"—as a still earlier verse says—includes "kings . . . captains . . . mighty men . . . horses and their riders . . . all men, both free and slave, both small and great" (v. 18). "All men" is all-inclusive.

[60]Mounce writes that "this figure of speech is . . . intended to . . . emphasize universality" (*The Book of Revelation*, NICNT, 362).

[61]Jay Adams speaks of premillennialism as "a system suffering from exegetical diplopia, i.e., double vision, wherein things get out of focus" (*The Time Is At Hand*, 7). "Exegetical diplopia" (an apt expression!) may also be illustrated in the case of those who view "Gog" and "Magog" as involved in *two* battles—before the Millennium and also at the end of it. According to Ezekiel 38 and 39, "Gog of the land of Magog" comes against Israel and is destroyed by fire—an event understood by many millennialists as happening *prior to* the Millennium. In Revelation 20, "Gog and Magog" (symbolic names of the nations that gather for battle) come against "the beloved city" and are also destroyed by fire—and this event is seen to *follow* the Millennium. Hence, it would seem that there must be *two* battles of Gog (and Magog), with destruction by fire each time! This indeed is "exegetical diplopia," a case of double vision, brought on by confusion about the Millennium.

[62]Recall note 48 in this connection.

Testament pictures, which exhibit an earthly fulfillment of blessing, do not fit well in Revelation 20. Verses 4–6 do not actually depict a time in which God's promised blessings abound on earth.[63] One may claim such for the thousand years, but without exegetical justification. Third, there is no suggestion in the Old Testament that the future messianic reign will occur *after* an overthrow of God's enemies and *before* a final destruction. The "day of the Lord" is the one eschatological day that leads to the eternal messianic reign. Fourth, Old Testament passages about such matters as the coming of the kingdom, the reigning of the Messiah, and the rebuilding of the temple[64] point either to the present gospel era or the eternal age to come, but not to an intervening thousand years. Fifth, those promises that point to a future age and call for an earthly fulfillment must be seen as fulfilled some day not on the *present* earth but on the *new* earth (in the new heaven and new earth). The Old Testament depiction of the future is far too earthly to be satisfied by the common view of a heaven to come devoid of all earthly substance. This is a strong reason why earthly millennial themes so often (even stubbornly) persist: heaven alone scarcely seems to satisfy. But when it is understood that God's ultimate purpose includes earth, the Old Testament concern is then totally fulfilled.

In summary, there definitely is a millennium, but it is not a future period of a thousand years during which Christ and the saints reign on earth. The millennium rather is a *historical* and *present* reality spanning the whole of the gospel era. Throughout this time, because of Christ's death on the cross and His triumph over Satan, the saints have been reigning with Him. It does not matter whether they, like their Lord, suffer trial and persecution even unto death. They are still "more than conquerors": they reign with the crucified and risen Christ!

But, finally, let us change the "they" to "we," for by His grace we have been raised from death to life, so that whatever has to be endured, we reign victoriously now and forever with Him. I close with the beautiful words of praise in Revelation 1:5–6 to our Lord:

> "To him who loves us and has freed us from our sins by his blood and made us a kingdom, priests to his God and Father, to him be glory and dominion for ever and ever. Amen."

EXCURSUS: POSTMILLENNIALISM AND PREMILLENNIALISM

Views about the Millennium have often gone in the direction of either postmillennialism or premillennialism.[65]

---

[63]Even if one were to hold that this is a future earthly period, nothing is said in Revelation 20 that would equate it with Old Testament descriptions of abundant blessings.

[64]E.g., the prophecy in Amos 9:11–12: "In that day I will raise up the tabernacle of David that is fallen . . . I will build it as in the days of old: that they may possess the remnant of Edom, and of all the heathen. . ." (KJV), which might suggest a future messianic period in which the temple is rebuilt, is interpreted in the New Testament as referring to the initial outreach of the gospel to the Gentiles, hence the present era (see Acts 15:12–18). Another example is the vision in Ezekiel about a future temple (chaps. 40–48), which is sometimes viewed as a physical temple to serve during the Millennium. However, since many of its features appear in the temple symbolism of Revelation 21–22, the fulfillment should rather be seen in "the new heaven and new earth." See the final chapter of this volume: "The Consummation."

[65]Some of this will already have been noted in my previous exposition, particularly in

A common theme in both is that the Millennium is a *future period on earth.* The figure of one thousand may be viewed symbolically or literally, but in either case the Millennium is seen as a coming time of blessing on earth. Thus the Millennium is understood to be an interim period on earth prior to the final consummation in the eternal age. Postmillennialism, however, holds that Christ will return *following* (post-) the Millennium; premillennialism affirms rather that Christ will return *before* (pre-) the Millennium.

I will quote some representatives of both camps, observe in more detail what the various positions are, and make a few additional comments.

Postmillennialism

A. H. Strong wrote at the end of the nineteenth century: "Through the preaching of the gospel in all the world, the kingdom of Christ is steadily to enlarge its boundaries, until Jews and Gentiles alike become possessed of its blessings, and a millennial period is introduced in which Christianity generally prevails throughout the earth."[66] Christ will return after this.

World Wars I and II signaled for many the demise of this way of thinking (at least, as some have said, postmillennialism became an "endangered species"!). However, Loraine Boettner wrote in 1957 that "the world eventually is to be Christianized, and the return of Christ is to occur at the close of a long period of righteousness and peace called the 'Millennium.' "[67] In his words the double motif of postmillennialism is clearly stated: a future period of blessing ("righteousness and peace") and then Christ will return. The Millennium, further, will be "a golden age of spiritual prosperity"; "the changed character of individuals will be reflected in an uplifted social, economic, political and cultural life of mankind"; "evil will be reduced to negligible proportions"; and "Christ will return to a truly Christianized world."[68] J. J. Davis has recently gone on record affirming postmillennialism as "a period of unprecedented revival in the church prior to the coming of Christ . . . the world as a whole is expected to experience conditions of significant peace and economic improvement."[69]

Postmillennialism has also enjoyed resurgence in the recent Reconstructionist[70] movement. R. J. Rushdoony, acknowledged leader of the movement, writes, "People out of every tongue, tribe, and nation shall be converted, and the word of God shall prevail and rule in every part of the earth."[71] Similarly David Chilton says: "It is a solid, confident, Bible-based assurance that before the Second Coming of Christ,

reference to premillennialism. However, I intend here to be more direct in presenting these alternative positions.

[66]*Systematic Theology*, 1008. The postmillennial viewpoint was common on the American scene in the nineteenth and early twentieth centuries. During that time other eminent conservative theologians such as C. H. Hodge, R. L. Dabney, and B. B. Warfield were also postmillennialists. Various Puritan scholars in the seventeenth century (e.g., John Owen) had earlier propounded a postmillennial viewpoint. The classical formulation was made by the Anglican scholar Daniel Whitby in 1703. In the eighteenth century Jonathan Edwards in America became an outstanding proponent of postmillennialism.

[67]*The Millennium*, 14.

[68]Ibid.

[69]*Christ's Victorious Kingdom: Postmillennialism Reconsidered*, 129.

[70]Leading figures are R. J. Rushdoony, Greg Bahnsen, Gary North, and David Chilton. Other terms, frequently used in addition to Reconstructionism, are Dominion Theology and Theonomy Movement.

[71]*God's Plan for Victory: The Meaning of Postmillennialism*, 12.

the gospel will be victorious throughout the entire world" (italics his).[72] Again, "through generations of obedience, the godly will increasingly become competent and powerful, while the ungodly will grow weak and impotent."[73] This idea of "the godly" becoming "competent and powerful" is a distinctive feature of Reconstructionist postmillennialism, which, unlike traditional postmillennialism, envisions Christians taking dominion over the structures of society.[74] Not only is the gospel to be universally victorious but also all of society will be governed by biblical law.

My basic observation is that postmillennialism represents an exaggerated optimism. Postmillennialism is a heady, even enthusiastic doctrine, and surely much better than a negative one of doom and gloom on every hand. Also, it undoubtedly captures an important aspect of New Testament teaching, namely, that the kingdom of God will grow continually. According to Matthew 13:31–33, "the kingdom of heaven is like a grain of mustard seed . . . it is the smallest of all seeds, but when it has grown it is the greatest of shrubs. . . . The kingdom of heaven is like leaven which a woman took and hid in three measures of meal, till it was all leavened."[75] Surely optimism is appropriate here, but there is also the needed balance of other statements in Matthew 13:24–50. Wheat and tares will "both grow together until the harvest" (v. 30), and the good fish and bad fish will only be sorted out "at the close of the age" (v. 49). The tares will not be increasingly rooted out, i.e., the world "eventually Christianized" (Boettner) or the Word of God prevailing and ruling "in every part of the earth" (Rushdoony) before Christ returns. To be sure, we are to proclaim the gospel to the ends of the earth and expect many to come to salvation, and surely by the power of the Holy Spirit much more can be done. But there is utterly no biblical assurance that the world will be converted to Christ before He returns (even less that there will be a reconstructed social order). We are to preach the gospel throughout the whole world as a *witness* to all the nations (Matt. 24:14), giving all peoples a chance to hear and believe. Then the end will come. Total evangelization to which we are indeed called does not equal total conversion!

Once postmillennialism leaves Matthew 13:31–33, the going gets rougher and rougher. For example, in Matthew 24 prior to the statement about the gospel being preached throughout the whole world, Jesus speaks of wickedness being multiplied and apostasy occurring ("most men's love will grow cold" [v. 12]). After that, great tribulation is depicted before Christ's return (vv. 15–30). In Luke 18:8 Jesus even asks, "When the Son of man comes, will he find faith on earth?" Paul speaks of "the apostasy" (2 Thess. 2:3 NASB) and then of the coming of "the man of sin" before Christ's return: "The Lord Jesus will slay him with the breath of his mouth and destroy him by his appearing and his coming" (v. 8). And the Book of Revelation climactically depicts an earth in which all except the faithful bow before the beast and the

[72] *Paradise Restored: A Biblical Theology of Dominion*, 5.

[73] Ibid., 223

[74] Chilton writes, "The Christian goal for the world is the universal development of Biblical theocratic republics, in which every area of life is redeemed and placed under the lordship of Christ and the rule of God's law" (ibid., 226).

[75] Chilton comments, "After looking at this parable [of the leaven], you might wonder how in the world anyone could deny a dominion eschatology" (ibid., 74). The problem, however, is that Chilton does not balance this parable with others, as I will point out.

false prophet, who are finally destroyed only when Christ returns (the climax in 19:17–21).

In regard to Revelation 19:17–21, postmillennialism demonstrates a very serious weakness. Postmillennialists generally view this section, *not* as the return of Christ in destruction of evil, but as the widespread propagation and victory of the gospel. Thus Boettner, for example, declares, "Revelation 19:11–21 describes not the Second Coming of Christ . . . rather it describes the progress of the church between the first and second comings of Christ . . . it results in an overwhelming victory for him and his church."[76] Chilton writes, "He [Christ] is riding out on His warhorse, followed by His army of saints, conquering the nations with the Word of God, the gospel, symbolized by a sword proceeding from His mouth. . . . This is not the Second Coming; rather, it is a symbolic declaration of hope, the assurance that the Word of God will be victorious throughout the world, so that Christ's rule will be established universally."[77] From such perspective, Revelation 20:1–6 represents the succeeding millennium of peace and prosperity to be followed by the return of Christ (as seen in Rev. 20:9). Thus the postmillennial scheme fits together—*except* for the fact that it is hard to avoid the scriptural evidence that Christ is already shown as returning in Revelation 19 and that the overall picture is not the victorious progress of the gospel but the final destruction of all who oppose it. Postmillennialism thus is weak in this critical area of the New Testament witness.

If postmillennialism is right, we are a long way from the Lord's return. Exhortations such as "Watch" and "Be alert" mean little: there can be no expectation of a soon return. But what if postmillennialism is blind to the signs of the times that may point to a return in the near future? Could this not be a misleading theology? Moreover, if things do not get better and evil rapidly increases, there would be little preparation for persecution and tribulation. Disillusionment could be the result. Optimism is much to be desired, but it surely needs the balance of a sober and valid biblical realism.

Finally, we should applaud postmillennial thinking in its concern to blanket the world with the gospel and to seek Christ's rule in every sphere of life. Christ *is* Lord, and His kingdom already established is growing with increasing witness to all peoples. However—and here is the needed balance—as surely as the gospel of the kingdom reaches further into the life of nations, there will be a counter thrust of evil. Indeed, evil forces will become even more virulent and antagonistic to all things Christian. But, praise God, when evil is released to do its worst and is thereby exposed in all its demonic nature, Christ will then return to destroy it utterly and consummate His glorious, eternal kingdom. At that time all that the postmillennialist has ever imagined—and far more—will come to pass—not in an earthly millennium but in a new heaven and a new earth!

Premillennialism

G. E. Ladd defines premillennialism thus: "Premillennialism is the doctrine stating that after the Second Coming of Christ, he will reign for a thousand years over the earth before the final consummation of God's redemptive

[76]R. G. Clouse, ed., *The Meaning of the Millennium*, 200.
[77]*Paradise Restored*, 191–92.

purpose in the new heaven and new earth of the Age to Come."[78]

Premillennialism has had a long and checkered history. Some of the early church fathers—including Justin Martyr, Irenaeus, and Tertullian—held a premillennial viewpoint.[79] This belief, at least in part, was a continuation of Jewish apocalyptic thinking that expected an earthly messianic kingdom, often depicted as a restoration of Paradise. However, Augustine, in his classic fifth century work *The City of God*, affirmed a nonfuturist view of the Millennium, holding instead that the Millennium refers to the present, ongoing rule of Christ in the church with the saints. Throughout the Middle Ages and the Reformation, Augustine's view largely prevailed, and premillennialism went into eclipse. In the seventeenth century there was some renewal of premillennialism, especially in England; however, postmillennialism soon came into prominence.[80] It was not until the nineteenth century that premillennialism once again became popular.

The dominant type of premillennialism through the influence of J. N. Darby came to be "dispensational." The Millennium was viewed as the final dispensation of the kingdom, which will follow the present dispensation of the church. Entirely separate programs for the church and for Israel came to be envisioned, including a secret pretribulation rapture of the church and a postponed kingdom for Israel. This kingdom will include a rebuilt temple and restoration of various Old Testament sacrifices. This dispensational form of premillennialism has been popularized through the Scofield Reference Bible and is now dominant in many evangelical circles. Presently a tension exists within the premillennial camp between those who hold to a more traditional church-centered premillennialism and those who subscribe to a dispensational formulation that highlights the rule of Israel in the Millennium.[81]

For dispensational premillennial thinking, the reign of Christ on earth in the Millennium is essential to the fulfilling of Old Testament prophecies for Israel. John F. Walvoord, for example, declares, "The millennium will fulfill literally the glowing expectations of Old Testament prophets for a kingdom of God on earth embracing all nations." Again, "Christ will reign on the throne of David on earth over a restored Israel as well as the Gentile world." Dispensational premillennialism thus tends to emphasize "the governmental and political character of the millennium itself."[82] (We may note here a certain parallel to the contemporary Restorationist brand of postmillennialism, which likewise has a strong governmental and political orientation [the

---

[78]*The Meaning of the Millennium*, 17.

[79]According to D. H. Kromminga, "The evidence is uniformly to the effect that throughout the years from the beginning of the second century till the beginning of the fifth chiliasm, particularly of the premillenarian type, was extensively found within the Christian church, but that it never was dominant, far less universal; that it was not without its opponents, and that its representatives were conscious of being able to speak only for a party in the Church" (*The Millennium in the Church*, 27–28).

[80]See the earlier discussion.

[81]For a helpful discussion of these similarities and differences, see the articles and responses by Ladd, entitled "Historic Premillennialism," and H. A. Hoyt, entitled "Dispensational Premillennialism," in Robert G. Clouse, ed., *The Meaning of the Millennium: Four Views*. This valuable book also contains articles and responses on postmillennialism by Boettner and amillennialism by A. A. Hoekema.

[82]Quotations from an article by Walvoord, "Dispensational Premillennialism," in Millard J. Erickson, ed., *The New Life*, 523.

two extremes meet!].) Ladd and other traditional (historical) premillennialists, whose basic concern is the church and not Israel, tend to emphasize more the spiritual blessings of the Millennium. They do not deny the political aspect but seek to avoid the strong dispensational Israelitish cast of the Millennium.

Before commenting on premillennialism in general, I want to emphasize that one should not simply identify its historic (or traditional) form with its dispensational form. *All dispensationalists are premillennialists, but not all premillennialists are dispensationalists*. For example, among contemporary scholarly commentators on the Book of Revelation who are premillennial almost all are nondispensational.[83] Unfortunately, because of the strong influence of dispensationalism in many circles, people frequently tend to identify dispensationalism with premillennialism. As we have seen, dispensationalism is a fairly recent nineteenth-century arrival on the scene, whereas historical premillennialism dates back to the early church. Dispensational motifs such as the sharp distinction between Israel and the church, the postponement of the kingdom, the secret coming of Christ for the church, a pre-tribulation rapture of believers, and a millennium in which temple sacrifices are reinstituted, have never been part of historical millennialism. So one may validly be a premillennialist without holding these accessory dispensational views. Having said this, I quickly add that the common thread uniting both forms of premillennialism is simply that Christ will return before the Millennium and reign on earth with His people. It will be a time of blessedness on this present earth before the final judgment and the dawn of the eternal kingdom.

Let me summarize the main points in premillennial teaching[84] in regard to Revelation 20.

1. Revelation 20 chronologically follows Revelation 19. The return of Christ and the destruction of evil (including the two beasts) will be followed by the establishment of Christ's millennial kingdom.

2. Satan at the outset of the thousand years will be bound, cast into the pit, and he will be so sealed off during this future period that he can "deceive the nations no more" (20:3). Since both of the beasts have already been thrown into "the lake of fire," this means an unparalleled era of freedom from evil on the earth.

3. Christ will then reign upon earth with His people. They will be on thrones and will include the martyrs and those who did not succumb to the beast. They all bodily "came to life" (20:4),[85] which is the same as "the first resurrection" (v. 5). Believers in their resurrected and glorified bodies will reign with Christ for a thousand years.

4. The millennial reign, while being a period of universal blessedness, will include "a rod-of-iron rule" by Christ and His saints. According to Revelation 19, "he [Christ] will rule them with a rod of iron" (v. 15). For in Revelation 2:26–27 Jesus had declared, "He who conquers and keeps my works until the end, I will give him power over the nations, and he shall rule them with a rod of iron." Rebellious nations will be sternly and totally kept in submission by Christ and His saints.

---

[83]I refer here to such recent commentators as R. H. Mounce, *The Book of Revelation*, NICNT; G. R. Beasley-Murray, *Revelation*, NCBC; Morton Kiddle, *The Revelation of St. John*; and George E. Ladd, *A Commentary on the Revelation of John*. John F. Walvoord, and his commentary *The Revelation of Jesus Christ*, is, of course, dispensational.

[84]This will follow the historical (traditional) pattern.

[85]Also NIV and NASB. The KJV and ASV translate the Greek word *ezēsan* as "lived."

5. Not until the close of the thousand years will unbelievers be raised from the dead. For, according to Revelation 20:5, "the rest of the dead did not come to life[86] until the thousand years were ended."

6. At the end of the Millennium Satan will be released to deceive and gather recalcitrant nations that are at the "four corners of the earth" to attack (v. 8) the beloved city. All the attacking nations will be destroyed and Satan cast into the lake of fire.

I will comment on each of these points:

1. If Revelation 19–20 actually teaches a return of Christ followed by a thousand-year millennial reign on earth, this seems to be at variance with all other biblical testimony. The Old Testament does indeed in many places depict a coming messianic reign. But it is by no means limited to a thousand years or any other temporal period: the kingdom will continue forever.[87] The New Testament undoubtedly distinguishes between this age and the one to come, but there is no mention elsewhere of an interim messianic kingdom. Christ in many statements declares His return, and with it He will bring about the final redemption of the righteous, the complete destruction of evil, the judgment of all people, and the beginning of the new age. But nowhere does He suggest an interim period between His return and the eternal kingdom.[88] The same is true for Paul. He often speaks about the return of Christ, but always Christ's return is for the purpose of bringing about the final consummation. For example, says Paul, after Christ returns, rather than reigning with Him a thousand years, "we shall always be with the Lord" (1 Thess. 4:17). Peter similarly speaks of the Parousia of Christ (2 Peter 3:4) as identical with "the day of the Lord" (v. 10), in which day the present heavens and earth will pass away and the new heavens and earth come into being (vv. 10–13). There is no place in this picture for a thousand-year period on earth between the return of Christ and eternal life in the new heavens and the new earth. Also—and this is quite significant—in the Book of Revelation itself there is no other possible reference to a millennium. For example, in Revelation 11:15 there is this joyous declaration: "The kingdom of the world has become the kingdom of our Lord and of his Christ, and he shall reign for ever and ever." "For ever and ever" precludes an interim, limited reign.

It is possible, of course, to argue, since Revelation 19–20 is near the close of the New Testament canon, that as a matter of progressive revelation a future thousand-year kingdom is at last unfolded and therefore should be affirmed regardless of its uniqueness in biblical witness. Surely one may rightly speak of progressive revelation, but if there is another possible interpretation other than the premillennial that is more harmonious with the rest of Scripture, it would surely seem wise to investigate that interpretation closely. Moreover, a

[86]As earlier noted, KJV translates this phrase as "lived not again"; ASV, "lived not."

[87]R. H. Charles writes, "Before the year 100 B.C. it was generally believed in Judaism that the messianic kingdom would last *for ever* on the present earth. . . . " (italics his). Thus it is that the idea of a limited period "is really a late and attenuated form of the old Jewish expectation of an eternal kingdom on earth" (*The Revelation of St. John*, ICC, 2:142). I will discuss the Old Testament view a little later.

[88]Recall Ladd's remark, "I can find no trace of the idea of either an interim earthly kingdom or of a millennium in the Gospels" (*The Meaning of the Millennium*, 38).

real danger in adopting the premillennial view is that relevant Scripture elsewhere may be forced into an uncongenial mold and accordingly be seriously distorted. Progressive revelation is one thing; misunderstood revelation is another.

One of the basic rules of biblical hermeneutics is that difficult and obscure passages should be viewed in the light of clear passages and the overall analogy of Scripture. This fundamental principle is sadly overlooked when a difficult and obscure passage becomes the determinant for biblical understanding elsewhere.

Having said all this, I am convinced that there is a better way of understanding Revelation 19–20, one that is more congenial to the overall biblical witness. I have earlier sought to demonstrate that this passage is in a nonchronological sequence: a succeeding vision, not a succeeding period. So I will not repeat my discussion here, except to emphasize that such an understanding is in full accord with other Scripture, including the overall witness of the Book of Revelation.

2. The binding, casting out, and sealing of Satan—again in harmony with the larger scriptural testimony—occurred through Christ's victorious life and death. As I have previously noted, Jesus spoke of binding Satan during His ministry and declared that on the night of His death Satan would be cast out. Also we have observed that Satan's inability after his sealing to deceive the nations refers to the new situation *after* Christ came: the gospel *will* get through to all the nations.

Incidentally, but importantly, Revelation 20:1–3 cannot chronologically follow Revelation 19:11–21 because those verses declare that all people on the earth have been slain (19:21), so there would be no nations left not to be deceived if the thousand years followed the destruction wrought by Christ!

3. Revelation 20:4–6 says nothing about Christ's reigning on earth. It tells of a reigning of the redeemed with Christ (vv. 4, 6), and the location is not given. Those who reign with Him are on "thrones," signifying their spiritual dominion: they are those who have experienced "the first resurrection," which is not a bodily resurrection but a spiritual one. They "lived" (better than "came to life")—even if put to death as martyrs—and will never know "the second death," namely, spiritual death, or hell. There is no reference in this passage to a second physical resurrection of unbelievers: they "did not live" (better than "did not come to life") refers to the spiritual condition of unbelievers throughout the whole gospel era. This passage accordingly has nothing to do with physical resurrections but totally relates to a spiritual resurrection both experienced and not experienced. It is a critical mistake therefore to speak of two physical resurrections separated by a thousand years. The Bible *never* depicts such. There is, to be sure, a separation in time between the spiritual resurrection of believers ("the first resurrection") and the later resurrection of both believers and unbelievers (recall John 5:21–25, 28–29), but a separation of bodily resurrections is contrary to both the total biblical witness and the teaching of Revelation 20.

Incidentally, if the first resurrection is thought of as the bodily resurrection of believers, and it is they who will reign on earth with Christ, this seems to leave out all believers who will not die but be translated when Christ returns. Surely they too will reign with Christ; however, they never experienced bodily resurrection.

4. The "rod of iron" rule during the thousand years is a total misunderstanding for several reasons. First, Christ's ruling the nations with a "rod of iron" in Revelation 19:15 does not mean to govern but to break and de-

stroy.[89] When Christ returns with His armies, He will smite the nations, the people of earth, so that all evil is destroyed. Hence during the succeeding thousand years there will be no nations to rule over with a "rod of iron." Second, if, however, there were such nations, it would hardly be a glorious messianic kingdom if both Christ and His saints are ruling over and holding in check rebellious peoples across the face of the earth. Indeed, it would be quite inglorious both for Christ after being glorified at the Father's right hand, and for the untold numbers of saints who have long known the glories of heaven, to return to this old earth still latent with rebellious forces. Third, this whole picture of a rod-of-iron rule on earth can by no means be coordinated with the view of the Millennium as a future golden age. Indeed, this picture is a reversion to the idea of an earthly messianic rule held by many in Jesus' own day, often including His own disciples. Fourth, as I earlier suggested, this is gross admixture of Christ and saints operating with spiritual bodies ruling over a world of people in their natural and physical bodies.

5. The premillennial idea of the resurrection of the unbelieving dead to follow after a thousand years is foreign to Scripture. Elsewhere the biblical witness unmistakably declares that the resurrection of both the righteous and the unrighteous occur on the same day of the Lord. The better translation for Revelation 20:5 is "the rest of the dead did not live [rather than 'did not come to life'] until the thousand years were ended." That is to say, all the way to the end of the present millennium unbelievers have remained spiritually dead. They did not experience "the first resurrection" to eternal life.

6. The final picture of Satan, after the thousand years of Christ's earthly reign, gathering "the nations" for battle—their number "like the sand of the sea"—to attack "the beloved city," is even more incredible. First of all, according to Revelation 19, Christ had already destroyed them all, so where will the nations come from? Second, this hardly sounds like the climax of a glorious reign of Christ on earth when evil people are so many as to be beyond numbering! With such a vast multitude of peoples it appears that, underneath, the Millennium will be a period of evil just as now; in fact, it appears that it will be even worse[90] than when Christ first returns. What is even more extraordinary, all this will transpire while the Devil is locked away in the bottomless pit! When Satan is released, evil multitudes long held in check will join his attack on "the beloved city." All of this strains credibility almost past limits.

Let me say a final word on chronological sequence. Premillennialists sometimes emphasize that when Satan is finally defeated, he will be "thrown into the lake of fire and brimstone where the beast and the false prophet [are]" (Rev. 20:10). Since the latter two were thrown into that same "lake of fire" at the return of Christ in Revelation 19:21 and are not referred to as functioning in Revelation 20 (only Satan is mentioned), then the thousand years must follow the return of Christ and precede the Millennium. The answer to

[89]See page 418, n.91.

[90]Actually there are some premillennialists who say this. Donald G. Barnhouse, for example, has been quoted as stating that "the millennial age will be the most iniquitous of all" (A. H. Lewis, *The Dark Side of the Millennium*, 15). John Phillips declares, "As children of believing parents today become glory hardened; so during the millennium many will become glory hardened; they will render only feigned obedience" (*Exploring Revelation*, 282; see Lewis, *Dark Side*, 16). What an inglorious situation!

this line of reasoning is the same as earlier suggested, namely, that Revelation 19:11–21 and 20:1–10 are chronological visions rather than chronological occurrences. The center of attention in Revelation 19 is the final destruction of Christ's and believers' enemies as represented by the first and second beast (or false prophet), whereas in 20:1–6 (and climaxing in vv. 7–10) the focus is on the inability of Satan to deceive the nations, hence the victorious witness of the gospel. Moreover, what occurs in Revelation 19:11–21 does *not* belong to a time prior to the Millennium, but to the last days when *after* the thousand years Satan is turned loose. Hence, Revelation 20:7–10 corresponds to Revelation 19:11–21 and is another (and last) depiction of the same final battle.[91]

Postmillennialism and premillennialism share a common fallacy that regards the Millennium as a future period in history. Because of this, neither system can adequately cope with the outbreak of evil at the end of the millennial period. Postmillennialism, which depicts a coming golden era of righteousness and peace, with evil reduced to negligible proportions, is hard-pressed to account for the violent resurgence of Satanic forces after that. Premillennialism is likewise hard-pressed to explain that same evil resurgence after Christ has been reigning on earth for a thousand years. The solution, however, is readily at hand when the Millennium is viewed as presently occurring and the reign of Christ as an ongoing reality.

Let me summarize this briefly. The Millennium is *now*. Christ is presently reigning, and His people reign with Him. In the words of Paul we "reign in life" (Rom. 5:17), or in the words of John we *are* "a kingdom" (Rev. 1:6) and sit on "thrones" (Rev. 20:4). This refers to all believers, including martyrs and those who have not "bowed to the beast": all have reigned, and do reign, victoriously with Christ. During this whole millennial era Satan has been "cast out" (John 12:31; Rev. 20:3) in the sense that he is utterly incapable of stopping the gospel from getting through to "the nations" (his former deception is over). Thus the gates of hell cannot "prevail" (Matt. 16:18) against the church's fulfilling the Great Commission (Matt. 24:14; 28:18–20). When at last the church has completed its task of witness, the Millennium will end and Satan will be released and allowed through deception to gather "the nations" for the final attack on Christ's spiritual kingdom. It is then that Christ will return—*after* the Millennium—to utterly destroy Satan and all his minions and to usher in the Day of Judgment and the age to come.

The interpretation of the Millennium that I have presented in the preceding pages is sometimes called "amillennialism." I am hesitant to use this nomenclature for two reasons.

First, the word may suggest negativity, i.e., "no millennium." This could imply that my position simply disregards Revelation 20. I surely do not—as should be fully apparent by now. One may more properly speak of many of the major creeds and confessions of Christendom as being amillennial, in that they make no reference to a millennium. The Apostles' Creed, for example, after affirming that Christ "sitteth on the right hand of God the Father Almighty" declares that "from thence he shall come to judge the quick and the dead." No reference is made to Christ's coming to establish a millennial kingdom prior to His judging. The Nicene

[91]Recall the previous discussion of how the same battle is described from different angles several times in the final chapters of Revelation.

Creed states, "He shall come again with glory to judge both the quick and the dead, whose kingdom shall have no end." The emphasis is on Christ's coming in judgment and the fact that His kingdom is eternal—nothing about an interim kingdom or period of time. The Westminster Confession of Faith in its last two chapters moves from "The Resurrection of the Dead" to "The Last Judgment," with nothing in between about a millennium. Such statements are "amillennial," not necessarily in denying a millennium but in making no reference to it. My position does not contradict such creedal and confessional statements, but rather goes beyond them in seeking to define the true biblical meaning of the Millennium. Since I vigorously affirm a millennium, I am not in this sense amillennial.

Second, some today who are known as amillennialists view the Millennium as having to do essentially with heaven not earth. While denying (as I do) a future millennium (either post- or pre-), they speak of the present reign of believers as that of departed saints in heaven. Over against premillennialists, who speak of "the first resurrection" as a bodily resurrection, these amillennialists claim that the expression refers to the "souls" of those who have passed on into glory. Thus the reign is in heaven, not upon earth. I have already made reference to this in notes 30 and 35. There I included quotations from William Hendricksen and Anthony A. Hoekema, both of whom hold this amillennial position.[92] In these footnotes I have commented that Scripture nowhere, including Revelation, depicts a heavenly reign of disembodied souls or spirits and that there is no adequate scriptural basis for viewing the believer's presence with the Lord in heaven as a resurrection. Nonetheless, this amillennial view, I submit, is much closer to the biblical picture than either postmillennialism or premillennialism for the reason that the Millennium is *not* viewed as a future interim kingdom.

I prefer to speak of a *present* and historical millennium on earth and not in heaven. To be sure, it is a heavenly existence while yet on this earth, for truly we are blessed "in Christ with every spiritual blessing *in the heavenly places*" (Eph. 1:3). Even now we "*reign in life* through the one man Jesus Christ" (Rom. 5:17). Throughout the whole Christian era, whatever their lot, the saints live and reign "with Christ a thousand years." A present millennium is totally other than "no millennium": it is the reality of the *present* kingdom of God.[93]

Truly in Christ we live and reign now—and shall throughout eternity.

---

[92]Some others who hold this amillennialist view are R. C. H. Lenski, *The Interpretation of St. John's Revelation*; Leon Morris, *Revelation* (TNTC); and Henry B. Swete, *Commentary on Revelation*. A somewhat modified position is found in Floyd Hamilton, *The Basis of Millennial Faith*.

[93]In the words of W. E. Cox, "The present phase of the kingdom and the millennium are synonymous terms. . . . The millennium, like the kingdom, was instituted by our Lord" (*Biblical Studies in Final Things*, 171). Although Cox speaks of himself as an amillennialist, his view is much more in accord with my own position.

14

The Last Judgment

Christ will return also for the purpose of rendering judgment: it will be the *Last Judgment*.[1] In Revelation 20, just following the picture of the destruction of the evil forces of mankind and Satan's being thrown into eternal torment (vv. 7–10), there occurs the scene of One seated on "a great white throne"—the throne of the Last Judgment (vv. 11–15). A similar picture is given in Matthew 25:31–46, which begins, "When the Son of man comes in his glory, and all the angels with him, then he will sit on his glorious throne" (v. 31). The throne so depicted is the seat of judgment, and the language of "great white"[2] and "glorious" designates it as the final judgment upon the world.[3]

I. THE JUDGE

The judge will be God in the person of Jesus Christ. Paul speaks of "the day when. . .God will judge the secrets of men through Christ Jesus" (Rom. 2:16 NASB). Again, in his address to the people of Athens Paul declares that God "has fixed a day in which He will judge the world in righteousness through a Man whom He has appointed, having furnished proof to all men by raising Him from the dead" (Acts 17:31 NASB). God will render final judgment through Jesus Christ.

There are also references in the New Testament simply to God's being the Judge. For example, Paul speaks directly of God as judge: "The day of wrath when God's righteous judgment will be revealed" (Rom. 2:5). Later in the same letter Paul states that "we shall all stand before the judgment seat of God" (14:10). In Hebrews reference is made to "a judge who is God of all" (12:23). Peter writes about the "Father . . . who judges each one impartially" (1 Peter 1:17). In the Book of Revelation is the declaration "Fear God and

[1]According to the Apostles' Creed, "He shall come to judge the quick and the dead." It is to this purpose that we now turn.

[2]"Great" points to power and majesty; "white," to holiness and purity—thus the rendering of judgment by the Almighty and All-Holy One.

[3]Earlier Jesus had said, "The Son of man is to come with his angels in the glory of his Father, and then he will repay every man for what he has done" (Matt. 16:27). Christ's coming will be glorious and, likewise, it will be His throne of judgment.

give him glory, for the hour of his judgment has come" (14:7).[4]

However, it is apparent in these passages that God the Father renders judgment through Jesus Christ. Indeed, Jesus Himself declares, "The Father judges no one, but has given all judgment to the Son" (John 5:22). Hence, Paul's language about "the judgment seat of God" that "we shall all appear before" is made more specific elsewhere in the similar statement that "we must all appear before the judgment seat of Christ" (2 Cor. 5:10). The judgment seat of God *is* the judgment seat of Christ.[5] Another direct reference to Christ the Lord as the judge is found in a statement of Paul to Timothy: "Henceforth there is laid up for me the crown of righteousness, which the Lord, the righteous judge, will award to me on that Day, and not only to me but also to all who have loved his appearing" (2 Tim. 4:8).

It is fitting, indeed, that Christ Himself will be the One who occupies the throne of judgment. As the Son of God, thus God Himself, He will be wholly qualified with all wisdom and knowledge, justice and mercy. Also, says Jesus on one occasion: "My judgment is true, for it is not I alone that judge, but I and he ['the Father'] who sent me" (John 8:16).[6] Hence the judgment, as that of Son and Father, will be absolutely just and true.[7] Also He will judge as the Son of man. Earlier Jesus had said that the Father had "given him authority to execute judgment, because he is the Son of man"[8] (John 5:27). He will do so with the inner knowledge of the human condition—the temptations, travails, even weaknesses of the flesh. This does not mean leniency, or an alleviation of judgment upon evil; rather, it means that the Son of man will have an intimate and personal knowledge of every human being.

[4]There are many Old Testament references to God as the Judge, beginning with Genesis 18:25: "Shall not the Judge of all the earth do right?"

[5]Hence, while it is true that in Revelation 14:7 "the hour of his judgment" simply mentions God, the "great white throne" scene depicted in Revelation 20:11, while not so stating it, suggests Christ. Note, e.g., the use of "white" in relation to Christ in earlier passages: Christ seated on "a white cloud" (14:14) and coming on "a white horse" (19:11). Some commentators hold, because of such a statement as "to him who sits upon the throne and to the Lamb" (5:13; cf. 6:16; 7:10)—differentiating the occupant of the throne from Christ—as well as such a declaration (quoted above) as "Fear God and give him the glory, for the hour of his judgment has come," that "him who sat upon" the "great white throne" must also be God (the Father). I am inclined, however, not only for the reason mentioned (i.e., the use of "white") but also by virtue of both the overall analogy of Scripture (e.g., it is "the Son of man" on "his glorious throne" in Matthew) and the wider picture in the Book of Revelation to view this Judge as Christ. For example, on the latter point, early in Revelation the throne of the Father is said by Christ to be occupied *also* by Him: "I myself conquered and sat down with my Father on his throne" (3:21). Since it is clearly Christ who will come to destroy all evil forces in Revelation 19, it follows that He will most likely occupy the throne of judgment, the event described immediately following.

[6]Although Jesus is not here referring to the final judgment, His words would surely, indeed supremely, apply to that event. Incidentally, these words of Jesus show that both He and the Father occupy the throne of judgment. This is set forth symbolically, I would suggest, in Revelation by the language of Christ's *also* sitting on the Father's throne.

[7]The Gospel of John emphasizes that Jesus "did not come to judge the world but to save the world" (12:47; cf. 3:17 [NASB]). However, Jesus does add, "He who rejects me, and does not receive my sayings has a judge; the word I have spoken will be his judge on the last day" (12:48). (See later discussion about the place of "the word" in the judgment of "the last day.")

[8]Literally, "son of man" or "a son of man." A literal translation all the more would stress His humanity. The translation "a son of man" is not unlike Paul's language that "God . . . will judge the world in righteousness by a man . . . " (quoted supra).

So it is that God Himself in the person of Jesus Christ, Son of God and Son of man, will sit upon the throne of judgment.[9]

Finally, that coming event will be awesome. Christ will sit upon "his glorious throne."[10] The word "glory" is an expression of His majesty, sublimity, and grandeur. Even as He will come in glory—"his glory and the glory of the Father and of the holy angels" (Luke 9:26)—so will be the glory of the throne upon which He will sit. The very appearance of Christ on that occasion will be so glorious in majesty that, as the Book of Revelation describes it, "from his presence earth and sky fled away, and no place was found for them" (20:11).[11] Indeed, the throne of Christ's glory will be utterly beyond all imagination.

II. SUBJECTS

The judgment will be of both angels and human beings. It will include all fallen angels as well as the whole of humanity. The very statement that this will happen further heightens the awesomeness of this occasion and its incalculable importance. Angels *and* people!

Regarding the angels, we are told in Scripture that "angels who did not keep their own domain, but abandoned their proper abode, He has kept in eternal bonds under darkness[12] for the judgment of the great day" (Jude 6 NASB). Similarly we read that "God did not spare the angels when they sinned, but cast them into hell[13] and committed them to pits of darkness, reserved for [or 'being kept for'] judgment" (2 Peter 2:4 NASB). We are not told in either passage of the time or circumstances of this angelic sin and fall,[14] but only that their present state is that of being kept in the darkness of hell for the coming day of judgment. In any event, these evil angels will be arraigned on that final day.

The focus of Scripture, however, is on mankind. On the day of judgment all persons—every human being—will be present. I have already quoted such Pauline statements as "[God] will judge the world in righteousness," and "we shall all appear before the judgment seat of God." In addition, Paul's statement about "the day of wrath when God's righteous judgment is revealed," continues: "For he will render to every man according to his works" (Rom. 2:6).

Let us also observe that "the Son of man is to come with his angels in the glory of his Father, and then he will repay every man for what he has done" (Matt. 16:27). Likewise, we now note that after Jesus said, "When the Son of man comes in his glory, and all the angels with him, then he will sit on his

---

[9]The role of believers in judging with Christ will be discussed later.

[10]The Greek phrase is *thronou doxēs autou*, literally "the throne of his glory."

[11]Recall that among the phenomena heralding "the day of the Lord," hence Christ's return, which the Book of Revelation earlier portrays, are these: "The sky was split apart like a scroll when it is rolled up; and every mountain and island were moved out of their places" (6:14 NASB). The Grand Assize of Christ results in still further movement of earth and sky: not simply "split apart" and "moved out of their places," but they will have totally "fled away" with "no place" at all for them!

[12]The Greek word here and in the next reference, 2 Peter 2:4, is *zophon*—"the Darkness of the nether regions" (BAGD).

[13]The Greek word for "cast into hell" is *tartarōsas*. Tartarus was "thought of by the Greeks as a subterranean place lower than Hades where divine punishment was meted out, [and] was so regarded in Jewish apocalyptic as well" (BAGD). The "abode of the wicked dead . . . answers to the Gehenna of the Jews" (Thayer).

[14]It is most likely that their sin and fall corresponds to that of Satan. However, there is no firm biblical reference to such.

glorious throne," He added, "Before him will be gathered all the nations [the *ethnē*]"[15] (Matt. 25:32). "Every man"—"all the nations,"[16] such phrases graphically show that the totality of humanity will be included.

In the final scene of the day of judgment in the Book of Revelation, John writes, "And I saw the dead, great and small, standing before the throne" (20:12). "The dead" refers comprehensively to all persons; and "great and small" includes everyone "standing before the throne," regardless of position or stature in life. All persons of all times and places—since the beginning of creation—will be present.

"The dead," accordingly, will consist of both unbelievers and believers, the lost and the saved. For Revelation continues, "And books were opened; and another book was opened, which is the book of life; and the dead were judged from the things which were written in the books" (v. 12 NASB). Furthermore, "if anyone's name was not found written in the book of life,[17] he was thrown into the lake of fire" (v. 15). These statements emphasize the presence of both the lost and the saved on the great day of judgment.[18]

Now, finally, I quote a statement of Jesus which emphasizes that all persons will be present on that day: "I tell you, on the day of judgment men[19] will render account. . ." (Matt. 12:36). The day of judgment will include all mankind.[20]

This leads me to speak for the first time of the resurrection of the unrighteous, the unbelieving dead. I have earlier discussed the resurrection of "the dead in Christ," which occurs at the return of Christ. Now I add that there will also be a resurrection of the unrighteous that they may also be present for the occasion of the Last Judgment. Further, since "the dead, great and small" stand before the throne, and as Revelation proceeds to say, "the sea gave up of the dead in it,

[15]*Ethnē* may also be translated "people," hence "all the people." "All the people" (Matt. 25:32) accordingly equals "every man" (Matt. 16:27).

[16]The error is sometimes made of assuming a separate judgment of the nations over against mankind in general. However, the two above texts in Matthew as well as Scriptures elsewhere make no such distinction.

[17]In Revelation believers are several times described as those whose names have been written in "the book of life." One "who conquers shall be clad thus in white garments, and I will not blot his name out of the book of life" (3:5); "the beast" is given authority over "every one whose name has not been written before the foundation of the world in the book of life of the Lamb that was slain" (13:8); and "the dwellers on earth whose names have not been written in the book of life from the foundation of the world, will marvel to behold the beast" (17:8).

[18]Accordingly, one cannot view this scene as the judgment of the unbelieving or unrighteous dead only. The statement that "the dead were judged from the things which were written in the books" is sometimes held to signify only the unbelieving dead by claiming that "the books" are other than "the book of life," hence only the unbelieving or unrighteous are in the scene. However, there is no reason why "the books" do not include "the book of life;" hence both unrighteous and righteous are judged. Indeed, if nothing else, the final statement that "if anyone's name [literally, 'if anyone'] was *not* found written in the book of life . . ." makes unambiguously clear that both the lost and the saved are present. The "not found written" presupposes the other category of persons at the judgment.

[19]Literally, "the men," that is, "the good man" and "the evil man" of verse 35.

[20]It is invariably "*the* day of judgment," never "days." Hence, the idea sometimes entertained that believers will have a prior judgment is out of the question. There is only *one* final occasion of judgment—as described in Matthew 25 and Revelation 20—at which *all* are present.

Death and Hades[21] gave up the dead in them" (20:13), it is apparent that there will also be a resurrection of the unrighteous.

An Old Testament presage of this is found in the Book of Daniel: "Multitudes who sleep in the dust of the earth will awake: some to everlasting life, others to shame and everlasting contempt [or 'abhorrence' NEB]" (12:2 NIV).[22] Hence, there will be both a resurrection to "life" and a resurrection to "shame" and "abhorrence." This points to the picture in Revelation of those whose names are in "the book of life," and thus have awakened, or been resurrected, to "everlasting life"; and others whose names not being found in the book of life are thrown into "the lake of fire" (20:15), hence have awakened to "everlasting abhorrence."

In this same connection we hear again the words of Jesus: "The hour is coming, in the which all that are in the graves shall hear his [Christ's] voice, and shall come forth; they that have done good, unto the resurrection of life; and they that have done evil, unto the resurrection of damnation"[23] (John 5:28–29 KJV). The parallel with the Book of Daniel and John's writings is obvious: "the resurrection of life" (John), "everlasting life" (Daniel), "the book of life" (Revelation); and "the resurrection of damnation" (John), "everlasting abhorrence" (Daniel), "the lake of fire" (Revelation). The unrighteous will also be resurrected. But unlike the "resurrection of life" for the righteous, it is a "resurrection of damnation," or "condemnation." The believer will by no means experience the latter, for Jesus also earlier said, "He that heareth my word, and believeth on him that sent me, hath everlasting life, and shall not come into condemnation;[24] but is passed from death unto life" (John 5:24 KJV). The unbeliever will "come into condemnation," for his resurrection on the day of judgment will be "the resurrection of damnation."

To summarize this section: On the day of judgment the subjects will be both angels and human beings. The angels will be those evil or fallen; the humans will include all persons. Righteous persons will already have been raised from the dead (or translated) and transformed into spiritual bodies; in-

[21]Hades is here "the abode of the unrighteous dead" (Mounce, *The Book of Revelation*, 366). Jeremias speaks of a "twofold use of *ἅδης* in the NT." It may refer to "the place of all the souls of the dead until the resurrection (Ac. 2:27, 31), whereas in others it denotes the place only of the souls of the ungodly (Lk. 16:23) or non-Christians (Rev. 20:13f.)" (TDNT 1:149). In Revelation 20, reference is definitely to non-Christians.

[22]In Daniel it is not clear that all the dead will "awake," since the term used is "multitudes," or "many." Christ makes it quite clear: *"all"* (see next paragraph in the text).

[23]The Greek phrase is *anastasin kriseōs*. This is translated "resurrection of judgment" in RSV and NASB. "Judgment" however may mislead, since it can suggest simply a resurrection for judgment, one way or the other, to be given. *Krisis* may indeed mean simply "judgment," but it can also carry the further meaning of "condemnation" (or "damnation" [KJV]). According to BAGD, "the word [*krisis*] often means judgment that goes against a person, *condemnation*, and the *punishment* that follows," (hence, again, "damnation"). Thus the best translation also for John 3:17–18 is not to use the neutral "judge" but "condemn" (or even "damn"!): "For God sent not his Son into the world to condemn [*krinē*] the world; but that the world through him might be saved. He that believeth on him is not condemned [*krinetai*]; but he that believeth not is condemned [*kekritai*] already, because he hath not believed in the name of the only begotten Son of God" (KJV). (It is interesting that here RSV has "condemned" rather than "judged," whereas NASB stays with "judged.")

[24]The Greek word is *krisin*. Again, it could be translated "damnation." "Judgment" (RSV, NASB, NEB) is misleading (NIV fortunately has "condemned"—"will not be condemned").

deed, they will also have come with Christ in His destruction of evil, and now stand before His throne. The unrighteous will likewise be raised from the dead and be present at the Great Assize. Such will be the vast multitude gathered before the throne of the Lord on the final day of judgment.

I append a brief word on the situation of the unrighteous dead before their resurrection. Those who have died before the return of Christ already are experiencing in some sense their coming condemnation. Two Scripture passages particularly bear on this matter: Luke 16:19–31 and 2 Peter 2:4–10.

In the Lukan passage Jesus speaks in a parable about a rich man who lived sumptuously, with no regard for the poor man Lazarus at his gate, and then died and was buried. The rich man's situation after death is described as "in Hades, being in torment"[25] (16:23). So he cries out to Abraham (in whose "bosom" Lazarus now was): "Send Lazarus to dip the end of his finger in water and cool my tongue; for I am in anguish in this flame" (v. 24). From this situation of torment and anguish, however, Abraham says there can be no relief and no crossing over the "great chasm" (v. 26) between. Thus the parable suggests that an unrighteous person, such as the rich man, after death experiences much pain and suffering: he is in a "place of torment" (v. 28).[26]

The passage in 2 Peter begins with words quoted earlier about how God did not spare the angels who sinned but cast them into hell to be kept there until the judgment. Then after an elaboration of God's not sparing the world in Noah's day while preserving a "herald of righteousness," and of His destroying Sodom and Gomorrah while rescuing "righteous Lot," Peter adds, "The Lord knows how to rescue the godly from trial, and to keep the unrighteous under punishment[27] until [or 'for'][28] the day of judgment, and especially those who indulge in the lust of defiling passion and despise authority" (2:9–10). Continuing punishment, accordingly, is the situation of the unrighteous until the day of judgment, though it seems from the use of the word "especially" that the amount or intensity varies with the evil committed before death.

This condition of suffering (Luke 16) or punishment (2 Peter) then applies to the situation of all the ungodly after death. It refers, of course, to their spirits, since their bodies, even as those of the righteous, decay in the grave. It will not be until the day of final judgment that they also will be raised and stand before the Lord.

III. PURPOSE

The purpose of the day of judgment will be, first, to exhibit the righteousness of God's judgment in the salvation of the righteous and the condemnation of the unrighteous. According to Paul, it will be the day "when God's righteous judgment will be revealed" (Rom. 2:5).

---

[25]The Greek word is *basanois*—plural, hence "torments" (as KJV).

[26]It is sometimes said that since this is a parabolic story, it should not be pressed into the service of doctrine. Perhaps, it may be suggested, the grimness of the account is only to make Jesus' later point that even if someone, informed about the torment to come, should proclaim repentance before it is too late, it would do no good (vv. 27–31). However, even though Jesus does build up to that point, there is little room to suppose that He was not serious about the lot of a person at death. Indeed, Jesus speaks many times about the perils of walking in the path that leads to destruction.

[27]Literally, "being punished," the Greek word is *kolazomenous*. The NIV translates the statement above in this way: "to hold the unrighteous for the day of judgment, while continuing their punishment."

[28]The Greek word is *eis*.

It will be a declaration of the sovereign justice and mercy of God in relation to the whole universe.

Accordingly, it is not the purpose of that day to decide the destinies of angels and men, but to show forth God's righteousness and justice in what has already been determined. Hence, fallen angels do not come to the day of judgment for a determination whether their time in the nether darkness will be changed to a different destiny; nor do persons stand before the throne of Christ for a decision about their ultimate lot.

In regard to human beings, this may be observed in the scenes of Christ on the throne of judgment in both Matthew and Revelation. Christ "on his glorious throne" (Matt. 25:31) "separates the sheep from the goats" (v. 32), and the former go "into eternal life," the latter "into eternal punishment" (v. 46). The purpose is *not* to decide who are sheep and who are goats, but to separate them and after that to make clear to all why they already belong in these distinct categories. In the "great white throne" scene (Rev. 20) the purpose is not to decide whose names belong in "the book of life"; that has long before been determined. Thus there will be no need on that day to discover whether or not one's name is inscribed in the book. A person's name is either in "the book of life" or in the other books: if not found in the former, he will be cast into "the lake of fire."[29]

The day of judgment will be a revelation of the righteousness of God's prior decision, and in each case this will be by an exhibition of the deeds done. Hence "sheep" are not sheep merely by an arbitrary decision of God, but are shown to be such by their acts of love and compassion (e.g., ministering to the thirsty and hungry, clothing the naked, visiting the sick and those in prison). "Goats" demonstrate their contrary nature by doing none of these things. Similarly, what is written about the deeds of persons in both "the book of life" and the other books—"the dead were judged by what was written in the books" (Rev. 20:12)—declares the righteousness of God's decision. But, to repeat, the names of persons are already in either "the book of life" or the other books; hence their ultimate destiny already has been set before the day of judgment.

Let me add a word about works (or deeds). Their importance should not be minimized in relation to one's eternal destiny. Let us hear further from Paul, for just after the words quoted earlier about the day "when God's righteous judgment will be revealed," Paul adds, "For he will render to every man according to his works: to those who by patience [or 'perseverance' NASB] in well-doing seek for glory and honor and immortality, he will give eternal life; but for those who are factious[30] and do not obey the truth, but obey wickedness, there will be wrath and fury" (Rom. 2:6–8). Works will therefore be very important on the day of judgment, not because they will then bring about a positive or negative judgment concerning a person's final destiny, but because God's judgment in Christ will be "according to" and in consonance with their concrete demonstration. Even as now we are saved by a living faith that is shown forth in good works, so on the

[29]Hence, as W. E. Cox puts it, "the judgment will not be for the purpose of determining men's destinies, but merely to manifest them" (*Biblical Studies in Final Things*, 148).

[30]The Greek word is *eritheias*. "Factious" or "contentious" (KJV) is possible; however, the further meaning of *eritheias* as "selfishness, selfish ambition" (BAGD) seems better to suit Paul's emphasis. The NIV has "self-seeking"; NASB, "selfishly ambitious"; NEB, "governed by selfish ambition."

day of judgment good or evil deeds will be the tangible demonstration of this faith or lack of it, which issues in eternal life or "wrath and fury."

The second purpose of the day of judgment is to reveal totally what is in every person. Paul writes, "Do not pronounce judgment before the time, before the Lord comes, who will bring to light the things now hidden in darkness and will disclose the purposes[31] of the heart" (1 Cor. 4:5). Again, judgment is not to determine the future state of a person, but to make manifest what is there: things hidden in this present life, the inner motives of the heart. Accordingly, the purpose of judgment is *revelatory*, and the essence of judgment is *coming to light*. It is like the function of X-ray—to pierce through the outward to the inward and to expose all the deep and hidden recesses of a person's being. Thus each one on the day of judgment will be revealed as he totally is.

There are, to be sure, areas of one's life—sins and evils—already both known to oneself and evident to others. They point to the coming judgment, but other dark spots will be disclosed at that time. So writes Paul: "The sins of some men are conspicuous, pointing to[32] judgment, but the sins of others appear later"[33] (1 Tim. 5:24). In this life many persons know that they have sins which, if they are honest enough to admit, will cause them to face a future judgment. Often there is a deep sense of apprehension over what is coming,[34] no matter how much people may try to suppress it or put it aside. But the day will come—it cannot be avoided—when not only known sins and evils will come to light, but also those now hidden. For, to use our Lord's own words, "Nothing is covered up that will not be revealed [i.e., 'uncovered'], or hidden that will not be known" (Luke 12:2).[35] The day of judgment, in summary, will be a disclosure of both open and hidden sins: it will be the day of total manifestation.

This revelation will include even the words that one has spoken. So says Jesus, "I tell you, on the day of judgment men will render account for every careless[36] word they utter; for out of[37] your words you will be justified, and out of your words you will be condemned" (Matt. 12:36–37). Like no other statement in the New Testament, this declaration of Jesus expresses the utter and total sensitivity to the minutest evil on the day of judgment. "Care-

[31]The Greek word is *boulas*; "motives" (NASB, NIV); "inward motives" (NEB); "counsels" (KJV).

[32]Or "going before." The Greek word is *proagousai*.

[33]Or "follow after." The Greek word is *epakolouthousin*.

[34]We may recall the fears of the Roman governor Felix as Paul spoke to him: "As he [Paul] was discussing righteousness, self-control, and the judgment to come, Felix became frightened" (Acts 24:25 NASB). It was talk of the coming judgment and doubtless a realization of his own lack of genuine "righteousness" and "self-control" that alarmed Felix.

[35]These words were spoken by Jesus to His disciples in the context of a warning concerning the "leaven of the Pharisees" (v. 1), and are not therefore directly words concerning the day of judgment. However, they point in that direction, as does much else in the same discourse (see especially vv. 5, 8).

[36]The Greek word is *argon*—usually translated "idle" (as in KJV). However, "careless" (RSV, NASB, NIV)—even "thoughtless" (NEB)—seems better to suit the context of *not* "speaking good" (v. 34). "Useless" (NASB mg.) is another possibility.

[37]Substituting "out of" (as in NEB) for "by" (RSV and others). "Out of" (for *ek*) seems preferable in light of verses 34 and 35 where *ek* three times is translated in all versions as "out of."

less" words may scarcely seem evil, yet Jesus had earlier declared, "Let what you say be simply 'Yes' or 'No' [literally, 'Yes, yes,' or 'No, no']; anything more than this comes from evil" (Matt. 5:37). Careless words, idle words, thoughtless words, even excessive words, are actually evil. For each one of these "men will render account" and "out of" them will be justification or condemnation, because God demands absolute integrity in human beings. Moreover, it is not the speech itself but what it represents, namely, the inner being or heart. "For," said Jesus just prior to His words about the day of judgment, "out of the overflow of the heart the mouth speaks" (Matt. 12:34 NIV). Hence, every single word has vital significance, and for every "careless" utterance persons will be accountable on the final day. This again demonstrates the total manifestation not only of inward motives, secret thoughts, and conspicuous sins but also of the verbalizations that occur every day. The words uttered are the outward evidence of one's real being.

Once more, this does not mean that on the day of judgment there will be a weighing of words (any more than deeds) to determine whether a person "makes it" to heaven or hell. For already by what one has spoken, i.e., the overflow of the heart whether evil or good,[38] the nature of the heart has been revealed. Thus whether it belongs to God or not—that is the determinant of one's final destiny. But still, as the outward manifestation of the inward condition of the heart, every careless word will be accounted for on the last day.

Thus on the day of judgment nothing will any longer be hidden. Motives, thoughts, imagination, words, deeds: all will be utterly and finally exposed. In the probing words of Hebrews, "Before him no creature is hidden, but all are open and laid bare to the eyes of him with whom we have to do" (4:13). On the day of judgment what is perceived even now will be made wholly manifest.

Before going farther, we may ask, But will there be no difference between the believer and the unbeliever on the day of judgment? Will the sins of one who belongs to Christ be declared the same as those of an unbeliever? Perhaps the best answer is that, while all sins will be disclosed, in the case of the believer they will be disclosed as *forgiven*. Since the great Judge will be Christ Himself who has borne the sins of the world, totally remitted the sins of His people, and perfected them in holiness, every sin, however small or great, as it is made manifest, will be wholly forgiven. Hence, there will be utterly no sense of guilt or condemnation: rather a fuller magnification than ever of the marvel of His grace. For only when the magnitude of what one has done is fully shown can there be complete rejoicing in His immeasurable love and mercy.[39]

And here these beautiful and reassuring words of Jesus come to mind: "Every one who acknowledges me be-

[38]"The good man out of his good treasure [i.e., the good heart] brings forth good [i.e., good words], and the evil man out of his evil treasure [i.e., the evil heart] brings forth evil [i.e., evil or careless words]" (Matt. 12:35). These words of Jesus immediately follow His statement that "out of the overflow of the heart the mouth speaks."

[39]The realization of the coming manifestation of all sin at the final judgment should also serve as an incentive to live purer lives now. For even though all sins will be manifest as forgiven, we should be challenged now not to add to their number. Anthony A. Hoekema puts it thus: "Believers have nothing to fear from the judgment—though the realization that they will have to give an account of everything they have done, said, and thought should be for them a constant incentive to diligent fighting against sin, conscientious Christian service, and consecrated living" (*The Bible and the Future*, 259).

fore men, I also will acknowledge before my Father who is in heaven" (Matt. 10:32). On the day of judgment, all who have truly acknowledged Christ before the world will likewise be acknowledged by Him who is on the throne. Sins will be manifest but totally forgiven; persons will be standing before the judgment seat but with no condemnation,[40] all acknowledged by the Son to the Father. Indeed, it will be glory!

Now we move on to a third purpose of the day of judgment—the giving of rewards and punishment. In one of the last statements in Revelation the Lord says, "Yes, I am coming soon, and bringing my recompense[41] with me, to requite everyone according to his deeds" (22:12 NEB). The return of Christ will bring the requiting of "everyone," hence good and bad, righteous and unrighteous, believers and unbelievers, each according to his works.

I am not referring to eternal life or death which, as has been noted, is determined in this present life, but to the giving of rewards and punishment for the life yet to come. In this connection the emphasis in Scripture mainly relates to the rewards of the righteous, those who are God's people. This is apparent from an earlier scene in Revelation where the elders in heaven cry forth to God, "The time has come for judging the dead, and for rewarding your servants the prophets and your saints and those who reverence your name, both small and great"[42] (11:18 NIV). This statement is obviously an inclusive one for all believers—and covers "both small and great."

The mention of "small and great" leads us to reflect on the fact that even as on this earth there are levels of Christians[43]—for example, some "least in the kingdom of heaven" and some "great"[44] (Matt. 5:19; cf. 11:11)—so will there be degrees of reward. All believers will equally share eternal life or, to use the language of Revelation, equally dwell in the "new heaven" and the "new earth" (21:1), but the rewards will vary. Jesus said, "In My Father's house are many dwelling places" (John 14:2 NASB). These "mansions" (KJV) could very well correspond to the varying rewards God has for His people. In any event, it is clear that rewards will differ.

Let us recount a few other Scriptures. In the Sermon on the Mount (Matt. 5–7), from which I just quoted the words about the "least" and the "great," Jesus several times speaks of reward.[45] In the first instance, He proclaims a blessing on those who are reviled, persecuted, and vilified on His account and then adds, "Rejoice and be

[40]This is the profound meaning of the statement of our Lord when He said, "He who hears my word and believes him who sent me has eternal life; he does not come into *krisin* [the judgment that condemns] but has passed from death to life."

[41]The Greek word is *misthos*. "Recompense" or "reward" (KJV, NIV, NASB) may refer to either blessing or punishment, though the former is more common in the New Testament. It is apparent in this verse that both are referred to. The background seems to be Isaiah 40:10: "Behold, the Lord God comes with might, and his arm rules for him; behold, his reward is with him, and his recompense before him" (cf. 62:11; Jer. 17:10).

[42]The sentence concludes, "And for destroying those who destroy the earth."

[43]It is noteworthy that in Revelation 11:18 "the prophets" are particularly called God's "servants." Perhaps they are viewed in the text as especially being among the "great."

[44]Of course all true believers equally share in salvation: it is "a great salvation" (Heb. 2:3) for all!

[45]Matthew 5:12, 46; 6:1, 2, 4–6, 16, 18. Incidentally, Jesus makes it clear that the true disciple does not seek a reward or work for one, but it is God's blessing on those who live without display and in faithful obedience.

glad, for your reward is great in heaven" (5:12). In the comparable Sermon on the Plain (Luke 6:17–49), Jesus declares in one place, "Love your enemies, and do good, and lend, expecting nothing in return; and your reward will be great" (6:35). Thus, summing up the two: there will be great reward for those who are persecuted for Christ's sake and those who love their enemies (even their persecutors) and do good, seeking nothing for themselves.

Also there are varieties of rewards. Jesus later declares, "He who receives a prophet because he is a prophet shall receive a prophet's reward, and he who receives a righteous man because he is a righteous man shall receive a righteous man's reward" (Matt. 10:41). There is both "a prophet's reward" and "a righteous man's reward": they are clearly not the same. Moreover, the former probably also signifies a great reward.[46] "A great reward" is promised in Hebrews: "Do not throw away your confidence, which has a great reward" (10:35).[47] Finally, John writes in 2 John about "a full reward": "Look to yourselves, that we lose not those things which we have wrought, but that we receive a full reward" (v. 8 KJV). There is "great reward" for maintaining confidence, and "full reward" in holding firm to what has been accomplished. Thus God has abundant reward for those who persevere in confidence to the very end.

One of the clearest statements about rewards is that set forth in the parable of the "pounds"[48] (Luke 19:11–27). Jesus tells about a nobleman who entrusted a pound each to ten of his servants, telling them, "Trade with [or 'do business with'] these till I come" (v. 13). When the nobleman received his kingdom, he returned and rewarded the servants according to their faithfulness and accomplishment. The servant who gained ten pounds more was told, "Well done, good servant! Because you have been faithful in a very little, you shall have authority over ten cities" (v. 17). Another servant who gained an additional five pounds was placed over five cities. Still another servant, who hid away the pound and earned nothing, was strongly condemned. The nobleman took away the pound and gave it to the servant who had earned the additional ten pounds. Then the nobleman said, "I tell you, that to every one who has will more be given; but from him who has not, even what he has will be taken away" (v. 26). That this parable is about Jesus Himself and His return is unmistakable; also it is clear He is affirming that rewards will be given at that time. The basis will be faithfulness in what has been entrusted to the individual by Christ; and the reward will

[46]Recall also Revelation 11:18, where, in speaking of giving rewards, the elders mentioned "the prophets" before "the saints" (the "righteous man" of Matthew 10?). If we view Revelation 11:18 from the perspective of Matthew 10:41, the prophets with their reward would seem to be in a unique, perhaps higher, category than "righteous" persons in general. (A higher category for the prophets was intimated in note 43 about "the prophets" and "the great.")

[47]That this reward refers to the time of the future advent of Christ is apparent from verse 37: "For yet a little while, and the coming one shall come and shall not tarry."

[48]Or "minas." A mina was worth approximately three months' wages of the ordinary laborer.

vary with the commitment and accomplishment of each person.[49]

Finally, on the matter of rewards at the day of judgment one other Scripture reference calls for attention: 1 Corinthians 3:10–15. In this passage Paul says that the believer's work[50] will be tested on the day of judgment, and if it survives, there will be a reward. The foundation, says Paul, is Jesus Christ, and how a person builds on that, whether "with gold, silver, precious stones, wood, hay, straw, each man's work will become evident; for the day will show it, because it is to be revealed with fire; and the fire itself will test the quality of each man's work.[51] If any man's work which he has built upon it remains, he shall receive a reward" (vv. 12–14 NASB). However, a person's work may be burned up, although he will himself still be saved: "If any man's work is burned up, he shall suffer loss; but he himself shall be saved, yet so as through fire"[52] (v. 15 NASB).

What is striking about this passage is that it depicts fire in relation to the believer. We have already observed that fire will finally consume all evil (the "afflicters," the "man of sin," "the nations" attacking the "beloved city"). But here fire will consume a believer's work if it is "wood, hay, straw"—and the believer himself barely escaping "so as through fire." Thus, if a person's work remains, there is a reward; if not, he can expect no reward.

This is a sobering note for all Christians. How is one building on the foundation of Christ? Are one's works outwardly impressive, but actually without enduring quality? Are they works that give glory to God, or are they works that are self-serving, whatever their semblance? Are they truly "good works" that God has ordained,[53] so that they will endure on that day when the believer stands before Christ? In Revelation a voice cries forth, " 'Blessed are the dead who die in the Lord hence-

[49]In the similar parable of the "talents" of money (Matt. 25:14–30), the servants were given differing amounts (in the parable of the "pounds" each was given the same)—five, two, and one. The first two servants who doubled their amount—to ten and four talents respectively—were rewarded equally: each being "set over much." Hence the stress here lies on faithfulness to the amount entrusted, with the rewards the same. So, unlike the parable of the "pounds," the parable of "talents" is not about varying rewards. However—I would add—the parable does end quite similarly, in that the servant who had hidden his one talent had it taken away and given to the servant who now had ten talents. So in that sense there is reward. Also note the similar words of Jesus: "For to everyone who has will more be given, and he will have abundance; but from him who has not, even what he has will be taken away" (v. 29).

Another parable of faithfulness, found in Matthew 24:45–51, is that of the servant who was set over his master's household. At the master's return he was found faithfully engaged in his responsibilities. Says Jesus, "Blessed is that servant whom his master when he comes will find so doing. Truly, I say to you, he will set him over all his possessions" (vv. 46–47). Thus the reward will be great.

[50]In 1 Corinthians 3:10–15 Paul refers to the believer who is engaged in the work of building (through teaching and other various forms of ministry) and warns against an inadequate building structure. Broadly speaking, Paul's words apply to all believers and the danger of false building or superficial works.

[51]A literal translation, namely, "of what sort each man's work is," may better convey the idea of whether the fire will find "gold, silver, precious stones" or "wood, hay, straw"—that is, "of what sort" it is.

[52]"As one escaping through the flames" (NIV). This translation vividly suggests the picture of a person in a burning house losing all his possessions, escaping with nothing but himself and, even that, "through the flames."

[53]Recall Ephesians 2:10: "good works, which God prepared beforehand, that we should walk in them."

forth.' 'Blessed indeed,' says the Spirit, 'that they may rest from their labors, for their deeds follow them!' " (14:13). Will those deeds that "follow" be "burned up" or remain?

To be saved, thus to meet the Lord as He returns, will indeed be glorious. But to make it only "as through fire" is scarcely God's intention or the believer's highest joy. Certainly if the works are of little or no worth, far better that they be totally burned up than to have them "follow" one any longer. Let even the memory of them be forever erased!

To summarize concerning the rewards of believers: there will be great rewards, lesser rewards, and—for some—no reward. Hence there will be much diversity, even though all will share in the blessedness of the world to come. Such is the grace and justice of the good Lord.

Now let us move on to the matter of recompense for the unrighteous. Are there likewise degrees of punishment? The answer, based on several Scripture passages, is yes.

First, some punishment will be "more tolerable" than other punishment. Jesus, in sending out His disciples, said to them, "If anyone will not receive you or listen to your words. . . . I say to you, it shall be more tolerable[54] on the day of judgment for the land of Sodom and Gomorrah than for that town" (Matt. 10:14–15). Similarly, Jesus, upbraiding the cities of Chorazin, Bethsaida, and Capernaum for their lack of repentance despite His many mighty works done among them, says to the former two: "Woe to you, Chorazin! woe to you, Bethsaida! for if the mighty works done in you had been done in Tyre and Sidon, they would have repented long ago in sackcloth and ashes. But I tell you, it shall be more tolerable on the day of judgment for Tyre and Sidon than for you" (Matt. 11:21–22). And then He reproaches Capernaum: "I tell you that it shall be more tolerable on the day of judgment for the land of Sodom than for you" (v. 24). The heavier judgment in all these cases will be because of their total indifference, even callousness, to the offer of the gospel and to the mighty works of God calling for repentance. As worldly and proud as mercantile Tyre and Sidon were, as morally depraved as the already-destroyed Sodom and Gomorrah were: on the day of judgment their punishment will be more tolerable than those who had been given the opportunity to receive the gospel and callously turned it away.

Second, the punishment of some is described as "greater" than that of others. Jesus warns, "Beware of the scribes,[55] who like to go about in long robes, and love salutations in the market places and the best seats in the synagogues and the places of honor at feasts, who devour widows' houses and for a pretense make long prayers. They will receive the greater condemnation" (Luke 20:46–47; cf. Mark 12:38–40). The scribes and Pharisees will receive greater condemnation than others because these religious leaders, whatever they say about God, are actually hypocrites. Constantly showing false piety, seeking the adulation of others, and being brutal in relation to human need, these persons already marked out for hell[56] will receive a "greater condemnation." The greater condemnation—it is important to stress—is not to be re-

[54]The Greek word is *anektoteron*, "bearable" (NIV, NEB).

[55]Or "scribes" and "Pharisees." Cf., e.g., Matthew 23:5–7, which is addressed to "the scribes and the Pharisees" (v. 2) and contains some of the same language.

[56]Jesus makes their destination clear in these words: "You serpents, you brood of vipers, how are you to escape being sentenced to hell?" (Matt. 23:33).

ceived by worldlings ("sinners" in the obvious sense of the immoral), but by the religious elite who underneath are veritable hypocrites. It does not take much imagination to hear the Lord today say, "Beware of the churchmen who. . . ." It is such who "will receive the greater condemnation."

Third, other Scripture lessons show that some will be punished far more severely than others. Jesus speaks of a servant who has been placed in charge of his master's household. But, thinking his master will not return soon, he begins to beat the other servants, and he himself eats and gets drunk. When the master unexpectedly returns, he (the master) will, first, "cut him to pieces and assign him a place[57] with the unbelievers" (Luke 12:46 NIV). Thus his future destination will be the same as that of "unbelievers," hence hell. Further, this servant who knew his master's will but did not get ready, or do it, "will be beaten with many blows," whereas another who did not know but still did things "deserving punishment will be beaten with few blows" (vv. 47–48 NIV). Thus there will be degrees of severity of punishment in the life to come. Again, when one projects this to the contemporary scene, it is apparent that this particularly applies to a church pastor whose very office is to administer his Lord's "household." Like the first servant, the pastor may know full well his master's will and purpose, even his promise of returning soon, yet heedlessly abuses the flock and gives himself over to self-indulgence. He will not only be destroyed and assigned the unbelievers' miserable lot: he will also be punished very severely. Another pastor, less aware of his master's will and purpose, while also abusing the flock and indulging himself, will receive lesser punishment.

To summarize: There is unmistakable biblical testimony to degrees of punishment. Punishment will be pronounced upon those who callously spurn the offer of the gospel and do not repent, even when God's mighty works are done before their eyes. Again, punishment will be great for those who make a pretense of religious commitment but inwardly are self-seeking and unconcerned about others: the hypocrites of the world. Finally, punishment will be quite severe for those who have a position of responsibility over the Lord's household but, rather than being concerned, are both abusive and negligent.

So we behold that both rewards and punishment will be rendered at the coming day of judgment. The Lord will give to everyone according to what his life and work shows forth. Surely, it is a challenge to all of us to live every day as servants of the Lord, and to be as ready as possible when He returns.

IV. STANDARD

I must now add something about the standard of judgment. What will be the norm by which persons will be judged on that day? Perhaps the briefest answer is to say that judgment will be in accordance with the revealed will and purpose of God. Let us now observe three aspects of this revelation.

A. God's Will as Revealed Inwardly to Every Person

All persons who have ever lived have an internal criterion of right and wrong, namely, that which stems from the law "written on the heart." They may not have the *L*aw (in the sense of the law

[57]Literally, "his lot." The Greek word is *meros*. Cf. Revelation 21:8: "as for the cowardly, the faithless, the polluted, as for murderers, fornicators, sorcerers, idolaters, and all liars, their lot [*meros*] shall be in the lake that burns with fire and brimstone, which is the second death."

given to Israel through Moses), but they have the *l*aw, and by that they will be judged. Let us hear Paul: "When Gentiles [*ethnē*], who do not have the law [i.e., the Law of Moses],[58] do by nature things required by the law, they are a law for themselves, even though they do not have the law, since they show that the requirements of the law are written on their hearts, their consciences also bearing witness,[59] and their thoughts now accusing, now even[60] defending them" (Rom. 2:14–15 NIV). "This will take place," Paul adds, "on the day when God will judge men's secrets through Christ Jesus" (v. 16 NIV). In other words, all people have the law of God—His central will and purpose—engraved on their hearts. To this their consciences will bear witness, and their thoughts will both accuse and defend them on the day of judgment when everything hidden will be brought to light. Thus mankind at large will be judged by the general, internal, revelation of God as their own consciences testify and their own thoughts act as prosecution and defense.[61]

All of this means, accordingly, that no one can escape the bar of judgment. To plead—as some might—that they were never given the Law of God as made known to Moses and Israel will be to no avail. They do have the law in their hearts, and they do have consciences, which are inward monitors; they are responsible for what they do. Moreover, on that final day their own thoughts will sufficiently accuse them and defend them. They will stand before the judgment seat of God self-judged—even as the hiddenmost secrets are probed by the awesome presence of the Lord.

B. God's Will as Revealed Specifically to Israel

Again, let us hear Paul: "All who have sinned without the law will also perish without the law, and all who have sinned under the law [the Law of Moses] will be judged by the law" (Rom. 2:12). Hence, the Jews who were "entrusted with the oracles of God" (3:2) will be responsible for the way in which each one measures up to that trust.

The Jews, or Israelites, therefore, have a far greater measure of responsibility than do the Gentiles, because they were uniquely chosen by God to be the recipients of His commandments. Moreover, the law of God written on the heart of man is not always clear. The conscience—the "fellow witness"—often becomes less and less sensitive, and people having no outward God-given law[62] may increasingly move farther and farther from the truth. In the midst of that human uncertainty God called a people, and through Moses He gave them His Word, His law, not only for themselves but also for the other nations. And since the Jews were

[58]The context shows that Paul is clearly referring to the Old Testament Law, since Jew and Greek are being compared (see Rom. 2:9–10). The NASB here capitalizes "law" as "Law," which, though not in the Greek, is proper. The NEB therefore takes the liberty of translating *nomos*, "law," as "the Law of Moses."

[59]Literally, "bearing witness with" (*symmartyrousēs*). Conscience, accordingly, is "fellow witness."

[60]Or "also"; Greek: *kai*.

[61]The NEB has an interesting translation of the latter part of verse 15: "Their conscience is called as witness, and their own thoughts argue the case on either side, against them or even for them."

[62]There are, of course, innumerable societal laws, and doubtless many bear a significant relationship to the inward law of conscience; however, such societal laws (however described) are not "the oracles of God."

so favored by God, they are also called to a far greater accountability.

On the day of judgment Israel will be judged by the very law God gave them. As Jesus Himself said to the Jews: "Do not think that I will accuse you before the Father; the one who accuses you is Moses, in whom you have set your hope" (John 5:45 NASB). So will Israel stand at the bar of judgment.[63]

C. God's Will as Revealed Through Jesus Christ

One of Jesus' most striking statements about the judgment of the last day is again found in the Gospel of John: "He who rejects me and does not receive my sayings has a judge; the word that I have spoken will be his judge on the last day" (12:48). This statement of Jesus, made just before His passion and directed to all people,[64] emphasizes that His "word," that is, the content of His message, will be the final judge. If a person rejects Christ and does not receive His "sayings," that is, His various words spoken, then the word that is going forth through every saying will be that person's judge on the Last Day.

Thus we now move beyond God's will as inscribed on the heart of every person and the Law given to Israel to the larger declaration that the words of Christ Himself will be the judge. In the Johannine passage this refers, as noted, to those who reject Christ; and this will surely include vast numbers who have spurned the gospel offer. But now, surely, we may add that the word of Christ will also be a judge for those who have accepted Him. Not only will that word judge those who do not receive Christ, but also those who have come to Him in true faith.

Truly Christ's words recorded in the New Testament will be a major criterion of judgment on the last day. The words of the Sermon on the Mount, which alone go far beyond the Old Testament commandments into inward thoughts and motives, will all the more probe the believer on the day of judgment. If the Jew will be judged by his adherence to the Law, which relates largely to external matters—murder, adultery, false vows, etc.—how much more will believers in Christ be judged by His word, which goes to the heart—anger, lust, no vows at all, etc. Even more, perhaps, Christ's words about love for enemies, praying for persecutors, rejoicing in suffering, and on and on, will sound forth on the judgment day. But, of course, the Sermon on the Mount is only a part of what Christ taught His disciples, and it will be His total word that will be heard on the final day. As Jesus said emphatically, "Heaven and earth will pass away, but my words will never pass away" (Matt. 24:35; Mark 13:31; Luke 21:33 NIV).[65] Surely, then, Christ's words will all the more reverberate around His throne as men and nations stand for judgment in His presence.

Beyond Christ's spoken words, as set forth in Scripture, there are also His

---

[63]Of course, I am not speaking here about salvation. No one will be saved by law—Gentile or Jew (or Christian, as I will discuss later). In Paul's words, "No human being will be justified in his [God's] sight by works of the law" (Rom. 3:20). Justification is one thing, judgment another; for although works (the law) cannot save, they are the measure of the judgment that will someday be given.

[64]In the preceding statement Jesus said, "I did not come to judge [or 'condemn'] the world, but to save the world" (v. 47). Thus He is speaking to the world at large.

[65]We may recall in the picture in Revelation, as Christ sits to judge at the Last Judgment, that from His presence "earth and heaven fled away" (20:11 NASB). After this the judgment of the dead occurs. Hence, although heaven and earth pass away, or flee away, Christ's words endure.

deeds. He was "a prophet mighty in deed and word" (Luke 24:19), and His mighty and compassionate deeds (or works) will stand supremely in judgment on that day. What He embodied in His life—total outgoing love for every person from the least to the greatest, friend and foe alike, even to His vicarious death on the cross, bearing the sin and punishment of the world—all this will continue to radiate from His throne. His total deed will be the judgment of all mankind.[66]

Of course, since Christ is the Word of God, it is the unity of word and deed in His person that will make for fullness of judgment. Hence, the ultimate standard, or criterion, will be the very presence of Christ. The Christ of total love and—now I must add—of total holiness will be on the throne. In the Book of Revelation Christ's eyes are described as being "like a flame of fire" (1:14; 19:12). Before those eyes aflame with holiness and love, righteousness and compassion, justice and mercy, all creation will be utterly probed.[67] It will be the presence of Christ—His eyes, His face, His total being—that will ultimately be the judgment of the world. There can be nothing beyond that.

This seems an appropriate place to reflect briefly on the matter of the saints judging the world. I have earlier spoken of the Judge as God in Christ[68]—and that cannot be emphasized too much. However, from Scripture it is also apparent that those who belong to Christ will somehow share in that judging. So in 1 Corinthians 6:2–3 Paul writes, "Do you not know that the saints will judge the world? . . . Do you not know that we are to judge angels?" According to Paul, saints will judge the world—humans and angels. "The world" here refers to those who are unrighteous; and "angels," to those who are evil. Both groups (as we have earlier noted) are reserved for judgment on the Last Day.

This is a staggering picture indeed: saints to judge unrighteous men and women and evil angels! Perhaps it seems out of order in the first place, for have we not already observed that all people—righteous and unrighteous, believers and unbelievers—must stand before the judgment seat of God in Christ? Are not believers objects of judgment rather than judges? The answer, perhaps strangely, is that both are true. I must quickly add, however, in regard to the first (i.e., believers as objects of judgment) that, as we have observed, theirs will be a different kind of judgment. For their sins will not come under the judgment that is condemnation, but under that which belongs to forgiveness. Moreover, they will be openly acknowledged by Christ;[69] and, to use the language of Matthew 25:33, they will be placed at His "right hand." Therefore, the situation of the righteous and that of the unrighteous will be quite different on the day of judgment. Similar to their coming with Christ and His angels in the final destruction of the evil of the world, believers will be with him—

[66]For example, the *words* of Christ about the sheep and the goats and how they are judged by deeds of love (for the hungry, the sick, the imprisoned) will carry all the more weight because of His *deeds*. In Himself Christ was the perfect embodiment of all that He said, and it is this fact that will put the world all the more under judgment.

[67]If it is true that even now "before him no creature is hidden, but all are open and laid bare to the eyes of him with whom we have to do" (Heb. 4:13), how much more will that be fulfilled on the final day of judgment.

[68]See earlier section "The Judge," pages 447–49.

[69]Recall Matthew 10:32: "So every one who acknowledges me before men, I also will acknowledge before my Father."

placed at His "right hand"—on the day of final judgment. Thus, in some way that Scripture does not fully relate, the saints will share in Christ's judgment of the world.

Let us pursue this a bit further. In the Book of Revelation are these words of Jesus: "He who conquers, I will grant him to sit with me on my throne, as I myself conquered and sat down with my Father on his throne" (3:21). We have already considered the latter part of this verse,[70] observing how the Father and the Son share in judgment (there is only one throne, not two). But now we recognize that the first part speaks of the victorious believer who will sit on Christ's throne. This means that he will share in judgment with the Son, even as the Son with the Father! For the throne, as we see it climactically in Revelation 20:11–15, is the throne placed for judgment. And although no one is specifically mentioned aside from "him who sat upon it" (v. 11), we may surely believe that even as Christ sits with the Father—"with my Father"—so will we sit with Him on His throne in fulfillment of His promise. This pictorial language of one throne upon which sits the Father, the Son, and believers is impossible to bring into focus. But when this is understood as symbolic language for sharing in judgment, everything becomes quite clear. Christ Himself will uniquely be the Judge, but somehow we will be associated with Him.

As I said before, the Scriptures do not relate how this judging by the saints will take place. So far as we can tell (to review for a moment), believers will at the outset stand with all other persons before the judgment seat. After they have given account and their sins have been declared forgiven, they will then be associated with the Lord, who is the Judge, in the judging of all others who are gathered in His awesome presence. How they will do this is simply not described. Let us, however, try humbly and reverently to surmise a bit.

First, remember that the saints who stand before the throne will already have been made perfect in holiness.[71] Thus they will have unimpeded discernment of all that is evil, and be able to join fully in Christ's judging. Even in this life, according to Paul, "the spiritual man judges all things, but is himself to be judged by no one . . . [for] we have the mind of Christ" (1 Cor. 2:15–16). How much more will this be a reality on judgment day when, with every trace of sin removed and therefore operating fully with "the mind of Christ," the believer "judges all things"!

Second, the righteous, the saints, who will share in Christ's judgment, were *all* once unrighteous, sinners away from God. They not only will have been tempted in every point as was their Lord but they will also have committed every sin known to mankind. On the same judgment day, as I have commented, the saints will have had to account for each and every sin. While gloriously proclaimed "forgiven," they will be quite aware of the sins and evils of the human race. Hence, they will have an experiential knowledge of every sin judged, and therefore will be able to add this dimension to the overall judgment of Christ.

Third, the judgment by the saints on that Last Day will not only be a matter of their discernment of all human evil so as to pronounce judgment verbally, but it will also be a matter of their very presence. In this life it is already a fact that in the presence of saints the unrighteous often sense themselves judged. We may recall the demoniacs

[70]See note 5.

[71]At their death or translation. See supra.

who cried out to Jesus, who had not spoken a word: "What have you to do with us, O Son of God? Have you come here to torment us before the time?"[72] (Matt. 8:29). Jesus' holy and righteous presence *was* their judgment already. He did not come to torment or condemn, but to save; yet His presence already was their judgment. So on the day of judgment it will, of course, be supremely true of Christ—from whose presence "earth and heaven fled away"—that there will be awesome judgment before any word is spoken.[73] In such a way, but of course to a lesser degree, all the unrighteous and unforgiven will be judged by the holy, pure, and righteous presence of the saints.

Now a final word about the angels and their judgment. "We are to judge angels" (1 Cor. 6:3), Paul declares. On first thought this may seem strange, even quite disproportionate: *humans* to judge *angels*? Are human beings not lower than angels by virtue of their creation? Would it not be more proper—if others than Christ are to be involved—for fellow angels to do the judging? For a vast host of blessed, unfallen angels indeed will have come with Christ to gather the elect and to wreak destruction on evil. Why would they not, then, along with the saints, be much involved on the day of judgment when both people and angels will be judged? Yet, despite such possible questions, angels simply are not depicted in the Bible as participating in the coming judgment.[74]

One further question may be asked: Since angels will not be involved in judging their fellow angels, why does not Christ judge angels alone without man? No scriptural answer is directly available; so here, even more than in the matter of how or why the saints will judge the world, we can only venture with much hesitation. I will suggest three answers. First, while it may seem inappropriate for saints to be judging angels, since human beings are on a lower level of creation, believers will be so changed on the day of resurrection as, in Jesus' words, to become "like angels in heaven" (Matt. 22:30). Hence, while lower *now*, believers will not be lower *then*.[75] They will be present in their spiritual bodies judging those who are spirits.[76] And since believers will be like Christ Himself, who will be present in His glorified body, they will stand with Him above the angels, bringing judgment to bear. Second, the saints will not be judging angels simply as

[72]I.e., before the coming day of judgment and punishment (see NASB mg.).

[73]Many standing there will also have experienced the coming of Christ in "flaming fire" (recall 2 Thess. 1:7) in their destruction; now raised from the dead, they will be facing the same Holy One again.

[74]Daniel writes, "As I looked, thrones were placed and one that was ancient of days [or 'the Ancient of Days'] took his seat, his raiment was white as snow, and the hair of his head like pure wool [cf. Rev. 1:14]; his throne was fiery flames . . . a thousand thousands served him, and ten thousand times ten thousand stood before him; the court sat in judgment, and the books were opened" (7:9–10). In this depiction of the day of judgment, angels—myriads of them—are shown to be present. But when it comes to judgment, this "was given to the saints" (v. 22 KJV). The angels serve and stand before "the Ancient of Days," but it is the court (i.e., the saints) that sits in judgment. Possibly "the thrones" that "were placed" likewise refers to the saints (see the earlier discussion of "throne" and "thrones").

[75]Hebrews 2:7 contains the words freely quoted from Psalm 8: "Thou didst make him [man] for a little while lower than the angels." If "a little while" (*brachu ti*)—as found in RSV, NASB, and NEB (also NIV mg.)—is the proper translation (both Thayer and BAGD concur that it is), then it is quite likely that the "little while" will end with the resurrection and glorification of the saints.

[76]In Hebrews 1:14 angels are called "spirits" (*pneumata*).

angels but as sinful and fallen angels. Thus whatever distance there might be between angels and people in their creation, there is no distance in relation to matters of sin and fall. The judging saints will be those who came from a fallen and sinful human race; thus they will have known experientially, not angelic nature, but angelic evil. And it is the latter, not the former, that will be the arena of judgment. Third, if the angels in their fall (as described in 2 Peter 2:4 and Jude 6) are the background for, and possible instigation of, the fall of man through Satan,[77] then they all the more deserve to stand not only before the judgment seat of Christ but also before redeemed humanity whom they formerly had helped to despoil. Their judgment and eternal punishment will show forth all the more vividly under the impact of having to be present before the saints at the throne of Christ.

V. SIGNIFICANCE

Finally, let me add a word about the significance of the Last Judgment. Here three statements are in order.

First, the very fact that it is called the Last Judgment implies former judgment. Indeed, this may be noted primarily by the fact that Christ in His first coming has already rendered a decisive judgment upon the world. "Now," declares Jesus, "is the judgment of this world" (John 12:31). Long before the Last Judgment, the world was being judged. Indeed, Jesus says, "For judgment I came into this world," adding, "that those who do not see may see, and that those who see may become blind" (John 9:39). While He was on the earth Jesus through His life and ministry brought about judgment. Many who had not seen before (i.e., were blinded by sin and evil) came to see; others who claimed to see, particularly the scribes and Pharisees, were blinded in their opposition. Thus a decisive judgment was rendered upon mankind in His first coming; the world was being judged by its reaction to Him. In regard to those who turned from Him, Jesus had earlier said, "This is the judgment,[78] that the light has come into the world, and men loved darkness rather than light, because their deeds were evil. For every one who does evil hates the light, and does not come to the light, lest his deeds should be exposed" (John 3:19–20). Evil persons were exposed already by their hatred of the light, namely Christ,[79] their judgment unto condemnation[80] being manifest in Jesus' presence among them. On the other hand, adds Jesus, "He who does what is true comes to the light, that it may be clearly seen that his deeds have been wrought in God" (John 3:21). By Jesus' first advent people were judged: those of evil deeds turned away from Him; those who practiced truth came to Him.[81] So did the ways divide; so did Christ bring judgment into the world.

---

[77]Jesus speaks of "the eternal fire prepared for the devil and his angels" (Matt. 25:41). The Devil is the head of the evil angels and therefore quite possibly led them in the rebellion in which they "did not keep their own domain" (Jude 6 NASB). It is that same spirit of pride and rebellion that entered into the human race at the beginning through Satan.

[78]Or "condemnation" (as in KJV). The Greek word again is *krisis* (see earlier footnote discussion). The "judgment" accordingly is a judgment to condemnation.

[79]Jesus declares in another place: "I am the light of the world" (John 8:12).

[80]See note 78.

[81]This does not mean that Christ's coming was *only* to make evil and good manifest. If that were the case, there would be no salvation: the dark would remain dark and the light light.

The climactic judgment of the world in Jesus' first advent came about in His crucifixion and death. His words "Now is the judgment of this world" were spoken just before His apprehension in Gethsemane, His trial before the Jewish high court and Roman authorities, and His torturous death on the cross. Men presumed to judge Christ as a blasphemer, an anarchist, and an evil force that had to be destroyed. But actually in the whole process they themselves were being judged, exposed by Him in all their abysmal evil. The Jews, the Romans, the Sanhedrin, Herod, and Pilate were on trial, not Christ, and proved that they, not Christ, deserved only condemnation and death. "*Now* is the judgment of this world."

And the world through its history, since Christ walked upon the earth, continues to be judged. It was not only to persons in Jesus' own time that He was speaking in John 3 and 9, but to people of every century since then. *The decisive judgment is rendered in this life* by the way people and nations respond to Christ, the Light of the world. The coming judgment on the last day, as emphasized before, will not be the determinant of people's destinies. That will already have been decided by their response to Christ in the present life. Thus the world is continually being judged,[82] even until the final day.

In a broad sense the entire world stands under the judgment of Jesus Christ. His whole manner of life—His total holiness and righteousness, His utter love and compassion, His constant truth and faithfulness, everything about Him including His words and His deeds—is a brilliant light that exposes the world in all its unholiness, lovelessness, and departure from truth. In a comprehensive way every moment, every occasion, every event in history stands before the bar of Christ: "Now"—every now—"is the judgment of this world."

Second, the Last Judgment will be the final separation of good from evil. Although judgment in this world has already occurred in the sense of ultimate decision having been made, it will only be at the Last Judgment that this will be fully manifest. During the present age, between Christ's first and second advent, good and evil remain intermingled; in Jesus' own imagery, the wheat with tares, the good fish with the bad. Indeed, there is no way we can know for certain which is which. Moreover, even if there were assured knowledge, and the righteous desired to remove the unrighteous, this would not be possible. In reference to the wheat and the tares and the question whether the latter should be gathered now, Jesus replied, "No; lest in gathering the weeds [tares] you root up the wheat along with them" (Matt. 13:29). Good and evil are so closely intermingled in every area of this world, including the church itself, that to extirpate all evil would also be to uproot the good! This does not mean there are no righteous ("the wheat"), for in Christ there surely are. But the righteous must live now in the matrix of an unrighteous world that cannot be removed or destroyed without detriment to their own existence.

Rather, those who through faith in Christ (John 3:16–18 precedes John 3:19–21!) come to the light are those who enter into eternal life; they thereby become "sons of light" (cf. John 12:36).

[82]Friedrich Schiller's words come to mind: "The history of the world is the judgment of the world." Not, I would submit, that *history* is the judge, but that throughout all history *judgment* is occurring.

Hence, the problem exists of not fully knowing who are the righteous and who are the unrighteous[83] and, even if this were known, of being able to separate the one from the other. Therefore, in the words of Jesus, "Let both grow together until the harvest" (Matt. 13:30).

Thus at the Last Day the separation will finally occur. We live now in the time of God's forbearance, of God's permitting the admixture to exist. But the day will come when total separation will be made: wheat from tares, good fish from bad fish, sheep from goats. Judgment will be discrimination and discernment manifested, but it will also be total and final separation.[84] The present state of uncertainty and inconclusiveness will be forever done away, and God will be wholly vindicated.[85]

On this latter point of God's vindication, we may sometimes wonder how and why God puts up so long with this continuing evil. How can He, in His holiness, bear it; why does He not end it all immediately? Has not evil been around long enough, ever seeking to corrupt the good? Why so much delay in the coming of the long-promised day of the Lord? Perhaps Peter speaks most directly to this line of questioning: "Do not ignore this one fact, beloved, that with the Lord one day is as a thousand years, and a thousand years as one day. The Lord is not slow about His promise as some count slowness, but is forbearing toward you, not wishing that any should perish, but that all should reach repentance. But the day of the Lord will come. . ." (2 Peter 3:8–10). The marvelous forbearance of the Lord, His longsuffering patience, His yearning for the repentance and salvation of all people—yes, He permits things to continue for a few "days" (= perhaps thousands of years)—but it will surely end someday. Then will come the judgment, the final separation of good from evil—and God will be glorified.

Third, and finally, every person should see vital significance in the prospect of the coming day of judgment. We live today in such an atmosphere of this-worldliness that many are deluded into thinking either that death ends it all, hence there is no judgment to come, or that God in His kindness will take everyone into bliss and happiness, hence no serious judgment is to be expected.[86] But we have seen how different the biblical picture is; both Old and New Testaments strongly emphasize the day of the Lord as the coming

[83]Of course, I speak from the human perspective. God fully knows those who are His own.

[84]*Krinō* means primarily to "separate, distinguish" (BAGD). *Krisis*, usually translated "judgment" or "condemnation" (supra), may also convey the note of separation. According to BAGD, *krisis* in John 3:19 "has in addition to the senses 'judgment' and 'condemnation' the clear connotation of 'separation, division.' "

[85]"Just as the resurrection puts an end to death, so judgment terminates the state of confusion and anxiety, of inconclusiveness . . . if there is no judgment, it means that God does not take his own will seriously" (Emil Brunner, *Eternal Hope*, 175).

[86]Popular thinking today seems to move between these two: either that there is nothing to fear after death because a person ceases to be, or that everything will be fine, even beauty and peace. In regard to the latter, one is reminded of many popular accounts today of presumed "after-death" experiences in which the spirit is said to hover for a time over the dead body, and after that—so some claim—goes through a dark tunnel but into light beyond that. Such illusions—for they are that—need to be done away in view of such scripture as we find in Hebrews 9:27: "It is appointed for men to die once, and after that comes judgment."

day of judgment.[87] Thus this should motivate us to urgently warn unbelievers of what will surely come to pass, that although God is now forbearing, repentance is needed before it is too late. Paul sharply challenges the person who may think lightly of God's kindness and pay little heed to the call for repentance and to the warnings of the severity of coming judgment: "Do you presume upon[88] the riches of his kindness and forbearance and patience? Do you not know that God's kindness is meant to lead you to repentance? But by your hard and impenitent heart you are storing up wrath for yourself on the day of wrath when God's righteous judgment will be revealed" (Rom. 2:4–5). In the spirit of Paul this should be our message to any who trifle with the things of God and their own ultimate accountability to Him.

But the last word I reserve for believers. What should the coming day signify to them? Primarily, it is a day to look forward to for a number of reasons: (1) Everyone who truly belongs to Christ—who hungers and thirsts after righteousness[89]—yearns for the day when righteousness will be wholly present and evil totally separated from it. (2) The Judge sitting in judgment will be none other than the One who has died for every person, even submitted Himself to the fearsome wrath of God the Father, and has become the believer's Savior and Lord; hence, there can be no fear or anxiety but only comfort[90] in the expectation of beholding Him on His glorious throne. (3) It will be a day of rewards for those who have remained faithful; therefore even now we may look forward with keen anticipation to what He will give. (4) Since believers will assist Christ in judging both unrighteous angels and human beings, this extraordinary fact, and the way it will be accomplished, is surely a matter of high expectation. (5) It will be the great transitional event that leads to the "new heaven" and "new earth," to the fulfillment of Christ's kingdom, and to dwelling with God perfectly and forever. To be present and a part of this vast transition is truly beyond all comprehension, but we can rejoice in the assurance that through God's great love we will share in it.

Now I must also speak of the other side—not to create fear or foreboding, but to emphasize the seriousness of the high calling as believers that God has given us now. Since He has entrusted much to us, He does expect faithfulness and commitment until the very end. As we have seen, the believer's works are very important: if they are "hay," "wood," or "straw," they will be burned up. Thus, even now in light of that future possibility, we should ever seek to do those things that give honor and glory to God. At the worst extreme,

---

[87]This was surely emphasized in the early church. As James Denney has well said, "It is impossible to overestimate the power of the final judgment, as a motive, in the primitive church" (*Studies in Theology*, 240–41).

[88]The Greek word is *kataphroneis*—"think lightly of" (NASB, NEB), "show contempt for" (NIV), "despise" (KJV).

[89]"Blessed are they which do hunger and thirst after righteousness" (Matt. 5:6 KJV).

[90]In the Heidelberg Catechism one of the questions (Q. 52) is, "What comfort does the return of Christ 'to judge the living and the dead' give you?" The answer: "That in all affliction and persecution I may wait with head held high the very Judge from heaven who has already submitted himself to the judgment of God for me and has removed all the curse from me; that he will cast all his enemies and mine into everlasting condemnation, but he shall take me, together with all his elect, to himself into heavenly joy and glory." This statement of over four hundred years ago well sums up some of the things said above, even if somewhat quaintly phrased!

if we are *knowingly* faithless to what God has given us (our responsibility in relation to the Lord's household, our stewardship of "talents" and possessions), there can only be the expectation of terrifying judgment: "a fearful prospect of judgment."[91] But of this, praise God, we need not fear if day by day we seek to remain His faithful disciples and fulfill His calling in our lives.

Someday the words will ring forth: "Fear God and give him glory, for the hour of his judgment has come" (Rev. 14:7). May we ever be ready for that announcement, and hail the occasion with joy and thanksgiving.

EXCURSUS: THE STATE OF THE LOST

Before leaving this discussion of the Last Judgment and beginning a consideration of the consummation in the new heaven and new earth, we should take a further look at the final state of the lost. Several times I have commented that the Last Judgment will not be for the purpose of determining that state; rather, it will be for the exhibition of the righteousness of God's prior decision in condemning the unrighteous, for the total revelation of what is in every person, and for the giving of rewards and punishment. The unrighteous are already lost before the day of judgment and will thereafter continue in that condition. Now let us reflect on their state.

Darkness and Fire

Two figures of speech are used to describe the state of the lost: *darkness* and *fire*. Let us consider each in turn.

A number of times Jesus speaks of "outer darkness." In the Gospel of Matthew He declares, "Many will come from east and west and sit at table with Abraham, Isaac, and Jacob in the kingdom of heaven, while the sons of the kingdom will be thrown into outer[92] darkness; there men will weep and gnash their teeth" (8:11–12). Here "sons of the kingdom" refers to unbelieving Jews, who, despite their traditional status as "sons," will be cast into the darkness outside the kingdom. Again, Jesus speaks of a certain man who came to a marriage feast without wearing a wedding garment. As a result, the king who gave the feast said to his servants, "Bind him hand and foot, and cast him into the outer darkness; there men will weep and gnash their teeth" (Matt. 22:13). The lack of a wedding garment signifies no appropriate repentance and change of life even though present at the feast of the Lord; such a person will be totally cast out. A third account is that of a man who buried the Lord's talent in the ground. About him the master will declare, "Cast the worthless servant into the outer darkness, there men will weep and gnash their teeth" (Matt. 25:30).

Before reflecting further on this "outer darkness," we should observe that the condition of natural man *already* is darkness. So Jesus declares, "I have come as light into the world, that whoever believes in me may not remain in darkness" (John 12:46). Not to believe in Christ, therefore, is to remain in darkness, both now and in the life to come. Paul says that God "has delivered us from the dominion of darkness and transferred us to the kingdom of his beloved Son" (Col. 1:13), and Peter describes God's people as "called . . . out of darkness into his marvelous light" (1 Peter 2:9). Clearly those not

---

[91]The language of Hebrews 10:27 relating to the believer.

[92]The Greek word is *exōteron*. BAGD translates it as "farthest, extreme," hence in relation to darkness, "the darkness farthest out."

"delivered" and "called out" are in darkness and by implication will remain there both now and in the world to come.

In specific reference to the future life Peter, describing people involved in a variety of debasing sins, says, "For them the nether gloom of darkness[93] has been reserved" (2 Peter 2:17). Jude similarly speaks of those "for whom the nether gloom of darkness has been reserved for ever" (Jude 13). This "nether gloom of darkness" is doubtless equivalent to the "outer darkness," the darkness farthest out, to which Jesus refers.

Incidentally, the word "outside" is used in the Book of Revelation to locate all people who are not finally found in the holy city:[94] "Outside are the dogs,[95] those who practice magic arts, the sexually immoral, the murderers, the idolaters and everyone who loves and practices falsehood" (22:15 NIV). The holy city is radiant with light and glory, while outside there is only darkness and gloom. Such is the final state of the lost.

What these Scriptures say is that the situation of the lost is one of continuing darkness, from this life into the next. Another word from Jesus: "I am the light of the world; he who follows me will not walk in darkness, but will have the light of life" (John 8:12). *Not* to follow Christ, who is the true light, is not only to walk in darkness now but also in the life to come. It means to continue in a state of separation from God; however, in the final state the separation will be total. Not a flicker of light will be there to relieve the utter darkness.

This darkness is far more than a physical reality. It is existence totally removed from God, from Christ. On one occasion Jesus declares that on the final day He will say to some of His own professed followers: "I never knew you; depart from me, you evildoers" (Matt. 7:23). Departure from Christ and estrangement from God is the state of the lost. It is to exist in "the nether gloom" of eternal darkness.

Jesus in His recorded teaching also speaks often of fire in connection with man's final condition. In the Sermon on the Mount Jesus warns against "the hell of fire": "Whoever says, 'You fool!' shall be liable to the hell[96] of fire" (Matt. 5:22). Later in His parable of the wheat and the tares (or weeds), Jesus speaks of "the furnace of fire": "Just as the weeds are gathered and burned with fire, so will it be at the close of the age . . . they [angels] will gather out of his kingdom all causes of sin and all evildoers, and throw them into the furnace of fire; there men will weep and gnash their teeth" (Matt. 13:40–42). Similarly in His parable of the dragnet, Jesus declares, "The angels will come out and separate the evil from the righteous, and throw them into the furnace of fire; there men will weep and gnash their teeth" (vv. 49–50). Yet again Jesus speaks about cutting off

---

[93]Or "black darkness" (NASB), "blackest darkness" (NIV, NEB). According to BAGD, in connection with Greek thought, "the Darkness of the nether regions."

[94]See the discussion of the holy city in the next chapter.

[95]The Greek word is *kynes*, literally "dogs"; however, according to Thayer, *kyōn* metaphorically is "a man of impure mind." Another possible meaning is "sodomites."

[96]The Greek word is *geenna*, often translated "gehenna" (Gehenna). The word *geenna* occurs twelve times in the New Testament, all except one (in James 3:6) being on the lips of Jesus in the Synoptic Gospels. Gehenna originally was the rubbish pit outside Jerusalem that was always burning, hence "the gehenna of fire." Thus it came to symbolize the final state of the unrighteous. Indeed, the word *geenna* may stand alone, without fire, as in some later statements of Jesus in Matthew 5:29–30 that speak of the "whole body" being "thrown into hell" or going "into hell."

one's hand or foot or plucking out one's eye if it causes one to sin rather than "with two hands or two feet to be thrown into the eternal fire" or "with two eyes to be thrown into the hell of fire" (Matt. 18:8–9). In the parallel Markan passage the fire is described as unquenchable: ". . . to go to hell, to the unquenchable fire . . . where their worm does not die, and the fire is not quenched" (9:44, 48). Finally, in Matthew are these words of Jesus concerning the day of judgment: "Then he will say to those at his left hand, 'Depart from me, you cursed, into the eternal fire prepared for the devil and his angels'" (25:41).

In the Book of Revelation is this vivid statement: "If any one worships the beast and its image, and receives a mark on his forehead or on his hand . . . he shall be tormented with fire and brimstone in the presence of the holy angels and in the presence of the Lamb. And the smoke of their torment goes up for ever and ever; and they have no rest, day or night" (14:9–11). Again: "If any one's name was not found written in the book of life, he was thrown into the lake of fire" (20:15). Finally: "The cowardly, the unbelieving, the vile, the murderers, the sexually immoral, those who practice magic arts, the idolaters and all liars—their place will be in the fiery lake of burning sulfur. This is the second death" (21:8 NIV).

All of these scriptures about fire—"the hell of fire," "the furnace of fire," "fire and brimstone," "the lake of fire"—unmistakably depict the state of the lost as one of torment.[97] It is obvious that a garbage pit (hell),[98] a furnace, and a lake are different figures and therefore cannot be taken literally. This, however, does not detract from what such imagery points to—a condition of vast misery. For "fire" is the constant in all these expressions, and fire signifies burning and torment.

These two terms, "darkness" and "fire," that point to the final state of the lost might seem to be opposites, because darkness, even black darkness, suggests nothing like fire or the light of blazing fire. Thus again we must guard against identifying the particular terms with literal reality, such as a place of black darkness or of blazing fire. Rather, darkness and fire are metaphors that express the profound truth, on the one hand, of terrible estrangement and isolation from God, and on the other, the pain and misery of unrelieved punishment. It is significant that Jesus in His portrayals of darkness and fire often adds the statement "There men will weep and gnash their teeth."[99] This weeping and gnashing (or "wailing and grinding" NEB) of teeth vividly suggests both suffering and despair. So whether the metaphor is darkness or fire, the picture is indeed a grim one, even beyond the ability of any figure of speech to express.[100]

---

[97]Recall also picture of the callous rich man described by Jesus as "in Hades, being in torment." "Hades" here signifies the intermediate condition of the unrighteous, whereas Gehenna invariably points to the final state. Nonetheless, whether after death or the final judgment, "torment" is the lot.

[98]See note 94.

[99]In regard to "outer darkness," recall Matthew 8:12; 22:13; 25:30. Regarding "fire," recall Matthew 13:42, 50.

[100]Calvin writes, "Because no description can deal adequately with the gravity of God's vengeance against the wicked, their torments and tortures are figuratively expressed to us by physical things, that is, by darkness, weeping, and gnashing of teeth . . . unquenchable fire, an undying worm gnawing at the heart. By such expressions the Holy Spirit certainly intended to confound all our senses with dread. . . . So we ought especially to fix our

One further word: both darkness and fire refer to the basic situation of the lost after the Last Judgment. However, we have already observed that there will be degrees of punishment, hence in some sense the darkness and fire will not be wholly the same. Some punishment will be more tolerable than other punishment: some people will receive a greater condemnation, while some (to change the figure) will be "beaten with few blows."[101] Thus we should not understand the overall picture of the state of the lost to exclude differences in degree of punishment. Even as for the righteous in the world to come, there will be varying rewards, so for the unrighteous the punishment will not be the same.

Eternal and Final

The state of the lost is an eternal one, and the condition is final.

Frequently the Bible stresses the *eternal* state of the lost. We have already noted various statements that reveal this eternal character, such as the "nether gloom of darkness . . . reserved for ever" and being "thrown into the eternal fire." Thus the state of the lost is everlasting.

This is borne out particularly in the concluding words of Christ at the Last Judgment as recorded in Matthew 25: "They [the unrighteous] will go away into eternal punishment, but the righteous into eternal life" (v. 46). The word "eternal"[102] is used for both the righteous and the unrighteous: even as the righteous are eternally blessed, so the unrighteous will undergo eternal punishment. One state is just as eternal as the other.

Next, let us observe that in speaking about "those who refuse to acknowledge God and . . . those who will not obey the gospel of our Lord Jesus," Paul adds, "They will suffer the punishment of eternal ruin,[103] cut off from[104] the presence of the Lord and the splendour of his might" (2 Thess. 1:8–9 NEB). The ruin that is eternal goes along with being cut off from the presence of the Lord. Rather than continuing blessedness in the life to come, there will be nothing but an existence of ongoing ruination and misery.

We now need to look at one statement of Jesus that might suggest, not eternal continuance, but annihilation at death. Jesus declares, "Do not fear those who kill the body, but are unable to kill the soul; but rather fear Him[105] who is able to destroy both soul and body in hell" (Matt. 10:28 NASB). However, the word translated "destroy"[106] is set in contrast to "kill," and means to

thoughts upon this: how wretched it is to be cut off from all fellowship with God" (*Institutes of the Christian Religion*, 3.25.12, Battles trans.).

[101]Luke 12:48 (NIV). Recall our earlier discussion on pages 457–58.

[102]The Greek word is *aiōnion*. The KJV translates the first *aiōnion* as "everlasting" and the second as "eternal." This may unfortunately give the impression that there is some kind of temporal difference between the two final states.

[103]The KJV, RSV, NIV, and NASB have "destruction." The Greek word is *olethron*. Thayer defines it as "ruin, destruction, death," then adds in relation to 2 Thessalonians 1:9: "the loss of a life of blessedness after death, future misery." *Olethron* therefore is better translated "ruin" or "ruination" rather than "destruction," which too readily suggests annihilation. "Eternal annihilation" is obviously self-contradictory.

[104]The RSV reads "and exclusion from"; NIV, "shut out from"; NASB, "away from"; KJV, "from." The Greek text simply has the word *apo*, "from"; however, the text does not mean that eternal ruin comes from the Lord (as KJV may suggest) but *away from* (cut off from, etc.).

[105]"Him" refers to God. Accordingly, NASB capitalizes it.

[106]The Greek word is *apolesai*, from *apollymi*.

"give over to eternal misery"[107] or to "subject to the torments of hell."[108] To view "destroy" as to annihilate is contrary to both the intention of Jesus' words and the larger context.[109]

I add here a word about "annihilationism." This is the view that the unrighteous, rather than having to endure everlasting punishment, will be annihilated (i.e., reduced to nonexistence) in the age to come. Such expressions as "destruction" and "second death" are understood as the obliteration of the unrighteous; hence there is no continuing lost condition.[110] Such a view lacks biblical support and has never had credal or confessional status in the church.[111]

One further comment about the word "destruction." I have previously discussed the purpose of the return of Christ for both "final redemption" and "total destruction."[112] "Total destruction," we have observed, refers to the slaying of all the "earth-dwellers," but

[107]Thayer, in relation to Matthew 10:28, so defines *apollymi*: "metaphorically, to devote or give over to eternal misery."

[108]H. R. Ridderbos, *Matthew*, 206. Ridderbos points out that "the words 'destroy in hell' do not mean annihilate," for "if they did, the word 'kill' in the first part of the verse would simply have been repeated" (p. 206).

[109]E.g., the verb *apollymi* is used in Matthew 9:17 where Jesus says, "Neither is new wine put into old wineskins; if it is, the skins burst, and the wine is spilled, and the skins are destroyed" (*apollyntai*). The wineskins surely are not annihilated. The NIV and NASB translation of *apollyntai* in Matthew 9:17 as "ruined" makes this much clearer. According to W. E. Vine, after stating that *apollymi* "signifies to destroy utterly," adds, "The idea is not extinction but ruin, loss, not of being, but of well-being" (*Expository Dictionary of New Testament Words*, 1:302). Robert A. Morey writes, "In every instance where the word *appollymi* is found in the New Testament, something other than annihilation is being described" (*Death and the Afterlife*, 90). It might also be pointed out that in Luke 12:5, the parallel passage to Matthew 10:28, the word *apollymi* is not used at all; rather, the language is "to cast into [*embalein*] hell."

[110]One form of annihilation is known as "conditional immortality." This view is that immortality will be granted only to those who believe in Christ; all others pass out of existence at death. Annihilationism proper, on the other hand, affirms the natural immortality of human beings, but declares that God will obliterate the unrighteous following the day of judgment and possibly after some time of punishment. Practically speaking, the two views end in the same result: there will be no eternal state of the lost.

Annihilationism is affirmed particularly by Jehovah's Witnesses and Seventh-day Adventists. A strong defense of annihilationism (designated as "conditionalism") may be found in E. W. Fudge, *The Fire That Consumes*. Some noted evangelicals have lately begun to favor some form of annihilationism. John Stott, for example, after exploring a number of relevant Scriptures, writes, "I . . . believe that the ultimate annihilation of the wicked should at least be accepted as a legitimate, biblically founded alternative to their eternal conscious torment" (David L. Edwards, *Evangelical Essentials: A Liberal Evangelical Dialogue*, with a Response from John Stott, 320). Philip E. Hughes speaks of "the abyss of obliteration" into which the wicked will plunge (*The True Image: The Origin and Destiny of Man in Christ*, 407). However, as much as one might like it to be so, neither annihilation nor obliteration is a biblical concept. For a careful study and refutation of annihilationism, see Morey, *Death and the Afterlife*, especially chapter 8, "Annihilationism." Some valuable brief comments contra annihilationism by J. I. Packer may be found in Kenneth S. Kantzer and Carl F. H. Henry, eds., *Evangelical Affirmations*, 123–26.

[111]For example, the Westminster Confession of Faith declares that, following the Last Judgment, "the wicked, who know not God, and obey not the gospel of Jesus Christ, shall be cast into eternal torments, and be punished with everlasting destruction from the presence of the Lord, and from the glory of his power" (chap. 33, "Of the Last Judgment").

[112]Chapter 12.

it does not mean their annihilation.[113] Like all others who previously have died and live on after death, so will they be raised for the Last Judgment and continue to live ever after. In summary, there is no annihilation of either the godly or the ungodly.

It follows that the condition of the lost is *final*. It is a situation of eternal estrangement and misery that has no possibility of future alteration. Accordingly, there can be no ultimate entering into salvation.[114]

Here I must speak about the matter of "universalism." Universalism is the view that ultimately all people will attain salvation. In a popular vein universalism is the outright denial of hell because God is viewed as too good to send anyone there; hence, if there is a heaven, He will surely take everyone in. In pantheistic philosophy, since man is viewed as a part of God or one with God, there is no possibility of a final and ultimate separation from Him. In Hindu religion and the New Age affirmation of reincarnation, there is no once-for-all Last Judgment with eternal consequences to follow. In the Christian tradition "liberal" thinking often moves in the direction of universal salvation, and may seek to claim biblical justification.[115]

In regard to scriptural evidence for universalism, texts frequently quoted are John 12:32: "I, when I am lifted up from the earth, will draw all men to myself"; Acts 3:21, which refers to the future "restoration of all things" (NASB); Romans 5:18, which speaks of "acquittal and life for all men"; 1 Corinthians 15:22: "as in Adam all die, so also in Christ shall all be made alive"; Ephesians 1:10 regarding "a plan for the fulness of time, to unite all things in him [Christ], things in heaven and things on earth"; Philippians 2:10–11: "that at the name of Jesus every knee shall bow, in heaven and on earth and under the earth, and every tongue confess that Jesus Christ is Lord"; Colossians 1:20: "through him to reconcile to himself all things, whether on earth or in heaven"; and Titus 2:11: "the grace of God has appeared for the salvation of all men." What such verses actually declare is *not* universal salvation,[116] but the universal outreach of the gospel (it is not limited to some), the universal applicability of the gospel to all people's need (their death in sin), the universal reconciliation and unity of all things in Christ (in heaven and on earth), and the universal acknowledgment of Jesus as Lord (whether by those in heaven, on earth, or under the earth). The last statement might seem to point to universal salvation, because it also includes those "under the earth"—an expression that

---

[113]See earlier NEB translation of 2 Thessalonians 1:8–9.

[114]This also excludes any idea of a "second chance" to hear the gospel and be saved. See J. M. Frame, "Second Chance," in the *Evangelical Dictionary of Theology*, 991–92.

[115]Universalism is particularly represented on the American church scene by the Unitarian Universalist Association (formed in 1961 by a merger of the Universalist Church of America and the American Unitarian Association). The first Universalist congregation was organized in 1779 in New England by a former Methodist preacher and grew in strength among liberal Congregational clergy. In 1803 Universalists adopted the Winchester Profession of Belief. Since then American universalism has become increasingly liberal in its view of Christ, its approach to other religions, and its close approximation to secular humanism.

[116]The words quoted in Acts 3:21 regarding the future "restoration" [*apokatastaseōs*] of all things have occasionally been regarded as including the universal salvation of mankind. Origen, an early church father, held that the *apokatastasis* included not only mankind but also Satan and his angels! Origen's view of restoration, later condemned by the church at large, has continued in various ways to be represented in universalism. (On *apokatastasis*, see EDT, 87.)

probably relates to the "nether" regions. However, even if the phrase does refer to the underworld of darkness, the acknowledgment of Christ's lordship is best understood as referring not to an act of faith and worship by believers, but to the recognition by even those below that Christ is Lord of all.[117]

Universalism must be faulted for a one-sided biblical approach. The texts just quoted *might* incline one in a universalist direction if there were not many other texts and passages that clearly do not point that way. Scriptures relating to eternal punishment, eternal destruction (or ruination), and the like, do not need to be repeated here.

Universalism is a kind of annihilationism in reverse. Rather than annihilating all the ungodly, the ungodly will all be saved! In neither case is the lost condition a final and eternal one. Actually both views detract from the seriousness of evil in this life. If all people will eventually be annihilated or eventually saved, what one does now makes little ultimate difference. But if the gospel is the good news of salvation *from* eternal perdition as well as into the glories of eternal life, there is much indeed to proclaim!

God's Character and Human Decision

Finally, the continuing state of the lost is the result of both God's character and human decision.

The foundational fact of God's character is His *holiness*.[118] Because of that fact, sin is abhorrent in His eyes. As primary evidence of this, when the first man and woman sinned, not only were they shut out from God's presence but also were all their descendants to the present day. *We* are Adam's sinful and guilty race, and even as we compound that sin, we are on our way to eternal condemnation. The holy God finds intolerable the sinful condition of humanity and reacts forever against it. This is the fundamental reason for the existence of the "outer darkness" to which the human race is consigned and the "eternal fire" of divine punishment. Even *one* sin (as Adam and Eve's one sin vividly attests) is sufficient to bar a person from the eternal presence of God. What more needs to be said about humanity's almost unlimited quantity? Hell is our due, not because God arbitrarily consigns us there, but because His very holy nature eternally repels all that is unholy—unrighteous, impure, unclean.

God also is a God of *love*.[119] It is a love so vast that in Christ God went all the way to save the world from its own self-destruction. "God so loved the world that he gave his only Son, that whoever believes in him should not perish but have eternal life" (John 3:16). The word translated "perish"[120] means "to be delivered up to eternal misery":[121] it was *that* world, *our* world, on the way to eternal darkness and misery that God loved so greatly as to send His Son to redeem it from perdition. In so doing, God in Christ paid the full price on the cross as He became totally identified with mankind's sin and misery, its lostness and continuing damnation. Christ suffered the ravages of God's holy judgment upon Himself—all the punishment that

---

[117]J. J. Müller summarizes Philippians 2:10–11 thus: "Angels and demons, the living and the dead, the saved and the lost will acknowledge Him as Lord, will recognize His Lordship, and confess that he is Lord even as God Himself" (*Epistles of Paul to the Philippians and to Philemon*, NICNT, 897).

[118]For more detail see "God Is Holy," *Renewal Theology*, 1:59–63.

[119]See *Renewal Theology*, 1:63–68.

[120]The Greek word is *apoletai*, again from *apollymi* (see earlier notes 106–7, 109).

[121]Thayer, in connection with John 3:16, so defines *apollymi*.

was our due—in order to set us free. Hence *there is nothing that mankind would ever have to endure that Christ has not already experienced Himself.* There is utterly no way that anyone can begin to contemplate the awful weight of the holy and righteous judgment that Christ took upon Himself. He has received it—in our place.

Thus God at unimaginable cost has done everything in Christ to make our final condition one of eternal joy and blessedness and not of eternal pain and misery. God is thereby *true*[122] to Himself in that both His holiness and His love have been fully and truly expressed through Christ who is "the way, and the *truth*, and the life" (John 14:6), and salvation has been opened to all mankind. Accordingly, in the words of Paul, God is one who "desires all men to be saved and to come to the knowledge of the truth" (1 Tim. 2:4). Such great salvation has made hell necessary for no person.

None of this, however, forecloses its possibility. Eternal separation from God may still recur. But the good and glorious news is that "whoever believes in" Christ will never have to face that grim reality. He will instead enter into eternal life.

I have done this brief review of the gospel to emphasize that a fuller picture of God's character puts all things in perspective. Sometimes the question is seriously raised, How can there be a hell if God is a loving God? If God is loving and compassionate, how could He possibly allow one person to perish forever? The answer should be clear. Although God is loving and compassionate to the uttermost, even to vicariously suffering our sin and punishment, He is also a God of total holiness and righteousness who cannot endure sin and unrighteousness, and therefore must finally banish it from His presence. Only when God is recognized in His full character as holiness and love and truth can both the total emancipation from hell and its continuing reality be understood.

The other side of this continuing state of the lost rests in human *decision*. God Himself has done all things necessary to keep any person from perishing, that is, going to destruction. The one crucial thing on our part is to accept what God has done in Christ as our Substitute, who bore our sin and guilt and fulfilled God's holy and righteous judgment in our place. In a word, it is to "believe" in Christ as our Savior from condemnation and destruction. For, as John 3:18 continues, "Whoever believes in him is not condemned, but whoever does not believe *stands condemned already* because he has not believed in the name of God's one and only Son" (NIV). Hence, one who does not believe in Christ remains under the final condemnation of God. A God of infinite love and holiness has truly wrought salvation for a lost human race. But a person must believe in Christ or else he still stands under condemnation. John 3 closes with these words: "Whoever believes in the Son has eternal life, but whoever rejects[123] the Son will not see life, for God's wrath remains on him" (v. 36 NIV). This statement makes it clear that to hear of Christ and then to reject Him is to stay under God's holy wrath. "God's wrath remains"—thus a fearsome prospect of coming condemnation and destruction.

Here we may ask, But what about

[122]See *Renewal Theology*, 1:68–70.

[123]The Greek word is *apeithōn* (participle), translated "does not obey" in RSV and NASB. However, the NIV rendering above is more likely. Thayer, in connection with John 3:36, translates *apeithōn* as "to refuse or withhold belief." The word "rejects" expresses this well.

those who have never had opportunity to hear about Christ? Do all stand under God's eternal condemnation? It is one thing to say that God's wrath remains on those who spurn what He has done in Christ to save the perishing, but another to say that those who have never heard will be condemned. Will hell be composed also of vast numbers of people who have never heard of Christ? The answer, I suggest, is twofold. First, the Scriptures are clear that there is no salvation outside of Christ. Jesus Himself declares, "I am the way, and the truth, and the life; no one comes to the Father, but by me" (John 14:6). Peter proclaims, "There is salvation in no one else, for there is no other name under heaven given among men by which we must be saved" (Acts 4:12). Paul writes, "There is one mediator between God and men, the man Christ Jesus" (1 Tim. 2:5). So the task and challenge of witnessing to the sole sufficiency of Christ must never be diminished. Second, we should also leave open the possibility of God's mercy in Christ being extended to some who do not outwardly know Him. I say, the *possibility*, based on such words as in John 1:9: "The true light that lightens every man was coming into the world," and 3:21: "He who does what is true comes to the light, that it may be clearly seen that his deeds have been wrought in God." These verses cannot mean that there is salvation outside of Christ. But they do suggest that the light of Christ in some sense lightens every person[124] whether Christ is outwardly known or not, and that there are those whose deeds have already "been wrought in God" prior to their coming to the light.[125] Thus God's grace may extend to persons outside the perimeter of overt gospel proclamation.[126]

Again, on the matter of human decision it is important to recognize that vast numbers of people turn from the light of Christ because of their preference for darkness. John 3 also states, "This is the condemnation, that light is come into the world, and men loved darkness rather than light, because their deeds were evil" (v. 19 KJV). This preference for darkness is seen throughout Jesus' ministry when many people turned against Him who is "the light of the world" (John 8:12). Figuratively speaking, they scurried away into the darkness so they could carry on their evil deeds.

Let us ponder this in terms of the final state of the lost. We have earlier noted that one description of this state is "outer darkness." Also, in several instances the picture is that of being thrown, or cast, into this darkness.

[124]F. F. Bruce writes that "whatever measure of truth men and women in all ages have apprehended has been derived from this source" (*The Gospel of John*, 35).

[125]On this latter point recall the Roman centurion Cornelius, described as "a devout man who feared God with all his household, gave alms liberally to the people, and prayed constantly to God" (Acts 10:2), to whom Peter said, "I perceive that . . . in every nation any one who fears him [God] and does what is right is acceptable to him" (vv. 34–35), and afterward proclaimed the message of salvation (vv. 36–43). The centurion's prior deeds had clearly been "wrought in God."

[126]I am aware of the possible hazards in such a statement, for it might seem to lessen the urgency of proclaiming Christ Himself as the only hope of salvation. However, on the other hand to state bluntly that the countless numbers of people who have never heard the gospel verbally are all consigned to hell seems to go beyond the New Testament message. I am, of course, not speaking here of anything like universal salvation, but rather of the possibility of God's grace *in Christ* reaching beyond the actual gospel proclamation. That this may be the case should not lessen the urgency of proclaiming the gospel, for not only are many far from the light but some who are doing "what is true" are all the more eager to come to the light of Christ when they hear the gospel!

However, the point now to reckon with is that for the lost this is not a new state; *it is rather a continuance in the state they are already in.*[127] To be sure, the condition will become still darker (recall "black darkness"), but it will not be a radical change or even necessarily a condition undesirable to the lost. If people have loved darkness rather than light in the present world, this will hardly change in the world to come. No matter how severe the biblical imagery of darkness, fire, and the weeping and gnashing of teeth, such a condition would be preferable to having to live in the presence of a holy God, holy angels, and holy people.

Strangely enough, hell may be viewed not only as the result of God's holy judgment upon the unsaved, but also as the consequence of His love and mercy. At the beginning of human history God "drove out" (Gen. 3:24) Adam and Eve from the garden of Eden because of their sin. It was an act of God's holiness that punished them with permanent exclusion from His presence. But beyond that, God's mercy was manifest in their exclusion. If man and woman had stayed in Eden, life would have been intolerable—always fleeing from the presence of God, always living in fear and shame. So God let them go—and their "hell" on earth (with drudgery and pain) was more bearable than life in the paradise of God. It follows that hell with all its misery will be less torment for still sinful persons than to have to live eternally in the presence of a holy God and of those who are continually praising His Name.

This may speak further to the relationship between God's holiness and His love. Some object that although the eternal continuance of hell may indeed represent God's holy vengeance against the vastness of evil, it seems to contradict His eternal love and compassion. To reply: a loving and merciful God will never force people into a heaven for which they are totally unfit. He would rather let them go into their own proper habitation. The punishment of hell, whatever its measure, will be far less than the punishment of being in the courts of heaven; the fire of Gehenna far more tolerable than the brilliance of God's face; the outer darkness of the nether world infinitely more bearable than the splendor of heaven's glory. Yes, in the midst of God's holiness His mercy will ever shine forth.

A final word about the love of God. We must always remember that God loves so vastly that in Christ He has already suffered the eternal punishment that is mankind's due, with its terrible darkness, its fiery pain and agony. Christ on the cross stripped and beaten, darkness enshrouding the awesome scene, the agonizing cry of "My God, My God, why hast thou forsaken me?"—all of this represents something of the terrifying reality of what God has endured. Verily, Christ "bore in his soul the tortures of condemned and ruined man."[128] Hell is no reality foreign to God: in Christ He has already experienced the worst that any person will ever have to endure. This truly is love beyond all comprehension.

---

[127]C. S. Lewis writes that a "bad man's perdition" should not be viewed "as a sentence imposed on him but as the mere fact of being what he is" (*The Problem of Pain*, 123).

[128]Words of Calvin (*Institutes*, 2,16.10, Beveridge trans.).

15

The Consummation

We move, finally, into a consideration of the consummation of all things. The topics will be, in turn, the renovation of the world, the fulfillment of the kingdom, and eternal life.

I. THE RENOVATION OF THE WORLD

The primary observation about the consummation is that there will be a *new world*. This is portrayed most vividly at the opening of Revelation 21: "Then I saw a new heaven and a new earth; for the first heaven and the first earth had passed away." The vision that unfolds follows the judgment scene and the casting of all evil into "the lake of fire," or "the second death" in Revelation 20. It will be a new heaven and earth, hence a new world, that will succeed the old. Similarly Peter speaks of "new heavens and a new earth in which righteousness dwells" (2 Peter 3:13). Thus the world to come will be both a renewed and a purified reality.

Let us look back for a moment to the Old Testament. The opening verse in Genesis refers to the original world: "In the beginning God created the heavens and the earth." And step by step this marvelous event of creation is described (Gen. 1:1–2:4). However, for all their substantiality, the heavens and earth, as originally made, will not last forever. In the words of the psalmist: "Of old thou didst found the earth; And the heavens are the work of Thy hands. Even they will perish, but Thou dost endure; And all of them will wear out like a garment; Like clothing Thou wilt change them, and they will be changed" (102:25–26 NASB).[1] Isaiah prophesies similarly, "Lift up your eyes to the heavens, and look at the earth beneath; for the heavens will vanish like smoke, the earth will wear out like a garment" (51:6). The latter example has an additional sense of this being related to salvation, for the passage continues, "And they who dwell in it will die like gnats; but my salvation will be for ever." Still further in Isaiah are these striking words: "Behold, I create new heavens and a new earth; and the former things shall not be remembered

[1]Cf. Hebrews 1:10–12. Luther expressed it in inimitable fashion: "The heavens have their work-day clothes on; hereafter they will have on their Sunday garments" (quoted in C. H. Hodge, *Systematic Theology*, 3:853. Hodge does not give the exact source; nor do I know).

or come into mind" (65:17). This extraordinary verse may well serve as the best link between Genesis 1 and Revelation 21—the passing from the old creation to the new heaven and earth.

A vivid picture of *how* this transition will occur is set forth in 2 Peter. Prior to the words about "new heavens and a new earth in which righteousness dwells" are a number of statements describing the present world as undergoing dissolution. First, there is reference to the original creation "by the word": "By the word of God heavens existed long ago, and an earth formed out of water and by means of water"; and later at the time of the Flood, "the world that then existed was deluged with water and perished" (3:5–6). Similarly, Peter says, "By the same word the present heavens and earth are reserved for fire, being kept for the day of judgment and destruction of ungodly men" (v. 7 NIV). What is to happen will occur at "the day of the Lord":[2] "The day of the Lord will come like a thief,[3] and then the heavens will pass away with a loud noise,[4] and the elements[5] will be dissolved[6] with fire,[7] and the earth and the works that are upon it will be burned up" (v. 10).[8] Peter adds that "all these things [the heavens, the elements, the earth] are thus to be dissolved," and repeats that "the heavens will be kindled and dissolved and the elements will melt with fire [or 'intense heat'[9]]"[10] (vv. 11–12).

The basic motif in this description is not annihilation of the heavens and the earth but dissolution,[11] albeit total, so that in the consuming of everything by

[2]Which is also "the day of judgment and destruction of ungodly men" (as we have seen).

[3]This is another way of describing the day of Christ's return. See the earlier discussion on *hēmera* in chapter 9. Also recall the words of 1 Thessalonians 5:2: "The day of the Lord will come as a thief in the night," the coming "as a thief" referring to the surprise element (see 5:4).

[4]The Greek word is *hroizēdon*, "roar" (NASB, NIV), "great rushing sound" (NEB), "great noise" (KJV).

[5]The Greek word is *stoicheia*, "elemental substances, the basic elements from which everything in the natural world is made, and of which it is composed" (BAGD). According to TDNT, this relates to "the Stoic idea of a cosmic conflagration in which the other elements will dissolve into the primal element of fire" (7:686).

[6]The Greek word is *lythēsetai*, "disintegrate" (NEB), "be destroyed" (NASB, NIV). The basic idea is that of being broken up and disintegrating. "To dissolve something coherent into parts" (Thayer).

[7]The Greek word is *kausoumena*, "with [by] intense heat" (NASB). According to EGT, it means "a violent consuming heat" (5:145).

[8]Or "laid bare" (NIV, NEB). In the Second Epistle of Clement (ca. A.D. 120–40) we find these interesting words: "But ye know that the day of judgment cometh even now as a burning oven, and the powers of heaven shall melt, and all the earth as lead melting on the fire, and then shall appear the secret and open works of men" (J. B. Lightfoot, *The Apostolic Fathers*, 50). The appearing of "the secret and open works of men" is parallel to the idea of being "laid bare" or "discovered." Since this destruction by fire is related to "the day of judgment," it could include the laying bare of "secret and open works" (as we have seen earlier). However, I believe the reference here is not primarily to the laying bare, hence judging of men's works, but to the physical destruction of all things upon the earth. If so, this will not be an occasion of judgment, but of transition to the new world.

[9]The Greek word is *kausoumena* (as in v. 10). See note 7.

[10]Peter writes these words in the context of his call to live "lives of holiness and godliness, waiting for and hastening the coming of the day of God, because of which the heavens will be kindled. . . ."

[11]See note 6 on *lythesētai*.

fire there will be the transformation[12] into the "new[13] heavens and a new earth in which righteousness dwells" (v. 13). Hence, a total renovation will occur both in terms of a new form for the present world and righteousness dwelling in it.

However, this does not mean that the new heaven and earth will be totally different from the present order. The form, to be sure, will be new,[14] and all evil that has permeated its existence will be radically done away with. But the essence, the substance, will be the same. There will still be heavens and earth, even if the old has "passed away"[15]—as Revelation 21 depicts. Thus it will not be the creation of heavens and earth as to their essential reality but as to their form, their mode of existence.[16]

Here we may ask whether there can be any connection between the fiery dissolution depicted in Peter's letter and the increasing technological possibility of worldwide conflagration. Is this holocaust to be viewed as a climactic result of the splitting of the atom and a nuclear chain reaction that would engulf the world in fire?[17] The "elements dissolved with fire" might seem to suggest that. However, the picture in 2 Peter goes far beyond any human capability in terms both of the power to execute and of the results attained. For it will be a *total* dissolution—the heavens themselves, the elements, the earth and the works upon it—which surely seems to go beyond man's utmost capacity. Indeed, according to Scripture, it will be accomplished by Almighty God Himself, by the word of His power. Since by the "word," says Peter, "the present heavens . . . are reserved for fire," it will be by that same word—the word of God, the word of Power—that the dissolution of the world will be brought about. But also—and this utterly transcends any human possibility—since the dissolution does not end with annihilation but with transformation, it must totally be of God. Man might destroy much of the old; but no man, no nation, no power on earth can bring about "a new heaven and a new earth"!

Now let us consider the *timing* of this transition from the old to the new creation. It seems that it will occur just following the Last Judgment. John in his vision saw the Majestic One sitting upon His throne in preparation for

---

[12]According to Calvin, "the elements of the world are to be consumed, only that they may be renovated, their substance still remaining the same" (*Commentary on The Second Epistle of Peter*, in loco). Similarly C. H. Hodge says, "Combustion is not a destruction of substance . . . it is merely a change of state or condition . . . destruction of the world by water and by fire are analogous events; the former was not annihilation, therefore the second is not" (*Systematic Theology*, 3:852).

[13]The word "new" in both 2 Peter and Revelation 21 is *kainos*. *Kainos* means what is "new in kind" (TDNT, 3:448); it "denotes the new primarily in reference to quality" (Thayer). Thus while remaining the same in substance, the heavens and earth will undergo a total qualitative change.

[14]Paul declares that "the form [*schēma*] of this world is passing away" (1 Cor. 7:31). *Schēma* means "figure, shape, fashion" (Thayer—under the discussion of *morphē* in which he is comparing *morphē*, "that which is intrinsic and essential," with *schēma*, "that which is outward and accidental").

[15]The "passing away" therefore refers only to its form, not its essence or substance.

[16]"There will not be a new, second creation, but a re-creation of what exists, a renaissance. Substantially, nothing will be lost" (C. G. Berkouwer, *The Return of Christ*, 221, in a paraphrase of a statement by Bavinck).

[17]Recall the earlier reflection on this point under "Total Destruction," pages 413–21. In this nuclear age we are surely closer than ever before to an all-consuming fiery end.

judgment, and "from his presence earth and sky [or 'heaven'][18] fled away, and no place was found for them" (Rev. 20:11). This may not only signify the vast awesomeness of the scene,[19] but also that the Last Judgment cannot be localized at any one place and that this is the next to last stage in the transition to the new.[20] On the latter point, the Book of Revelation early depicts a vast shaking and moving of heaven (or sky) and earth (6:14), and now a fleeing away with no place to be (20:11), hence, quite possibly, the next to last stage before total dissolution occurs. It seems likely that this dissolution will occur after the judgment, in view of the fact that the next scene is that of "a new heaven and a new earth" (21:1). Also the succeeding words are "for the first heaven and the first earth had passed away."[21] The "passing away" (final stage)—which is more than "fleeing away"—would correspond to the "passing away"[22] in 2 Peter 3:10, which, as noted, occurs "with a loud noise" and "by fire." Thus between Revelation 20 and 21, it would follow, is the fiery transition described in 2 Peter.[23]

Now let us reflect upon another question: not how or when this transition will happen, but *why*—surely this is far more important. At least three answers may be given.

The first relates to the fact that the present world is *aging*. In some scriptural words already noted, the heavens and earth will "wear out like a garment"; hence there will be the need for a change of "clothing." Like the human body that wears out no matter how healthy it is now, so also the heavens and the earth will wear out. To be sure, their life is vastly longer than man's few years, but eventually they will wear out and need to be changed. This fact we may seldom reflect upon because of the great age of the world and its seeming unending continuance. Still there may come a time when even the world will grow old, and, like everything finite and creaturely, it will simply wear out. Hence, a change will be much in order.

---

[18]*Ouranos* may be translated either "heaven" (KJV, NASB, NEB) or "sky" (RSV, NIV). *Ouranos* is the word translated "heaven" (all versions) in "new heaven" (Rev. 21:1) and in "new heavens" (2 Peter 3:13). "Sky" in Rev. 20:11 scarcely seems strong enough, though it does convey the proper note that the Scripture is not here describing "heaven" in the ultimate sense as the spiritual, presently invisible, realm beyond earth. (We will observe this meaning of "heaven" in discussing Revelation 21:2.) It is rather the expanse beyond earth with all things visible in it.

[19]Recall the earlier discussion of this.

[20]Some commentators understand the words of Revelation 20:11 as referring to the transition from the old order to the new creation (e.g., G. E. Ladd in his *Commentary on the Revelation of John*, 272; W. Hendriksen in *More Than Conquerors*, 235; R. H. Mounce in *The Book of Revelation*, NICNT, 364–65). However, I have difficulty finding this meaning in the language of Revelation; moreover, it seems incongruous to view the transition as having occurred before "Death and Hades" have been done away (at the end of the event of judgment in Rev. 20:14). For in the new order death will be no more.

[21]The Greek word is *apēlthon*, "vanished" (NEB).

[22]The word there is *pareleusontai*. Both words (from *aperchomai* and *parerchomai*) have basically the same meaning. *Pareleusontai* is likewise found in Jesus' statement "Heaven and earth will pass away" (Matt. 24:35; Mark 13:31; Luke 21:33).

[23]Incidentally, if my understanding is correct that this transition will occur at the conclusion of the Last Judgment, it is all the more apparent that people can have nothing to do with the act of dissolution. All ungodly persons will have been slain already and raised from the dead for judgment; all righteous ones will have been raised or translated, shared with Christ in His total victory over the evil of the world, and afterward also been present for the judgment. Indeed, since the very heavens and earth will have "fled away," the final act in relation to them will—and must—be totally of God.

A second answer relates to the fact that the world itself is in bondage to *corruption*. With the sin and fall of man, nature came under a curse: "Cursed is the ground because of you" (Gen. 3:17). In the language of Paul, "The creation[24] was subjected to futility,[25] not of its own will, but because of Him who subjected it, in hope that the creation itself also will be set free from its slavery to corruption[26] into the freedom of the glory of the children of God" (Rom. 8:20–21 NASB). Creation, for all its outward vitality and beauty, lies under the curse of man's evil. His sin has infected all,[27] so that creation is dominated by "thorns and thistles" (Gen. 3:18), by "nature red in tooth and claw." Even though man may cultivate and domesticate, creation still is basically intractable and constantly ready to revert to its "fallen" state of corruption. Thus creation has lost its original, pristine significance—it has been "subjected to futility" and frustration—and lies in bondage to corruption. But this will not be forever: there is hope (God-given) of a future glorious freedom, which will accompany the finally liberated children of God!

Let us continue with Paul as he states the background of his words about creation: "I consider that the sufferings of this present time are not worth comparing with the glory[28] that is to be revealed to us" (Rom. 8:18). This glory, of course, refers to the glory that will be revealed at the return of Christ and in the age to come. Immediately following the statement just quoted are these extraordinary words: "For the anxious longing[29] of the creation waits eagerly[30] for the revealing of the sons of God. For the creation was subjected to futility. . ." (v. 19–20 NASB). Along with this anxious longing and eager waiting there is a deep inner agony. "We know," Paul later adds, "that the whole creation has been groaning in travail together until now" (v. 22). Thus creation yearns for that coming day of liberation from bondage, which will occur at the revealing of the sons of God, that is, when at the consummation those who belong to Christ are made manifest.

I referred earlier to Isaiah 65:17: "Behold, I create new heavens and a new earth; and the former things shall not be remembered or come into mind." Several verses later is this memorable statement: "'The wolf and the lamb shall feed together, the lion shall eat straw like the ox; and dust shall be the serpent's food. They shall not hurt or destroy in all my holy mountain,' says the LORD" (v. 25). In this idyllic picture of the new world, the corruption of the animal world is done away, and creation is at peace. In a related pas-

[24]The Greek word is *ktisis*. It can also be translated "creature" (as KJV); however, "creation" (all modern translations) is doubtless better in this context. It is also apparent that *ktisis* here refers to creation below man, thus the world of animate and inanimate nature.

[25]The Greek word is *mataiotēti*, "vanity" (KJV), "frustration" (NIV, NEB), "futility" (RSV, NASB).

[26]The Greek word is *phthoras*, "ruin, destruction, dissolution, deterioration, corruption" (BAGD). "Decay" (RSV, NIV) does not as adequately capture the result of the curse on nature.

[27]"You cannot divide the created order into distinct and independent sections. What happens in one section will have repercussions in all. If there is any unity in the universe, a disaster in one realm will have repercussions on all" (IB, in loco).

[28]Literally, "the coming glory"—*mellousan doxan*.

[29]The Greek word is *apokaradokia*, "to watch with head erect or outstretched" (Thayer). What a vivid picture this is of creation personified, straining ahead, watching for the future!

[30]The Greek word is *apekdechetai*, "assiduously and patiently to wait for" (Thayer). The very form of creation is that of expectant, eager waiting.

sage in Isaiah, following the language about the One who will "smite the earth with the rod of his mouth, and with the breath of his lips . . . slay the wicked"[31] (11:4), there is an even fuller picture of nature at peace: not only wolf with lamb but also leopard with kid, lion with calf, bear with cow, asp with small child. The climax: "They shall not hurt or destroy in all my holy mountain; for the earth shall be full of the knowledge of the LORD as the waters cover the sea" (v. 9). Here indeed is a glorious picture of the new world with all the fierceness and wildness of nature at last done away, and the knowledge of God filling all the earth![32]

One further picture in Isaiah may be mentioned. Isaiah 34 is largely a portrayal of the destruction of the evil world. All the people of the nations will be slain: "He will totally destroy them" (v. 2 NIV), and the heavens will collapse: "All the stars of the heavens will be dissolved and the sky rolled up like a scroll; all the starry host will fall. . ." (v. 4 NIV). This is the Lord's "day of vengeance" (v. 8). In chapter 35 a beautiful scene follows: "The desert and the parched land will be glad; the wilderness will rejoice and blossom . . . water will gush forth in the wilderness and streams in the desert" (vv. 1, 6 NIV). Hence, not only will the ferociousness of wild beasts be no more, but also the recalcitrance of the earth will be transformed into the glory of a new world.[33]

This actually means, then, the redemption of creation, which—I may now add—corresponds to the redemption of our bodies. Following his statement about the whole creation's groaning and travailing together, Paul writes, "And not only this, but also we ourselves, having the first fruits of the Spirit, even we ourselves groan within ourselves, waiting eagerly for our adoption as sons, the redemption of our body" (Rom. 8:23 NASB). Since "the redemption of our body" refers to our bodies' being redeemed from corruption and decay, and since this will not occur until the Day of the Lord—the same day when the old heavens and earth are consumed to make way for the new—it is apparent that even as we receive new bodies, so will all creation become new. Thus creation, at last free from corruption and decay, will enter into "the freedom of the glory of the children of God."[34]

A third answer to the question of why there will be a new heaven and earth relates to the fact that this will be a proper dwelling for the *new humanity*. Since those who belong to Christ will have been transformed in their bodies, and so entered a new dimension of spiritual corporeality, they will be able to function better in a realm more suited to their new mode of existence. The new humanity will have transcended the old spatio-temporal order of existence (even as Christ did in His resurrection appearances) and hence will need a

---

[31]Recall the previous discussion of this as occurring at the return of Christ.

[32]Some biblical interpreters (e.g., Scofield; see the Scofield Reference Bible) hold that this Isaianic picture refers to a messianic reign of Christ on the present earth. However, F. Delitzsch, I believe, puts it well in saying that "the full realization [of this prophecy] is conditioned no doubt by a revolution in creation, and therefore belongs to the new earth under the new heaven" (*Biblical Commentary on the Prophecy of Isaiah*, 248).

[33]It would be a mistake to view Isaiah 35 as referring to the presently constituted earth. The background (in chap. 34) of total destruction of the nations and the dissolution of the heavens is preparatory (as we have before observed) to the coming of a new creation. The prophet is speaking about a *renovated* earth.

[34]"The creation itself shall in a glorious sense be delivered into the freedom from debility and decay in which the children of God, when raised up in glory, shall expatiate" (W. E. Biederwolf, *The Second Coming Bible Commentary*, 416).

higher, and different, arena of activity. So it is that the new heaven and the new earth will provide the appropriate setting for the age to come.

It is important to recognize that the new world will no more be a purely spiritual realm than will humanity's existence be purely spiritual. To be sure, until the day of resurrection and translation, all believers who have died are present only as spirits in heaven. But because on the day of Christ's return all believers, both living and dead, will have been given spiritual bodies, their future appropriately lies in a spiritual/corporeal realm. And God will provide this in the new heaven and earth!

This will mean, further, that the new humanity will dwell neither in the present creation—"the first heaven and the first earth" (Rev. 21:1)—nor in a realm that is totally other than heaven and earth, although it will be a "new heaven and a new earth" (Rev. 21:1). Spiritual corporeality would not fit the former (the present world) because the realm would be too material for its proper functioning; it would not fit the latter (a totally other realm) because the realm would be too spiritual. Hence, views of a future existence for spiritual bodies on the present earth, even if for a limited time,[35] or of an existence that is so ethereal (or heavenly) that the earthly has no place at all,[36] are both inadequate.

I need to say also that the new humanity will be more than a return to a "pre-fallen" human existence. It will surely be as sinless as was humanity in its originally created state, but it will also be a new form of humanity that has never existed before. To speak of Revelation 21 and 22 as simply picturing a "return to Eden" is not enough. Eden belongs to the "first heaven and the first earth" which, for all its pristine beauty, cannot approximate the new that is yet to come. For in the age to come, there will be redeemed, glorified saints in bodies suited for that age—all the more truly to glorify God and to worship and serve Him forever.

The pattern of history—as we earlier observed—moves from creation to consummation, and—as I now emphasize—the latter is far more than a return to the former. There is "renovation" to be sure, and this includes all that Eden originally was; but it is a renovation that is far beyond anything humanity, even in Adam, has ever before known. It is a re-novation that is also a re-creation—"I create new heavens and a new earth";[37] a re-creation that is also re-novation—"I saw a new heaven and a new earth." Truly, it is beyond all present imagination.

Here let us pause to note two further New Testament terms that express this future realm. The first is often translated "restoration"; the second, "regeneration."

[35]As, for example, in a millennialism that posits resurrected saints dwelling on the present earth for a thousand years.

[36]As in much popular Christianity that envisions only a future heaven far beyond this earth. Hoekema writes, "Are we to spend eternity somewhere off in space, wearing white robes, plucking harps, singing songs, and flitting from cloud to cloud while doing so? On the contrary, the Bible assures us that God will create a new earth on which we shall live to God's praise in glorified, resurrected bodies" (*The Bible and the Future*, 274). Hoekema's final chapter (20), "The New Earth" (274–87), may go too far on the earthly side, but he undoubtedly speaks an important word (see also G. C. Berkouwer's *The Return of Christ*, chap. 7, with the same title, "The New Earth").

[37]We actually need both terms, "renovation" and "recreation," since the former without the latter may suggest too little, the latter without the former too much. (I chose the former word, "renovation," for this section heading, realizing that it is not altogether satisfactory.)

In Peter's address to a gathered throng of Jews, he declared, "Repent . . . that your sins may be wiped away, in order that times of refreshing may come from the presence of the Lord; and that He may send Jesus, the Christ appointed for you, whom heaven must receive until the period of restoration[38] of all things about which God spoke by the mouth of His holy prophets from ancient time"[39] (Acts 3:19–21 NASB). The "restoration" of which Peter spoke is unmistakably connected with the return of Christ; further, it will be the restoration of "all things."

This restoration patently involves far more than a people or nation. The apostles (including Peter himself) had shortly before asked the risen Jesus, "Lord, will you at this time restore the kingdom to Israel?" (Acts 1:6). Later, in his message to the Jews, Peter spoke not of a national but a universal restoration:[40] it will be "the restoration of all things." Hence this restoration primarily refers to the situation of the present world, which has fallen away from its original harmony between God and man, and between man and the natural world. It is this primeval situation of the brokenness of the world, as depicted by "prophets from ancient time," especially recorded in the Book of Genesis, that will be restored to its original unity.

We must carefully observe that this restoration will occur only against the background of the work of the gospel—repentance, forgiveness of sins, and renewal ("times of refreshing"). This is in itself spiritual restoration, but it is also preparation for the return of Christ ("that He may send Jesus") and the final total restoration.

One further matter: the word translated "restoration" does, however, contain more than the idea of a return to the original situation of the world.[41] It also means to establish[42] or, perhaps

[38]The Greek word is *apokatastaseōs*, "restitution" (KJV), "establishing" (RSV), "restoration" (NEB), "restore" (NIV). "Restoration" is the translation given in BAGD and Thayer. This is the only use of the noun *apokatastasis* in the New Testament. Cf. other passages where the verb form *apokathistēmi* is used: Mark 3:5 (cf. Matt. 12:13; Luke 6:10); 8:25; 9:12 (cf. Matt. 17:11); Acts 1:6; Hebrews 13:19.

[39]The Greek phrase is *ap' aiōnos*, "from eternity."

[40]Jesus' earlier reply to the apostles also implies a universal restoration: "It is not for you to know times or seasons which the Father has fixed by his own authority. But you shall receive power when the Holy Spirit has come upon you; and you shall be my witnesses in Jerusalem and in all Judea and Samaria and *to the end of the earth*" (Acts 1:7–8). Jesus' words not only are a reproof about trying to fix "times" and "seasons" but they also imply a much wider, even different, fulfillment, namely, that by the proclamation of the gospel in the power of the Holy Spirit the kingdom of God, not the restoration of Israel as a kingdom, will be brought near. It is about *this* kingdom that Jesus had been speaking with the apostles: "during forty days . . . speaking of the kingdom of God" (Acts 1:3). It is significant that after the apostles had this last conversation with Jesus before His ascension, when Peter again used the words about "restoration," it was no longer concerning Israel but "all things." Henceforward in Acts there is no reference anywhere to a national restoration of Israel; moreover, the kingdom as proclaimed throughout the book invariably relates only to the spiritual kingdom into which one enters through faith in Christ (see Acts 8:12; 14:22; 19:8; 20:25; 28:23, 31). It is this, and this alone, that prepares the way for the restoration of all things at the return of Christ.

[41]In the Stoic philosophy of endless recurrence the word *apokatastasis* is used to express a cyclical return to the original state—"everything is restored exactly as it was before" (TDNT, 1:390).

[42]As noted before, RSV translates *apokatastaseōs* as "establishing." F. F. Bruce writes, "αποκαταστάσις may here be rendered 'establishment,' 'fulfilment,' referring to the

better, fulfill what has never before been brought to its consummation. Thus, what the prophets of old saw at the end of the age concerning "all things" (for example, "the earth shall be full of the knowledge of the Lord as the waters cover the sea"),[43] while in one sense a return to man's pristine condition, will have a far greater, indeed richer, fulfillment in that which is yet to come.

The other word, "regeneration," is to be found in Jesus' words in Matthew 19:28: "Truly I say to you, that you who have followed Me, in the regeneration[44] when the Son of Man will sit on His glorious throne, you also shall sit upon twelve thrones, judging [or ruling][45] the twelve tribes of Israel" (NASB). It is immediately noteworthy that here the idea of regeneration applies not to an individual,[46] but to something larger and in the future.

It follows that "the regeneration" refers to the rebirth of the world—thus "the new world" (RSV)—and belongs to the time when Christ will have returned and been seated on His throne of glory. That the apostles will sit on thrones in this "new world" forbids any viewing of this activity as occurring in the present world or age. It will happen only when the "new heavens and the new earth"—"the regeneration"—have come into being.

We may observe again, as in the case of "restoration," that "regeneration" is not simply a return to the past, whatever its goodness and beauty, but signifies a new reality. There is continuity with the old world in its first generation, but there is also discontinuity: the same world but in a new and higher form.[47]

II. THE FULFILLMENT OF THE KINGDOM

The consummation will bring the fulfillment of the kingdom of God. It is this kingdom of which Jesus speaks when He says, "Come, O blessed of my Father, inherit the kingdom prepared for you from the foundation of the world" (Matt. 25:34). The "blessed" are those who before the "glorious throne" of the returned Christ have been set at His "right hand" and will go "into eternal life" (vv. 31–33, 46). Those who have ministered to "the least"—the naked, the sick, the impris-

---

fulfilment of all OT prophecy, culminating in the establishment of God's kingdom on earth" (*The Acts of the Apostles*, 112). Bruce does not rule out "restoration": "The sense of 'restoration' should perhaps not be entirely excluded." TDNT brings together the idea of both "restoration" and "establishment": "These ('all things') are restored, i.e. brought back to the integrity of creation, while the promise itself is established or fulfilled" (1:391).

[43]Isaiah 11:9 (cf. Hab. 2:14).

[44]The Greek word is *palingenesia*, "the new world" (RSV), "the renewal of all things" (NIV), "the world that is to be" (NEB). Both NASB and KJV translate it "regeneration." The only other New Testament usage of *palingenesia* is in Titus 3:5: "the washing of regeneration" (KJV, RSV), "rebirth" (NIV, NEB). *Palingenesia* means, literally, "again-birth," thus "re-generation."

[45]The Greek word is *krinontes*. According to TDNT, "The sense 'to rule' rather than 'to judge' occurs at Mt. 19:28; Lk. 22:30" (3:923).

[46]As, e.g., in John 3:3–8. The language about being "born again" (or "anew," "from above") does not use the word *palingenesia*. Rather, in various forms, it is a combination of *gennaō* and *anōthen*.

[47]According to TDNT, *palingenesia* "means 'new genesis' either in the sense of a. 'return to existence,' 'coming back from death to life,' or of b. 'renewal to a higher existence'. . ." (1:646). It is this latter meaning that is particularly contained in the picture of a coming "new world."

oned, and so to Christ Himself (vv. 35–40)—will inherit the kingdom.[48]

Before proceeding further, it is important to recall that Christ in His first coming established the kingdom[49] and that all who belong to Him are already participants in that kingdom. The power of Satan over the world was broken in Christ's victory so that—in the words of Paul—"He has delivered us from the dominion of darkness and transferred us to the kingdom of his beloved Son" (Col. 1:13). Accordingly, even now we are "sons of the kingdom" (Matt. 13:38), Christ is reigning, and we know such kingdom blessings as "righteousness and peace and joy in the Holy Spirit" (Rom. 14:17).[50] Although Christ won a decisive victory through His life, death, and resurrection, thereby establishing His kingdom and bringing many sons and daughters into it, the kingdom will not be complete until He destroys all enemy forces. "He must reign until he has put all his enemies under his feet," writes Paul, adding, "The last enemy to be destroyed is death" (1 Cor. 15:25–26). This destruction of all enemies will happen only at the return of Christ. Only then will the kingdom be consummated.

Let us contemplate the fuller picture. In the context of speaking about the future resurrection, Paul declares, "For as in Adam all die, so also in Christ shall all be made alive. But each in his own order: Christ the first fruits, then at his coming [*parousia*] those who belong to Christ. Then comes the end, when he delivers the kingdom to God the Father after destroying every rule and every authority and power" (1 Cor. 15:22–24).[51] The sequence, accordingly, is: the return of Christ, the resurrection of the dead in Christ and the translation of the living, the destruction of all evil, and the delivering of the kingdom to the Father. It is then that the saints will—in the language of Christ—"inherit the kingdom prepared . . . from the foundation of the world."

We may here also recall the words of Christ about "the close of the age": "Then shall the righteous shine forth as the sun in the kingdom of their Father" (Matt. 13:43 KJV). This will follow the return of Christ: "The Son of man will send his angels, and they will gather out of his kingdom all causes of sin and all evildoers, and throw them into the furnace of fire; there men will weep and gnash their teeth" (Matt. 13:41–42). Then come the words quoted about the righteous in the kingdom.

Turning again to the Book of Revelation, it is apparent that the kingdom to come will belong to the order of "the new heaven and the new earth." Earlier in the book there is this joyous declaration: "The kingdom of the world has become the kingdom of our Lord and of his Christ, and he shall reign for ever and ever" (11:15). The background for this declaration is found in the thanksgiving that follows: "We give thanks to thee, Lord God Almighty, who art and who wast, that thou has taken thy great power and begun to reign. The nations

---

[48]In the similar judgment scene found in Revelation 20:11–15, the "blessed" ones are undoubtedly the same as those whose names are found in "the book of life" (v. 12). They—like all others—"were judged by what they had done" (v. 13).

[49]See the earlier discussion in chapter 8.

[50]Paul's definition of the kingdom of God. His complete statement is this: "For the kingdom of God does not mean food and drink but righteousness and peace and joy in the Holy Spirit."

[51]This delivery signifies that the Son has completed His work of abolishing every alien power, and at last presents the perfected kingdom to God the Father. This by no means signifies that Christ ceases to reign, but that He, so to speak, offers up the victory to the Father. The kingdom will forever be "the kingdom of Christ and of God" (Eph. 5:5).

raged, but thy wrath came, and the time for the dead to be judged, for rewarding thy servants, the prophets and saints, and those who fear thy name, both small and great, and for destroying the destroyers of earth'' (11:17–18). Hence in an anticipatory vision, the final judgment—as portrayed later in Revelation 20—has just occurred: thus the joyous affirmation that ''the kingdom of our Lord and of his Christ'' has come. Accordingly, what immediately follows is a depiction of that kingdom, beginning with John's words in Revelation 21: ''Then I saw a new heaven and a new earth.''

A. God's Immediate Presence

In the kingdom to come God will be immediately present with His people. This is the primary fact declared in the Book of Revelation. ''I heard a great voice from the throne saying, 'Behold, the dwelling of God is with men. He will dwell with them, and they shall be his people, and God himself will be with them' '' (21:3).[52] No longer—as in this present age—will God dwell in heaven, but will (marvelous to relate!) Himself dwell among His people. Even now, to be sure, the people of God know His indwelling by the Holy Spirit[53]—and this is a wondrous present fact and experience. But a future further action will occur in which, through the bridging of heaven and earth, God will be in immediate relationship with His redeemed people. And this, of course, means with *all* people, since no one else will be in the new heaven and the new earth except those who belong to God.

This points to the truth, first, that there will be a glorious fulfillment of the relationship between God and man as it was known in the beginning. In the original Eden God was personally present with man. Genesis 2 describes how He formed man from the earth itself, breathed the breath of life into him, placed him in the garden, brought the animals to him for naming, shaped out of his rib a woman and brought her to him that they might be one flesh. All such actions—including ''walking in the garden in the cool of day'' (Gen. 3:8)—bespoke the immediate and personal presence of God. But tragically, all this was lost through mankind's sin: Adam and Eve were driven out and no longer knew the wonder of divine immediacy. The whole of Scripture from Genesis 1 and 2 to Revelation 21 and 22 basically recounts the history of man's alienation from God and His action to restore the divine-human relationship. Centrally, there is the event of the divine Incarnation in which God came in human flesh. Hence God was again with man; but He was present in hidden fashion for the gracious purpose of overcoming man's alienation and restoring him to Himself. Through Christ God was *with* man; through the Holy Spirit He dwells *in* and *among* His people. But until all evil is eliminated and the new order of heaven and earth instituted, God will not establish His dwelling *within* the human sphere. Finally the end will come as a marvelous fulfillment of the beginning: God with man in a relationship that will go on forever!

---

[52]This declaration actually follows a vivid statement concerning the ''holy city . . . coming down out of heaven from God, prepared as a bride adorned for her husband'' (v. 2). However, since the theme of the holy city and bride is not elaborated until verses 9ff., whereas verses 3–4 depict God's dwelling with people, the primacy of the latter is apparent. The ''great voice from the throne,'' declaring God's dwelling with people, lends further weight to its great significance.

[53]Recall, e.g., Paul's words about how Jew and Gentile believers are members of ''the household of God . . . a holy temple . . . a dwelling place of God in the Spirit'' (Eph. 2:19–22).

But also, in the second place, the end will be far more than a reconstitution of the beginning. For one thing, in the kingdom to come—the new heaven and new earth—man will be in his new spiritual body and thus have a direct relationship to God that transcends anything presently known. Again, in the kingdom to come, Jesus Christ, the Savior and Redeemer of mankind, will be bodily present. This will produce an intensity of joy and fellowship that could not have been experienced in the beginning, nor at any time by the redeemed people of God prior to the consummation. Further, in the kingdom to come there will never again be a temptation to evil—no Satan to get into Paradise, for he will have been consigned to "the lake of fire" (Rev. 20:10). All will be in perfect accord.

One of the truly beautiful touches in the Book of Revelation depicting God's immediate and personal presence is in the statement following the words "God himself will be with them," namely, "He will wipe away every tear from their eyes, and death shall be no more, neither shall there be mourning nor crying nor pain any more, for the former things have passed away" (21:4). How tender is God's personal presence: wiping away every teardrop of the past (tears that possibly came through suffering persecution for the sake of Christ and tears shed in deep sorrow for sin), so that not a trace remains! How wonderful to realize that death is forever gone[54]—indeed, there will only be life! How joyful to know that never again will there be any sorrow or pain,[55] for the old, hurtful things will be totally done away!

It is also marvelous to realize that God's immediate presence will mean the bodily presence of Jesus Christ in the coming kingdom. Christ, who is now known on earth by faith and in heaven by sight, will be present with all the saints forever in the kingdom to come! Earlier in Revelation one of the elders before the throne made this memorable statement: "The Lamb in the midst of the throne will be their shepherd, and he will guide them to springs of living water" (7:17). And then in words almost identical with those in Revelation 21, he added, "And God will wipe away every tear from their eyes" (also v. 17). The Lamb/Shepherd will guide them to springs of water, and God the Father will wipe away all tears![56] Thus there will be the intimate presence of both Father and Son.

Although Jesus did not utilize the Apocalyse's imagery of Lamb as Shepherd in his earthly ministry, He did speak of the coming kingdom as the time when He would have close fellowship with His disciples. Following the memorable occasion of the Last Supper, Jesus declared, "I tell you I shall not drink again of this fruit of the vine until that day when I drink it new with you in my Father's kingdom" (Matt. 26:29). Hence, each celebration of the Lord's Supper is, for all its rich present meaning, also a looking forward to the coming kingdom where Christ will be immediately present to "drink it new" with all who belong to Him. Shortly

---

[54]Recall Revelation 20:14: "Death and Hades were thrown into the lake of fire."

[55]Here truly is the ultimate fulfillment of these beautiful words in Isaiah: "And the ransomed of the LORD shall return, and come to Zion with singing; everlasting joy shall be upon their heads; they shall obtain joy and gladness, and *sorrow and sighing shall flee away*" (35:10).

[56]God the Father will not only wipe away tears but also, according to Revelation 21:6, give His people water to drink—from the very springs the Lamb/Shepherd has led them to: "To the thirsty I will give water without price from the fountain [or 'spring'] of the water of life." Thus closely associated again are Father and Son.

after the Last Supper, Jesus also declared to the Twelve: "You are those who have continued with me in my trials; as my Father appointed a kingdom for me, so do I appoint for you that you may eat and drink at my table in my kingdom"[57] (Luke 22:28–30). That such fellowship at the Lord's table will by no means be limited to the apostles is clear from other words of Jesus: "And men will come from east and west, and from north and south, and sit at table in the kingdom of God"[58] (Luke 13:29).

These portrayals of Christ's presence with His people all refer to the kingdom to come in the new age. This will occur, therefore, not on the present earth or in some heaven beyond the earth, but in the world constituted by the new heaven and the new earth. In that world to come, which will transcend our present spatio-temporal sphere,[59] Christ will have close fellowship with all, and the "table" will be of such proportions that all the saints will be gathered in His personal presence and in intimate relationship with one another!

Now, returning to the Book of Revelation, we hear these powerful words from the throne: "Behold, I make all things new. . . . It is done! I am the Alpha and the Omega, the beginning and the end" (21:5–6). This mighty proclamation follows all that has just been said about God Himself dwelling with His people (tears wiped away, death no more, pain forever gone). Although this is the future for us, it is already done in God's sight! But then once again, despite the august voice of Almighty God from the throne, there is immediately the personal and intimate touch: "To the thirsty I will give water without price from the fountain of the water of life. He who conquers shall have this heritage, and I will be his God and he shall be my son" (vv. 6–7).

In the kingdom to come God will be immediately and personally present with His people—forever.

B. A Radiant People

We have earlier noted the statement about the coming kingdom: "Then shall the righteous shine forth as the sun in the kingdom of their Father" (Matt. 13:43 KJV). Thus there will be a radiance, like the sun itself, about God's people dwelling in the new heaven and the new earth.

The Book of Revelation describes this radiance through the imagery of a *holy city* and a *bride adorned*. After seeing the vision of a new heaven and a new earth, John declares, "And I saw the holy city, new Jerusalem, coming down out of heaven from God, prepared as a bride adorned for her husband" (21:2). In this extraordinary double figure of the holy city and the adorned bride, John portrays the people of God in the age to come.

Let us look first at the imagery of an adorned bride. In doing so we may, at the outset, look back into the parable of Jesus about the kingdom that begins,

---

[57]The verse concludes, ". . . and sit on thrones judging [or 'ruling'—*krinontes*; see n. 45] the twelve tribes of Israel." Recall the prior discussion of this in relation to the "regeneration" to come. According to N. Geldenhuys, "*krinein* here does not mean 'to judge' but 'to rule' " and "the expression 'the twelve tribes of Israel' is not intended literally, but is a conventional expression for the members of the kingdom" (*The Gospel of Luke*, NICNT, 565). Thus the apostles will continue to have a leadership role in the fulfilled kingdom.

[58]In the preceding verse Jesus speaks of "Abraham and Isaac and Jacob and all the prophets in the kingdom of God" (v. 28). Hence, the "table" will include Old Testament worthies before Christ as well as those who have come to personal faith in Him since His Incarnation.

[59]See the prior discussion of this.

"Then the kingdom of heaven will be comparable to ten virgins, who took their lamps, and went out to meet the bridegroom" (Matt. 25:1 NASB). The parable relates that the bridegroom returned after a lengthy delay, and those who were ready with oil "trimmed[60] their lamps" (v. 7) and went into "the wedding feast" (v. 10) with him. Jesus Himself is unmistakably the bridegroom, the return is His final Parousia, and the virgins with trimmed lamps—thus radiant with light—are those prepared for His arrival. No bride is mentioned in the parable; however, we may understand that the prepared virgins represent the bride awaiting the bridegroom,[61] namely, Christ in His return.

We observe, next, that the apostle Paul speaks of the church as the bride of Christ: "Christ loved the church and gave himself up for her, that he might sanctify her, having cleansed her by the washing of water with the word, that he might present the church to himself in splendor" (Eph. 5:25–27). This is said against the background of the statement "Husbands, love your wives as. . . ." The ultimate intention of Christ is to have a bride "in splendor"[62] ("a radiant church" NIV), who is "without spot or wrinkle or any such thing, that she might be holy and without blemish" (v. 27). This, as surely as Christ intended it, will be fulfilled in the coming kingdom.

Again we come to the Book of Revelation and now hear these memorable words in chapter 19: " 'Hallelujah! For the Lord our God the Almighty reigns. Let us rejoice and exult and give him the glory, for the marriage of the Lamb has come, and his Bride has made herself ready; it was granted her to be clothed with fine linen, bright[63] and pure'—for the fine linen is the righteous deeds of the saints" (vv. 6–8). Here one beholds the heavenly bride in her adornment "bright and pure," once again radiant and holy. Then occur the words "Blessed are those who are invited to the marriage supper of the Lamb" (v. 9). The marriage has not yet taken place, but the bride is now ready for the event.[64]

Thus the New Testament portrays a series of images of the radiant bride. The climactic one in Revelation 21 shows "a bride adorned for her husband." The word "adorned" conveys a sense of beauty and radiance while also recalling all the previous imagery about virgins with "lamps trimmed,"[65] a church "in splendor," a bride "bright and pure." Now—at long last—the consummation is to occur as the radiant bride comes down "out of heaven."

The significance of this is that in the kingdom to come the people of God—the church—will be a radiant and holy people. As such, they will be "wed" to Christ forever. Later in Revelation 21, the bride is designated as "the wife of the Lamb" (v. 9), and there is no

[60]The word translated "trimmed" is *ekosmēsan*, a form of *kosmeō*, often meaning "adorn." In the picture of "the bride adorned" (Rev. 21:2), the word for "adorned" is a form of *kosmeō* (*kekosmēmenēn*).

[61]Recall that Jesus was described by John the Baptist as a bridegroom (John 3:29) and that Jesus referred to Himself in similar fashion (Matt. 9:15; Mark 2:19–20; Luke 5:34–35).

[62]The Greek word is *endoxon* (from *doxa*), "glorious," "splendid," "radiant."

[63]The Greek word is *lampron*. "Bright (*lampros*) is the color of radiant whiteness that depicts glorification" (Alan F. Johnson, *Revelation*, EBC, 12:571).

[64]It would be a mistake to assume that the marriage feast occurs in heaven. Revelation 19 is a picture of the preparation of the bride for the feast yet to come. Her brightness and purity beautifully represent the saints in heaven who have gone to be with the Lord (whether by death or rapture). This is final preparation for the consummation of the marriage in the kingdom to come (Rev. 21).

[65]See note 61.

suggestion of this marriage ever ending! The radiant bride has become the radiant wife—and with her glorious Lord will live forever.

Thus the imagery of the radiant bride and wife depicts the beauty and holiness of the people of God as finally fulfilled in the kingdom to come: the bride "comes down" out of heaven. But since this is imagery (however meaningful), the people of God may also be described (as we have observed) as "the righteous [who] shine forth as the sun in the kingdom of their Father." Although there is no nuptial imagery in this description, the picture of the righteous "shining forth" is basically the same. In the kingdom to come, God's people will radiate the holiness and glory of God.

Second, let us consider the radiant people of God under the imagery of the holy city. It is a striking, perhaps surprising, thing to observe how easily the imagery shifts back and forth between the adorned bride and the holy city. Let us recall again John's words: "And I saw the holy city, new Jerusalem, coming down out of heaven from God, prepared as a bride adorned for her husband" (Rev. 21:2). In such language there may be a seeming incongruity: a city and a bride compared! What have they in common? Later, in verses 3–8,[66] there is no direct reference to either. But then an angel gives an invitation to John: "Come, I will show you the Bride, the wife of the Lamb" (v. 9). But when John looks to behold the bride, he is shown a city! Then John says, "And in the Spirit he [an angel] carried me away to a great, high mountain, and showed me the holy city Jerusalem coming down out of heaven from God"[67] (v. 10). Again, one may wonder at the comparison—until the next words: "having the glory of God, its radiance[68] like a most rare jewel, like a jasper, clear as crystal" (v. 11). Ah, now it comes together: the radiant bride, the radiant city—each reflecting the glory of God!

The bridal imagery, for all its beauty, is now transformed into city imagery because the people of God may also be likened to a holy and radiant city. Further, no matter how beautifully a bride may be described in her adornment,[69] what John afterward sees in regard to the holy city goes far beyond what he has seen before. The splendor that is now unfolded dazzles even the heights of human imagination.

But first the holy city is identified as the people of God. There are twelve gates inscribed with the names of the twelve tribes of Israel, and twelve foundations with the names of the twelve apostles of Christ. This unmistakably designates the holy city as the people of God in continuity from the Old Testament to the New. Second, the vast size and shape of the city are next measured out: twelve thousand stadia (about 1,500 miles) in length, breadth, and height—an area far greater in length and breadth than any present earthly city, and in height utterly beyond the reach of any present city on earth—thus in shape a perfectly symmetrical

[66]The verses we earlier considered in relation to God's dwelling with people.

[67]Cf. Ezekiel 40:1–2. Ezekiel declares, "The hand of the LORD was upon me, and brought me in the visions of God into the land of Israel, and set me down upon a very high mountain, on which was a structure like a city opposite me." Following this, in chapters 40–48, much of what is described by Ezekiel is evidently a foregleam of what John beholds of the holy city in Revelation 21 and 22.

[68]The Greek word is *phōstēr*, "splendor, radiance" (BAGD). The word *phōstēr* conveys the idea of a glittering radiancy. NASB and NIV translate *phōstēr* as "brilliance."

[69]As briefly in Revelation 19:8: "It was granted her to be clothed with fine linen, bright and pure."

cube. The vastness of size suggests the enormous number of saints, and the perfect symmetry suggests the Holy of Holies of the Old Testament temple,[70] hence a people in perfect holiness.

Once again the unspeakable radiance of the city, the people of God, is set forth: the wall "built of jasper," hence clear as crystal, the city itself "pure gold, clear as glass," the foundations of the wall (representing the twelve apostles) "adorned with every jewel" (twelve jewels are named), the gates (representing the twelve patriarchs) made of twelve pearls (each a single pearl), and the street of the city "pure gold, transparent as glass" (21:18–21). All this beggars the imagination: incomparable beauty, glistening brilliance, shimmering radiance—none of which any city of earth could ever approximate. Such is the holy city come down out of heaven from God.

It is of utmost importance to recognize that this holy city represents the holiness of the people of God in the age to come. As Jesus had said, "Then shall the righteous *shine forth* as the sun in the kingdom of their Father." The holy city in all its glorious luster is that shining forth of "the righteous." It is they who will be a "holy city."[71] It is *not* that the people of God *will dwell* in the holy city, but they *will be* the holy city. Even now believers are to "shine as lights in the world" (Phil. 2:15)—a world that is full of darkness—but in the kingdom to come there will be a total radiance.

Here we pause to consider the fact that the redeemed people of God, the church of Jesus Christ, even now reflects something of this radiance. In 2 Corinthians 3:7, Paul recalls how Moses came down from the mountaintop with his face so radiating the glory of God that the Israelites could not look upon it; however, that glory soon faded away. But now in the dispensation of the Holy Spirit, Paul adds, believers without any veil over their face not only reflect the glory of God, but will go on from glory to glory: "And we, who with unveiled faces all reflect[72] the Lord's glory, are being transformed into his likeness with ever-increasing glory, which comes from the Lord, who is the Spirit"[73] (3:18 NIV). Already in this present age those who belong to the Lord are a radiant people; they reflect His glory in their faces—indeed their whole life. But it is only the beginning! On and on we are to move "from glory to glory,"[74] more and more to be changed into His image, until—praise God!—in the kingdom to come we will totally show forth His glory.

Truly in the coming kingdom, the people of God, whether depicted as a bride or a city, will be a wholly radiant people. This means, further, that sin and evil will never again have a place. The people of God will be a *holy* bride—"without spot or wrinkle . . .

---

[70]The Holy of Holies, or "inner sanctuary" was likewise a perfect cube: "twenty cubits long, twenty cubits wide, and twenty cubits high" (1 Kings 6:20).

[71]Even as they will be a "bride adorned" in purity.

[72]The Greek word is *katoptrizomenoi*, "reflecting." The KJV, NASB, and RSV translate it as "beholding" (KJV, "beholding as in a glass"; NASB, "beholding as in a mirror"); RSV has "reflecting" in the margin. Either "reflecting" or "beholding" is exegetically and linguistically possible; however, the broader context, including Moses, points, I believe, to the translation of "reflects" or "reflecting as a mirror." So one commentator puts it, "As Moses reflected temporarily the glory of Yahweh which he had seen, our faces reflect continually the brilliance of Christ" (P. E. Hughes, *Second Epistle to the Corinthians*, NICNT, 118, n.19, quoting E. B. Allo).

[73]That is, by the Holy Spirit ("the Spirit of the Lord" KJV).

[74]Second Corinthians 3:18, KJV and NASB translation.

holy and without blemish."[75] As a *holy* city, "nothing unclean and no one who practices abomination and lying, shall ever come into it" (Rev. 21:27 NASB). Forever sin-free, the people of God will be a radiant people throughout eternity!

C. The Light and the Glory

The climactic reality in the kingdom to come is the light and the glory of God that illumines all.

First, not only is the city itself resplendent and radiant, but it is also suffused throughout with the light and glory of God. Already the city come down from heaven was shown as "having the glory of God" (Rev. 21:11). This city was later described as dazzlingly radiant—foundations of precious stones, gates made wholly of pearl, the city itself of pure and transparent gold. Truly the holy city in every way will reflect the glory of God. But now the climax is even more wondrous: "And I saw no temple in the city, for its temple is the Lord God the Almighty and the Lamb.[76] And the city has no need of sun or moon to shine upon it, for the glory of God is its light[77] and its lamp is the Lamb" (vv. 22–23). The city—the radiant, holy city—is illumined from within by the glory of God!

Let us pause to reflect and rejoice. What all this magnificently declares is that the people of God, as the holy city, need never again to seek God in an earthly sanctuary or dwelling. For God Himself and the Lamb will be the temple in their midst. In this luminous presence all the lights of the heavens will be far surpassed; nor will there be need to look beyond to the heaven above the heavens for the light of God to come streaming down. The holy city—the new heaven and the new earth—will be suffused by the light and glory of God. The Lord God Almighty and the Lamb will be there,[78] and the people of God will be showing forth His eternal glory.

Second, John here moves beyond the city to the surrounding earth (the "new earth"), declaring, "By its light shall the nations walk; and the kings of the earth shall bring their glory into it" (Rev. 21:24). The light of the city itself, which comes from the indwelling glory of God, is so vastly luminous that the nations of earth walk by it. In keeping with the glory radiating outward, the

---

[75]Ephesians 5:27. Recall that the bride will be "clothed with fine linen, bright and pure" (Rev. 19:8).

[76]Earlier I mentioned Ezekiel 40–48 as a foregleam of Revelation 21–22. Here the revelation to John goes far beyond that given to Ezekiel, for in Ezekiel, although the city is spoken of, the main vision concerns the temple: its measurements, its priestly service, etc. But for John the temple—for all its earthly beauty—has been wholly transcended and replaced by God Himself! "For John there is no temple because symbol [i.e., in Ezekiel] has given way to reality" (Mounce, *The Book of Revelation*, NICNT, 383). The city is no longer Jerusalem but the glorified people of God, and the temple is no longer a structure built by man but the presence of God Almighty and the Lamb.

[77]Cf. Isaiah 60:19: "The sun shall be no more your light by day, nor for brightness shall the moon give light to you by night, but the LORD will be your everlasting light, and your God will be your glory." What a glorious fulfillment of this prophecy is found in Revelation 21:22–23! Isaiah, to be sure, depicts this in terms of the earthly Jerusalem of "Zion" (v. 14), and a people who "shall possess the land for ever" (v. 21), but in the revelation to John all of this is transcended in the glory of the New Jerusalem "out of heaven from God," a "land" that is "the new heaven and the new earth," and a possession that is eternal life (see following).

[78]The magnificent climax of Ezekiel 40–48, after the description of temple and city, is found in these words: "And the name of the city from that time on will be: THE LORD IS THERE" (48:35 NIV). What words could better declare the reality of the coming holy city, the radiant people of God: "THE LORD IS THERE"!

kings of the earth bring their glory within, as John shortly after adds: "They [the kings] shall bring into it the glory and the honor of the nations"[79] (v. 26).

From this it is apparent that the kingdom to come truly will have arrived on earth. The "nations" will no longer be the "earth-dwellers"[80] who walk contrary to the light of God; the "kings of the earth" will no longer be those who oppose God and the Lamb.[81] Indeed, *they will all be God's people*—nations[82] and kings alike—and at long last the ancient word from God Himself will have been fulfilled: "Truly, as I live . . . all the earth shall be filled with the glory of the Lord" (Num. 14:21).

It is important to recognize that both the holy city and the nations of earth represent the kingdom of God. The "holy city" is a depiction of the radiant holiness of God's people; "the nations" walking in God's light with the "kings of the earth" bringing glory and honor portray the universal centering of everything in God. It is *not* that some people will live in the city whereas others will be outside, for the city will not be the dwelling place of man but of God ("Behold, the dwelling of God is with men"). God's presence there will give *all* persons immediate access to Him. For, as John further relates about the city: "Its gates shall never be shut by day—and there shall be no night there" (Rev. 21:25).[83] Thus there will be both immediate and continuous access to the presence of the Lord God and the Lamb.

Let us try further to apprehend this magnificent portrayal of the kingdom to come. The people of God will be a holy and radiant people, as all the dazzling imagery of the holy city declares. The people of God will also be a people constantly giving God glory and honor, as the vivid imagery of nations and kings sets forth. Between these two pictures is one of Almighty God and the Lamb totally illuminating the city ("no need of sun or moon to shine upon it") and the nations ("by its light shall the nations walk"). This is the kingdom to come: God henceforth will dwell in the midst of a holy and radiant people who forever render Him glory and honor!

III. ETERNAL LIFE

Finally, the consummation will bring eternal life. Already in this age the believer has entered into life eternal. In the words of Jesus, "He who hears my word and believes him who sent me, *has* eternal life; he . . . has passed from death to life" (John 5:24). This present eternal life is the result of the transition from spiritual death into spiritual life. Although physical death may yet have to be faced, spiritual life will never end. Indeed, it is only in the age to come that believers will know its completeness.

Eternal life in its consummation signifies far more than continuance. For there is also a continuance for those who do not know eternal life; however, they will experience a different kind of eternity. Jesus speaks of those who "will go away into eternal punishment" (Matt. 25:46), and Paul speaks of "the punishment of eternal destruction" (2 Thess. 1:9). Hence, eternity itself is

[79]Cf. Isaiah 60:3: "And nations shall come to your light, and kings to the brightness of your rising."

[80]Recall the earlier references in Revelation to the "earth-dwellers."

[81]Recall Revelation 19:19 and elsewhere.

[82]The KJV, in translating Revelation 21:24, has "the nations of them which are saved," emphasizing that the nations are the people of God. Although the basis for such a textual addition is weak, the KJV, I believe, is correct in its understanding.

[83]Cf. Zechariah 14:7: "And there shall be continuous day (it is known to the LORD), not day and not night, for at evening time there shall be light."

not what the believer looks forward to, but an eternity that is life. The conclusion of Jesus' statement, following His words concerning eternal punishment, is that "the righteous [will go] into eternal life." Thus the key word is not "eternal" but "life"—eternal life both now and in the age to come.

Returning to the Book of Revelation, we observe the picture of eternal life in 22:1–5. The character of the life to come, depicted in these verses, is that of eternal blessedness, fullness of the worship of God, and reigning throughout eternity.

A. Eternal Blessedness

First, there will be *eternal blessedness*. This is vividly portrayed in "the water of life" and "the tree of life" with their blessings:

> Then he showed me the river of the water of life, bright as crystal, flowing from the throne of God and of the Lamb through the middle of the street of the city; also, on either side of the river, the tree of life with its twelve kinds of fruit, yielding its fruit each month; and the leaves of the tree were for the healing of the nations. (Rev. 22:1–2)

The very expressions "the river of the water of life" and "the tree of life" recall the Garden of Eden: "a river flowed out of Eden to water the garden" and "the tree of life [was] also in the midst of the garden" (Gen. 2:9–10). The purpose of both the "water" and the "tree" was for "life," the former to enliven the garden of man's habitation, and the latter to enable him to "live forever."[84] Since man disobeyed God, ate of another tree—the "tree of the knowledge of good and evil" (2:9)—and was expelled from Eden, he could no longer benefit from the river nor partake of the tree of immortality. "Paradise lost," consequently, in the consummation will be "Paradise regained," or perhaps better, "Paradise fulfilled." Indeed, earlier in the Book of Revelation the future tree of life is spoken of as being in "the paradise of God": "To him who conquers I will grant to eat of the tree of life, which is in the paradise of God" (2:7).

Both "the river of the water of life" and "the tree of life" also call to mind the visionary temple, portrayed by Ezekiel, with water pouring forth and trees on both sides of the river (Ezek. 47). Ezekiel beholds "water . . . issuing from below the threshold of the temple" (v. 1) until it becomes a river bringing freshness to the land eastward so that "everything will live where the river goes" (v. 9). Also, the prophet declares, "on the banks, on both sides of the river, there will grow all kinds of trees for food . . . they will bear fresh fruit every month. . . . Their fruit will be for food, and their leaves for healing" (v. 12). The parallel with Revelation is unmistakable, although the temple from which the water issues is here seen as "the throne of God and the Lamb" who are the temple in the age to come.[85] Rather than flowing through the land, the water flows "through the middle of the street of the city"; rather than many trees, only one, "the tree of life," is depicted (though it is "on either side of the river"!). What these differences in Revelation declare is immensely important: God Himself, that is, God and the Lamb, is the continuing source of the river that provides not merely physical life but life eternal; and since the water flows through the middle of

[84]Genesis 3:22. God spoke these words after Adam and Eve had sinned so that man had to be banished "lest he put forth his hand and take also of the tree of life, and eat, and live forever." Although Genesis 2 does not state that the "tree of life" made eternal life possible, this is so specified in Genesis 3.

[85]Recall Revelation 21:22.

the street of the city, which is none other than the holy city, the glorified people of God, it is they, not merely a land, who will be blessed eternally by God's refreshing presence. Moreover, this very river makes possible the tree of life, whose manifold and continuing fruit is not merely for physical strengthening but for eternal life.

Before going further, we should observe that "the river" may well refer to the Holy Spirit. Jesus declares on one occasion, "He who believes in me, as the scripture has said, 'Out of his heart shall flow rivers of living water' "—to which the Gospel adds, "Now this he said about the Spirit, which those who believed in him were to receive" (John 7:38–39). Also, Isaiah equates water and Spirit in this prophecy: "I will pour water on the thirsty land, and streams on the dry ground; I will pour my Spirit upon your descendants, and my blessing on your offspring" (44:3). Moreover, to return to the New Testament and particularly to the Gospel of John, Jesus also declares that the Spirit "proceeds from the Father" (John 15:26). The Greek word translated "proceeds from"[86] is the same as that used in Revelation 22:1 regarding the water "flowing from"[87] "the throne of God and of the Lamb." In both cases (the Gospel and Revelation) the source is God, whether depicted as the "Father" or "the throne of God and the Lamb."[88]

Hence we may conclude that "the river" represents the Holy Spirit,[89] and "the water of life" is that eternal life which His flowing forth makes ever actual and enduring. At the consummation, the Holy Spirit, along with Father and Son, is involved in making available "the water of life." Let me add that although the Holy Spirit is not mentioned by name in this passage, He later with the Bride gives a moving invitation: "The Spirit and the Bride say, 'Come.'. . . And let him who is thirsty come, let him who desires take the water of life without price" (Rev. 22:17). This invitation is all the more compelling against the background of the Holy Spirit as the river from which the water of life comes.

"The river of the water of life" not only points to eternal life but also suggests a special component of that life, namely, *joy and gladness*. The river "bright as crystal" sparkles as it flows forth, bringing pleasure and freshness in its flow. The Book of Psalms draws this vivid picture: "There is a river whose streams make glad the city of God, the holy habitation of the Most High" (46:4). This clearly anticipates Revelation 22—the river flowing through the city, the holy city—but also declares that the water "makes glad." One thinks also of Psalm 36:8: "Thou givest them drink from the river of thy delights." The river, it seems, is a joy, first of all to God, and then to man. Hence, in the age to come there will be joy and gladness, as from an ever-flowing, sparkling river. Surely, in the words of Jesus, this is that to which the faithful saint can look forward: "Enter thou into the joy of thy Lord" (Matt. 25:21 and 23 KJV).

Although in this life we may experience joy, even fullness of joy,[90] it pales

[86]The word is *ekporeutai*.

[87]The word is *ekporeuomenon*. The KJV translates it "proceeding out of."

[88]The Lamb is shown in Revelation sitting on the throne of the Father: "I myself conquered and sat down with my Father on his throne" (3:21). Thus there is only one throne and one God.

[89]Swete calls it "the river of the life-giving Spirit" (*Commentary on Revelation*, 298).

[90]We may recall that Jesus said, "These things I have spoken to you, that my joy may be

in comparison with the joy to be known in what lies beyond.[91] For it is the joy of the Lord—the joy that is first of all His—that we will find overflowing to us as we dwell in His personal presence. It is the joy, again, that can be known only when all of life's sorrows and anguish are forever a thing of the past. In the words of Revelation 21:4, "He [God] will wipe away every tear from their eyes, and death shall be no more, neither shall there be mourning nor crying nor pain any more, for the former things have passed away." Truly this will be joy beyond all that the present life can contain: it will be joy in the personal, intimate presence of the eternal God.[92]

Looking again at "the tree of life," we observe a number of extraordinary features. First, it is "on either side of the river" (Rev. 22:2). What seems practically impossible–one tree on both sides of a river—is spiritually a beautiful symbol of the eternal life that is present wherever the river of God flows. Also, this one tree has "twelve kinds of fruit"[93] (v. 2), signifying the variety and diversity of the eternal supply of fruit,[94] and that in the age to come one will feast on the richness of God's bountiful supply. Again, the tree, far beyond any earthly tree's ability, will yield its fruit "each month" (v. 2), thus portraying in vivid manner the constancy of God's blessing.

We may pause to reflect on the blessedness exhibited in "the tree of life" and its fruit. Regarding the tree itself: before sin entered the world, man could have partaken of the tree of life, that is, lived in accordance with God's command, walked in communion with his Maker, and thereby lived forever. But since the Fall, "the tree of life" has been closed off to him. Even now in this present life, although there is the possibility of entrance into eternal life, death still looms for all people. Thus, "the tree of life" lies yet beyond. What a joy to know that there will be no "tree of the knowledge of good and evil" in the age to come, for all evil will be utterly done away! The *only* tree—in all its marvelous multiplicity—will be the tree of eternal life.

What is depicted regarding the twelve kinds and monthly yield of the fruit of the tree surely is the blessedness of God's ever-varied and ever-continuing bounty. This highlights the *abundance* of God's supply in the new heaven and

in you, and that your joy may be full" (John 15:11). Peter speaks of a present "unutterable and exalted joy" (1 Peter 1:8).

[91]C. S. Lewis writes, "All your life an unattainable ecstasy has hovered just beyond the grasp of your consciousness" (*The Problem of Pain*, 136). It is this "unattainable ecstasy," then attained, that will highlight the age to come.

[92]A final note on the theme of the coming joy: The prophet Isaiah, speaking for the Lord, declares, "Behold, I create new heavens and a new earth; and the former things shall not be remembered or come into mind." (Observe the unmistakable parallel with Revelation 21:1.) Then follows "But be glad and rejoice for ever . . . for behold, I create Jerusalem a rejoicing, and her people a joy" (Isa. 65:17–18). The immediate reason for this coming joy: "No more shall be heard in it the sound of weeping and the cry of distress" (v. 19). (Note the parallel with Revelation 21:4.) "No more shall there be in it an infant that lives but a few days . . . for the child shall die a hundred years old" (v. 20). How much greater the joy to come in the "new Jerusalem" where life is not only extended but will never come to an end!

[93]Literally, "twelve fruits" (*karpous dōdeka*). The NASB also adds "kinds"; KJV, "manner"; NIV and NEB, "crops." "Kinds" or "manner," suggesting diversity, seems to be the more likely translation of the Greek text.

[94]Hence "the tree of life" is the composite and ultimate fulfillment of the words in Genesis 2:9: "And out of the ground the LORD God made to grow every tree that is pleasant to the sight and good for food, the tree of life also in the midst of the garden."

the new earth. We can scarcely imagine what all this signifies, for "no eye has seen, nor ear heard, nor the heart of man conceived, what God has prepared for those who love him" (1 Cor. 2:9). So it is with this marvelous fruit of the tree of life. We may sense the blessedness of what it signifies; but until the new age dawns, we can by no means begin to comprehend it all.

Also there is the blessing of *rest* in the world to come. In the Book of Revelation, a voice is heard proclaiming, "Blessed are the dead who die in the Lord henceforth. 'Blessed indeed,' says the Spirit, 'that they may rest from their labors' " (14:13). Rest is also mentioned in the Book of Hebrews: "So then, there remains a sabbath rest for the people of God; for whoever enters God's rest also ceases from his labors as God did from his" (Heb. 4:9–10). After all the labors of this earth and even the "sabbath's rest" intermittently enjoyed, there still awaits[95] an eternal rest for those who belong to Christ.

Let me further clarify this. For the present life God established a pattern of rest from human labors in the provision of the Sabbath: one day in seven to desist from work. Further, the provision of rest for the generation of those who left Egypt, while not fulfilled for them because of their sin, has been fulfilled with those who believe the gospel—"we who have believed enter that rest" (Heb. 4:3). In this connection we may recall these words of Jesus: "Come to me, all who labor and are heavy laden, and I will give you rest . . . for I am gentle and lowly in heart, and you will find rest for your souls" (Matt. 11:28–29). Accordingly, there is provision for both physical and spiritual rest in this life—and for both we are profoundly grateful. Yet, despite such rest, work is frequently tedious and toilsome,[96] labor often results in pain and weariness. From all such burdens there will be total deliverance in the new heaven and new earth.

It is possible that the picture of the tree of life, with its multiple and continuing yield of fruit—"twelve kinds . . . each month"—points in the direction of this rest. Since man's labor on earth is for earning his daily bread, and this in the sweat[97] of his face, the depiction of the world to come is all the more meaningful. There will be total rest from this kind of labor, as God Himself provides bountiful fruit for all to enjoy. Truly there will be blissful rest from toil in the coming Paradise of God.[98]

One final feature of the tree of life is that "the leaves of the tree were for the healing of the nations" (Rev. 22:2). This vivid picture should be set alongside that of God's wiping away tears from the eyes of His people. For not only will tears of mourning and pain be done away, but also the wounds due to long-held division and strife between various peoples will be forever healed. Hence,

[95]The NEB translates Hebrews 4:9: "Therefore, a sabbath rest still awaits the people of God. . . ."

[96]Originally man in Eden knew nothing of toil. He was, indeed, responsible for cultivating the garden—"to till it and keep it" (Gen. 2:15). Thus there was work to be done. After the Fall, toil becomes man's lot: "Cursed is the ground because of you; in toil you shall eat of it . . . and in the sweat of your face" (Gen. 3:17, 19). It is from the work that has become toil (not from work itself) that rest will be complete in the age to come.

[97]See note 96.

[98]Worth quoting here are some beautiful words from noncanonical 2 Esdras 8:52–54: "It is for you that paradise is opened, the tree of life is planted, the age to come is prepared, plenty is provided, a city is built, rest is appointed, goodness is established and wisdom perfected beforehand. The root of evil is sealed up from you, illness is banished from you, and death is hidden; hell has fled and corruption has been forgotten; sorrows have passed away, and in the end the treasure of immortality is made manifest."

all personal sorrow will pass away, and all causes of strife will be totally gone.[99]

Surely here also is the suggestion of universal *peace*. The same Old Testament passage that speaks of the sun being no more and the Lord instead being an "everlasting light" (Isa. 60:19) also affirms that "violence shall no more be heard in your land, devastation or destruction within your borders" (v. 18). Hence, peace will be on every hand in the future age. Isaiah 65:17, which speaks of the coming creation of a new heaven and a new earth, also declares about wild animals: "They shall not hurt or destroy in all my holy mountain" (v. 25).[100]

It is of course true that at the heart of the gospel is the message of peace and its realization through Christ. There is deep personal peace as well as opportunity for growth in that peace; both are true regardless of the world situation. Indeed, it is a peace the world cannot give or take away. Also, Christ has made peace possible between Jew and Gentile by being the one way for both to the Father. "He [Christ] is our peace, who has made us both one" (Eph. 2:14). Yet, by no means has universal peace come in this world, nor will it come until evil has been utterly destroyed and the new age has dawned.

Truly in the new world—to use the words of Isaiah—"nation shall not lift up sword against nation, neither shall they learn war any more" (2:4).[101] For all nations will be the holy people of God, and perfect peace will prevail. There may be memories of past bitterness and disappointment, of wars and bloodshed; but those memories, however poignant, will be healed. For the tree of life from which all people will be nourished will also be a tree of healing—"The leaves of the tree were [perhaps better 'will be'!] for the healing of the nations."

To summarize thus far: Eternal life in the world to come means the perfection of blessedness. The water of life and the tree of life—both its fruit and its leaves—point to the final fulfillment of joy and gladness, of rest and peace. All of this will come from the throne of God (Father, Son, and Holy Spirit); for it is in His presence that they will become complete.

B. Fullness of the Worship of God

A second aspect of the character of the life to come, as pictured in Revelation 22:1–5, is that there will be the *fullness* of the worship of God. In verses 3–4 we read, "There shall no more be anything accursed, but the throne of God and of the Lamb shall be in it, and his servants shall serve[102] him; they shall see his face, and his name shall be on their foreheads."

The curse that has been upon the world since man's fall into sin will be forever gone.[103] For God's throne will

---

[99]"The nations" are to be understood as in Revelation 21:24, 26. See the previous section. They are none other than God's people whose tears will be wiped away (Rev. 21:4), but now viewed not in terms of individual hurts and pains but of collective wounding and strife.

[100]Recall the prior reference to this verse on pages 483–84.

[101]The same words are found in Micah 4:3.

[102]Instead of "worship" as found in both RSV and NEB. The Greek verb is *latreusousin* from *latreuō*, which primarily means the total service one offers to God. Thus, it may also mean "worship," as the highest possible service to God. However, I believe it best to keep the broader meaning, "serve," in the translation (as do KJV, NASB, and NIV). Incidentally, the one other use of *latreuo* in Revelation 7:15 is translated as "serve" in the RSV ("minister" in NEB), also in KJV, NASB, and NIV. See the comment on Revelation 7:15 infra.

[103]The words "There shall be no more anything accursed"—more literally, "There shall

be in the holy city to sanctify it totally. In that beautiful and holy situation, several things will take place.

There will be, first of all, the *unending service* of God: "His servants shall serve Him." Earlier in Revelation is the heavenly scene of the saints who have come out of "the great tribulation" and whose robes were washed "white in the blood of the Lamb" (7:14). These words follow: "Therefore are they before the throne of God, and serve him day and night within his temple; and he who sits upon the throne will shelter them with his presence" (7:15). In the new world, as we have observed, there will be no temple, for God Himself and the Lamb will replace it. Also there will be no night and day. Nonetheless, what is said about the tribulation saints doubtless will apply even more vividly to the redeemed in the world to come, namely, they will continually be in the service of God. They will serve Him throughout eternity!

One marvelous aspect of the eternal service of God will be the freedom and capacity to do this totally. The believer in this world is likewise dedicated to serve God faithfully, though such service is, in part, always inadequate. Both the frailty of human life and the residue of sin stand in the way of that perfect service. We are called upon now to present ourselves as "a living sacrifice, holy and acceptable to God" (Rom. 12:1). But this we can never fully do because of our imperfect holiness. We may yearn for total devotion to the Lord, but we never completely attain it. Thus, one of the most striking aspects of eternal life will be that of free and total unending service.

Climactically, at the heart of all service in the coming age will be the worship of God. At every moment, in whatever aspect of service, there will be the continuing praise and worship of God. It will be joyful, obedient service—whatever the Lord commands—and always with the heart fixed on God. Service and worship actually become one,[104] for *all* things will be done for the glorifying of God.

Again, there will be the *direct vision* of God: "they shall see his face." In these simple but profound words is declared the ultimate blessedness: beholding the face of God! Remember that Moses once said to God, "I pray thee, show me thy glory," and God replied, "You cannot see my face; for man shall not see me and live" (Exod. 33:18, 20). Even Moses, who had intimate communication with God and doubtless yearned to behold God in totality, was not permitted the ultimate vision. Indeed, it would have caused his destruction, for mortal flesh cannot bear the full weight of the divine glory. Likewise the apostle Paul, although testifying of many "visions and revelations of the Lord," even to being "caught up into Paradise" (2 Cor. 12:1, 3), was constrained to speak of God as one who "dwells in unapproachable light, whom no man has ever seen or can see" (1 Tim. 6:16). The sheer brilliance of God's presence makes such sight presently impossible.

But—it may be rejoined—was not the Incarnation the very revelation of God Himself? For John wrote, "No one has ever seen God; the only Son, who is in the bosom of the Father, he has made him known" (1:18). Does not this imply that God, invisible before, became visible through Christ, so that those who beheld the face of Christ beheld the face of God? Is this not further confirmed by

no longer be any curse" (NASB)—go back to Zechariah 14:11: "There shall be no more curse." The prophecy of Zechariah, continuing with the words "Jerusalem shall dwell in security," refers in Revelation to the new Jerusalem of the world to come.

[104]As noted before, the Greek word *latreuō* contains the note of both service and worship.

Jesus' own words, "He who has seen me has seen the Father" (John 14:9)? To reply: Christ, the Incarnate One, was truly the mediator of God's presence, so that God the Father was seen in Him. However, for all its glory and grace, His presence was still a mediation in the flesh. The direct vision of God remains beyond—and in the age to come we shall so behold Him!

Actually, there is nothing, absolutely nothing, that people so yearn to behold as the face of God. The psalmist speaks the heart cry of mankind: "My soul thirsts for God, for the living God. When shall I come and behold the face of God?" (42:2).

For "the face of God" means the shining forth of God's own being, the splendor of His glorious person. It has been truly said, "Life has but one failure: not to see God." For to see God in all His glory is the highest possible good;[105] to miss that is ultimately to miss everything. While seeing God is not possible in this mortal and sinful flesh, the wonder, the marvel is that the day is coming when in our transformed bodies we shall see His face! Then the weight of God's glory will not simply overwhelm and crush our human existence; rather, it will shine forth upon a humanity prepared to receive it.

The glorious vision of God! The angels in heaven always see the face of God;[106] the four living creatures that stand around the throne of God continually behold Him;[107] the twenty-four elders on surrounding thrones constantly fall down and worship the Lord, casting their crowns before Him.[108] Likewise, the living creatures and elders prostrate themselves before the Lamb who stands near the throne of God, giving Him similar worship. Their worship joins that of the "myriads of myriads and thousands of thousands" of angels and every creature in heaven, and earth, and under the earth.[109] All this that is transpiring even now anticipates the glory to come in the new heaven and the new earth. No longer will God be on the throne and the Lamb near at hand; rather it will be "the throne of God *and* of the Lamb"[110] (Rev. 22:3). And it is He (not they) who will be seen: "They shall see *his* face." Although God the Father and the Son will forever remain distinct persons, the vision will merge, the faces becoming gloriously one, and in that one face will be united all the glory of God the Creator and God the Redeemer. His face they will see, His being they will worship—throughout eternity!

What this vision of God in the age to come will be far transcends our human imagination. For in the one vision—the one "face"—will be seen all the glory and the grace of both God the Father and God the Son. It will be the face of the One who brought us forth out of nothing but also saved us from final destruction. It will be the face of complete holiness and purity, but also the face of total mercy and compassion. Such glory, such grace—also such beauty, such truth—"*they* shall see."

---

[105]The summum bonum of which philosophers often have spoken.

[106]Jesus in reference to "these little ones" said, "Do not despise [them]; for I tell you that in heaven their angels always behold the face of my Father who is in heaven" (Matt. 18:10).

[107]The four living creatures are described in Revelation 4:8 as "full of eyes all round and within" (hence, total vision); moreover, "day and night they never cease to sing, 'Holy, holy, holy, is the Lord God Almighty, who was and is and is to come!' "

[108]Revelation 4:9–11; compare 11:16; 19:4. Although one cannot be certain, the twenty-four elders probably represent the glorified church.

[109]Revelation 5:11–14. The climax: "The elders fell down and worshiped" (v. 14).

[110]Even as the temple will be "the Lord God the Almighty and the Lamb" (Rev. 21:22).

But let us change the pronoun to we—"*we* shall see his face"[111]—and, so seeing, will worship and praise Him throughout eternity.

Once again, there will be an *intimate relationship* between God and man: "His name shall be on their foreheads" (Rev. 22:4). This vivid picture recalls the Old Testament passage where Moses tells Aaron and his sons to bless Israel: "The LORD bless you and keep you: The LORD make his face to shine upon you, and be gracious to you: The LORD lift up his countenance upon you, and give you peace" (Num. 6:24–26). Then follows this promise of God: "So shall they put my name upon the people of Israel, and I will bless them" (v. 27). "My name upon the people of Israel" signifies that Israel belonged to God in a special way and that all the blessings mentioned, including God's face shining upon them, were intended for His people. In a far more abundant way God's name will be upon His redeemed people in the age to come, for we are totally His[112] forever.

A similar picture is described earlier in the Book of Revelation of the 144,000 with the Lamb on Mt. Zion who have "his name and his Father's name written on their foreheads" (14:1).[113] They, likewise, are the redeemed—"these have been redeemed from mankind as first fruits for God and the Lamb" (v. 4). The two names (Christ's and the Father's) of Revelation 14[114] merge into the one name of Revelation 21, because the redemption of all has now occurred so that even as they see God's face in eternity, His one name is upon them. Surely God's name upon His people in the new heaven and new earth bespeaks an intimate relationship flowing out of the fullness of worship in which His very face is seen. For those who see the face of God will have His name on their foreheads, not only as a sign of their being possessed by Him and having His blessings on them, but also doubtless as a reflection of His glory.[115]

Paul says that even now we "with unveiled faces all reflect the Lord's glory," and in this way "are being transformed into his likeness with ever-increasing glory" (2 Cor. 3:18 NIV).[116] If indeed in this life we reflect God's glory and are being gradually changed into His likeness from glory to glory, how much more will this be when we will not

[111]There comes to mind this gospel chorus:
O that will be glory for me,
Glory for me, glory for me;
When by His grace
I shall look on His face
That will be glory, be glory for me.
Charles H. Gabriel

[112]"The redeemed shall be perfectly possessed by God" (Ladd, *A Commentary of the Revelation of John*, 288).

[113]Incidentally, this strikingly contrasts with Revelation 13, where the "earth-dwellers" have the mark of the beast on their foreheads (v. 16). Also, compare 14:9, where reference is again made to the beast's mark on the forehead. In between these two "beastly" passages is the beautiful picture of Revelation 14:1.

[114]Still earlier, in Revelation 3:12, there are three names. In the message to the church of Philadelphia Jesus declares, "He who conquers I will make him a pillar in the temple of my God; never shall he go out of it, and I will write on him the name of my God, and the name of the city of my God, the New Jerusalem which comes down from my God out of heaven, and my own new name."

[115]Mounce puts it well: "The faces of those who have experienced the beatific vision will reflect the unmistakable likeness of their heavenly Father" (*The Book of Revelation*, NICNT, 388).

[116]Recall the earlier discussion of this verse on pages 496–97.

just reflect God's glory but also behold His face! The transformation will be complete, the believers will be glorified, and their whole being will radiate a divine glory that will *never* fade away.[117]

"His name shall be on their foreheads." How incomprehensible is the picture of this intimate relationship with the Lord God! We will be marked not with our own name but with God's name, the name of Him whose face is beheld in glory, and will bear that name throughout eternity! Blessed by Him beyond measure, possessed by Him in totality, changed wholly into His likeness—so shall it be in the age that is yet to come.

But let us end this section as we began, emphasizing that everything focuses on the fullness of the worship of God. Whether we speak of unending service, the direct vision of God, or the intimate relationship between God and the redeemed, the background is "the throne of God and the Lamb." The only possible attitude before this glorious throne is worship and adoration. So whether serving Him, beholding His face, or reflecting His likeness, it will all be in the context of overflowing praise. It will be praise—eternally!

C. Reigning Forever

Third, and finally, there will be an *eternal reign*. We may now hear this climactic prophecy: "And night shall be no more; they need no light of lamp or sun, for the Lord God will be their light, and they shall reign for ever and ever" (Rev. 22:5). With these words the vision of the consummation comes to an end.

To appreciate better the eternal reign of the saints, let us consider a number of truths.

1. From the beginning man was made by God to rule. The first recorded words of God to newly created man were these: "Be fruitful and multiply, and fill the earth, and subdue it; and rule over the fish of the sea and over the birds of the sky, and over every living thing that moves on the earth" (Gen. 1:28 NASB). The psalmist echoes these words, saying, "Thou dost make him to rule over the works of Thy hands; Thou hast put all things under his feet" (8:6 NASB). The writer of Hebrews, after quoting from Psalm 8, declares, "Now in putting everything in subjection to him [man], he left nothing outside his control" (2:8).

2. Man does not fully exercise this rule. The words in Hebrews 2:8 continue: "As it is, we do not yet see everything in subjection to him." The point, then, is that this dominion, or rule, by man is not complete—indeed, it is far from complete because of the inroads of sin, death, and the power of Satan.

3. The focus shifts to Jesus: "But we see Jesus," who was victorious over all that prevents man's rule, "crowned with glory and honor" (v. 9). So Jesus, by His victory on the cross and His elevation to heaven, now rules over all principalities and powers.

4. Those who belong to Christ also rule, or reign, now because of Him. Paul writes, "If, because of one man's trespass, death reigned through that one man, much more will those who receive the abundance of grace and the free gift of righteousness reign in life through the one man Jesus Christ" (Rom. 5:17). We

[117]I should not fail to mention Moses, who with "unveiled face" had such an exposure to God's glory (for forty days and nights, praying and fasting atop a mountain, communing with God, and receiving the Ten Commandments) that when he came down, "the skin of his face shone because he had been talking with God" (Exod. 34:29). That glory faded in time, but not so for the inner glory of the believer, who is being continuously changed in this life and will be completely transformed in the age to come. The glory is there—forever.

"reign in life" even now. As Paul later adds, "We are more than conquerors through him who loved us" (Rom. 8:37)—and this includes life, death, principalities, things present, things to come: there is no limit.[118] In the Book of Revelation, John writes, "To him who loves us and has freed us from our sins by his blood and made us a kingdom, priests to his God and Father, to him be glory and dominion for ever and ever" (1:5–6). We have been made a kingdom and therefore rule even now, just as we are also now priests to God.

5. Although Christ now reigns, He has not yet destroyed all the forces of evil; their power is broken, but their end has not yet come. Paul, looking ahead to the Parousia of Christ, writes, "Then comes the end, when he delivers the kingdom to God the Father after destroying every rule and every authority and power" (1 Cor. 15:24). Paul adds that Christ "must reign[119] until he has put all his enemies under his feet" (v. 25). For this final destruction and subjection, Christ will return to inflict "eternal destruction" (2 Thess. 1:9) upon His enemies and to "destroy" (2 Thess. 2:8) utterly the "man of sin."[120] According to the Book of Revelation, this will be the time when a loud voice in heaven cries forth: "The kingdom of the world has become the kingdom of our Lord and of his Christ, and he shall reign for ever and ever" (11:15).[121] Thus, after all foes are destroyed, Christ will reign eternally.

6. Although we reign now, the reign is not complete, since there is still sin and evil, death and Satan. But once they have all been destroyed, and the new age entered into, there will no longer be any hindrance. Recall Daniel's prophecy in which the "horn[122] made war with the saints, and prevailed over them, until the Ancient of Days came, and judgment was given for the saints of the Most High, and the time came when the saints received the kingdom" (7:21–22). It is further said that "his [the 'horn's'] dominion shall be taken away, to be consumed and destroyed[123] to the end. And the kingdom and the dominion and the greatness of the kingdoms under the whole heaven shall be given to the people of the saints of the Most High; their[124] kingdom shall be an everlasting kingdom, and all dominions shall serve and obey them" (vv. 26–27).[125] Looking forward from Daniel, we hear again the climactic note of the Book of Revelation: "They shall reign for ever and ever."

It is clear that the saints will reign

---

[118]Paul adds that none of these things can "separate us from the love of God in Christ Jesus our Lord" (v. 39). The very fact that they cannot separate us demonstrates that we are "more than conquerors."

[119]This refers to Christ's present reign. For the view of those who understand this to mean a future millennial reign, see the Excursus in chapter 13, "The Millennium," pages 437–46.

[120]Recall the earlier discussion.

[121]Later the twenty-four elders say that the time came for "destroying the destroyers of the earth" (v. 18). It is against this background that the victorious reign "for ever and ever" is pronounced.

[122]The "horn" represents the same anti-God, anti-Christian evil force as "the beast" (Rev. 13:7).

[123]Note the parallel with the theme of destruction in the preceding paragraph.

[124]The NASB (cf. NIV) has "His." The pronoun is singular, so it could point to the Messiah (see 7:14); however, the present context suggests that the "his" refers to the saints. Accordingly, RSV and NEB translate it as "their." The KJV has "whose kingdom," thus, like RSV and NEB, referring back to the "saints of the Most High."

[125]This agrees with Daniel 7:18: "The saints of the Most High shall receive the kingdom . . . for ever, for ever and ever."

with Christ throughout eternity, for both "he" and "they" "shall reign for ever and ever" (Rev. 11:15; 22:5). But if we ask, "Over what shall the saints reign?" the answer is not clear. According to Daniel, as was quoted, "All dominions shall serve and obey them."[126] Perhaps this refers to angelic dominions or sovereignties—the various beneficent principalities, authorities, and powers.[127] Since Christ reigns over them, we may share in that reign. Since the saints are to judge angels at the judgment day,[128] it seems quite possible that we may somehow also reign over them.

But the reign of believers could also be over other spheres. We may again refer to Jesus' parables of the talents (Matt. 25:14–30) and pounds (Luke 19:11–27).[129] Each of these parables depicts the return of the Lord after a long period of time and His settling accounts with His servants who had been entrusted with various amounts of money. In the former parable, the two servants who doubled their amount are told, "You have been faithful with a few things; I will put you in charge of many things" (NIV). In the latter parable, the two servants who increased their amount are given a greater sphere of authority: "You shall have authority over ten cities. . . . You are to be over five cities." We have earlier observed how these parables relate to different rewards in the age to come; here we note that the rewards consist of spheres of rule and authority. On the basis of these parables we may conclude that in the coming age the reign of believers will be wide-ranging ("in charge of many things") and varied (some "over ten cities," some "over five cities"). What these "many things" are is not described, nor is it clear how there can be "cities" in the age to come. Since *the* "holy city" alone is portrayed in the Book of Revelation, where may other "cities" be found? Of course, since these are parables and the main point in each case concerns faithfulness rather than a later reward, we should be hesitant to draw too many detailed conclusions. However, it seems possible to say this much: the saints will have spheres of authority in the world to come—whether or not these are "cities" in a literal sense. The saved will be over "many things."

In line with this, it may well be that we will reign fully in those areas over which the Lord has already given us authority and responsibility in this life. This could signify the fullest possible expansion of our abilities and experience, the uniqueness of each person preserved and multiplied beyond measure. "Reigning" does not need to be understood only as over authorities and powers but over every aspect of what God has made us to do and to accomplish. It hardly seems possible that all we have been given by God at birth and in the experience of our lives will simply be a thing of the past with no relation to the future world. If this were true, why does God both preserve us in our entirety (body, soul, and spirit) and glorify what He has made in the age to come? His purpose surely must be that we carry forward to an ultimate degree what has begun on this present earth. We may not—indeed do not—reign completely now; moreover, death cuts us short. *But* in the new heaven and the new earth, by God's grace, we shall reign forever.

Whatever the full nature or scope of our future reign, we may greatly rejoice

[126]Assuming as above that this text refers to the rule of the saints.

[127]As mentioned in Ephesians 1:21; Colossians 1:16; 1 Peter 3:22.

[128]Recall the previous discussion.

[129]See the earlier discussion, pages 455–56.

that it will be a shared reign with our Lord Jesus Christ. And as surely as Christ and the Father are one God, and there is only one throne of God and the Lamb, our reign will be with the Lord of the whole universe. Moreover, it will not be at a distance, for God Himself will be dwelling with us, His Son guiding us, and His Spirit refreshing us. Our reign will be in the glorious presence of Him whose face we shall at every moment behold.

Praise God! So shall we reign—for ever and ever!

BIBLIOGRAPHY

Abbot, Walter M., gen. ed. *The Documents of Vatican II*. New York: Guild Press, 1966.

Adams, Jay. *The Time Is at Hand*. Nutley, N.J.: Presbyterian and Reformed, 1966.

Aland, Kurt. *Did the Early Church Baptize Infants?* London: SCM, 1963.

Allen, Willoughby C. *Gospel According to St. Matthew*. ICC. New York: Scribner, 1925.

Amos, Gary T. *Defending the Declaration*. Brentwood, Tenn.: Wolgemuth and Hyatt, 1989.

Augustine. *On Baptism, Against the Donatists*.

________. *The City of God*.

________. *John's Gospel*. NPNF VII.

Aulén, Gustaf. *The Faith of the Christian Church*. Philadelphia: Muhlenberg Press, 1948.

Bahnsen, Greg L. *Theonomy in Christian Ethics*. Nutley, N.J.: Craig Press, 1977.

Barrett, C. K. *The Epistle of the Romans*. HNTC. New York: Harper, 1957.

________. *The First Epistle to the Corinthians*. HNTC. New York: Harper & Row, 1968.

Barrett, David. *World Christian Encyclopedia*. Oxford: Oxford Unversity Press, 1982.

Barth, Karl. *Church Dogmatics*. Edinburgh: T. & T. Clark, 1936–69.

________. *Credo*. London: Hodder and Stoughton, 1936.

________. *The Teaching of the Church Regarding Baptism*. London: SCM, 1948.

Barth, Marcus. *Ephesians 4–6*. AB. Garden City, N.Y.: Doubleday, 1974.

Bauer, Walter, William F. Arndt, F. Wilbur Gingrich, and Frederick W. Danker. *A Greek-English Lexicon of the New Testament*. Chicago: University of Chicago Press, 1979.

Beasley-Murray, G. R. *Baptism in the New Testament*. Exeter, England: Paternoster, 1972.

________. *Ezekiel*. NBC. Edited by Donald Guthrie. Rev. ed. Grand Rapids: Eerdmans, 1970.

________. *Jesus and the Kingdom of God*. Grand Rapids: Eerdmans, 1986.

________. *The Book of Revelation*. NCBC. Grand Rapids: Eerdmans, 1981.

Beckwith, I. T. *The Apocalypse of John*. Grand Rapids: Baker, 1979.

Berkhof, Louis. *Systematic Theology*. Grand Rapids: Eerdmans, 1941.

Berkhouwer, G. C. *Studies in Dogmatics: The Return of Christ*. Grand Rapids: Eerdmans, 1972.

________. *Studies in Dogmatics: The Sacraments*. Grand Rapids: Eerdmans, 1969.

Biederwolf, W. E. *The Second Coming Bible Commentary*. Grand Rapids: Baker, 1985.

Blackstone, W. E. *Jesus Is Coming*. Chicago: Revell, 1916.

Boettner, Loraine. *The Millennium*. Philadelphia: Presbyterian and Reformed, 1957.

Bonhoeffer, Dietrich. *Ethics*. Translated by Neville H. Smith. London: SCM, 1955.

Bright, John. *The Kingdom of God*. Nashville: Abingdon, 1953.

Brooke, Tal. *When the World Will Be as One: The Coming New World Order in the New Age*. Eugene, Ore.: Harvest House, 1989.

Brown, William Adams. *Christian Theology in Outline*. Edinburgh: T. & T. Clark, 1907.

Bruce, F. F. "Antichrist in the Early Church." In *A Mind for What Matters: Collected Essays*. Grand Rapids: Eerdmans, 1990.

________. *1 & 2 Thessalonians*. WBC. Waco: Word, 1982.

________. *Acts of the Apostles*. Grand Rapids: Eerdmans, 1950.

________. *The Book of the Acts,* rev. ed. NICNT. Grand Rapids: Eerdmans, 1988.

________. *The Canon of Scripture*. Downers Grove, Ill.: InterVarsity, 1988.

________. *The Epistle of Paul to the Romans*. TNTC. Grand Rapids: Eerdmans, 1964.

________. *The Epistle to the Hebrews. NICNT*. Grand Rapids: Eerdmans, 1964.

________. *The Epistles of John*. Grand Rapids: Eerdmans, 1970.

________. *The Epistles to the Colossians, to Philemon, and to the Ephesians*. NICNT. Grand Rapids: Eerdmans, 1984.

________. *The Gospel of John*. Grand Rapids: Eerdmans, 1983.

Brunner, Emil. *Eternal Hope*. Westport, Conn.: Greenwood Press, 1972.

________. *The Christian Doctrine of the Church, Faith, and the Consummation, Dogmatics*. Vol. 3. Philadelphia: Westminster, 1962.

Brunner, Peter. *Worship in the Name of Jesus*. St. Louis: Concordia, 1968.

Bultmann, Rudolf. *Kerygma and Myth*. London: SPCK, 1953.

Buswell, J. Oliver. *A Systematic Theology of the Christian Religion*. Grand Rapids: Zondervan, 1962.

Caird, G. B. *A Commentary on the Revelation of St. John the Divine*. HNTC. New York: Harper & Row, 1966.

Calvin, John. *Commentaries*. Translated by Beveridge. Grand Rapids: Eerdmans, 1948–50.

________. *Institutes of the Christian Religion*. Translated by Beveridge. Grand Rapids: Eerdmans, 1957. Translated by Battles. Library of Christian Classics, vol. 20. Philadelphia: Westminster, 1960.

Carson, D. A. *Matthew*. EBC. Grand Rapids: Zondervan, 1976.

Chafer, L. S. *Systematic Theology*. Dallas: Dallas Seminary Press, 1947.

Charles, R. H. *The Revelation of St. John*. ICC. New York: Scribner, 1920.

Chilton, David. *Paradise Restored: A Biblical Theology of Dominion*. Tyler, Texas: Reconstruction Press, 1985.

Clement. *The Letter of the Romans to the Corinthians*, in *The Apostolic Fathers*. Edited by Michael W. Holmes. Grand Rapids: Baker, 1989.

Clouse, Bonnidell, and Robert G. *Women in Ministry: Four Views*. Downers Grove, Ill.: InterVarsity, 1989.

Clouse, Robert, G., ed. *The Meaning of the Millennium: Four Views*. Downers Grove, Ill.: InterVarsity, 1977.

Cole, Alan. *The Gospel According to St. Mark*. TNTC. Grand Rapids: Eerdmans, 1961.

Cox, W. E. *Biblical Studies in Final Things*. Philadelphia: Presbyterian and Reformed, 1966.

Cranfield, C. E. B. *Romans: A Shorter Commentary*. Grand Rapids: Eerdmans, 1985.

Creme, Benjamin. *The Reappearance of Christ and the Masters of Wisdom*. Tara Center, 1988.

Cullmann, Oscar, and Leenhardt, F. J. *Essays on the Lord's Supper*. Richmond: John Knox, 1958.

________. *Baptism in the New Testament*. London: SCM, 1950.

________. *Immortality of the Soul or Resurrection of the Dead?* London: Epworth, 1958.

________. *The State in the New Testament*. New York: Scribner, 1956.

Damsteegt, P. G., et al. *Seventh-day Adventists Believe*. Washington: Ministerial Association, General Conference of Seventh-day Adventists, 1988.

Davis, J. J. *Christ's Victorious Kingdom: Postmillennialism Reconsidered*. Grand Rapids: Baker, 1986.

Delling, Gerhardt. *Worship in the New Testament*. Philadelphia: Westminster, 1962.

Denney, James. *Studies in Theology*. Reprint. Grand Rapids: Baker, 1976.

Dodd, C. H. *Gospel and Law: The Relation of Faith and Ethics in Early Christianity*. New York: Columbia University Press, 1951.

________. *The Apostolic Preaching and Its Development*. New York: Harper & Row, 1964.

________. *The Parables of the Kingdom*. London: Nisbet, 1936.

Duddy, Neil T. *The God-Men: An Inquiry into Witness Lee and the Local Church*. Downers Grove, Ill.: InterVarsity, 1981.

Dunn, James D. G. *Jesus and the Spirit*. London: SCM, 1975.

________. *Romans 9–16*. WBC. Dallas: Word, 1988.

Edwards, David L. *Essentials: A Liberal Evangelical Dialogue*. London: Hodder and Stoughton, 1988.

Eliot, T. S. "Choruses from 'The Rock,'" *The Complete Poems and Plays, 1909–1950*. New York: Harcourt, Brace and World, 1971.

English, E. Schuyler. *Rethinking the Rapture*. Traveler's Rest, S.C.: Southern Bible Bookhouse, 1954.

Erickson, Millard, J. *Contemporary Options in Eschatology*. Grand Rapids: Baker, 1977.

Erickson, Millard, J., ed. *The New Life*. Grand Rapids: Baker, 1979.

Eusebius. *Ecclesiastical History*. Cambridge: Harvard University Press, 1926–32.

Fee, Gordon. *1 and 2 Timothy, Titus*. NIBC. San Francisco: Harper & Row, 1984.

________. *The First Epistle to the Corinthians*. NICNT. Grand Rapids: Eerdmans, 1987.

Feinberg, Charles. *Millennialism: The Two Major Views*. Chicago: Moody, 1982.

Ford, J. M. *Revelation*. AB. Garden City, N.Y.: Doubleday, 1975.

Fox, Matthew. *The Coming of the Cosmic Christ*. San Francisco: Harper & Row, 1988.

Frame, J. M. "Second Chance." *Evangelical Dictionary of Theology*. Edited by Walter A. Elwell. Grand Rapids: Baker, 1984.

France, R. T. *The Gospel According to Matthew*. TNTC. Grand Rapids: Eerdmans, 1985.

Fudge, E. W. *The Fire that Consumes*. Houston: Providential Press, 1982.

Geldenhuys, Norval. *The Gospel of Luke*. NICNT. Grand Rapids: Eerdmans, 1951.

Gilmour, S. M. *Luke*. IB. New York: Abingdon-Cokesbury, 1951–57.

Gloer, W. Hulitt. *Eschatology and the New Testament*. Peabody, Mass.: Hendrickson, 1988.

Goldingay, John. *Daniel*. WBC. Dallas: Word, 1989.

Gordon, A. J. *The Ministry of the Spirit*. Minneapolis: Bethany Fellowship, 1964.

Green, Michael, ed. *The Truth of God Incarnate*. Grand Rapids: Eerdmans, 1977.

________. *The Second Epistle of Peter and the Epistle of Jude*. TNTC. Grand Rapids: Eerdmans, 1968.

Groothuis, Douglas, R. *Unmasking the New Age*. Downers Grove, Ill.: InterVarsity, 1986.

Gundry, Robert, H. *Matthew: A Commentary on His Literary and Theological Art*. Grand Rapids: Eerdmans, 1982.

________. *The Church and the Tribulation*. Grand Rapids: Zondervan, 1973.

Haenchen, Ernst. *Acts of the Apostles*. Oxford: Blackwell, 1971.

Hamilton, Floyd E. *The Basis of Millennial Faith*. Grand Rapids: Eerdmans, 1955.

Hamon, Bill. *Prophets and the Prophet Movement*. Shippensburg, Pa.: Destiny Image, 1990.

Harper, Michael. *Let My People Grow*. Plainfield, N.J.: Logos International, 1977.

Harrison, Everett, F. *Romans*. EBC. Grand Rapids: Zondervan, 1976–88.

Harrison, Norman B. *The End: Rethinking the Revelation*. Minneapolis: Harrison, 1941.

Hemer, Colin. *The Letters to the Seven Churches of Asia in Their Local Setting*. Sheffield: JSOT, 1986.

Hendriksen, William. *I & II Timothy and Titus*. NTC. London: Banner of Truth Trust, 1957.

________. *More Than Conquerors*. Grand Rapids: Baker, 1982.

———. *The Gospel of Matthew*. NTC. Edinburgh: Banner of Truth Trust, 1974.
Henry, Carl F. H., ed. *Basic Christian Doctrines*. Grand Rapids: Baker, 1962.
Herbert, A. S. *Worship in Ancient Israel*. Richmond: John Knox, 1959.
Hicks, John, ed. *The Myth of God Incarnate*. London: SCM, 1977.
Hiebert, D. E. *Titus*. EBC. Grand Rapids: Zondervan, 1978.
Higgins, A. J. B. *The Lord's Supper in the New Testament*. London: SCM, 1952.
Hodge, C. H. *Systematic Theology*. 3 vols. Grand Rapids: Eerdmans, 1970.
Hoekema, Anthony A. *The Bible and the Future*. Grand Rapids: Eerdmans, 1979.
Holmes, M. W., ed. *The Apostolic Fathers*. Grand Rapids: Baker, 1989.
Hoyt, Karen. *New Age Rage*. Old Tappan, N.J.: Revell, 1987.
Hughes, Philip, E. *The Book of Revelation*. Grand Rapids: Eerdmans, 1990.
———. *The Second Epistle to the Corinthians*. NICNT. Grand Rapids: Eerdmans, 1962.
———. *The True Image: The Origin and Destiny of Man in Christ*. Grand Rapids: Eerdmans, 1989.
Ignatius. *Letter to the Smyrnaeans*.
———. *Letter to Polycarp*.
———. *Letter to the Philadelphians*.
Irenaeus. *Against Heresies*.
Jehovah's Witnesses. *Let God Be True*. Brooklyn: Watch Tower Bible and Tract Society, 1952.
Jeremias, J. *Infant Baptism in the First Four Centuries*. Philadelphia: Westminster, 1962.
———. *The Eucharistic Words of Jesus*. London: SCM, 1966.
———. *The Parables of Jesus*. Translated by S. H. Hooke. 3rd ed. London: SCM, 1972.
Jewett, Paul. *Infant Baptism and the Covenant of Grace*. Grand Rapids: Eerdmans, 1978.
Josephus, F. *The Complete Works*. Translated by William Whiston. Grand Rapids: Kregel, 1960.
Justin Martyr. *First Apology*.
Käsemann, Ernst. *Commentary on Romans*. Grand Rapids: Eerdmans, 1980.
Kaufmann, Yehezkel. *History of the Religion of Israel*. Vol. 4. New York: Kiev, 1977.
Keil, C. F., and F. Delitzch. *Commentary on the Old Testament*, 10 vols. Reprint. Grand Rapids: Eerdmans, 1983.
Kelly, J. N. D. *A Commentary on the Pastoral Epistles*. HNTC. New York: Harper, 1963.
Kiddle, Morton. *The Revelation of St. John*. MNTC. London: Hodder and Stoughton, 1940.
Kidner, Derek. *Psalms 1–72: An Introduction and Commentary*. TOTC. London: Inter-Varsity, 1973.
Kik, J. Marcellus. *An Eschatology of Victory*. Nutley, N.J.: Presbyterian and Reformed, 1971.
———. *Church and State in the New Testament*. Grand Rapids: Baker, 1962.
Kistemaker, S. J. *Acts*. NTC. Grand Rapids: Baker, 1953–80.
Kromminga, D. H. *The Millennium in the Church*. Grand Rapids: Eerdmans, 1945.
Küng, Hans. *The Church*. London: Search Press, 1971.
Ladd, George E. *A Commentary on the Revelation of John*. Grand Rapids: Eerdmans, 1972.
———. *The Blessed Hope*. Grand Rapids: Eerdmans, 1956.
———. *The Presence of the Future*. Grand Rapids: Eerdmans, 1974.
Leith, John. *Creeds of the Churches*. Richmond: John Knox, 1973.
Lenski, R. C. H. *The Interpretation of St. John's Revelation*. Minneapolis: Augsburg, 1963.
———. *The Interpretation of St. Luke's Gospel*. Minneapolis: Augsburg, 1961.
———. *The Interpretation of St. Matthew's Gospel*. Minneapolis: Augsburg, 1961.
———. *The Interpretation of St. Paul's Epistles to the Colossians, Thessalonians, Timothy, Titus, Philemon*. Minneapolis: Augsburg, 1961.

________. *The Interpretation of the Acts of the Apostles*. Minneapolis: Augsburg, 1961.

Lewis, A. H. *The Dark Side of the Millennium*. Grand Rapids: Baker, 1980.

Lewis, C. S. *Screwtape Letters*. Philadelphia: Fortress, 1980.

________. *The Problem of Pain*. New York: Macmillan, 1944.

Lightfoot, J. B. *The Apostolic Fathers*. Grand Rapids: Baker, 1956.

Lightner, Robert, P. *The Last Days Handbook*. Nashville: Nelson, 1990.

Lindsey, Hal. *The Rapture: Truth or Consequences*. New York: Bantam, 1983.

________. *There's a New World Coming*. Santa Ana, Calif.: Vision, 1973.

________. *When Is Jesus Coming Again?* Carol Stream, Ill.: Creation House, 1974.

Lipnack, Jessica, and Jeffery Stamps. *Networking Book*. New York: Viking, Penguin, 1988.

Lock, Walker. *The Pastoral Epistles*. ICC. Edinburgh: T. & T. Clark, 1924.

Luther, Martin. *Luther's Small Catechism*. St. Louis: Concordia, 1965.

________. *Works of Martin Luther*. Philadelphia: A. J. Holman, 1915–32.

MacLaine, Shirley. *Dancing in the Light*. New York: Bantam, 1986.

________. *It's All in the Playing*. New York: Bantam, 1988.

________. *Out on a Limb*. New York: Bantam, 1983.

Marcel, Pierre Ch. *The Biblical Doctrine of Infant Baptism*. London: J. Clark, 1953.

Marshall, I. Howard. *1 Peter*. Downers Grove, Ill.: InterVarsity, 1991.

________. *Last Supper and Lord's Supper*. Grand Rapids: Eerdmans, 1981.

________. *The Acts of the Apostles*. TNTC. Grand Rapids: Eerdmans. 1980.

________. *The Gospel of Luke*. NIGTC. Grand Rapids: Eerdmans, 1978.

Martin, Ralph P. *The Worship of God*. Grand Rapids: Eerdmans, 1982.

Martin, Walter. *The Kingdom of the Cults*. Minneapolis: Bethany, 1985.

________. *The New Age Cult*. Minneapolis: Bethany, 1989.

McNeile, A. H. *The Gospel According to St. Matthew*. London: Macmillan, 1949.

Meyer, H., and L. Vischer. *Growth in Agreement: Reports and Agreed Statements of Ecumenical Conversations on a World Level*. Mahwah, N.J.: Paulist, 1982.

Michaels, J. Ramsey. *1 Peter*. WBC. Waco, Texas: Word, 1988.

Mickelsen, Alvera, ed. *Women, Authority and the Bible*. Downers Grove, Ill.: InterVarsity, 1986.

Micklem, E. R. *Our Approach to God: A Study in Public Worship*. London: Hoddard & Stoughton, 1934.

Minear, Paul S. "The Wounded Beast," *The Journal of Biblical Literature*, vol. 72, 1953.

________. *Christian Hope and the Second Coming*. Philadelphia: Westminster, 1954.

________. *Images of the Church in the New Testament*. Philadelphia: Westminster, 1960.

Morey, Robert A. *Death and the Afterlife*. Minneapolis: Bethany, 1984.

Morris, Leon. *Hebrews*. EBC. Grand Rapids: Zondervan, 1988.

________. *Epistle to the Romans*. Grand Rapids: Eerdmans, 1988.

________. *The First Epistle of Paul to the Corinthians*. TNTC. Rev. ed. Grand Rapids: Eerdmans, 1956–83.

________. *The First and Second Epistles to the Thessalonians*. NICNT. Grand Rapids: Eerdmans, 1959.

________. *The Gospel According to John*. NICNT. Grand Rapids: Eerdmans, 1971.

________. *The Revelation of St. John*. TNTC. Rev. ed. Leicester, England: Inter-Varsity, 1976.

Mounce, Robert H. *The Book of Revelation*. NICNT. Grand Rapids: Eerdmans, 1977.

Müller, J. J. *Epistles of Paul to the Philippians and to Philemon*. NICNT. Grand Rapids: Eerdmans, 1955.

Murray, John. *The Epistle to the Romans*. NICNT. Grand Rapids: Eerdmans, 1968.

Otto, Rudolf. *The Kingdom of God and the Son of Man*. Grand Rapids: Zondervan, n.d.

Pache, René. *The Return of Jesus Christ*. Chicago: Moody, 1955.

Packer, J. I. *Evangelical Affirmations*. Edited by Kenneth S. Kantzer and Carl F. H. Henry. Grand Rapids: Zondervan, 1990.

Payne, J. Barton. *Encyclopedia of Biblical Prophecy*. Grand Rapids: Baker, 1980.

Pentecost, J. Dwight. *Things to Come*. Grand Rapids: Zondervan, 1958.

Phillips, John. *Exploring Revelation*. Chicago: Moody, 1987.

Piper, John, and Wayne Grudem, eds. *Recovering Biblical Manhood and Womanhood*. Wheaton, Ill.: Crossway, 1991.

Rattenbury, J. Ernest. *The Eucharistic Hymns of John and Charles Wesley*. London: Epworth, 1948.

Rauschenbusch, Walter. *A Theology for the Social Gospel*. New York: Macmillan, 1917.

———. *Christianity and the Social Crisis*. New York: Hodder and Stoughton, 1907.

Rea, John. *The Holy Spirit in the Bible*. Lake Mary, Fla.: Creation House, 1990.

Reiter, Richard, R., ed. *The Rapture: Pre-, Mid-, or Post-Tribulation?* Grand Rapids: Zondervan, 1984.

Richardson, D. W. *The Revelation of Jesus Christ*. Richmond: John Knox, 1957.

Ridderbos, Herman N. *Matthew*. BSC. Grand Rapids: Zondervan, 1987.

Robertson, Pat. *The Secret Kingdom*. Nashville: Nelson, 1982.

Rosenthal, Marvin. *The Pre-Wrath Rapture of the Church*. Nashville: Nelson, 1990.

Rushdoony, R. J. *God's Plan for Victory: The Meaning of Postmillennialism*. Fairfax, Va.: Thoburn Press, 1977.

Ryrie, C. C. *Dispensationalism Today*. Chicago: Moody, 1965.

———. *Revelation*. Chicago: Moody, 1968.

Satin, Mark. *New Age Politics*. New York: Dell, 1979.

Schweitzer, Albert. *The Quest for the Historical Jesus*. New York: Macmillan, 1968.

Schweizer, Eduard. *Church Order in the New Testament*. Naperville, Ill.: Allenson, 1961.

Scott, E. F. *The Pastoral Epistles*. MNTC. London: Hodder and Stoughton, 1936.

Slosser, Bob G. *Changing the Way America Thinks*. Dallas: Word, 1989.

Spangler, David. *Revelation: The Birth of a New Age*. Middletown, Wis.: Lorian, 1976.

Sparks, Jack. *The Mindbenders: A Look at Current Cults*. Nashville: Nelson, 1977.

Stanton, Gerald B. *Kept from the Hour: A Systematic Study of the Rapture in Bible Prophecy*. Grand Papids: Zondervan, 1957.

Stevens, William. *Doctrines of the Christian Religion*. Nashville: Broadman, 1967.

Stott, John R. W. *The Epistles of John*. TNTC. London: Tyndale House, 1964.

Strong, A. H. *Systematic Theology*. Old Tappan, N.J.: Revell, 1907.

Swete, Henry B. *Commentary on Revelation*. Grand Rapids: Kregel, 1977.

Synan, Vinson. *In the Latter Days: The Outpouring of the Holy Spirit in the Twentieth Century*. Ann Arbor, Mich.: Servant, 1984.

———. *The Twentieth-Century Pentecostal Explosion*. Altamonte Springs, Fla.: Creation House, 1987.

Tertullian. *Apology*.

———. *On Baptism*.

Thayer, Joseph H. *Greek-English Lexicon of the New Testament*. New York: Harper, 1899.

Titus, Herbert W. *The Biblical Basis of Public Policy*. Chesapeake, Va.: National Perspectives Institute, 1986.

Trevelyan, George. *A Vision of the Aquarian Age*. Walpole, N.H.: Stillpoint Publishing, 1984.

Tucker, Ruth. *Another Gospel: Alternative Religions and the New Age Movement*. Grand Rapids: Zondervan, 1989.

Vine, W. E. *Expository Dictionary of New Testament Words*. London: Oliphants, 1952.

Vos, Geerhardus. *The Pauline Eschatology*. Grand Rapids: Eerdmans, 1930.

________. *The Teaching of Jesus Concerning the Kingdom of God and the Church*. Phillipsburg, N.J.: Presbyterian and Reformed, 1972.

Wagner, Gunter. "The Future of Israel: Reflections on Romans 9–11." In Hulitt W. Gloer, ed. *Eschatology and the New Testament*. Peabody, Mass.: Hendrickson, 1988.

Walvoord, J. F. *The Blessed Hope and the Tribulation*. Grand Rapids: Zondervan, 1976.

________. *The Millennial Kingdom*. Grand Rapids: Zondervan, 1981.

________. *The Rapture Question*. Grand Rapids: Zondervan, 1977.

________. *The Revelation of Jesus Christ*. Chicago: Moody, 1966.

Watson, David. *I Believe in the Church*. Grand Rapids: Eerdmans, 1979.

Watts, John, D. W. *Isaiah 1–33*. WBC. Waco, Texas: Word, 1985.

Webster's Ninth New Collegiate Dictionary. Springfield, Mass.: Merriam-Webster, 1986.

Webster's Third New International Dictionary. Springfield, Mass.: G. & C. Merriam, 1981.

Welch, Claude. *The Reality of the Church*. New York: Scribner, 1958.

Weymouth, R. F. *New Testament in Modern Speech*. London: James Clarke, 1909.

White, R. E. O. *The Biblical Doctrine of Initiation*. Grand Rapids: Eerdmans, 1960.

Williams, J. Rodman. *Renewal Theology: God, the World and Redemption*. Vol. 1. Grand Rapids: Zondervan, 1988.

________. *Renewal Theology: Salvation, the Holy Spirit and Christian Living*. Vol. 2. Grand Rapids: Zondervan, 1990.

________. *The Era of the Spirit*. Plainfield, N.J.: Logos, 1971.

________. *The Pentecostal Reality*. Plainfield, N.J.: Logos, 1972.

________. *The Gift of the Holy Spirit Today*. Plainfield, N.J.: Logos, 1980.

Williams, N. P. *The Ideas of the Fall and of Original Sin*. New York: Longmans, Green, 1927.

Wimber, John. *Power Evangelism*. San Francisco: Harper & Row, 1986.

Wright, G. Ernest. *The Rule of God*. Garden City, N.Y.: Doubleday, 1960.

Young, E. J. *The Prophecy of Daniel: A Commentary*. Grand Rapids: Eerdmans, 1949.

INDEX OF PERSONS

Adams, Jay, 313n.51, 433n.61
Aland, Kurt, 233n.56, 236n.74
Alford, Henry, 235n.70
Allen, Willoughby C., 60n.48
Allo, E. B., 494n.72
Amos, Gary T., 269n.16
Antiochus Epiphanes, 355, 355nn.174, 176, 178–79, 356n.182
Archer, Gleason L. Jr., 375, 376
Arnett, William M., 297n.1
Augustine, 35n.41, 177n.76, 239n.86, 424n.18, 427n.34, 428n.38, 438
Augustus, Caesar, 343n.120, 365n.219
Aulén, Gustaf, 234n.61

Bahnsen, Greg L., 277n.44, 435n.70
Barnhouse, Donald, 442n.90
Barrett, C. K., 189n.132, 259n.162, 275nn.32–33
Barrett, David, 322n.17
Barth, Karl, 18n.18, 43n.81, 90n.20, 231n.46, 233n.56, 237n.78, 241n.102
Barth, Marcus, 174n.67, 178n.78
Bavinck, Herman, 481n.16
Beasley-Murray, G. R., 56n.34, 231n.47, 294n.16, 343n.120, 347n.140, 367n.228, 369n.233, 439n.83
Beckwith, I. T., 344nn.122–123, 357n.185, 367n.228
Berkhof, Louis, 42n.77, 337n.89
Berkouwer, G. C., 231n.49, 481n.16, 485n.36
Bernard of Clairvaux, 246n.124
Biederwolf, W. E., 309n.39, 310nn.40, 42, 318n.4, 340n.97, 484n.34
Blackstone, W. E., 370n.241, 373n.259
Boettner, Loraine, 435, 438n.81
Bonhoeffer, Dietrich, 336n.88
Bright, John, 291n.3
Brooke, Tal, 332n.64
Brown, William Adams, 315n.60
Bruce, A. B., 60n.49
Bruce, F. F., 19nn.23–24, 25n.2, 34n.38, 41n.73, 56n.32, 61n.56, 80n.121, 81n.125, 116n.115, 121n.138, 164n.22, 168n.41, 177n.76, 178n.78, 198n.181, 202nn.198, 199, 227n.29, 242nn.106, 109, 243nn.110–112, 269n.13, 324n.29, 331nn.56, 61, 336n.83, 355n.178, 410nn.60–61, 476n.124, 487n.42
Brunner, Emil, 319n.7, 402n.22, 466n.85
Brunner, Peter, 103n.67
Bultmann, Rudolf, 315n.58, 333n.66
Buswell, J. Oliver, 375, 376

Caird, G. B., 309n.36, 353n.160
Caligula, 336n.83, 343n.120
Calvin, John, 23, 41n.73, 178n.78, 195n.155, 214n.261, 228n.38, 232n.55, 234n.62, 235n.69, 236nn.72, 73, 239n.90, 241nn.98, 103–104, 246n.122, 249n.131, 250n.133, 252n.136, 253n.140, 256n.152, 262n.182, 267n.5, 271n.21, 273n.27, 291n.5, 420n.98, 470n.100, 477, 481n.12
Carson, D. A., 60, 48, 237n.79, 278n.47, 310n.40
Chafer, L. S., 292n.9
Charles, R. H., 440n.87
Chilton, David, 435, 435n.70, 436nn.74–75
Claudius, 343n.120
Clement, 162–163, 163n.18, 206, 274n.30, 480n.8
Clouse, Bonnidell and Robert G., 216n.273
Clouse, Robert G., 429n.45, 437n.76, 438n.81
Cole, Alan, 156n.265
Cox, W. E., 424n.18, 444n.93, 451n.29
Cranfield, C. E. B., 133n.200, 324n.29
Creme, Benjamin, 333n.65
Cullmann, Oscar, 230n.43, 231n.48, 233nn.55, 56, 247n.128, 268n.8, 401n.17
Cyril of Jerusalem, 177n.76

Dabney, R. L., 435n.66
Darby, J. N., 370n.239, 438
Dart, John, 334n.71
Darwin, Charles, 338
Davis, J. J., 435
Delling, Gerhardt, 90n.15
Denney, James, 467n.87
Dibelius, M., 21n.31
Diocletian, 340n.101
Dodd, C. H., 293n.13, 293n.14, 314n.57
Domitian, 343n.120, 347n.141, 350n.151
Duddy, Neil, 40n.69
Dunn, James D. G., 93n.27, 128nn.163, 170, 129n.172, 129n.174, 130n.183, 192n.142, 208n.242, 275n.31

Edwards, David L., 472n.110
Edwards, Jonathan, 435n.66
Eliot, T. S., 90n.18
English, E. Schuyler, 330n.52
Erickson, Millard J., 370n.238, 376n.279
Eusebius, 364n.217

Fausset, A. R., 349n.146
Fee, Gordon, 150n.239, 169n.50, 192n.142, 213n.258, 259n.62, 308n.34
Feinberg, Charles, 372n.254, 373n.259, 374, 374nn.262, 268, 375

Feinberg, Paul, 371, 371nn.243–44, 247, 373, 373n.259, 378, 379n.291
Ferguson, Marilyn, 332n.64, 339, 339n.94
Foh, Susan, 214n.265, 216n.73
Ford, J. M, 353n.160
Fox, Matthew, 333n.67
Frame, J. M., 473n.114
France, R. T., 60n.48, 156n.266, 279n.48, 327n.38
Freud, Sigmund, 338
Fudge, E. W., 472n.110

Galba, 343n.120
Gabriel, Charles H., 504n.111
Geldenhuys, Norval, 156n.267, 364n.217, 491n.57
Gilmour, S. M., 156n.267
Gloer, W. Hulitt, 324n.26
Goldingay, John, 352n.158
Gordon, A. J., 393n.31
Graham, Billy, 46
Green, Michael, 333n.68, 420n.98
Groothuis, Douglas R., 332n.64
Gundry, Robert H., 60n.48, 74n.102, 330n.52, 366n.224, 408n.15, 410n.61
Guthrie, Donald, 206n.222, 214n.265

Haenchen, E., 243n.110
Hamilton, Floyd E., 424n.18, 444n.92
Hamon, Bill, 173n.63
Harper, Michael, 161n.11, 173n.65
Harrison, Everett F., 126n.159, 275n.34, 324n.28
Harrison, Norman B., 375, 375n.275, 376
Hemer, Colin, 347n.139
Hendriksen, William, 195n.196, 211n.255, 382n.301, 409n.54, 424n.18, 426n.30, 444, 482n.20
Herbert, A. S., 85n.2, 87n.6
Hiebert, D. E., 276n.40
Higgins, A. J. B., 242n.109, 260n.167
Hippolytus, 260n.171
Hitler, Adolf, 348, 350n.152
Hobbs, Edward, 334n.71
Hodge, C. H., 435n.66, 481n.12
Hoekema, Anthony A., 424n.18, 427n.35, 428n.38, 429n.44, 438n.81, 444, 453n.39
Holmes, M. W., 206n.221
Hoyt, H. A., 438n.81
Hoyt, Karen, 332n.64
Hughes, Philip E., 148n.234, 422n.3, 472n.110, 494n.72

Ignatius, 230n.45
Irenaeus, 36n.51, 38n.58, 343n.120, 350n.151, 438
Irving, Edward, 167n.36

Jerome, 177n.76
Jeremias, J., 73n.100, 74n.104, 233nn.55, 56, 235n.70, 236nn.72–74, 242nn.107, 109, 243n.111, 449n.24
Jewett, Paul, 232n.51, 234n.60, 236n.74, 237n.76
John XXIII, Pope, 44
Josephus, F., 313nn.53–54, 355n.178, 383n.302, 355nn.175, 178
Julius Caesar, 343n.120, 350n.151
Justin Martyr, 438

Käsemann, E., 129n.172, 170n.51
Kaufmann, Yehezkel, 197n.166
Keil, C. F. and F. Delitzsch, 318n.3, 355n.179, 484n.32
Kelly, J. N. D., 183nn.103, 104, 192n.142, 202n.200, 210n.248, 213n.261, 214n.265
Kiddle, Morton, 439n.83
Kidner, Derek, 87n.7
Kik, J. Marcellus, 266n.1, 426n.28
Kistemaker, S. J., 200n.186
Kromminga, D. H., 438n.79
Küng, Hans, 49n.2, 67n.76, 78n.115

Ladd, George E., 293n.14, 307n.31, 341n.104, 343n.116, 365n.220, 366n.224, 368n.230, 379n.293, 382n.301, 410n.61, 423n.12, 429nn.44–46, 437, 438n.81, 439n.83, 440n.88, 482n.20, 504n.112
Lee, Witness, 40n.69
Leenhardt, F. J., 247n.128
Leith, John, 26n.3
Lenski, R. C. H., 200n.186, 201n.192, 204n.16, 309n.39, 348n.142, 421n.3, 424n.18, 444n.92
Lewis, A. H., 442n.90
Lewis, C. S., 21n.34, 477n.127, 499n.91
Lightfoot, J. B., Harmer, J. R. and Holmes, M. W., 228n.37
Lightner, Robert P., 376n.279
Lindsey, Hal, 309n.35, 371, 374, 378, 391n.22
Lipnack, Jessica and Jeffrey Stamps, 332n.64
Lock, Walker, 210n.248
Luther, Martin, 234n.63, 239n.89, 241n.104, 249n.131, 283, 350n.152, 479n.1

MacLaine, Shirley, 332n.64, 339, 399nn.95–96
Madonna, 358n.186
Maitreya, Lord, 332nn.62–63, 391n.24
Marcel, Pierre Ch., 232n.53
Marshall, I. Howard, 226n.25, 237n.80, 238n.81, 242nn.106, 109, 243nn.110–112, 259n.162, 276n.41, 294n.16
Martin, Ralph P., 88n.11, 90n.20
Martin, Walter, 332n.64, 358n.188
Marx, Karl, 338
McNeile, A. H., 60n.48
McCall, Thomas S., 381n.297
Medved, Michael, 358n.187
Meyer, H. and L. Vischer, 45n.88
Michaels, J. Ramsey, 89n.13
Mickelsen, Alvera, 216n.273
Micklem, E. R., 90n.19
Minear, Paul S., 312n.50, 341n.103, 386n.5
Moo, Douglas J., 213n.260, 377n.284
Morey, Robert A., 472nn.109–10
Morris, Leon, 43n.82, 129n.172, 226n.27, 259n.162, 336n.83, 343n.119, 353n.160, 388n.14, 410n.56, 422n.5, 424n.20, 444n.92
Mounce, Robert H., 340n.101, 341n.108, 343n.116, 344n.122, 352n.157, 368n.230, 383n.304, 418n.91, 424n.20, 429n.42, 430n.46, 433n.60, 439n.83, 449n.24, 482n.20, 495n.76, 504n.115
Müller, J. J., 474n.117
Murray, John, 20n.27, 129n.172

Neander, Joachim, 92n.25
Nero, 340n.101, 343n.120, 350n.151
Nerva, 343n.120

Napoleon, 350n.152
North, Gary, 435n.70

Origen, 473n.116
Otto, Rudolf, 242n.109
Owen, John, 435n.66

Pache, René, 366n.224, 370n.240
Packer, J. I., 472n.110
Paul VI, Pope, 44
Payne, J. Barton, 310n.40
Pentecost, J. Dwight, 375, 375n.270
Phillips, John, 442n.90
Piper, John and Wayne Grudem, 216n.273

Rattenbury, J. Ernest, 254n.144
Rauschenbusch, Walter, 153n.252
Rea, John, 78n.114
Reiter, Richard R., 370n.238
Richardson, D. W., 369n.234, 424n.18, 430n.17
Ridderbos, Herman N., 472n.108
Robertson, Pat, 293n.12
Rosen, Moishe, 325n.31
Rosenthal, Marvin, 376n.279
Rushdoony, R. J., 435, 435n.70
Ryrie, C. C., 292n.9, 371n.246, 374, 380

Satin, Mark, 332n.64
Schiller, Friedrich, 465n.82
Schlier, 329n.50
Schreck, Alan, 257n.156
Schweitzer, Albert, 315n.59
Schweizer, E., 192n.142
Scofield, C. I., 484n.32
Scott, E. F., 276n.40
Short, Stephen, S., 134n.201
Slosser, Bob G., 271n.20
Spangler, David, 332n.64, 339n.96
Sparks, Jack, 40n.69
Stanton, Gerald B., 371n.242
Stevens, William, 245n.119
Stott, John R. W., 202n.198, 331n.56, 472n.110
Strong, A. H., 38n.61, 225n.7, 227n.30, 257n.155, 295n.17, 326n.34, 435
Swete, Henry B., 347n.139, 422n.5, 444n.92, 498n.89
Synan, Vinson, 318n.5

Ten Boom, Corrie, 381n.296
Tersteegen, Gerhardt, 58n.43
Tertullian, 125n.153, 236n.75, 438
Thomas, Robert L., 388n.14
Tiberius, 343n.120
Titus, Emperor, 343n.120, 355
Titus, Herbert W., 277n.43
Trevelyan, George, 332n.4
Tucker, Ruth, 332n.64, 358n.188

Vespasian, 343n.120, 350n.151
Vos, Geerhardus, 292n.7, 293n.14, 295n.17, 319n.8, 430n.46

Wagner, Günter, 324n.26
Wagner, Peter, 322n.18
Walvoord, J. F., 292n.9, 370, 370n.241, 371, 371nn.244, 246–47, 372, 372n.248, 373, 373nn.255, 257, 260, 374–75, 378–79, 438, 439n.83
Warfield, B. B., 435n.66
Watson, David, 69n.84, 78n.116, 161n.11, 214n.265
Watts, John D. W., 62n.57
Welch, Claude, 69n.83
Wesley, John, 214n.262
Wesley, John and Charles, 254n.144
West, Kenneth S., 330n.52
Westcott, B. F., 42n.73
Whitby, Daniel, 435n.66
White, R. E. O., 227n.33, 233n.57
Williams, J. Rodman, 318n.5
Williams, N. P., 237n.77
Wimber, John, 150n.240
Wright, G. Ernest, 318n.6

Young, E. J., 356n.181

Zwingli, Ulrich, 245n.119

INDEX OF SUBJECTS

Amillennialism, 443–44
Apostasy, 28
Apostles, 60–61, 165–170
Apostles' Creed, 43n.80, 82n.127
Apostolic succession, 36–38, 38n.60, 167
Athanasian Creed, 29; 29n.13
Baptism: as part of the Great Commission, 136–39; formula, 222–23; infant baptism, 229–31; "Jesus only," 139n.219; miscellaneous 237; mode, 225–28; ordinance of baptism, 222–41; pouring and sprinkling, 228; relationships, 223; significance, 223–25
Bride adorned, 74
Church: apostolicity, 35–38, 37n.54; body of Christ, 65–71; bride of Christ, 72–77; building of Christ, 59–65; as "called," 16–20; city, 40–41, 40n.69; catholicity, 34–35, 34n.40; community of the Holy Spirit, 77–84; the communion of saints, 82–83; composite people, 51–52; cornerstone, 61–64; definition, 15–23; description, 49–84; ecumenical, 34, 34n.39; of the 'first-born,' 41nn.72-73; foundation, 59–61; fullness of Christ, 71–72; functions, 85–157; God indwelt, 57–58; holiness, 30–34; house, 38–40; as "invisible," "visible" 23–24; as local, 38–41; living stones, 64–65; militant and triumphant, 42, 42n.77; a new people, 52–57; Old Testament background, 15–16; oneness, 26–30; the people of God, 49–58; regional, 41; scope, 25–48; as spiritual and social, 20–23; transcendent, 41–43; as universal, 25–26
Church and civil government, 265–85; church beyond civil government, 278–85; duties toward civil government, 272–78; function of civil government, 267–72; two spheres, 265–67;
Church government, 216–20; local autonomy, 216–17; plural leadership, 217–19
Church of Scotland, 232n.55
Circumcision and baptism, 231–32
Confession, 94–95
Consistent eschatology, 315n.59
Consultation on Church Union (COCU), 45n.88
Consummation, 479–508; bride adorned and holy city, 491–94; eternal life, 496–508; fulfillment of the kingdom, 487–96; renovation of the world, 479–87
Council of Chalcedon, 37
Council of Constantinople, 37
Council of Nicea, 37
Council of Trent, 161n.12, 222n.3, 235n.66, 238n.84. 249n.131, 262nn.182–83
Dancing to the Lord, 108–9
Deaconesses, 210–11
Deacons, 207–10, 217–19; ordination, 209–10; responsibility, 208–9
Deeds of love, 117
Demythologized eschatology, 315n.58
Discipline 120–23
Dispensationalism, 370n.239, 438–39
Docetism, 21n.35
Doctrine, soundness of, 182
Eastern Orthodox Church, 44, 244n.117
Ecumenical movement, 43–48
Ekklēsia, 15–24, 15n.2, 16n.2, 16n.9, 17n.12, 19n.25, 39n.64
Elders: 196–207, 217–19; nomenclature, 202–3; ordination, 205–7; qualifications, 203–5
Episcopal Book of Common Prayer, 241n.99, 258n.161
Equipping gifts, 109
Evangelical Lutheran Church in America, 45n.90
Evangelical Presbyterian Church, 233n.59, 250n.134
Evangelists, 174–77
Faith and Order Conference, 43, 45
Footwashing, 221n.2
Freedom and order, 104–6
Functional gifts, 69–70, 125–33
Great Tribulation, 363–70
Humanist Manifestos I and II, 338
Interim state, 400–401, 450
Israel: as God's people, 49–51; future salvation, 323–263; worship in, 85–87
Kingdom of God, 289–96; background, 289–90; completion, 293–96, 487–96; establishment, 291–93; preparation, 290–91
Last Judgment, 445–68; the judge, 445–47; subjects (angels and human beings), 447–50; purpose, 450–58; saints judging world and angels, 461–64; significance, 464–68; standard, 458–61
Lausanne II, 46
Local Church movement, 40n.69
Lord's Prayer, 96–98
Lord's Supper, 241–63; concomitance, 262n.182; consubstantiation, 249n.131; meaning, 244–54; observance, 254–63; self-examination, 258–59; terminology, 241–44; transubstantiation, 249n.131
Manila Manifesto, 153n.253

Manner of Christ's return, 385–96; accompaniments, 388–90; clouds of heaven, 385–88; personal and corporeal, 392–94; sudden and unexpected, 394–96; total visibility, 390–92
Mark of the beast, 350–51
Midtribulationism, 375–76
Millennium: 421–44; binding of Satan, 422–25; final destruction, 430–34; millennium as present, 429–30, 443–44; reigning with Christ, 425–30
Ministers: all Christians, 159–60; clergy, 162–64; priests, 160–62
Ministry of the word, 181–96; ordination, 191–96; quality of life, 186–91
Missionary strategy, 145–46
National Association of Evangelicals, 45–46
National Council of Churches, 45, 46n.92
New Age movement, 332nn.62–65, 339nn.94–96
New heaven and earth, 479-87
Nicene Creed, 26n.3, 103n.65
Ordinances (sacraments), 221–63
Outreach: the Great Commission, 133–40; enabling of the Holy Spirit, 141-51; whole human condition, 151–54
Pastors and teachers, 177–81
Pentecost, 78
Postmillennialism, 435–37; in reconstructionism, 435–36
Prayer, 95–98
Premillennialism, 437–43; in dispensationalism, 438–39
Presbyterian Church (U.S.A.), 45n.90, 238n.84, 259n.161, 262n.179, 329nn.46, 48, 333n.70
Presbyterian Church of New Zealand, 240n.97
Presbytery, 194
Pretribulationism, 370–81
Prophecy, 127–28
Prophets, 170–74
Purgatory, 400n.10
Purpose of Christ's return, 397–420; final redemption, 397–413; fire, 414–17; gathering, 397–99; glorification, 412–13; resurrection, 399–405; translation, 405–10; total destruction, 413–20; word and breath, 417–20
Rapture, 407–8, 409n.55
Rapturism, partial and pre-wrath, 376n.279
Realized eschatology, 314n.57
Reconstructionism, 277n.44, 435–36
Redemption, final, 411
Restoration and regeneration 485-86
Resurrection, believers, 399–405, 426–27; unbelievers, 448–50
Return of Christ, 297-316; Christian attitude, 297–302; the comings of Christ, 309–14; language of the return, 302–9; real event, 314–16
Reverence, 91–92
Rewards and punishment, 454–58
Roman Catholic Church, 32n.23, 35, 44–45, 244n.117, 246n.122, 255n.146, 262n.182, 281n.56
Roman Catholic-Pentecostal dialogue, 45n.87
Salt, Christians as, 154–57
Salvation, final, 411–12
Scripture, importance, 184–86
Second Helvetic Confession, 160
Signs, the abomination of desolation, 353–60; the Antichrist, 330; end time, 317–84; outpouring of the Holy Spirit, 317–20; gospel to all the world, 320–26; increase of evil, 326–27; the man of sin, 334–39; religious apostasy, 327–30; the two beasts, 339–53; great tribulation, 360–70; extraordinary phenomena, 381–84
Social gospel, 153–54
Southern Baptist Church, 329n.49
State of the lost: 468–77; annihilationism, 472–73; universalism, 473–74
Supernatural manifestations, 146–51
Teaching, 109–17, 129, 139–40, 180–81
Thanksgiving, 92–94
Translation, 405–10
Trinity, 101–4
Two witnesses and the beast, 351–53
United Church of Christ, 45n.90
United Methodist Church, 45n.90
Upbuilding: by the Word, 109–17; by deed, 117; word and deed, 125–33
Vatican Council II, 37n.53, 44, 44nn.85–86, 161n.13, 246n.122, 255n.146, 260n.166
Westminster Confession, 28n.11, 82n.127, 90n.17, 228n.39, 235n.69, 241n.98, 271n.18, 277n.42, 283n.63, 472n.411
Women, ministry of, 210–16
World Council of Churches, 44–45, 46n.92, 47
World Missionary Conference, 43
Worship: its character, 90–101; its primacy, 87–90; way of worship, 101–9

SCRIPTURE INDEX

Genesis
1 .....289, 405, 418, 480, 489
1:1–2 479
1:1 289
1:4 479
1:12 183
1:28 505
1:29–30 183
2 .....289, 489
2:7 .....77, 419
2:9–10 497
2:9 .....499n.94
2:15 .....500n.96
2:18 .....82, 213
2:22–24 183
2:24 75
3:5–12 480
3:8 489
3:15 341
3:17–19 .....500n.96
3:17 483
3:22 .....497n.84
3:24 477
5:24 .....406n.33
9:6 .....280n.53
12:7–8 85
13:18 .....85n.3
14:17–20 .....98n.48
17:10–12 232
17:12 .....232n.51
18–19 .....119n.124
18:25 .....446n.4
28:20–22 .....98n.48
35:1–7 .....85n.3
50:7 .....196n.161

Exodus
3:5 91
3:12 86
7–12 .....353n.161
7–11 .....367n.229
12:21–28 .....196n.163
12:21–27 .....243n.114
12:27 86
15:2 86
19:5–6 .....160, 290
19:9–20 386
19:16–19 390
20:1 .....182n.97
20:3–4 .....101n.56
21:24 .....115n.112, 278n.46, 280n.53
22:28 282
24:15–18 386
25:8 57
30:34–35 .....154n.257
33:18 502
33:20 502
34:5 386
34:29 .....505n.11
40:34 386
40:35 387

Leviticus
2:13 ..154n.258, 155n.261
12:3 .....232n.52
19:18 .....125n.152
24:19–20 .....278n.46
24:20 .....115n.112
26:3 57
26:12 57
27:30–33 .....98n.48

Numbers
6:24–27 504
11:16–17 196
14:21 496
18:19 .....155n.262
18:21–32 .....98n.48
22:7 .....196n.161

Deuteronomy
4:24 91
4:31 .....132n.194
5:7–9 101
6:4 101
6:5 .....109n.83
6:8 .....350n.148
8:3 .....116, 181n.88
10:21 86
12:5–19 .....98n.48
14:22–29 .....98n.48
16:18–20 267
18:15 170
19:11–13 .....196n.164
19:15 .....352n.160
19:21 .....115n.112, 278n.46, 280n.53
26:12–15 .....98n.48
30:4 398
33:5 290

Joshua
2:22 .....329n.50
5:15 .....91n.22

Judges
5:4–5 .....313n.51
5:20 .....313n.51

1 Samuel
8:4–5 197

2 Samuel
6:14 .....109n.83

1 Kings
6:20 .....494n.70
8:10 386
8:11 387
8:27 58
11:1 .....86n.6
12:1 324
17:1 .....353n.161
18:20–39 .....347n.136
20:7–8 197

2 Kings
1:10–12 .....353n.161
2:11–12 406
2:20–22 156
5:14 .....222n.5
16:4 156

1 Chronicles
16:4–9 86
16:29–37 86

2 Chronicles
5:13–14 86
7:1–3 86
13:5 .....155n.263
19:5–7 268
20:15–22 87
29:19 .....329n.50
29:28–29 87
31:4–12 .....98n.48

Ezra
6:7 .....197n.166
10:8 .....197n.166
10:14 .....197n.166

Nehemiah
1:4–11 .....95n.30
10:36–39 .....98n.48
12:44 .....98n.48
12:46 87
13:5 .....98n.48
13:12 .....98n.48

Job
6:6 154

Psalms
2:8–9 ....417, 418n.91
2:10–12 ....284n.67
2:11 91
8:6 505
18 ....312n.49
18:9–10 312
19:5 107
22:3 95
29:2 87
29:7 419
33:3 ....104n.70
36:8 498
38:3 ....294n.16
40:3 104
42:2 503
44:22 361
46:1–2 381
46:4 498
46:8 381
46:11 381
47:1 108
50:3 ....414n.74, 419
51:17 94
54:6 98
66:4 87
68:18 ....164n.22
76:2 57
90:5 ....400n.14
95:2 93
95:6 ....91, 92
96 ....86n.5
96:1 ....104n.70
96:4 92
96:8 98
96:8–9 85
96:10 290
97:3 ....414n.74, 419
98:1 104
99:9 87
102:1 ....294n.16
102:18 87
102:21–22 87
102:25–26 479
103:1 108
103:8 ....132n.194
103:13 290
104:1–3 ....386n.4
104:3 ....312, 409n.50
105:1–15 ....86n.5
106:1 ....86n.5
106:47–48 ....86n.5
106:47 398
106:48 107
107 ....93, 93n.29
108:22 ....294n.16
117:1 ....263n.184
118:22–23 62
118:22 ....62n.59
119:105 117
132:7 87
135:20 91
136 ....93, 93n.29
145:13 290
147:2 398
148:1–3 107
148:11 107
148:13 107
149:1 ....104n.70
149:3 108
150:4 108
150:6 92
150:16 108

Proverbs
3:6 ....185n.110
8:15–16 267
8:22–31 ....267n.6
25:21 ....279n.49

Isaiah
2:4 501
6:3 91
6:8 100
8:7 ....62n.58
8:13–15 ....62, 63n.64
9:6–7 290
9:6 ....291n.4
9:7 268
11:4 ...416, 418n.91, 484
11:9 ....487n.43
13:1–22 ....383n.305
13:6 413
13:9–11 383
14:12–14 ....336n.82
17:12 ....340n.97
19:1 312
24:3–4 94
26:20–21 ....387n.290
28:16 ....61, 63n.64
28:17 62
30:27–28 417
30:33 ....418, 419
34–35 ....484n.33
34:1–8 484
34:2–5 ....313n.51
35:1–6 484
35:10 ....490n.55
40:7 ....418n.93
40:10 ....454n.41
42:10 ....104n.70
42:12 ....88n.10
43:15 290
43:21 ....88n.10
44:3 498
45:1 266
49:2 ....418n.92
51:6 479
53:7–8 ....114, 177
54:5 72
56:8 398
57:4 ....335n.79
57:15 94
60:3 ....496n.79
60:14 ....495n.78
60:19 ......495n.78, 501
60:21 ....495n.78
61:6 162
61:10 74
62:5 73
62:11 ....454n.41
63:7 ....88n.10
65:17 ......479, 483, 501
65:17–20 ....499n.92
65:25 ....483, 501
66:15–16 414

Jeremiah
2:2 72
2:19 ....329n.50
3:20 73
4:23–24 ....313n.51, 383n.303
5:14 ...353n.161, 414n.74
9:26 142
17:10 ....454n.41
23:24 71
24:6 59
25:9 266
27:6 ....266, 281n.57
31:4 ....59n.44
43:10 266
49:36 ....397n.1

Ezekiel
1:4 386
9:4–6 ....367n.229
16 73
16:8 72
22:30 274
28:2 ....336n.82
32:2–11 312
32:7–8 ....383n.303
34:23 ....57n.36
36:25 ....228n.40
37:5–14 77
37:9 .....77n.112, 397n.1
37:10 419
37:23–24 57
37:27–28 57
38–39 ....433n.61
40–48 .....434, 493n.67, 495n.76, 495n.78
40:1–2 ....492n.67
43:23–24 ....154n.258
47:1–12 497
48:35 ....495n.78

Daniel
2:20–21 266
2:21 ....281n.58
3:17–21 281
3 ....347n.138
4:17 266
7 ....345n.126
7:2 ....397n.1
7:3–7 ....340n.98
7:7–8 ....341n.105
7:8 ....336n.82, 342n.108
7:9–10 ....463n.74
7:11–13 ....385n.1
7:14 ....506n.124
7:18 ....506n.125
7:21 ....341n.110
7:22 ....463n.74
7:25 ..342n.108, 357, 357
8:8 ....397n.1
8:9–14 ....352n.157
9:3–19 ....95n.30
9:24 ....356n.182
9:26 ....356n.181
9:27 354
11:4 ....397n.1
11:31 ......354, 356n.181
11:36–37 ....336n.82
12:1 ....388n.12

12:2 ....400n.14, 449
12:6–7 357
12:7 ....342n.108, 353n.157, 357
12:11 .....353n.158, 354, 356n.181

Hosea
2:16 73
2:19–20 73
2:19 76

Joel
1:15 413
2:28–31 ....313n.51
3:14–15 383

Amos
3:2 313
4:4 ....98n.48
8:2–9 ....313n.52
8:11 ....116n.117
9:11–12 ....434n.63

Micah
4:3 ....501n.101

Nahum
1:6 ....414n.74

Habakkuk
2:14 ....487n.43
2:20 92

Zephaniah
1:14–18 414
1:18 416

Zechariah
2:6 ....397n.1
3 ....353n.159
4:6–14 353
4:7 ....62n.59
6:5 ....397n.1
12:10 ....314n.56
14:7 ....496n.83
14:11 ....502n.103
19:37 ....314n.56

Malachi
3:8 ....98n.48
3:10 ....98, 98n.48
4:1 414
4:5–6 ....414n.73

Matthew
1:20 ....408n.45
2:11 102
3:11 ....227n.32
3:12 ....398, 414
3:16 ....226n.22
4:1 ....98n.46
4:4 ....116, 181
4:8–9 ....284n.79
4:19 176
4:23 150
5–7 ....140, 140n.223
5:3 ....292, 362
5:3–13 154
5:6 ....467n.89
5:11 454
5:12 ....454n.45, 455
5:13 156
5:14–16 ....157n.268
5:17 ....36n.48, 278
5:22 469
5:23–24 ....97n.44
5:29–30 ....469n.96
5:37 453
5:38–45 279
5:38–40 278
5:38–39 ....115n.112
5:45 152
5:46 ....454n.45
6 ....96n.39
6:1–2 ....454n.45
6:2–4 99
6:4–6 ....454n.45
6:7 ....96n.37
6:8–13 ....96n.36
6:9–10 ....96, 290
6:9 92
6:12–13 97
6:14–15 ....97n.44
6:16 ....454n.45
6:18 ....454n.45
6:24 250
6:33 ....291n.6
7:11 96
7:23 469
7:24 59
8:11–12 468
8:12 ....470n.99
8:28 ....326n.35
8:29 463
9:9 ....276n.38
9:15 ....73, 492n.61
9:17 ....472n.109
9:36 ....150n.242
10:1–23 310
10:1–2 ....165n.30
10:14–15 457
10:23 ....310, 310n.40
10:28 .....471, 472n.107, 472n.109
10:30 97
10:32 ....454, 461n.69
10:40 ....169n.46
10:41 ....455, 455n.46
11:9 ....171n.56
11:11 454
11:15 ....182n.97
11:21–24 457
11:28–29 500
11:28 120
12:13 ....486n.38
12:18 ....294n.16
12:28 292
12:29 422
12:33 ....153n.249
12:34 453
12:34–35 ....452n.37
12:35 ....453n.38
12:36–37 452
12:36 448
13:9 ....182n.97
13:24–50 436
13:24–33 322
13:24–30 ....22, 295
13:29 465
13:30 ....414, 466
13:31–33 ..294, 379n.294
13:36–43 ....22, 295
13:38 ....293, 488
13:39 ....398n.4
13:40–42 ....414, 469
13:41–43 488
13:41 ....416n.83
13:42 ....470n.100
13:43 ....398, 491
13:47–50 295
13:49–50 ....415, 469
13:50 ....470n.100
13:57 ....171n.55
14:33 102
14:34–35 156
16:16–18 59
16:18 .....15n.5, 21, 25, 64n.70, 125, 216, 423n.15, 443
16:27 ......307, 388n.10, 445n.3, 447, 448n.15
16:28 309
17:1–8 ....309n.39
17:1 ....408n.45
17:5 386
17:11 ....486n.38
17:17 ....312n.48
17:24–25 275
17:27 ....275n.36
18:8–9 470
18:15–18 120
18:16 ....352n.160
18:17 ..15n.5, 21, 41n.70, 59n.45, 216
18:20 ....41n.70
18:23–35 ....97n.43
19:5 ....75n.106
19:9 ....204n.207
19:19 ....125n.152
19:28 ....487, 487n.45
20:17 ....408n.45
21:5 309
21:11 ....171n.54
21:23 ......197, 197n.167
21:43 ......292, 323, 377
22:1–14 73
22:13 ....468, 470n.99
22:14 ....377n.283
22:17–21 276
22:28 402
22:29 404
22:30 ....403, 463
22:32 ....404, 404n.27
22:37 108
23:2 ....457n.55
23:5–7 ....457n.55
23:8 ....163n.19
23:23 99
23:25 ....335n.79
23:26 ....294n.16
23:28 ....334n.72
23:33 ....457n.56
23:35–38 ....311n.44
23:37–38 398
23:38 313

23:39 325
24 ....311n.44, 313, 323, 372n.254
24:1–3 302
24:2 311
24:3 317
24:4–30 .....317n.1
24:9–21 363
24:9 362
24:12–30 436
24:12–13 327
24:12 .....334n.72, 353
24:13 362
24:14–15 425
24:14 ..34, 320, 353, 424, 443
24:15–29 354
24:15–16 355
24:21–22 ...364, 372, 377
24:21 .....360, 373
24:22 .....377n.283
24:23–27 .....331, 391
24:24 117
24:27 .....302, 384n.309
24:29–31 372
24:29–30 ...360, 373, 382
24:29 .....312, 365
24:30–31 397
24:30 .....307, 311, 383, 384, 385, 387, 390
24:31 .....389, 411
24:34 ..311, 312, 312n.48
24:35 .....460, 482n.22
24:36–43 394
24:36 .....306, 413
24:37–42 408
24:37 302
24:39 .....302, 413
24:40–41 .....408n.44
24:40 311
24:42 ...299n.9, 306, 379
24:45–51 .....456n.49
24:50 306
25 .....448n.20
25:1–13 74
25:1–10 492
25:6–10 410
25:6 .....410n.61
25:13 .....299, 300, 306
25:14–30 ...456n.49, 507
25:19 379
25:21–23 300
25:21 498
25:23 498
25:26 301
25:30 ..300, 468, 470n.99
25:31–46 445
25:31–34 487
25:31–32 451
25:31 307
25:32 .....448, 448n.15
25:33 461
25:34–40 152
25:34 295
25:35–40 488
25:36 306
25:41 .....464n.77, 470
25:46 .....153, 451, 471, 487, 496
26:3 .....197n.167
26:18 180
26:26–28 261
26:26–27 .....221, 248
26:26 .....66, 242
26:27–28 246
26:29–30 263
26:29 .....253, 261n.178, 295, 490
26:31 .....178n.80
26:47 .....197n.167
26:52 .....342n.112
26:52–53 280
26:63–64 310
26:64 ..310n.42, 310n.43, 311, 325n.30
27:1 .....197n.167
27:25 325
27:41 325
27:47 246
27:52 .....400n.14
28 ...135, 135n.205, 207, 138
28:9 102
28:16–17 237
28:16 .....134n.202
28:18–20 .....134, 443
28:18–19 424
28:18 284
28:19–20 ...109, 221, 320
28:19 .....220, 222
28:20 .....20n.30, 80

Mark
1:9–10 .....225, 226, 226n.25
1:14–15 .....150n.241
1:14 174
1:15 291
1:17 176
2:19–20 .....492n.61
2:19 73
3:5 .....486n.38
3:14–15 191
3:26–27 .....422n.10
3:31–35 .....82n.126
4:9 .....182n.97
4:23 .....182n.97
6:4 .....171n.55
6:30 .....165n.30
6:34 .....178n.80
8:25 .....486n.38
8:38 .....307, 388
9:12 .....486n.38
9:37 .....169n.46
9:44 470
9:48 470
9:50 ..155, 156, 156n.265
10:1 180
10:13 .....233n.57
10:14–16 232
10:45 159
12:10 62
12:29 101
12:31 .....125n.152
12:38–40 457
12:43–44 131
13 .....311n.44, 311n.45
13:4 303
13:9 .....362n.204
13:11 .....320, 320n.10
13:14 .....354n.168
13:20 .....364n.214
13:22 331
13:24–25 312
13:24 .....3630n.193
13:26 ...299n.8, 311, 385, 387
13:27 ...397n.2, 399, 411
13:30 .....311, 312n.48
13:31 .....460, 482n.22
13:32–37 299
13:32 306
13:33 .....299n.9, 394
14:14 180
14:22–24 221
14:22–23 260
14:22 66
14:25–26 263
14:25 .....261n.178
14:31 142
14:62 .....310n.41
15:1 .....197n.168
15:34 246
15:40–42 211
16 ....135, 135n.205, 136
16:9–20 .....134n.200
16:14 .....134n.202
16:15–16 .....134, 221
16:16 .....225n.20, 234
16:17–20 148

Luke
1:31–33 291
1:32 57
1:33 .....429n.41
1:44 .....234n.64
1:46–55 .....93n.26
1:46–47 104
1:68–79 .....93n.26
2:1 .....365n.219
2:8 .....303, 304
2:10–11 291
2:21–23 .....233n.58
2:29–32 .....93n.26
2:37 .....90n.16
2:39 138
3:11 .....130n.183
3:13 276
3:16 .....227n.32
3:21–23 .....233n.58
4:5 .....34n.37
4:16 .....182n.98
4:18 .....169n.46, 174
4:24 .....171n.55
4:43 .....169n.46, 174
5:3 180
5:31 .....182n.101
5:34–35 .....492n.61
5:34 73
6:10 .....486n.38
6:13 .....35, 165
6:17–49 455
6:20 .....291n.6
6:38 99
7:3–5 197

7:3 ....197n.167
7:10 ....182n.101
7:26 ....171n.56
8:3 211
8:8 ....182n.97
9:26 ....387, 447
9:48 ....169n.46
10:1 191
10:16 ....37n.53
10:29–37 132
11:4 ......97n.41, 97n.42
11:21–22 ....422n.10
11:42 ....99, 99
12:1 ....452n.35
12:2 452
12:5 ...452n.35, 472n.109
12:7 97
12:8 ....223, 452n.35
12:32 ....178n.80
12:35–40 ....299n.10
12:37–40 307
12:37 308
12:46–47 458
12:48 ....471n.101
12:50 227
13:14 197
13:29 491
13:33 ....171n.55
14:35 ....182n.97
15:3–7 ....178n.80
15:11–12 ....268n.10
15:27 ....182n.101
16:19–24 250
16:23 ....449n.21
16:27–31 ....450n.26
17:20–21 294
17:24 306
17:26–27 ....408n.46
17:30 305
18:7 ....268n.9
18:8 ....307, 436
18:12–14 99
18:15 ....232n.54
18:22 99
19:8 ....276n.39
19:11–27 ....297n.2, 455, 507
19:13 300
19:14 ....429n.41
19:17 300
19:22 ....301n.15
20:1 197
20:17–18 62
20:46–47 457
21 ......311n.44, 311n.45
21:1–4 98
21:7 303
21:12–19 ......362n.204
21:12 310
21:15 154
21:20 310
21:21–23 364
21:22 .....363, 363n.210
21:25–26 ....312, 382
21:27 ....311, 385
21:28 ......390, 397, 411
21:32 ....312n.48
21:33 ....460, 482n.22
21:36 371
21:37 311
22:7–8 243
22:11 180
22:14–27 ......248n.130
22:15 ....243, 247
22:16–18 253
22:17–19 ..221, 260n.170
22:17 244
22:18 ....261n.178
22:19–20 ......261n.174
22:19 ...71, 66, 244, 245
22:20 246
22:26 132
22:27 ....70, 123, 207
22:28–30 491
22:28 ....491n.58
22:30 ....491n.57
22:66 ......197, 197n.167
23:34 280
23:43 ....400, 400n.11
24 135
24:19 461
24:27 114
24:30–31 247
24:31 403
24:33 ....134n.202
24:36–43 403
24:39 ....247n.129
24:44 114
24:46–47 134
24:48–49 141
24:49 ......137n.216, 320

John

1 ....405, 418
1:6 ....169n.46
1:7 ....353n.162
1:8–9 ....54n.21
1:9 476
1:11 309
1:14 ...58, 114, 330, 332
1:17 76
1:18 502
1:21 171
1:26 ....294n.16
1:33 227
2:19 ....58n.41
2:21 ....58n.21
2:23–25 ....149n.238
3:3–8 ....487n.46
3:3–7 292
3:3 21
3:5 ....223, 225n.20, 229n.42
3:7–8 ....78n.113
3:7 21
3:16–21 ....465n.81
3:16 ..100, 474, 474n.121
3:17–18 ....370n.237, 449n.23
3:17 .....169n.46, 446n.7
3:18 475
3:19–21 464
3:19 ....466n.84, 476
3:21 476
3:22–23 ....227n.34
3:23 226
3:29 ....73, 492n.61
3:34 ....169n.46
3:36 ..370, 475, 475n.123
4:1–2 ....227n.34
4:10 248
4:21–24 106
4:23 102
4:24 ....80, 250n.132
4:38 ....169n.46
4:39 211
4:44 ....171n.55
4:53 230
5:21–25 441
5:21 ...404, 427, 427n.37
5:22 446
5:24–25 .....427, 427n.37
5:24 ...427n.32, 449, 496
5:25 ....405, 428
5:27 446
5:28–29 ...405, 427, 441, 449
5:28 ....387n.7
5:36 ....169n.46
5:39 114
5:45 460
6:35 248
6:39 ....31n.19
6:40 ....399, 399n.7
6:44 ....399, 399n.7
6:53–54 248
6:54 ....399, 399n.7
6:57 ....169n.46
6:61–63 248
6:63 ....77, 181
7:28 180
7:29 ....169n.46
7:38–39 498
8:1 248
8:11 ....269n.12
8:12 ...464n.79, 469, 476
8:16 446
8:42 ....169n.46
8:44 ....335n.79
9:39 464
10:1 180
10:8–9 180
10:9 248
10:11 ....178, 426n.26
10:14–16 26
10:14 178
10:15 ....426n.26
10:17 ....426n.26
10:35 36
10:36 ....169n.46
11:11 ....400n.12
11:23–26 399
11:25–26 427
11:42 ....169n.46
11:43 404
11:50–52 398
12:21 ....423n.14
12:25 ....426n.26
12:26 ....70, 207
12:31–32 ...423, 423n.14
12:31 ....443, 464
12:32 473
12:36 ....465n.81
12:46 468
12:47–48 ....446n.7

12:47 ....460n.64
12:48 460
13:1–20 ....248n.130
13:1 125
13:13 180
13:14–15 ....221n.2
13:34 ......120n.129, 125
13:37 ....426n.26
13:38 ....426n.26
14:1–3 393
14:2–3 408
14:2 454
14:6 ..103, 107, 180, 475, 476
14:9 503
14:15–16 141
14:15 140
14:26 ......113, 123n.143
15:5 66
15:6 ....417n.90
15:11 ....499n.90
15:13 ....125, 426n.26
15:16 191
15:26 ......123n.143, 498
16:2 ....90n.16
16:7 ....123n.143
16:8 78
16:14 ....346n.134
16:33 360
17:3 ....169n.46
17:6 30
17:8 ....169n.46
17:12 ....335n.78
17:15 ....377n.281
17:18 ....135n.206
17:21–23 28
17:21 ...96, 169n.46, 219
17:23 ....46n.93, 169n.46
17:25 ....169n.46
18:11 ....342n.112
18:36 ....293, 432n.58
19:11 ....266, 276n.37
20:12 66
20:19 ....309, 403
20:21 ..134, 135, 169n.46
20:22 ....77, 419
20:23 134
20:29 ....134n.202
20:30–31 ....150n.238
20:31 ....115n.111
21:12–13 247
21:15–17 178
21:15 ....115n.108
21:16 203
21:17 ....115n.108
21:22 307

Acts

1:1–26 78
1:1 ....114n.106
1:2 ....36n.44, 81
1:3 ....486n.40
1:4–5 ....137n.216
1:5 ....19, 81
1:6–11 301
1:6 ....486, 486n.38
1:7–8 ....486n.40
1:8 ....141, 211, 320, 322n.16, 379n.294
1:9–11 386
1:11 392
1:14 ....80, 211, 212
1:15 ....78n.115, 81
1:22 ....36n.45, 166
1:24–26 165
1:24–25 167
1:26 ....162n.15
2–13 ....61n.53
2 ....17, 134n.203, 142
2:1 81
2:2 395
2:4 88
2:6 146
2:11 ....88, 146
2:16–21 ....313n.51
2:17–18 ....215, 228n.40, 317, 326n.36
2:17 ....128, 202n.199, 212, 236
2:19–20 ....382n.300
2:22–36 ......88, 449n.21
2:22 147
2:31 ....449n.21
2:33 ....137n.216
2:37–38 28
2:38–41 136
2:38–39 ....235, 235n.70, 236
2:38 ....222, 222n.7, 223, 225n.20, 234
2:40–42 28
2:40 ....16, 17
2:41 .....17, 19, 78, 229, 237
2:42–47 19
2:42 ...36, 109, 139, 242, 242n.107, 243n.110, 244n.115, 247n.127
2:44–47 81
2:44 39
2:45 123
2:46–47 39
2:46 ....242, 242n.109, 243n.110, 254, 255
2:47 ....88, 247n.127
3:1–8 88
3:10 147
3:19–21 ....392, 486
3:19 ....137n.213, 147
3:21 ....473, 473n.116
3:22 171
4:4 147
4:10–11 63
4:12 476
4:24–31 88
4:29–31 ....147, 175
4:29 143
4:32 117
4:33–35 123
4:33 143
4:36 ..119n.127, 130, 167
5:1–10 ....122n.140
5:11 ..17n.17, 39n.64, 40
5:12 147
5:20–21 144
5:29 282
5:42 ....39, 110, 175
6 ....200n.186
6:1–7 117
6:1–6 .....123, 175, 199, 207, 208
6:2 ....123n.144, 165n.32, 199n.185
6:3 ...143, 176, 201n.192, 209
6:4 ....161, 182n.96
6:5 ....143, 176
6:8–7:61 ....209n.243
6:8 147
6:12 197
7:7 ....90n.16
7:37 171
7:38 ....15, 15n.3, 16, 59
7:48–50 ....58n.39
7:59 ....400n.11
7:60 ....400n.14
8:1 .....18, 40, 198n.175, 216
8:3 40
8:4–40 ....209n.243
8:4 215
8:6–7 147
8:6 176
8:7–12 175
8:12 ......136n.210, 137, 229, 231, 238, 486n.40
8:14–17 318
8:14 ....198n.175
8:16 ....222, 222n.7, 318n.2
8:17 137
8:18 177
8:26–29 144
8:29 176
8:35–39 175
8:35 ....114, 177, 229
8:36–37 ....235n.65
8:38–39 226
8:38 ..136n.210, 229, 238
8:39 ....177, 407n.40
8:40 176
9:15–17 191
9:15 ....143, 166
9:17 143
9:18 ....136n.210, 222n.8
9:20–21 323
9:26–27 ....192n.145
9:27 ...130n.181, 198n.75
9:32 ....176n.72
9:36–39 133
9:36 ....176n.72, 212
10:2–48 230
10:2–45 ....138n.218
10:2 ....476n.125
10:13–20 144
10:34–48 54
10:34–43 ....476n.125
10:38 151
10:44–47 318
10:45 ....238, 318n.2
10:48 ...222, 222n.7, 229, 238
11:1 ....198n.175
11:12 144

11:22–26 ....192n.145
11:22–23 ....130n.181
11:22 28
11:27–30 220
11:27 171
11:28 ....34n.37
11:29–30 ..192n.145, 198
11:30 199
12:1–2 ....167n.35, 198n.179
12:12 212
12:17 ....198n.179
12:25 ....192n.145
13:1–3 220
13:1–2 171
13:1 .....18, 40, 192, 216
13:2–4 144
13:2–3 ....89, 193
13:15 ....181n.93
13:36 ....400n.14
13:52 ....177n.77
14:1–3 148
14:7 175
14:14 ....165n.32, 167
14:15 53
14:17 152
14:21 175
14:22 ..360, 362, 486n.40
14:23 ....37, 191, 199, 200n.186, 218
14:26 220
15 220
15:2 ....198, 198n.176
15:4 ....198n.176
15:6 ..198, 198n.176, 218
15:7–12 145
15:7 ....163n.19
15:9 54
15:12–18 ....434n.64
15:19 ......198, 217, 219
15:22 ......171, 173, 198, 198n.176, 220
15:23 ....198n.176
15:27 173
15:28 145
15:32 ....119n.127, 168n.40, 171, 173, 220
15:35 110
15:37 ....130n.181
16:1 195
16:4 ....198, 198n.176
16:6–8 144
16:9 145
16:10 175
16:14–15 229
16:15 .....136n.210, 212, 222n.8, 238
16:25–30 89
16:31–33 229
16:32–34 230
16:33–34 ....230n.44
16:33 ....222n.8, 238
16:37–39 ....266n.2
16:40 ....119n.127
17:27–29 ....186n.121
17:31 445
18:6 323
18:8 ....136n.210, 222n.8, 229, 238
18:26 212
18:27 ....119n.127
19 16
19:1–7 318
19:1–6 ....239n.91
19:2 143
19:4–5 229
19:5–6 137
19:5 ......136n.210, 222, 222n.7
19:6 ....128, 318n.2
19:8 ....486n.40
19:10 146
19:19 ....329n.50
19:21 ....145n.228
19:32 ....15n.3, 16
19:39 ....15n.3, 16
19:41 ....16, 18
20:7–8 255
20:7 ......242, 243n.110, 247n.127
20:11 .....243, 243n.110, 247n.127
20:17–38 200
20:17 ....179, 218
20:22–23 ....145n.228
20:23 ....145n.227
20:25 ....486n.40
20:28 ....25, 179, 202
20:29–30 180
20:32 ....110, 115
21:4 ....145n.228
21:8 ...147, 175, 176n.72
21:9 ....128, 212
21:10–11 171
21:11 ....145n.228
21:17–18 198
21:20–25 199
22:5 ....194n.148, 197
22:16 ....222n.8
22:25 266
23:5 282
23:11 ....145n.227
23:27 ....266n.2
24:14 ....90n.16
24:16 187
24:25 452
24:53 80
26:16 191
26:18 162
27:24 ....145n.228
27:35–36 243
28:1–6 ....148n.232
28:15 ....410, 410n.61
28:23 ....486n.40
28:30–31 110
28:31 ....486n.40

Romans

1–11 ....100n.53
1:1 ....114n.106, 166n.33
1:4–5 167
1:5–6 20
1:7 ....30n.28
1:11–12 119
1:11 ....130n.183
1:12 130
1:15 ....175n.69
1:16 323
1:18–32 ....280n.52, 415n.80
2:4–5 467
2:5 ....445, 450
2:6–8 451
2:6–7 ....153n.249
2:6 447
2:9–10 ....459n.58
2:12 459
2:14–16 459
2:15 ....187, 272n.23, 272n.24, 283n.62, 459n.61
2:16 445
2:29 55
3:2 459
3:20 ....460n.63
4:7 ....334n.72
4:11 ....224, 232
5:1–5 361
5:5 328
5:9 ....371, 371n.247
5:17 ..293, 426, 443, 444, 505
5:18 473
6:3–4 ....223, 225n.20
6:3 222
6:4 ....226, 229
6:13 ....100n.54
6:19 ....334n.72
7:1–3 ....204n.207
7:4 66
8 363
8:3–4 55
8:6-8 70
8:9 ....32n.27
8:11 405
8:14 103
8:17 412
8:18–22 483
8:18 387
8:23 ..367n.230, 404, 484
8:29 ....41n.72
8:30 20
8:33 ....377n.283
8:35–37 361
8:37 ....429, 506
8:38–39 362
8:39 ....506n.118
9:4 ....90n.16, 100n.53
9:24–27 51
9:33 ....64n.70
10:18 ....34n.37, 34n.38
11:1 51
11:2 324
11:5 51
11:11–12 323
11:13 ....28n.10
11:15 325
11:18 ....506n.121
11:20–22 28
11:23 324
11:24 325
11:25–26 ....51, 323
11:25 ....428n.38
11:26–27 324

11:29 30
11:32 ....132n.194
12 131–33
12:1 ....90n.16, 100, 130, 162n.14, 502
12:3 128
12:4–8 173
12:4 127
12:5 ....69, 68, 68, 65
12:6–8 .....126, 164n.26, 215
12:6 128
12:7–8 192
12:7 ....114n.105, 208
12:8 ....119n.127, 131n.186, 131n.187, 132n.195, 200n.190
12:10 118
12:13 ....118, 123
12:15 120
12:18 130
12:19 ....280n.50
12:20–21 279
12:21 ....152n.247
13:1–7 282
13:1–2 272
13:1 ....266, 337n.89
13:3 271
13:4 ....268, 269, 280
13:5–7 275
13:5 272
13:7 ....272, 506n.122
13:30 326
14:1 123
14:2 ....124n.148
14:10 445
14:14 ....124n.148
14:15 124
14:17 ....295n.18, 488
14:19 118
14:21 124
15:1 ....123n.146
15:2–3 124
15:5–6 118
15:5 ....119n.127, 130
15:18–19 149
15:25–28 ....220n.286
15:27 ....88n.12
16:1–2 212
16:1 18
16:3–5 39
16:5 ....39n.62
16:7 167
16:11 ....163n.19
16:12 212
16:16 ....20n.28, 26
16:17 252

1 Corinthians
1:1–2 ....166n.33
1:1 ....21n.33
1:2 ...17, 18, 20, 21n.33, 30, 31, 31n.18, 38, 216, 220n.285, 266n.3
1:7–8 305
1:7 298
1:8 ....306, 306n.31
1:9 ....20, 80
1:10–13 ....33n.30
1:10–12 117
1:12–13 27
1:14 ....238n.82
1:16–19 39
1:16 ....231, 238n.82
1:17 ....175n.69, 225n.20
1:24–30 ....267n.6
1:30 31
2:4 ....150n.239
2:9 500
2:15–16 462
2:46 ....255n.149
3:1–4 ....33n.30
3:1–3 ....112, 118
3:3 117
3:5 ....160, 207
3:9–18 ....32n.25
3:9 60
3:10–15 .....456, 456n.50
3:11–12 ....38n.60
3:11 60
3:16–17 32
4:5 452
5 ....269n.9
5:1–5 ....113n.99
5:1–2 252
5:2–13 122
5:5 ....33n.30, 306
5:7 ....243, 243n.113
5:11 ....251, 257
6 ....269n.9
6:2–3 461
6:3 463
6:11 30
6:16–17 75
6:18–20 ....32n.26
7:31 ....406n.36, 481n.14
8 ....124n.148
9:1 ....36n.45, 166
9:2 167
9:5 212
9:31 41
9:32–33 63
10:1–2 226
10:16 ....83, 244, 246
10:17 .....251, 259n.162, 261
10:19–21 250
10:21 244
10:24 152
10:32n.10 51
11:20n.1 15
11:3 ....213, 215n.271
11:4–5 ....128n.168
11:5 ....212, 214n.263
11:9 213
11:16 ....21n.33, 26
11:18–26 252
11:18–20 255
11:18 18
11:20 242
11:22 256
11:23–26 242
11:24–25 221
11:24–26 245
11:24 261
11:25 ......246n.120, 261
11:26 ......253, 307, 308
11:27–28 258
11:27 ....259n.162
11:28 257
11:29 259
11:31–32 259
12–14 105
12 ....148n.235
12:4 ....126n.158
12:7–10 ...126n.158, 173
12:7 70
12:8–10 .....164n.26, 215
12:8 ....129n.175, 298n.5
12:10 ......127, 128, 148
12:12 ...66n.72, 259n.162
12:14–26 68
12:27 65
12:28 ....26, 132, 161, 164n.25, 164n.27, 165, 170, 170n.54, 172, 208, 208n.242
12:40 105
14:1 127
14:3 ...127, 171n.57, 173
14:23 ....40n.23
14:26 ......105, 108, 129, 129n.174
14:30 ....174n.66
14:33–34 ....214n.263
14:33 105
14:40 238
15:5–8 168
15:5 165
15:6 ....400n.14
15:8–9 166
15:12–57 ....185n.111
15:20 ....403n.25
15:22–26 488
15:22 473
15:23 ....303, 303n.20
15:23–26 ....429n.46
15:24–26 295
15:24–25 506
15:28 295
15:37–38 ....405n.32
15:43 412
15:44 402
15:51–53 406
15:52 ......389, 399, 411
15:52–53 404
16:22 ....394n.34
16:1 ....220n.286
16:12 ....163n.19
16:15 231
16:19 ....39n.63, 41, 212
16:22 ..253, 298, 308n.33
18:11 110
19:10 110
20:20 110
20:27 110

2 Corinthians
1:1 ....18, 166n.33
1:14 306
2:12 ....175n.69
2:16 369
3:3 56
3:7 494
3:14 ....324n.24

3:17 ....104, 106n.75
3:18 ....413, 494, 504
4–5 160
4:4 ....294, 122n.139
4:16 ....401n.16
5:4 ....401n.19
5:8 400
5:10 446
5:14 321
5:15 75
6:14–15 251
6:14 ....334n.72
6:16 ....336n.83, 57
7:6 302
8–9 ..123n.145, 220n.286
8:1–2 ....131n.185
8:1 216
8:2 ....131n.184
8:19 ..200n.186, 220n.287
9:6–7 98
9:6 131
9:7 133
9:11 ....131n.184
9:13 ....131n.184
9:15 93
9:18–23 168
11:2–4 76
11:2 74
11:3 ..130n.184, 214n.265
11:5–13 ....148n.234
11:13 117
12:1 502
12:2 ....407n.40
12:3 ....400n.8
12:11–12 148
13:1 ....352n.160
13:14 ....79, 79n.118, 82

Galatians

1:1 166
1:2 ....41, 216
1:4 17
1:10 ....124n.149
1:11–12 166
1:11 ....175n.69
1:12 ....36n.47
1:13 ......21n.33, 266n.3
1:16 166
1:18–19 167
1:19 ....199n.182
1:22 ....41, 216
2:8 167
3 ....148n.235
3:5 148
3:20 101
3:27–28 223
3:27 ...222, 225n.20, 229
3:28 ....64, 215
4:6 405
5:1 105
5:13 123
5:14 ....120n.129
5:18 103
6:1 123
6:2 120
6:10 ....152n.247

Ephesians

1:1–13 66
1:1 ....19, 25, 166n.33
1:3–14 110
1:3 444
1:7 397
1:20–23 71
1:20–22 284
1:21 507
1:22–23 ....31, 285
1:22 25
1:23 ....66n.72
2:2 ....410n.56
2:4 ....132n.194
2:10 ....456n.53
2:12 ....51n.7
2:13 64
2:14 ....63, 501
2:16 ....66n.72
2:18 79
2:19–22 ..33, 58, 489n.53
2:19–20 ....60, 63
2:20 .....38n.60, 64n.68, 169, 169n.49, 170n.54, 172
2:21–22 ....65, 336n.83
2:21 64
2:22 ..56, 64n.69, 58n.38, 79
3:4–6 .....26n.5, 324n.25
3:4–5 ....170, 174
3:4 ....60n.52
3:5 ....169, 169n.49, 170n.54, 172
3:6 ....68, 66n.72
3:10 25
3:19 72
3:21 ....72, 25, 66
4 ......174n.67, 215n.270
4:1–3 27
4:2 ....117n.118, 118
4:3 117
4:4–6 26
4:4 ....66n.72
4:8 ....126n.158, 164
4:10 71
4:11–15 109
4:11–12 ...126n.158, 164
4:11 ....60n.52, 161, 164n.25, 170n.54, 178n.79, 203
4:12 .....66n.72, 68, 159, 159n.4, 207
4:13–14 117
4:13 114
4:14 180
4:15–16 68
4:16 ....117, 117n.118
4:28 ....130n.183
4:32 118
5:5 ....488n.51
5:6 ....371n.247
5:14 ....93n.26
5:18–19 92
5:18 103
5:19 104
5:20 ....93, 103
5:23–24 67
5:23 66
5:25–33 72
5:25–27 ..26, 32, 75, 492
5:25–26 54
5:25 ....20, 74, 431n.554
5:27 ..42, 42n.75, 67n.78, 72n.94, 495n.75
5:30 ....67, 66n.72
5:31–32 75
6:4 116
6:5 ....131n.184
6:6 ....124n.149
6:17 281
6:19 ....175n.69
6:21–22 130
6:21 207
6:22 ....119n.127

Philippians

1:1 ...161, 207, 217, 218
1:6 306
1:10–11 ....299n.7
1:10 306
1:21–23 400
1:26 302
2:1 ....79n.119
2:3 124
2:6–11 ....93n.26
2:7–8 70
2:10–11 ...473, 474n.117
2:12 302
2:15 494
2:16 306
2:22 ....176n.73
2:25–30 168
3:3 ....55, 90n.16, 103
3:10–11 ....361n.196
3:10 ....82n.130
3:20–21 ....393, 406, 409n.51, 412
3:20 ....21, 266, 298
4:2–3 212
4:15–16 208

Colossians

1:1 ....166n.33
1:7 207
1:12 ....66n.72, 162
1:13–14 ....292, 468, 488
1:15–20 ....93n.26
1:15 ....41n.72
1:18 ......26, 41n.72, 66, 71n.92, 219, 403n.25
1:20 473
1:23 ....34n.38, 159
1:24 26
1:27–29 ....113n.101
2:2 ....119n.127
2:6–7 ....65, 115
2:7 ....64n.69, 93
2:9 ....72n.95
2:10 ....71n.92, 284
2:11–12 231
2:12 ...222, 223, 225n.20, 226, 229
2:15 ....284n.66
2:19 ....66n.72, 67
3:3 389
3:4 ....303, 303n.21, 319, 388, 412

3:6 ....371n.247
3:12 119
3:16 ...104n.69, 113, 121
3:21 ....116n.115
3:22 ..124n.149, 131n.184
4:5–6 154
4:7–8 ....130n.182
4:8 ....119n.127
4:15–16 39
4:15 ....39n.62
4:16 ....182n.98

1 Thessalonians
1:1 ....18, 168
1:5 78
1:9–10 ....412n.65
1:10 ..298, 371n.247, 371
2:4 ....124n.149
2:8 ....130n.183
2:9 ....175n.69
2:11 ....119n.127
2:13 ....111n.91, 186
2:14 ....21n.33, 26
2:19 ....303n.20
3:2 ....119n.127, 207
3:3 360
3:13 ....299n.7, 303, 303n.20, 388, 401
4 391
4:13–18 ....376n.280
4:13 ....400n.14, 407n.39
4:14–16 401
4:14–17 ...371n.245, 407
4:14 ....388, 389n.15
4:15–17 379
4:15 ....303n.20
4:16–17 ....379n.292
4:16 ....387n.7, 388, 389, 390n.19, 399, 404, 411
4:17 ....408n.43, 440
5:1–2 300
5:2–8 306
5:2–4 ....480n.3
5:2–3 413
5:2 394
5:3 372
5:4–6 394
5:9 ...371n.247, 371, 377, 411
5:11 119
5:12–13 131
5:12 ..200n.190, 218n.277
5:14 ....119, 121, 123
5:15 152
5:20 ..128n.168, 193n.147
5:23–24 413
5:23 .....299n.7, 303n.20
5:24 413

2 Thessalonians
1:1 18
1:4–5 361
1:4 ....21n.33, 26
1:5–6 363
1:6–10 305
1:6–9 415
1:7–10 417
1:7 ....388, 388n.11, 463n.73
1:8–9 ......471, 473n.113
1:9 ....471, 496, 506
1:10 ...306, 388, 388n.14, 412
2 ....353n.165, 419
2:1–3 329
2:1 ....303, 399, 408n.47
2:2 ....303n.20, 306
2:3–10 425
2:3–4 ....335, 345
2:3 ....306, 334, 334n.72, 335n.77, 371n.247, 416n.82, 436
2:4 345
2:6–7 336
2:8–11 337
2:8 ....303, 303n.20, 334, 335n.76, 335n.81, 345, 379, 388n.9, 416, 416n.83, 419, 432n.55, 436, 506
2:9–10 351
2:9 ...151, 302, 335, 345
2:17 ....152n.247
3:6 121
3:14–15 121

1 Timothy
1–3 ....168n.40
1:1–2 ....166n.33
1:2 ....168n.41
1:3 ....181n.90
1:5 ....187, 189
1:6–7 193
1:10 ....110n.87, 182
1:14 190
1:17 ....93n.26, 101
1:18–19 ....187, 193
1:19–20 188
1:20 ....183n.105
2:1–2 ..96, 270, 270n.17, 274
2:3–4 275
2:4 ....321, 475
2:5 476
2:7 191
2:8–11 ....213n.261
2:8 ....213n.258
2:10 ....152n.247
2:11–12 ....213n.258
2:11 214
2:12 ....213, 214n.262
2:13–14 ....213n.258
2:13 214
2:14 ....214n.265
3:1–10 207
3:1–7 ......196, 203, 214
3:1–2 202
3:1 ...131, 200n.191, 217
3:2–7 205
3:2 ....111n.94, 204
3:5 ....21n.33, 131
3:8–13 ....129n.171, 199n.185, 210
3:8–10 209
3:11 ..211, 211n.252, 212
3:12–23 207
3:12–13 209
3:12 132
3:15 ....21n.33
3:16 ....93n.26, 188
4:1–6 183
4:1–2 ......328, 330n.51
4:1 319
4:2 188
4:5–6 186
4:6 ....187, 328
4:7 188
4:8–10 189
4:8 ....186n.118
4:12 189
4:13 ......110, 130n.178, 181, 182n.98, 182n.100, 192
4:14 ....191, 192n.142, 194, 194n.148, 195, 200, 217
4:15 196
4:16 ..192, 196n.158, 328
5:2 190
5:3–16 210
5:9–10 ....211n.252
5:10 ....211, 212
5:17 ......161, 200, 202, 205n.210, 218
5:19 ......152n.247, 200, 218n.280
5:20 201
5:22 ....190, 205
5:24 452
6:1 130
6:2 ....181n.94
6:3 ....110n.87, 182,
6:5 189
6:6 188
6:9–10 189
6:11 ....186n.119
6:12 ....193, 328
6:14 ....299n.6, 304
6:16 502
6:20 184

2 Timothy
1:1 ....166n.33
1:3 ....90n.16, 187
1:5 ....116, 186, 194
1:6 ....37, 194, 196
1:9 17
1:12 306
1:13–14 184
1:13 ....182, 190
1:18 306
2:1 ....193n.146
2:2 ....37, 110
2:9 20
2:10 ....377n.283
2:11–13 ....93n.26
2:14 ....185n.112
2:15–18 185
2:17 ....183n.105
2:18 ....188n.127
2:19 22
2:21–22 190
3:1–5 326
3:1 ....330n.51
3:5 189

3:12 ....189, 360
3:13 326
3:15–17 185
3:15–16 36
3:15 ....111n.90, 116
3:16–17 111
3:16 ....115n.113
4:2–3 110
4:1–2 ....301, 304
4:2 ....176n.74
4:3 ....182, 183n.106
4:5 176
4:8 ...298, 304, 306, 446

Titus
1:1 ....166n.33, 377n.283
1:5–9 ....196, 203
1:5–7 202
1:5 .....37, 181n.91, 191, 201, 201n.192, 218
1:6–9 205
1:6–7 ......204, 204n.205
1:7 37
1:9 ....110n.87, 130n.179, 205n.214
2:1 ....110, 182
2:3–5 211
2:7 ....152n.247
2:11 473
2:12–13 304
2:12 188
2:13–14 ....52, 53
2:13 ....297, 297n.4, 378, 387
2:14 ....152n.247
2:15 130
3:1 ....152, 272, 276
3:5 ....75n.109, 223, 225n.20, 229n.42, 487n.44
3:8 152
3:9 ....111n.94
3:10–11 252
3:14 ..131n.187, 152n.247

Philemon
1–2 ....39, 39n.62

Hebrews
1:2 ....326n.36
1:6 ....41n.72
1:10–12 479
1:12 ....406n.34
1:14 ....463n.76
1:16 ....34n.37
2:3 ....454n.44
2:4 318
2:7 ....463n.65
2:8–9 505
2:12 ....15, 15n.4, 16
2:14 423
3:1 ....35, 165
3:2–3 59
3:2 191
3:13 ....119n.127
4:3 500
4:9–10 500
4:9 ....500n.95
4:13 ....453, 461n.67
4:14 160
5:10 ....112n.98
5:11–14 112
5:12 ....129n.173
6 ....113n.99
6:5 ....151, 319
7:4–10 99
8:6 54
8:8 54
8:10 ....55n.26
9:1 ......90n.16, 100n.53
9:6 ....90n.16
9:9 ....53, 90n.16, 91n.21
9:12–14 53
9:15 ......54n.23, 54n.24
9:21 ....90n.16
9:26 239
9:27 ....466n.86
9:28 ....298, 411
10 ....104n.68
10:2 ....91n.21
10:11 ....88n.12
10:14 54
10:17 ....334n.72
10:19–22 103
10:19 ....54, 187
10:22 ....54, 187, 226, 228n.40, 229n.42
10:23–25 119
10:24 ....152n.247
10:25–27 417
10:27 ....468n.91
10:35 455
11:5 ....406n.33
11:10 ....431n.54
12:1–2 ....43n.82
12:14 299
12:22–23 ....41, 400
12:23 ...42n.73, 412, 445
12:24 ....54n.23
12:28–29 91
12:28 293
12:29 416
13:1–2 119
13:15–16 161
13:15 ....89, 124, 263
13:17 ....68n.80, 218
13:19 ....486n.38
13:20 178

James
1:5 ....131n.184
1:13 ....97n.45
1:18 ....367n.230
2:15–17 ....124n.147
2:15–16 124
3:1 ...114n.105, 129n.173
3:15 ....346n.128
5:7 ....298, 303n.20
5:8 ....303n.20
5:14–15 201

1 Peter
1–2 202
1:1 ....17, 20, 201
1:2 30
1:3 ....132n.194
1:6–8 63
1:7 305
1:8 ....394, 499n.90
1:13 297
1:17 445
1:18–19 53
1:23–25 ....112n.95
1:25 175
2:1–9 160
2:2 112
2:4–5 ....33, 64
2:4 ....64n.70
2:5 ....89, 161
2:8 ....64n.70
2:9–10 .....162, 201n.196
2:9 ...17, 20, 30, 33, 51, 87, 89, 161n.10, 468
2:12 152
2:13–14 273
2:13 283
2:14 ....269, 271
2:15 276
2:16 ....273n.25
2:17–18 273
2:17 ....282, 469
2:25 178
3:1 273
3:8 119
3:15 155
3:16 187
3:18–19 ....401n.16
3:20 ....426n.26
3:21 ....225n.20, 229
3:22 507
4:8–9 119
4:10 ....70, 125
4:11 126
4:13 ....387, 305
4:14 320
5:1–4 ......179, 203n.202
5:1–3 162
5:1 ...194, 199n.184, 201, 204n.207, 218, 218n.280, 413
5:2–3 ....68n.81
5:3 ....162n.17
5:4 ....178, 303, 303n.21
5:5 ....124n.151

2 Peter
1:16 ....303n.20
1:17 387
1:20–21 36
2:1 117
2:4–10 450
2:4 ....447, 447n.12, 464
3:4 ....303n.20, 440
3:7 ....335n.78, 413
3:8–10 466
3:8 298
3:9 299
3:10–13 440
3:10 ....306, 394
3:11–13 307
3:12 306
3:13 ...479, 481, 481n.13, 482n.18
3:15 ....163n.19
3:16 .....36n.50, 111n.91, 112n.97, 186n.117

1 John
1:3 ....79, 80
1:5–6 80
1:7 80
1:9 94
2:18 ...330, 330n.55, 331
2:20 113
2:22 ....330, 330n.55
2:27 113
2:28 ...299, 303, 303n.20, 303n.21
3:2 ....303, 303n.21
3:16 ....125, 425n.26
3:17–18 ....124n.147
4:3 ....330, 330n.55, 331n.61, 336n.85
4:13 ....80n.120

2 John
1 ....202, 218n.280
7 ..330, 330n.55, 331n.61
8 455

3 John
1 ....202, 218n.280

Jude
3 ....328n.44
4 ....252n.138
6 ....464, 464n.77
9 ....388n.12
13 469
14 ....388n.14
14–15 ....420n.98
17–19 ....326n.37
24–25 413

Revelation
1 430
1:1 ....114n.106
1:3 ....172, 341n.111
1:4 ....216, 344n.120, 350n.153, 362
1:5–6 ....162, 428, 429, 506
1:5 ....41n.72, 284, 403n.25
1:6 ....293, 443
1:7 ...307, 314, 383n.304, 385, 390
1:8 101
1:9 ...172, 345n.125, 362, 428
1:10 ....15, 172n.60
1:13 ....220n.289
1:14 ....461, 463n.74
1:17 ....102n.58
1:20 ....352n.160
2–19 370
2–3 ....69n.86, 217, 341n.111, 377
2 18
2:1 ....18, 58
2:2 ....400n.8
2:3–5 327
2:8 ....102n.58
2:9–10 362
2:19–24 363
2:26–7 439
3 ....18, 366
3:5 ....448n.17
3:10–11 365
3:10 ....34n.37, 365n.220, 365n.221, 371n.247, 376
3:12 ....504n.114
3:20 251
3:21 ....101, 446n.5, 462, 498n.88
4–19 ....372, 376, 377
4:1–2 366
4:1 ...371, 371n.246, 377, 422n.5
4:2 ....172n.60
4:4 ....43n.79
4:8–10 ....89, 91
4:8 ....503n.106
4:9–11 ....503n.17
4:9–10 ....43n.79
4:11 ....93n.26
5 430
5:6 ...340n.100, 346n.131
5:8–10 ....43n.79
5:8–9 284
5:8 ....372n.249
5:9–10 429
5:9 ....35, 53, 104
5:10 ....429n.41
5:12–14 89
5:12 ....340n.100
5:13 ....42n.79, 93n.26, 101, 446n.5
5:14 102
6–19 ....380, 381n.299
6 ....305n.30, 383
6:2–7 284
6:8 368
6:9–11 ....400, 426n.30
6:9–10 368
6:9 ....367n.228
6:10 ..341n.106, 365n.200
6:12–16 382
6:14 ....447n.11, 482
6:15 416
6:16–17 ....368n.232
6:16 ....446n.5
6:17 ....371, 377, 380
6:9–11 ....359n.189
7 ....368n.230
7:1–8 378
7:3–4 ....349n.146
7:3 367
7:4 367
7:9–17 ....366, 375
7:10 ....446n.5
7:11 ....89n.14
7:12 ....93n.26
7:13–14 ....43n.82
7:14–15 502
7:14 ....363n.209, 369, 378n.286
7:15 ..366n.227, 501n.102
7:17 ....366n.227, 490
8:3–4 ....372n.249
8:3 ....400n.12
8:7–9:19 368
8:9 ....425n.26
8:12 ....369n.233
8:13 ..341n.106, 365n.220
9:3–4 367
9:4–6 ....378n.288
9:4 ....349n.146
9:13 ....400n.12
10:6–7 389
11 352
11:1 ....89n.14
11:2–3 ....341n.108
11:3 ....353n.162
11:5–6 ....353n.161
11:7 ..353, 368n.331, 424
11:10 ....341n.106, 365n.220
11:11–12 ..353n.164, 409, 409n.55
11:12 376
11:15 ....267, 295, 345, 389, 440, 488, 506, 507
11:16–18 ....43n.79
11:16 ...89n.14, 503n.107
11:17–18 489
11:18–19 422
11:18 ....172n.59, 368n.232, 372n.249, 375, 414, 416n.88, 454, 454n.4, 455n.46
12 422
12:1 ....422n.6
12:3 ....340, 342n.114
12:5–17 ....422n.7
12:5 ....407n.40, 421n.3
12:6 ....341n.108
12:7–17 ....423n.15
12:7 ....388n.12, 423n.12
12:9 ..340n.99, 341n.102, 423n.15
12:11 ..368n.231, 425n.26
12:14 ....342n.108, 343n.115, 356
12:17 339
13 ...344, 345n.126, 352, 422n.7
13:1–3 340
13:1 339
13:2 ..340n.98, 341n.107, 345
13:3–8 341
13:3 ....340n.101, 343n.115, 346n.135
13:4–5 345
13:5–10 342
13:5–7 ....359n.191
13:5 425
13:6–7 283
13:6 345
13:7–15 353
13:7 ....368n.231, 372n.249, 376
13:8 ....340n.100, 346n.133, 365n.220, 448n.17
13:9 372
13:10 ....366n.223, 372n.249

13:11 339
13:12 ....341n.106, 365n.220
13:13–15 347
13:13–14 351
13:14 ....340n.101, 341n.106, 365n.220, 426n.27
13:16–17 349
13:16 ....504n.113
13:17–18 350
14:1–5 ....367n.230
14:1 ....349n.146, 504, 504n.113
14:3 104
14:4 504
14:6 ..341n.106, 365n.220
14:7 ..89n.14, 91, 446n.5, 446, 468
14:8 375
14:9–11 ....350, 470
14:9 ....504n.113
14:10 375
14:12 ....372n.249
14:13 ....368n.231, 426n.30, 457, 500
14:14–16 .....385n.2, 399
14:14 .....387n.8, 446n.5
14:18 ..368n.232, 400n.12
14:19 ....375, 423n.12
15:1 375
15:4 ....89n.14
15:5 ....422n.5
15:7 ....368n.232, 375
16:1–10 368
16:1 ....368n.232, 375
16:3 ....425n.26
16:6 ...172n.59, 372n.249
16:7 ....375, 400n.12
16:8–9 369
16:8 ....369n.233
16:13–14 432
16:13 ....347n.136, 349n.144
16:14–15 307
16:14 ....306, 432n.53
16:15 ....300, 394
17 352
17:1 375
17:2 ..341n.106, 365n.220
17:3 ....172n.60, 342
17:5–6 ....342n.113
17:5 ....314n.55, 431n.54
17:6 ....372n.249
17:8–11 ...343, 365n.220, 448n.17
17:9 ....314n.55
17:11–12 346
17:11 ......345, 351n.156
17:12–14 ...344, 432n.56
17:14 ..345, 389n.16, 420
17:15 ....340n.97
17:18 ....341n.106, 342n.113, 429n.41, 431n.54
18:1 ....422n.5
18:10–19 ....344n.124
18:10 375
18:20 ....172, 172n.61, 372n.249
18:24 ....172n.59, 368n.231, 372n.249
19 ...419, 422, 433, 439, 440, 441, 442, 446n.5
19:2 375
19:4–5 ....43n.79
19:4 ....89n.14, 503n.107
19:6–9 492
19:6–7 74
19:7–8 42
19:7 ....77, 254
19:8 ....76, 389, 493n.69
19:9 ....74, 77, 254
19:10 ...89n.14, 353n.162
19:11–21 ...417, 420n.99, 421, 437, 441, 443
19:11 ....387, 446n.5
19:12 461
19:13 ....368n.232
19:14 ..388, 389, 420n.99
19:15 ....368n.232, 418n.91, 441
19:18 ....433n.59
19:19–21 432
19:19 ..420n.100, 496n.81
19:20–21 369
19:20 ....343n.117, 347n.136, 349n.144, 432n.55
19:21 ..433n.59, 441, 442
20 ....422, 430n.47, 433, 433n.61, 439, 440, 441, 442, 448n.20, 479, 482, 489
20:1–15 421
20:1–10 ....422, 443
20:1–9 437
20:1–3 .....424, 431, 441
20:1 ..367n.228, 423n.12, 423n.15
20:2–3 423
20:2 ....422n.8
20:3 ....423n.13, 439
20:4–6 ....425, 430, 434, 441
20:4–5 439
20:4 ....425n.25, 426n.30, 427n.32
20:5 ....427, 440, 442
20:6 ....426, 428
20:7–15 445
20:7–10 ....430, 432
20:7–9 431
20:7 ....337n.90
20:8 ....432n.52, 432n.53, 440
20:9 ....352n.157
20:10 ....347n.136, 349n.144, 421n.3, 432n.55, 442, 490
20:11–15 ...462, 488n.48
20:11 ....446n.5, 447, 460n.65, 482, 482n.18, 482n.20
20:12 ....448, 451
20:13 ....449, 449n.21
20:14–15 ....426n.30
20:14 ...482n.20, 490n.54
20:15 ......448, 449, 470
20:7–9 416
21–22 ..430n.48, 434n.64
21 ...289, 366, 480, 481, 482, 485, 489, 492n.64, 493n.67, 495n.76, 504
21:1 ....42n.74, 289, 403, 454, 479, 481n.13, 482, 482n.18, 485, 489, 499n.92
21:2–11 493
21:2–4 ....489n.52
21:2 .....42, 74, 482n.18, 491, 492, 492n.60
21:3 489
21:4 ......366n.227, 490, 499, 499n.92
21:5–7 491
21:6 ..102n.58, 366n.227, 490n.56
21:8 ....458n.57, 470
21:9 ....74, 492
21:10–11 ....352n.157
21:10 ....172n.60
21:11 ....74, 495
21:12–14 ....43n.79
21:12 ....38, 61
21:14 ....38, 61
21:18–21 494
21:19 ....352n.157
21:22–24 495
21:22–23 ....495n.77
21:22 ....497n.85
21:24 ...496n.82, 501n.99
21:25 496
21:26 ......496, 501n.99
21:27 495
22 ...289, 366, 485, 489, 493n.67, 495n.76
22:1–5 ....497, 501
22:1 498
22:2 ....499, 500
22:3 ......89n.14, 90n.16, 366n.227, 503
22:4 504
22:5 ....429, 505, 507
22:6 172
22:7 497
22:9 ....89n.14, 172
22:12–13 101
22:12 454
22:13 405
22:15 469
22:17 ....26, 74, 498
22:20 ....307, 314

Extrabiblical Literature

1 Maccabees

1:54 ....355n.175
4:52–59 ....355n.177

2 Esdras

8:52–54 ....500n.98